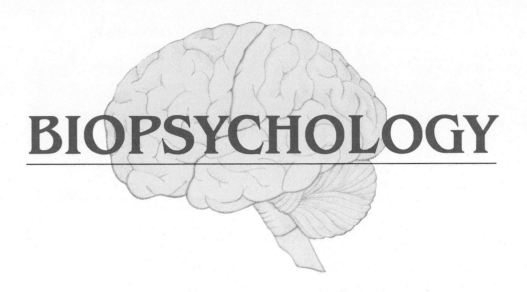

BIOPSYCHOLOGY

John P. J. Pinel

THE UNIVERSITY OF BRITISH COLUMBIA

ALLYN AND BACON

BOSTON LONDON SYDNEY TORONTO

To the memory of Donald Olding Hebb (1904–1985)
for his contributions to biopsychology

AND

To Maggie *and* Greg *for their*
love and support

Series editor: Diane McOscar
Developmental editor: Alicia Reilly
Editorial assistant: Laura Frankenthaler
Cover administrator: Linda Dickinson
Copy editor: Kathleen Smith
Editorial-production service: Deborah Schneck
Composition buyer: Linda Cox
Manufacturing buyer: William Alberti
Production administrator: Elaine Ober
Cover designer: Lynda Fishbourne

Library of Congress Cataloging-in-Publication Data

Pinel, John P. J.
    Biopsychology.

    Includes bibliographical references.
    1. Psychobiology.   I. Title.
QP360.P463 1990   152   89-18091
ISBN 0-205-12052-0

Printed in the United States of America

10 9 8 7 6 5 4 3 2 1   90 91 92 93 94

Contents

17

Preface

This book is intended for use as a primary text in one- or two-semester undergraduate courses in biopsychology (variously titled Biopsychology, Physiological Psychology, Brain and Behavior, Psychobiology, Behavioral Neuroscience, Behavioral Neurobiology, etc.). Because most of the students who enter undergraduate biopsychology courses have had little previous exposure to neuroscientific topics, I have attempted to tailor *Biopsychology* to the needs of the beginning student. *Biopsychology* is a book that focuses on fundamentals rather than details; a book that clearly and carefully develops each topic from primary principles; and a book that never forgets that scientific material is more easily digested with a dash of humor, a sprinkling of enthusiasm, and a dollup of personal implication. The following are some of the general approaches and good intentions that guided its preparation.

Increasing the Emphasis on Behavior

In many biopsychology textbooks the coverage of neurophysiology, neurochemistry, and neuroanatomy subverts the coverage of behavioral research. This prejudice is often most obvious in the obligatory chapter on research methods, where the various neuroanatomical, neurophysiological, and neurochemical research methods are typically described at great length while behavioral technology receives short shrift. In contrast, *Biopsychology* gives behavior top billing: It stresses that neuroscience is a team effort and that the unique contribution made by biopsychologists to this team is their behavioral expertise. Half the research methods chapter (chapter 4) is dedicated to methods for studying behavior, and half is dedicated to methods for studying the nervous system.

Increasing the Coverage of Human Research

Biopsychology provides more than the customary coverage of case studies and experiments involving brain-damaged and healthy human subjects. However, despite this increased attention to human research, controlled experiments in laboratory species provide the backbone for most of the chapters. A point of view that pervades *Biopsychology* is that diversity is a major strength of biopsychological research and that major advances have often resulted from the convergence of research involving human and nonhuman subjects.

Helping Students Learn

The diversity of information to which the beginning biopsychology student must be introduced makes the task of both the teacher and the student difficult. Accordingly, I have incorporated in *Biopsychology* features expressly designed to help students learn the material. Five are particularly noteworthy.

- First are the lists of key terms and definitions that appear at the end of each chapter; these are expressly designed to help students prepare for examinations. My students tell me that they are very helpful.

- Second are the study exercises that punctuate the text. Rather than appearing at the end of each chapter, these exercises occur at key transition points, where students can benefit greatly by pausing to consolidate their understanding of preceding fundamentals before proceeding to new material.

- Third are the food-for-thought discussion questions at the end of each chapter.

- Fourth are the many demonstrations, anecdotes, analogies, and case studies that I have used to illustrate important principles and generate interest in them.

- Fifth are the illustrations.

Improving the Illustrations

Because biopsychology is such a highly visual discipline, particular attention was paid to the design of the illustrations in this book. Each was carefully designed and annotated to clarify central ideas raised in the body of the text. One of the major strengths of the illustrations is that they are produced in full color. In this respect, *Biopsychology* represents a first: It is the first biopsychology textbook to be produced in full color from cover to cover. The decision to produce *Biopsychology* in full color was motivated by pedagogical, rather than cosmetic, objectives. There were three of them.

- First, I wanted to be able to illustrate at appropriate points in the text the color-coded brain scans and selective neural staining and labelling procedures that play such a central role in current biopsychological research.

- Second, I wanted to use color to simplify what is the most difficult task faced by many beginning biopsychology students—learning the three-dimensional structure of the brain from a series of two-dimensional drawings. It is remarkable how much a neuroanatomical drawing can be clarified by color labelling its key structures.

- Third, I wanted to be able to lead each student through the section of the text on color vision by illustrating the key phenomena under investigation.

Generating an Appreciation for the Scientific Method

Woven through the fabric of many chapters are important messages about the scientific method. The following are four recurring themes: (1) The scientific method is a method of answering questions that is as applicable to daily life as it is to the biopsychology laboratory. (2) The scientific method is fun—it is virtually the same method that detectives use to solve unwitnessed crimes or that treasure hunters use to infer the location of sunken galleons. (3) Widely accepted scientific theories are current best guesses rather than statements of absolute fact. (4) Even theories that ultimately prove to be wrong can contribute greatly to the progress of science.

Making Biopsychology Personal

One sure way to interest students in biopsychology and to improve their level of performance is to relate what they are learning to their own lives. Several chapters in *Biopsychology*—particularly those on eating, sleeping, sex, and drug abuse—carry strong personal messages. Many of the food-for-thought questions at the end of each chapter are designed to encourage students to consider the implications of biopsychological research for life in the real world. Some of these questions are excellent topics for classroom discussion.

How to Use the Text

An important feature of *Biopsychology* from a course-design perspective is that each chapter is written so that it is as independent as possible from other chapters. When a technical term is encountered that has been explained earlier in the text, it is briefly redefined, and the reader is referred to the relevant previous chapter. Thus, it is quite feasible to omit certain chapters or to vary their sequence. Further flexibility in course design is provided by the appendices. These appendices summarize detailed information that is appropriate for some kinds of students and courses, but not for others. For example, there are appendices illustrating the projections of the cranial nerves, the location of each hypothalamic nucleus, and the hormonal correlates of the human female menstrual cycle. By putting these details in appendices, each instructor can decide whether to assign them or not. There is a table in the Instructor's Manual that suggests sample syllabi for courses with five different profiles.

Ancillary Materials Available with Biopsychology

The ancillary materials available with *Biopsychology* differ from those available with comparable texts in several ways; the most obvious is that they have been prepared entirely by me, the author of the text. I understand why authors do not often choose to write the ancillary material for texts that they have just finished writing, but my commitment to teaching did not allow me to take this route. I believe that students and instructors deserve ancillary material that is written with the same tone, orientation, and care as the text.

Study Guide

Each chapter of the study guide includes three sections. Section I is composed of the so-called "jeopardy study items"—named after the popular television quiz show. The jeopardy study items are arranged in two columns on the page with questions on the left and answers on the right. Sometimes there is nothing in the space to the right of a question and the student's task is to write in the correct answer (with reference to the text). Sometimes there is nothing in the space to the left of an answer and the student's task is to write in the correct question (again with reference to the text). When the jeopardy study items are completed, the student has a list of questions and answers that summarize all of the main points in the chapter, and they are conveniently arranged for bidirectional studying—students can study with one half of each page covered and then the other.

Section II of each study guide chapter is composed of essay study questions. Spaces are provided for the student to write outlines of the correct answers to each question (with reference to the text). These essay study questions encourage students to consider broader issues in their studying.

Section III of each study guide chapter is a practice examination, which is designed to be written after most, but not all, of the studying has been completed. It is recommended that students write the practice examination at least twenty-four hours before the scheduled time of their formal examination so that the results of the practice examination can be used to guide the last stages of their studying. The practice final examination is composed of multiple-choice questions, fill-in-the-blanks questions, short-answer questions, true-and-false questions, and diagram questions. The correct answers appear at the end of each study guide chapter.

Test Bank

Provided to the instructor of each class using *Biopsychology* is an extensive multiple-choice test bank. From the student's perspective, one of the most important parts of any textbook is the test bank—the clarity, difficulty, and focus of the test bank have a substantial effect on the degree to which those students who have learned the material well will be rewarded for their efforts. My intention in preparing the multiple-choice test bank was to supply enough good test items—1327 by last count—of varied focus and difficulty that every instructor can tailor examinations to the specific needs of her or his class without having to invest a substantial amount of time in test construction.

Instructor's Manual

The instructor's manual for *Biopsychology* provides the instructor with two things: a set of lecture notes that complement the text and a set of over-head transparency masters to accompany each lecture. There are notes for two one-hour lectures to accompany each chapter of the text, and there are two or three overhead masters to go along with each lecture.

Each page of the instructor's manual is divided in two columns: a left column which covers two-thirds of the page, and a right column, which covers one-third. The lecture notes are printed in the left column and the right column is left blank for each instructor to make her or his own insertions.

I expect that the lecture notes in the instructor's manual will be used in three different ways. Some instructors might use them as sources for preparing their own lectures in a separate book; other instructors might add their own personal touches in the right-hand columns and lecture directly from the manual; and still others might find that they can lecture effectively directly from the manual notes with few additions—at least on those few occasions when they are caught short of preparation time.

Acknowledgments

Many people have contributed to the successful completion of this book. Particularly instrumental in my decision to begin writing were Bill Barke, Philip Curson, Boris Gorzalka, Fred Regan, and Jerry Kraus. During the writing phase, many colleagues and students provided me with information and feedback, and put up with my predictable cycles of enthusiasm and despair as I neared the completion of one chapter and then became mired in middle of the next. These supporters include, in no particular order, Maggie Edwards, Rod Cooper, Michael Mana, Jon Druhan, Jim Pfaus, Tim Harpur, Scott Mendelson, Boris Gorzalka, Tess O'Brien, Eric Eich, Bob Hare, Don Wilkie, Janet Werker, Jack Kelly, Cathy Rankin, Dave Mumby, Wolfgang Linden, Tony Phillips, Roy Wise, Steve Woods, Peter Graf, Dave Albert, Kwon Kim, Christine Beck, Emma Wood, Mel Goodale, Craig Jones, Harvey Weingarten, Henry Koopmans, Ralph Mistlberger, Steve Petersen, Beverley Charlish, Dennis Paul, Jim Blackburn, Robert Bolles, Geoff Carr, Jill Becker, and Stanley Coren. Although I have never met them, the following instructors deserve special thanks for reviewing early drafts of the manuscript and exposing its weaknesses to me. Being able to see my efforts through their critical eyes, led to significant improvements in all of the chapters.

John F. Axelson   Neil Rowland
College of the Holy Cross   *University of Florida*

Anthony R. Caggiula
University of Pittsburgh

Sally Haralson
*California State University
at Long Beach*

Charles Kutscher
Syracuse University

Joan B. Lauer
*Purdue University at
Indianapolis*

George V. Rebec
Indiana University

Virginia F. Saunders
*San Francisco State
University*

Cheryl Sisk
Michigan State University

Paul J. Wellman
Texas A & M University

Jeffrey Wilson
*Indiana University–Purdue
University at Fort Wayne*

Thomas B. Wishart
University of Saskatchewan

The amount of graphic, typographic, and clerical work that went into the preparation of this book was prodigious. Six people carried this burden for me, and thus allowed me to focus on writing. Michael Mana, Lucille Hoover, and Christine Beck located and photocopied all of the cited articles, plus many more—a stack over seven feet tall. Christine Beck prepared the reference list, and she helped prepare the glossaries at the end of each chapter. Maggie Edwards produced first versions of many dozens of original drawings and graphs, and she also obtained permission for me to reprint those obtained from other sources. Liz McCririck transformed my scrawl into typed copy, which she had to revise again and again and again (sorry Liz).

I would like to express my gratitude to the members of the Allyn and Bacon publishing team for their exceptional efforts in bringing this project to fruition. I am in awe of their ability to transform my typed pages into the striking volume that you have in front of you. My thanks go to Bill Barke, Diane McOscar, Alicia Reilly, Laura Frankenthaler, Judy Hauck, Elaine Ober, Anne Marie Fleming, Deborah Schneck, and Kathy Smith who were largely responsible for the editing, design, and production of this book.

Finally, I would like to thank you, the reader. It is you, and only you, who make my efforts and the efforts of all those acknowledged above worthwhile.

To the Student

In the 1960s, I was, in the parlance of the times, "turned on" by an undergraduate course in biopsychology. I could not imagine anything more interesting than a field of science dedicated to studying the relation between psychological functioning and the brain. This initial fascination has been nourished by twenty-five years as a student, teacher, and researcher of biopsychology. *Biopsychology* is my effort to share this fascination with you.

I have tried to make *Biopsychology* a different kind of textbook, a textbook that includes clear, concise, well-organized explanations of the key points but is still interesting to read—a book from which you might suggest a suitable chapter to an interested friend or relative. To accomplish this goal, I thought a bit about what kind of textbook I would have liked when I was a student, and I decided immediately to avoid the stern formality and ponderousness of conventional textbook writing. What I wanted was a more relaxed and personal style. To accomplish this, I imagined that you and I were chatting as I wrote and that I was telling you—usually over a glass of something—about the interesting things that go on in the field of biopsychology. Imagining these chats kept my writing from drifting back into conventional "textbookese," and it never let me forget who I was writing this book for. I hope that *Biopsychology* teaches you much, and I hope that reading it manages to generate for you the same personal feeling that writing it did for me. If you are so inclined, please write; I welcome your comments and suggestions. You can write to me at the Department of Psychology, University of British Columbia, Vancouver, B.C., Canada V6T 1Y7.

1

Biopsychology as a Neuroscience

The appearance of the human brain is far from impressive (see Figure 1.1). It is a squishy, wrinkled, walnut-shaped hunk of tissue weighing little more than 1.5 kilograms—about 3 pounds. It looks like something that you might find washed up on a beach rather than like one of the wonders of the world—which it surely is. Despite its unprepossessing external appearance, the human brain is a wonderfully complex cellular network comprising an estimated 100 billion highly specialized cells called **neurons,** which receive and transmit complex electrochemical signals. Contemplate for a moment the complexity of the brain's neural circuits. Consider the 100 billion neurons in complex array, each receiving direct input from dozens of neurons and passing on its output to dozens more; consider the estimated 100 trillion connections between them; and consider the infinite number of paths that a neural signal could follow through this morass.

Although the complexity of the human brain is truly amazing, it would be even more amazing if the human brain were not so complex. It is inconceivable that an organ capable of creating a Mona Lisa, an artificial heart, and a supersonic aircraft; of traveling to the moon and to the depths of the sea; and of experiencing the wonder of an alpine sunset, a newborn infant, and a reverse slam dunk would itself not be complex. Paradoxically, **neuroscience** (the study of the nervous system) may prove to be the brain's

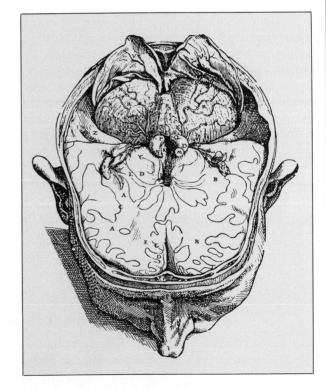

ultimate challenge: Does the brain have the capacity to understand something as complex as itself?

There is only one way for scientists to study something as complex as the brain. It is to study it bit by bit, from this perspective and that in the hope that it may eventually be possible to combine specific pieces of information into

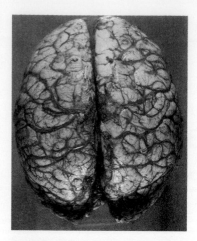

FIGURE 1.1 *A human brain viewed from above. (Courtesy of Kenneth Berry, Head, Neuropathology, Vancouver General Hospital.)*

a broader understanding. For example, some neuroscientists study the physiological basis of memory by analyzing the transmission of neural signals between two particular neurons in the abdominal ganglion of the *Aplysia*, a large marine mollusk; others study it by assessing the memory deficits of human patients with brain damage; and still others study it by assessing effects of drugs on the ability of rats to remember mazes. Although it is unlikely that any single research approach will ever reveal how memories are stored in the brain, there is reason for optimism if you consider that neuroscien-

tists are currently studying the neural basis of memory in hundreds of different ways. It is out of the convergence of different approaches that important answers are likely to come.

Given the diversity of neuroscientific research, it is safe to say that no two neuroscientists take exactly the same approach to their subject matter. It is possible, however, to group approaches with certain features in common into various neuroscientific subdisciplines. As its title indicates, this book is about one such subdiscipline: biopsychology. The primary purpose of this first chapter is to introduce you to biopsychology. To accomplish this, it deals with the following six questions:

1.1 What Is Biopsychology?

1.2 What Is the Relation Between Biopsychology and the Other Disciplines of Neuroscience?

1.3 What Types of Research Characterize the Biopsychological Approach?

1.4 What Are the Four Divisions of Biopsychology?

1.5 How Do Biopsychologists Use Observational Methods to Study the Unobservable?

1.6 What Is Bad Science, and How Do You Spot It?

1.1 What Is Biopsychology?

Biopsychology is the branch of neuroscience concerned with how the brain and the rest of the nervous system (including the endocrine system) control behavior. Of course, one could, as some have done, refer to this field as ''psychobiology'' or ''behavioral biology'' or ''behavioral neuroscience,'' but I prefer the term *biopsychology* because it puts the emphasis on psychology (behavior), which is the emphasis that distinguishes biopsychology from the other subdisciplines of neuroscience. ''Biopsychology'' denotes a biological approach to the study of psychology; the alternatives denote a psychological approach to the study of biology. Psychology commands center stage in this text. Psychology can be defined as the study of behavior, if the term *behavior* is used in its broadest sense to refer to all overt activities of the organism as well as the psychological processes that are presumed to underlie them (e.g., learning, memory, motivation, perception, and emotion).

The study of the nervous system and behavior has a long history, but biopsychology did not coalesce into a major neuroscientific discipline until this century. Although it is not possible to specify its exact date of birth, the publication of the *Organization of Behavior* in 1949 by D.O. Hebb played a key role in its emergence (see Milner & White, 1987). Prior to 1949, there were some scientists engaged in biopsychological research—most notably Hebb's teacher, Karl Lashley, who is regarded by some as the father of the field—but the publication of Hebb's book triggered a rapid expansion of the discipline. In his book, Hebb (see Figure 1.2) developed the first comprehensive theoretical account of how complex psychological phenomena, such as perceptions, emotions, thoughts, and memories, might be produced by brain activity. By this account, Hebb did much to discredit the then prevalent view that psychological functioning is too complex to have its roots in the physiology and chemistry of the brain. Hebb based his conclusions on experiments involving both humans and laboratory animals, on clinical case studies, and on logical arguments developed from his own insightful observations of daily life. As you will soon learn, this eclectic approach has become a hallmark of biopsychological inquiry.

In comparison to other sciences that you may have studied, such as physics, chemistry, or biology, biopsychology is an infant: a raucous, healthy, rapidly growing infant, but nonetheless an infant. In this book, you will reap the benefits of biopsychology's youth. Because biopsychology does not have a long and complex history, you will have the luxury of moving quickly to the excitement of current biopsychological research.

1.2 What Is the Relation Between Biopsychology and the Other Disciplines of Neuroscience?

There is a healthy competition among the various disciplines of neuroscience. Scientists are a dedicated lot, so it is only natural that they would be at least slightly chauvinistic about their own approach to research. However, the predominant inclination in neuroscience is cooperation—not competition. This cooperation is facilitated by the fact that the primary purpose of some of its subdisciplines is to synthesize information from other subdisciplines. Biopsychology is such an integrative subdiscipline.

As its name implies, biopsychology is a synthesis of two general approaches, the biological and the behavioral. Biopsychologists are above all else psychologists (persons dedicated to behavioral research); but they are psychologists who, like other neuroscientists, bring to their research a knowledge of the biology of the organisms under investigation. Thus, their primary contribution to neuroscientific research is a knowledge of behavior and of the methods of behavioral research. The fundamental integrative nature of biopsychology is reflected in the organization of this book. Although its focus is strictly biopsychological, that is, on the interface between brain and behavior, there is not a single chapter in which information provided by other neuroscientific disciplines does not come into play. The following are some of the fields of neuroscience that are touched on in this book:

Biological Psychiatry study of the biological bases of psychiatric disorders and their treatment through the manipulation of the brain (see Chapter 6)

Biopsychology study of the biological bases of behavior; how the brain and the rest of the nervous system control behavior and other psychological processes

FIGURE 1.2 *D.O. Hebb.
(Photograph courtesy of
Jane Hebb-Paul.)*

Developmental Neurobiology study of how the nervous system changes as an organism matures and ages; **neurobiology** is a general term roughly equivalent to neuroscience (see Chapter 15)

Neuroanatomy study of the structure of the nervous system (see Chapter 2)

Neurochemistry study of the chemical bases of neural activity, particularly those that underlie the transmission of signals through and between neurons (see Chapters 3 and 6)

Neuroethology study of the relation between the nervous system and behavior that occurs in the animal's natural environment (Camhi, 1984; Hoyle, 1984); in contrast, biopsychologists prefer to study behavior in controlled laboratory situations (see Chapter 4)

Neuroendocrinology study of the interactions of the nervous system with the endocrine glands and the hormones that they release (see Chapter 10)

Neuropathology study of nervous system disorders (see Chapter 5)

Neuropharmacology study of the effects of drugs on the nervous system, particularly those influencing neural transmission (see Chapters 6 and 16)

Neurophysiology study of the responses of the nervous system, particularly those involved in transmission of electrical signals through and between neurons (see Chapter 3)

Some scientists who are involved in research programs that require a synthesis of material from several subdisciplines of neuroscience coin terms to characterize their particular approach. They string together appropriate modifiers in sequence to create a label for what they do. The possibilities are limitless and at times almost humorous. What type of research do you think would interest a developmental psychoneuroendocrinologist?

Another way of characterizing the discipline of neuroscience and the place of biopsychology in it is to consider the professional environments in which neuroscientists are trained and conduct their research. To do this, I selected at random 224 neuroscientists from a recent membership directory of the **Society for Neuroscience** and recorded the departmental affiliation of each. The results are presented in Table 1.1. In the present context, the most noteworthy point made by Table 1.1 concerns the relative contribution of biopsychologists to the research effort in neuroscience. Clearly the contribution is substantial; about 16 percent of the members of the Society

Table 1.1 *Departmental Affiliations of Members of the Society for Neuroscience*

DEPARTMENTAL AFFILIATION	PERCENTAGE OF SAMPLE
Psychology	16.1
Physiology	14.3
Pharmacology	12.5
Biology	11.2
Anatomy	11.2
Neurology	6.7
Psychiatry	5.8
Neuroscience/Neurobiology	5.3
Neurosurgery	3.1
Pathology	3.1
Veterinary Medicine	1.8
Others	8.9
	100.0

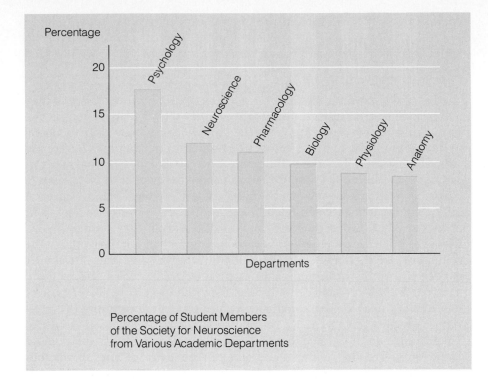

Percentage of Student Members
of the Society for Neuroscience
from Various Academic Departments

FIGURE 1.3 *The departmental affiliation of graduate-student members of the Society for Neuroscience. Only academic departments contributing over 5% of the graduate-student members are listed. (Adapted from Davis et al., 1988.)*

for Neuroscience listed psychology as their primary departmental affiliation. A recent analysis of the graduate-student members of the Society for Neuroscience confirms this conclusion (Davis, Rosenzweig, Becker, & Sather, 1988)—see Figure 1.3.

1.3 What Types of Research Characterize the Biopsychological Approach?

The complexity of the nervous system and the behavior that it produces dictates the diversity of the research approaches that biopsychologists use to study the relation between the two. To characterize this diversity, this section discusses three important dimensions along which biopsychological research can vary. Biopsychological research can involve either human or nonhuman subjects; it can take the form of either formal experiments or nonexperimental studies; and it can be either pure or applied.

Human and Nonhuman Subjects

Both human and nonhuman animals are the subject of biopsychological research. Of the nonhumans, rats are, without question, the most common subjects; however, mice, cats, dogs, and nonhuman primates are also widely used.

Humans have several advantages as experimental subjects: They can follow instructions, they can report their subjective experiences, and their cages are easier to clean. I am joking, of course, but the joke does serve to draw attention to one advantage that humans have over other species of experimental subjects: Humans are often cheaper. Because only the highest standards of animal care are acceptable, the cost of maintaining an animal laboratory can be prohibitive for all but the most well-funded researchers.

Of course, the greatest advantage that humans have as subjects in a field aimed at understanding the intricacies of human brain function is that they have human brains. In fact, you might wonder why biopsychologists use nonhuman subjects at all. How can the study of laboratory animals reveal anything about human brain function? The answer lies in the evolutionary continuity between the brains of humans and related species. The neurons composing the nervous systems of various species appear to be the same, as do the mechanisms by which the neurons interact. There are even striking similarities between related species in the gross structure of their nervous systems. Other than the obvious difference in size, human brains differ substantially from the brains of their mammalian relatives only in the proliferation of their neocortical tissue. In other words, the differences between the brains of humans and those of related species appear more quantitative than qualitative, and thus many of the principles of human brain function may be extrapolatable from the study of nonhumans (e.g., Kolb & Whishaw, 1989).

Nonhuman animals have three advantages as subjects in biopsychological research. The first is that the brains and behavior of nonhuman subjects are more simple than those of human subjects. Hence, the study of nonhuman species is often more likely to reveal basic principles of brain-behavior interaction. The second is that insights frequently arise from a **comparative approach,** the comparison of brain-behavior relations in different species. For example, comparing the behavior of species that do not have a cerebral cortex with that of species that have a cerebral cortex can provide valuable clues about cortical function. The third is that it is possible to conduct research on laboratory animals that, for ethical reasons, is not possible on human subjects. This is not to say that the study of nonhuman animals is not governed by a rigid code of ethics—it is—but there are fewer ethical constraints on the study of laboratory species than on the study of human subjects. In my experience, most biopsychologists display considerable concern for their subjects whether they are of their own species or not.

It is difficult to impartially weigh the potential benefits of one's own research with the distress that it might entail for one's subjects. Accordingly, the task of judging the morality of a given project is usually handled by independent committees, rather than being left to the discretion of the individual investigator.

Experiments and Nonexperiments

Biopsychological research involves both experiments and nonexperimental studies.

Experiments   The experiment is the method used by scientists to find out what causes what, and as such, it is almost single-handedly responsible for our modern, "high-tech" way of life. It is somewhat paradoxical that a method capable of such complex feats is itself so simple. To conduct an experiment involving living subjects, the experimenter first designs two or more conditions under which the subjects will be tested. Usually a different group of subjects is tested under each condition (**between-subject design**), but sometimes it is possible to test the same group of subjects under each condition (**within-subject design**). The experimenter assigns the subjects to conditions, administers the treatments, and measures the outcome in such a way that there is only one relevant difference between the conditions being compared. This difference between the conditions is called the **independent variable.** The variable that is measured by the experimenter to assess the effect of the independent variable is called the **dependent variable.**

Why is it critical that there be no differences between conditions other than the independent variable? The reason is that when there is more than one difference, it is not possible to determine with absolute certainty whether it was the independent variable or the unintended difference—called a **confounded variable**—that led to effects on the dependent variable. If there is only one difference between experimental conditions, that difference must be responsible for any difference in the dependent variable; there is no other possibility. Although the experimental method seems simple—and it is, conceptually—eliminating all potential sources of confounded variables can sometimes be quite difficult. Readers of research papers must be constantly on the alert for confounds that have gone unnoticed by the experimenters themselves.

A recent experiment by Lester and Gorzalka (1988) provides an interesting illustration of the experimental method in action. The experiment was a demonstration of the so-called Coolidge effect in females. The **Coolidge effect** refers to the fact that once males become incapable of copulating with one sex partner, they often begin copulating with renewed vigor if a new sex partner becomes available. Before your imagination starts running wild, I should mention that the subjects in Lester and Gorzalka's experiment were female hamsters, not students from the undergraduate subject pool.

Lester and Gorzalka argued that the lack of evidence of a Coolidge effect in female animals was not attributable to the fact that males and females are fundamentally different in this respect; they attributed the lack of evidence to the fact that it is more difficult to conduct well-controlled Coolidge-effect experiments in females. The confusion, according to Lester and Gorzalka, stemmed from the fact that the males of most mammalian species become sexually fatigued more readily than do the females. As a result, attempts to demonstrate the Coolidge effect in females are often confounded by the fatigue of the males. When, in the midst of copulation, a female is provided with a new sex partner, the increase in her sexual receptivity could be either a legitimate Coolidge effect or a reaction to the increased vigor of the new male. Because female mammals usually display little sexual fatigue, this confound is not a serious problem in demonstrations of the Coolidge effect in males.

Lester and Gorzalka devised a clever procedure to control for this confound. At the exact time that each subject was copulating with one male (the familiar male), the other male to be used in the test (the new male) was copulating with another female. Then, both males were given a rest while the female was copulating with a third male. Finally, the female subject was tested with either her original partner (the familiar male) or with the new male. The dependent variable was the amount of time that the female displayed **lordosis** (i.e., the arched-back, rump-up, tail-diverted posture of female rodent sexual receptivity) during each sex test. As illustrated in

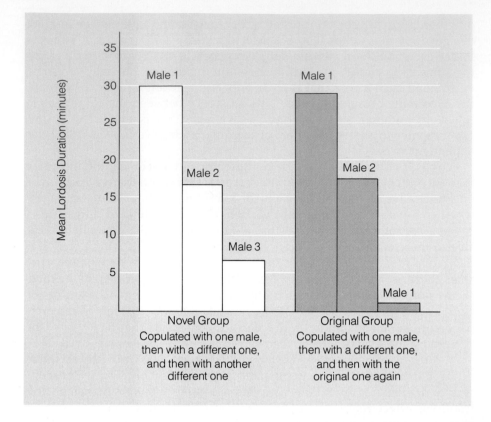

FIGURE 1.4 *The experimental design and results of Lester and Gorzalka (1988). On the third test, the female hamsters were more sexually receptive to novel males than they were to the males with which they had copulated on the first test.*

Figure 1.4, the females responded more vigorously to the new males than they did to the familiar males, despite the fact that both the new and familiar males were equally fatigued. This experiment illustrates the importance of good experimental design and a theme that dominates Chapter 10—that males and females are more similar than most people appreciate.

Correlational Studies   It is not possible for biopsychologists to bring the experimental method to bear on all problems of interest to them. There are frequently physical or ethical impediments that make it impossible to assign subjects to particular conditions or to administer the conditions once the subjects have been assigned to them. For example, experiments on the nature of alcohol-produced brain damage in humans are not feasible. Although many individuals consume alcohol on a regular basis, it would clearly not be ethical for an experimenter to assign a subject to a condition that involves years of alcohol consumption and the attendant risk of brain damage. Some of you may even be concerned with the ethics of assigning subjects to a control condition that requires years of continuous sobriety. In such prohibitive situations, biopsychologists conduct what are called natural or **correlational studies.** If they cannot assign subjects to the conditions that they wish to study, then they must find subjects in the real world who have, in a sense, already assigned themselves to these very conditions.

Consider, for example, the question of the relation between alcohol and brain damage. Although it would not be ethical to assign a subject to an experimental condition involving chronic alcohol consumption, it is possible to find individuals who have been chronic consumers of alcohol through much of their adult lives. For example, one team of researchers compared 100 detoxified, male alcoholics from an alcoholism treatment unit with 50 male nondrinkers obtained from various sources (Acker, Ron, Lishman, & Shaw, 1984). The alcoholics as a group performed more poorly on various tests of perceptual, motor, and cognitive ability, and their brain scans revealed extensive brain damage.

Although this correlational study seems like an experiment in several respects, it is not. Because the subjects themselves decided what group they would be in—by drinking alcohol or not—the researchers had no means of ensuring that alcohol consumption was the only variable that distinguished the two conditions. Can you think of other differences that could reasonably be expected to exist between a group of alcoholics and a group of abstainers that might contribute to the neuroanatomical or intellectual differences between them? There are several. For example, alcoholics as a group tend to be more poorly educated, more prone to accidental head injury, more likely to use other drugs, and more likely to have poor diets. Any of these differences, or any combination of them, could have contributed to the deficits found in the alcoholics. Moreover, in correlational studies it is usually difficult to determine the direction of causation. Did the alcohol cause the intellectual deficits or did they exist prior to the alcohol abuse and contribute to it? Hence, the demonstration that brain damage and behavioral deficits are more prevalent in alcoholics than in nondrinkers does not prove that alcohol caused the brain damage and behavioral deficits (see Wilkinson, 1982). Only experiments can provide a sound basis for identifying causal effects.

There is, in fact, strong evidence that at least some of the brain damage found in alcoholics is the consequence of their typically poor diets. Because alcohol is such a rich source of calories, many alcoholics consume little food and suffer from a variety of vitamin deficiencies. Two lines of clinical evidence suggest that a thiamine (vitamin B_1) deficiency contributes to the brain damage observed in alcoholics (Tuck, Brew, Britton, & Loewy, 1984); injections of thiamine reduce many of the behavioral deficits observed in chronic alcoholics, and many of the symptoms of alcohol-related brain pathology have been observed in nonalcoholic individuals with thiamine-deficient diets. The fact that alcohol has been shown to produce brain damage in laboratory animals even when they are maintained on a nutritionally complete diet (Walker, Barnes, Zornetzer, Hunter, & Kubanis, 1980) suggests that human alcoholics are exposed to a double-edged sword.

Case Studies **Case studies** are studies that focus on a single case or subject. A major problem with case studies has to do with their **generalizability,** that is, with the degree to which the results of the study of one subject can be applied to other cases. Because humans differ markedly from one another in both their brain function and behavior, it is important to be skeptical of any general theory based on a few case studies.

Despite the limitations of correlational and case studies, they can be a valuable complement to a program of experimental research. For example, interest in the neuropathological effects of alcohol began with case study reports of individual alcoholics who showed evidence of brain damage and behavioral impairment. Then, correlational studies confirmed that brain damage and the attendant behavioral deficits were more common in alcoholics than in nondrinkers of the same age. And finally, controlled experiments on laboratory animals confirmed that alcohol does indeed damage the brain in at least two ways, directly by its **neurotoxic** (poisonous to neural tissue) effect and indirectly by its effect on nutrition.

Pure and Applied Research

Biopsychological research can be either applied or pure. Pure and applied research differ in a number of respects, but they can be distinguished less by their own attributes than by the motives of the individuals involved in their pursuit. **Pure research** is motivated primarily by the curiosity of the researcher—it is done for the purpose of contributing knowledge. In contrast, **applied research** is intended to bring about some direct benefit to humankind.

Many scientists believe that pure research often proves to be of more practical benefit than applied research. Their view is that applications flow readily from an understanding of basic principles and that attempts to short-circuit this process by moving directly to application without first gaining a basic understanding of the relevant issues is counterproductive. Of course, it is not necessary for a research project to be completely pure or completely applied; many research programs have elements of both approaches.

One important difference between pure and applied research is that pure research is more vulnerable to the vagaries of political regulation because politicians and the voting public frequently have difficulty understanding why research of no obvious practical benefit should be supported. If the decision were yours, would you be willing to grant the hundreds of thousands of dollars required to support the study of the motor neurons of the squid; learning in recently hatched geese; the activity of single nerve cells in the visual systems of monkeys; the hypothalamic hormones of pigs and sheep; or the function of the corpus callosum, a large neural pathway that connects the left and right cerebral hemispheres? Which, if any, of these projects would you consider worthy of support? If it surprises you to learn that each of these seemingly esoteric projects was supported, you will be even more surprised to learn that each earned a Nobel Prize for its author. Table 1.2 lists the Nobel Prizes awarded for research involving the brain and behavior (Wilhelm, 1983).

1.4 What Are the Four Divisions of Biopsychology?

Biopsychology can be viewed as comprising four main divisions: (1) **physiological psychology,** (2) **psychopharmacology,** (3) **neuropsychology,** and (4) **psychophysiology.** All are characterized by an interest in the relation between neural function and behavior, but each involves a different approach to the topic. They are described here to illustrate biopsychology's diversity. For simplicity, they are presented as distinct approaches, but in reality they are not distinct. There is much overlap between them, and many biopsychologists regularly follow more than one of the four approaches in their research. In fact, the approaches work best when used in combination.

Physiological Psychology

The research of physiological psychologists focuses on the manipulation of the nervous system through surgical, electrical, and chemical means in strictly controlled experimental settings (see Shuttlesworth, Neill, & Ellen, 1984). As a result, the subjects of physiological psychology research are almost always laboratory animals; the nature of the subject matter and the

Table 1.2 *Nobel Prizes Awarded for Studies of the Nervous System and/or Behavior*

NOBEL WINNER	DATE	ACCOMPLISHMENT
Ivan Pavlov	1902	Research on the physiology of digestion
Camillio Golgi and Ramón Y Cajal	1906	Research on the structure of the nervous system
Charles Sherrington and Edgar Adrian	1932	Discoveries regarding the functions of neurons
Henry Dale and Otto Loewi	1936	Discoveries relating to the transmission of nerve impulses
Joseph Erlanger and Herbert Gasser	1944	Research on the functions of single nerve fibers
Walter Hess	1948	Research on the role of the brain in controlling behavior
Egas Moniz	1949	Development of frontal lobotomy in the treatment of psychosis
Georg Von Békésy	1961	Research on the auditory system
John Eccles, Alan Hodgkin, and Andrew Huxley	1963	Research on the ionic basis of neural transmission
Ragnor Granit, Haldan Hartline, and George Wald	1967	Research on the chemistry and physiology of the visual system
Bernard Katz, Ulf Von Euler, and Julius Axelrod	1970	Discoveries concerning the mechanisms of synaptic transmission
Karl Von Frisch, Konrad Lorenz, and Nikolaas Tinbergen	1973	Studies of animal behavior
Roger Guillemin and Andrew Schally	1977	Discoveries concerning hormone production by the brain
Roger Sperry	1981	Research on the differences in behavioral function of the two cerebral hemispheres
David Hubel and Torsten Wiesel	1981	Research on information processing in the visual systems
Rita Levi-Montalcini and Stanley Cohen	1986	Discovery and study of nerve and epidermal growth factors

focus on formal experimentation precludes the use of human subjects in most instances. There is also a tradition of pure research in physiological psychology; the emphasis is often on research that contributes to the development of theories of the neural control of behavior, rather than on research that can be of immediate practical benefit.

Psychopharmacology

Psychopharmacology is similar to physiological psychology in most respects. In fact, many of the early psychopharmacologists were simply physiological psychologists who moved into drug research, and many of today's biopsychologists identify with both approaches. However, the study of the effects of drugs and behavior has expanded so rapidly in recent decades that psychopharmacology is regarded by many as an independent discipline. Psychopharmacologists are primarily concerned with the effects of drugs on behavior and how these effects are mediated by changes in neural activity.

A substantial portion of psychopharmacological research is applied. Although drugs are frequently used by psychopharmacologists to study the basic principles of brain-behavior interaction, the purpose of many psychopharmacological experiments is to develop therapeutic drugs (see Chapter 6) or to reduce drug abuse (see Chapter 16). Psychopharmacologists study the effects of drugs on laboratory species—and on humans, if the ethics of the situation permits it (see McKim, 1986; Meltzer, 1987).

Neuropsychology

Neuropsychology is the study of the behavioral deficits produced in humans by brain damage. Obviously, such effects are not normally amenable to study by experimentation; human subjects cannot ethically be exposed to experimental treatments that endanger normal brain function just for the sake of research. As a result, neuropsychology deals almost exclusively with case studies and correlational studies of patients with brain damage resulting from disease, accident, or neurosurgery. Because it is the outer layer of the cerebral hemispheres, the **neocortex,** that is most likely to be damaged by accident and is most accessible to surgery, the discipline has focused almost exclusively on this important part of the brain.

Neuropsychology is the most applied of the biopsychological subdisciplines; the neuropsychological assessment of human patients, even when part of a program of pure research, is almost always done with an eye toward benefiting them in some way. Neuropsychological tests of brain-damaged patients frequently facilitate diagnosis and thus help the attending physician prescribe an effective treatment; they can also be an important basis for patient care and counseling. Kolb and Whishaw (1985) describe such an application.

> Mr. R., a 21-year-old left-handed man, had struck his head on the dashboard in a car accident two years prior to our seeing him. He was unconscious for a few minutes, but other than a cut on the right side of his forehead and amnesia for the period just before and after the accident, Mr. R. appeared none the worse for his mishap. Prior to his accident Mr. R. was an honor student at a university, with plans to attend professional or graduate school. However, a year after the accident he had become a mediocre student who had particular trouble completing his term papers on time, and although he claimed to be studying harder than he had before the accident, his marks had fallen drastically in courses requiring memorization. He was referred for a neurological exam by his family physician, but it proved negative and an EEG and a CT scan failed to demonstrate any abnormality. He was referred to us for neuropsychological assessment, which revealed several interesting facts. First, Mr. R. was one of about one-third of left-handers whose language functions are represented in the right rather than left hemisphere. This discovery was significant not only in interpreting his difficulties but also in the event that Mr. R. should ever require neurosurgery, since the surgeon would want to respect the speech zones of the neocortex. In addition, although Mr. R. had a superior IQ, his verbal memory and reading speed were low average, which is highly unusual for a person of his intelligence and education. These deficits indicated that his right temporal lobe may have been slightly damaged in the car accident, resulting in an impairment of his language

skills. On the basis of our neuropsychological investigation we were able to recommend vocations to Mr. R. that did not require superior verbal memory skills, and he is currently studying architecture. (pp. 112–113)[1]

Psychophysiology

Psychophysiologists study the relation between physiology and behavior by recording the physiological responses of human subjects (see Andreassi, 1980; Furedy, 1983). Because the subjects of psychophysiological research are human, the recording procedures employed by psychophysiologists are noninvasive; that is, the measures are taken from the surface of the body. The usual measure of brain activity is the scalp **electroencephalogram** (**EEG**). Also commonly recorded in psychophysiological experiments are measures of muscle tension, eye movement, and **autonomic nervous system** (see Chapter 2) activity, such as heart rate, blood pressure, pupil dilation, and electrical conductance of the skin.

Most psychophysiological research focuses on understanding the physiology of basic psychological processes, such as attention, emotion, and information processing, but there have also been a number of interesting clinical applications of psychophysiological data (see Iacono, 1985). For example, as illustrated in Figure 1.5, recent evidence has suggested that

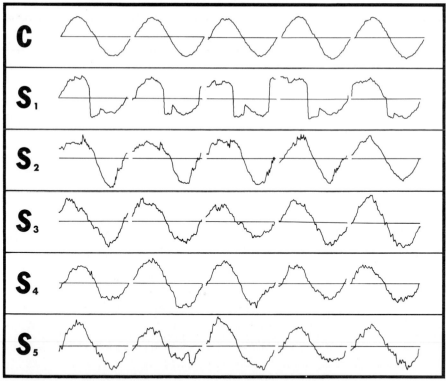

FIGURE 1.5 *Visual tracking of a pendulum by a normal subject (top) and by schizophrenics.*

From "Features That Distinguish the Smooth-Pursuit Eye-Tracking Performance of Schizophrenic, Affective-Disorder, and Normal Individuals" by W. G. Iacono and W. G. R. Koenig, 1983, *Journal of Abnormal Psychology, 92,* p. 39. Copyright 1983 by the American Psychological Association. Reprinted by permission.

---

[1]From *Fundamentals of Human Neuropsychology,* 2nd Edition by Bryan Kolb and Ian Q. Whishaw. Copyright © 1980, 1985 W. H. Freeman and Company. Reprinted with permission.

schizophrenics have difficulty visually tracking a regularly moving object, such as a pendulum (Iacono and Koenig, 1983), and so do many of their parents (Holzman, Solomon, Levin, & Waternaux, 1984).

Because none of the four biopsychological approaches to research is without its shortcomings, major biopsychological issues are rarely resolved by a single experiment or even by a series of experiments taking the same general approach. Progress is most rapid when different approaches are focused on a single problem in such a way that the strengths of one approach compensate for the weaknesses of others; this is called **converging operations.** Consider, for example, the relative strengths and weaknesses of neuropsychology and physiological psychology in the study of the psychological effects of damage to the human neocortex. The strength of the neuropsychological approach in this instance is that it deals directly with human patients; its weakness is that its focus on human patients precludes experiments. In contrast, physiological psychologists can bring the power of the experimental method and neuroscientific technology to bear on the question because their research involves nonhuman animals; the weakness here is that the relevance of research on laboratory animals to the neuropsychological deficits of human patients is always subject to question. Clearly these two approaches complement one another well. Together they can provide strong evidence for points of view that neither can defend individually. The point is that the strength of biopsychology is in its diversity. Although some individual biopsychologists dogmatically adhere to

---

To make sure that you understand the distinctions between these four biopsychological approaches, fill in each of the following blanks. If you have difficulty, review the preceding section before continuing.

1. A biopsychologist who studies the memory deficits of human patients with brain damage would likely identify with the subdivision of biopsychology termed _____.

2. Psychologists who study the physiological correlates of psychological processes by recording physiological signals from the surface of the human body are often referred to as _____.

3. The biopsychological research of _____ frequently involves the direct manipulation or recording of the neural activity of laboratory animals by various invasive surgical, electrical, and chemical means.

4. The subdivision of biopsychology that focuses on the study of the effects of drugs on behavior is often referred to as _____.

The answers to the preceding review questions are: (1) neuropsychology, (2) psychophysiologists, (3) physiological psychologists, and (4) psychopharmacology.

particular approaches in their own research, it is rare to encounter a major biopsychological issue that cannot be fruitfully approached from more than one perspective.

1.5 How Do Biopsychologists Use Observational Methods to Study the Unobservable?

Paradoxically, although the scientific method, in essence, is a system of finding out things by careful observation, many of the processes studied by scientists cannot be directly observed. Surprisingly, the scientific study of the unobservable is not as difficult a problem as it first appears. Scientists routinely use their empirical (observational) methods to study processes, such as ice ages, gravity, evaporation, neural inhibition, thinking, electricity, nuclear fission, and evolution, all of which for various reasons are not accessible to direct observation; the effects of these processes can be observed, but the processes themselves cannot. And biopsychology is no different from the other sciences in this respect—the main task is to characterize through observation the unobservable neural processes by which the nervous system controls behavior.

The method that biopsychologists and other scientists use to study the unobservable is called **scientific inference.** They carefully measure relevant events that can be observed and use these measures as a basis for logically inferring the properties of those that cannot. Like a detective carefully gathering clues to recreate an unwitnessed crime, a biopsychologist carefully gathers data—relevant measures of behavior and neural activity—from which to infer the nature of the neural processes regulating particular classes of behavior.

Because scientific inference is such an integral aspect of biopsychological inquiry, the way that it is utilized in biopsychological research can be illustrated with reference to almost any successful research project in the field. I have selected for illustrative purposes a research project in which you can participate both as a subject and as an experimenter. By making a few simple observations of your own visual abilities under different conditions, you will be able to discover for yourself one of the basic principles by which the brain perceives motion.

How does your brain translate the movement of images on your retinas into perceptions of movement? One feature of the mechanism is immediately obvious. If you look at your hand in front of your face and then move its image across your retinas by moving your eyes, by moving your hand, or by combining both activities, you will notice immediately that your brain works in a very adaptive way. Only movements of the retinal image produced by the movement of objects in the visual field are translated into visual perceptions of motion; movements of the retinal image produced by your own eye movements are not. Obviously, there must be a part of the brain that monitors the movement of the retinal image and subtracts from the total those movements of the retinal image produced by your own eye movements, leaving the remainder to be perceived as motion in the visual field.

Let's carry this analysis a bit further and try to characterize in more detail the nature of the information about eye movement used by the brain in its perception of motion. Try the following experiment. Shut one eye and rotate your other eye slightly upward by gently pressing on your lower eyelid with your fingertip. What do you see? What you should see is all of the objects in the visual field moving downward.

Why, when the eye is passively rotated, do you perceive movement in the opposite direction? One possibility is that the brain mechanism responsible for perceiving motion does not consider eye movement per se; it may consider only those eye movements actively produced by neural signals from the brain to the eye muscles, and not those passively produced by external means. Because the passive upward rotation of the eye produces a shift in the retinal image that is like what would be produced in a stationary eye by a downward shift of the entire visual field (see Fig. 1.6), a mechanism insensitive to passive movement would assume that the eye had remained stationary and thus that the entire visual field had moved downward.

It is possible to trick the visual system in the opposite way; instead of moving the eyes when no active signals have been sent to the eye muscles, the eyes can be held stationary despite the brain's attempts to move them. Because this experiment involves paralyzing the eye muscles, you cannot participate. Hammond, Merton, and Sutton (1956) injected *d*-tubocurarine, the active ingredient of the paralytic substance with which some South American natives coat their blow darts, into the eye muscles of their subject—which was Merton himself. What do you think Merton saw when he tried to move his eyes? Merton saw the stationary visual world moving in the same direction as his attempted eye movements. If a visual object is focused on part of your retina and it stays focused there despite the fact that you have moved your eyes to the right, it too must have moved to the right. Consequently, when Merton sent signals to his eye muscles to move the eyes to the right, the brain assumed that the movement was carried out, and it perceived stationary objects as moving to the right. It is clear

FIGURE 1.6 *The perception of motion under four different conditions.*

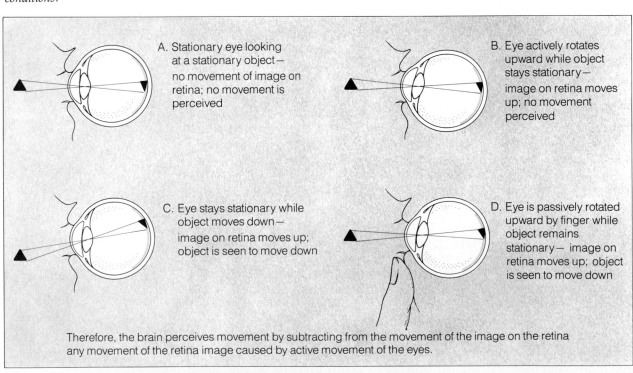

A. Stationary eye looking at a stationary object— no movement of image on retina; no movement is perceived

B. Eye actively rotates upward while object stays stationary— image on retina moves up; no movement perceived

C. Eye stays stationary while object moves down— image on retina moves up; object is seen to move down

D. Eye is passively rotated upward by finger while object remains stationary— image on retina moves up; object is seen to move down

Therefore, the brain perceives movement by subtracting from the movement of the image on the retina any movement of the retina image caused by active movement of the eyes.

from these observations that the visual system bases its perception of motion on a comparison between movements of the image on the retina and the commands sent from the brain to the eye muscles, rather than with the eye movements themselves. The point of this all—if you have forgotten—is that biopsychologists and other neuroscientists can learn much about the activities of the brain without directly observing them.

A physician inferring the internal causes of a disease from overt symptoms, a successful treasure hunter inferring the site of a sunken galleon from archival documents, and a skilled bridge player inferring the location of the lone unplayed trump card from the pattern of play all use scientific inference. Has it occurred to you that you use scientific inference? You may not be as good at it as a scientist or as the other aforementioned experts, but you use it nonetheless. Think of the last time that you misplaced your wallet or your keys. After your initial frenzied search, you undoubtedly tried to bring your powers of inference to bear on the problem; you accumulated as much relevant information as possible, and from it you tried to infer the location of the missing item. If you consider the great feeling of satisfaction that you get when you successfully use your powers of inference to solve such everyday problems, you will appreciate the attraction of scientific research as a career.

1.6 What Is Bad Science, and How Do You Spot It?

Scientists, like other people, make mistakes, and biopsychologists are no exception in this respect. In fact, two features of biopsychological inquiry make it particularly susceptible to error. The first is that biopsychological research has such a wide appeal that it tends to invite the participation of those who have had little or no first-hand experience with its complexities. The second is that it is often difficult to remain objective when studying biopsychological issues. Whether we realize it or not, we all bring to the analysis of biopsychological issues many preconceptions about the brain and behavior that can be major impediments to its objective analysis. You might wonder why a book about biopsychology would dwell, even momentarily, on errors in biopsychological research. There are two reasons. One is that an understanding of such errors provides important insights into what biopsychology is—the standards and methods—and why. The standards and methods of a discipline frequently grow out of its mistakes. As certain lines of logic are found wanting, as certain research designs are shown to have inherent confounds, and as certain lines of research are found to be unfruitful, they are phased out and the discipline evolves. Another reason for dwelling on errors is to encourage you to become good consumers of science. Individuals familiar with examples of scientific error are less likely to be passive consumers of science; that is, they are less likely to accept without question any statement credited to a scientist, and they are more likely to have the basic skills necessary to evaluate for themselves the validity of various claims. In other words, one purpose of this final section of Chapter 1 is to improve your B.S. detection skills—B.S., in this context stands for bad science.

Following are the descriptions of two well-known examples of biopsychological analysis that are seriously flawed.

Case 1

José Delgado demonstrated to a group of newspaper reporters a remarkable new procedure for controlling aggression. Delgado strode into a Spanish bull ring carrying only a red cape and a small radio transmitter. With the transmitter he could activate a battery-powered stimulator that had previously been mounted on the horns of the other inhabitant of the ring. As the raging bull charged, Delgado calmly activated the stimulator and sent a weak train of electrical current from the stimulator through an electrode that had been implanted in the *caudate nucleus* of the bull's brain. The bull immediately veered from its charge. After a few such interrupted charges, the bull stood tamely as Delgado walked about the ring. According to Delgado, this demonstration marked a significant scientific breakthrough—the discovery of the caudate taming center and the fact that stimulation of this structure could eliminate aggressive behavior, even in bulls specially bred for their ferocity.

To those present at this carefully orchestrated event and to most of the millions who subsequently read about it, Delgado's conclusion was a compelling one. Surely if caudate stimulation could stop the charge of a raging bull, the caudate must be a taming center. It was even suggested that caudate stimulation through implanted electrodes might be an effective treatment for human psychopaths. What do you think?

Analysis of Case 1

The fact of the matter is that Delgado's demonstration provided little or no support for his conclusion. It should have been obvious to anyone who did not get caught up in the provocative nature of Delgado's media event that there are numerous ways in which brain stimulation can abort a bull's charge, most of which are more simple, and thus more probable, than the one suggested by Delgado. For example, the stimulation may have simply rendered the bull confused, dizzy, nauseous, sleepy, or temporarily blind rather than nonaggressive; or the stimulation could have been painful. Clearly, any observation that can be interpreted in so many different ways provides little support for any one interpretation. When there are several possible interpretations for a behavioral observation, the rule is to give precedence to the most simple, rather than to the most complex and provocative. This rule is called **Morgan's Canon**. The following comments of Valenstein (1973) provide a more reasoned view.

> . . . actually there is no good reason for believing that the stimulation had any direct effect on the bull's aggressive tendencies. An examination of the film record makes it apparent that the charging bull was stopped because as long as the stimulation was on it was forced to turn around in the same direction continuously. After examining the film, any scientist with knowledge in this field could conclude only that the stimulation had been activating a neural pathway controlling movement. (p. 98)
> . . . he [Delgado] seems to capitalize on every individual effect his electrodes happen to produce and presents little, if any, experimental evidence that his impression of the underlying cause is correct. (p. 103)
> . . . his propensity for dramatic, albeit ambiguous, demonstrations has been a constant source of material for those whose purposes are served by exaggerating the omnipotence of brain stimulation. (p. 99)

Case 2

In 1949, Dr. Egas Moniz was awarded the Nobel Prize in Physiology and Medicine for the development of the **prefrontal lobotomy** (cutting connections between the prefrontal lobes and the rest of the brain) as a treatment for mental illness. Moniz's discovery was based on the report that Becky, a chimpanzee that frequently became upset when she made errors during the performance of a food-rewarded task, did not do so following a large, bilateral (both sides of the brain) lesion of her prefrontal cortex. After hearing Jacobsen mention this

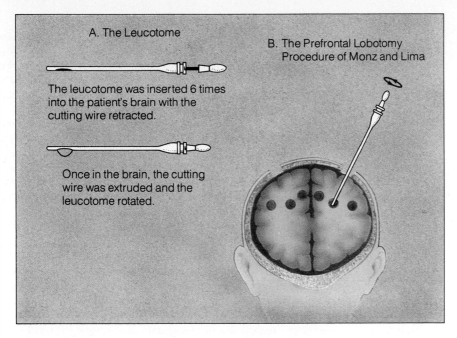

A. The Leucotome

The leucotome was inserted 6 times into the patient's brain with the cutting wire retracted.

Once in the brain, the cutting wire was extruded and the leucotome rotated.

B. The Prefrontal Lobotomy Procedure of Monz and Lima

FIGURE 1.7 *The original prefrontal lobotomy procedure developed by Moniz.*

isolated observation at a scientific meeting in the summer of 1935, Moniz persuaded neurosurgeon Almeida Lima to operate on a series of his (Moniz's) psychiatric patients. The first prefrontal lobotomy, performed in November of the same year, involved cutting out six large cores of prefrontal tissue with a device called a **leucotome** (see Figure 1.7).

Following Moniz's claims that the prefrontal surgery was therapeutically successful and had no significant side effects, there was a rapid proliferation of various forms of prefrontal psychosurgery (see O'Callaghan & Carroll, 1982; Valenstein, 1980). One such variation was the **transorbital lobotomy** popularized in the United States by Walter Freeman in the late 1940s. It involved inserting an icepick-like device under the eyelid, driving it through the orbit (the eye socket) with a few taps of a mallet, and pushing it into the frontal lobes, where it was waved back and forth to sever the connections between the prefrontal area and the rest of the brain (see Figure 1.8). This operation was frequently performed in the surgeon's office.

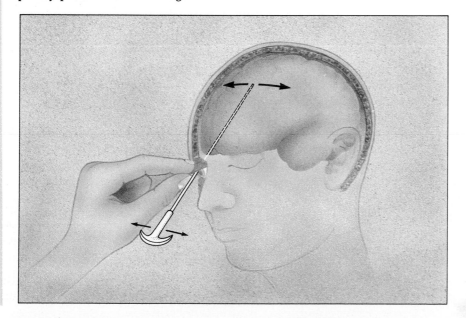

FIGURE 1.8 *The transorbital procedure for performing prefrontal lobotomy.*

Analysis of Case 2

Incredible as it may seem, Moniz initiated his program of psychosurgery based on the observation of a single chimpanzee, thus displaying a complete lack of appreciation for the great diversity of brain and behavior, both within and between species. No program of psychosurgery should ever be initiated without first assessing the effects of the surgery on a large sample of subjects from various nonhuman mammalian species.

A second major weakness in the scientific case for prefrontal psychosurgery was the failure of Moniz and others to carefully evaluate the consequences of the surgery in the first patients to undergo the operation. There were some early reports that the operation was therapeutically successful, but these were based, for the most part, on the general impressions of the very individuals who were least objective—the physicians who had prescribed the surgery. Patients were frequently judged as improved if they were more manageable, and little effort was made to evaluate more important aspects of psychological adjustment or to document the existence of adverse side effects.

Few lobotomies have been performed since the 1950s. The accumulation of reports that it was of no real therapeutic benefit and that it produced a wide range of undesirable side effects, such as amorality, lack of foresight, emotional unresponsiveness, epilepsy, and urinary incontinence, led to its eventual abandonment—but not before over 40,000 patients had been lobotomized in the United States alone. Some regard the fundamentals of scientific protocol

> as unduly strict: as unnecessary obstacles in the path of patients seeking treatment and therapists striving to provide it. However, the barely discarded practices of purging and blood-letting [and prefrontal lobotomy] should caution us against abandoning science for expediency. . . . Only by insisting on careful and controlled study . . . and only by observing the rules of science can the public be protected from inappropriate and bogus [scientific claims and clinical remedies] (Carroll, 1984, p. 109).

There is a particularly somber postscript to this story. Dr. Moniz was shot by one of his lobotomized patients and was rendered *paraplegic* (paralyzed below the waist) by the bullet, which became lodged in his spine.

Conclusion

The general purpose of this chapter is to introduce you to the field of biopsychology and to whet your appetite for more of it. You learned that biopsychology is the study of the nervous system and behavior, that it is one component of a massive and diverse neuroscientific research effort, and that it in turn comprises four fundamentally different approaches: physiological psychology, psychopharmacology, neuropsychology, and psychophysiology. And finally, you were provided with examples of both good and bad biopsychology: the good examples illustrated the ways in which biopsychologists use the scientific method to answer questions about the brain and behavior, and the bad examples demonstrated the importance of adhering to the fundamental principles of scientific inquiry and of greeting claims of major scientific breakthroughs with a healthy degree of caution and skepticism.

You are about to enter a world of amazing discoveries and intriguing ideas: the world of biopsychology. I hope that you enjoy it, and I hope that it challenges and stimulates you.

1. In retrospect, the entire prefrontal lobotomy episode is shocking. How could physicians, who are intelligent, highly educated, and dedicated to helping their patients, participate in such a travesty? How could somebody win a Nobel Prize for developing a form of surgery that left over 40,000 mental cripples in the United States alone? Why did this happen? Could it happen today?

2. Chapter 1 tells you in general conceptual terms what biopsychology is. Another, and perhaps better, way of defining biopsychology is to describe what biopsychologists do. If you are using this book as a text, ask your instructor to describe what she or he did to become a biopsychologist and what activities dominate her or his work day. I think that you will be surprised. Is she or he predominantly a physiological psychologist, a psychopharmacologist, a neuropsychologist, or a psychophysiologist?

ADDITIONAL READING

Each of the following provides an excellent introduction to one of the four biopsychological disciplines:

Andreassi, J. L. (1980). *Psychophysiology*. New York: Oxford.

Carlson, N. R. (1986). *Physiology of behavior* (3rd ed.). Boston, Massachusetts: Allyn and Bacon.

Kolb, B., & Whishaw, I. Q. (1989). *Fundamentals of human neuropsychology* (3rd ed.). New York: Freeman.

McKim, W. A. (1986). *Drugs and behavior: An introduction to behavioral pharmacology*. Englewood Cliffs, New Jersey: Prentice-Hall.

This book of readings provides an excellent overview of the topic of psychosurgery:

Valenstein, E. S. (1980). *The psychosurgery debate: Scientific, legal, and ethical perspectives*. New York: Freeman.

The following article is a good discussion of what biopsychology is and how it is related to the other neurosciences:

Davis, H. P., Rosenzweig, M. R., Becker, L. A., & Sather, K. J. (1988). Biological psychology's relationships to psychology and neuroscience. *American Psychologist, 43,* 359–371.

KEY TERMS

To help you study the material in this chapter, all of the key terms—those that have appeared in bold type—are listed and briefly defined here.

Applied research. Research that is intended to bring about some direct benefit to humankind.

Autonomic nervous system. The part of the peripheral nervous system that participates in the regulation of the internal environment.

Between-subject design. An experimental design in which a different group of subjects is tested under each condition.

Biological psychiatry. Study of the biological bases of psychiatric disorders and their treatment through the manipulation of the brain.

Biopsychology. A subdiscipline of neuroscience concerned with how the brain and the rest of the nervous system control behavior.

Case study. A study of a single case or subject.

Comparative approach. Research focusing on the comparison of different species.

Confounded variable. An additional, unintended difference between conditions in an experiment.

Converging operations. The use of several research approaches to solve a single problem.

Coolidge effect. When males incapable of copulating with one sex partner begin copulating with a new sex partner.

Correlational study. A study in which subjects are not assigned to conditions, but are studied in their various real-world conditions.

Dependent variable. The variable measured by the experimenter; the variable on which the independent variable acts.

Developmental neurobiology. Study of how the nervous system changes as an organism matures and ages.

Electroencephalogram (EEG). A measure of the general electrical activity of the brain, often recorded through the scalp.

Generalizability. The degree to which the results of a study can be applied to other individuals or situations.

Independent variable. The difference between experimental conditions that is arranged by the experimenter.

Leucotome. Any one of the various surgical devices used for performing lobotomies—*leucotomy* is another word for lobotomy.

Lordosis. The arched-back, rump-up, tail-diverted posture of female rodent sexual receptivity.

Morgan's Canon. Of several possible interpretations for a behavioral result, the most simple should be given precedence.

Neocortex. The layer of neural tissue covering the cerebral hemispheres of humans and other mammals.

Neuroanatomy. The study of the structure of the nervous system.

Neurobiology. Neuroscience.

Neurochemistry. The study of the chemical bases of neural activity.

Neuroendocrinology. The study of the interaction of the nervous system with the endocrine system.

Neuroethology. The study of the relation between the nervous system and behavior of animals that occurs in their natural environment.

Neurons. Cells of the nervous system that are specialized for receiving and transmitting electrochemical signals.

Neuropathology. The study of nervous system disorders.

Neuropharmacology. The study of the effects of drugs on the nervous system.

Neurophysiology. The study of the responses of the nervous system, particularly those involved in transmission of electrical signals through and between neurons.

Neuropsychology. The study of behavioral deficits produced in humans by brain damage.

Neuroscience. The scientific study of the nervous system; neurobiology.

Neurotoxic. Poisonous to neural tissue.

Physiological psychology. Research that focuses on the direct manipulation of the nervous system of animal subjects in controlled experimental settings.

Prefrontal lobotomy. Cutting the prefrontal lobes from the rest of the brain as a treatment for mental illness.

Psychopharmacology. The study of the effects of drugs on behavior.

Psychophysiology. The study of the relation between behavior and physiological signals recorded from the surface of the human body.

Pure research. Research motivated primarily by the curiosity of the researcher.

Scientific inference. The logical process by which observable events are used to infer the properties of unobservable events.

Society for Neuroscience. An international association of neuroscientists.

Transorbital lobotomy. A prefrontal lobotomy performed with an instrument inserted through the eye socket.

Within-subject design. An experimental design in which the same subjects are tested in each condition.

2

The Anatomy of the Nervous System

You learned in Chapter 1 that biopsychology is an integrative enterprise. It is a discipline that has taken up the ultimate challenge of neuroscience by focusing squarely on the interaction between the nervous system and behavior. Because of the fundamental duality of biopsychological research, biopsychologists must keep their feet firmly planted in two camps. They must bring to their studies, in addition to their primary commitment to the study of behavior and psychological processes, a sound knowledge of the nervous system. You must do the same.

This chapter is about the anatomy of the nervous system. It has three purposes: to give you a general idea of the structure of the human nervous system, to describe some of the methods that are commonly used to study neuroanatomy, and to provide you with a basic vocabulary that you can use to refer to the nervous system's major components. Many people react to the last objective with some apprehension. There is no disguising the fact that in order to acquire a basic neuroanatomical vocabulary, you are going to have to engage in some good old-fashioned rote memorization. However, I can assure you of two things. First, it is necessary. There is no way to discuss most biopsychological topics without knowing the names of their major components. Second, the number of neuroanatomical terms introduced in this chapter has been kept to a minimum. The purpose of this chapter is to provide you with a general introduction—more detail is provided at those points in the book where it is directly relevant and in the appendices at the end of the book (see Appendices I to IV).

The anatomy of the nervous system and some of the methods used to study it are discussed in seven separate sections:

2.1 **General Layout of the Nervous System**

2.2 **Neurons and Glia: The Building Blocks of the Nervous System**

2.3 **Neuroanatomical Directions and Planes**

2.4 **The Spinal Cord**

2.5 **The Five Major Divisions of the Brain**

2.6 **Major Structures of the Brain**

2.7 **Finding Out What Is Connected to What: Neuroanatomical Tracing**

2.1 General Layout of the Nervous System

The Major Divisions of the Nervous System

The nervous system has two major divisions: the **central nervous system** (CNS) and the **peripheral nervous system** (PNS). The CNS is the portion of the nervous system that is contained within the bony central core of the body (the skull and the spine), and the PNS is the portion that is not. Figure 2.1 illustrates the human CNS and PNS.

The CNS is itself composed of two divisions: the brain and the spinal cord. The *brain* is the part of the CNS that is contained within the skull, and the *spinal cord* is the part that is contained within the spine.

The PNS is also composed of two major divisions: the somatic nervous system and the autonomic nervous system (*ANS*). In general, the **somatic nervous system** is the part of the PNS that interacts with the external environment. It is composed of **afferent nerves,** which carry sensory input from receptors in the skin, joints, eyes, and ears, etc. to the central nervous system, and **efferent nerves,** which carry signals from the central nervous system out to the skeletal muscles, which produce overt behavior. In general, the **autonomic nervous system** is that part of the PNS that participates in the regulation of the internal environment. Accordingly, afferent nerves of the ANS carry signals from the organs of the body to the CNS, and efferent nerves of the ANS carry signals from the CNS back out to the organs. You will not get the terms *afferent* and *efferent* confused if you remember that many words that involve the idea of *going toward* something begin with an "a" (e.g., advance, approach, arrive) and that many words that involve the idea of *going away* from begin with an "e" (e.g., exit, embark, escape).

The autonomic nervous system has two kinds of efferent nerves: sympathetic nerves and parasympathetic nerves. In general, the **sympathetic nerves** stimulate, organize, and mobilize energy resources to deal with threatening situations, whereas the **parasympathetic nerves** generally act to conserve energy. Most organs receive input from both the sympathetic and parasympathetic arms of the autonomic nervous system, and thus, their activities are controlled by the relative levels of sympathetic and parasympathetic activity. For example, heart rate is increased by signals from sympathetic nerves and decreased by signals from the parasympathetic nerves. The distribution of sympathetic and parasympathetic fibers is illustrated in Appendix I.

You have probably already noticed that the nervous system is a system of twos. If you haven't, you will when you inspect Figure 2.2, which schematically summarizes the major divisions of the nervous system.

Most of the nerves of the peripheral nervous system extend from the CNS at the level of the spinal cord, but there are 12 exceptions: the 12 pairs of **cranial nerves,** which extend from the brain and which are numbered in sequence from top to bottom. These include purely sensory (afferent) nerves such as the *olfactory nerves* (the first cranial nerves) and the *optic nerves* (the second cranial nerves), but most contain both sensory and motor fibers. The longest cranial nerve is the *vagus nerve* (the tenth cranial nerve), which carries sensory and motor fibers to and from the gut and is considered to be a branch of the parasympathetic nervous system. The 12 pairs of cranial nerves and their targets are illustrated in Appendix II.

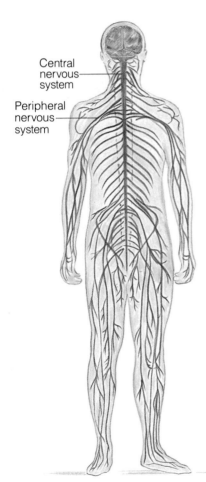

Central nervous system

Peripheral nervous system

FIGURE 2.1 *The human central nervous system (CNS) and peripheral nervous system (PNS).*

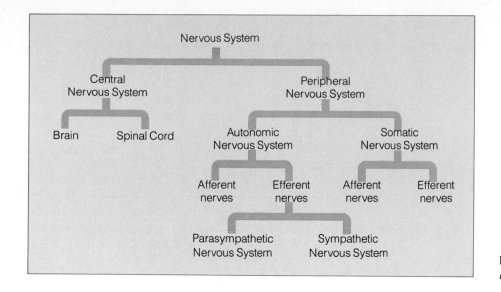

FIGURE 2.2 *The major divisions of the nervous system.*

The Meninges, the Ventricles, and the Cerebrospinal Fluid

The brain and spinal cord are the most protected organs in the body. In addition to being encased in bone, they are swaddled in three protective membranes, the **meninges** (pronounced MEN in gees). The outer menynx (which, believe it or not, is the singular of meninges) is a tough membrane called the **dura mater** (tough mother). Immediately inside the dura mater is the spongy **arachnoid membrane.** Beneath the arachnoid membrane is a space called the **subarachnoid space,** which contains the large blood vessels. The innermost menynx is the delicate **pia mater** (pious mother), which adheres to the surface of the CNS tissue itself.

Also protecting the central nervous system is a bath of colorless fluid, the **cerebrospinal fluid** (*CSF*), which fills the subarachnoid space and the spaces in the core of the brain and spinal cord. There is a small CSF-filled passage called the **central canal,** which runs down the core of the spine; and there are four large CSF-filled internal chambers or **ventricles** in the brain: the two *lateral ventricles,* the *third ventricle,* and the *fourth ventricle.* The four cerebral ventricles, central canal, and the *cerebral aqueduct,* which connects the third and fourth ventricles, are illustrated in Figure 2.3.

The brain actually floats in the cerebrospinal fluid, and the fluid's buoyancy provides the brain with considerable protection from mechanical injury. The important role played by the cerebrospinal fluid in supporting and cushioning the brain is all too apparent to patients who have had some of their cerebrospinal fluid drained away. They suffer raging headaches, and they experience stabbing pains each time they suddenly move their heads.

Cerebrospinal fluid is continuously produced by networks of capillaries (small blood vessels), called **choroid plexuses,** which protrude into the ventricles from their pia mater lining. The excess cerebrospinal fluid is continuously absorbed from the subarachnoid space into large blood-filled spaces or *sinuses,* which run through the dura mater and drain into the large jugular veins of the neck. Figure 2.4 illustrates the absorption of

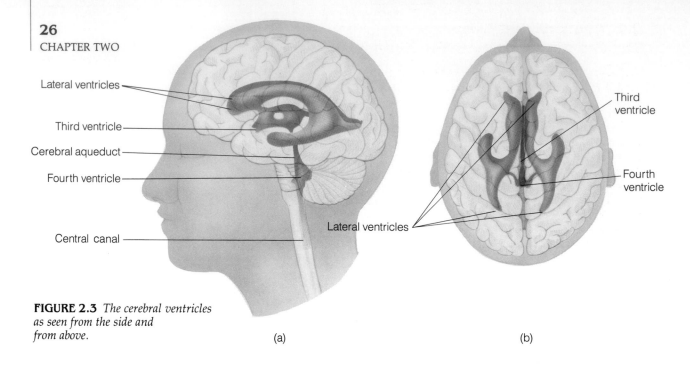

Lateral ventricles

Third ventricle

Cerebral aqueduct

Fourth ventricle

Central canal

Third ventricle

Fourth ventricle

Lateral ventricles

FIGURE 2.3 *The cerebral ventricles as seen from the side and from above.*

(a)

(b)

cerebrospinal fluid from the subarachnoid space into the large **superior sagittal sinus,** which runs in the dura mater along the top of the brain between the two hemispheres.

Occasionally the flow of cerebrospinal fluid from the lateral ventricles is blocked—usually by a tumor at one of the narrow channels, called **foramens,** that link the ventricles. The build-up of fluid in the ventricles causes the walls of the ventricles, and thus the entire brain, to expand, producing a condition called *hydrocephalus* (literally "water head"). Hydrocephalus is treated by draining the excess fluid from the ventricles and trying to remove the obstruction.

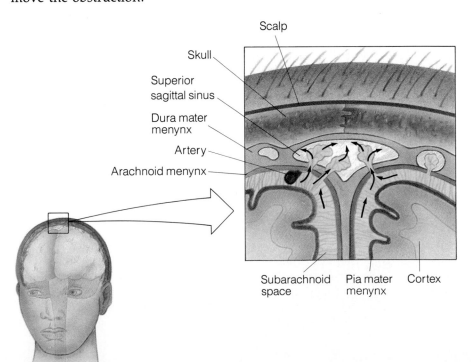

Scalp

Skull

Superior sagittal sinus

Dura mater menynx

Artery

Arachnoid menynx

Subarachnoid space

Pia mater menynx

Cortex

FIGURE 2.4 *The absorption of cerebrospinal fluid from the subarachnoid space into the superior sagittal sinus. Note the three meninges.*

2.2 Neurons and Glia:
The Building Blocks of the Nervous System

When did neurons and nervous systems first appear during the course of evolution—and why? These questions have proven extremely difficult to answer.

> The problem is that nerve cells seem to have sneaked into phylogeny: they are much like other cells, with attributes all cells share. For one thing, all cells are irritable: almost any stimulus—mechanical prodding, heat or cold, electricity—can trigger a local change in the membrane forming the envelope of the cell, so that the membrane's permeability to various ions is altered. In this way, currents of ions are made to flow through the membrane; thus the concentration of ions on each side of the membrane changes, and with it the voltage difference across the membrane. In the second place, all cells are conductive: a local alteration in permeability can advance along the membrane, so that an altered bioelectric potential spreads over the surface of the cell. Although nerve cells or neurons have developed these attributes notably well—neurons are exquisitely irritable and exquisitely conductive—the universality of their most characteristic properties makes investigations into neural phylogeny extremely problematic. (Nauta & Feirtag, 1986, pp. 4–5)

One of the most significant events in the study of the nature and evolution of the nervous system was the accidental discovery of the **Golgi stain** by Golgi (pronounced GOLE gee), an Italian physician, in the early 1870s. According to one of his laboratory assistants, Golgi was trying to stain the meninges by exposing a block of neural tissue first to potassium dichromate and then to silver nitrate, when he noticed the most amazing thing. For some still unknown reason, the silver chromate created by the chemical reaction between the potassium dichromate and the silver nitrate invaded only a few cells in each slice of tissue, and it stained each invaded cell entirely black. This fortuitous discovery made it possible to see the shape of individual neurons for the first time (see Figure 2.5). Stains that dye all of the neurons on a given slide in their entirety reveal nothing of the

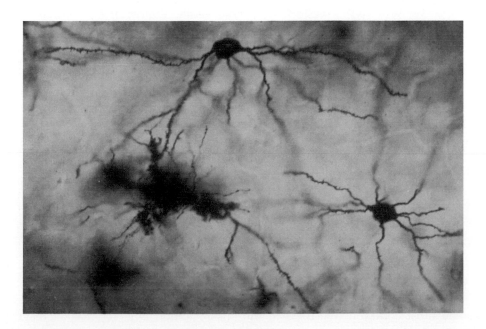

FIGURE 2.5 *Neural tissue stained by the Golgi method. Because only a few cells are stained, their silhouettes are revealed in great detail. Usually only part of a neuron is captured in a single slice. (Courtesy of Steven Vincent, Kinsmen Laboratory of Neurological Research, University of British Columbia.)*

structure of individual neurons because neurons are so tightly woven together. Accordingly, the accidental discovery of the mysterious selectivity of the Golgi stain unquestionably ranks as one of the greatest blessings to befall neuroscience in its early years.

Early in this century, Golgi-stain studies of the tissues of primitive animals provided several insights into the evolution of the nervous system (Parker, 1919). In sea anemones, the most simple organism studied by Parker, each neural circuit involves only a single neuron. Emanating from each *epithelial cell* (a cell of the surface layer of tissue or epithelium) of the tentacles surrounding the mouth is a single neural filament, which projects to a muscle fiber of the same tentacle. Thus, every time a tentacle is touched by a particle floating in the water, the tentacle contracts and brings the particle into contact with the digestive processes of the mouth. Although this single-neuron circuit is well suited to its one simple function, it lacks the flexibility of more complex neural circuits.

Certain simple jellyfishes have a slightly more complex neural arrangement. In these creatures, neural fibers that project from *sensory neurons* in epithelial tissue do not terminate directly on muscle fibers. Instead, they terminate on an array of neurons, which in turn terminate on muscle fibers (neurons terminating on muscle fibers are called *motor neurons*). These two-neuron circuits provide the potential for some flexibility. In this two-neuron scheme, the activation of a motor neuron can depend on the interaction between signals from various sensory neurons impinging on it. Such two-stage nervous systems involving sensory (afferent) and motor (efferent) neurons required, for the first time in evolutionary history, functional interactions between neurons. These interactions occur at points, called **synapses,** where the fibers of one neuron come into close proximity to another. At these points, the sensory neurons release a chemical, called a **neurotransmitter,** that stimulates the motor neurons.

The third evolutionary advance noted by Parker was identified in complex jellyfishes and mollusks. In these creatures, there was a complex intermediate nerve net intervening between the sensory and motor neurons. In a sense, this third evolutionary step in nervous system evolution is the final step. The nervous systems of all "higher" organisms share with these complex jellyfishes and mollusks the fact that their nervous systems comprise only three basic kinds of neurons: sensory neurons, motor neurons, and *interneurons* (the neurons of the great intermediate nerve net). Hence, the development of the three-stage nervous system seems to have occurred quite early in evolutionary history. Figure 2.6 illustrates the evolution of the three-stage nervous system—note the synapses, through which interneuronal communication takes place.

The Structure of Neurons

The fact that the Golgi technique stains only a few neurons on a slide, but stains them completely, is both its strength and its weakness. Although it provides an excellent view of the silhouette of the few neurons that take up the black stain, it provides no indication of the total number of neurons in an area or of the details of their inner structure. The first neural staining procedure to circumvent these shortcomings was the **Nissl stain,** which was developed by Franz Nissl in the 1880s and is still widely used today. The most common dye used in the Nissl method is *cresyl violet.* Cresyl

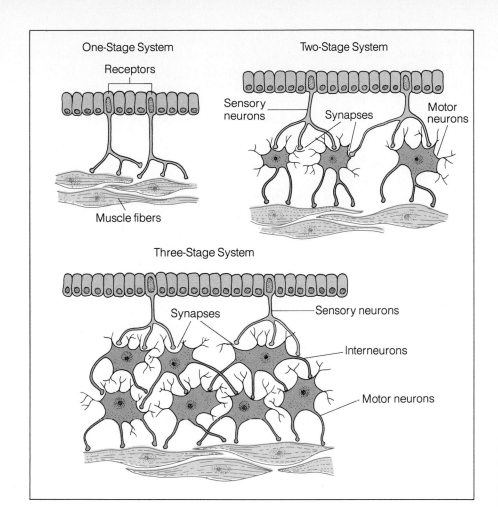

FIGURE 2.6 *A schematic illustration of Parker's three stages of nervous system evolution: the one-stage circuit, the two-stage circuit, and the three-stage circuit.*

violet and other Nissl dyes penetrate all cells on a slide, but they bind densely only to structures in the **cytoplasm** (internal fluid of the cell) of the **cell bodies** (metabolic centers of cells, also called the *somas*) of neurons. In the early years, these neuronal structures to which Nissl stains bound were referred to as *Nissl bodies,* but now we know that these structures are, in fact, aggregations of **ribosomes,** the intracellular structures that assemble amino acids into proteins under the direction of strands of messenger ribonucleic acid (**messenger RNA or mRNA**). The manufacture of proteins by ribosomes in the neuron cell body is illustrated schematically in Figure 2.7. Ribosomes are present in all cells, but only in neuronal cell bodies do they aggregate so densely, and thus stain so darkly.

Presented in Figure 2.8 is a photograph of a slice of tissue cut from a brain structure called the hippocampus and stained with the cresyl violet. Notice how only the well-defined cell-body layers stain densely.

Another neuroanatomical procedure that has provided a great deal of information about neuronal structure is **electron microscopy** (pronounced my CROSS cuh pee). Because of the nature of light, the limit of magnification in light microscopy is 1500 times, which is not sufficient to reveal the fine anatomical details of neurons. Greater detail can be obtained by coating thin slices of neural tissue with an electron-absorbing substance that is taken up by different parts of neurons to different degrees. Then a beam of electrons is passed through the tissue onto a photographic film, and the

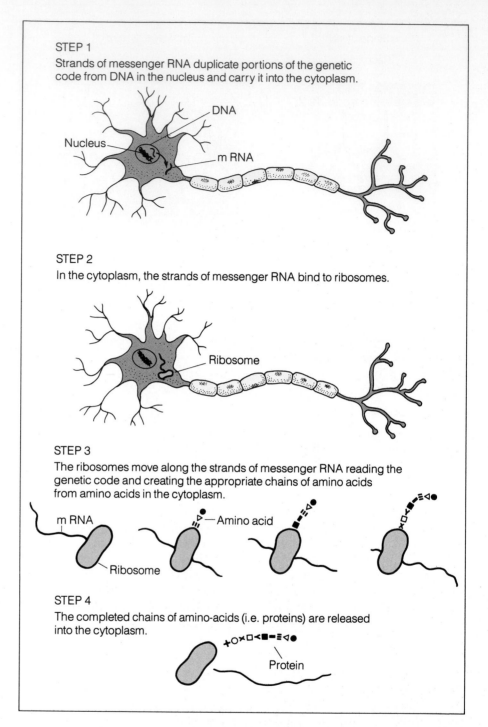

STEP 1
Strands of messenger RNA duplicate portions of the genetic code from DNA in the nucleus and carry it into the cytoplasm.

STEP 2
In the cytoplasm, the strands of messenger RNA bind to ribosomes.

STEP 3
The ribosomes move along the strands of messenger RNA reading the genetic code and creating the appropriate chains of amino acids from amino acids in the cytoplasm.

STEP 4
The completed chains of amino-acids (i.e. proteins) are released into the cytoplasm.

FIGURE 2.7 *A schematic illustration of the synthesis of proteins from amino acids in the neuron cell body by ribosomes under the direction of messenger RNA.*

result is an *electron micrograph,* which is capable of revealing neuronal structure in exquisite detail (see Figure 3.13). Although the *scanning electron microscope* is not capable of as much magnification, it provides beautiful electron micrographs in three dimensions (see Figure 2.9).

With an arsenal of neuroanatomical techniques at their disposal (e.g., the Golgi stain, the Nissl stain, and electron microscopy), each providing a different view of neural tissue, neuroanatomists have been able to characterize the structure of neurons in great detail. The most important rule to

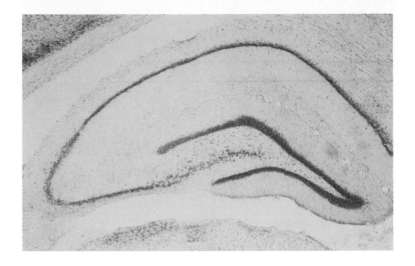

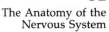

FIGURE 2.8 *A Nissl-stained section (slice) of the hippocampus, a structure that you will be learning much about in Chapters 14 and 15 because of its important role in learning and memory. Notice the well-defined cell-body layers. (Courtesy of Steven Vincent, Kinsmen Laboratory of Neurological Research, University of British Columbia.)*

remember about the structure of neurons is that there are no firm rules: Neurons come in an incredible assortment of different shapes and sizes.

Many of the neurons in the mammalian nervous system are comparable in major respects to the one illustrated schematically in Figure 2.10. Note the following labeled structures:

cell membrane   the semipermeable membrane that encloses the neuron

cytoplasm   the liquid of the neuron's interior

cell body   (*soma*) the metabolic center of the neuron, which contains the nucleus

nucleus   the structure in the cell body that contains the genetic material or **deoxyribonucleic acid** (DNA)

dendrites   the short processes emanating from the cell body, which, along with the cell body itself, receive most of the synaptic contacts from other neurons

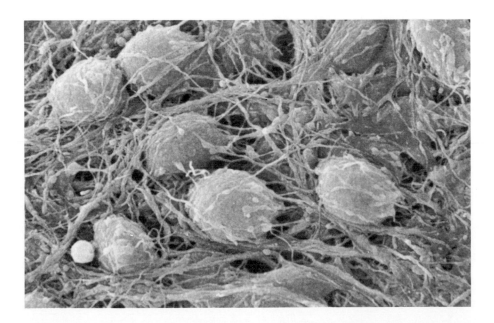

FIGURE 2.9 *A scanning electron micrograph of a cluster of neuron cell bodies, studded with terminal buttons (Phototake/Scott).*

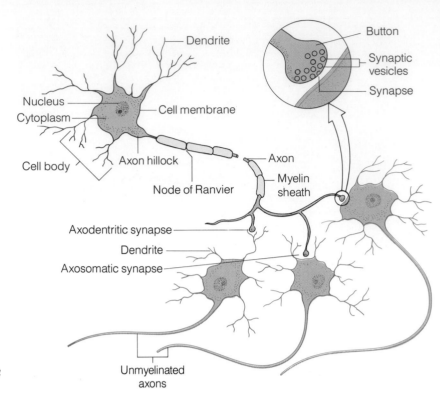

FIGURE 2.10 *A schematic diagram of a multipolar neuron.*

axon   the long, narrow process that leaves the cell body

axon hillock   the cone-shaped region where the axon leaves the cell body

myelin sheath   segments of fatty insulation found around many axons

nodes of Ranvier (pronounced ron vee yay)   the *unmyelinated* gaps between sections of myelin

buttons   the swollen endings of the axon branches, which synapse on the postsynaptic cells

synaptic vesicles   tiny packets containing neurotransmitter molecules, which are stored near synapses in the presynaptic neuron

axosomatic synapses   synapses between axons and cell bodies

axodendritic synapses   synapses between axons and dendrites

Figure 2.11 illustrates some of the diversity of neural structure. A simple way to classify a neuron is to count the number of processes emanating from its cell body. Most neurons, like the one in Figure 2.10, have many processes extending from the cell body, and are thus classified as **multipolar neurons.** Neurons with one process extending from the cell body are classed as **unipolar,** and those with two are classed as **bipolar.** Neurons that do not have axons or that have very short ones typically function as interneurons.

Many of the nervous system structures that you will be introduced to later in this chapter are clusters of neural cell bodies. In the CNS, these clusters are called **nuclei**—not to be confused with the nucleus inside each cell body—and in the PNS, they are called **ganglia** (singular is "ganglion"). Similarly, many axons travel through the body in large axon bundles. These bundles of axons are called **tracts** in the CNS and **nerves** in the PNS.

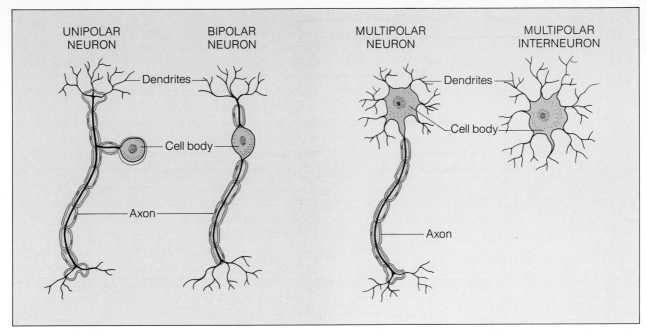

UNIPOLAR NEURON   BIPOLAR NEURON   MULTIPOLAR NEURON   MULTIPOLAR INTERNEURON

Dendrites — Cell body — Axon — Dendrites — Cell body — Axon

FIGURE 2.11 *Unipolar neurons, bipolar neurons, multipolar neurons, and interneurons.*

Glial Cells and Satellite Cells

Neurons are not the only inhabitants of the nervous system. In the central nervous system, there are also cells called **glial cells,** *neuroglia,* or just plain *glia.* They are thought to outnumber neurons 10 to 1. The term *neuroglia* literally means "nerve glue," and it alludes to the role of glial cells in providing a matrix that holds CNS neurons together. This supportive function is performed in the PNS by similar cells called **satellite cells.**

The largest glial cells are called **astroglia** or astrocytes because they are star-shaped (from the Greek *astron,* meaning *star*). Astroglia form most of the matrix in which neurons are embedded, but they also appear to serve another important function. Because their processes envelop blood vessels coursing through the brain, it has been hypothesized that they play a role in the selective transfer of substances from blood to neurons. Accordingly, they are thought to be one of the mechanisms of the so-called **blood-brain barrier,** which keeps certain toxic substances in the blood from penetrating the neural tissue.

Other glial cells, called **oligodendroglia** or oligodendrocytes, send out myelin-rich processes that wrap around and around the axons of many of the neurons in the CNS. As you will learn in Chapter 3, the **myelin** sheaths formed by these processes increase the speed and efficiency of axonal transmission. A similar function is performed by **Schwann cells** (a class of satellite cells) in the PNS. In Chapter 5, there is a discussion of *multiple sclerosis,* a disease that disrupts axonal transmission by attacking myelin. The myelination of a PNS axon is illustrated in Figure 2.12.

One of the main differences between Schwann cells and oligodendroglia is that only the former can guide axonal *regeneration* (regrowth) after damage. Accordingly, there is normally no axonal regeneration in the mammalian CNS (see Chapter 15).

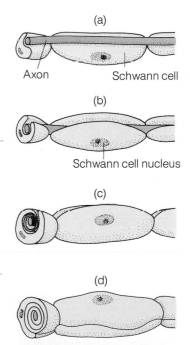

(a)

Axon   Schwann cell

(b)

Schwann cell nucleus

(c)

(d)

FIGURE 2.12 *The myelination of a PNS axon. The Schwann cells wrap themselves around and around the axon.*

2.3 Neuroanatomical Directions and Planes

Locations in the nervous system are usually described in relation to the orientation of the spinal cord. The system is straightforward for most animals. As indicated in Figure 2.13, the nose end of such animals is referred to as the **anterior** end, and the tail end is referred to as the **posterior** end. These same coordinates are sometimes referred to as **rostral** (toward the beak) and **caudal** (toward the tail), respectively. The back is referred to as the **dorsal** surface, and the stomach is referred to as the **ventral** surface. **Medial** means toward the midline, and **lateral** means away from the midline.

We humans complicate this simple three-dimensional (anterior-posterior, ventral-dorsal, medial-lateral) system of neuroanatomical directions by insisting on walking around on our hind legs, thus changing the orientation of our brains in relation to our spines. However, you can save yourself some confusion if you remember two things: first, that the system was originally designed for animals whose normal spine and brain orientation is horizontal, and second, that it was adapted for use in primates in such a way that the terms used to describe the positions of various parts of the nervous system are the same as in non-upright animals. The fundamental comparability of the system of neuroanatomical coordinates in upright and nonupright organisms is illustrated in Figure 2.14. Notice that the neuroanatomical directions on a standing dog or human refer to the same parts of the anatomy as they do on a dog in its normal position. For example, notice that the stomach and the bottom of the head are referred to as ventral regardless of the animal's posture. Similarly, the front of the head is always anterior. In primates, the terms **superior** and **inferior** are often used to refer to the top and bottom of the head, respectively.

In the next few pages, you will be seeing drawings of *sections* (slices) of the brain cut in one of three different planes: **horizontal, coronal (frontal),**

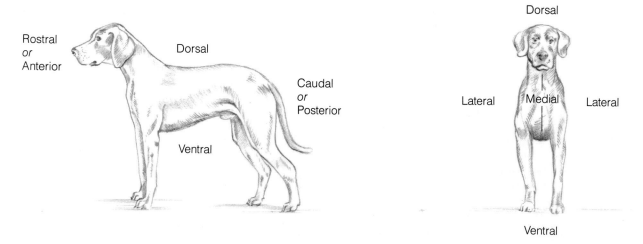

FIGURE 2.13 *Anatomical directions on a four-legged animal.*

or **sagittal.** These three planes are illustrated in Figure 2.15. A section cut down the center of the brain, between the two hemispheres, is called a *midsagittal section*. A section of tissue cut at a right angle to any long, narrow structure, such as the spinal cord or a nerve, is called a **cross section.**

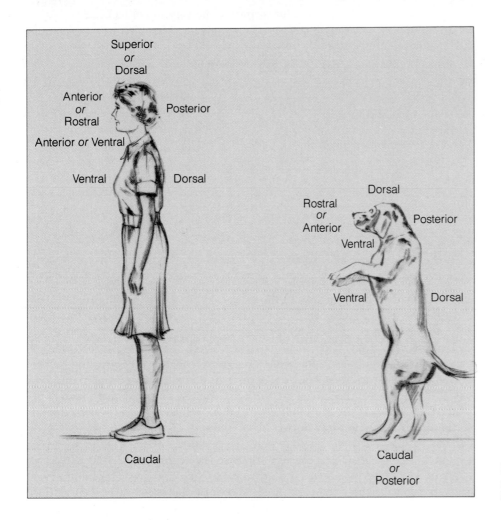

FIGURE 2.14 *A comparison of neuroanatomical directions in humans and dogs.*

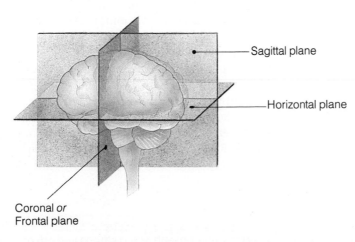

FIGURE 2.15 *The orientation of horizontal, coronal (frontal), and sagittal sections in the human brain.*

To test your comprehension of neuroanatomical directions, review the preceding section and fill in the following blanks:

1. The nose of a dog is _____ and _____ (or rostral) to the very top of its head.

2. The nose of a human is _____ (or inferior) and _____ to the very top of his or her head.

3. A slice taken in the _____ plane will expose both the nose and the throat.

4. A slice taken in either the _____ (or frontal) or the _____ plane will expose both eyes.

2.4 The Spinal Cord

The spinal cord is a hollow cylinder of neural tissue that is housed within the protective confines of the spine. In cross section (Figure 2.16), it is apparent even from casual inspection that it can be divided into two different areas: an inner H-shaped core of gray matter and a surrounding area of white matter. The gray matter is largely composed of cell bodies and small, unmyelinated interneurons, whereas the surrounding white matter is largely composed of ascending and descending myelinated axons. It is the myelin that gives the white matter its glossy white sheen. The four arms of the spinal gray matter are often referred to as the two **dorsal horns** and the two **ventral horns.**

Pairs of *spinal nerves* pass between the vertebrae of the spine and enter the spinal cord—one from the left and one from the right—at 31 different levels of the spine. As shown in Figure 2.16, each of these 62 spinal nerves splits in two as it nears the cord, and its axons enter the cord via one of two roots: the *dorsal root* or the *ventral root.*

All the axons of the dorsal root are sensory. Most of them are axons of sensory receptors of the skin, muscles, and joints. The cells of the dorsal roots are all unipolar neurons with their cell bodies grouped together just outside the cord to form the *dorsal root ganglia* and their synaptic terminals in the dorsal horn of the spinal cord gray matter (see Figure 2.17). In contrast, the neurons of the ventral root are all multipolar neurons with their cell bodies in the ventral horn. Those that are part of the somatic nervous system project to skeletal muscles, whereas those that belong to the autonomic nervous system leave the cord and travel to a ganglion (a group of cell bodies in the PNS), at which point they synapse on other

The answers to the preceding review questions are: (1) ventral; anterior; (2) ventral; anterior; (3) midsagittal; and (4) coronal; horizontal.

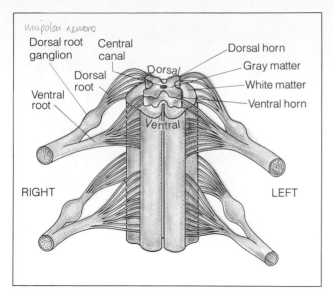

unipolar neurons

Dorsal root ganglion
Central canal
Dorsal root
Ventral root
Dorsal
Ventral
Dorsal horn
Gray matter
White matter
Ventral horn

RIGHT
LEFT

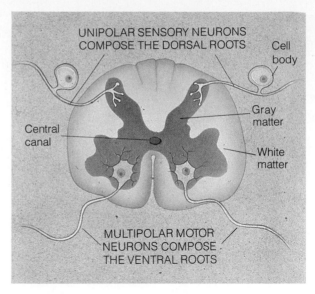

UNIPOLAR SENSORY NEURONS COMPOSE THE DORSAL ROOTS
Cell body
Central canal
Gray matter
White matter
MULTIPOLAR MOTOR NEURONS COMPOSE THE VENTRAL ROOTS

FIGURE 2.16 *The peripheral nerves associated with two sections of the spinal cord.*

FIGURE 2.17 *A schematic cross section of the spinal cord illustrating the sensory and motor neurons.*

multipolar neurons that project to the target organ (e.g., heart, stomach). Accordingly, the neurons of the autonomic nervous system are classified as either *preganglionic* or *postganglionic* (before the ganglion or after the ganglion); see Appendix I.

2.5 The Five Major Divisions of the Brain

The vertebrate nervous system is considered to have five major divisions. In sequence from caudal (tail) to rostral (beak), these are the **myelencephalon,** the **metencephalon,** the **mesencephalon,** the **diencephalon,** and the **telencephalon** (*encephalon* means *within the head*). These five divisions reflect the changes that the brain goes through during its embryological development. In the developing vertebrate embryo, the tissue that will eventually develop into the CNS is first noticeable as a simple fluid-filled tube (see Figure 2.18). The first indications of the developing brain are three swellings that occur at the rostral end of this tube. These are the antecedents of the *forebrain*, the *midbrain* (mesencephalon), and the *hindbrain*.

In higher vertebrates, it is the forebrain that undergoes the most extensive development. Large lateral outgrowths occur on the rostral end of the forebrain and these eventually develop into the cerebral hemispheres, the division of the forebrain that is known as the telencephalon. The more caudal part of the forebrain, which does not develop into the cerebral hemispheres, is known as the diencephalon. It is also conventional to divide the hindbrain into two divisions. Swellings develop on the dorsal and ventral surface of the rostral portion of the hindbrain, and this portion is known as the metencephalon. The remaining, caudal portion of the hindbrain is the myelencephalon, also known as the *medulla*. The portion of the brain caudal to the telencephalon is often referred to as the **brain stem**—it is the stem from which the two hemispheres branch.

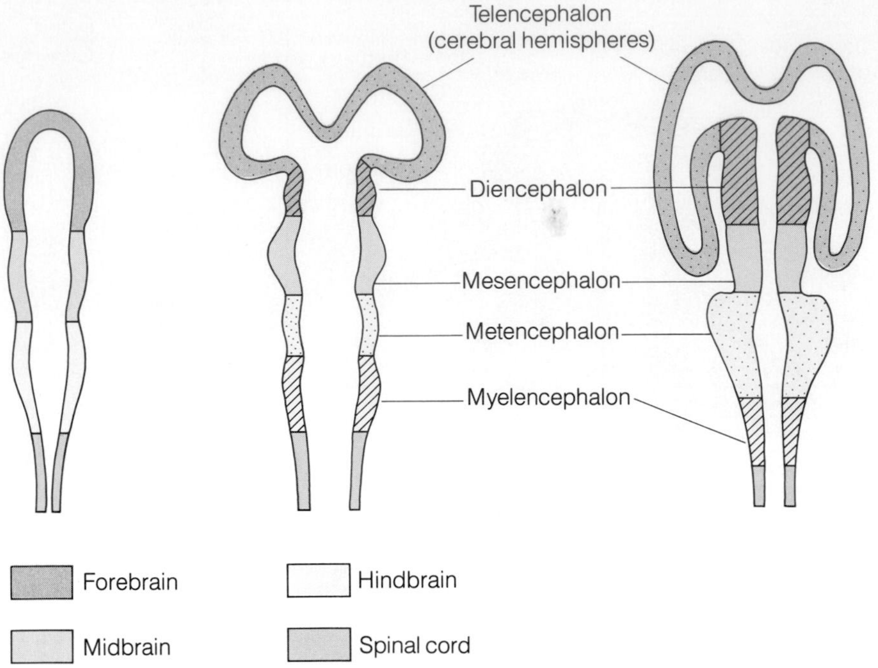

Telencephalon
(cerebral hemispheres)

Diencephalon

Mesencephalon

Metencephalon

Myelencephalon

Forebrain   Hindbrain

Midbrain   Spinal cord

FIGURE 2.18 *A schematic illustration of the early development of the mammalian brain, drawn from the top. Compare this figure with Figure 2.19, which is a sagittal schematic view of the adult mammalian brain color-coded according to the same scheme.*

2.6 The Major Structures of the Brain

The major structures of the brain that are about to be described are illustrated in the simplified schematic sagittal section of a generalized mammalian brain presented in Figure 2.19. Examine it carefully before proceeding. You will also find it useful for review purposes.

Myelencephalon

Not surprisingly, the myelencephalon (medulla), the most caudal division of the brain, is composed almost entirely of tracts (bundles of axons in the CNS) carrying signals between the rest of the brain and the body. In addition, it contains the nuclei of the cranial nerves that leave the brain at this level (see Appendix II).

An interesting part of the myelencephalon from a psychological perspective is the reticular formation. The **reticular formation** is a complex, loosely defined network of about 100 tiny nuclei and their interconnections that occupies the central core of the brain stem from the caudal boundary of the myelencephalon to the rostral boundary of the midbrain. Early neuroanatomists gave it this name because of its net-like appearance—*reticulum* means "little net." Sometimes the reticular formation is referred to as the *reticular activating system* (RAS) because parts of it seem to play a role in arousal; however, recent research suggests that the nuclei of the reticular formation are involved in a variety of specific, unrelated functions, including sleep, attention, movement, muscle tone, and various cardiac, circulatory, and respiratory reflexes. Accordingly, referring to this collection of nuclei as a "system" is somewhat misleading.

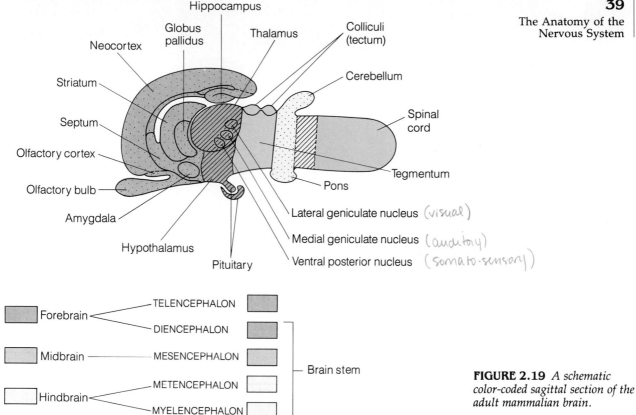

Neocortex
Striatum
Septum
Olfactory cortex
Olfactory bulb
Amygdala
Hippocampus
Globus pallidus
Thalamus
Colliculi (tectum)
Cerebellum
Spinal cord
Tegmentum
Pons
Lateral geniculate nucleus (visual)
Medial geniculate nucleus (auditory)
Ventral posterior nucleus (somato-sensory)
Hypothalamus
Pituitary

Forebrain — TELENCEPHALON
DIENCEPHALON
Midbrain — MESENCEPHALON
Hindbrain — METENCEPHALON
MYELENCEPHALON
Brain stem

FIGURE 2.19 *A schematic color-coded sagittal section of the adult mammalian brain.*

Metencephalon

The metencephalon, like the myelencephalon, houses many ascending and descending tracts, the nuclei of several cranial nerves, and part of the reticular formation. These structures create a bulge, called the **pons,** on the brain stem's ventral surface. The other division of the metencephalon is the **cerebellum** (meaning *little brain*), the large convoluted structure clearly visible on its dorsal surface. The cerebellum is an important structure of the sensorimotor system (see Chapters 9 and 15).

Mesencephalon

The most obvious external feature of the mesencephalon or midbrain is the layer of tissue called the **tectum.** The word *tectum* means *roof*, and the tectum is the roof or dorsal surface of the midbrain. In mammals, the tectum forms two pairs of bumps or colliculi (little hills). In higher vertebrates the more caudal pair, which have an auditory function, are called the **inferior colliculi,** and the more rostral pair, which have a visual function, are called the **superior colliculi.** In lower vertebrates, the tectum is composed of only a single pair of bumps, and it is referred to as the *optic tectum* because its function is entirely visual.

Figure 2.20 is a drawing of a cross section taken through the human midbrain. The area of the midbrain ventral to the tectum is generally referred to as the **tegmentum.** In addition to the reticular formation, cranial

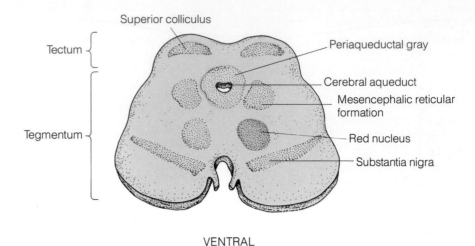

DORSAL

Superior colliculus

Tectum

Periaqueductal gray

Cerebral aqueduct

Mesencephalic reticular formation

Tegmentum

Red nucleus

Substantia nigra

VENTRAL

FIGURE 2.20 *A drawing of a cross section through the mammalian mesencephalon or midbrain.*

nerves, and tracts of passage, the tegmentum has three structures that have been of particular interest to biopsychologists: the periaqueductal gray, the substantia nigra, and the red nucleus. The *periaqueductal gray* is the gray matter situated around the **cerebral aqueduct,** the small duct connecting the third and fourth ventricles. The periaqueductal gray is of special interest because of its role in mediating the *analgesic* (pain-reducing) effects of opiate drugs (see Chapter 8). Both the **substantia nigra** and the **red nucleus** are important components of the sensorimotor system (see Chapter 9).

Diencephalon

The diencephalon is composed of two major structures: the **thalamus** constitutes its dorsal portion, and the **hypothalamus** constitutes its ventral portion. The thalamus is a large two-lobed structure that is the top of the human brain stem (see Figure 2.21). One lobe sits on each side of the third ventricle. The two lobes of the thalamus are joined by the **massa intermedia,** which is a small **commissure** (a tract joining the left and right cerebral hemispheres) that runs right through the third ventricle. Surprisingly, many apparently normal people have been found to lack a massa intermedia.

The thalamus comprises many different pairs of nuclei, most of which project to the cortex. Some of the nuclei of the thalamus are sensory processing stations for specific sensory systems. They receive signals from sensory receptors, process them, and then transmit them to the appropriate areas of the sensory cortex. For example, the **lateral geniculate nuclei,** the **medial geniculate nuclei,** and the **ventral posterior nuclei** are important processing stations in the visual, auditory, and somatosensory systems, respectively. Those thalamic nuclei that are not sensory processing stations project either specifically to particular areas of the cortex that do not have a sensory function, or they project diffusely to vast areas of cortex. The various thalamic nuclei are illustrated in Appendix III.

Although the hypothalamus is a small structure (*hypo* means *less than*), only about one-tenth the size of the thalamus in humans, it has been shown to play an important role in the regulation of several motivated behaviors. In part, it exerts its effects by regulating the release of hormones from the **pituitary gland** (see Chapter 10), which dangles from it on the ventral surface of the brain. The literal meaning of pituitary gland is *snot gland*. Because the early anatomists who first described it found it behind the nose in a somewhat decomposed, gelatinous condition in an unembalmed cadaver, they incorrectly assumed that it was the main source of nasal mucus and named it accordingly.

Also clearly visible on the inferior (ventral) surface of the brain (see Figure 2.22), just in front of the pituitary, is an X-shaped structure called the **optic chiasm.** The optic chiasm is the point at which the *optic nerves* (the second cranial nerves) from each eye come together. The X-shape is created because some of the axons of the nerve **decussate** (cross over to the other side of the brain) at this point. The decussating fibers are said to be **contralateral** (projecting from one side of the body to the other), and the nondecussating fibers are said to be **ipsilateral** (staying on the same side of the body). The tiny pair of spherical structures clearly visible just posterior to the pituitary are the **mammillary bodies,** two prominent nuclei of the hypothalamus. The mammillary bodies and the other nuclei of the hypothalamus are illustrated in Appendix IV.

Telencephalon

The telencephalon is the largest division of the human brain, and it subserves the most complex functions. It initiates voluntary movement, interprets sensory input, and mediates various cognitive processes such as learning, language, and problem solving. Not surprisingly, it is the portion of the brain that is of most interest to many psychologists.

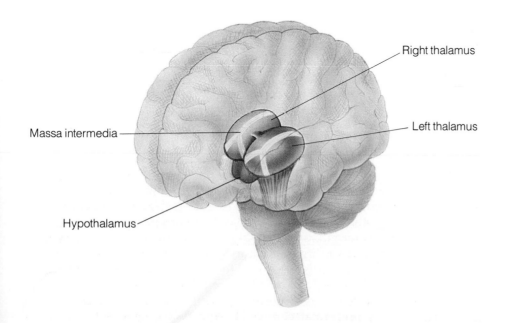

FIGURE 2.21 *The location of the human diencephalon.*

Right thalamus

Left thalamus

Massa intermedia

Hypothalamus

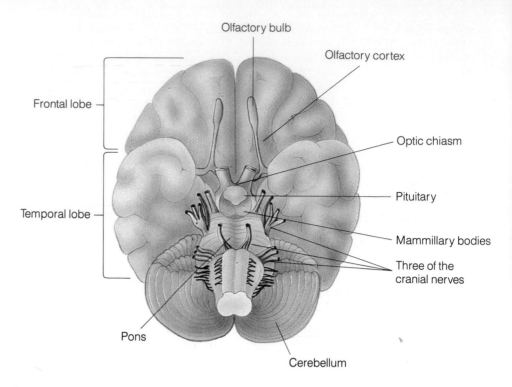

FIGURE 2.22 *The inferior surface of the human brain.*

Cortex The cerebral hemispheres are covered by a layer of tissue called the **cerebral cortex** (literally *cerebral bark*). In humans, the cortex is deeply furrowed. This furrowing has the effect of increasing the amount of cerebral cortex without increasing the overall volume of the brain—the surface area of the cerebral cortex is estimated at 1.5 square feet. Not all mammals have furrowed cortices; for example, rats (see Figure 2.8) and some New World monkeys such as squirrel monkeys are *lissencephalic* (smooth-brained). Because the human brain is so highly convoluted, it is widely believed that the degree of cortical convolution is directly related to an animal's intellectual development; however, the degree of convolution appears to be related more to an animal's size. Every large mammal has a deeply convoluted cortex.

The large furrows in a convoluted cortex are called **fissures,** and the small ones are called **sulci** (singular *sulcus*). The ridges between fissures and sulci are called **gyri** (singular *gyrus*). The convolutions of the human brain and the degree to which they increase the area of cerebral cortex are illustrated in Figure 2.23; Notice that the cerebral hemispheres are almost completely separated by the **longitudinal fissure.** The hemispheres are joined by a few tracts called commissures. The largest is the **corpus callosum,** which is visible in Figure 2.23; most are quite small.

As indicated in Figure 2.24, the major landmarks on the surface of the human cortex are four deep fissures, the two **central fissures** and the two **lateral fissures,** and their adjacent gyri (gyruses). The **precentral gyri** serve a motor function, the **postcentral gyri** are **somatosensory** (i.e., receive input from sensory receptors of the skin, joints, and muscles), and the **superior temporal gyri** are largely auditory. These major fissures serve as a basis for dividing each hemisphere into four lobes: the **frontal lobe,** the **parietal lobe,** the **temporal lobe,** and the **occipital** (pronounced awk SIP i tul) **lobe.** It is common to refer to the anterior, nonmotor cortex of the frontal lobe as the **prefrontal cortex.** The function of the cortex of the occipital lobe is entirely visual (see Chapter 8).

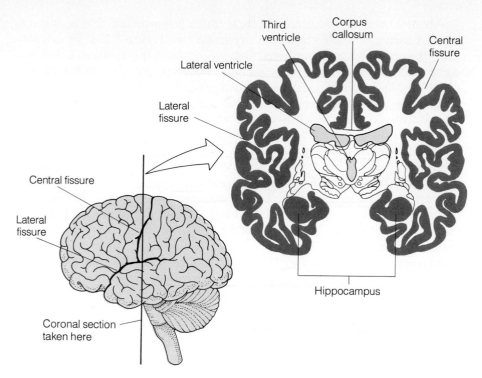

FIGURE 2.23 *A drawing of a frontal (coronal) section of the human brain. Notice the location and shape of the hippocampus.*

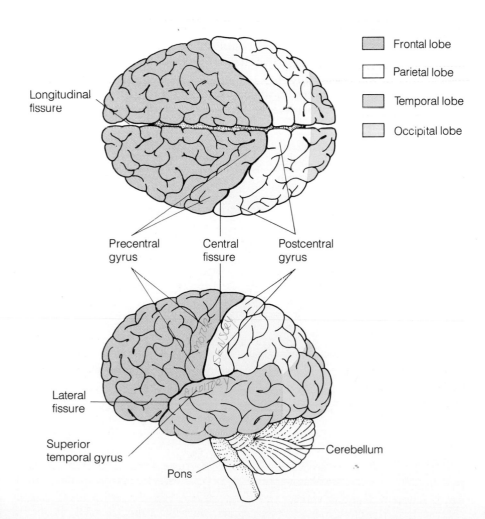

FIGURE 2.24 *The lateral and dorsal surfaces of the human cerebral hemispheres.*

About 90 percent of human cerebral cortex is **neocortex;** that is, it is six-layered cortex of relatively recent evolution (see Figure 2.25). By convention, the six layers are numbered, beginning from the surface. Layer 1 is composed almost entirely of axons and dendrites, and thus is not readily visible in Nissl-stained sections. In mammals, two areas of cerebral cortex lack the six-layer structure characteristic of neocortex. One of these areas is the **olfactory cortex,** which is on the ventral surface of the frontal lobes, adjacent to the olfactory bulbs (see Figure 2.22). The olfactory cortex has three cell layers—two with cell bodies and one without. Almost all of the cerebral cortex of fish and most of the cerebral cortex of reptiles and birds is olfactory cortex. The other area of cerebral cortex in humans that is not neocortex is the hippocampus. The **hippocampus** is formed at the inferior, medial edge of the cortex as it folds back on itself in the medial temporal lobe. Notice in Figure 2.23 that this folding produces a shape that when viewed in frontal section is somewhat reminiscent of a sea horse—*hippocampus* means *sea horse.* The hippocampus has only two cell layers, one with cell bodies and one without. Olfactory cortex and hippocampal cortex are often referred to as **paleocortex** (literally *old cortex*) because of their early phylogenetic (evolutionary) origins.

The Limbic System and the Basal Ganglia   Although most of the subcortical portion of the telencephalon is taken up by fibers of passage, there are several large nuclear groups of importance. Most of them are considered to be part of either the limbic system or the basal ganglia motor system. Don't be misled by the word *system* in this context; it implies a level of certainty that is unwarranted. It is not entirely clear exactly what these hypothetical systems do, exactly what structures should be included in them, or even if it is appropriate to view them as unitary systems. Nevertheless, if not taken too literally, the concepts of a limbic system and a basal ganglia motor system provide a useful means of conceptualizing the organization of the subcortex.

The *limbic system* is a group of interconnected telencephalic and diencephalic structures that are believed to be involved in the regulation of

FIGURE 2.25 *The six layers of the neocortex; a drawing of a Nissl-stained section viewed under low magnification.*

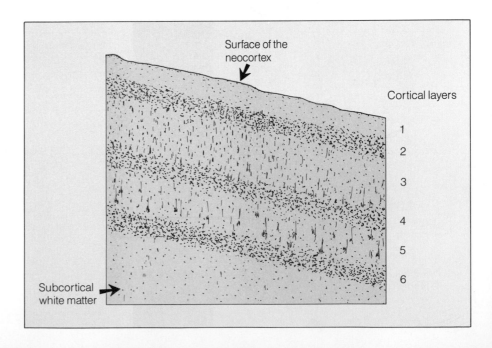

Surface of the neocortex

Cortical layers

1

2

3

4

5

6

Subcortical white matter

motivated behaviors—including the four F's of motivation: fleeing, feeding, fighting, and sexual behavior. (This joke is as old as biopsychology itself, but it is a good one.) In addition to several structures about which you have already read (the hypothalamus and mammillary bodies, the anterior nuclei of the thalamus, and the hippocampus), the amygdala, the cingulate cortex, the septum, and the fornix are commonly considered to be part of the limbic system. The **amygdala** (meaning "almond") is a large group of nuclei situated in each temporal lobe just anterior to the hippocampus, and the **septum** is situated on the midline just below the front of the corpus callosum and in front of the hypothalamus. The **cingulate cortex** is in a gyrus (the **cingulate gyrus**) that is hidden from external view in the longitudinal fissure just above the corpus callosum. The **fornix** (meaning "arch") is the major pathway of the system; it projects in an arc from the hippocampus along the edge of the third ventricle and then to the anterior nuclei of the thalamus, septum, and hypothalamus. The major structures of the limbic system are presented in Figure 2.26.

The basal ganglia of the left hemisphere are presented in Figure 2.27. There is the **globus pallidus,** which sits just lateral to the thalamus in each hemisphere; the **putamen** (pronounced pyou TAY men), which is just lateral to the globus pallidus; the **caudate,** which is a long, curved structure that sweeps out of the anterior end of the putamen; and the *amygdala* (pronounced a MIG duh luh), which sits in the temporal lobe at the end of the caudate. The amygdala, you will recall, is also considered to be a component of the limbic system. The caudate and putamen together are known as the **striatum.**

The basal ganglia are thought to play a major role in the performance of voluntary motor responses. Of major interest in his respect is a pathway that projects from the substantia nigra of the midbrain to the striatum. *Parkinson's disease,* a disorder of the motor system characterized by rigidity, tremors, and a poverty of voluntary movement is associated with the deterioration of this pathway (see Chapter 5).

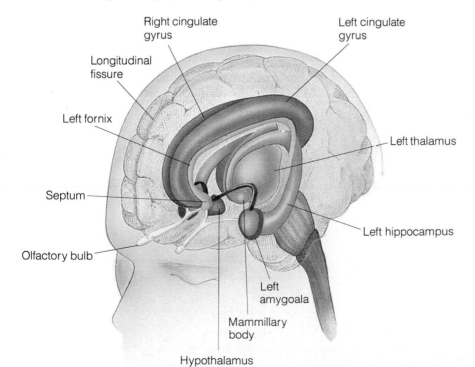

Right cingulate gyrus
Left cingulate gyrus
Longitudinal fissure
Left fornix
Left thalamus
Septum
Left hippocampus
Olfactory bulb
Left amygoala
Mammillary body
Hypothalamus

FIGURE 2.26 *The major structures of the limbic system: the anterior thalamus, the hypothalamus and mammillary bodies, the hippocampus, the amygdala, the septum, the fornix, and the cingulate cortex. Also illustrated are the olfactory bulbs, which are connected to several limbic structures.*

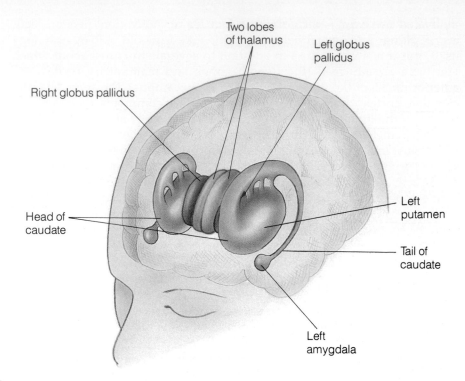

FIGURE 2.27 *The basal ganglia: stratum (caudate plus putamen), globus pallidus, and amygdala.*

Review of the Gross Anatomy of the Brain

If you have not previously studied the gross anatomy of the brain, your own brain is probably straining under the burden of new neuroanatomical terms. It is time to pause and assess your own progress. Test your knowledge of the brain by labeling the following (Figure 2.28) midsagittal section of the human brain. The correct answers are presented at the end of this chapter.

FIGURE 2.28 *A midsaggital view of the human brain.*

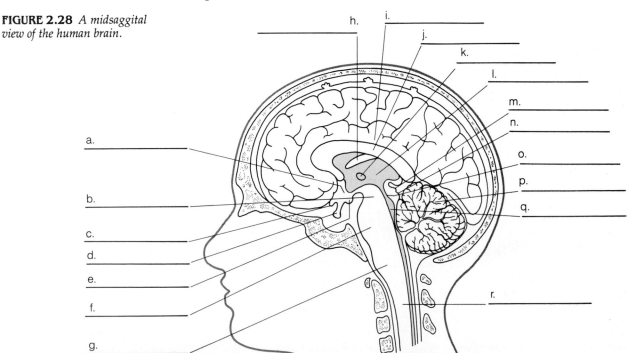

2.7 Finding Out What Is Connected to What: Neuroanatomical Tracing

Although most of this chapter has dealt with the positions and names of groups of cell bodies in the nervous system (i.e., with nuclei), understanding how nuclear structures are connected is prerequisite to gaining an insight into their function. This chapter concludes with a description of several neuroanatomical procedures that have proven useful in studying neural connections.

The Nissl and Golgi stains, which you have already learned about, are of little use in determining the connections between nuclei. Nissl stains are of no help because they leave axons completely unstained. Golgi stains, in contrast, do stain axons; they stain a few of the neurons on each slide in their entirety. The problem with the Golgi stain as a method of mapping axonal projections is that unless an axon is exceedingly short, it is very unlikely that more than a small portion of it would be present in a given slice of neural tissue. You might think that it would be possible to track a particular axon through the brain by following it through a series of Golgi-stained slices, but unfortunately a neuron in one slice that takes up the stain is not likely to take up the stain in the other slices.

The first stain designed expressly for studying axons was developed by Weigert in the 1880s. The **Weigert stain** selectively stains the sheaths of myelinated axons. Figure 2.29 is a Weigert-stained coronal section. Notice how the subcortical white matter is heavily stained, while the cortex and various subcortical nuclear groups are not.

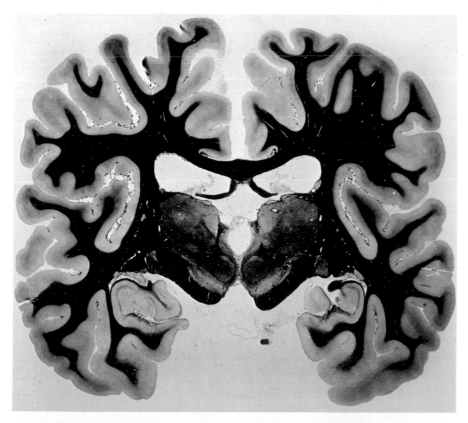

FIGURE 2.29 *A Weigert-stained frontal section of the human brain. Notice that white matter is stained black and the cortex and other nuclear groups are relatively unstained.*

From *Fundamental Neuroanatomy* by Walle J. H. Nauta and Michael Feirtag. Copyright © 1986 W. H. Freeman and Company. Reprinted with permission.

There are three reasons why the Weigert method is not very useful for tracking axonal projections through the brain. First, it is of no use in tracking unmyelinated axons. Second, because the initial segment and terminal branches of myelinated axons are not myelinated, the Weigert stain cannot reveal exactly where a particular axon originates or where it terminates—the two most crucial pieces of information. And third, because the Weigert method stains all myelinated axons indiscriminately, once a myelinated axon (or group of axons) becomes intermingled with others, it is impossible to track it through a series of slices.

Modern staining procedures have overcome these difficulties in a spectacular fashion. Two kinds of procedures have been developed: anterograde (forward) tracing methods and retrograde (backward) tracing methods. *Anterograde tracing methods* are used to determine where the axons originating in a particular structure terminate; *retrograde tracing methods* are used to determine where those axons terminating in a particular structure originate. These methods are based on the fact that some substances are taken up by cell bodies and transported down their axons to their terminal buttons, whereas others are taken up by the terminal buttons and transported back to the cell body.

Anterograde Tracing

Most current anterograde tracing studies employ a technique called **autoradiographic tracing.** This technique takes advantage of the fact that amino acids are absorbed from the extracellular medium by cell bodies, incorporated into proteins, and transported throughout the neuron. First, an amino acid is labeled with *tritium,* the radioactive isotope of hydrogen, and injected into the site whose anterograde projections are under investigation. Several days later, the brain is removed, hardened, and sliced; and the slices are coated with a photographic emulsion. Then the coated slides are stored in light-tight containers for several weeks. During this period, radioactive particles given off by the tritiated amino acid react with the photographic emulsion. The slides are then developed like a film to reveal the whereabouts of the tritiated amino acid at the time that the animal was killed. These locations indicate the positions of axons and buttons of the neurons whose cell bodies are near the site of injection.

Retrograde Tracing

The most widely used technique of retrograde tracing is the **horseradish peroxidase** (HRP) technique. In the 1970s, it was discovered that horseradish peroxidase, an enzyme found in horseradish and various other plants, is readily taken up by the terminal buttons of axons and then transported back to their cell bodies at a rate of between 200 to 300 millimeters per day. Accordingly, to discover the origins of the neural inputs into a site of interest, neuroscientists inject a minute quantity of horseradish peroxidase into it and wait for a day or two. Then they slice the brain and expose the sections to a stain that dyes the horseradish peroxidase. The location of the horseradish peroxidase reveals the positions of the cell bodies of the neurons whose terminal buttons took up the horseradish peroxidase at the site of the injection.

Figure 2.30 illustrates how anterograde and retrograde techniques have been used to identify a source of input to the amygdala and one of the

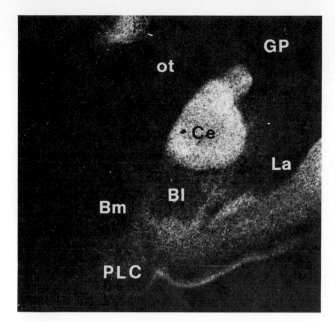

Panel A   Panel B

FIGURE 2.30 *Illustration of autoradiographic tracing (Panel A) and horseradish peroxidase tracing (Panel B). Illustrated in Panel A is the accumulation of radioactivity in the central amygdala following injection of a radioactive amino acid into the frontal cortex. Illustrated in Panel B is the accumulation of HRP in the substantia nigra following its injection into the amygdala.*

Panel A is reprinted with permission from *Neuroscience, 15,* 336, B. S. Kapp, J. S. Schwaker, and P. A. Driscoll, "Frontal Cortex Projections to the Amygdaloid Central Nucleus in the Rabbit." Copyright 1985 Pergamon Press, Elmsford, NY. Panel B is reprinted courtesy of Bruce S. Kapp.

targets of its output. In Panel A, you can see accumulated in the terminal buttons of the central amygdala, the radioactive amino acid that was injected into the frontal cortex (Kapp, Schwaber, & Driscoll, 1985). Panel B shows the accumulation of HRP in the cell bodies of the substantia nigra after it was injected into the central amygdala.

Conclusion

This chapter has summarized the overall organization of the nervous system; it has introduced you to a basic vocabulary of neuroanatomical terms; and it has described a few of the techniques that have been used to identify the location and structure of nuclear groups and the connections between them.

It is fitting to end this introduction to neuroanatomy with the story of Ramón y Cajal, the person who is regarded by many as the father of the discipline. His words ring as true today as they did then.

In 1892 he assumed the Chair of Normal Histology and Pathological Anatomy at Madrid. It was a time, he later remembered, of "devouring activity," as he "hunted cells with delicate and elegant forms, the mysterious butterflies of the soul, the beatings of whose wings may some day—who knows?—clarify the secret of mental life." By that time his investigations centered on cerebral cortex. In particular, he extended his studies to the human cerebral cortex, seeking to find a qualitative difference between the brains of people and animals; suspecting otherwise, it seemed to him, was "a little unworthy of the dignity of the human species." He began with the primary visual cortex; later came studies of other cortical fields. "The functional superiority of the human brain," he finally decided, "is intimately linked up with the prodigious abundance and unaccustomed wealth of forms of the so-called neurons with short axons." It is linked, that is, to the intricate interconnections of local-circuit neurons. That was the essence of the problem of cerebral cortex. "I desired to determine as far as possible its fundamental plan. But, alas! my optimism deceived me. For the supreme cunning of the structure of the gray matter is so intricate that it defies and will continue to defy for many centuries the obstinate curiosity of investigators." (Nauta & Feirtag, 1986, p. 309)

_ Food for Thought _

1. Which of the following extreme conditions do you think is closer to the truth? (a) The primary goal of all psychological research should be to relate psychological phenomena to the anatomy of neural circuits. (b) Psychologists should leave the study of neuroanatomy to neuroanatomists.

2. Perhaps the most famous and fortunate mistake in history was made by Olds and Milner (see Chapter 16). They botched an electrode implantation operation on a rat, and the tip of the stimulation electrode ended up in an unintended structure. When they subsequently tested the effects of electrical stimulation of this unknown structure, they made a fantastic discovery; the rat seemed to find the brain stimulation extremely pleasurable. In fact, the rat would press a lever for hours at an extremely high rate if every press produced a brief stimulation to its own brain through the electrode. If you had accidentally stumbled on this intracranial self-stimulation phenomenon, what neuroanatomical procedures would you have used to identify the stimulation site and the neural circuits involved in the pleasurable effects of the stimulation?

ADDITIONAL READING

For those interested in a more thorough introduction to neuroanatomy than that provided by this chapter, I recommend two books. One is a particularly clear and enjoyable introduction to neuroanatomy by Nauta and Feirtag and the other is the classic collection of neuroanatomical illustrations drawn by Frank Netter.

Nauta, W. J. H., & Feirtag, M. (1986). _Fundamental neuroanatomy._ New York: Freeman.

Netter, F. H. (1962). _The CIBA collection of medical illustrations: Volume 1, the nervous system._ New York: CIBA.

KEY TERMS

To help you study the material in this chapter, all of the key terms—those that have appeared in bold type—are listed and briefly defined here.

Afferent nerves. Nerves that carry signals toward the CNS.

Anterior. Toward the nose end of the animal.

Arachnoid membrane. The menynx between the dura mater and the pia mater.

Astroglia. Large, star-shaped glial cells that play a role in the blood-brain barrier and form the supportive matrix for CNS neurons.

Autonomic nervous system (ANS). The portion of the PNS that participates in the regulation of the internal environment.

Autoradiographic tracing. An anterograde tracing technique in which a tritiated amino acid is injected into the site of interest.

Axodendritic synapses. Synapses between axons and dendrites.

Axon. The long, narrow process that leaves the cell body of many neurons.

Axon hillock. The cone-shaped region where the axon leaves the cell body.

Axosomatic synapses. Synapses between axons and cell bodies.

Bipolar neurons. Neurons with two processes extending from the cell body.

Blood-brain barrier. Mechanism that keeps certain toxic substances in the blood from penetrating the neural tissue.

Brain stem. The brain caudal to the telencephalon—the stem from which the two hemispheres branch.

Buttons. The bulbous endings of axon branches, which release neurotransmitters into synapses.

Caudal. Toward the tail end of an animal.

Cell body (soma). The metabolic center of the cell, which contains the nucleus.

Cell membrane. The semipermeable membrane that encloses neurons and other cells.

Central canal. The small CSF-filled passage that runs through the core of the spine.

Central nervous system (CNS). The portion of the nervous system within the skull and spine.

Cerebrospinal fluid (CSF). The protective colorless fluid that fills the subarachnoid space and the spaces in the core of the brain and spinal cord.

Choroid plexuses. The networks of capillaries that protrude into the ventricles and continuously produce CSF.

Commissures. Tracts joining the left and right cerebral hemispheres (e.g., the corpus callosum).

Contralateral. Projecting from one side of the body to the other.

Coronal section (frontal section). A slice of tissue as viewed from the front of the brain.

Corpus callosum. The largest commissure.

Cranial nerves. The twelve pairs of nerves extending from brain (e.g., the optic nerves, the olfactory nerves, and the vagus nerves).

Cytoplasm. The clear, internal fluid of the cell.

Decussate. Cross over to the other side of the brain.

Dendrites. The short processes emanating from cell body.

Deoxyribonucleic acid (DNA). The molecules that carry the genetic information.

Dorsal. Toward the back or toward the top of the brain.

Dorsal horns. The two dorsal arms of the spinal gray matter; where the dorsal roots enter.

Dura mater (tough mother). The outer menynx.

Efferent nerves. Nerves that carry signals away from the CNS.

Electron microscopy. A neuroanatomical procedure for studying the fine details of neural structure.

Fissures. The large furrows in the neocortex of humans and other animals with convoluted brains; sulci are small fissures.

Foramens. Narrow channels that link the ventricles.

Ganglia (singular: ganglion). Clusters of neuronal cell bodies in the PNS.

Glial cells (neuroglia). The supportive cells of the CNS (e.g., astroglia and oligodendroglia).

Golgi stain. A neural stain that invades only a few of the cells in each slice of tissue.

Gyri (singular: gyrus). The ridges in the cerebral cortex between the sulci and the fissures.

Horizontal section. A horizontal slice of brain tissue as viewed from the top of the brain.

Horseradish peroxidase (HRP). An enzyme that is readily taken up by the terminal buttons of axons and then transported back to their cell bodies.

Inferior. Toward the bottom of the brain in primates.

Interneurons. Neurons that do not have axons or that have very short axons.

Ipsilateral. On the same side of the body.

Lateral. Away from the midline.

Longitudinal fissure. The fissure that separates the two cerebral hemispheres.

Medial. Toward the midline.

Meninges (singular: menynx). The three protective membranes that swaddle the brain and spinal cord.

Messenger ribonucleic acid (mRNA). Molecules that copy the genetic code from the DNA in the nucleus and use it to direct the manufacture of proteins in the cytoplasm.

Multipolar neurons. Neurons that have more than two processes emanating from their cell bodies.

Myelin. A fatty insulation that is found around many axons.

Nerves. Large bundles of axons in the PNS.

Neurotransmitter. A chemical that is released into synapses from the buttons of an active neuron and that stimulates the neurons on the other side of the synapses.

Nissl stain. A neural staining procedure that stains neural cell bodies (e.g., *cresyl violet*).

Nodes of Ranvier. The unmyelinated gaps between sections of myelin on myelinated axons.

Nucleus. The structure in the cell body that contains the DNA; or, a cluster of neuronal cell bodies in the CNS.

Oligodendroglia (oligodendrocytes). Glial cells that myelinate CNS axons.

Paleocortex (old cortex). The olfactory cortex and the hippocampus; cortex of early phylogenetic origin.

Parasympathetic. Nerves of the ANS whose activity tends to conserve the body's energy resources.

Peripheral nervous system (PNS). The portion of the nervous system outside the skull and spine.

Pia mater (pious mother). The delicate, innermost menynx.

Posterior (caudal). Toward the tail end of an animal or to the back of the head.

Ribosomes. Intracellular organelles that assemble amino acids into proteins under the direction of strands of messenger ribonucleic acid (mRNA).

Rostral (anterior). Toward the nose end of an animal.

Sagittal section. Slice of tissue as viewed from the side of the brain.

Satellite cells. Cells that provide a structural matrix for the neurons in the PNS.

Schwann cells. Satellite cells that send out glial cells in the PNS that send out myelin-rich processes that wrap around axons of neurons in the PNS.

Somatic nervous system. The portion of the PNS that interacts with the external environment.

Somatosensory. Referring to sensations from the body —for example from receptors in the skin, joints, and muscles.

Subarachnoid space. The space beneath the arachnoid membrane, which contains the large blood vessels that are visible on the surface of the brain.

Sulci (singular: sulcus). Small fissures in the cerebral cortex.

Superior. Toward the top of the brain in primates.

Superior sagittal sinus. A sinus that runs in the dura mater along the top of the brain between the two hemispheres.

Sympathetic. Nerves of the ANS whose activity tends to mobilize energy resources and prepare the body for action.

Synapses. The sites where neurons interact with one another.

Synaptic vesicles. Tiny packets of neurotransmitter chemical, which are stored near the presynaptic membrane.

Tracts. Bundles of axons in the CNS.

Unipolar neurons. Neurons with one process emanating from the cell body.

Ventral. Toward the stomach of an animal or toward the bottom of the brain.

Ventral horns. The two ventral arms of spinal gray matter.

Ventricles. The four large, CSF-filled internal chambers of the brain; the two lateral ventricles, the third ventricle and the fourth ventricle.

Weigert stain. Selectively stains the sheaths of myelinated axons.

Answers to the Neuroanatomical Quiz on Page 46.

a. hypothalamus
b. tegmentum
c. optic chiasm
d. pituitary
e. mammillary body
f. pons

g. medulla (myelencephalon)
h. fornix
i. cingulate gyrus
j. corpus callosum
k. massa intermedia
l. third ventricle

m. superior colliculus
n. inferior colliculus
o. cerebral aqueduct
p. cerebellum
q. fourth ventricle
r. spinal cord

Table of Key Neuroanatomical Terms

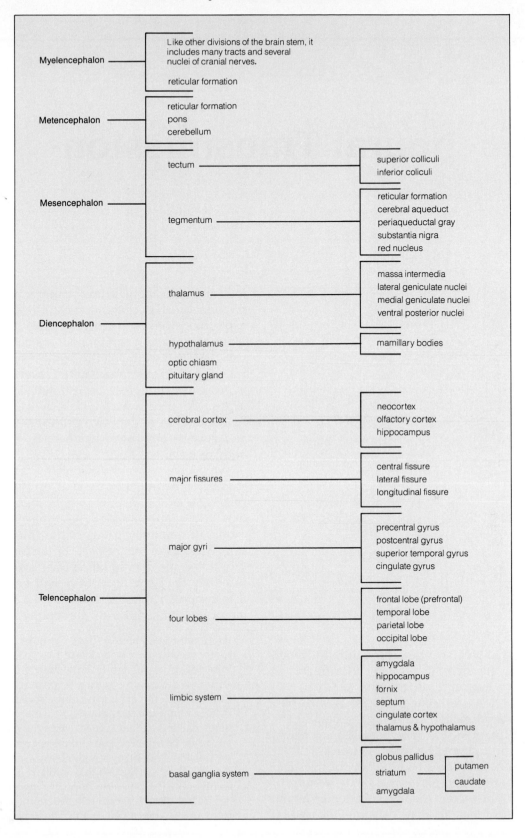

Myelencephalon — Like other divisions of the brain stem, it includes many tracts and several nuclei of cranial nerves.

reticular formation

Metencephalon —
reticular formation
pons
cerebellum

Mesencephalon —
tectum — superior colliculi
inferior coliculi

tegmentum — reticular formation
cerebral aqueduct
periaqueductal gray
substantia nigra
red nucleus

Diencephalon —
thalamus — massa intermedia
lateral geniculate nuclei
medial geniculate nuclei
ventral posterior nuclei

hypothalamus — mamillary bodies

optic chiasm
pituitary gland

Telencephalon —
cerebral cortex — neocortex
olfactory cortex
hippocampus

major fissures — central fissure
lateral fissure
longitudinal fissure

major gyri — precentral gyrus
postcentral gyrus
superior temporal gyrus
cingulate gyrus

four lobes — frontal lobe (prefrontal)
temporal lobe
parietal lobe
occipital lobe

limbic system — amygdala
hippocampus
fornix
septum
cingulate cortex
thalamus & hypothalamus

basal ganglia system — globus pallidus
striatum — putamen
caudate
amygdala

3

Neural Transmission

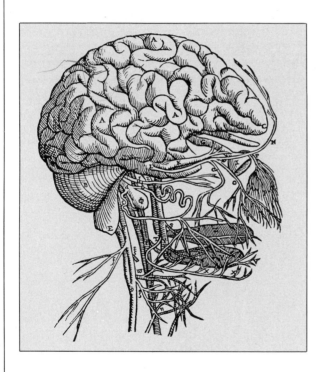

Chapter 3 continues the introduction to the nervous system that began in Chapter 2. In contrast to Chapter 2, however, Chapter 3 deals with nervous system function rather than structure. The topic of Chapter 3 is the transmission of neural signals through and between neurons.

Neurons come in a wide variety of sizes and shapes, and they perform a wide variety of functions; however, the investigation of neural transmission has, to a large degree, focused on just one class of neurons: **motor neurons.** A motor neuron is a multipolar neuron with a long axon that projects to receptive sites on muscle fibers. Accordingly, motor neurons directly control the contraction of the body's muscles by releasing their neurotransmitter, **acetylcholine,** in response to signals transmitted down their axons. Motor neurons are classified as multipolar because more than two processes (one axon and several dendrites) emanate from the cell body of each.

Why have neurophysiologists focused their studies of neural transmission on motor neurons? One of the main reasons is their large axons. Although all motor neurons have large axons, the motor neurons of the squid are the clear winners in this respect. When Mother Nature rolled the first squids off her evolutionary assembly line, she must have had neuroscientists in mind because she produced a sample of motor neurons with truly gigantic axons.

An invention of nature, once we have learned to appreciate it, may facilitate the progress of knowledge more significantly than a new instrument devised by human ingenuity. Such is the case with the giant axon of the squid. In the living animal the usefulness of this large-sized nerve cable is demonstrated when the creature suddenly changes course and darts away by jet propulsion. An array of giant axons activate the muscles that furnish this auxiliary mode of locomotion. In the laboratory the investigator can easily dissect a convenient length of axon from the tissues of a squid. The transparent tubelike axon up to a millimeter in diameter gives him [or her] a nerve fiber that he [or she] can handle and study with far greater ease than the tenuous fibers, 50 to 1,000 times thinner, available from most animals. (Keynes, 1958, p. 83)

In view of the uniqueness of squid motor neurons, it is reasonable to question whether information obtained through their study can reveal much about the function of other neurons—those of the human brain, for example. Fortunately, the answer is yes. Despite their unparalleled size, they seem to function in much the same way as many other neurons. Hence, the squid motor neuron has played, and continues to play, an important role in the advancement of our understanding of the general principles of neural transmission. These principles are discussed in this chapter under the following headings:

3.1 The Neuron's Resting Membrane Potential

The key to understanding the function of the neuron is its **membrane potential,** the difference in electrical charge that exists between the inside and the outside of the cell. To measure this difference, it is necessary to position the tip of one recording electrode inside the neuron and the tip of another recording electrode outside the neuron in the extracellular fluid. Although the size and shape of the extracellular electrode are not critical, it is paramount that the tip of the intracellular electrode be fine enough to pierce the neural membrane without severely damaging it. The tips of such intracellular **microelectrodes,** as they are called, are about 0.5 of a nanometer in diameter—0.5 millionth of a millimeter—much too small to be seen by the naked eye.

To construct a microelectrode, each end of a fine glass tube is fastened to one of the "arms" of an automated **microelectrode puller,** and the center of the tube is heated. When the center reaches the melting point, the two ends are rapidly drawn apart by the puller—just as a child might pull apart a piece of toffee—and the infinitesimally small, but still hollow, point at which the tube separates serves as the electrode tip. Glass pipettes thus created are then filled with a concentrated salt solution through which neural signals can be recorded. As illustrated in Figure 3.1, the construction of the microelectrode is completed by inserting a wire into the solution through the larger end of the pipette and then sealing it to fix the wire in position and to prevent leakage of the solution. The solution does not leak from the electrode tip because the hole in the tip is too small to permit it.

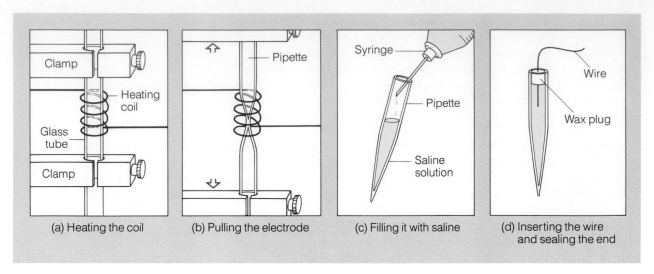

| (a) Heating the coil | (b) Pulling the electrode | (c) Filling it with saline | (d) Inserting the wire and sealing the end |

FIGURE 3.1 *The construction of a microelectrode.*

Recording the Membrane Potential

To record the membrane potential of a neuron, the wires leading from an intracellular electrode and an extracellular electrode are each attached to an **oscilloscope,** a device that displays the changes in the membrane potential over time as vertical displacements of a spot of light as it sweeps from left to right across a fluorescent screen. Because the spot of light on an oscilloscope screen is produced by a beam of electrons, which has little inertia to overcome, an oscilloscope can accurately display even the most rapid changes in the membrane potential. Mechanical recording devices that plot neural activity with a pen on chart paper are convenient, but they are much too cumbersome to faithfully respond to the rapid changes in membrane potential that occur in an active neuron. Figure 3.2 is an illustration of how a membrane potential is recorded using an oscilloscope.

When both electrodes are in the extracellular fluid, the voltage difference recorded between them is close to zero. However, when the tip of the intracellular electrode is inserted into a neuron, a steady potential of about −70 millivolts (mV) is registered on the oscilloscope screen. This indicates that the potential inside the resting neuron is about 70 mV less than that outside the neuron, which by convention is considered to be zero. This steady membrane potential of about −70 mV is called the neuron's **resting potential.** In its resting state, with the −70 mV charge built up across its membrane, a neuron is said to be *polarized.*

The Ionic Basis of the Resting Potential

Why are resting neurons polarized? Like all salts in solution, the salts in neural tissue separate into positively and negatively charged particles called **ions.** The resting potential results from the fact that the ratio of negative to positive charges is greater inside the neuron than outside. Why this unequal distribution of charges occurs can be understood in terms of the interaction of four factors: two forces that act to distribute ions equally throughout the intracellular and extracellular fluids of the nervous system, and two features of the neural membrane that counteract these homogenizing influences.

The first of the two homogenizing forces is random motion. The ions in neural tissue are in constant random motion, and particles in random motion tend to become evenly distributed because it is more likely that they will move from areas of high concentration, down their concentration gradients, to areas of low concentration. The second force that promotes the even distribution of ions is electrostatic pressure. Any accumulation of particular charges, positive or negative, in one area tends to be dispersed by the repulsion of like charges in the vicinity and the attraction of opposite charges concentrated elsewhere.

The homogenizing effects of these two forces can be illustrated by a simple analogy. Assume that it is mating season and that, as a result, the birds living in an aviary are highly excited and flying about in a more-or-less random fashion, except that they have an attraction for members of the opposite sex and an aversion for members of their own. In such a situation, the two forces of random movement and sexual preference would tend to distribute both male birds and female birds equally in all parts of the aviary and keep it that way by immediately dispersing any concentrations of male or female birds that begin to build up. Consider what would happen if, for example, females began to congregate in one half of the aviary. The concentration of females would be dispersed by their random movement because there would be more of the randomly moving females available to move out of the half in which they had become concentrated than would be available to move in. If you have difficulty understanding this statistical

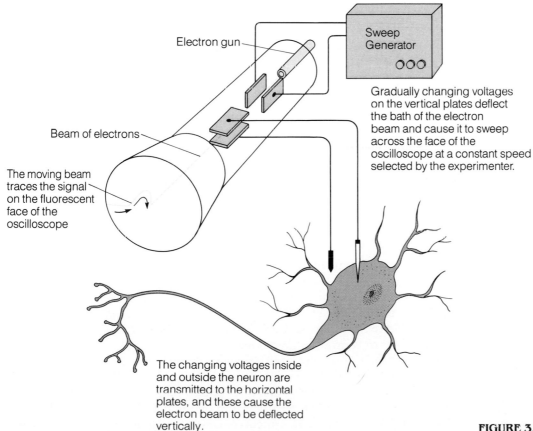

FIGURE 3.2 *How a membrane potential is recorded.*

concept, think of the most extreme case; think of the case in which all of the females are concentrated in one half. In this situation, it is obvious that the random movement of the female birds would invariably reduce the number of birds on the crowded side, rather than increasing it, because there would be no females on the vacant side to move in. Any concentration of female birds would also be dispersed by the force of their sexual preference. As soon as females began to congregate, they would tend to be dispersed by their repulsion for each other and their attraction for the increased proportion of males in other parts of the aviary. In much the same way, the forces of random movement and electrostatic pressure constantly act to distribute each class of ions equally throughout the fluid medium of the nervous system.

Despite the continuous homogenizing effects of random movement and electrostatic pressure, no single class of ions is distributed equally on the two sides of the neural membrane. There are three major classes of ions that diffuse through neural membranes in sufficient quantities to effect major changes in the resting potential: sodium ions (Na^+), potassium ions (K^+), and chloride ions (Cl^-). The concentration of both Na^+ and Cl^- is greater outside a resting neuron than inside, whereas K^+ ions are more concentrated on the inside. See Figure 3.3.

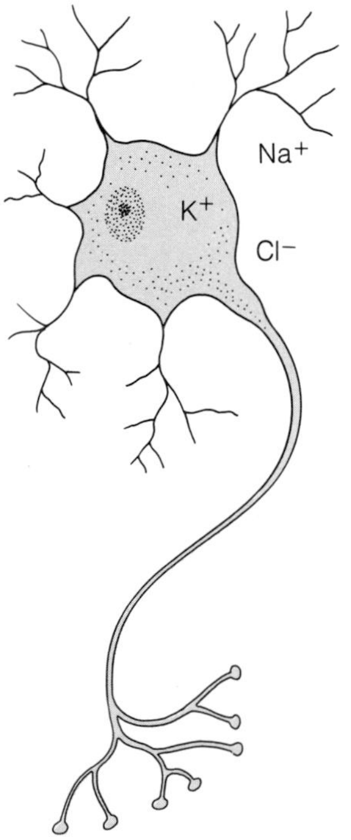

Two properties of the neural membrane are responsible for this unequal distribution of Na^+, K^+, and Cl^- ions in resting neurons. One of these properties is passive, that is, it does not involve the consumption of energy; whereas, the other is active, and does. The passive property of the neural membrane that contributes to the unequal disposition of ions is its differential permeability to Na^+, K^+, and Cl^- ions. Both K^+ and Cl^- ions readily diffuse through the neural membrane, whereas there is considerable resistance to the passage of Na^+ ions. Ions pass through the neural membrane only at specialized pores called **ion channels.** There are many kinds of ion channels, and each is specialized to some degree for the passage of particular ions.

Evidence that an energy-consuming mechanism plays an important role in maintaining the membrane potential was provided by Hodgkin and Huxley in the 1950s. First, they measured the intracellular and extracellular concentrations of Na^+, K^+, and Cl^- ions. They found each of these classes of ions to be unequally distributed between the two sides of the membrane of a resting neuron, and they concluded that there must be pressure for each kind of ion to move down its concentration gradient to the side of lesser concentration. Why then do the concentrations of ions inside and outside of the neuron stay unequal when the neuron is at rest? The answer was clear; there must be some force or forces offsetting the tendency for ions to move down their concentration gradients. Could the electrostatic pressure of -70 mV built up across the membrane be the force responsible for maintaining the unequal distribution of ions? To answer this question, Hodgkin and Huxley calculated for each of the three ions the electrostatic charge that would be required to offset the pressure for them to move down their concentration gradients.

For Cl^- ions, this calculated value was about -70 mV, the same as the actual resting potential. Hodgkin and Huxley thus concluded that when neurons are at rest, the unequal distribution of Cl^- ions across the neural membrane is maintained in equilibrium by the balance between the 70-mV force driving Cl^- ions down their concentration gradient into the neuron and the 70 mV of electrostatic pressure driving them out. The situation was

FIGURE 3.3 *In its resting state, more Na^+ and Cl^- ions are outside the resting neuron that inside, and more K^+ ions are inside the neuron than outside.*

different for the K$^+$ ions. Hodgkin and Huxley calculated that about -90 mV of electrostatic pressure would be required to keep intracellular K$^+$ ions from moving down their concentration gradient and leaving the neuron. However, because the resting potential is only about -70 mV, some 20 mV less, there is not enough electrostatic pressure to keep K$^+$ ions from leaking out of the cell. The case of Na$^+$ ions was similar to that of K$^+$ ions, but more extreme because the forces of both the concentration gradient and the electrostatic gradient are in the same direction. In the resting neuron, the concentration of Na$^+$ ions outside the neuron creates 50 mV of pressure for Na$^+$ ions to move down their concentration gradient into the neuron, and this is added to the -70 mV of electrostatic pressure for them to move in the same direction.

According to Hodgkin and Huxley's measurements and calculations, Na$^+$ ions are continuously forced into resting neurons and K$^+$ ions are continuously forced out. Why then do the intracellular and extracellular concentrations of Na$^+$ and K$^+$ and the membrane potential remain constant in resting neurons? Hodgkin and Huxley concluded that there must be active mechanisms in the membrane to counteract the influx (in flow) of Na$^+$ ions by pumping them out as rapidly as they leak in and to counteract the efflux (out flow) of K$^+$ ions by pumping them in as rapidly as they leak out. Figure 3.4 summarizes Hodgkin and Huxley's conclusions.

Subsequent research has confirmed that the neural membrane contains active mechanisms for the transport of Na$^+$ and K$^+$ ions. For example, Hodgkin and Keynes (1955) measured the active transport of sodium ions out of the squid motor neuron by loading it with a radioactive isotope of sodium and measuring the accumulation of radioactivity in the extracellular fluid. Because the number of sodium ions that can passively diffuse

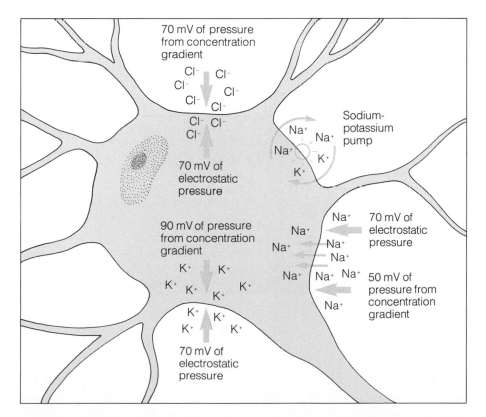

FIGURE 3.4 *The passive and active forces acting on the distribution of Na$^+$, K$^+$, and Cl$^-$ ions across the neural membrane. Because passive forces from the electrostatic and concentration gradients act to continuously drive K$^+$ ions out of the resting neuron and Na$^+$ ions in, K$^+$ ions must be actively pumped in and Na$^+$ ions must be pumped out to maintain the resting equilibrium.*

from resting neurons against the concentration and electrostatic gradients is negligible, they concluded that the steady accumulation of radioactivity outside the neuron could result only from the active sodium-pumping action of the membrane. To provide evidence that this pumping process was active, that is, energy consuming, Hodgkin and Keynes showed that temporarily blocking the supply of energy to the neuron by bathing it in the metabolic poison, **dinitrophenol (DNP)**, blocked the steady efflux of radioactive sodium. This study is illustrated in Figure 3.5.

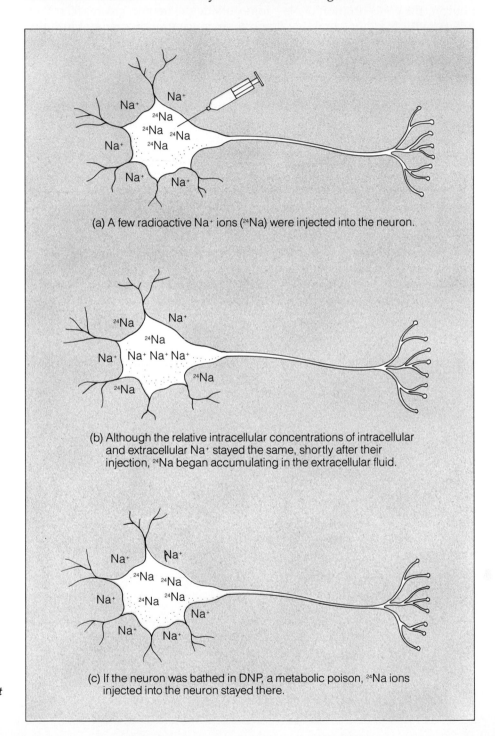

(a) A few radioactive Na$^+$ ions (^{24}Na) were injected into the neuron.

(b) Although the relative intracellular concentrations of intracellular and extracellular Na$^+$ stayed the same, shortly after their injection, ^{24}Na began accumulating in the extracellular fluid.

(c) If the neuron was bathed in DNP, a metabolic poison, ^{24}Na ions injected into the neuron stayed there.

FIGURE 3.5 *Inhibition of the active transport of Na$^+$ ions out of the squid motor neuron by dinitrophenol (DNP).*

Table 3.1 *The Factors Responsible for the Differences in the Intracellular and Extracellular Concentrations of Ions in Resting Neurons*

ION	SUMMARY OF FACTORS INFLUENCING THE DISPOSITION OF IONS
Na^+	Na^+ ions are driven into the neuron by both the high concentration of Na^+ ions outside the neuron and the negative internal resting charge of -70 mV. However, the membrane is resistant to the passive diffusion of Na^+, and the sodium-potassium pump is thus able to maintain the high external concentration of Na^+ ions by pumping them out at the same slow rate as they leak in. *(3 are pumped out)*
K^+	K^+ ions are driven out of the neuron by their high internal concentration, although this pressure is to a large degree offset by the internal negative charge. Despite the minimal pressure for the K^+ ions to leave the neuron, they do so at a substantial rate because the membrane offers little resistance to their passage. To maintain the high internal concentration of K^+ ions, they are pumped into neurons at the same rate as they diffuse out. *(2 are pumped in)*
Cl^-	There is little resistance in the neural membrane to the passage of Cl^- ions. Thus, Cl^- ions are readily forced out of the neuron by the negative internal charge. As chloride ions begin to accumulate on the outside, there is increased pressure for them to move down their concentration gradient back into the neuron. When the point is reached where the electrostatic pressure for Cl^- ions to move out of the neuron is equal to the pressure for them to move back in, the distribution of Cl^- ions is held in equilibrium. This point of equilibrium occurs at -70 mV. *also PO_4^{-2} SO_4^{-2} Pr^-*

There is considerable evidence that the active transport of Na^+ ions out of neurons and the active transport of K^+ ions into them are not independent processes. It is widely held that active sodium and potassium transport is carried out by a common mechanism that exchanges Na^+ ions inside the neuron for K^+ ions outside—a mechanism commonly referred to as the **sodium-potassium pump.** Because sodium ions can be transported out of the neuron at a rate that is 50 percent more than the rate at which potassium ions can be transported in, it is assumed that under optimal conditions sodium-potassium pumps exchange three NA^+ ions for every two K^+ ions.

Table 3.1 summarizes the factors that are responsible for the differences between the intracellular and extracellular concentrations of Na^+, K^+, and Cl^- ions in resting neurons—and hence for the resting membrane potential itself. Now that you understand these basic properties of the resting neuron, you are prepared to consider how neurons respond to stimulation.

3.2 The Generation and Transmission of Postsynaptic Potentials

When neurons fire, they usually release from their terminal buttons chemicals called **neurotransmitters,** which diffuse across the synaptic clefts and interact with specialized postsynaptic receptor molecules on the receptive membranes of the next neurons in the circuit. The effect of this interaction is often a change in the membrane potential at the postsynaptic receptor sites. This is the somewhat arbitrary starting point for the following account of the events involved in the transmission of signals through a neural network. This section of the chapter deals with the generation of signals in the postsynaptic neurons. The following sections explain how such postsynaptic signals can trigger an action potential, how such action potentials are then transmitted down the axon, and finally how the arrival of an action potential at a terminal button initiates the release of neurotransmitter molecules, which affect the next neuron in the circuit and begins the cycle once again.

When neurotransmitter molecules bind to postsynaptic receptors, they have one of two effects, depending on the structure of both the neurotransmitter and the receptor in question. They may **depolarize** the receptive membrane (decrease the resting membrane potential from -70 to -67 mV, for example) or they may **hyperpolarize** it (increase the resting membrane potential from -70 to -72 mV, for example). The postsynaptic depolarizations are called **excitatory postsynaptic potentials** (**EPSPs**) because, as you will soon learn, they increase the likelihood that the neuron will fire (that an action potential will be generated). The postsynaptic hyperpolarizations are called **inhibitory postsynaptic potentials** (**IPSPs**) because they decrease the likelihood that the neuron will fire. Both EPSPs and IPSPs are **graded responses.** This means that the amplitudes of EPSPs and IPSPs are proportional to the intensity of the signals that elicit them; weak signals elicit small postsynaptic potentials, whereas strong signals elicit large ones.

EPSPs and IPSPs travel passively from their sites of generation at synapses, usually on the dendrites or cell body, in much the same way that electrical signals travel through a cable. Accordingly, the transmission of postsynaptic potentials has two important characteristics. First, it is rapid—so rapid that it can be assumed to be instantaneous for most purposes. It is important not to confuse the duration of EPSPs and IPSPs with their rate of transmission; although the duration of EPSPs and IPSPs can vary considerably, they are all, whether brief or enduring, transmitted at great speed. Second, the transmission of EPSPs and IPSPs is decremental. EPSPs and IPSPs generated at points on the receptive membrane decrease in amplitude as they travel through the neuron, just as an electrical signal weakens as it travels through a long cable or as a sound grows fainter as it travels through air.

3.3 The Integration of Postsynaptic Potentials and the Generation of Action Potentials

The postsynaptic potentials created by the activities at a single synapse typically have little effect on the firing of the postsynaptic neuron. The receptive areas of most neurons are covered with literally thousands of synapses, and whether or not a neuron fires is determined by the net effect of their activity. More specifically, whether or not a neuron fires depends on the balance between the excitatory and inhibitory signals reaching the **axon hillock,** the conical structure at the junction between the cell body and the axon. The graded EPSPs and IPSPs created by the action of neurotransmitters at particular receptive sites on the neural membrane are conducted instantly and decrementally to the axon hillock. If the sum of all of the depolarizations and hyperpolarizations reaching the axon hillock is sufficient to depolarize the membrane to a level referred to as its **threshold of excitation**—about -65 mV for many neurons—an **action potential** (**AP**) will be generated at the axon hillock. In other words, the neuron will fire.

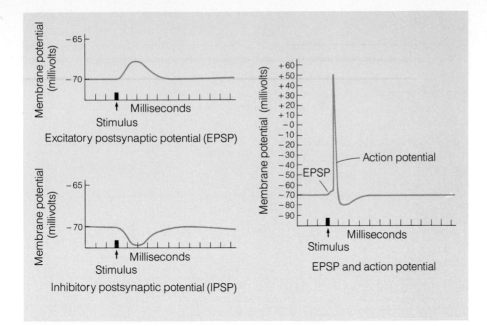

FIGURE 3.6 *A record of the membrane potential of a neuron illustrating EPSPs, IPSPs, and APs.*

As its name implies, the action potential is the most vigorous neural response. As soon as the axon hillock is depolarized to its threshold of excitation, the negative membrane potential is suddenly reversed, from −65 mV to about +50 mV, for about 1 millisecond. This momentary reversal of the resting potential is the action potential. Unlike postsynaptic potentials, action potentials are not graded responses; their magnitude is not related in any way to the intensity of stimuli that elicit them. They are **all-or-none responses;** that is, they either occur full-blown, or they do not occur at all. See Figure 3.6 for an illustration of EPSPs, IPSPs, and APs.

In effect, each multipolar neuron adds together all of the graded excitatory and inhibitory postsynaptic potentials reaching its axon hillock and it "makes its decision" to fire or not to fire on the basis of their sum. Adding or combining a number of individual signals into one overall signal like this is called **integration**. Neurons integrate their postsynaptic potentials in two ways: over space and over time. Figure 3.7 illustrates the experimental procedure for demonstrating the three types of **spatial summation.** It illustrates: (1) how local EPSPs that are produced simultaneously on different parts of the receptive membrane sum to form a greater EPSP, (2) how simultaneous IPSPs sum to form a greater IPSP, and (3) how simultaneous EPSPs and IPSPs sum to cancel one another out.

Figure 3.8 illustrates the experimental procedure for demonstrating **temporal summation;** that is, how postsynaptic potentials produced in rapid succession at the same synapse can sum to form a greater signal. The reason that stimulations of a neuron can be summated over time is that the postsynaptic potentials that they produce outlast them. Thus, if a particular synapse is activated, and then it is activated again before the original postsynaptic potential has dissipated, the effect of the second stimulus will be superimposed on the lingering postsynaptic potential produced by the first. Accordingly, it is possible for a brief excitatory stimulus that does not produce a large enough EPSP to fire a neuron to do so if it is administered twice in rapid succession. In the same way, an inhibitory synapse activated

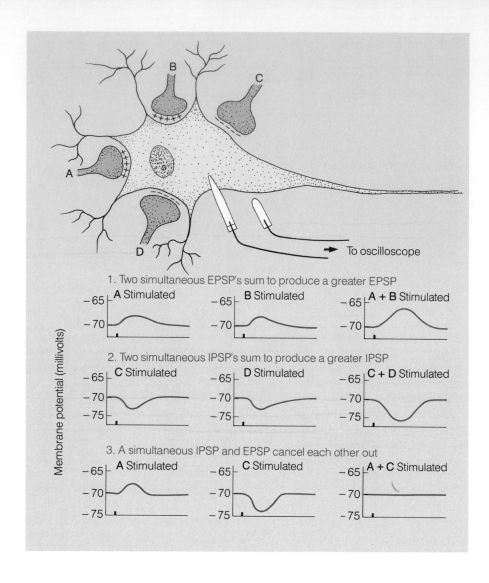

FIGURE 3.7 *The three combinations of spatial summation.*

twice in rapid succession can produce a greater IPSP than that produced by a single stimulation at the same intensity.

It is important not to be misled by the way in which neural integration is studied in the laboratory. Spatial summation is studied independently of temporal summation by administering two discrete stimuli to different sites at exactly the same time, and temporal summation is studied independently of spatial summation by stimulating one site twice in rapid succession. However, the normal operating conditions of most neurons are quite different; most neurons continuously integrate signals over both time and space as the neuron is continually bombarded with stimuli through the thousands of synapses covering its dendrites and cell body. Remember that although schematic diagrams of neural circuitry rarely include neurons with more than a few representative synaptic contacts, the real situation is much more complex. For example, each mammalian motor neuron receives about 10,000 synaptic contacts.

The location of a synapse on a receptive membrane is an important factor in determining its potential to influence neural firing. Because EPSPs

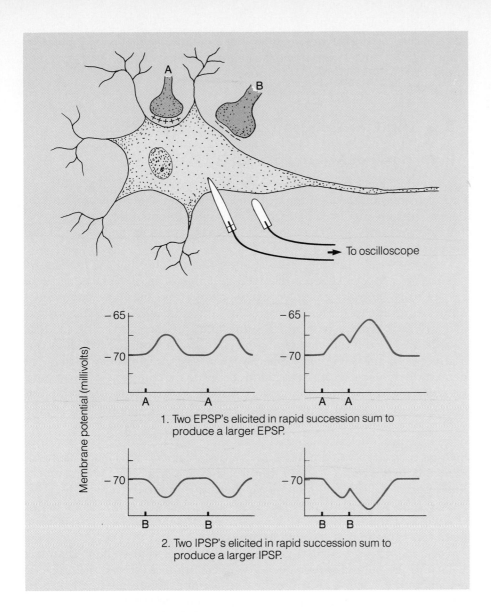

Membrane potential (millivolts)

To oscilloscope

−65

−70

A   A

1. Two EPSP's elicited in rapid succession sum to
   produce a larger EPSP.

−65

−70

A A

−70

B   B

2. Two IPSP's elicited in rapid succession sum to
   produce a larger IPSP.

−70

B B

FIGURE 3.8 *The two
combinations of temporal
summation.*

and IPSPs are transmitted decrementally, those synapses near the hillock
trigger zone have the most influence on the firing of the neuron. This may
explain why synaptic contacts tend to be segregated, that is, why synaptic
contacts from a particular source or from a particular class of neurons tend
to be located on a particular part of the target neuron. For example, axons
from one part of the brain might all synapse on the cell body of the target
neuron, whereas those from another area might favor dendritic target
sites.

In some ways the firing of a neuron is like the firing of a gun. Both are
all-or-none reactions triggered by their own graded responses to stimulation. As a trigger is squeezed, it responds by gradually moving back until it
causes the gun to fire. Similarly, as depolarizing stimulation of gradually
increasing intensity is applied to a neuron, the neuron becomes less and
less polarized until the threshold of excitation is reached, and the neuron
fires. And like the firing of a gun, neural firing is an all-or-none event; just

as squeezing a trigger harder does not make the bullet travel faster or farther, stimulating a neuron more intensely does not increase the speed or amplitude of the resulting action potential.

3.4 The Transmission of Action Potentials

Ionic Basis of Action Potentials

What ionic mechanisms underlie the generation of action potentials and their transmission through the neuron? As you are about to learn, both of these events are mediated by the action of **voltage-gated ion channels,** ion channels that open and close in response to changes in the voltage of the membrane potential.

You may recall from the first section of this chapter that the membrane potential of a neuron at rest is relatively constant despite the fact that there is force from both the external positive charge and the high external sodium concentration for Na^+ ions to flow into the cell. The Na^+ ions are held in check by the relative impermeability of the membrane to their passage and by the active pumping mechanism that pumps Na^+ ions out of the cell at the same slow rate as they leak in. However, when the membrane potential at the axon hillock drops to the threshold of excitation, the voltage-gated sodium channels in the hillock membrane open briefly, and Na^+ ions adjacent to the membrane rush into the neuron, driving the membrane potential from -70 to almost $+50$ mV. The rapid change in the membrane potential associated with the *influx* of Na^+ ions triggers the brief opening of voltage-gated potassium channels, and K^+ ions near the membrane are driven out of the cell through these channels by their relatively high internal concentration and by the positive internal charge. The positive internal charge also draws some Cl^- ions into the cell. Both the *efflux* of K^+ ions and the influx of Cl^- ions partially counteract the effects on the membrane potential of the sodium influx.

Once the action potential has reached its peak, the sodium channels close, and the neuron is repolarized by the continued efflux of K^+ ions. In fact, enough K^+ ions exit before the potassium channels are finally closed that the neuron is left hyperpolarized for a brief period of time. After the action potential, the intracellular and extracellular concentrations of Na^+, K^+, and Cl^- ions return to their resting levels. The flow of ions during the action potential is illustrated in Figure 3.9.

FIGURE 3.9 *The flow of Na^+ and K^+ ions through an axonal membrane axon during an action potential.*

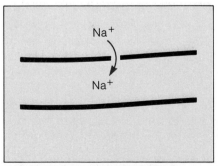

1. Sodium channels open and Na^+ ions rush in

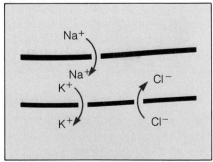

2. This draws Cl^- ions into the neuron and momentarily opens potassium channels to allow K^+ ions to flow out and briefly hyperpolarize the neuron.

The number of ions that flow through the membrane is extremely small in relation to the total number inside and around the neuron. It involves only a few ions right next to the membrane. Therefore, an action potential has little effect on the overall concentrations of Na^+ and K^+ ions in the cytoplasm and extracellular fluid, and the concentration of gradients of sodium and potassium across the membrane are rapidly re-established by the random movement of ions both inside and outside the neuron. The sodium-potassium pump plays only a minor role in the re-establishment of the resting potential. If the sodium-potassium pump is blocked by dinitro-phenol (DNP), thousands of action potentials can occur before the extracellular concentrations of Na^+ ions and the intracellular concentrations of K^+ ions become so low that no more action potentials can be elicited.

To check that you understand the ionic basis of action potentials, a difficult topic for many students, fill in the following blanks.

1. When the membrane potential at the axon hillock drops to the threshold of excitation, the voltage-gated ___ion___ channels in the hillock membrane open briefly.

2. During an action potential, the membrane potential is driven from -70 mV to about $+50$ mV by the influx of ___Na⁺___ ions.

3. The influx of ___Na⁺___ ions triggers the brief opening of voltage-gated potassium channels.

4. When the potassium channels open, potassium ions are driven out of the neuron by their relatively high ___intracellular___ concentration and the ___pos.___ internal charge.

5. The effects on the membrane potential of the influx of sodium ions are partially counteracted by the efflux of ___K⁺___ ions and the influx of ___Cl⁻___ ions.

Refractory Periods

There is a brief period of about 1 to 2 milliseconds after the initiation of an action potential during which it is impossible to elicit another one. This period is called the **absolute refractory period.** The absolute refractory period is followed by a period called the **relative refractory period,** during which it is possible to fire a neuron only if higher than normal levels of stimulation are applied. The end of the relative refractory period is the point at which the amount of stimulation necessary to fire a neuron returns to baseline.

−65 mv

The answers to the preceding review questions are: (1) sodium, (2) Na^+, (3) Na^+, (4) internal; positive internal, and (5) K^+; Cl^-.

The refractory period is responsible for two important characteristics of neural activity. First, it is responsible for the fact that action potentials normally travel along axons in only one direction. Because the portions of an axon over which an action potential has traveled are left momentarily refractory, an action potential on any part of the axon cannot spread back over portions of the axon through which it has just traveled. Second, it is responsible for the fact that the rate of neural firing is related to the intensity of the stimulation that triggers it. If a neuron is subjected to an extremely high continual level of stimulation, it fires and then fires again as soon as the absolute refractory period is over—a maximum of about 1,000 times per second. However, if the level of stimulation is of an intensity just sufficient to fire the neuron when it is at rest, the neuron does not fire again until both the absolute and relative refractory periods have run their course. And of course, intermediate levels of stimulation produce intermediate rates of neural firing.

Transmission of Action Potentials

The transmission of action potentials along an axon differs from the transmission of EPSPs and IPSPs in two important ways. First, the transmission of action potentials along an axon is *nondecremental;* action potentials do not grow weaker as they travel along the axonal membrane. The second difference is that action potentials are transmitted along the axonal membrane more slowly than postsynaptic potentials.

The reason for these differences is that the axonal transmission of action potentials, rather than being solely passive, involves the active participation of the neural membrane. Once an action potential has been generated at the axon hillock, it travels passively along the axonal membrane to the adjacent voltage-gated sodium channels, which have yet to open. The arrival of the signal opens these channels, thus allowing Na^+ ions to rush into the neuron and generate a full-blown action potential on this portion of the membrane. This signal is then conducted passively to the adjacent sodium channels, where another action potential is triggered. These events are repeated again and again until a full-blown action potential is triggered in the terminal buttons. Because the ion channels on the axonal membrane are so close together, it is usual to think of axonal transmission as a single wave of excitation spreading at a constant speed along the axon, rather than as a series of discrete events. The wave of excitation triggered by the generation of an action potential on the hillock membrane also spreads back through the cell body and dendrites of the neuron; however, because the sodium channels of the cell body and dendrites are not voltage-gated channels, the conduction of action potentials back through the cell body and dendrites is purely passive.

The following analogy illustrates several important features of axonal transmission. Consider a row of mouse traps on a wobbly shelf, each set and ready to be triggered. Each trap stores energy by holding back its striker against the pressure of the spring just as each sodium channel holds back Na^+ ions, which are under pressure to move down their concentration and electrostatic gradients into the neuron. When the first trap is triggered, the vibration from this event is transmitted passively through the shelf, and the next trap is sprung—and so on down the line. The nondecremental nature of action potential transmission is readily apparent from this analogy; the last trap to be triggered strikes with no less intensity than the first. The analogy also illustrates the critical role of repolarization in neural transmission; a trap cannot respond again until it has been reset, just as a section of axon cannot fire again until it has been repolarized. Finally, a row of traps, like an axon, can transmit in both directions. If stimulation of sufficient intensity is applied to the terminal end of an axon, an action potential will be generated that will travel along the axon back to the cell body. This is called **antidromic** transmission, whereas axonal transmission in the natural direction, that is from cell body to terminal buttons, is called **orthodromic.**

Transmission in Myelinated Axons

You may remember from Chapter 2 that the axons of many neurons are insulated from the extracellular fluid by segments of fatty tissue called *myelin.* Because these myelin segments effectively prevent the exchange of ions between the neuron and the extracellular fluid, ion flow in myelinated axons can occur only at the gaps between the segments, which are called **nodes of Ranvier** (pronounced ron vee yay). How then are action potentials transmitted in myelinated axons?

When an action potential is generated across the hillock membrane of a myelinated axon, the signal is transmitted passively, that is instantly and decrementally, along the axon to the first node of Ranvier. Although the signal is somewhat diminished by the time it reaches the first node, it is still strong enough to open its voltage-gated sodium channels and to generate another full-blown action potential. This action potential is transmitted passively to the next node, where another full-blow action potential is elicited, and so on.

Although it may initially seem counterintuitive, the reduction of ion flow by myelination actually improves axonal transmission in two important ways. The first advantage of myelination is that it increases the speed of transmission. Because the transmission along the myelinated segments of the axon is passive, it occurs instantly, and the signal, in a sense, "jumps" down the axon from node to node. There is, of course, a slight delay at each node of Ranvier while the action potential is actively regenerated, but the transmission in myelinated axons is still much faster than in unmyelinated axons in which passive conduction plays a less prominent role. The transmission of action potentials in myelinated axons is called **saltatory conduction,** from the Latin *saltare,* which means *to dance.* The second advantage of myelination is that it conserves energy. Because Na^+ ions enter the neuron and K^+ ions leave the neuron only at the nodes of Ranvier, it requires less energy for the sodium-potassium pump to re-establish the resting concentration gradients.

The Velocity of Axonal Transmission

At what speed are action potentials transmitted along an axon? The answer to this question depends to a large degree on two properties of the axon in question. Transmission is faster in axons of large diameter, and—as you have just learned—it is faster in those that are myelinated. Mammalian motor neurons are myelinated and have diameters of up to 0.015 millimeter, and thus they can conduct at speeds of up to 100 meters per second (about 224 miles per hour). In contrast, small unmyelinated axons conduct action potentials at only about 1 meter per second. Squid giant motor neurons, which are unmyelinated and have diameters of about 0.7 millimeter, conduct at a rate of about 25 meters per second.

It is a simple matter to determine the velocity of axonal conduction with the precise recording equipment available today. One simply measures the time that it takes an action potential to travel from one point on an axon to another and divides that figure by the distance between them. However, the ingenuity of the scientists who long ago estimated the rate of axonal transmission without the benefit of today's sophisticated neuroscientific technology is just as impressive. Why don't you take a few minutes from your reading to match wits with these early neuroscientists? It will certainly help you to appreciate their ingenuity. Your task is to devise a way of estimating the rate of transmission in the large, myelinated sensory nerves of the human arm, which carry information from the skin to the spinal cord. Your subjects are 20 healthy humans, and your single piece of equipment is a good stopwatch. I will be generous and also allow you to use a pencil and a piece of paper to record your measurements and to perform simple calculations, but no other devices are permitted or required. The solution follows, but don't peek until you have made a serious effort to solve the problem yourself.

Demonstration

To solve this problem, have the subjects join hands to form a ring. Then instruct them to practice transmitting signals around the ring as fast as they can by squeezing the hand of the person to their left as soon as their right hand is squeezed. Once the subjects feel comfortable with this procedure, record to the nearest 0.01 second the amount of time that it takes for a signal to travel around the ring. Repeat this 10 times, and use the fastest time as the measure. This measure is obviously of little use by itself because it reflects numerous processes in addition to the time that it takes for the signal to be conducted along the axons of the sensory neurons of the right hand, but it is not as useless as it might first appear. It is possible to estimate the amount of time attributable to the axonal transmission in sensory neurons by subtracting from this overall measure an estimate of the amount of time taken by all the other processes contributing to the total time. To accomplish this, have the subjects form a ring as pictured in Figure 3.10, with the left hand of each subject on the right shoulder of the person to his or her left. Then use exactly the same method as before to determine the time that it

FIGURE 3.10 *In order to estimate the speed of axonal transmission in the sensory neurons in the arm, the time that it takes to transmit a signal around circle B is subtracted from the time that it takes to transmit a signal around circle A.*

takes a signal to travel around this shorter ring. In effect, this reduces by about 50 centimeters the distance that the signal travels over the axons of sensory neurons in each subject. You will find that it takes the signal approximately 0.1 second less to complete this shorter circuit. The speed of axonal transmission can then be determined by the following simple calculations:

Circumference of the larger ring − Circumference of the smaller ring = 20 × 50 cm = 1,000 cm

Time to travel the larger ring − Time to travel the smaller ring = about 0.1 second

Speed of axonal transmission $= \dfrac{\text{Distance}}{\text{Time}} = \dfrac{1{,}000 \text{ cm}}{0.1 \text{ sec}}$ = about 100 meters per second

3.5 Synaptic Transmission: The Transmission of Signals Between Neurons

You have already learned in this chapter how excitatory and inhibitory postsynaptic potentials are generated on the receptive membrane; how these graded potentials are transmitted passively to the axon hillock; how the sum of these graded potentials triggers all-or-none action potentials; and how these all-or-none action potentials are actively transmitted down the axon to the terminal buttons. In this section, the cycle is completed. You will learn about how action potentials arriving at terminal buttons lead to the transmission of signals across synapses to the next neurons in the circuit. The focus here is on the general aspects of synaptic transmission. Specific neurotransmitters and their role in mental illness is the subject of Chapter 6.

The Neuromuscular Junction

Current views of synaptic transmission are based to a large degree on the study of transmission between motor neurons and muscle fibers. Just as the study of squid giant motor neurons provided the first insights into the mechanisms of axonal transmission, it was the study of **neuromuscular junctions,** primarily in frogs, that laid the foundation for our understanding of chemical synapses.

> The synapse of the motor neuron on skeletal muscle provides a particularly convenient preparation for studying the synaptic actions of neurotransmitters. Because muscle cells are large, they can accommodate several microelectrodes for electrophysiological measurements. . . . one can visualize the region of nerve-muscle contact and precisely locate the postsynaptic membrane. Moreover, a single muscle fiber usually is innervated by only one motor axon, and the transmitter [*acetylcholine*] is known. These technical advantages have made the study of this synapse particularly fruitful. (Kandel & Siegelbaum, 1985, p. 94)

Structure of the Synapse

Figure 3.11 is a schematic representation of a terminal button. The most obvious structures in the cytoplasm of the terminal button are the **synaptic**

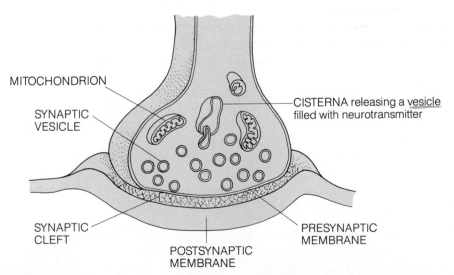

FIGURE 3.11 *A schematic diagram of a synapse.*

MITOCHONDRION

SYNAPTIC VESICLE

CISTERNA releasing a vesicle filled with neurotransmitter

SYNAPTIC CLEFT

POSTSYNAPTIC MEMBRANE

PRESYNAPTIC MEMBRANE

vesicles near the *presynaptic membrane;* the **mitochondria,** which are important sources of energy; and **cisternas,** which are neurotransmitter packaging plants similar to the Golgi apparatus of the cell body. Also apparent in Figure 3.11 is the web-like material that is present in some **synaptic clefts** (the gaps between presynaptic membranes and *postsynaptic membranes*).

Mechanisms of Synaptic Transmission

For the purpose of discussion, synaptic transmission can be divided into five somewhat independent processes: (1) synthesis of the neurotransmitter and the synaptic vesicles; (2) release of the neurotransmitter; (3) generation of postsynaptic potentials; (4) deactivation of the neurotransmitter; and (5) recycling of the membranes of the synaptic vesicles. Each of these five steps is discussed in the following paragraphs.

1. *Synthesis of the neurotransmitter and the synaptic vesicles.* Synaptic vesicles are manufactured from proteins in the cytoplasm of the cell body by the **Golgi apparatus.** When the vesicles are released from the Golgi apparatus, they leave the cell body and travel through the axon to the buttons. Materials are transported from the cell body to the buttons in two different ways; that is, there are two different mechanisms of **anterograde** (forward-acting) **axonal transport.** Synaptic vesicles travel along **microtubules** in the axonal cytoplasm at a rate of about 400 millimeters per day; this is called **fast anterograde axonal transport**. Other materials from the cell body ooze along the axon in the cytoplasm at a speed of less than 10 millimeters per day; this is called **slow anterograde axonal transport.**

Some neurotransmitters are short chains of amino acids called **peptides**—they are in effect simple proteins, which are long chains of amino acids. Like neural proteins, peptide neurotransmitters are manufactured in the cell body by ribosomes. Peptide neurotransmitters are packaged in their vesicles in the cell body by the Golgi apparatus before being transported to the buttons. In contrast, nonpeptide neurotransmitters are often synthesized and packaged in the cytoplasm of the neuron (in the button, for example). The synaptic vesicles protect neurotransmitters from degradation by enzymes in the cytoplasm.

2. *Release of the neurotransmitter.* How does the arrival of an action potential trigger the release of neurotransmitter molecules from the terminal buttons? There is good evidence that the critical mediating event is the opening of calcium channels produced by the arrival of an action potential at the terminal button. The opening of the calcium channels allows Ca^{++} ions to enter the button and to trigger the release of neurotransmitter. If the concentration of Ca^{++} ions in the extracellular fluid is artificially reduced, the release of neurotransmitter is also reduced. Conversely, increasing the extracellular concentration of Ca^{++} ions enhances transmitter release.

The mechanism of neurotransmitter release is illustrated by Figure 3.12. Neurotransmitter release begins with a vesicle moving toward the presynaptic membrane and fusing with it. At the point of contact, the membrane opens, the neurotransmitter is released into the cleft, and the vesicle becomes part of the presynaptic membrane. Figure 3.13 is a photomicrograph of a synaptic vesicle apparently caught in the act of **exocytosis,** the act of releasing its neurotransmitter into the synaptic cleft (Heuser, 1977). Once

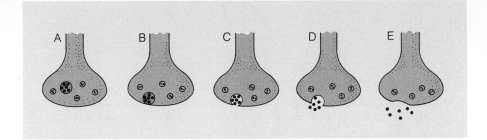

FIGURE 3.12 *A schematic representation of neurotransmitter release.*

the neurotransmitter molecules have been released, they move quickly across the cleft and combine with receptor molecules on the external surface of the postsynaptic membrane to initiate a postsynaptic potential.

3. *Generation of postsynaptic potentials.* How does the binding of a neurotransmitter to its postsynaptic receptor result in a postsynaptic potential? Although the exact mechanism by which this is accomplished depends on the particular synapse under consideration, the principle appears to be the same in all cases: the binding of a neurotransmitter with a postsynaptic receptor protein influences **chemically gated ion channels** in the receptive membrane. There are, however, two different mechanisms by which these chemically gated channels can be influenced: one direct and one indirect. The binding of the neurotransmitter to its receptor can directly open or close the chemically gated channels in the immediate vicinity, or it can initiate a series of chemical changes in the molecules of the cytoplasm that indirectly influence the status of the chemically gated ion channels of the postsynaptic neuron. In the latter case, the molecules created in the cytoplasm by the binding of a neurotransmitter to a receptor molecule are called **second messengers**. The second messenger in many neurons is **cyclic adenosine monophosphate (cAMP)**. It is created when the binding

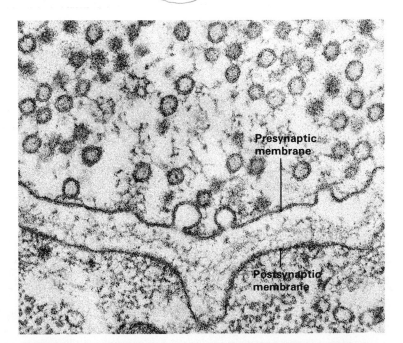

Presynaptic membrane

Postsynaptic membrane

FIGURE 3.13 *A photomicrograph of a terminal button captured in the act of exocytosis.*

of a neurotransmitter to a receptor causes the enzyme *adenylate cyclase* to be released into the cytoplasm of the postsynaptic neuron. The adenylate cyclase then causes adenosine triphosphate (ATP) to be converted to cyclic AMP. The effect of the cyclic AMP on the ion channels of the postsynaptic neuron is only brief because it is destroyed by the cytoplasmic enzyme *phosphodiesterase*. Other second messengers have long-lasting effects.

What ion channels are involved in the generation of postsynaptic potentials? The answer to this question depends on the particular class of neurons under consideration. For example, the EPSPs produced in the mammalian motor neuron appear to result from the opening of a class of chemically gated channels that permit the simultaneous flow of both Na^+ and K^+ ions. Because the pressure for Na^+ ions to move into the neuron is greater than the pressure for the K^+ ions to move out of the neuron, the overall effect of the opening of these channels is a depolarization. In other neurons, EPSPs are produced by the closing of K^+ channels that are normally open while the neuron is at rest, thus reducing the internal negativity of the neuron by decreasing the efflux of K^+ ions. IPSPs are usually produced by the opening of K^+ channels to permit an efflux of K^+ ions.

4. *Deactivation of the neurotransmitter*. There are two well-documented means by which the postsynaptic effects of a neurotransmitter are terminated. The more common of these is reuptake of the neurotransmitter molecules from the synaptic cleft by the presynaptic neuron. The advantage of this method of deactivation is that it allows the presynaptic neuron to recycle neurotransmitter molecules, that is, to package and release them again. Less commonly, enzymes in the membrane of the postsynaptic neuron deactivate the neurotransmitter by cleaving it into its constituent parts.

5. *Recycling of the vesicular membrane*. Vesicular membranes are recycled (Miller & Heuser, 1984). As each synaptic vesicle fuses with a presynaptic membrane to release its contents into the synaptic cleft, the terminal button tends to grow larger and larger. However, this growth is counteracted by the fact that pieces of excess presynaptic membrane pinch off and return to the cytoplasm. These pieces may be formed into new vesicles in the button and refilled with a nonpeptide neurotransmitter available in the cytoplasm. This is accomplished by cisternas, structures much like the Golgi apparatus of the cell body. Other pieces of excess membrane in the cytoplasm of the button are transported back to the cell body by **retrograde** (backward-moving) **axonal transport** mechanisms at a speed of just over 200 millimeters per day. In the cell body, they may be refilled with neurotransmitter by a Golgi apparatus, or they may be broken down and their molecules recycled.

3.6 The Diversity of Neural Transmission

As neuroscientists have delved more and more deeply into the intricacies of neural transmission, the diversity of neural function has become more and more apparent. It is beyond the scope of this book to describe this diversity in depth. At the same time, however, it would be misleading to leave the topic of neural transmission without providing you with at least some appreciation of its diverse nature. That is the purpose of this final section.

The investigation of neural transmission has concentrated on neurons with axons, primarily because they are large and accessible. This focus sometimes creates the misconception that all neurons have axons and that transmission in the nervous system occurs almost entirely in the all-or-none code of action potentials. They do not, and it does not. There are many neurons in the mammalian nervous system without axons—particularly in the complex interneuronal circuits that appear to play important roles in the control of complex activities such as learning, memory, motivation, and perception. Action potentials are the means by which neural messages are carried nondecrementally along axons, and thus action potentials do not occur in neurons without axons.

Not All Synapses Between
Neurons Are Axodendritic or Axosomatic!

As you have already learned, *axodendritic synapses* (synapses between the axon terminals of the presynaptic neuron and the dendrites of the postsynaptic neuron) and *axosomatic synapses* (synapses between the axon terminals of the presynaptic neuron and the *soma* or cell body of the postsynaptic neuron) are common. However, there are many other kinds of synapses. Axon terminal buttons often synapse on the axons of other neurons; axon shafts sometimes make direct synaptic contact with the dendrites or axons of other neurons; and some dendrites transmit signals across synapses to other dendrites or axons. It is also important to be aware of the fact that not all synapses are one-way streets. Some *dendrodendritic synapses* are **reciprocal synapses;** that is, they are capable of transmitting signals in either direction. Furthermore, many neurons are able to stimulate themselves; they have receptors, called **autoreceptors,** which are sensitive to their own transmitter substance. The activation of autoreceptors often reduces the subsequent synthesis and release of the neurotransmitter. Axodendritic synapses frequently occur on little specialized buds on the dendrite called **dendritic spines.**

Axoaxonic synapses have been shown to mediate **presynaptic inhibition.** Presynaptic and **postsynaptic inhibition** are compared in Figure 3.14. The major functional difference between the two is that postsynaptic inhibition reduces a neuron's responsiveness to all synaptic inputs, whereas presynaptic inhibition selectively reduces a neuron's responsiveness to only one input.

Not All Synapses Are Chemical!

The transmission at some synapses, called **gap junctions,** is electrical rather than chemical. Gap junctions are extremely narrow clefts—2 nanometers as opposed to the usual 30 nanometers—which are spanned by channels called **connexons** through which electrical current can flow. Transmission across gap junctions is rapid and inflexible, and thus gap junctions are frequently involved in the mediation of the rapid, stereotypical responses of lower organisms. Gap junctions are rare in the mammalian nervous system.

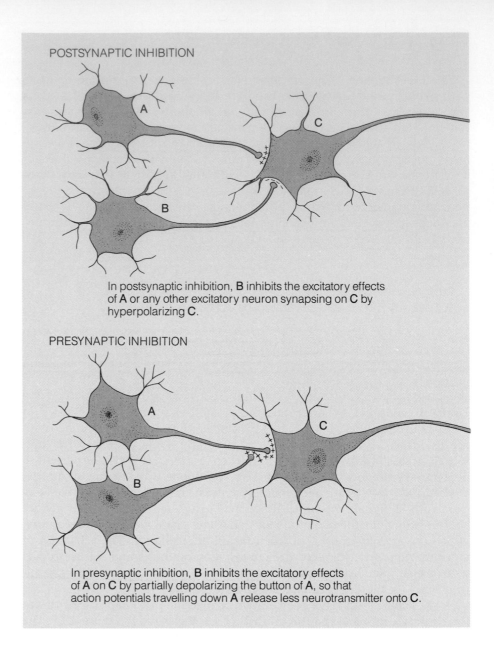

POSTSYNAPTIC INHIBITION

In postsynaptic inhibition, **B** inhibits the excitatory effects of **A** or any other excitatory neuron synapsing on **C** by hyperpolarizing **C**.

PRESYNAPTIC INHIBITION

In presynaptic inhibition, **B** inhibits the excitatory effects of **A** on **C** by partially depolarizing the button of **A**, so that action potentials travelling down **A** release less neurotransmitter onto **C**.

FIGURE 3.14 *A schematic illustration of presynaptic and postsynaptic inhibition.*

Not All Chemical Synapses Are Directed!

So far, only **directed synapses** have been discussed; these are synapses in which the presynaptic membrane and the receptive area of the postsynaptic cell are in close apposition. However, there are also many **nondirected synapses** in the nervous system; these are synapses at which the site of transmitter release from the presynaptic neuron is not so close to the target receptors. For example, the postganglionic neurons of the autonomic nervous branch diffusely as they approach their target structure (see Figure 3.15), and each branch has a series of swellings or varicosities, which gives them the appearance of strings of beads. Neurotransmitter is released from these varicosities into the extracellular fluid and has relatively widespread effects on the surrounding neurons. The neurons of the

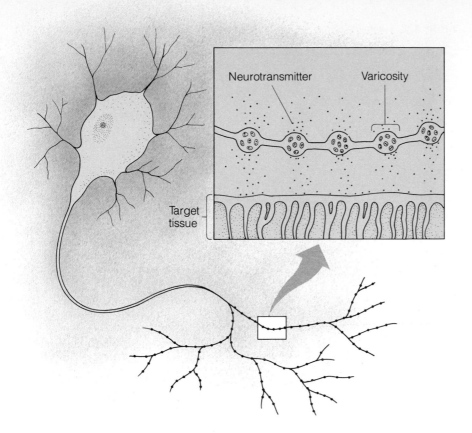

Neurotransmitter   Varicosity

Target
tissue

FIGURE 3.15 *A schematic illustration of nondirected neurotransmitter release. The neurotransmitter released from the varicosities is widely dispersed to various target sites.*

neuroendocrine system are the most nondirected of all neurons; they release their neurotransmitters directly into the blood, and thus they can influence sites throughout the organism.

Not All Neurons Remain at Rest Until Excited!

Motor neurons remain inactive unless they are excited, but this is not true of most neurons of the central nervous system. Most central nervous system neurons are almost always active. Some fire continually at a regular rate; some fire in bursts separated by regular intervals; and still others fire frequently, but irregularly. In the complex circuits of the mammalian CNS, it is difficult to determine the source of this activity; however, research on the simple nervous systems of invertebrates has suggested that many neurons fire spontaneously, that is, without being stimulated. The fact that so many neurons of the central nervous system are continually active may explain why inhibitory synapses are so prevalent.

Spontaneously active neurons have one major advantage over those that remain at rest until activated. Spontaneously active neurons have the capacity to transmit information in two ways: either by increasing or by decreasing their firing rates. Obviously the latter option is not open to neurons that do not fire unless stimulated.

Conclusion

The function of the nervous system, like the function of any circuit, depends on how signals are transmitted through it. Accordingly, an understanding of the basic principles of neural transmission is prerequisite to the study of the neural bases of behavior. This chapter has introduced you to these basic principles. They are summarized in Table 3.2.

Table 3.2 *Summary of the Events Associated with the Transmission of Signals through a Multipolar Neuron and Across a Directed Chemical Synapse*

SITE	EVENT
Postsynaptic membranes on dendrites and cell body	When the neurotransmitter binds to post-synaptic receptors, postsynaptic potentials are created either by the direct opening of chemically gated ion channels or by the synthesis of second messengers in the cytoplasm of the postsynaptic neuron.
Dendrites and cell body	Postsynaptic potentials are conducted instantly and decrementally to the axon hillock, which automatically sums or integrates them.
Axon hillock	If the integrated postsynaptic potential is a depolarization sufficient to drive the axon hillock membrane to its threshold of excitation, an all-or-none action potential is generated by the brief opening of voltage-gated sodium channels on the hillock membrane.
Axon	The action potential is nondecrementally transmitted down the axon. If the axon is myelinated, conduction is saltatory.
Terminal buttons	When an action potential arrives at a terminal button, it triggers an influx of Ca^{++} ions through voltage-gated calcium channels, and this in turn triggers the release of the neurotransmitter.
Postsynaptic membranes	The neurotransmitter moves across the synaptic cleft, where it generates postsynaptic potentials, thus beginning the next cycle of neural transmission.
Presynaptic neuron	The neurotransmitter and synaptic vesicles are subsequently taken back into the cytoplasm of the button and recycled.

Food for Thought

1. Just as computers operate on binary (yes-no) signals, the all-or-none action potential is the basis of neural communication. The human brain is thus nothing more than a particularly complex computer. Discuss.

2. How have the findings described in this chapter changed your concept of brain function?

ADDITIONAL READING

For a systematic introduction to neurophysiology that is more detailed than that provided by this chapter, the first 150 pages of the following text are hard to beat.

Kandel, E. R., & Schwartz, J. H. (Eds.). (1985). *Principles of neural science*. New York: Elsevier.

Scientific American is one of the few scientific journals that can be purchased at your local newstand. It specializes in making the research of the world's greatest scientists accessible to the educated public in beautifully illustrated, well-written articles. The following are several that are relevant to this chapter.

Dunant, Y., & Israël, M. (1985). The release of acetylcholine. *Scientific American, 252,* 58–66.

Gottlieb, D. I. (1988). GABAergic neurons. *Scientific American, 258,* 82–89.

Keynes, R. D. (1979). Ion channels in the nerve-cell membrane. *Scientific American, 240,* 126–135.

Llinás, R. R. (1982). Calcium in synaptic transmission. *Scientific American, 247,* 56–65.

Schwartz, J. H. (1980). The transport of substances in nerve cells. *Scientific American, 242,* 152–171.

Snyder, S. H. (1985). The molecular basis of communication between cells. *Scientific American, 253,* 132–141.

To help you study the material in this chapter, all of the key terms—those that have appeared in bold type—are listed and briefly defined here.

Absolute refractory period. A brief period (1 to 2 milliseconds) after the initiation of an action potential during which it is impossible to elicit another action potential in the same neuron.

Acetylcholine. A neurotransmitter.

Action potential (AP). The firing of a neuron; a momentary change in the membrane potential from -70 mV to $+50$ mV.

All-or-none responses. Responses that are not graded; responses, such as action potentials, that occur full blown or not at all.

Anterograde axonal transport. Transport of materials from the cell body down the axon to the terminal buttons by either slow or fast transport mechanisms.

Antidromic. An adjective that refers to signals traveling from axon terminals toward the cell body.

Autoreceptors. Receptors, often on the presynaptic membrane, that are sensitive to a neuron's own neurotransmitter.

Axon hillock. The site at which the axon leaves the cell body and at which action potentials are normally generated.

Chemically gated ion channels. Ion channels that are opened and closed by chemical changes.

Cisternas. Intracellular organelles that fill synaptic vesicles in the terminal buttons with neurotransmitter available in the cytoplasm.

Connexons. The channels that span gap junctions.

Cyclic adenosine monophosphate (cAMP). The second messenger in many neurons.

Dendritic spines. Specialized buds on dendrites at which axodendritic synapses often occur.

Depolarize. To decrease the membrane potential (e.g., from -70 mV to -60 mV).

Dinitrophenol (DNP). A metabolic poison.

Directed synapses. Synapses at which the site of neurotransmitter release and the receptor sites on the postsynaptic membrane are in close proximity.

Excitatory postsynaptic potentials (EPSPs). Graded postsynaptic depolarizations.

Exocytosis. The act of releasing the neurotransmitter into the synaptic cleft.

Gap junctions. The sites of electrical transmission between neurons.

Golgi apparatus. The structure in the cell body of a neuron that manufactures synaptic vesicles.

Graded response. A response whose magnitude is related to the magnitude of the stimulus.

Hyperpolarize. To increase the membrane potential (e.g., from -70 mV to -75 mV).

Inhibitory postsynaptic potentials (IPSPs). Postsynaptic hyperpolarizations, which decrease the likelihood that an action potential will be generated.

Integration. Adding or combining a number of signals into one overall signal.

Ion. A positively or negatively charged particle.

Ion channels. Pores in cellular membranes through which ions pass.

Membrane potential. The difference in electrical charge between the inside and the outside of a cell.

Microelectrode puller. A device that pulls apart hot fine glass tubes to form very fine hollow pipettes that are used to make microelectrodes.

Microelectrodes. Intracellular recording electrodes.

Microtubules. Fine tubes in the cytoplasm responsible for intracellular transport of various materials.

Mitochondria. Structures in the cytoplasm responsible for the conversion of certain molecules into ATP (adenosine triphosphate), the source of energy for all cells.

Motor neurons. Multipolar neurons with large axons that project to receptive sites on muscle fibers.

Neuromuscular junction. The synapse of a motor neuron on a muscle.

Neurotransmitters. Various chemicals that mediate the communication between neurons; they are typically released by the presynaptic neuron into the synaptic cleft, where they bind to receptors on the postsynaptic membrane.

Nodes of Ranvier. The regular gaps in the axonal myelin.

Nondirected synapses. Synapses at which the site of neurotransmitter release and the target site are not close together.

Orthodromic. From the cell body down the axon toward the terminal buttons.

Oscilloscope. A device that displays the changes in the membrane potential over time as vertical displacements of a spot of light as it sweeps from left to right across a fluorescent screen.

Peptides. Short chains of amino acids, some of which function as neurotransmitters.

Postsynaptic inhibition. A form of inhibition that reduces a neuron's responsiveness to all excitatory synaptic inputs.

Presynaptic inhibition. A form of inhibition that selectively reduces a neuron's responsiveness to specific synaptic inputs; it is mediated by axoaxonal synapses.

Reciprocal synapses. Synapses capable of transmission in both directions.

Relative refractory period. A period after the absolute refractory period during which a higher than normal amount of stimulation is necessary to make a neuron fire.

Resting potential. The steady membrane potential of about -70 mV of a neuron at rest.

Retrograde axonal transport. Transport of materials from the buttons up the axon to the cell body.

Saltatory conduction. Conduction of an action potential from node to node down a myelinated axon.

Second messengers. Molecules that are created in the cytoplasm of the postsynaptic cell in response to the activation of postsynaptic receptors; once created, second messengers influence the membrane potential of the postsynaptic cell.

Sodium-potassium pumps. Active transport mechanisms that pump Na^+ ions out of the cell and K^+ ions into the cell.

Spatial summation. The integration of signals that occur at the same time, but at different sites on the neuron.

Synaptic cleft. The extracellular space between the presynaptic membrane and the postsynaptic membrane.

Synaptic vesicles. Small spherical membranes that store neurotransmitter molecules and release them into the synaptic cleft.

Temporal summation. The integration of neural signals that occur at different times.

Threshold of excitation. The level of depolarization at the axon hillock necessary to generate an action potential, usually about -65 mV.

Voltage-gated ion channels. Ion channels that open and close in response to changes in the membrane potential.

4

Research Methods of Biopsychology

In Chapter 1, you were introduced to the discipline of biopsychology. You learned that biopsychology focuses on the interaction between the nervous system and behavior; you learned some of the "dos" and "don'ts" of biopsychological research; and you learned that biopsychology is a diverse discipline encompassing a variety of different research approaches. In Chapters 2 and 3, the introduction of biopsychology was temporarily curtailed while prerequisite background material in neuroanatomy and neurophysiology was presented. This chapter marks a return to biopsychology. However, unlike Chapter 1, which introduced biopsychology in terms of the general interests and approaches that characterize

it, this chapter gets down to the specific day-to-day activities of the biopsychology laboratory. It is intended to broaden your understanding of how biopsychologists do their research by introducing you to some of the specific research techniques that they use.

The organization of this chapter reflects biopsychology's intrinsic duality. It has two major parts: one dealing with methods for studying the nervous system and the other dealing with methods for studying behavior.

Part 1: Methods of Studying the Nervous System

Part 2: Behavioral Research Methods of Biopsychology

NEUROTRANSMITTERS TAKE A HOLIDAY

4.1 Methods of Visualizing Human Brain Damage

Neuropsychological researchers study the relation between the brain and behavior by comparing their assessment of a patient's behavioral deficits with information about the location, nature, and extent of the underlying brain damage. If the patient is one who has undergone neurosurgery, a description of the damage is often provided by the neurosurgeon's report; or, if the patient dies, precise information about the damage can be obtained by postmortem examination. Otherwise, one of the following methods must be used for visualizing the living brain: X-ray photography, contrast X-rays, computerized axial tomography, magnetic resonance imaging, and positron emission tomography.

X-ray Photography

To take an X-ray photograph, an X-ray beam is passed through the test object. As each portion of the beam passes in a straight line through the test object, each of the molecules through which it passes absorbs some of the radiation. The unabsorbed portion of the beam leaving the test object is projected onto a photographic plate. Standard X-ray photography is effective in characterizing internal structures that differ substantially from the surrounding medium in the degree to which they absorb X-rays—for example, a revolver in a suitcase full of clothes or a bone in flesh. Accordingly, a standard X-ray photograph of the head can reveal the location of a skull fracture, but it is of little use in visualizing the various structures of the brain. By the time an X-ray beam passes through the numerous overlapping structures of the brain, which differ only slightly from one another in their ability to absorb X-rays, it carries little information about the shape of the individual structures through which it passed.

Contrast X-rays

One way to increase the usefulness of X-ray technology in the study of brain pathology is to highlight parts of the brain by introducing a substance that readily absorbs X-rays. The structures in which the *radio-opaque substance* accumulates stand out from other structures on X-ray photographs.

There are two such **contrast X-ray** techniques that have been widely used to study the brain. **Pneumoencephalography** involves temporarily replacing some of the cerebrospinal fluid with air. Because air is radio-opaque, the ventricles and fissures of the brain are clearly visible in the subsequent contrast X-ray, which is called a *pneumoencephalogram*. A local deformation of a ventricle or a fissure may indicate the location of a tumor, and a general increase in the size of ventricles or fissures is indicative of diffuse brain damage. **Angiography** is a procedure for visualizing the cerebral circulatory system by infusing a radio-opaque dye through a cerebral artery during X-ray photography (see Figure 4.1). *Angiograms* are most useful in identifying the location of vascular damage, but the displacement of blood vessels from their normal position can be used to infer the location of a tumor.

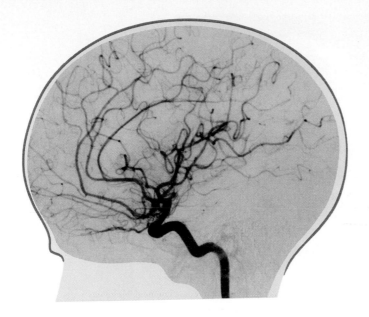

FIGURE 4.1 *A cerebral angiogram of a healthy subject.*
(Courtesy of William Robertson, Department of Radiology, Vancouver General Hospital.)

Computerized Axial Tomography

Computerized axial tomography (CAT) is a computer-assisted X-ray procedure for visualizing the brain in three dimensions. The procedure provides a series of X-ray photographs of horizontal sections of the living brain, which characterize its three-dimensional structure when viewed in sequence. During computerized axial tomography, the neurological patient lies with his or her head positioned in the center of a large cylinder as depicted in Figure 4.2. On one side of the cylinder is an X-ray tube that

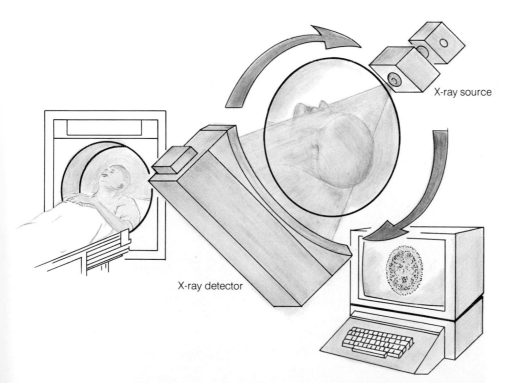

X-ray source

X-ray detector

FIGURE 4.2 *Computerized axial tomography.*

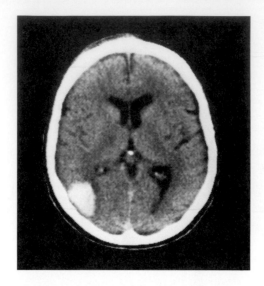

FIGURE 4.3 *A CAT scan section. Notice the tumor in the occipital lobe.*

Courtesy of J. McA. Jones Good Samaritan Hospital and Medical Center, Portland, Oregon.

projects an X-ray beam through the head of the patient to an X-ray detector mounted on the other side. The X-ray tube and detector automatically rotate around the head of the subject at one level of the brain, taking a series of individual measurements as they rotate. These are combined by the computer to generate one section of the *CAT scan* (see Figure 4.3). Then, the X-ray tube and detector are moved along the axis of the patient's body to another level of the brain, and the process is repeated. Scans of eight or nine horizontal brain sections are usually obtained from each patient.

Magnetic Resonance Imaging

Despite the technological sophistication of computerized axial tomography, it is not the last word in techniques for providing three-dimensional images of the brain. **Magnetic resonance imaging** (MRI) has even higher powers of resolution (see Figure 4.4). MRI is not an adaptation of X-ray

FIGURE 4.4 *An MRI scan.*

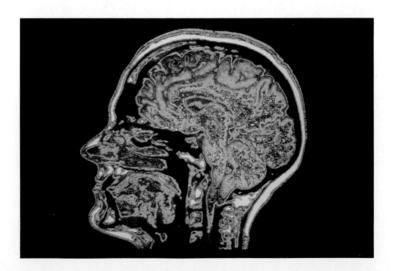

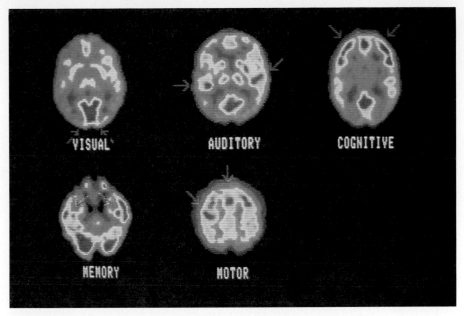

From "Positron Tomography: Human Brain Function and
Biochemistry" by Michael E. Phelps and John C. Mazziotta, May 17, 1985,
Science, 228 (4701), p. 804. Copyright 1985 by the AAAS.
Reprinted by permission. Courtesy of Drs. Michael E. Phelps and
John Mazziotta, UCLA School of Medicine.

FIGURE 4.5 *A color photograph of a PET scan. High levels of activity are indicated by reds and yellows.*

photography; instead, the images are constructed from the measurement of waves that hydrogen atoms emit when they are activated by radio-frequency waves in a magnetic field. The clarity of MRI stems from the fact that the concentration of hydrogen atoms in different neural structures varies substantially.

Positron Emission Tomography

Another technique for viewing the living human brain is **positron emission tomography (PET).** Unlike CAT and MRI scans, *PET scans provide information about the metabolic activity of the brain.* In the most common version of PET, the patient is injected with radioactive **2-deoxyglucose (2-DG).** Because of its similarity to glucose, the primary metabolic fuel of the brain, 2-deoxyglucose is taken up more rapidly by active (i.e., energy-consuming) neurons. However, unlike glucose, 2-deoxyglucose cannot be metabolized, and it thus accumulates in active neurons until it can be gradually broken down and released. Thus, if PET is performed on a patient while he or she is engaged in an activity such as reading, the PET scan will indicate the areas of the brain most active during the activity (see Figure 4.5).

4.2 Recording Psychophysiological Activity from the Surface of the Human Body

In this section of the chapter, five of the most widely studied psychophysiological measures are introduced: one measure of brain activity (the scalp EEG), two measures of somatic nervous system activity (muscle tension and eye movement), and two measures of autonomic nervous system activity (skin conductance and cardiovascular activity).

Scalp Electroencephalography

The *electroencephalogram* (EEG) is a gross measure of the electrical activity of the brain and it is recorded by a device called an **electroencephalograph** or EEG machine. In experiments on human subjects, each channel of EEG activity is usually recorded between two large, disk-shaped electrodes, about half the size of a dime, that are taped to the scalp. There are two basic variations of **electroencephalography**. In *monopolar recording*, one electrode is placed at the target site and the other electrode is attached to the subject at a point of relative electrical silence—for example, an earlobe. In *bipolar recording*, the EEG signal is recorded between electrodes placed at two active sites.

The scalp EEG activity reflects the sum of electrical events throughout the head. These include the action potentials and postsynaptic potentials (EPSPs and IPSPs) generated by neurons and electrical signals from skin, muscles, blood, and eyes. Thus, the utility of the scalp EEG clearly does not lie in its ability to provide an unclouded view of neural activity. Its value as a research and diagnostic tool rests on the fact that some recognizable EEG wave forms are associated with particular states of consciousness or particular types of cerebral pathology. A few examples of EEG wave forms and their psychological correlates are presented in Figure 4.6.

Because EEG signals decrease in amplitude as they spread from their source, a comparison of signals recorded from various sites can sometimes indicate their origin. On the following page is a classic problem encountered by clinical electroencephalographers. How would you solve it?

Event-Related Potentials and Signal Averaging

In some cases, psychophysiologists are more interested in the EEG waves that accompany certain events than they are in the background EEG signal (e.g., Hillyard & Kutas, 1983). These accompanying waves are gen-

FIGURE 4.6 *Some typical electroencephalograms and their psychological correlates.*

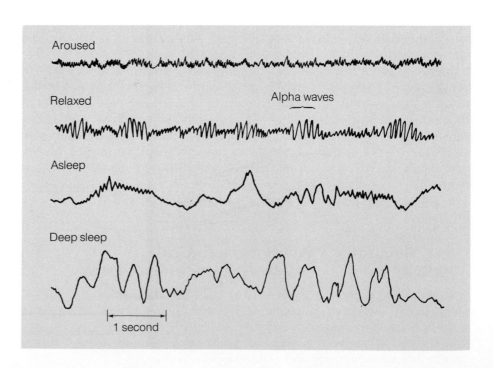

You are serving as a research assistant in a psychophysiology laboratory, and your task is to conduct a pilot study on several of your classmates. The first step of the experiment is to record two channels of bipolar EEG activity, and to do this you attach four electrodes—A, B, C, and D—to the scalp of one of your friends. You then set the dials on the EEG machine so that electrodes A and B are compared on the first channel of EEG activity, and electrodes C and D are compared on the second. You are alarmed to notice epileptic spikes in your friend's EEG. Upon more careful inspection, you determine that all of the epileptic spikes are being displayed on the first channel. This indicates that your friend has a focus of epileptic activity near A, near B, or near both. How can you determine which of these three possibilities is correct? When you solve this basic problem, you will have discovered your friend's epileptic focus and discovered on your own the electroencephalographic technique called **triangulation** (see Figure 4.7).

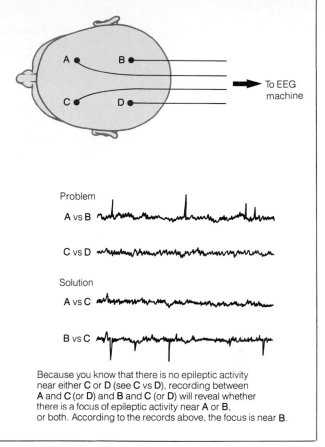

Because you know that there is no epileptic activity near either C or D (see C vs D), recording between A and C (or D) and B and C (or D) will reveal whether there is a focus of epileptic activity near A or B, or both. According to the records above, the focus is near B.

FIGURE 4.7 *The triangulation problem.*

erally referred to as **event-related potentials (ERPs)**. One commonly studied type of event-related potential is the **sensory evoked potential,** the change in the cortical EEG signal elicited by the momentary presentation of a sensory stimulus. As illustrated in Figure 4.10, the cortical EEG recorded following a sensory stimulus has two components: the response to the stimulus (i.e., the signal) and the ongoing background EEG activity (i.e., the noise). The *signal* is the part of any recording that is of interest; the *noise* is the part that isn't. The problem is often that the noise of the background EEG is so great that the sensory evoked potential is almost completely masked—measuring a sensory evoked potential can be like measuring a whisper at a rock concert. The method used to reduce the noise of the background EEG is called **signal averaging.** First, a subject's response to a stimulus, such as a click, is recorded many—let's say, 1,000—times. Then a computer identifies the millivolt value of each of the 1,000 traces at their starting points (i.e., at the click) and calculates the mean of these 1,000 scores. Next, it considers the value of each of the 1,000 traces 1 millisecond (msec) from their start, for example, and calculates the mean of these values. Then, it repeats this process at the 2-msec mark, the 3-msec mark, and so on. When these averages are plotted, the average responses evoked by the click are more apparent because the random background EEG is canceled out by the averaging. See Figure 4.8.

The analysis of *average evoked potentials* (AEPs) usually focuses on the various peaks or waves in the averaged signal. Each wave is characterized

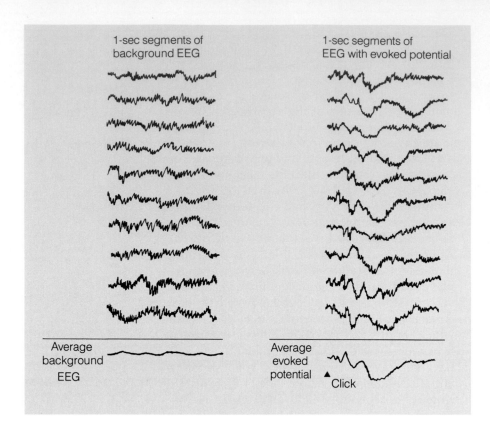

1-sec segments of
background EEG

1-sec segments of
EEG with evoked potential

Average
background
EEG

Average
evoked
potential ▲
Click

FIGURE 4.8 *The averaging of
an auditory evoked potential.*

by whether it is positive or negative and by its latency. For example, the
P300 wave illustrated in Figure 4.9, is the positive wave that usually occurs
about 300 msec after a momentary stimulus only if it has considerable
meaning for the subject (Sutton, Teuting, Zubin, & John, 1967). In contrast, the small waves recorded in the first few milliseconds after a stimulus
are not easily influenced by changing the meaning of the stimulus. These
small waves are called **far-field potentials** because, although they are recorded from the scalp, they originate in the sensory nuclei of the brain
stem (Jewett, Romano, & Williston, 1970; Jewett & Williston, 1971).

FIGURE 4.9 *An average auditory evoked response showing
the P300 wave. By convention,
positive EEG waves are always
shown as downward deflections.*

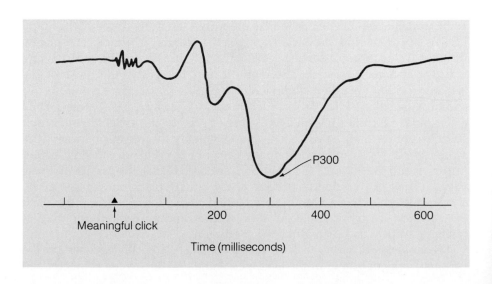

P300

Meaningful click

200   400   600

Time (milliseconds)

Electromyography

Skeletal muscles are each composed of millions of thread-like muscle fibers. Each muscle fiber contracts in an all-or-none fashion when activated by the motor neuron that innervates it. At any given time, a few fibers in each muscle are likely to be contracting, thus maintaining the overall tone of the muscle. Movement results when a large number of fibers contract at the same time. Under normal conditions, the impulses reaching a muscle are staggered so that the all-or-none responses of individual muscle fibers combine to produce fluid responses of the muscle as a whole.

Electromyography is a procedure for measuring the electrical discharge of muscles. The resulting record is called an *electromyogram* (EMG). EMG activity is usually recorded between two electrodes taped to the surface of the skin over the muscle of interest. An EMG record is presented in Figure 4.10. You will notice from this figure that the main correlate of an increase in muscle contraction is an increase in the amplitude of the EMG signal, which reflects the number of fibers contracting at any one time. Most psychophysiologists do not work with the raw EMG signal; they convert it to a more workable form by a process called *signal integration*. The signal is fed into a computer that calculates the total amount of EMG spiking per unit of time—in consecutive 0.1-second intervals, for example. The total EMG activity per unit of time is then plotted, and the result is a smooth curve, the amplitude of which is a simple, continuous measure of level of muscle contraction over time (Figure 4.10).

Eye Movement

The electrophysiological technique for recording eye movements is called **electrooculography,** and the resulting record is called an *electrooculogram* (EOG). Electrooculography is based on the fact that there is a steady potential difference between the front (positive) and back (negative) of the eyeball. Because of this steady potential, when the eyes move, a change in the electrical potential can be recorded between electrodes placed around the eye. It is usual to record EOG activity between two electrodes placed on each side of the eye to measure its horizontal movements, and between two electrodes placed above and below the eye to measure its vertical movements (see Figure 4.11).

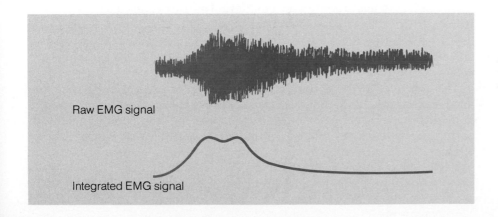

Raw EMG signal

Integrated EMG signal

FIGURE 4.10 *The relation between the raw EMG signals and the integrated EMG of a subject suddenly tensing and gradually relaxing the muscle beneath the electrodes.*

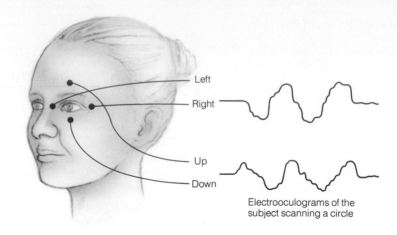

FIGURE 4.11 *The typical placement of electrodes around the eye for electrooculography, and an electrooculogram produced by the subject's scanning a circle.*

Left

Right

Up

Down

Electrooculograms of the subject scanning a circle

Electrodermal Activity

It was first reported in the the last century that increases in the ability of the skin to conduct electricity were associated with emotional thoughts or experiences. The two most commonly employed indices of electrodermal activity are the **skin conductance level** (**SCL**) and the **skin conductance response** (**SCR**). The SCL is a measure of the steady background level of skin conductance associated with a particular situation, whereas the SCR refers to transient changes in the SCL caused by discrete experiences. The physiological bases of skin conductance changes are not fully understood, but there is considerable evidence implicating the sweat glands. Although the main function of these glands is to cool the body, they tend to become active in emotional situations—as you are almost certainly aware. Although sweat glands are distributed over most of the body surface, it is those of hands, feet, armpits, and forehead that are particularly responsive to emotional stimuli. Few young lovers have escaped the dreaded duo: clammy hands and hircismus. (I recommend *Mrs. Byrnes Dictionary of Obscene, Obscure, and Preposterous Words* for those of you who collect unusual words such as the latter, which by the way means underarm odor.)

Cardiovascular Activity

The presence in our language of terms such as "chicken-hearted," "heartache," "white with fear," and "blushing bride" indicates that modern psychophysiologists were not the first to recognize the relation between *cardiovascular activity* and emotion. The cardiovascular system has two parts: the blood vessels and the heart. The blood vessels distribute oxygen and nutrients to the tissues of the body, remove metabolic wastes, and serve as pathways of hormonal communication. The heart pumps the blood through the blood vessels.

The output of the heart responds immediately to general increases in the need for energy, and the dispersal of blood throughout the system is immediately adjusted in response to changes in the energy requirements of particular tissues. Blood can be distributed preferentially to various tissues because the cardiovascular system, rather than being a single closed loop of vessels, is connected in parallel, as illustrated in Figure 4.12. The selective distribution of blood to various tissues is accomplished by the activity of *sphincter muscles* (any muscles whose contraction closes a bodily canal) in

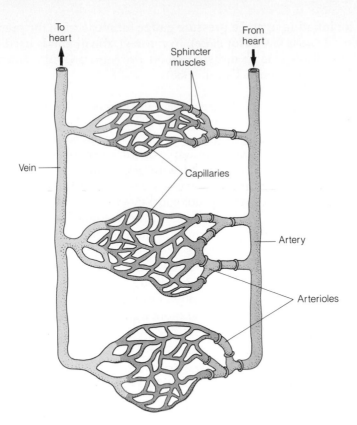

FIGURE 4.12 *A schematic representation of the parallel organization of the circulatory system. Blood flow is directed by the arteriole sphincters.*

the walls of the arterioles. Constriction of particular arterioles reduces the blood flowing to areas of the body supplied by them, whereas dilation increases it. Three different measures of cardiovascular activity are frequently employed in psychophysiological research: heart rate, arterial blood pressure, local blood volume.

Heart Rate   The electrical signal generated by the heart during each heartbeat can be recorded through electrodes placed on the chest. The recording obtained in this manner is called an **electrocardiogram** (abbreviated either **ECG,** for obvious reasons, or **EKG,** from the original German). The average resting heart rate of a healthy adult is about 70 beats per minute, but it increases abruptly at the sound or thought of a dental drill.

Blood Pressure   Measuring arterial blood pressure involves two independent measurements: a measurement of the peak pressure during the periods of heart contraction, the *systoles,* and a measurement of the minimum pressure during the periods of relaxation, the *diastoles.* Blood pressure is usually expressed as a ratio of systolic over diastolic blood pressure in mmHg (millimeters of mercury). The normal resting blood pressure for an adult is about 130/70 mmHg. A blood pressure of more than 140/90 mmHg is viewed as a serious health hazard and is called **hypertension.** When no simple physiological cause for the hypertension can be identified, it is commonly assumed to be caused by excessive psychological stress and it is termed **essential hypertension.**

I am sure that most of you have had your blood pressure measured with a *sphygmomanometer,* an archaic device composed of a hollow cuff, a rubber bulb for inflating it, and a pressure gauge for measuring the pressure in the cuff (*sphygmos* is Greek for *pulse*). In contrast, the methods used by modern psychophysiologists to measure blood pressure are fully automated (see for example, Linden & Estrin, 1988).

Blood Volume *Plethysmography* is the general term used to refer to the various techniques for measuring changes in the volume of blood in a particular part of the body (from the Greek *plethysmos*, meaning *an enlargement*). The most well-known example of such a change is the engorgement of the genitals that is associated with sexual arousal in both males and females, but changes in the flow of blood to other areas of the body occur in association with other psychological events. One method of measuring these changes is to record changes in the volume of the target tissue by wrapping a strain gauge around it. Although this method has utility in measuring blood flow in fingers or in similarly shaped organs, the possibilities of employing it are somewhat restricted. Another plethysmographic method is to shine a light through the tissue under investigation and to measure the amount of the light that is absorbed by it—the more blood there is in a structure, the more light will be absorbed.

4.3 Invasive Physiological and Pharmacological Research Methods

Attempts to study the neural bases of human behavior are seriously impeded by the necessity of adhering to lines of research involving no direct interaction with the organ of interest, that is, the nervous system. We turn now from a consideration of the noninvasive techniques employed in research on human subjects to a consideration of more direct procedures. This section introduces basic physiological and pharmacological methods employed in biopsychological studies of laboratory animals.

Most techniques used in biopsychological research on laboratory animals fall into one of four categories: lesion methods, electrical stimulation methods, invasive recording methods, and psychopharmacological methods. Each of these four methods is discussed in this section of the chapter, but first there is a description of stereotaxic surgery, the first step in many biopsychological experiments on laboratory animals.

Stereotaxic Surgery

The first step in lesioning, stimulating, or recording from a subcortical structure is to insert the lesioning, stimulating, or recording device so that its "working end" is positioned at the target site. *Stereotaxic surgery* is the means by which this is accomplished. Stereotaxic surgery requires two things: an atlas to provide directions to the target site and an instrument for getting there. The **stereotaxic atlas** is used to locate structures in much the same way that a geographic atlas is used to locate a geographic landmark. There is, however, one important difference; in contrast to the surface of the earth, which has only two dimensions, the brain has three. Accordingly, the brain is represented in a stereotaxic atlas by a series of individual maps, one per page, each representing the structure of a single, two-dimensional coronal brain slice. In stereotaxic atlases, all distances are given in millimeters from a designated reference point. In some rat atlases,

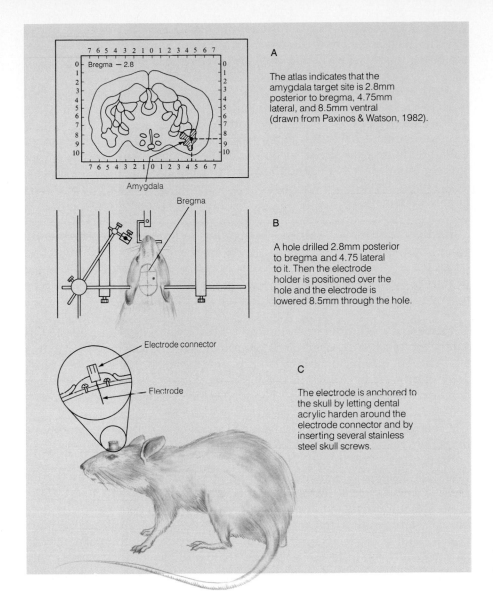

A

The atlas indicates that the amygdala target site is 2.8mm posterior to bregma, 4.75mm lateral, and 8.5mm ventral (drawn from Paxinos & Watson, 1982).

B

A hole drilled 2.8mm posterior to bregma and 4.75 lateral to it. Then the electrode holder is positioned over the hole and the electrode is lowered 8.5mm through the hole.

C

The electrode is anchored to the skull by letting dental acrylic harden around the electrode connector and by inserting several stainless steel skull screws.

FIGURE 4.13 *Implanting an electrode in the rat amygdala.*

the reference point is **bregma,** a point on the skull where two *sutures* (seams) intersect. The **stereotaxic instrument** has two parts: a *head holder,* which firmly holds each subject's brain in the prescribed position and orientation, and an *electrode holder,* which holds the device to be inserted. The electrode holder can be moved in three dimensions: anterior-posterior, dorsal-ventral, or lateral-medial (front-back, up-down, or side to side, respectively) by a system of precision gears. The implantation of an electrode in the amygdala of a rat is illustrated in Figure 4.13.

Lesion Method

Those of you with an unrelenting drive to dismantle objects to see how they work will appreciate the lesion method. In the lesion method, a part of the brain is removed, damaged, or destroyed; then, the behavior of the subject is carefully assessed to determine the functions of the lesioned structure. Four lesion methods are discussed here: aspiration lesions, radio-frequency lesions, knife cuts, and cryogenic blockade.

Aspiration Lesions   When a lesion is to be made in cortical tissue that is accessible to the eye and instruments of the surgeon, **aspiration** is frequently the method of choice. The cortical tissue is drawn off by suction created in a hand-held glass pipette. Because the underlying white matter is slightly more resistant to suction than the cortical tissue itself, a skilled surgeon can delicately peel off the layers of cortical tissue from the surface of the brain, leaving the underlying white matter and major blood vessels largely undamaged.

Radio-Frequency Lesions   Subcortical lesions are most frequently made by passing high-frequency (radio-frequency) current through the target tissue from the tip of a stereotaxically positioned electrode. It is the heat from the current that destroys the tissue. The size of the lesion can be regulated by controlling current duration and intensity.

Knife Cuts   Cutting or sectioning is used to eliminate transmission in a nerve or tract. A tiny, well-placed cut can unambiguously accomplish this task without producing extensive damage to surrounding tissue. How does one insert a knife into the brain to make a cut without severely damaging the overlying tissue? The method is depicted in Figure 4.14.

Cryogenic Blockade   **Cryogenic blockade** is an attractive alternative to the other lesion techniques. When coolant is pumped through the tip of an implanted *cryoprobe* such as the one depicted in Figure 4.15, the surrounding tissue is cooled and the firing of neurons in the vicinity is suppressed. Moreover, if the tissue temperature is kept well above 0°C, there is no structural damage and normal neural function returns to the area once its temperature returns to normal. A cryogenic blockade is functionally similar to a lesion in that it eliminates the contribution of a particular area of the brain to the ongoing behavior of the subject. This is why cryogenic blockades are sometimes referred to as functional or *reversible lesions* even though no structural damage is produced if the technique is properly applied. Similar reversible lesions can be produced with microinjections of local anesthetics into particular brain sites.

Interpreting Lesion Effects   Before you leave this section on lesions, a word of caution is in order. Lesion effects are deceptively difficult to interpret. Because the structures of the brain are so small, so convoluted, and so tightly packed together, even a highly skilled surgeon cannot completely destroy a structure without producing significant damage to adjacent structures. There is, however, an unfortunate tendency to lose sight of this fact. For example, a lesion that leaves major portions of the amygdala intact and damages an assortment of neighboring structures, comes to be thought of simplistically as an *amygdaloid lesion.* Such an apparently harmless abstraction can be very misleading. If you believe that lesions referred to as amygdaloid lesions involve no other tissue, you will incorrectly attribute all of the behavioral effects of such lesions to amygdala damage; and conversely, if you believe that so-called amygdaloid lesions involve the entire amygdala, you will incorrectly conclude that the amygdala does not participate in behaviors uninfluenced by the lesion.

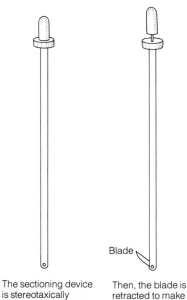

The sectioning device is stereotaxically positioned in the brain.

Then, the blade is retracted to make the cut.

Blade

FIGURE 4.14 *A device for performing subcortical "knife" cuts.*

Electrical Stimulation

Clues about the function of a neural structure can be obtained by stimulating it with electrical current. It is usual to administer electrical stimulation to the nervous system across the two tips of a *bipolar electrode*—two insulated wires wound tightly together and cut at the end. Even very weak pulses of current produce an immediate increase in the firing of neurons near the tip of the electrode. As you will learn in the forthcoming chapters, such stimulation can elicit a number of very interesting behavioral reactions (e.g., sexual behavior, attack, seizures, sleep, and eating), which provide an indication of the functions of the stimulation site. Often electrical stimulation of a particular site produces effects opposite to those produced by a lesion to the same general area.

Invasive Recording Methods

Intracellular Unit Recording *Intracellular unit recording* was discussed at length in Chapter 3; it is the most effective method of studying the electrophysiological responses of individual neurons. Its main advantage is that it provides a moment by moment measure of graded fluctuations in the membrane potential; see Figure 3.6. Most studies using this recording procedure are performed on chemically immobilized animals because it is extremely difficult to keep the tip of a microelectrode positioned inside a single neuron in a freely moving animal.

Extracellular Unit Recording It is possible to record the action potentials of a neuron through a microelectrode whose tip is positioned in the extracellular fluid next to it. Each time the neuron fires, a blip is recorded on the oscilloscope. Accordingly, *extracellular unit recording* provides a record of the firing rates of neurons (see Figure 7.15), but they provide no information about the value of the membrane potential. It is difficult, but not impossible, to record extracellularly from a single neuron in a freely moving animal without the electrode tip shifting away from the neuron (e.g., Siegel, 1983).

Multiple-Unit Recording In *multiple-unit recording*, the electrode tip is larger than that of a microelectrode, and thus it picks up signals from the many neurons near it—the larger the electrode, the more neurons contribute to the signal. The action potentials picked up by the electrode are fed into an integrating circuit, which adds them together and displays for the experimenter a record of the changes in the overall level of firing in the general area around the electrode tip as a function of time.

Invasive EEG Recording In laboratory animals, EEG signals are recorded through large implanted electrodes rather than through scalp electrodes. Cortical EEG signals are frequently recorded through stainless steel skull screws, whereas subcortical EEG signals are typically recorded through stereotaxically implanted bipolar electrodes constructed of two twisted insulated wires.

Psychopharmacological Methods

The major research strategy of psychopharmacology is to administer drugs that either increase or decrease the effects of particular neurotransmitters and to observe the behavioral consequences. You will be introduced to many of these selective drugs in Chapter 6 (Neurotransmitters,

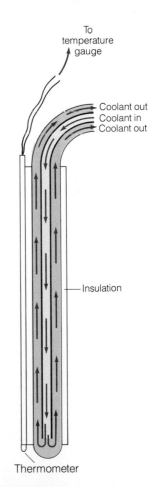

To temperature gauge

Coolant out
Coolant in
Coolant out

Insulation

Thermometer

FIGURE 4.15 *A cryoprobe.*

Drugs, and Mental Illness). Described here are the various routes of drug administration, several methods of using chemicals to make selective brain lesions, and three methods of measuring the chemical activity of the brain that are particularly useful in biopsychological research.

Routes of Drug Administration In most psychopharmacological studies, drugs are administered peripherally by feeding them to the subject; by injecting them through a tube into the stomach (*intragastrically*, IG); or by injecting them hypodermically into the peritoneal cavity of the abdomen (*intraperitonally*, IP), into a large muscle (*intramuscularly*, IM), into the fatty tissue beneath the skin (*subcutaneously*, SC), or into a large surface vein (*intravenously*, IV). A problem with peripheral routes of administration is that many drugs do not readily pass through the blood-brain barrier. To overcome this problem, drugs can be injected in small amounts through a fine, hollow needle, called a **cannula,** which has been stereotaxically implanted in the brain. Such microinjections can be made directly into neural tissue, or if more widespread exposure of the brain to a drug is desired, larger volumes can be injected into the ventricles through an *intraventricular cannula.*

In some cases, researchers wish to study the effects of chronic drug exposure. This can be done by implanting beneath the skin drug pellets, which gradually enter general circulation over a period of days. A more controllable method of chronic drug administration is to deliver the drug through an implanted cannula from a tiny, battery-operated infusion pump mounted on the skull of the subject (e.g., Blackshear, 1979).

Selective Chemical Lesions The effects of surgical, electrolytic, and cryogenic lesions are frequently difficult to interpret because they affect all neurons in the target site. In some cases, it is possible to make more selective lesions by injecting toxic chemicals that have an affinity for certain components of the nervous system. There are several such selective **neurotoxins.** For example, when *kainic acid* and *ibotenic acid* are administered by microinjection, they are preferentially taken up by cell bodies at the tip of the cannula and destroy those neurons, while leaving neurons with axons passing through the area largely unscathed. Another widely used selective neurotoxin is **6-hydroxydopamine (6-OHDA)**, which is selectively taken up by neurons that release the neurotransmitters *norepinephrine* or *dopamine*. Thus, 6-hydroxydopamine can be injected into a site known to contain such neurons, and they will be selectively destroyed.

Measuring the Chemical Activity of the Brain There are many procedures for measuring the chemical activity of the brain (see Iversen, Iversen, & Snyder, 1982). The following are three that have proven to be particularly useful in biopsychological research. First is the 2-deoxyglucose (2-DG) technique. An animal subject injected with radioactive 2-DG is placed in a test situation where it must engage in the activity of interest. Because 2-DG is similar in structure to glucose, the brain's main source of energy, neurons active during this test absorb it at a high rate, but they do not metabolize it. The subject is then killed, and its brain is removed and sliced. The slices are subjected to **autoradiography;** that is, they are coated with a photographic emulsion, stored in the dark for a few days, and then developed much like film. Areas of the brain that absorbed high levels of the radioactive 2-DG during the test appear as spots on the slides. See Figure 13.18.

Two neurochemical procedures have been developed for measuring neurochemical changes in behaving experimental animals (Fillenz, MacDonald, & Marsden, 1986; Myers & Knott, 1986). By using these techniques, it is possible to study moment-by-moment correlations between the experiences of experimental subjects and their brain chemistry. One of these techniques, **transcerebral dialysis,** involves passing a fine tube

---

The research methods of biopsychology illustrate a psychological disorder suffered by many scientists; I call it "unabbreviaphobia," the fear of leaving any term unabbreviated. As a means of reviewing the first half of this chapter, write out the following definitions in full.

1. CAT: _____

2. MRI: _____

3. PET: _____

4. 2-DG: _____

5. EEG: _____

6. ERP: _____

7. AEP: _____

8. EMG: _____

9. EOG: _____

10. SCL: _____

11. SCR: _____

12. ECG: _____

13. EKG: _____

14. IP: _____

15. IM: _____

16. IV: _____

17. SC: _____

18. 6-OHDA: _____

The answers to the preceding questions are: (1) computerized axial tomography, (2) magnetic resonance imaging, (3) positron emission tomography, (4) 2-deoxyglucose, (5) electroencephalogram, (6) event-related potential, (7) average evoked potential, (8) electromyogram, (9) electrooculogram, (10) skin conductance level, (11) skin conductance response, (12) electrocardiogram, (13) electrocardiogram, (14) intraperitoneal, (15) intramuscular, (16) intravenous, (17) subcutaneous, and (18) 6-hydroxydopamine.

through the brain. The tube has a short semipermeable section that is positioned at the site of interest so that neurochemicals from the site diffuse into the tube and are carried by a solution flowing through the tube directly to an automated *chromatograph* (a device for measuring the chemical constituents of blood and other liquids and gases) for continuous, on-line analysis. The other technique is **in vivo voltammetry,** a procedure for inferring the changes in the extracellular concentration of specific chemicals at the tip of a carbon-based electrode from changes in the flow of current as the voltage across the electrode is gradually increased. The technique takes advantage of the fact that some chemicals are readily oxidized at characteristic current intensities, thus releasing a flow of electrons.

PART 2: THE BEHAVIORAL RESEARCH METHODS OF BIOPSYCHOLOGY

We turn now from the methods used by biopsychologists to study the nervous system to those that deal with the behavioral side of biopsychology. As you progress through this section of the chapter, it will become apparent that a fundamental difference between behavior and the nervous system is reflected in the nature of the methods used in their investigation. This difference is one of visibility. The nervous system and its activities are not ordinarily observable, whereas behavior is continually on display in all its diversity and complexity. In essence, behavior is the overt expression of covert neural activity. Because of the inherent invisibility of neural activity, the primary objective of the methods used in its investigation is to render the unobservable observable. In contrast, the major objectives of behavioral research methods are to control, to simplify, and to objectify. A single set of such procedures developed for the investigation of a particular behavioral phenomenon is commonly referred to as a **behavioral paradigm.** Each behavioral paradigm normally comprises a method for producing the behavioral phenomenon under investigation and a method of objectively measuring it.

There is an unfortunate tendency to underestimate both the critical role that effective behavioral paradigms play in the progress of neuroscience and the ingenuity and effort required to develop them. Perhaps this is a consequence of behavior's visibility—we all seem to undervalue the familiar. Do not make this mistake! Remember that behavior is the ultimate and most complex manifestation of nervous system activity. In the final analysis, the purpose of all neural activity is the production of behavior. Measuring it is no simple matter (see Jacobs et al., 1988; Whishaw, Kolb, & Sutherland, 1983).

4.4 Neuropsychological Testing

A patient suspected of suffering from some sort of nervous system dysfunction is usually referred to a *neurologist* for an assessment of simple sensory and motor function. However, neurological examinations often do not reveal subtle changes in emotional, motivational, or intellectual function. This is the domain of the neuropsychologist.

Because of the diversity and complexity of the psychological function, a thorough neuropsychological assessment typically requires several hours, spread over 2 or 3 days. As a result of the onerous nature of neuropsychological assessment, it is prescribed in only selected cases. Neuro-psychological tests are normally administered: (1) to serve as a basis for diagnosis, particularly in cases in which the results of computerized axial tomography (CAT), electroencephalography (EEG), and neurological testing have proven equivocal; (2) to serve as a basis for counseling and caring for neurological patients whose problems cannot be treated; or (3) to evaluate the effectiveness of treatment. This section introduces some of the tests commonly employed in the neuropsychological assessment of general intelligence, language lateralization, memory, language, and perceptual-motor function.

Tests of General Intelligence

Most neuropsychological assessments begin with a so-called test of general intelligence such as the **Wechsler Adult Intelligence Scale** (**WAIS**). The overall intelligence quotient (IQ) is a notoriously poor measure of brain damage; however, a skilled neuropsychologist can draw inferences about a patient's neuropsychological dysfunction from the pattern of deficits on the various subtests. For example, low scores on subtests of verbal ability tend to be associated with left hemisphere damage; whereas, right hemisphere damage tends to reduce scores on the performance subtests. The 11 subtests of the WAIS are illustrated in Table 4.1.

Table 4.1 *The eleven subtests of the WAIS in chronological order. The Verbal Scale comprises the information, digit span, vocabulary, arithmetic, comprehension, and similarities subtests. The Performance Scale comprises the picture completion, picture arrangement, block design, object assembly, and digit symbol subtests (Wechsler, 1981).*

Information Twenty-nine questions of general information are read to the subject; for example, "Who was the president of the United States during the Civil War?"

Picture Completion The subject must identify the important part missing from 20 drawings; for example, a door with no doorknob.

Digit Span Three digits are read to the subject at 1-second intervals and the subject is asked to repeat them in the same order. Two trials are given at three digits, four digits, five digits, and so on until the subject fails both trials at one level.

Picture Arrangement Ten sets of cartoon drawings are presented to the subject, and the subject is asked to arrange each set so that they tell a sensible story.

Vocabulary The subject is asked to define a list of 35 words ranging in difficulty from "bed" to "tirade."

Block Design The subject is presented with blocks that are red on two sides, white on two sides, and half red and half white on the other two. The subject is shown pictures of nine patterns and is asked to duplicate them by arranging the blocks.

Arithmetic The subject is presented with 14 arithmetic questions and must answer them without the benefit of pencil and paper.

Object Assembly The subject is asked to put together the pieces of four jigsaw-like puzzles to form familiar objects.

Comprehension The subject is asked 16 questions that test the ability to understand general principles; for example, "Why should people pay taxes?"

Digit Symbol The subject is presented with a key that matches each of a series of symbols with a different digit. On the lower part of the page is a series of digits, and the subject is given 90 seconds to write the correct symbol next to as many digits as possible.

Similarities The subject is presented with a pair of items and is asked to explain how the items in each pair are similar.

Tests of Language Lateralization

It is usual for one hemisphere to participate more than the other in language-related abilities. There are two tests that are commonly used to determine which hemisphere predominates: the **sodium amytal test** (Wada, 1949) and the **dichotic listening test** (Kimura, 1973). The sodium amytal test involves injecting sodium amytal, which is an anesthetic, into either the left or right carotid arteries of the neck. This temporarily blocks the function of the ipsilateral hemisphere, while leaving the contralateral hemisphere largely unaffected. While the brain is partially anesthetized, several tests of language function are quickly administered to the patient. Later, the entire process is repeated for the other side. When the injection is made on the side dominant for speech—the left for most people— the patient is completely mute for about 2 minutes. When the injection is on the nondominant side, there are typically just a few minor speech problems.

In the standard version of the dichotic listening test, patients hear three spoken digits presented in sequence to one ear through a set of stereo headphones, and at the same time three different digits are presented to the other ear. After a brief delay, the patients are asked to report as many of the six digits as they can. Kimura found that the superior ear on the dichotic listening test was normally the ear contralateral to the dominant hemisphere for speech, as determined independently by the sodium amytal test—the right ear for most people.

Tests of Memory

Brain damage can have extremely specific effects on different aspects of memory. Thus, a variety of tests are needed to properly assess the memorial deficits of neurological patients. A battery of tests called the *Wechsler Memory Scale* is widely employed to assess memory dysfunction. It includes a brief survey of orientation in space and time and of awareness of current public information (Where are you? What day is it? Who is the mayor?), a test of the ability to read and to recall logical stories; a **digit-span test** (see Table 4.1); and a test of the memory for both related (motor-car) and unrelated (wagon-shampoo) paired associates. In the **paired-associate test,** pairs of words are read to the patient, and the patient's memory for the pairs is subsequently tested by assessing his or her ability to respond to the first word of each pair with the appropriate second word. Unfortunately, because of its predominantly verbal character, the Wechsler Memory Scale is inadequate for assessing memory for nonverbal material or for assessing the memorial abilities of patients with serious language-related deficits.

Tests of Language

Language is one of the most complex human abilities, and the deficits that occur in various aspects of language production and comprehension reflect this complexity. As a result, it is usual to administer a brief screening test of language abilities and to follow it up with a more extensive testing if deficits are revealed by the initial screening. One screening test for language-related problems is the **token test,** which is surprisingly effective in view of its simplicity. Twenty tokens of two different shapes (squares or circles), two different sizes (large or small), and five different colors (white, black, yellow, green, and red) are placed on a table in front of the subject. The task of the patient is to touch the tokens as instructed. The test begins with simple instructions, such as "touch a red square," being read by the examiner, and progresses to more difficult instructions, such as "touch the small, round circle and then the large, green square." Finally, the subject may be asked to read the instructions aloud and follow them.

Tests of Perceptual-Motor Function

Most patients referred for neuropsychological testing will have already had their basic sensory-motor abilities evaluated by a neurologist. The neurologist will have assessed the ability of patients to detect the presence of simple stimuli and their ability to control each major voluntary muscle of the body. In addition, basic aspects of sensory-motor coordination will have been evaluated by checking the status of various reflexes, such as the pupillary and patellar (knee-jerk) reflexes, and various reflexively regulated voluntary behaviors, such as walking and balancing. However, in some instances, the problems experienced by neurological patients in their everyday lives are not attributable to deficits in the sorts of simple sensory-motor abilities tested by neurologists. In such cases, neuropsychological testing is often prescribed.

One commonly used neuropsychological test of complex visuospatial ability is the *block-design subtest* of the WAIS (see Table 4.1). The **Rey-Osterrieth Complex Figure Test** is another. In the Rey-Osterrieth Complex Figure Test, the subject is asked to copy the Rey-Osterrieth Figure onto a sheet of paper with a pencil; this task is no problem for normal subjects. The value of this test stems from the fact that people with right hemisphere damage and those with left hemisphere damage often make different types of errors. Patients with right hemisphere lesions tend to copy all of the details, but they link them together inappropriately; those with damage to the left hemisphere tend to get the overall configuration correct, but they omit the details. Asking a subject to draw the figure from memory is a means of assessing nonverbal memory. Figure 4.16 illustrates the performance on the block-design test and the Rey-Osterrieth Complex Figure Test of a subject who suffered a stroke in the right hemisphere (Goodglass & Kaplan, 1979). Why don't you give the memory version of the test a try?

Semmes and her colleagues have devised tests of both personal and extrapersonal visuospatial orientation. In the *personal orientation test,* patients are presented with five diagrams of the front and back of a human body with numbers at various points on the body, and they are asked to touch their own bodies in sequence at the points represented by the numbers. The patient's task in Semmes' *extrapersonal orientation test* is to walk the routes between a 3 × 3 matrix of dots on the floor of the test room by following a series of five hand-held maps.

There is a group of perceptual-motor tests that assess the patient's ability to inhibit incorrect motor responses. The best known of such tests is the **Wisconsin Card Sorting Test,** which is illustrated in Figure 4.17. On each of the Wisconsin cards is from one to four identical symbols (either triangles, stars, circles, or crosses) of the same color (either red, green, yellow, or blue). The subject is confronted with four stimulus cards that differ from one another in form, color, and number. The task of the patient is to correctly sort cards from a deck into piles in front of the stimulus cards;

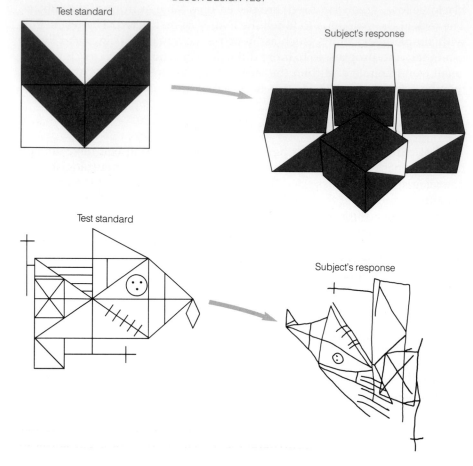

FIGURE 4.16 *The performance of a patient with right hemisphere damage on the Block-Design and Rey-Osterrieth Complex Figure Tests.*

Test standards are from *Wechsler Adult Intelligence Scale.* Copyright © 1955 by The Psychological Corporation. Reproduced by permission. All rights reserved.
   Subject's responses are from ''Assessment of Cognitive Functions in the Brain Injured Patient,'' by H. Goodglass and E. Kaplan in *Handbook of Behavioral Neurobiology,* Vol. 2 (p. 20) by M. Gazzaniga (Ed.), 1979, New York, Plenum Publishing Corporation. Copyright 1982 by Plenum Publishing Corporation. Reprinted with permission.

FIGURE 4.17 *The Wisconsin Card Sorting Test.*

however, he or she does not know whether to do this by sorting according to form, color, or number. The patient begins by guessing and is told after each card is sorted whether it was sorted correctly or incorrectly. At first, the task of the patient is to learn to sort by color, but as soon as the patient makes several consecutive correct responses, the sorting principle is changed, without any indication other than the fact that previously correct responses become incorrect. And once this new principle is learned, the sorting principle is changed again. Patients with frontal lobe lesions often continue for 100 or more trials to sort on the basis of color after this strategy becomes incorrect. The tendency to keep making previously appropriate responses when they become inappropriate is termed **perseveration.**

4.5 The Behavioral Methods of Psychophysiology

The defining feature of psychophysiology is its focus on the recording of electrophysiological signals from the surface of the human body, and the behavioral methods of psychophysiological research tend to be those that are compatible with such recording procedures. Described in this section are behavioral methods used in the psychophysiological investigation of (1) emotion, (2) lie detection, and (3) biofeedback.

The Pattern Approach and the Study of Emotion

In early psychophysiological research, psychophysiological measures were often taken as indices of general *arousal*. Mildly arousing stimuli, such as "the F word," were found to produce a slight increase in cardiovascular, electrodermal, and electromyographic activity and a transient *desynchronization of the EEG* (a lowering of its amplitude and an increase in its frequency). More arousing stimuli, such as hypodermic needles, final examinations, and electric shocks were found to have similar, but greater, effects. In most of the early studies, a single psychophysiological measure was taken while the experimenter attempted to induce in the subjects a single emotional state. In this approach, neither the particular emotion under investigation nor the particular psychophysiological measure was considered to be of much consequence because all emotional experiences were assumed to produce the same general pattern of psychophysiological changes.

It was Ax (1955) who first demonstrated the utility of the *pattern approach* in the study of emotion—measuring the profiles of psychophysiological responses over a range of measures that are associated with an emotion. He measured various aspects of electrodermal, electromyographic, cardiovascular, and respiratory activity during the induction of both fear and anger in the same subjects. Volunteer subjects were told that they were participating in a study of hypertension, and they were asked to lie quietly on a couch while the measures were being taken. While the electrodes were being attached, it was casually mentioned that the regular technician, who usually operated the polygraph in the adjacent room, was sick and that a man who had recently been fired for incompetence and arrogance was filling in for him. After a few minutes, during which baseline measures were recorded, one of the two conditions of the experiment was administered; half were tested first in the "anger condition" and then in the "fear condition," while the other subjects received the two treatments in the opposite order. In the "anger condition," the technician, who was in reality an actor, entered the test room and spent 5 minutes checking the wiring. During this period, the technician jostled the subject, he criticized the attending nurse, and he blamed the subject for creating an equipment malfunction. In the fear condition, a continuous mild shock was administered to the finger of the subject with no word of warning or explanation, and its intensity was gradually increased until the subject complained. When the subject did complain, the experimenter expressed surprise and, unbeknownst to the subject, pressed a button that caused sparks to jump. Ax analyzed 14 different psychophysiological measures and found that the changes in 7 of them were significantly different in the two conditions. It was the pattern of responses that told the story, not individual measures. As influential as Ax's experiment has proven to be, such methods of inducing fear and anger would not be permitted by today's strictly enforced ethical codes. Fortunately, it has proven unnecessary to take such extreme measures; Weerts and Roberts (1976) found that patterns of psychophysiological activity similar to those reported by Ax could be produced simply by asking subjects to imagine that they were in situations that made them angry or afraid.

A study by Schwartz, Fair, Salt, Mandel, and Klerman (1976) is an example of the effective use of the pattern approach in the study of facial expression and emotion. Subjects sat quietly in a darkened room and imagined various emotional experiences while EMG activity was recorded from various facial sites. The major conclusion of this study was that it is the pattern of facial EMG activity that reveals an emotion, not the activity of a single facial muscle. Because facial expression has been shown to be a more accurate reflection of subjective experience than a subject's own verbal report (e.g., Craig & Patrick, 1985), and because changes in facial EMG can be recorded even in the absence of noticeable changes in expression, the measurement of patterns of facial EMG provides a particularly sensitive measure of human emotional experience.

Psychophysiological Methods of Lie Detection

Lie detection or **polygraphy** involves monitoring various autonomic nervous system (see Chapter 2) indices of emotion during interrogation and using them to infer the veracity of the subject's responses. Polygraph tests administered by skilled examiners can be useful additions to normal interrogation procedures, but they are far from infallible (Iacono & Patrick, 1987). The main problem involved in evaluating the effectiveness of any particular polygraphic technique is that it is rarely possible in real-life situations to determine whether a polygrapher's verdict is correct. Because of this difficulty, many studies of lie detection have employed the **mock-crime procedure;** volunteer subjects participate in a mock crime and are then subjected to a polygraph test by an examiner who is unaware of their "guilt" or innocence. The interrogation method used by many polygraphers in laboratory and real-life situations is the **control-question technique.** The physiological response to the target question (Did you steal that purse?) is compared to the responses to a variety of control questions whose answers are known (What is your name? Have you ever been in jail before?). The average success rate in various mock-crime studies using this control-question technique is about 80 percent.

There are two problems with the mock-crime, control-question studies. One is that, unlike real suspects, the subjects are under no particular threat. In real life, the question, "Did you steal that purse?" is likely to elicit an emotional reaction from all suspects, regardless of their guilt or innocence, making it much more difficult to detect deception. The lie detector does not detect lies; it detects arousal. Lykken (1959) developed the **guilty-knowledge technique** to circumvent this problem. In order to use this technique, the *polygrapher* must have a piece of information concerning the crime that would be known to the subject only if he or she were guilty. The polygrapher, rather than attempting to catch the suspect in a lie, simply assesses his or her reaction to a list of actual and contrived details of the crime. Innocent parties, because they have no knowledge of the crime, will react to all such items in the same way; the guilty will react differentially. For example, in one of Lykken's (1959) experiments, "guilty" subjects waited until the occupant of an office went to the washroom. Then they entered her office, stole her purse from her desk, removed the money, and hid the purse in a locker. The critical part of the interrogation went something like this. "We know where the thief hid the purse. Where do you think that we found it? In the washroom? . . . In a locker? . . . Hanging on a coat rack? . . ." Even though electrodermal activity was the only measure used in this study, 44 of 50 mock criminals were correctly identified, and none of the 48 "innocent" parties was judged guilty. Patrick (1987) found that a group of psychopathic prison inmates were no better than control subjects at deceiving a professional polygrapher.

The EEG may prove to be a useful addition to the conventional ANS polygraphic indices. Forth, Hart, Hare, and Harpur (1988) measured the ERPs (event-related potentials) evoked by brief presentations of slides, some of which contained words whose relation to the mock crime were known to only the guilty parties. The guilty parties responded to these test items with particularly large **P300 waves**.

The Biofeedback Method

Biofeedback refers to the method of supplying subjects with continuous feedback about their own biological processes, particularly feedback about processes of which they would normally not be aware. The basic idea is that such feedback may allow a person to bring these normally unconscious biological processes under control. The impetus for the use and study of biofeedback came from two developments in the late 1960s. One was the claim that human subjects supplied with information about their own EEG **alpha waves** (see Figure 4.6) could voluntarily increase their occurrence, and in so doing quickly bring about a state of meditative bliss. The other was the report (DiCara, 1970; Miller, 1969) that rats could be trained with rewards and punishments to control their own autonomic nervous system activity. Reports of these findings in the popular press triggered a frenzy of pseudoscience among the general public. According to these reports, the day was at hand when lasting contentment could be achieved by a few alpha biofeedback training sessions and when nervous system dysfunction could be corrected without drugs by teaching the patient to control the misbehaving system through biofeedback. However, the reaction of the scientific community to these claims was more measured. The enthusiasm engendered by the early reports was balanced by a substantial degree of caution, which has—as is usually the case in such

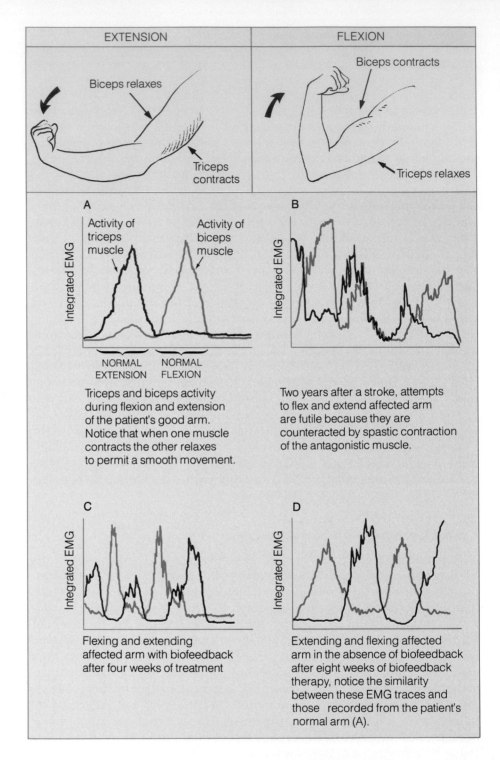

FIGURE 4.18 *The progress of a patient with right spastic hemiparesis during biofeedback treatment. (Adapted from Brudny, 1978.)*

situations—proven to be appropriate. Several of the early reports proved to be unreplicable (see Dworkin & Miller, 1986), and others proved too slight to be of practical significance. Nevertheless, psychophysiological researchers have persisted in their study of the biofeedback procedure, carefully defining its limits, searching for its underlying mechanisms, and exploring the possibilities for its practical application.

It is in the field of EMG biofeedback where the progress in biofeedback research has been greatest, and it is the work of Brudny (1982) and his colleagues that best illustrates this progress. Brudny treats the movement disorders of brain-damaged patients by providing them with feedback in the form of integrated EMG activity from their dysfunctional muscles. The cornerstone of Brudny's procedure is the monitoring and retraining of antagonistic muscle groups—pairs of muscle groups, such as the *biceps* and *triceps*, that work in opposition. By observing on a video monitor displays of integrated EMG activity during attempted normal movement, patients try to bring their muscle activity more in line with the desired pattern. A tone sounds when slight improvements have been achieved, to signal subtle improvements. From three to five such 45-minute training sessions are typically administered each week.

The series of integrated EMG traces presented in Figure 4.18 illustrates the progress made by one of the many hemiparetic patients who have been treated by Brudny and his colleagues, a patient with right spastic hemiparesis. *Hemiparesis* refers to a partial paralysis of one side of the body, and *spasticity* refers to involuntary increases in muscle tension that interfere with normal movement.

Of the 70 hemiparetic patients treated by Brudny and his colleagues in one study, a remarkable 61 percent gained meaningful use of their dysfunctional arm. By "meaningful," I mean that a lasting improvement was carried over into everyday life. When you consider that Brudny treats only those patients who have failed to respond to conventional forms of therapy, these figures are extremely impressive. But even more impressive than the figures themselves is what they represent. Can you imagine the joy felt by a patient who is able to walk for the first time in years? Can you imagine the sense of accomplishment felt by Brudny and his colleagues?

4.6 Biopsychological Paradigms of Animal Behavior

In contrast to neuropsychologists and psychophysiologists, physiological psychologists and psychopharmacologists focus much of their research on nonhuman laboratory species. One advantage of studying laboratory animals rather than humans is that there are many fewer restrictions. As a consequence, the behavioral research methods used in physiological psychology and psychopharmacology are extremely diverse. Illustrative examples are provided here under three separate headings: (1) procedures for the assessment of species-common behaviors, (2) traditional conditioning paradigms, and (3) seminatural animal learning paradigms. In each case, the focus is on methods used to study the behavior of the laboratory rat; however, most of these methods have been adapted for use with other species.

Assessment of Species-Common Behaviors

Some behavioral tests used by physiological psychologists and psychopharmacologists are designed to evaluate the effects of nervous system manipulations on **species-common behaviors;** these are behaviors such as grooming, scratching, walking, exploring, swimming, eating, drinking, copulating, fighting, and nest building that are displayed by virtually all members of a species or at least by all members of the same sex. Considered here are the open-field test, tests of aggressive and defensive behavior, and tests of sexual behavior.

Open-Field Test   The **open-field test** involves scoring the behavior of a subject in a large, barren chamber. It is usual to measure general activity, either by drawing lines on the floor of the chamber and counting the number of line-crossings during the test or by using one of the numerous automated devices designed for the purpose. It is also common in the open-field test to count the number of *boluses*, that is, pieces of excrement, dropped by an animal during the test. Low activity scores and high bolus counts are frequently used as indicators of fearfulness. Fearful rats are highly **thigmotaxic,** that is, they rarely venture away from the walls of the test chamber, and they rarely engage in such activities as rearing and grooming. As you might expect, rats typically appear fearful when they are first placed in a strange open field, but this fearfulness normally declines with repeated exposure to the same apparatus.

Aggressive and Defensive Behavior   Typical patterns of aggressive and defensive behavior can be observed during combative encounters between the dominant male rat of an established colony and a smaller male intruder (see Blanchard & Blanchard, 1988). The behaviors of the dominant male are considered to be aggressive, and those of the hapless intruder, defensive. The dominant male of the colony moves sideways toward the intruder, with its hair bristling. When it nears the intruder, it tries to push it off balance, and it tries to deliver bites to the back and flanks. The defender tries to protect its back and flanks by rearing up on its hind legs and by pushing the attacker away with its forepaws, or by rolling onto its back. In view of these observations, piloerection, lateral display, and flank and back biting indicate conspecific aggression in the rat; whereas freezing, boxing, and rolling over indicate defensiveness.

Some tests of rat defensive behavior assess reactivity to the experimenter, rather than to another rat. The test developed by Albert (e.g., Albert, Walsh, Zalys, & Dyson, 1986) is a good example of such a test. The rat is confronted in the test box by a sequence of test stimuli: a pencil held in front of its nose, a tap on the back with a pencil, a poke in the side with a pencil, a gloved hand in front of the nose, a gloved hand grasping its tail, and a hand around its abdomen. The response to each stimulus is rated on a scale from 0 (no response) to 3 (defensive attack). Rats with bilateral septal lesions are notoriously reactive to these stimuli.

Sexual Behavior   Most attempts to study the physiological bases of rat sexual behavior have focused on the copulatory act itself. The male mounts the female from behind and clasps her hindquarters. If the female is receptive, she responds by assuming the **lordosis** posture; that is, she sticks her hindquarters in the air by bending her back in a U, and she deflects her tail to the side. During some mounts the male inserts his penis into the female's vagina—this act is called **intromission.** After intromission, the male dismounts by jumping backwards. He then returns a few seconds later to mount and intromit once again. Following about 10 such cycles of mounting, intromitting, and dismounting, the male mounts, intromits, and **ejaculates,** that is, deposits his sperm (Dewsbury, 1967; McClintock, 1984). The number of mounts required to achieve intromission, the number of intromissions required to achieve ejaculation, and the interval between ejaculation and the reinitiation of mounting are three common measures of male sexual behavior. The intensity of the female's response is frequently scored in terms of the proportion of mounts that produce lordosis (i.e., her **lordosis quotient**) and how much her back bends during lordosis.

Mendelson and Gorzalka (1987) have developed a special test chamber for studying rat sexual behavior that has advantages over the conventional small cylindrical chambers. Because the *Mendelson box* is extremely narrow (see Figure 4.19), it insures that all interactions between the rats will be observable from the most revealing angle (i.e., from the side), and because it contains a series of ledges, it permits the subjects to engage in approach and avoidance behaviors by moving vertically through the apparatus.

Traditional Conditioning Paradigms

Learning paradigms have always played a major role in physiological psychology and psychopharmacology for three basic reasons. The first reason is that learning has long been a phenomenon of primary interest to psychologists. The second reason is that learning paradigms have provided a technology for producing and controlling animal behavior—because animals cannot follow instructions from the experimenter, it is often necessary to train them to behave in a fashion consistent with the goals of the experiment. The third reason is that it is possible to infer much about the sensory, motor, motivational, and cognitive state of an animal from its ability to learn various tasks and to perform various learned responses.

FIGURE 4.19 *Rats in a Mendelson box. (Courtesy of Scott Mendelson & Boris Gorzalka.)*

If you have taken a previous course in psychology, or even if you have not, you will likely be familiar with the **Pavlovian** and **operant conditioning** paradigms. In the Pavlovian conditioning paradigm, the experimenter pairs an initially neutral stimulus called a *conditional stimulus* (e.g., a tone or a light) with an *unconditional stimulus* (e.g., meat powder), a stimulus that elicits a reflexive or *unconditional response* (e.g., salivation). As a result of these pairings, the conditional stimulus eventually acquires the capacity, when administered alone, to elicit a *conditional response* (e.g., salivation), a response that is usually similar to the unconditional response. In operant conditioning, the rate at which a particular voluntary response (such as a lever press) is emitted is increased or decreased by *reinforcing* it or *punishing* it, respectively. One of the most widely used operant paradigms in biopsychology is the **self-stimulation paradigm** in which animals press a lever to administer reinforcing electrical stimulation to certain so-called "pleasure centers" in their own brains (e.g., Fibiger & Phillips, 1986).

Although conventional Pavlovian and operant conditioning paradigms are still widely employed in physiological psychology and psychopharmacology, the discovery of a form of learning called *conditioned taste aversion* (e.g., Garcia & Koelling, 1966) in the 1950s stimulated the development of laboratory learning paradigms that mimicked important features of situations that an animal might encounter in its natural environment. The 50s was a time of sock hops, sodas at Al's, crewcuts, and drive-in movies. In the animal behavior laboratory, it was a time of lever presses, keypecks, and shuttles made in response to flashing lights, tones, and geometric patterns. Then along came rock 'n roll and conditioned taste aversion, and things have not been the same since.

Seminatural Animal Learning Paradigms

Conditioned Taste Aversion   **Conditioned taste aversion** refers to the observation that rats and many other animals develop an aversion for tastes that have been followed by illness. In the standard conditioned taste aversion experiment, rats exposed to an *emetic*—a nausea-inducing drug—after their first experience with a highly palatable saccharin solution, subsequently refuse to drink the solution. The ability of rats to readily learn the relation between taste and subsequent illness unquestionably increases their chances of survival in their natural environment, where potentially edible substances are not routinely screened by government agencies. Rats and many other animals are *neophobic* (afraid of new things); thus, when they first encounter a new food, they consume it in only small quantities. If they subsequently become ill, they will not consume it again. Humans also develop conditioned taste aversions. Cancer patients have been reported to develop aversions to foods consumed before nausea-inducing chemotherapy (Bernstein & Webster, 1980). Also, many of you will be able to testify on the basis of personal experience about the effectiveness of conditioned taste aversions. I still have vivid memories of a batch of laboratory punch that I overzealously consumed after eating a . . . but that is another story.

Research on conditioned taste aversion challenged three principles of learning (see Revusky & Garcia, 1970) that had grown out of research on traditional operant and classical conditioning paradigms. First, it challenged the view that animal conditioning is always a gradual step-by-step process; enduring taste aversions are routinely established in only a single

trial. Second, it showed that *temporal contiguity* is not essential for conditioning; rats acquire taste aversions even when they are not rendered ill until several hours after exposure to the critical taste. Third, it challenged the principle of equipotentiality, the view that conditioning proceeds in basically the same manner regardless of the particular stimuli and responses under investigation; rats appear to be genetically prepared to learn associations between tastes and illness, but it is only with difficulty that they learn relations between the color of food and nausea or between taste and footshock. Accordingly, the laboratory investigation of conditioned taste aversion encouraged the development of other seminatural laboratory paradigms that focused on forms of learning for which the subjects seemed specially prepared.

Radial Arm Maze   The **radial arm maze** taps the well-developed spatial abilities of rodents. The survival of rats in the wild depends on their ability to navigate quickly and accurately through their environment and to learn which locations in it are likely to be sources of food and water. This task is much more complex for a rodent than it is for us. Most of us obtain food from locations where the supply is continually replenished—we go to the market confident that we will find enough food to satisfy our needs. In contrast, the foraging rat must learn, and retain, a complex pattern of spatially coded details. It must learn those places in its environment where morsels of food are likely to be found, and it must remember which of these sites it has recently stripped of their booty so as not to revisit them too soon. The radial arm maze was designed by Olton and Samuelson (1976) to demonstrate and study these special spatial abilities. The radial arm maze (see Figure 4.20) is a central platform with an array of arms—usually eight or more—radiating from it. At the end of each arm is a tiny food cup, which may or may not be baited, depending on the purpose of the experiment. In one version of the test, rats are placed each day in a radial arm maze that has all arms baited. After a few days of experience, rats rarely visit the same arm twice in the same day, even when control procedures make it impossible for them to recognize odors left during previous visits to an arm or to make their visits in a systematic sequence. Because the arms are identical, the rats orient themselves in the maze with reference to external room cues, and thus their performance can be disrupted by rotating the maze or by changing the appearance of the room.

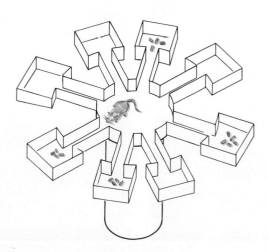

FIGURE 4.20 *A radial arm maze.*

Morris Water Maze   Another seminatural learning paradigm that has been designed to study the special spatial abilities of rats is the **Morris water maze** (Morris, 1981). The rats are placed in a circular, featureless pool of cool milky water, and they must swim until they discover the escape platform, which is invisible just beneath the surface of the water. The rats are allowed to rest on the platform before being returned to the water for another trial. Despite the fact that the starting point of the rats is varied from trial to trial, the rats learn after only a few trials to swim directly to the platform, presumably by using spatial cues from the room as a reference. Adaptations of this task have proven extremely useful for assessing the navigational skills of lesioned or drugged animals (Sutherland & Dyck, 1984).

Conditioned Defensive Burying   Yet another seminatural learning paradigm that has proven useful in biopsychological research is the **conditioned defensive burying paradigm** (e.g., Pinel & Mana, 1989; Pinel & Treit, 1978). In the conditioned defensive burying paradigm, rats receive a single aversive stimulus (e.g., shock, airblast, or odor) from an object mounted on the wall of the chamber just above the floor, which is littered with bedding material. After a single trial, almost every rat learns that the test object is a threat and responds to it by spraying the bedding material at it with their head and forepaws (see Figure 4.21). Because many subjects completely cover the source of aversive stimulation during the test period, this response has been termed conditioned defensive burying. Treit has shown that antianxiety drugs reduce the amount of conditioned defensive burying and has used the paradigm to study the neurochemistry of anxiety (e.g., Treit, 1987).

Paradigms of Avian Memory   With the growing awareness of the remarkable abilities of animals to learn and remember things that are important to them in their natural environments, biopsychologists have shown an increasing interest in the memorial capacities of birds. For example, there has been considerable interest in the abilities of some species

FIGURE 4.21 *Rats burying a test object. (From Pinel, Ladak, & Gorzalka, 1981.)*

Photography by Jack Wong.

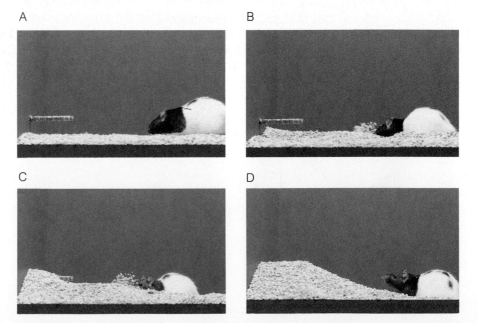

of birds to sing as adults a song that they heard for only a brief period during their infancy (Marler, 1984); to follow specific migration routes after making only a single trip with adult birds (Baker, 1982); and to retrieve seeds from thousands of different cache sites (Shettleworth, 1983). Laboratory paradigms have been designed for the investigation of each of these phenomena.

Conclusion

You have now been introduced to the research methods of biopsychology: to its neural methods in Part 1 of the chapter and to its behavioral methods in Part 2. Before leaving the chapter, it is extremely important that you appreciate how these methods work together. Seldom, if ever, is an important biopsychological issue resolved by a single set of methods. The reason for this is that neither the methods used to manipulate the brain nor the methods used to assess the behavioral consequences of these manipulations are totally selective; there are no methods of manipulating the brain that change only a single aspect of brain function, and there are no methods of measuring behavior that do not reflect a variety of psychological processes. Thus, any experiment that uses a single set of methods can be interpreted in more than one way, and it cannot provide unequivocal evidence for any one interpretation. Problems are solved only when several methods are brought to bear on a single problem in such a way that all interpretations but one can be ruled out. This approach is called **converging operations,** and you will encounter it frequently in the following chapters.

__ Food for Thought __

1. The current rate of progress in the development of new and better brain scanning devices will soon render behavioral tests of brain damage obsolete. Discuss.

2. You are taking a physiological psychology laboratory course, and your instructor gives you two rats: one rat with a lesion in an unknown structure and one normal rat. How would you test the rats to determine which has the lesion? How would your approach differ from what you might use to test a human patient suspected of having brain damage?

ADDITIONAL READING

The following are provocative discussions of two different behavioral testing strategies:

Jacobs, W. J., Blackburn, J. R., Buttrick, M., Harpur, T. J., Kennedy, D., Mana, M. J., MacDonald, M. A., McPherson, L. M., Paul, D., & Pfaus, J. G. (1988). Observations. *Psychobiology, 16,* 3–19.

Whishaw, I. Q., Kolb, B., & Sutherland, R. J. (1983). The analysis of behavior in the laboratory rat. In T. E. Robinson (Ed.), *Behavioral approaches to brain research.* New York: Oxford University Press.

An interesting, colorful, and simple introduction to modern brain imaging techniques is provided by:

Sochurek, H., & Miller, P. (1987). Medicine's new vision. *National Geographic, 171,* 2–41.

To help you study the material in this chapter, all of the key terms—those that have appeared in bold type—are listed and briefly defined here.

Alpha waves. Eight-to-twelve-per-second, high-amplitude EEG waves, which frequently occur during relaxed wakefulness.

Angiography. A contrast X-ray technique that involves infusing a radio-opaque dye through a cerebral artery.

Aspiration. A lesion technique in which the tissue is drawn off by suction through the tip of a hand-held glass pipette.

Autoradiography. The radiation released from a radioactively labeled substance such as 2-DG is photographically developed so that regions of high uptake are visible on a brain slice.

Behavioral paradigm. A single set of procedures developed for the investigation of a particular behavioral phenomenon.

Biofeedback. The method of supplying subjects with continuous feedback about their own biological processes so that the subjects may try to bring them under control.

Bregma. A landmark on the surface of the skull commonly used as a reference point in stereotaxic surgery.

Cannula. A tube or hypodermic needle that is implanted in the body for the purpose of introducing or extracting substances; for example, an intraventricular cannula.

Computerized axial tomography (CAT). A computer-assisted X-ray procedure for visualizing the brain in three dimensions.

Conditioned defensive burying. A paradigm in which the subject responds to an aversive stimulus by burying its source.

Conditioned taste aversion. The aversion developed by animals to tastes that have been followed by illness.

Contrast X-ray techniques. X-ray techniques involving the injection of a radio-opaque substance.

Control-question technique. A lie detection technique in which the polygrapher compares the suspect's psychophysiological responses associated with answers to questions about his or her guilt with the psychophysiological responses associated with answers to various control questions.

Converging operations. Solving a scientific question by using several methods to rule out all interpretations but one.

Cryogenic blockade. Temporarily eliminating neural activity in a particular part of the brain by cooling it with a cryoprobe.

2-deoxyglucose (2-DG). A substance similar to glucose; it is taken up by active neurons and accumulates in them because, unlike glucose, it cannot be used by neurons as a source of energy.

Dichotic listening test. A test of speech lateralization in which patients hear different sequences of digits simultaneously presented to two ears.

Digit-span test. A classic test of verbal short-term memory.

Ejaculation. Ejection of sperm.

Electrocardiogram (ECG or EKG). A recording of the electrical activity of the heart.

Electroencephalography. Recording the gross electrical activity of the brain through large electrodes; in humans, EEG electrodes are often taped to the surface of the scalp.

Electromyography. A procedure for measuring the electrical discharge of muscles.

Electrooculography. The technique for recording eye movements through electrodes placed around the eye.

Essential hypertension. High blood pressure assumed to be caused by excessive psychological stress.

Event-related potentials (ERPs). The EEG waves that regularly accompany certain psychological events.

Far-field potentials. EEG signals recorded in an attenuated form at a distance from their source.

Guilty-knowledge technique. A lie detection technique that assesses psychophysiological responses of the suspect to information known to only the guilty party.

6-hydroxydopamine (6-OHDA). A neurotoxin that selectively destroys those neurons that release norepinephrine or dopamine.

Hypertension. Chronically high blood pressure.

Intromission. Insertion of the penis into the vagina.

In vivo voltammetry. A procedure for inferring the changes in the extracellular concentration of specific chemicals at the tip of a carbon-based electrode from changes in the flow of current as the voltage across the electrode is gradually increased.

Lordosis. The female rat's arched-back posture of sexual receptivity.

Lordosis quotient. The proportion of mounts that produce lordosis.

Magnetic resonance imaging (MRI). A procedure in which high-resolution images of the structures of the brain are constructed from the measurement of waves that hydrogen atoms emit when they are activated by radio-frequency waves in a magnetic field.

Mock-crime procedure. A procedure used in the study of lie detection in which subjects participate in a mock crime and then undergo a lie detection test.

Morris water maze. A pool of milky water with a submerged goal platform.

Neurotoxins. Neural poisons; some neurotoxins (such as kainic acid, ibotenic acid, and 6-OHDA) are selective, that is, they destroy specific parts of the brain.

Open-field test. Scoring the behavior of a subject in a large barren chamber.

Operant conditioning. The rate at which a particular voluntary response is emitted is increased or decreased by reinforcing it or punishing it, respectively.

P300 wave. The positive EEG wave that usually occurs about 300 milliseconds after a momentary stimulus that has meaning for the subject.

Paired-associate test. Pairs of words are read to the subject, and the subject's memory is subsequently tested by assessing his or her ability to respond to the first word of each pair with the appropriate second word.

Pavlovian conditioning. A paradigm in which the experimenter pairs an initially neutral stimulus (conditional stimulus) with a stimulus (unconditional stimulus) that elicits a reflexive response (unconditional response); after several pairings the neutral stimulus elicits a response (conditioned response).

Perseveration. The tendency to keep making previously appropriate responses after they have become inappropriate.

Plethysmography. Measuring changes in the volume of blood in a part of the body.

Pneumoencephalography. A contrast X-ray technique that involves temporarily replacing some of the cerebral spinal fluid with air.

Polygraphy. Lie detection.

Positron emission tomography (PET). A technique for visualizing the metabolic activity in the brain by measuring the accumulation of radioactive 2-deoxyglucose (2-DG).

Radial arm maze. A multiple-arm maze designed to test spatial ability in rats.

Rey-Osterrieth Complex Figure Test. A neuropsychological test of complex visuospatial ability.

Self-stimulation paradigm. A paradigm in which animals press a lever to administer reinforcing electrical stimulation to their own brains.

Sensory evoked potential. A change in the electrical activity of the brain that is elicited by the momentary presentation of a stimulus.

Signal averaging. A method used to reduce the noise of the background EEG when trying to measure event-related potentials.

Skin conductance level (SCL). A measure of the steady level of skin conductance associated with a particular situation.

Skin conductance response (SCR). A measure of the transient changes in skin conductance associated with brief experiences.

Sodium amytal test. A test involving the anesthetization of one hemisphere and then the other to determine which hemisphere plays the dominant role in language.

Species-common behaviors. Behaviors that are performed in the same manner by all members of species.

Stereotaxic atlas. A series of two-dimensional maps that provide a three-dimensional representation of the brain.

Stereotaxic instrument. A device for performing stereotaxic surgery; it is composed of two parts, a head holder and an electrode holder.

Thigmotaxic. Tending to stay near the walls of an open field.

Token test. A test for aphasia that involves following verbal instructions to touch or move tokens of different colors and shapes.

Transcerebral dialysis. A method for recording moment-by-moment changes in brain chemistry in behaving animals; a fine tube with a short semipermeable section is passed through the brain and into an automated chromatograph for on-line analysis of neurochemicals diffusing through the semipermeable section.

Triangulation. A standard bipolar electroencephalographic technique for determining which of the two sites being compared on a channel of abnormal EEG is the source of abnormality observed in the channel; both suspect sites are individually compared with a site known to be normal.

Wechsler Adult Intelligence Scale (WAIS). A popular test of general intelligence.

Wisconsin Card Sorting Test. A neuropsychological test that evaluates a patient's ability to inhibit previously correct motor responses.

5

Human Brain Damage and Animal Models

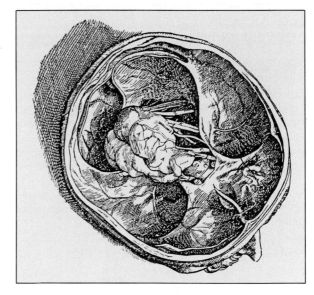

Much of what we know about human brain function has been learned from the study of its dysfunction; the behavioral anomalies associated with particular patterns of brain damage provide important insights into the normal behavioral functions of the afflicted structures. This chapter provides a systematic introduction to the topic in three sections:

5.1 Causes of Brain Damage
5.2 Neuropsychological Diseases
5.3 Animal Models of Human Neuropsychological Diseases

To make you more aware of the personal tragedy underlying the academic discourse that follows, the chapter begins with a look at the life of a neurological patient named Jimmie G. The case of Jimmie G. was described by Sacks (1985) in his provocatively titled and written book, *The Man Who Mistook His Wife for a Hat and Other Clinical Tales*.[1]

> [In 1975] Jimmie was a fine-looking man, with a curly bush of grey hair, a healthy and handsome forty-nine-year-old. He was cheerful, friendly, and warm.
> 'Hiya, Doc!' he said. 'Nice morning! Do I take this chair here?' . . . He spoke of the houses where his family had lived. . . . He spoke of school and school days, the friends

> he'd had, and his special fondness for mathematics and science. . . . he was seventeen, had just graduated from high school when he was drafted in 1943. . . . He remembered the names of the various submarines on which he had served, their missions, where they were stationed, the names of his shipmates. . . . But there for some reason his reminiscences stopped. . . .
> . . . I was very struck by the change of tense in his recollections as he passed from his school days to his days in the navy. He had been using the past tense, but now used the present . . .

116

A sudden, improbable suspicion seized me.

'What year is this, Mr. G.?' I asked, concealing my perplexity under a casual manner.

'Forty-five, man. What do you mean?' He went on, 'We've won the war, FDR's dead, Truman's at the helm. There are great times ahead.'

'And you, Jimmie, how old would you be?' . . .

'Why, I guess I'm nineteen, Doc. I'll be twenty next birthday.'

Looking at the grey-haired man before me, I had an impulse for which I have never forgiven myself . . .

'Here,' I said, and thrust a mirror toward him. 'Look in the mirror and tell me what you see.' . . .

He suddenly turned ashen and gripped the sides of the chair. 'Jesus Christ,' he whispered. 'Christ, what's going on? What's happened to me? Is this a nightmare? Am I crazy? Is this a joke?'—and he became frantic, panicked. . . .

. . . I stole away, taking the hateful mirror with me.

Two minutes later I re-entered the room. . . . 'Hiya, Doc!' he said. 'Nice morning! You want to talk to me—do I take this chair here?' There was no sign of recognition on his frank, open face.

'Haven't we met before, Mr. G?' I asked casually.

'No, I can't say we have. Quite a beard you got there. I wouldn't forget *you*, Doc!' . . .

. . . 'Where do you think you are?'

'I see these beds, and these patients everywhere. Looks like a sort of hospital to me. But hell, what would I be doing in a hospital—and with all these old people, years older than me. . . . Maybe I *work* here. . . . If I don't work here, I've been *put* here. Am I a patient, am I sick and don't know it, Doc? It's crazy, its scary. . . .'

On intelligence testing he showed excellent ability. He was quick-witted, observant, and logical, and had no difficulty solving complex problems and puzzles—no difficulty, that is, if they could be done quickly. If much time was required, he forgot what he was doing. . . .

Homing in on his memory, I found an extreme and extraordinary loss of recent memory—so that whatever was said or shown to him was apt to be forgotten in a few seconds' time. Thus I laid out my watch, my tie, and my glasses on the desk, covered them, and asked him to remember these. Then, after a minute's chat, I asked him what I had put under the cover. He remembered none of them—or indeed that I had even asked him to remember. I repeated the test, this time getting him to write down the names of the three objects; again he forgot, and when I showed him the paper with his writing on it he was astounded . . .

'What is this?' I asked, showing him a photo in the magazine I was holding.

'It's the moon,' he replied.

'No, it's not,' I answered. 'It's a picture of the earth taken from the moon.'

'Doc, you're kidding! Someone would've had to get a camera up there! . . . how the hell would you do that?' . . .

He was becoming fatigued, and somewhat irritable and anxious, under the continuing pressure of anomaly and contradiction, and their fearful implications . . . And I myself was wrung with emotion—it was heartbreaking . . . to think of his life lost in limbo, dissolving.

He is, as it were . . . isolated in a single moment of being, with a moat . . . of forgetting all round him . . . He is a man without a past (or future), stuck in a constantly changing, meaningless moment. (pp. 22–28)

Remember Jimmie G. There is more about his tragic case later in the chapter.

5.1 Causes of Brain Damage

This section of the chapter provides an introduction to six causes of brain damage: tumors, cerebrovascular disorders, closed-head injuries, infections of the brain, neurotoxins, and genetic factors.

Brain Tumors

A **tumor** or *neoplasm* (literally, *new growth*) is a mass of cells that grows independently of the rest of the body. About 20% of tumors found in the human brain are **meningiomas** (see Figure 5.1), tumors that grow between the *meninges* (the three membranes that cover the CNS). All meningiomas are **encapsulated tumors;** that is, they grow within their own membrane. As a result, they are particularly easy to identify on a CAT scan; they can influence the function of the brain only by the pressure they exert on surrounding tissue; and they are almost always **benign**—that is, they can be surgically removed with little risk of further tumor growth. Unfortunately, encapsulation is the exception, rather than the rule when it comes to brain tumors. With the exception of meningiomas, most brain tumors are infiltrating. **Infiltrating tumors** are those that grow diffusely through normal tissue, and as a result, they are almost always **malignant.** That is, it is almost impossible to remove them completely, and any cancerous tissue that remains after surgery continues to grow.

About 10% of all brain tumors do not originate in the brain. They grow from tumor fragments carried to the brain by the bloodstream from some other part of the body—the brain seems to be a particularly fertile ground for tumor growth. These are called **metastatic tumors**—*metastasis* is a general term that refers to the transmission of disease from one organ to another. Most metastatic brain tumors originate as cancers of the lungs. Obviously the chances of recovering from a cancer that has already attacked two or more separate sites is slim at best. Figure 5.2 illustrates the ravages of metastasis.

Cerebrovascular Disorders

The term *stroke* refers to any severe, sudden attack. Because brain damage from disorders of the cerebral circulatory system frequently occurs

FIGURE 5.1 *A meningioma. (Courtesy of Kenneth Berry, Head, Neuropathology, Vancouver General Hospital.)*

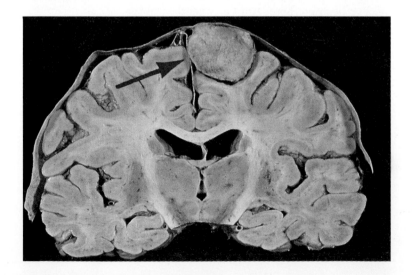

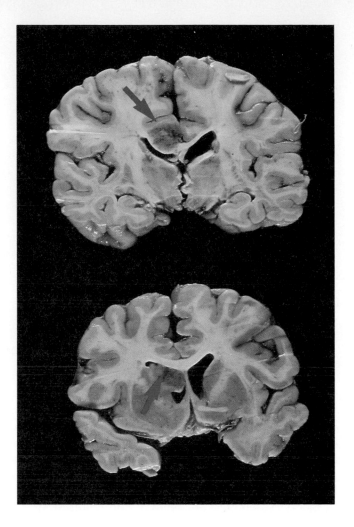

FIGURE 5.2 *Multiple metastatic brain tumors. (Courtesy of Kenneth Berry, Head of Neuropathology, Vancouver General Hospital.)*

with great suddenness and severity, stroke is commonly used as a syn-onym for *cerebrovascular disorder*. However, not all cerebrovascular disor-ders are characterized by sudden onset, and not all cerebral disorders of sudden onset are vascular in origin.

There are two main types of cerebrovascular disorders. One, termed *intracerebral hemorrhage* (bleeding), occurs when a cerebral blood vessel is ruptured and blood seeps into the surrounding neural tissue and damages it. Aneurysms are a common cause of intracerebral hemorrhage. An **aneu-rysm** is a pathological balloon-like dilation that forms in the wall of a blood vessel at a point where the elasticity of the vessel wall is defective. These are points of weakness in the cerebrovascular system, and they sometimes burst. Aneurysms can be **congenital**—that is, present at birth—or they can result from exposure to vascular poisons or infection. Individuals who have aneurysms should make every effort to avoid high blood pressure.

The second type of cardiovascular disorder, termed **cerebral ischemia,** is a disruption of the blood supply to an area of the brain, which eliminates its supply of glucose and oxygen and kills it. An area of ischemic brain damage is called an **infarct.** There are three main causes of infarcts: throm-bosis, embolism, and arteriosclerosis. In **thrombosis,** a plug called a *throm-bus* is formed and blocks blood flow at the site of its formation. A thrombus

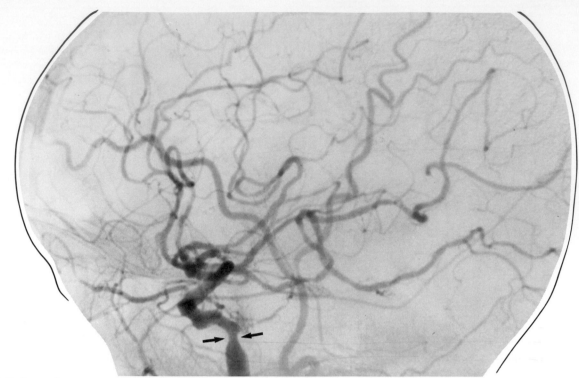

FIGURE 5.3 *An angiogram illustrating narrowing of a major cerebral artery (see arrow). Compare with the normal angiogram in Figure 4.1. (Courtesy of William D. Robertson, Department of Radiology, Vancouver General Hospital.)*

may be composed of a blood clot, fat, oil, an air bubble, tumor cells, or any combination thereof. **Embolism** is similar except the plug, called an *embolus* in this case, is carried by the blood from a larger vessel, where it was formed, to a smaller one, where it becomes lodged—in essence, an embolus is just a thrombus, that has taken a trip. In **arteriosclerosis,** the walls of blood vessels thicken, often as the result of fat deposits, and this produces narrowing of the vessels, which may eventually lead to complete blockage. Figure 5.3 is an angiogram (see Chapter 4) illustrating such narrowing of the carotid artery in the neck.

Closed-Head Injuries

The most serious brain injuries are those produced by high velocity projectiles, such as bullets or shrapnel fragments, that penetrate the skull and underlying neural tissue. However, it is not necessary for the skull to be penetrated for the brain to be seriously damaged. In fact, any heavy blow to the head should be treated with extreme caution, particularly when confusion, sensory-motor disturbances, or loss of consciousness ensue.

Contusions are closed-head injuries involving damage to the cerebral circulatory system. Such damage produces internal hemorrhaging, which results in a **hematoma,** a localized collection of clotted blood in an organ or tissue—in other words, a bruise. It is paradoxical that the very hardness of the skull, which protects the brain from penetrating injuries, is frequently a major factor in the development of contusions. Many contusions occur when the brain slams against the inside of the skull. As illustrated in Figure 5.4, blood from such injuries can accumulate in the *subdural space*, the space between the dura mater and arachnoid membrane, and severely distort the

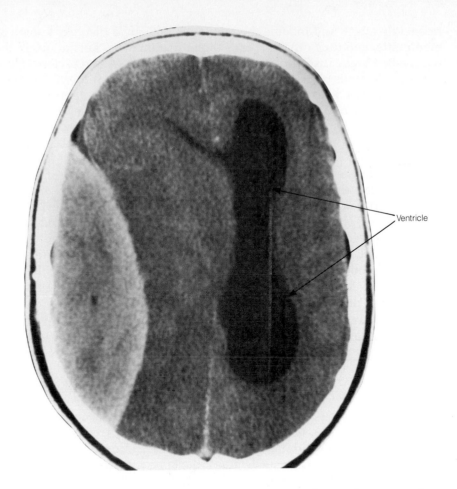

Ventricle

FIGURE 5.4 *A CAT scan of a subdural hematoma. Notice that pressure from the hematoma has displaced the ipsilateral lateral ventricle. (Courtesy of William D. Robertson, Department of Radiology, Vancouver General Hospital.)*

surrounding neural tissue. It may surprise you to learn that contusions frequently occur on the side of the brain opposite the side struck by a blow. The reason for such so-called **contrecoup injuries** is that the blow causes the brain to strike the inside of the skull on the other side of the head.

When there is a disturbance of consciousness following a blow to the head and there is no evidence of a contusion or other structural damage, the diagnosis is **concussion.** It is commonly assumed that concussions entail a temporary disruption of normal cerebral function with no long-term damage. However, the punch-drunk syndrome suggests otherwise. The **punch-drunk syndrome** refers to the **dementia** (general intellectual deterioration) and cerebral scarring observed in boxers and other individuals experiencing repeated concussions. If there were no damage associated with a single concussion, the effects of many concussions could not summate to produce severe damage. One of the most dangerous aspects of concussion is the complacency with which it is regarded—flippant references to it, such as "having one's bell rung," do little to communicate its hazards.

Infections of the Brain

When an invasion of the brain by microorganisms produces damage, it is referred to as a brain infection, and the inflammation associated with brain infection is commonly referred to as **encephalitis.** Bacteria and viruses are two kinds of organisms that commonly invade the brain. Bacteria frequently attack and inflame the meninges, causing a disorder known as **meningitis,** and they can also cause the formation of pockets of pus in the brain called **brain abscesses.** *Syphilis* is the most well-known bacterial brain infection. Syphilis bacteria are passed from infected to noninfected individuals via contact with genital sores; the infecting bacteria then go into a dormant stage; and finally, several years later, they become virulent and attack many parts of the body, including the brain. The syndrome of insanity and dementia resulting from a syphilitic infection is called **general paresis.**

Syphilis has a particularly interesting history. The first Europeans to visit America stripped the natives of their gold and left smallpox in return. But the deal was not totally one-sided; the booty carried back to Europe by the sailors of Columbus and the adventurers that followed included a cargo of syphilis bacteria. Until then, syphilis had been restricted to the Americas, but it was quickly distributed to the rest of the world. Penicillin and other antibiotics are no panacea for bacterial brain infections; they can eliminate the infection, but they cannot reverse brain damage that has already been produced.

There are two types of viral infections of the nervous system: **neurotropic** infections, which have a particular affinity for neural tissue, and **pantropic** infections, which attack neural tissue, but do not attack it preferentially. Rabies is a well-known example of a neurotropic viral infection, which is usually transmitted through the bite of a rabid animal. The fits of rage caused by the virus's effects on the brain increase the probability that rabid animals that normally attack by biting (e.g., dogs, cats, raccoons, bats, mice, etc.) will spread the disorder. Although the effects of the rabies virus on the brain are ultimately lethal, it does have one redeeming feature. The rabies virus does not usually attack the brain for at least a month after it has been contracted, thus allowing time for a preventive vaccination. The *mumps* and *herpes* viruses are common examples of pantropic viruses; they typically attack other tissues of the body, but they can spread into the brain with dire consequences.

Neurotoxins

The nervous system can be damaged by exposure to any one of a variety of toxic chemicals, which can enter general circulation from the gastrointestinal tract, from the lungs, or through the skin. For example, heavy metals such as mercury and lead can accumulate in the brain and permanently damage it, thus producing a **toxic psychosis** (chronic insanity produced by a neurotoxin). Have you ever wondered why Alice in Wonderland's Mad Hatter was a mad hatter and not a mad something else? In eighteenth and nineteenth century England, hatmakers were commonly driven mad by the mercury that they used in the preparation of the felt that they used to make hats. In a similar vein, the word "crackpot" originally referred to the toxic psychosis observed in people—primarily the British poor—who steeped their tea in cracked ceramic pots with lead cores.

Sometimes the very drugs used to treat neurological disorders prove to be neurotoxins. Some of the antipsychotic drugs introduced in the early 1950s provide an example of distressing scope. By the late 1950s, literally millions of psychotic patients were being chronically maintained on these drugs. However, the initial enthusiasm for antipsychotic-drug therapy was tempered by the discovery that many of the patients developed a motor disorder termed **tardive dyskinesia** (**TD**). Its primary symptoms are involuntary smacking and sucking movements of the lips, thrusting and rolling of the tongue, lateral jaw movements, and puffing of the cheeks. Unfortunately, tardive dyskinesia is not responsive to treatment. Once it has developed, even lowering the dose of the offending drug does not help; in fact, it sometimes makes the symptoms worse.

Brain damage from the neurotoxic effects of recreational drugs is also a serious problem. The case of Jimmie G., with which the chapter began, is a prime example. You see, Jimmie's memory problems resulted from his long-term consumption of alcoholic beverages. Many heavy drinkers eventually develop the same memory disorder, which is called **Korsakoff's syndrome.** There is much more about Korsakoff's syndrome in Chapter 14, Memory and Amnesia.

An important point to remember about neurotoxins is that they do not necessarily come from outside the body; that is, they are not necessarily **exogenous.** In some cases, the body makes toxins that destroy its own nervous system. Multiple sclerosis, which you will learn about in the next section of the chapter, is an example of a neural disorder produced by **endogenous** (produced in the body) toxins.

Genetic Factors

The cells of normal humans have 23 pairs of chromosomes. Twenty-two of these pairs are composed of two similarly shaped chromosomes and are the same in both males and females. The twenty-third pair, the *sex chromosomes*, controls sexual development, and thus differs in males and females. Females have a pair of X-shaped sex chromosomes, whereas males have one X-shaped sex chromosome and one Y-shaped sex chromosome. However, sometimes accidents of cell division occur, and the fertilized egg ends up with an abnormal chromosome or with an abnormal number of normal chromosomes. Then, as the fertilized egg divides and redivides, these chromosomal anomalies are duplicated in every cell of the body. A common example of a disorder caused by such a genetic accident is **Down's syndrome,** which occurs in 0.15% of all live births. Down's syndrome is associated with an extra chromosome in pair 21. The consequences of the superfluous chromosome 21 are disastrous. In addition to the characteristic disfigurement—flattened skull and nose, folds of skin over the inner corners of the eyes, and short fingers (see Figure 5.5)—the Down's child is severely retarded and often dies before reaching adulthood. The probability of giving birth to a child with Down's syndrome increases markedly with advancing maternal age.

Unlike Down's syndrome, most neurological diseases of genetic origin are not the result of faulty chromosomal duplication. They are caused by *genes* that are passed from parent to offspring. Genes control the manufacture of the body's proteins, which are the building blocks of the nervous system and regulate all of its chemical reactions. Thus, a faulty gene can have far-reaching effects on the structure and function of the brain and the behavior that it produces.

Some traits are controlled by a single pair of genes, which are always located at the same position on both chromosomes of a pair. Sometimes one gene of a pair dominates the other. For example, a person with one gene for brown eyes and one gene for blue eyes will have brown eyes. Thus, the gene controlling the development of brown eyes is said to be

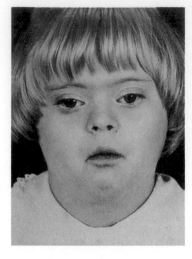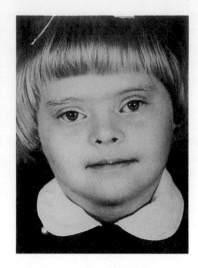

FIGURE 5.5 *A child with Down's syndrome before and after stigma-reducing plastic surgery.*

Before corrective surgery   After corrective surgery

dominant, and the gene controlling the development of blue eyes is said to be *recessive*. The only time blue eyes occur in humans is when both eye-color genes inherited by an individual are the genes for blue eyes. When genetic disorders are associated with recessive genes on the X sex chromosome, they occur more frequently in males than in females. Males have only a single X chromosome, and thus an abnormal recessive gene on the X chromosome is always expressed because there is never a dominant normal counterpart to override it. This is not the case in females because they have two X chromosomes.

There are some inherited neurological disorders that have been shown to be the product of a single anomalous gene. Perhaps the best understood of these disorders in **phenylketonuria** (**PKU**). PKU, like blue eyes, is transmitted by a recessive gene. Thus, the disorder manifests itself only in those cases in which both chromosomes of the pair carry the PKU gene. Individuals with PKU lack the critical enzyme that normally metabolizes the amino acid, *phenylalanine*. As a result, phenylalanine accumulates and disrupts neural function. If left untreated, PKU can result in mental retardation, schizophrenic-like behavior, tremors, and muscle rigidity; however, once the disorder is diagnosed, its development can be arrested by a diet low in phenylalanine. Thus, the expression of PKU, like the expression of many neurological disorders, depends on an interaction between heredity and environment.

Genetic abnormalities are rarely related to dominant genes. If they were, every individual carrying the gene would develop the disorder; and, because they would be at a severe survival and reproductive disadvantage, the abnormal genes would be eliminated from the human genetic pool during the course of evolution. However, there is an exception to this general rule. If the dominant abnormal gene is not expressed until an individual is well past puberty, it will be passed from generation to generation. As you will learn in the next section of this chapter, Huntington's disease is such a disorder.

Before leaving the topic of the inheritance of neurological disorders, it is important that you understand an important methodological point. The fact that a disorder runs in families does not necessarily mean that it has a genetic basis. The reason is that the members of a family are likely to be exposed to many of the same environmental influences, such as deficient diet, chemical pollutants, or infections. There are two common ways of proving that disorders that run in families are, in fact, genetic: (1) by showing that children adopted at a young age tend to have the same disorder as their biological parents, but not their adopted parents, and (2) by showing that **monozygotic twins** (identical twins), which develop from the same fertilized egg and are thus genetically identical, are more likely to have the same disorder than **dizygotic twins** (*fraternal twins*), which develop from two different fertilized eggs and are thus no more genetically similar than any pair of *siblings* (offspring of the same parents).

5.2 Neuropsychological Diseases

Our discussion of neuropsychological dysfunction continues in this section. However, the focus here is on the neuropsychological diseases themselves, rather than on their causes.

It is not always easy to decide whether an individual has a neuropsychological disease. There is no doubt that an individual with a normal body who cannot see, walk, or talk is suffering from some kind of neurological dysfunction. But what about an individual who performs poorly on intelligence tests, sleeps longer than most, or is very aggressive? Is such an individual suffering from a disorder of the brain, or does he or she simply represent the extreme of normal biological function? The problem of *differential diagnosis*—that is, the problem of deciding which particular neural disorder a patient has—is even more thorny. Neuropsychological patients display an incredible array of complex behavioral symptoms, and although each patient's pattern of symptoms is unique, there are similarities among them. Physicians and scientists search for these similarities. When they find a number of symptoms that tend to occur together, they coin a term to summarize them; this label comes to refer to what most of us commonly think of as a neuropsychological disease or disorder. The hope of scientists and physicians is that all patients with a particular neuropsychological disease will prove to have the same underlying neural pathology caused by the same factors. As more is found out about the patients with a particular cluster of neuropsychological symptoms, it is usually necessary to redefine the disorder—perhaps by excluding some cases, including others, or dividing the disorder up into subtypes. The more that is known about the causes and neural bases of a neuropsychological disorder, the more accurately it can be diagnosed; and the more accurately it can be diagnosed, the more readily its causes and neural bases can be identified. Epilepsy, Parkinson's disease, Huntington's disease, multiple sclerosis, and Alzheimer's disease are the disorders discussed in this section of the chapter.

Epilepsy

The primary symptom of epilepsy is the epileptic seizure, but not all persons who suffer seizures are considered to have epilepsy. It is not uncommon for otherwise healthy persons to have a seizure during temporary illness or following exposure to a convulsive agent. The label *epilepsy* is applied to only those patients whose seizures appear to be generated by their own chronic brain dysfunction. About 1% of the population will be diagnosed as epileptic at some point in their lives.

In view of the fact that epilepsy is characterized by epileptic seizures—or more accurately, by spontaneously recurring epileptic seizures—you might think that the task of diagnosing epilepsy would be an easy one. But you would be wrong. The task is made difficult by the diversity and complexity of the various forms that an epileptic seizure can take. You are probably familiar with those seizures that take the form of **convulsions** (motor seizures), which involve tremors (*clonus*), rigidity (*tonus*), and/or a loss of both balance and consciousness. But many seizures do not take this form; instead, they involve subtle changes of thought, mood, or behavior that are not readily distinguishable from normal ongoing activity. In such cases, the diagnosis of epilepsy rests heavily on electroencephalographic evidence.

The value of scalp electroencephalography in suspected cases of epilepsy stems from the fact that epileptic seizures are produced by bursts of high-amplitude EEG spikes, which are often apparent in the scalp EEG during an attack (see Figure 5.6), and from the fact that individual spikes often punctuate the scalp EEG of epileptics between attacks. Although the observation of spontaneous epileptic discharges is incontrovertible evidence of epilepsy, the failure to observe them does not mean that the patient is not epileptic. It could mean that the patient is epileptic but did not happen to experience epileptic discharges during the test, or that epileptic discharges did occur during the test but were not recorded through the scalp electrodes.

Once an individual has been diagnosed as epileptic, it is usual to assign him or her to one of two general categories, partial or generalized, and then to one of their respective subcategories. The various seizure types are so different from one another that there are many who believe that epilepsy is best viewed not as a single disease, but as a number of different, but related, diseases. Supporting this view is the fact that epilepsy has no single cause; almost any kind of brain disturbance can cause seizures.

Partial Seizures A **partial seizure** is one that does not involve the entire brain. For reasons unknown, the epileptic neurons at a focus begin to discharge together in bursts, and it is this synchronous bursting of neurons (see Figure 5.7) that produces epileptic spiking in the EEG. This synchronous activity may stay restricted to the focus until the seizure is over, or it may spread to other, healthy, areas of the brain—but, in the case of partial seizures, not to the entire brain. The specific behavioral symptoms of a partial epileptic seizure depend on where the disruptive discharges begin and into what structures they spread. Because partial seizures do not involve the entire brain, they are not accompanied by a complete loss of consciousness or equilibrium.

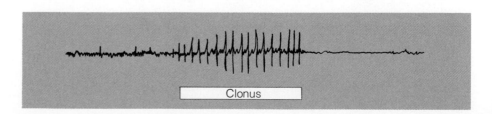

FIGURE 5.6 *EEG activity before and during a seizure.*

FIGURE 5.7 *The bursting of an epileptic neuron.*

There are two major categories of partial seizures: simple and complex. **Simple partial seizures**—first described by Hughlings Jackson, and thus commonly referred to as *Jacksonian seizures*—are those partial seizures whose symptoms are primarily sensory and/or motor. As the epileptic discharges spread through the sensory or motor areas of the brain, the symptoms spread through the body. In contrast, **complex partial seizures** are usually restricted to the temporal lobes, and those who experience them are said to have *temporal lobe epilepsy.* Complex partial seizures typically begin with an aura, which may or may not develop into a **psychomotor attack.** In psychomotor attacks, the patients engage in compulsive, repetitive, simple behaviors commonly referred to as *automatisms* (e.g., doing and undoing a button) or in more complex behaviors that appear almost normal. The diversity of psychomotor attacks is illustrated by the following four cases reported by Lennox (1960):

> A war veteran subject to many automatisms read in the newspaper about a man who had embraced a woman in a park, followed her into a women's toilet, and then boarded a bus. From the description given, he realized he was the man.

> One morning a doctor left home to answer an emergency call from the hospital and returned several hours later, a trifle confused, feeling as though he had experienced a bad dream. At the hospital he had performed a difficult . . . [operation] with his usual competence, but later had done and said things deemed inappropriate.

> A young man, a music teacher, when listening to a concert, walked down the aisle and onto the platform, circled the piano, jumped to the floor, did a hop, skip, and jump up the aisle, and regained his senses when part way home. He often found himself on a trolley [bus] far from his destination.

> A man in an attack went to his employer and said, "I have to have more money or [I] quit." Later, to his surprise, he found that his salary had been raised. (pp. 237–238)

Although patients appear to be conscious throughout their psychomotor attacks, they usually have little or no subsequent recollection of them. About half of all cases of epilepsy are of the complex partial variety—the temporal lobes are particularly susceptible to epileptic discharges.

Generalized Seizures Generalized seizures are those that involve the entire brain. Some generalized seizures begin as focal discharges that gradually spread into more and more structures until the entire brain is involved. In other cases, the discharges seem to begin almost simultaneously throughout the brain. Such sudden-onset generalized seizures may result from diffuse pathology, or they may begin focally in a structure, such as the thalamus, that projects to many parts of the brain.

Like partial seizures, generalized seizures occur in many different forms. One is the **grand mal** (literally, *big trouble*) seizure. The primary symptoms of a grand mal seizure are loss of consciousness, loss of equilibrium, and a violent *tonic-clonic convulsion*—that is, a convulsion involving both tonus and clonus. Tongue biting, urinary *incontinence*, and *cyanosis* (turning blue from excessive extraction of oxygen from the blood during the convulsion) are common accompaniments of grand mal convulsions. It is important to note that the shortage of oxygen in the blood (**hypoxia**) associated with grand mal convulsions can itself cause brain damage. In contrast, **petit mal** (literally, *small trouble*) generalized seizures are not associated with convulsions. Instead, the primary behavioral symptom is the *petit mal absence*, a cessation of ongoing behavior accompanied by a disruption of consciousness. Without warning, there is a sudden immobility and a vacant look in the eyes, which may be accompanied by blinking and by slight 3-per-second jerks of the arms. The EEG of petit mal is different than that of other seizures; it is a bilaterally symmetrical **3-per-second spike-and-wave** (see Figure 5.8). Petit mal seizures are most common in children, and they often disappear at the onset of puberty. Because petit mal attacks are difficult to diagnose without an EEG test, some children with petit mal epilepsy are labeled "daydreamers" by their parents and teachers—or, less generously, "space cadets" by their playmates.

Some epileptics experience peculiar psychological changes just before a convulsion. These changes, called **epileptic auras,** may take many different forms: for example, a bad smell, a specific thought, a vague feeling of familiarity, a hallucination, or a tightness of the chest. Epileptic auras are important for two reasons. First, the nature of the auras provides clues concerning the location of the epileptic focus. Second, because the epileptic auras experienced by a particular patient tend to be the same from attack to attack, they warn the patient of an impending convulsion. For most people, the warning of an impending convulsion is an advantage, but for some it can become an experience of great dread, as the normal parts of their brains struggle to keep in touch with reality. Witness author Margiad Evans' (1953) description of the early stages of her own seizures.

Parkinson's Disease

Parkinson's disease or parkinsonism is a movement disorder that affects about 1% of the population, usually in adulthood. Its initial symptoms are mild—perhaps no more than a stiffness or tremor of the fingers—but they

FIGURE 5.8 *The bilaterally symmetrical 3-per-second spike-and-wave discharge of a petit mal attack recorded from frontal and temporal cortex.*

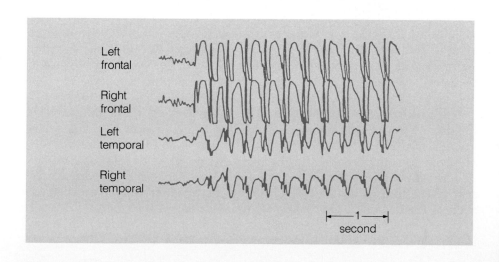

gradually increase in severity with advancing years. The most common symptoms of the full-blown disorder are: (1) a tremor that is pronounced during inactivity but is suppressed during both voluntary movement and sleep, (2) muscular rigidity, (3) continual involuntary shifts in posture (*cruel restlessness*), (4) slowness of movement (*bradykinesia*), and (5) a shuffling, wide-based gait with a forward-leaning posture that frequently leads to *festination*, the tendency to take faster and faster steps to keep from falling forward. There is usually no intellectual impairment. Like epilepsy, Parkinson's disease has no single cause; brain infections, strokes, tumors, traumatic brain injury, and neurotoxins have all been implicated in specific instances. However, in the majority of cases, no cause is obvious, and there is no family history of the disorder.

Although the causes of the neural changes underlying Parkinson's disease remain a mystery, the nature of the changes is well understood. There is obvious degeneration of the *substantia nigra*, the midbrain nucleus whose neurons project via the **nigrostriatal pathway** to the **striatum** of the basal ganglia (see Chapter 2). Dopamine is the neurotransmitter synthesized by the neurons of the substantia nigra, and there is almost a total lack of dopamine in the striatums of long-term Parkinson's patients. Because Parkinson's disease was the first neuropsychological disorder to be linked to a specific neurotransmitter (i.e., dopamine), it has been the focus of a massive research effort. In the next chapter, you will learn how neurochemicals are used to correct the dopamine deficiency associated with the disorder; and in Chapter 15, you will learn about the recent attempts to alleviate Parkinson's disease by transplanting healthy dopaminergic tissue.

Huntington's Disease

Like Parkinson's disease, **Huntington's disease** is a progressive disorder of motor function; but unlike Parkinson's disease, it is relatively rare, it has a strong genetic basis, and it is always associated with severe dementia. The first motor symptoms take the form of increased fidgetiness, but they slowly grow worse until the behavior of the patient is characterized by the incessant involuntary performance of a variety of rapid, complex, jerky movements that involve entire limbs rather than individual muscles. Huntington's disease is sometimes called *Huntington's chorea* because the twisting, writhing, grimacing movements displayed by some Huntington's patients have a dance-like quality—*chorea* is from the Greek word for *dance*, as is "chorus line" and "choreography."

Huntington's disease is passed from generation to generation by a single dominant gene; thus, all of the individuals carrying the gene develop the disorder, as do about half their offspring. The Huntington's gene is readily passed from parent to child because the first symptoms of Huntington's disease do not appear until the parent is well past his or her peak reproductive years (at about 45 years of age). There is no cure; death occurs approximately 15 years after the appearance of the first symptoms. Autopsy reveals gross degeneration of the striatum and diffuse thinning of the cerebral cortex.

If one of your parents were to develop Huntington's disease, the chance would be 50/50 that you too would develop it. If you were in such a situation, would you want to know your fate? Medical geneticists have discovered the location of the lethal Huntington's gene, and they have developed a test that can tell the relatives of Huntington's patients whether or not they are carrying it (Martin, 1987). One advantage of the test is that it permits the relatives of Huntington's patients who have not inherited the gene to have children without the fear of passing on the disorder.

Much of the early research on Huntington's disease was aimed at tracing the family trees of those with the disorder. The first recorded cases of the disease were reported in 1630 in the town of Bures, England (Vessie, 1932). At that time, entire families containing afflicted individuals were judged to be witches and executed. The history of the disease in North America can be traced to two families who fled Bures and sailed to North America. Once in North America, these poor unfortunates were dealt with more humanely—only one of them was hanged. In the last few decades, the number of those afflicted has declined as the result of genetic counseling.

Multiple Sclerosis

Multiple sclerosis (MS) typically begins in early adult life. It is a progressive disease of CNS myelin. First, there are microscopic areas of degeneration on axon sheaths, but eventually there is a complete breakdown of both the myelin and the associated axons, along with the development of many areas of hard scar tissue—*sclerosis* literally means *hardening*. Figure 5.9 illustrates degeneration in the white matter of a patient with multiple sclerosis.

The diagnosis of multiple sclerosis in terms of specific behavioral symptoms is difficult because the nature of the disorder depends on the number, size, and position of the sclerotic lesions. In almost all cases there are periods of remission, which may last up to 2 years; however, these happy interludes are but oases in the cruel progression of the disorder. Common symptoms of multiple sclerosis are urinary incontinence, visual disturbances, weakness, numbness, tremor, and **ataxia** (loss of motor coordination).

Epidemiological studies of multiple sclerosis have provided evidence that both environmental and genetic factors influence its development (McDonald, 1984). **Epidemiology** is the study of the various factors, such as diet, geographic location, age, sex, and race, that influence the distribution of a disease in the general population. Evidence that environmental factors influence the development of multiple sclerosis comes from the finding that the incidence of multiple sclerosis is far greater in cooler climates. However, multiple sclerosis is rare among certain groups, such as gypsies and orientals, even when they live in environments in which the

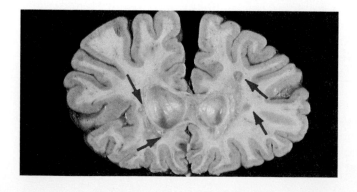

FIGURE 5.9 *Areas of sclerosis (see arrows) in the white matter near the ventricles of a patient with MS. (Courtesy of Kenneth Berry, Head, Neuropathology, Vancouver General Hospital.)*

incidence is high in others. The existence of a genetic factor in the disease has been established by comparisons of the concordance of the disease in monozygotic (about 36%) and dizygotic (about 12%) twins in several studies (e.g., Currier & Eldridge, 1982; McFarland, Greenstein, McFarlin, Eldridge, Xu, & Krebs, 1984).

A model of multiple sclerosis can be induced in laboratory animals by injecting them with myelin and a preparation that stimulates the body's immune reaction. Because the resulting disorder, termed **experimental allergic encephalomyelitis,** is similar in some respects to multiple sclerosis, it has led to the view that multiple sclerosis results from a faulty immune reaction that attacks the body's own myelin as if it were a foreign substance. Some researchers believe that this faulty autoimmune reaction is the result of a viral infection.

Alzheimer's Disease

Alzheimer's disease is the most common cause of *dementia* (Wurtman, 1985). It is estimated that one-third of all nursing-home beds in North America are filled by individuals suffering from this disorder. Alzheimer's disease is a disease of the aged. The disease sometimes appears in individuals as young as 40, but the likelihood of manifesting it becomes greater with advancing years. About 5% of the general population over the age of 65 suffer from Alzheimer's disease, and the proportion is 11% in those over 85. Alzheimer's disease is progressive. Early Alzheimer's is characterized by depression and a general decline in cognitive ability; the intermediate stages are marked by irritability, anxiety, and complete loss of speech; and in its advanced stages, the patient deteriorates to the point that even simple responses such as swallowing and bladder-control are difficult. Alzheimer's disease is terminal.

Alzheimer's disease is characterized by neurons that contain tangles of *neurofibrils* (thread-like structures in the cytoplasm), by a loss of neurons, and by multiple plaques (clumps of degenerating neurons interspersed with abnormal proteins collectively referred to as **amyloid**). Figure 5.10 is a section of the brain of a patient who died of Alzheimer's disease; the section has been treated with a stain that has an affinity for amyloid

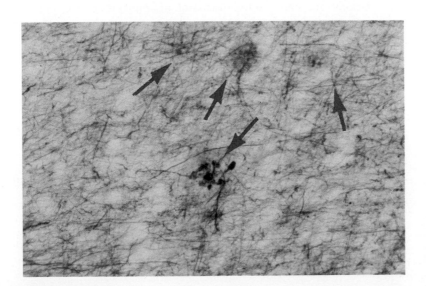

FIGURE 5.10 *Amyloid placques (see arrows) in the brain of a patient with Alzheimer's disease. (Courtesy of Steven Vincent, Kinsmen Laboratory of Neurological Research, University of British Columbia.)*

placques. Recent studies have suggested that Alzheimer's disease preferentially attacks neurons in which *acetylcholine* is the neurotransmitter (Summers, Majovski, Marsh, Tachiki, & Kling, 1986).

Although the cause of Alzheimer's disease has not been unequivocally demonstrated, its association with Down's syndrome has provided an important clue. You may recall from earlier in the chapter that Down's syndrome is the result of a genetic accident that creates an extra chromosome 21 in each cell—three rather than two. The fact that almost all Down's patients surviving to middle age develop Alzheimer's disease suggests that Alzheimer's disease also results from a genetic anomaly associated with chromosome 21. This has recently been proven to be the case. The gene associated with forms of Alzheimer's disease that runs through families was found to be on chromosome 21 (St. George-Hyslop et al., 1987), as was the gene that controls the production of amyloid proteins (Goldgaber, Lerman, McBride, Saffiotti, & Gajdusek, 1987; Tanzi et al., 1987).

Psychiatric Disorders

The concept of mental illness originally implied that behavioral disorders are of two basic kinds: diseases of the brain (neurological disorders) and diseases of the mind (mental disorders). However, recent progress in identifying the neural bases of the so-called mental illnesses has eliminated any need for a special category of disorders that are assumed to have no neuropathological basis. The designation *mental illness*—and its modern equivalent, *psychiatric disorder*—are used for historical and professional reasons, but the disorders to which they refer are not fundamentally different from other neuropsychological disorders. They are simply neuropsychological disorders whose primary behavioral symptoms reflect particularly complex intellectual, motivational, and emotional deficits whose expression is greatly influenced by the experiences of the patient. Two of the most prevalent categories of psychiatric disorder—schizophrenia and affective disorder (depression and mania)—are the focus of the next chapter.

Before proceeding to the discussion of animal models of neuropsychological disorders, test your knowledge of the disorders themselves by filling in the following blanks.

1. The two major categories of epileptic seizures are
   _____ and _____ seizures.

2. The disorder characterized by tremor at rest, bradykinesia, cruel restlessness, and festination is _____.

3. _____ is passed from generation to generation by a single dominant gene.

4. Parkinson's disease is associated with degeneration in the _____ dopamine pathway.

5. Experimental allergic encephalomyelitis is an animal model of

_____.

6. The most common cause of dementia is _____.

7. _____ attacks are complex partial seizures that are similar in many respects to normal behavior.

8. Alzheimer's disease is associated with _____ syndrome.

5.3 Animal Models
of Human Neuropsychological Diseases

The first two sections of this chapter focused on neuropsychological diseases (Section 5.2) and their causes (Section 5.1), but they also provided some revealing glimpses into the various ways in which researchers have attempted to solve the various puzzles of neurological dysfunction. This section focuses on one of them: the experimental investigation of animal models. Because the laboratory experimentation necessary to identify the neuropathological basis of human neuropsychological disorders is seldom possible on the patients themselves, animal models of the disorders play a particularly important role in their investigation.

Three different types of animal models are used in medical research (Kornetsky, 1977). There are **homologous animal models,** which are diseases in animals that duplicate the human disorder; the etiology, symptoms, and prognosis of the model resemble those of the human disorder in every major respect. There are **isomorphic animal models,** which resemble the human disorder, but are artificially produced in the laboratory in a way that does not reflect normal etiology. And finally, there are **predictive animal models,** which do not resemble the human disorder in key respects, but are of value in predicting some aspect of the disorder, such as its response to various drugs. In a sense, the three types of animal models represent a hierarchy: a predictive model enables one to make certain predictions about the disorder that it models; an isomorphic model permits predictions, and it allows one to study underlying mechanisms; and a homologous model serves as a basis for studying all aspects of a disorder, including its causes. Accordingly, to understand a model's potential uses and limitations, it is important to recognize which type of model it is. One difficulty in this respect is that we currently do not understand the mechanisms underlying most neuropsychological disorders well enough to assess the degree to which they are faithfully mirrored by an animal model. Another difficulty is that even the best animal models seem to represent only some aspects of a disorder. Consequently, animal models must be employed with caution. Studying an animal model is like exploring a section of an unknown maze. One enters an unfamiliar section with little more than a hope that its exploration will prove fruitful, and it is only after each of its arms have been carefully explored that it is possible to know whether the decision to enter the section was wise. In the same way, it is not possible to evaluate the numerous models of neuropsychological dysfunction currently under investigation until each has been thoroughly explored. Surely, only a few models will lead toward the goals of understanding and prevention, but only time and effort can tell which ones these are.

Completing this chapter is a discussion of three animal models that are currently the focus of intensive investigation.

The Kindling Model of Epilepsy

In 1969, Goddard, McIntyre, and Leech delivered one mild electrical stimulation per day to rats through implanted amygdaloid electrodes. There was no behavioral response to the first few stimulations, but soon each stimulation began to elicit a convulsive response. The first convulsions were mild, involving a slight tremor of the face; however, with each subsequent stimulation, the elicited convulsion became more generalized until each convulsion involved the entire body. Each of these generalized kindled convulsions was characterized in rats by the following progression of symptoms: facial tremor, rhythmic jaw movements, rhythmic head nodding, forelimb clonus, rearing up on the hind legs, and falling (e.g., Racine, 1972). This effect became known as the **kindling phenomenon.**

Although kindling is most frequently studied in rats subjected to repeated amygdaloid stimulation, it is a remarkably general phenomenon. For example, kindling has been reported in mice (Leech & McIntyre, 1976), rabbits (Tanaka, 1972), cats (Goddard & Morrell, 1971), dogs (Wauquier, Ashton, & Melis, 1979), and various primates (Wada, Osawa, Wake, & Corcoran, 1975). Moreover, kindling can be produced by the repeated stimulation of many brain sites other than the amygdala, and it can be produced by the repeated application of initially subconvulsive doses of convulsive drugs (e.g., Pinel & Cheung, 1977).

There are many interesting features of kindling (see Racine, 1978; Racine & Burnham, 1984), but two warrant emphasis. The first is that the neural changes underlying kindling are permanent. A subject that has been kindled and then left unstimulated for several months still responds to each low-intensity stimulation with a generalized convulsion (Goddard et al., 1969; Wada & Sato, 1974). The second is that kindling is produced by distributed, as opposed to massed, stimulations. If the intervals between successive stimulations are shorter than an hour or two, it usually requires many more stimulations to kindle a subject, and under normal circumstances no kindling at all occurs at intervals of less than about 20 minutes (Racine, Burnham, Gartner, & Levitan, 1973).

Much of the interest in kindling stems from the fact that it models epilepsy in two ways. First, the convulsions elicited in kindled animals are similar in many respects to those observed in some types of human epilepsy. Second, the kindling phenomenon itself is comparable to the **epileptogenesis** (the development or genesis of epilepsy) that can follow a head injury—some individuals who at first appear to have escaped serious injury after a blow to the head begin to experience convulsions a few weeks later, and these convulsions sometimes begin to recur more and more frequently and with greater and greater intensity. Accordingly, many studies have been conducted in order to determine which drugs block the kindling of motor convulsions and which block the elicitation of convulsions in animals that have already been kindled. The study of Racine, Livingston, and Joaquin (1975) is a good example of the latter approach. They found that an anticonvulsant commonly used in the treatment of human epileptics, *diphenylhydantoin* (Dilantin), blocked convulsions elicited in kindled rats by neocortical stimulation, but not those elicited by amygdaloid stimulation. Conversely, another commonly used anticonvulsant, *diazepam* (Valium), blocked kindled convulsions elicited by amygdaloid stimulation, but had no effect on neocortical kindled convulsions. These data suggest that the response of human epileptics to various anticonvulsant drugs may depend on the location of the epileptic focus.

It must be stressed that the kindling model as it is applied in most laboratories is not isomorphic. You will recall from earlier in this chapter that epilepsy is a disease in which epileptic attacks recur spontaneously; in contrast, kindled convulsions are elicited. However, a model that overcomes this shortcoming has been developed. If subjects are kindled for a very long time—about 300 stimulations in rats—a syndrome can be induced that is truly epileptic in the sense that the subjects begin to display spontaneous seizures and continue to display them even after the regimen of stimulation is curtailed (e.g., Pinel, 1981; Wada, Sato, & Corcoran, 1974).

Amphetamine Model of Schizophrenia

Amphetamine abuse can lead to a syndrome called **amphetamine psychosis,** which is similar in many respects to schizophrenia (e.g., Connell, 1958)—the abuse of other stimulant drugs (e.g., cocaine) can have a similar effect. The symptoms of amphetamine psychosis include compulsive pacing, stereotypic touching and picking of the face and extremities, repeated assembling and disassembling of objects, distortion of time and space, extreme reactivity, olfactory and tactile hallucinations, and paranoia. Fortunately, once individuals displaying amphetamine psychosis stop taking the drug, these symptoms dissipate in a day or two, but sometimes they do not dissipate completely. There are frequently residual delusions and mannerisms that persist long after amphetamine abuse has stopped, and a full-blown psychotic episode can sometimes be reinstated by a single dose of the drug after long periods of abstinence (Bell, 1973). Amphetamine and other stimulants have been found to exacerbate the schizophrenic symptoms of psychotic patients (Janosky, Huey, & Storms, 1977), and antischizophrenic drugs have been shown to counteract the symptoms of amphetamine psychosis (Angrist, Rotrosen, & Gershon, 1980).

Although the behavioral effects of amphetamine are not the same in each species, in mammals there is always a general increase in locomotor activity (pacing) and other repetitive, apparently functionless, behaviors (e.g., Haber, Barchas, & Barchas, 1981; Schiorring, 1979). Because these so-called *behavioral stereotypies* resemble behaviors commonly associated with amphetamine psychosis in humans, they have been widely used as an animal model of human schizophrenia. The following is a description of the amphetamine-induced open-field behavior of the rat.

Doses that range from 0.3 to 1.5 mg/kg (*d*-amphetamine injected subcutaneously) produce an increase in forward locomotion. . . . This ambulation persists for approximately 40 to 90 minutes, depending on the dose, and is followed by a period of sleep. Administration of higher doses elicits a multiphasic response pattern that consists of early and late phases of ambulation, and an intermediate phase of focused stereotypy during which locomotion is absent. The focused stereotypy phase is characterized by sniffing, repetitive head and limb movements, and oral behaviors (e.g., licking, biting and/or gnawing) expressed over a small area of the cage floor. Although these behaviors are most prominent during the focused stereotypy phase, they may appear intermittently during other phases of the drug response. The time course of each phase is dose-dependent: with increasing doses, the initial locomotor phase decreases in duration as the animal spends progressively more time in focused stereotypy and in the last phase of locomotion. In fact, at doses of 5.0 to 10.0 mg/kg the total duration of the resonse may exceed 5 or 6 hours before the animal goes to sleep. (Rebec & Bashore, 1984, p. 154)

Because many of the drugs effective in the treatment of human schizophrenia attenuate the stereotypies induced in laboratory animals by amphetamine, the amphetamine model has been widely used to assess the efficacy of various antischizophrenic drugs and to study their mechanisms of action. However, Rebec and Bashore (1984) have argued that progress in this area of research has been impeded by the lack of precise behavioral assessment. Most investigators lump the complex behavioral changes observed during the course of a test into one or two scores—for example, a single measure of locomotor activity and a single measure of stereotypy—but Rebec and Bashore contend that a more selective behavioral approach is warranted. They have offered the following lines of evidence in support of their contention: (1) Some of the behavioral symptoms of amphetamine psychosis in humans occur in individuals who chronically use amphetamine but do not become psychotic. (2) Although amphetamine psychosis typically occurs only after long-term amphetamine abuse, some of the behavioral effects of amphetamine in laboratory animals, such as the oral stereotypies (licking and biting), actually decline with repeated exposure. (3) Some clinically effective antischizophrenic agents block some of the stereotypical behaviors elicited in animals by amphetamine but leave others, such as the oral stereotypies, unaffected (Costall & Naylor, 1977; Iversen & Koob, 1977). On the basis of the preceding observations, Rebec and Bashore concluded that the amphetamine-produced locomotion, but not oral stereotypy, models amphetamine psychosis, and they stressed the need for careful and independent assessment of each of the behavioral aspects of the amphetamine model.

MPTP Model of Parkinson's Disease

Parkinson's disease . . . rarely occurs before the age of 50. It was somewhat of a surprise then to see a group of young drug addicts at our hospital in 1982 who had developed symptoms of severe and what proved to be irreversible parkinsonism. The only link between these patients was the recent use of a new 'synthetic heroin.' They exhibited virtually all of the typical motor features of Parkinson's disease, including the classic triad of bradykinesia (slowness of movement), tremor and rigidity of their muscles. Even the subtle features, such as seborrhea (oiliness of the skin) and micrographia (small handwriting), that are typical of Parkinson's disease were present. After tracking down samples of this substance, the offending agent was tentatively identified as 1-methyl-4-phenyl-1,2,3,6-tetrahydropyridine or **MPTP**. . . . After nearly two and a half years, there has been no sign of remission, and most are becoming increasingly severe management problems. (Langston, 1985, p. 79)

Researchers immediately tried to turn the misfortune of these few to the advantage of many by developing a much-needed animal model of Parkinson's disease (Langston, 1986). It was quickly established that various nonhuman primates responded to MPTP like humans (Burns, Chiueh, Markey, Ebert, Jacobowitz, & Kopin, 1983; Jenner, et al., 1986; Langston, Forno, Robert, & Irwin, 1984), but attempts to develop a rodent model have been less successful. A parkinsonian-like syndrome can be produced in some mice, but, unlike Parkinson's disease and the MPTP syndrome in humans, it does not persist for more than a few weeks (Duvoisin, Heikkila, Nicklas, & Hess, 1986).

The study of the brains of primates exposed to MPTP has revealed highly selective damage to the substantia nigra. Although the brain damage in Parkinson's patients is somewhat more diffuse, the MPTP data suggest that cell loss in the substantia nigra is responsible for the motor symptoms of the disease. Considering that the substantia nigra is the major source of the brain's dopamine, it is not surprising that the level of this transmitter is greatly reduced in both the MPTP model and in the naturally occurring disorder.

Conclusion

This chapter commenced with the tragic case history of Jimmie G., and then it proceeded to the causes of brain damage, common neuropsychological disorders, and the study of animal models. The following case history of a 30-year-old woman poisoned by MPTP (Ballard, Tetrud, & Langston, 1985) completes the circle.[2]

> During the first 4 days of July 1982, . . . [she] used 4½ grams of a "new synthetic heroin." The substance was injected IV [intravenously] three or four times daily and caused a burning sensation at the site of injection. . . .
>
> She had brief auditory hallucinations and visual distortions with larger doses. After 3 days of use, she felt "weak" and "slow," but used the drug for another day. Four days later, she was described by family as sitting quietly without moving all day, staring into space "like a zombie." She later said that she felt fully alert during this period and was aware of the environment, but had difficulty initiating speech and could move only with great effort. She also noted intermittent "shaking" of the left arm. Her family provided total care for her, including all dressing, feeding, and bathing.
>
> On July 21, 1982, she was admitted to our neurobehavioral unit. She had the appearance of a "wax doll," sitting immobile with head and arms held in flexion. General examination [revealed] . . . facial seborrhea [oiliness] . . . , a breakdown of horizontal smooth [visual] pursuit, . . . infrequent blinking, continuous drooling, . . . and difficulty initiating speech. Tongue protrusion was slow, limited to about 1 cm. Voluntary movements were profoundly slowed. Left to herself, she remained motionless. . . . A resting tremor of 5 to 6 Hz in the right hand and foot disappeared on volitional movement. . . . She

---

[2]From "Permanent Human Parkinsonism Due to 1-methyl-4-phenyl-1,2,3,6-tetrahydropyridine (MPTP): Seven Cases" by P. A. Ballard, J. W. Tetrud, and J. W. Langston, 1985, *Neurology*, 35, 949–956. Reprinted by permission.

could not rise from a chair without assistance. Gait was shuffling, with small steps, loss of associated movement . . . and loss of postural reflexes. Sensation was normal. The remainder of the neurologic examination was normal, including mental status. . . .

After 2 years of treatment, there has been no improvement in her parkinsonism, and she has suffered a variety of therapeutic complications. (pp. 949–951)

Before leaving this chapter, pause for a moment to contemplate the plight of this woman and of others who suffer from MPTP poisoning or from advanced parkinsonism. These are intelligent, sensitive, alert people—people just like you—who are trapped for the rest of their lives in a body that does not work.

Food for Thought

1. An epileptic is brought to trial for assault. The lawyer argues that her client is not a criminal and that the assaults in question were psychomotor attacks. She points out that her client takes her medication faithfully, but that it does not help. The prosecution lawyer argues that the defendant has a long history of violent assault and must be locked up. What do you think that the judge should do?

2. Describe a bizarre incident that you have observed that you think in retrospect might have been a psychomotor or petit mal attack.

3. The more that is known about a disorder, the easier it is to diagnose; and the more accurately it can be diagnosed, the easier it is to find things out about it. Explain and discuss.

ADDITIONAL READING

I strongly recommend the following two texts on neuropsychological disorders. The book by Chusid is a clearly written and well-illustrated summary of nervous system disorders for medical students. The book by Sacks is a collection of highly entertaining and personal descriptions of neuropsychological patients whom he has studied.

Chusid, J. G. (1985). *Correlative neuroanatomy and functional neurology.* Los Altos, California: Lange Medical Publications.

Sacks, O. (1985). *The man who mistook his wife for a hat and other clinical tales.* New York: Summit Books.

KEY TERMS

To help you study the material in this chapter, all of the key terms—those that have appeared in bold type—are listed and briefly defined here.

Amphetamine psychosis. A psychotic state similar to schizophrenia that is produced by amphetamine abuse.

Amyloid. A type of protein found in clumps of degenerating neurons in Alzheimer's patients.

Aneurysm. A balloon-like dilation that forms in the wall of a blood vessel at a point where the elasticity of the vessel wall is defective.

Arteriosclerosis. A condition in which the walls of the blood vessels thicken and narrow.

Ataxia. Loss of motor coordination.

Benign. A tumor is benign if it can be removed without leaving vestiges of it that continue to grow in the body.

Brain abscess. Pocket of pus in the brain.

Cerebral ischemia. A damage-producing disruption of the blood supply to an area of the brain.

Complex partial seizures. Seizures that are characterized by various complex psychological phenomena and are thought to result from temporal lobe discharges.

Concussion. When there is a disturbance of consciousness following a blow to the head with no cerebral bleeding or obvious structural damage.

Congenital. Present at birth.

Contracoup injury. A contusion that occurs on the side of the brain opposite to the side of the blow.

Contusion. A closed-head injury that involves bleeding.

Convulsions. Motor seizures.

Dementia. General intellectual deterioration.

Dizygotic twins (fraternal twins). Twins that developed from two different fertilized eggs.

Down's syndrome. A disorder associated with the presence of an extra chromosome in pair 21 resulting in disfigurement and mental retardation.

Embolism. When a plug forms in a larger blood vessel and is carried to a smaller one where it blocks the passage of blood.

Encapsulated tumor. A tumor that grows within its own membrane.

Encephalitis. The inflammation associated with brain infection.

Endogenous. Produced inside the body.

Epidemiology. The study of factors that influence the distribution of a disease in the general population.

Epileptic aura. A psychological symptom that precedes the onset of a convulsion.

Epileptogenesis. Development of epilepsy.

Exogenous. From outside the body.

Experimental allergic encephalomyelitis. A model of multiple sclerosis that can be induced in laboratory animals by injecting them with myelin and a preparation that stimulates the body's immune system.

Generalized seizures. Seizures that involve the entire brain.

General paresis. The insanity and intellectual deterioration resulting from syphylitic infection.

Grand mal. A seizure whose symptoms are loss of consciousness, loss of equilibrium, and a violent tonic-conic convulsion.

Hematoma. A bruise.

Homologous animal model. A disorder in animals that duplicates a human disorder in every respect.

Huntington's disease. A progressive disorder of motor and intellectual function that is produced in adulthood by a dominant gene.

Hypoxia. Shortage of oxygen in the blood.

Infarct. An area of ischemic brain damage.

Infiltrating tumor. A tumor that grows diffusely through surrounding tissue.

Isomorphic animal model. A disorder in animals that resembles a human disorder, but is artificially produced in the laboratory.

Kindling phenomenon. The progressive intensification of convulsions elicited by a series of distributed low-intensity stimulations—most commonly by daily electrical stimulations to the amygdala.

Korsakoff's syndrome. A memory disorder associated with chronic heavy alcohol consumption.

Malignant. A tumor is malignant if it cannot be surgically removed without continued growth in the body.

Meningiomas. Tumors that grow between the meninges.

Meningitis. Inflammation of the meninges caused usually by bacterial infection.

Metastatic tumors. Tumors that originate in one organ and spread to another.

Monozygotic twins (identical twins). Twins that develop from the same fertilized egg.

MPTP. A neurotoxin that produces a disorder in primates that is similar to Parkinson's disease.

Multiple sclerosis (MS). A progressive disease of the CNS myelin.

Neurotropic. Viral infections that have a particular affinity for neural tissue.

Nigrostriatal pathway. The pathway along which the neurons from the substantia nigra project to the striatum.

Pantropic. Viral infections that can infect brain tissue, but have no preference for it.

Parkinson's disease. A movement disorder associated with degeneration of neurons in the substantia nigra and a dopamine deficiency in the striatum.

Partial seizure. A seizure that does not involve the entire brain.

Petit mal. A generalized seizure accompanied by a disturbance of consciousness and a 3-per-second spike-and-wave discharge.

Phenylketonuria (PKU). A genetic dysfunction caused by the absence of the enzyme necessary to metabolize phenylalanine.

Predictive animal model. A model that does not resemble the human disorder in key respects, but is of value in predicting some aspect of the disorder.

Psychomotor attack. An epileptic attack in which the patient engages in compulsive behaviors that, although inappropriate, have the appearance of normal behaviors.

Punch-drunk syndrome. The mental disturbances resulting from repeated concussions.

Simple partial seizure. Partial seizures in which the symptoms are primarily sensory and/or motor.

Tardive dyskinesia (TD). A motor disorder associated with chronic use of certain antipsychotic drugs.

3-per-second spike-and-wave. The characteristic EEG of the petit mal seizure.

Thrombosis. When a plug blocks blood flow at the site of its formation.

Toxic psychosis. Psychiatric disturbance caused by exposure to toxic chemicals.

Tumor (neoplasm). A mass of cells that grows independently of the rest of the body.

6

Neurotransmitters, Drugs, and Mental Illness

This chapter deals with three different topics: neurotransmitters, drugs, and mental illness—three ostensibly different topics that together constitute a single, exciting field of research. The primary goal of many of the researchers who work in this field is the identification of the neurochemical dysfunctions associated with various psychiatric disorders and the development of drugs to treat them, but the field does not focus exclusively on dysfunction. It can't. The study of function and dysfunction are inextricably related. The definition of one is the absence of the other. One is what the other isn't. In this chapter, you will encounter instances in which the investigation of normal neurochemical and behavioral function has provided a framework for the analysis and correction of dysfunction; and conversely, you will encounter instances in which the study of dysfunction has provided insights into normality.

This chapter comprises four sections:

6.1 A Brief Historical Introduction
6.2 How Neurotransmitters Are Studied
6.3 The Neurotransmitters
6.4 The Chemistry and Pharmacology of Schizophrenia and Affective Disorders

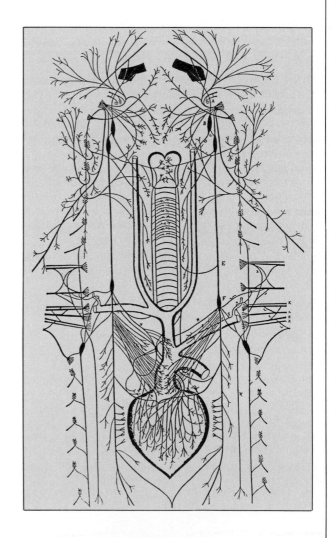

6.1 A Brief Historical Introduction

Early brain researchers envisioned the nervous system as a continuous, web-like network of neural processes. It was not until the beginning of this century that the Spanish neuroanatomist Ramón y Cajal discovered, using the then recently developed *Golgi stain* (see Chapter 2), that the nervous system is actually composed of many individual neurons that do not come into direct physical contact with one another. Cajal's important discovery is referred to as the *neuron doctrine*.

A fundamental implication of the neuron doctrine is that the key to understanding brain function lies in the study of how individual neurons communicate with one another. The first inkling of how such communication takes place was provided by an elegantly simple study conducted in 1921 by Otto Loewi, a German pharmacologist (see Figure 6.1). Loewi placed the beating heart of a frog in a saline bath and stimulated the *vagus nerve* (the tenth cranial nerve), which innervates it. As expected, this caused the beating heart to slow down. The important finding was that when a second frog heart was exposed to the saline bath in which the first heart had been stimulated, it also slowed down. This suggested that the electrical stimulation of the vagus neurons innervating the first heart released some chemical into the bath that retarded the beating of both hearts. This neurochemical was subsequently isolated and found to be **acetyl-choline.** A similar series of experiments involving stimulation of the *accelerans nerve*, which, as its name implies, increases heart rate, led to the isolation of a second neurochemical, **norepinephrine** (sometimes referred to as *noradrenaline*). Neurons that release acetylcholine are said to be *cholinergic;* those that release norepinephrine are said to be *nonadrenergic*.

In the years after Loewi's revolutionary discovery, the mechanisms of synaptic transmission in the peripheral nervous system were gradually elucidated (see Chapter 3); however, studies of synaptic transmission

FIGURE 6.1 *The classic experiment by Loewi, which provided the first evidence that synaptic transmission is chemically mediated.*

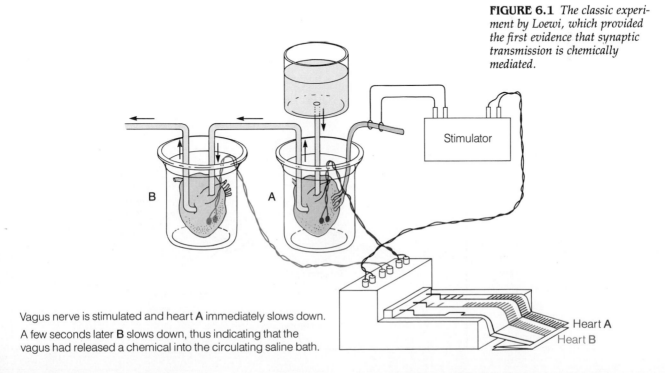

Stimulator

B

A

Heart A
Heart B

Vagus nerve is stimulated and heart **A** immediately slows down.

A few seconds later **B** slows down, thus indicating that the vagus had released a chemical into the circulating saline bath.

in the CNS were rare. By the mid-1950s, a full 35 years after Loewi's breakthrough, the function of only one class of CNS synapses could be confidently ascribed to a particular neurotransmitter—these were the cholinergic synapses between the terminal buttons of motor neuron **collaterals** (fibers branching off from the main motor neuron axon) and small inhibitory interneurons called **Renshaw cells** in the spinal cord (see Figure 6.2).

In the early 1950s, three independent developments set the stage for subsequent breakthroughs in the study of CNS synaptic transmission (see Carlsson, 1987). The first was the discovery in the brain of norepinephrine and three other neurochemicals with similar structures: **epinephrine** (adrenaline), **serotonin,** and **dopamine.** Each of the four is created through minor modification of an amino acid molecule, and thus each belongs to the class of neurochemicals called *monoamines* (literally, *one amine*). Much of the early research on neurotransmission in the CNS focused on these monoamines, and all four were subsequently proven to be bona fide neurotransmitters. The second stage-setting event of the early 1950s was the development of several new biochemical procedures for detecting minute quantities of **putative neurotransmitters** (suspected neurotransmitters) in tissue samples. Not the least of these procedures was **spectrophotofluorimetry,** a procedure for establishing the concentration of monoamines in a tissue sample by measuring its fluorescence (Eränkö, 1955). This procedure takes advantage of the fact that monoamines exposed to formalin fixative yield a compound that fluoresces when illuminated by ultraviolet light. The third stage-setting development of the early 1950s was the explosion of interest in psychopharmacology. This was triggered by the increasing recreational use of psychoactive drugs such as LSD, mescaline, and marijuana, and by the discovery that **chlorpromazine** and **reserpine** alleviate the symptoms of schizophrenia.

FIGURE 6.2 *The cholinergic synapse of motor neuron collaterals on Renshaw cells in the ventral horn of the spinal gray matter.*

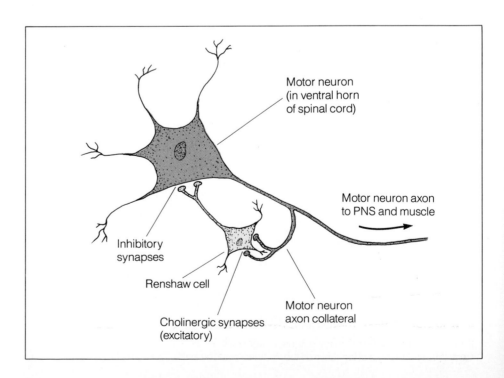

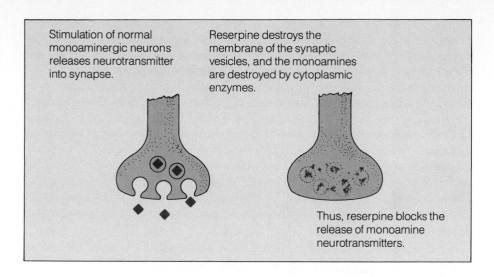

Stimulation of normal monoaminergic neurons releases neurotransmitter into synapse.

Reserpine destroys the membrane of the synaptic vesicles, and the monoamines are destroyed by cytoplasmic enzymes.

Thus, reserpine blocks the release of monoamine neurotransmitters.

FIGURE 6.3 *The mechanism of action of reserpine.*

In the late 1950s, the combined impact of these developments led to two major breakthroughs in the study of CNS neurotransmission. The first was the discovery that the antischizophrenic drug reserpine disrupts transmission at monoaminergic synapses. Reserpine was shown to cause monoamine neurotransmitters to leak from their synaptic vesicles into the cytoplasm of the presynaptic cell, where they are broken down by enzymes (e.g., Carlsson, Lindqvist, & Magnusson, 1957; Carlsson, Lindqvist, Magnusson, & Waldeck, 1958; Shore, Silver, & Brodie, 1955)—see Figure 6.3. This was the first evidence of an interaction between a psychoactive drug and a putative neurotransmitter.

The second 1950s breakthrough in the study of CNS synaptic transmission came just as the decade was coming to a close. Postmortem examination of the brains of people with Parkinson's disease revealed that they contained almost no dopamine (Ehringer & Hornykiewicz, 1960)—you may recall from the preceding chapter that *Parkinson's disease* is a disorder characterized by tremor at rest, muscular rigidity, and poverty of movement. This suggested that Parkinson's disease results from a disruption of dopaminergic transmission in the striatum, the structure that normally contains most of the brain's dopamine (Bertler & Rosengren, 1959; Carlsson, 1959). Within two years, reports confirmed that the symptoms of Parkinson's disease are alleviated by injections of **L-DOPA,** the chemical from which dopamine is synthesized (Birkmayer & Hornykiewicz, 1962). Dopamine itself proved ineffective because, unlike L-DOPA, it does not pass through the blood-brain barrier (see Chapter 2).

Both of these early breakthroughs in the study of CNS neurotransmitters were important for the same reasons. Both illustrated how the psychological effects of drugs can be understood in terms of their effects on CNS neurotransmitters, and both illustrated the therapeutic spin-offs from the study of such interactions.

6.2 How Neurotransmitters Are Studied

It is not an easy matter to prove beyond the shadow of a doubt that a particular neurochemical functions as a neurotransmitter in the CNS. This process often begins with the publication of the hypothesis that a particular chemical is a neurotransmitter, usually on the basis of quite flimsy evidence. This often stimulates attempts to test the hypothesis, and if evidence accumulates in favor of it, many researchers begin to refer to the chemical as a *putative neurotransmitter*. This acknowledges that they consider the evidence to be strong, but not yet conclusive. As still more positive evidence accumulates, more and more researchers are willing to drop the qualifier, "putative" (suspected) and refer to the chemical as a bona fide neurotransmitter. Whether or not a particular neurochemical should be considered a putative neurotransmitter or a neurotransmitter is a matter of individual judgment, but most experts agree that there are currently about 9 neurotransmitters and another 40 or so putative neurotransmitters. The following are seven kinds of observations that are often offered as evidence that a particular chemical is a neurotransmitter at a particular population of synapses.

Lines of Evidence That Establish the Identity of a Neurotransmitter at a Particular Synapse

1. *Location in the Terminal Button.* Proving that a particular chemical is present in the neurons suspected of releasing it is often the first step in establishing that the chemical is a neurotransmitter. If the chemical can be shown to reside in synaptic vesicles (see Chapter 3), the evidence is even stronger.

2. *Presence of Appropriate Enzymes.* Further support for the hypothesis that a particular chemical is a neurotransmitter is provided by evidence that the enzymes necessary for its synthesis and breakdown reside in the neurons that are thought to release it.

3. *Release from the Presynaptic Membrane.* Evidence that the suspect chemical is released by the neurons that contain it greatly strengthens the case that can be made for its being a neurotransmitter. Unfortunately, this important criterion is extremely difficult to meet in the CNS. In the PNS, where organs are commonly innervated by large, accessible bundles of axons that all release the same neurotransmitter, it is possible to stimulate the axon bundles (i.e., nerves) and collect analyzable samples of the released substance. For example, substantial quantities of acetylcholine can be collected from the neuromuscular junctions of a stimulated motor nerve. However, in the CNS the intricacy and inaccessibility of the neural circuits usually makes this method impractical.

4. *Effect on the Postsynaptic Cell.* In order to prove that a substance is a neurotransmitter, it is necessary to show that it influences the activity of the postsynaptic cell. Such evidence is obtained by recording intracellularly from the postsynaptic neuron while molecules of the candidate neurotransmitter are deposited on its receptive surface. It is also important to show that the response of the postsynaptic cell to the deposition of the substance is the same as that produced by stimulation of the presynaptic cell.

5. *Existence of Receptors in the Postsynaptic Membrane.* There are specialized outward facing proteins in the postsynaptic membrane that are designed to bind neurotransmitter molecules released by the presynaptic neuron. Demonstrating that there are receptor proteins in the postsynaptic membrane that bind the suspect neurotransmitter greatly strengthens the case.

6. *A Mechanism of Deactivation.* Once a neurotransmitter has been released, it acts for only a short time. So far, two methods of neurotransmitter deactivation have been identified: reuptake by the presynaptic cell and its degradation in the synapse by an enzyme. The demonstration of either of these deactivating mechanisms for a particular neurochemical adds weight to the argument that it is a neurotransmitter.

7. *Predictable Pharmacologic Effects.* Drugs that are known to influence a particular neurochemical can be used to test the hypothesis that the neurochemical is the neurotransmitter released by a particular class of neurons. For example, because reserpine is known to deplete neurons of monoamine neurotransmitters, evidence that reserpine reduces transmission at a particular synapse suggests that the neurotransmitter at the synapse is a monoamine.

How Drugs Affect Synaptic Transmission

Drugs have two fundamentally different kinds of effects on synaptic transmission: they facilitate it, or they inhibit it. Drugs that facilitate the activity of the synapses of a particular neurotransmitter are said to be **agonists** of that neurotransmitter. Drugs that inhibit the activity at the synapses of a particular neurotransmitter are said to be its **antagonists.**

In order to understand how drugs exert their agonistic and antagonistic effects, it is important to understand the mechanisms of normal synaptic transmission. You may recall these from Chapter 3, but they are summarized here just in case you do not. First, neurotransmitter molecules are synthesized from chemical precursors in the cytoplasm under the influence of particular enzymes. They are then stored in synaptic vesicles near the presynaptic membrane, and any neurotransmitter that leaks from the vesicles is destroyed by enzymes. When an action potential arrives at the synaptic button, the vesicles fuse with the synaptic membrane, and the neurotransmitter molecules are released into the synaptic cleft. In the synaptic cleft, they bind to receptors on the membrane of the postsynaptic neuron; and in so doing, they affect its activity. Some presynaptic membranes have receptors for their own neurotransmitter (*autoreceptors*), and when the neurotransmitter binds to these, subsequent release of the neurotransmitter is inhibited. The action of the neurotransmitter is terminated by mechanisms that draw the neurotransmitter back into the presynaptic neuron, or by enzymes in the synaptic cleft that break it down. Figure 6.4 illustrates these basic mechanisms of neurotransmitter synthesis, storage, release, and deactivation and how drugs can interact with these mechanisms to produce agonistic and antagonistic effects.

Mechanisms of Agonistic Drug Effects   Illustrated in Figure 6.4 are six mechanisms by which agonistic drugs have been shown to increase synaptic transmission: (1) by increasing the amount of neurotransmitter that is synthesized; for example, you have already learned that L-DOPA alleviates Parkinson's disease by increasing dopamine levels; (2) by deactivating the enzymes that normally break down the neurotransmitter in the cytoplasm of the presynaptic neuron; (3) by increasing the release of the neurotransmitter from the presynaptic neuron into the synaptic cleft; (4) by binding to autoreceptors and blocking their inhibitory action; (5) by binding to the neurotransmitter's postsynaptic receptors and activating them;

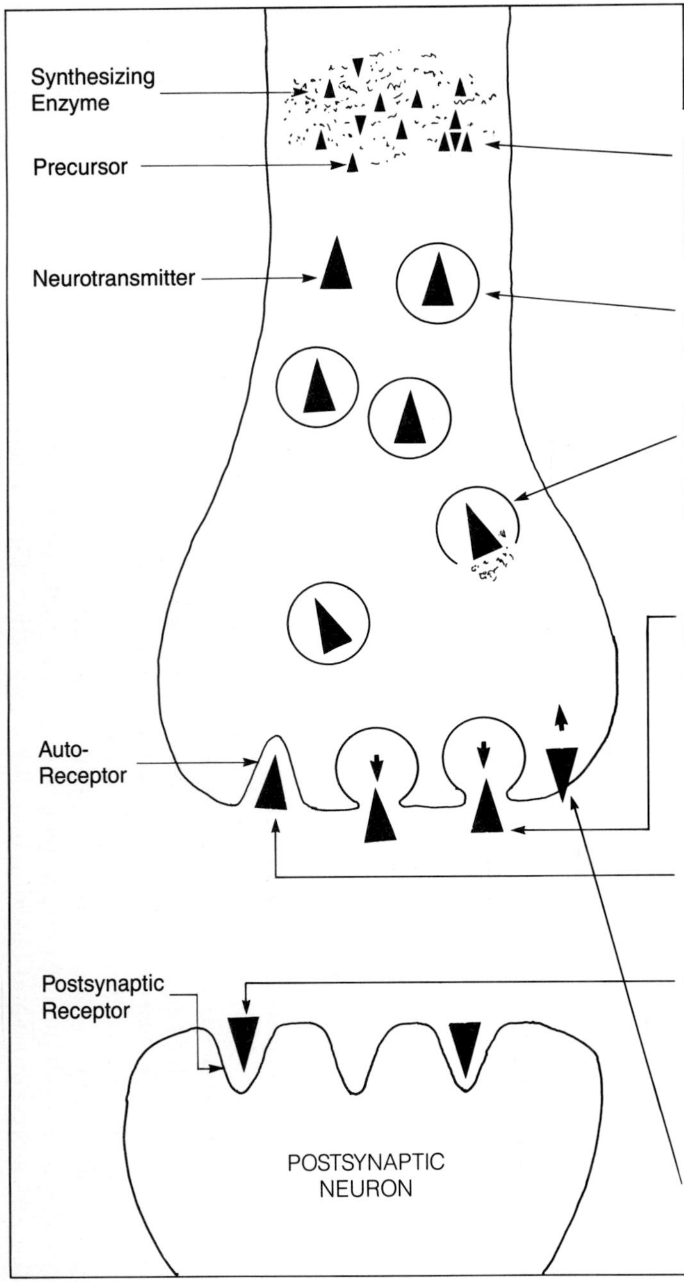

Mechanisms of Neurotransmitter Action	Mechanisms of Agonistic Drug Effects	Mechanisms of Antagonistic Drug Effects
Neurotransmitter is synthesized from precursors under influence of enzymes.	Drug increases synthesis of neurotransmitter (e.g. by increasing the amount of precursor).	Drug blocks synthesis of neurotransmitter (e.g., by destroying synthesizing enzymes).
Neurotransmitter is stored in vesicles.		Drug causes neurotransmitter to leak from vesicles.
Any neurotransmitter leaking from vesicles is destroyed by enzymes.	Drug increases amount of neurotransmitter by destroying degrading enzymes.	
When impulse arrives, vesicles fuse with presynaptic membrane and release neurotransmitter.	Drug increases amount of neurotransmitter released.	Drug blocks release of the neurotransmitter from the presynaptic neuron.
Neurotransmitter decreases subsequent neurotransmitter release by exciting autoreceptor.	Drug binds to autoreceptors and blocks their activity.	Drug activates autoreceptors.
Neurotransmitter activates postsynaptic receptor	Drug binds to postsynaptic receptors and activates them.	Drug is a false transmitter; it binds to postsynaptic receptors and blocks access of the neurotransmitter.
Neurotransmitter is deactivated by reuptake or enzymatic degradation	Drug blocks deactivation by blocking degradation or re-uptake.	

Synthesizing Enzyme

Precursor

Neurotransmitter

Auto-Receptor

Postsynaptic Receptor

POSTSYNAPTIC NEURON

FIGURE 6.4 *Mechanisms by which drugs can exert agonistic and antagonistic effects on synaptic transmission.*

or (6) by blocking the degradation of the neurotransmitter in the synaptic cleft or its reuptake from the cleft into the presynaptic neuron.

Mechanisms of Antagonistic Drug Effects   Illustrated in Figure 6.4 are five mechanisms by which drugs have been shown to inhibit synaptic transmission: (1) by blocking the synthesis of the neurotransmitter; for example, by disrupting the actions of enzymes that play a critical role in its synthesis; (2) by causing the neurotransmitter to leak from its vesicles and to be broken down by enzymes in the cytoplasm; (3) by disrupting the mechanism of neurotransmitter release; (4) by activating autoreceptors which normally inhibit neurotransmitter release; or (5) by acting as **false transmitters.** Like the wrong keys jammed in locks, false transmitters bind to the postsynaptic receptors and keep the natural neurotransmitter from performing its function.

Methods of Locating Neurotransmitters in the CNS

Although simple introductions to complex, highly technical areas of research such as neurotransmission and neuropharmacology can be a blessing, they are often a mixed blessing. A case in point is the preceding discussion of neurotransmitters, agonists, and antagonists. The very generality and simplicity that I hope has made your journey to this point in the chapter a smooth one has obscured your view of the amazing technical sophistication required to study particular neurotransmitters within the morass of central nervous system neurons. For example, the preceding parts of this chapter treat locating a particular neurotransmitter in the synaptic vesicles of a terminal button and depositing a few molecules of a neurotransmitter on a postsynaptic membrane as if they were as easy as tying one's shoelaces. This subsection of the chapter is an attempt to correct this false impression by briefly describing four influential neurochemical techniques that have enabled neurochemists to accomplish the seemingly impossible.

The Histofluorescence Technique   Major advances in the study of monoamine neurotransmitters followed the development of the **histofluorescence technique** by Falck and Hillarp (Falck, Hillarp, Thieme, & Torp, 1962). It had been shown that monoamines exposed to a formalin fixative glow when exposed to fluorescent light, and Falck and Hillarp reasoned that it might be possible to adapt the procedure to reveal the location of monoamines in the brain. After several failures, Falck and Hillarp exposed thinly sliced tissue specimens known to contain norepinephrine and serotonin to formaldehyde vapor; and low and behold, when they viewed the slices in a *fluorescence microscope,* the glowing outlines of the monoaminergic neurons were clearly recognizable (see Figure 6.5). The histofluorescence technique was the first to permit the visualization of specific neurotransmitter systems in the brain.

One drawback of the histofluorescence technique is that it does not discriminate between norepinephrine, dopamine, and epinephrine—all three fluoresce a bright green. Additional studies are required to determine which of these three monoamines is contained in a system of green-fluorescing neurons. Serotonin-containing neurons are readily identifiable because they fluoresce a bright yellow.

FIGURE 6.5 *Neural tissue exposed to formaldehyde vapor and viewed by a fluorescence microscope reveals the position of monoamine-containing neurons.*

Receptor Binding Autoradiography Receptor binding autoradiography is a conceptually simple, but technically difficult, procedure. First, a neurotransmitter or drug that binds to the receptor of interest is labeled with a radioactive isotope. Then, slices of neural tissue are exposed to the labeled *ligand* (any molecule that binds chemically to the target), the excess (unbound) radioactivity is washed away, and the slide is coated with a photographic emulsion, which reacts to the radioactivity, thus revealing the location of the receptors. Unfortunately, most ligands bind to the receptor only briefly, and most show some degree of affinity for molecules other than the receptor under investigation. Accordingly, in order for the binding to be selective, researchers must develop specific procedures to increase the strength of the binding of the radioactive ligand with the receptor and/or to decrease nonspecific binding.

Monoclonal Antibody Immunohistochemistry Monoclonal antibody immunohistochemistry is based on the discovery that mouse lymphocyte cells can be fused with mouse bone-marrow cancer cells to produce hybrid cells that have the characteristics of both ancestors (see Milstein, 1980). Like **lymphocytes,** they secrete **antibodies;** and like cancer cells, they divide forever if they are maintained in a suitable medium.

The monoclonal antibody immunohistochemical technique is illustrated in Figure 6.6. First, a sample containing the neural protein of interest is injected into a mouse; it is not necessary for the sample to be pure, but the purer that it is the better. The mouse will produce a variety of antibodies to the impure injected material; however, each lymphocyte produces only a single kind of antibody. Next, the lymphocytes are harvested from the mouse's spleen and fused to bone-marrow cancer cells. Then, the individual fused cells are separated from one another, and as each divides it creates a colony of *clones* (a colony in which each cell is identical to the others). Each colony of clones manufactures only a single antibody, and each divides indefinitely if properly maintained; thus, each is potentially an immortal source of exquisitely pure antibody. Finally, the antibody produced by each colony is labeled by dyes or by radioactive or fluorescent material, and the binding patterns of each colony on sample tissue are evaluated until a colony is discovered that binds to the protein under investigation. Once a culture has been developed to produce an antibody to a particular protein, the antibody can be produced in almost limitless quantities.

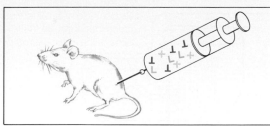

A solution containing an antigen (e.g. a protein) of interest is injected into a mouse (⊥).

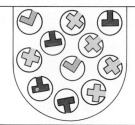

Mouse lymphocytes begin to produce antibodies to the antigen of interest (⊥) and to the other proteins in the solution. The lymphocytes are harvested from the mouse spleen.

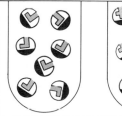

The lymphocytes, which each produce only a single antibody, are fused to individual cancer cells.

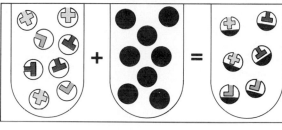

The hybrid cells are separated from one another and grow into a colony of clones, each of which produces a supply of pure antigen.

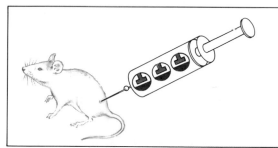

The antigen produced by each colony is radioactively labeled and is injected into a subject, where it binds to its antigen, thus revealing the antigens location in the brain. Each colony is tested until the colony that produces the antibodies to the protein of interest is identified.

FIGURE 6.6 *The monoclonal antibody immunohistochemistry technique.*

Microiontophoresis   In order to establish that a particular chemical serves as a neurotransmitter, it is necessary to show that the postsynaptic neuron responds to it. This is accomplished by **microiontophoresis,** which employs a *double-barreled micropipette*. A double-barreled micropipette consists of two micropipettes, one inside the other. As illustrated in Figure 6.7, the tip of the inner *pipette* is filled with saline and inserted into the postsynaptic neuron so that the intracellular voltage can be recorded through the saline. The space between the inner and outer micropipette contains a solution of the ions of the neurochemical under investigation. By passing a weak current through the ion solution, a few ions are deposited on the

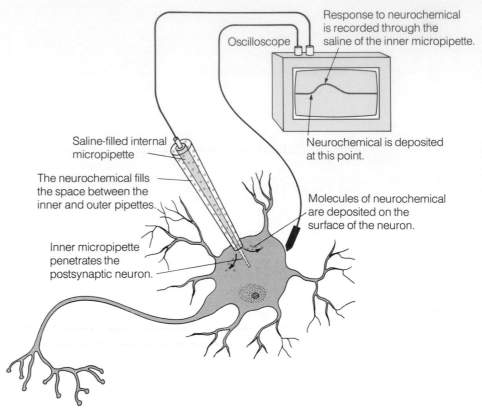

Oscilloscope

Response to neurochemical is recorded through the saline of the inner micropipette.

Saline-filled internal micropipette

The neurochemical fills the space between the inner and outer pipettes.

Inner micropipette penetrates the postsynaptic neuron.

Neurochemical is deposited at this point.

Molecules of neurochemical are deposited on the surface of the neuron.

FIGURE 6.7 *Microiontophoresis. A small amount of electrical current passed between the inner and outer pipettes deposits a few molecules of neurochemical onto the surface of the neuron, and the response of the neuron is recorded through the saline solution filling the inner pipette. By using this technique, it is possible to find out which neurotransmitters change the resting potential of the neuron.*

neuron's membrane, and their effect on the resting potential of the neuron can be recorded through the saline of the inner pipette. Excitatory neurotransmitters reduce the normal resting potential of the postsynaptic neuron and increase its firing rate; inhibitory neurotransmitters increase the resting potential of the postsynaptic neuron and decrease its rate of firing (see Chapter 3). *Multiple-barreled micropipettes* work on the same principle, but they permit the testing of a variety of putative neurotransmitters on the same neuron.

6.3 The Neurotransmitters

There are three major classes of neurotransmitters: the amino acid neurotransmitters, the monoamine neurotransmitters, and the neuropeptides. In addition, there is acetylcholine, which is in a class by itself. Late professors, too, are often in a class by themselves.

The Amino Acid Neurotransmitters

The neurotransmitters used in a vast majority of fast-acting, point-to-point synapses in the central nervous system are **amino acids,** the molecular building blocks of proteins. There are four that have proven to be neurotransmitters to the satisfaction of most experts: **glutamate, aspartate, glycine,** and **gamma-aminobutyric acid (GABA)**. The first three are common in the proteins that we consume, whereas GABA is synthesized by a simple modification of the structure of glutamate. Of these four amino acids, GABA has been the most thoroughly investigated. It is present in all regions of the brain and spinal cord, mainly in local inhibitory interneurons. Because the microiontophoretic administration of GABA inhibits most CNS neurons, it is thought to be the most prevalent inhibitory transmitter in the CNS.

The Monoamine Neurotransmitters

In contrast to the fast point-to-point effects of the amino acid neurotransmitters, the four monoamine neurotransmitters—**norepinephrine, epinephrine, dopamine,** and **serotonin**—have slower, more diffuse effects (e.g., Iversen, 1987). The monoamines are present in small groups of neurons whose cell bodies are, for the most part, found in the brain stem. These neurons often have long, highly branched axons with many *varicosities* or swellings, which give the axons a string-of-beads appearance. The monoamine neurotransmitters are widely dispersed from the varicosities.

Monoamines are commonly subdivided into two groups, **catecholamines** and **indolamines,** on the basis of their structure. Dopamine, norepinephrine, and epinephrine are all catecholamines. They are all synthesized from the amino acid *tyrosine* as part of the same synthetic pathway. Tyrosine is converted to *L-DOPA,* which is in turn converted to dopamine. Noradrenergic neurons have an extra enzyme not present in dopaminergic neurons, and this enzyme converts the dopamine in them to norepinephrine. Similarly, adrenergic neurons have all the enzymes present in dopaminergic and noradrenergic neurons, along with an extra one, which converts norepinephrine to epinephrine (see Figure 6.8). Because the catecholamines have similar structures and a common synthetic pathway, drugs that affect one of them often affect them all. In contrast to the other monoamines, serotonin (also called *5-hydroxytryptamine,* or *5-HT*) is synthesized from the amino acid *tryptophan* and is classed as an *indolamine.*

Acetylcholine

Neurotransmitters are often considered to be of two distinct types: small-molecule neurotransmitters and large-molecule neurotransmitters. Both the amino acids and the monoamines are small-molecule neurotransmitters. So too is **acetylcholine** (Ach), but unlike the others, it is neither an amino acid nor a simple modification of one. It is created by adding an *acetyl group* to a *choline molecule,* which is a constituent of the fats that we eat and is also manufactured by the liver. Acetylcholine is the neurotransmitter at neuromuscular junctions, at most of the synapses in the autonomic nervous system (norepinephrine is the transmitter at the others), and at synapses throughout the central nervous system. It is deactivated in the synaptic cleft by being broken down in the synapse by the enzyme, **acetylcholinesterase.**

Neuropeptides

Nine small-molecule transmitters have been discussed so far: the four amino acids (glutamate, aspartate, glycine, and GABA), the four monoamines (dopamine, norepinephrine, epinephrine, and serotonin), and

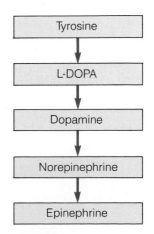

FIGURE 6.8 *The steps in the synthesis of catecholamines from tyrosine.*

acetylcholine. These are the nine for which the evidence is largely complete—the nine that are accepted as bona fide neurotransmitters by even the most skeptical neuroscientists. The rapid accumulation of evidence that peptides also serve as neurotransmitters ranks as one of the major advances in neuroscience in the last decade. Peptides are at once both large and small; they are large for neurotransmitters, but they are small for proteins. **Peptides** are short chains of amino acids; thus, they are larger than the small-molecule neurotransmitters, which comprise only a single amino acid, but they are smaller than **proteins,** which by definition are chains of amino acids that comprise 100 or more amino acids. About 40 or so peptides currently qualify as putative CNS neurotransmitters (Iversen, 1987), and the list is growing rapidly (see Appendix VI).

Some neuropeptides have been known and studied for a long time as hormones, not as neurotransmitters. First, these peptides were shown to be released into the bloodstream by endocrine glands, and it was assumed that their role was restricted to the endocrine system. Then, one by one, each of the peptide hormones was shown to be present in neural tissue. Initially, it was assumed that various neural structures simply served as the targets for hormones synthesized and released by endocrine glands, but it is now clear that these peptide hormones are synthesized and released by neurons as well as by endocrine glands.

Small-molecule neurotransmitters can be synthesized in the cytoplasm of the terminal buttons; but neuropeptides, like all proteins, are synthesized in the cell body. Although the diversity of neuropeptides is enormous, current evidence suggests that they are all synthesized from only a few different **polypeptides,** chains of amino acids that are longer than peptides, but shorter than proteins (i.e., polypeptides are between 10 and 100 amino acids in length). All neurons synthesize the same few polypeptides, but those that manufacture a particular neuropeptide contain specific enzymes that cleave one of the polypeptides apart at the appropriate sites along its length to release the neuropeptide embedded in it. The neuropeptide is then stored in vesicles and transmitted to the terminal buttons.

Recent Changes in the Concept of Neurotransmission

In the early years of neurotransmitter research, it was assumed that each neuron has one kind of neurotransmitter (**Dale's principle**); that each neurotransmitter has only one kind of receptor; that all neurotransmitter receptors are in postsynaptic membranes; and that, when released, all neurotransmitters produce an immediate, brief change in the ionic permeability of the postsynaptic neuron. It is now clear that some of these four assumptions are true (e.g., Snyder, 1984).

First, the study of peptide neurotransmitters has led to the rejection of *Dale's principle,* the widely accepted assumption that each neuron releases only a single neurotransmitter. Because each neuron releases only one small-molecule neurotransmitter, Dale's principle seemed valid when only small-molecule neurotransmitters were known. But since the discovery of neuropeptides, there have been several well-documented reports of **coexistence,** the residence of two neurotransmitters in the same neuron. So far, all documented cases of coexistence involve a small-molecule neurotransmitter and a neuropeptide.

Second, we now know that virtually every neurotransmitter acts on more than one kind of receptor. The different classes of receptors acted on by a particular neurotransmitter are referred to as the *receptor subtypes* of that neurotransmitter. For example, there are two acetylcholine receptor subtypes, nicotinic receptors and muscarinic receptors. The *nicotinic receptors* are those cholinergic receptors to which the drug nicotine binds, and the *muscarinic receptors* are those cholinergic receptors to which the drug muscarine binds. The receptors of the neuromuscular junction are all nicotinic and the receptors on the organs innervated by the parasympathetic nervous system are all muscarinic. Both cholinergic subtypes are found in the CNS. Psychoactive drugs that act specifically on a receptor subtype *are*, strictly speaking, agonists and antagonists of the receptor subtype, rather than to the neurotransmitter in general.

Third, it is now well established that, although the postsynaptic membrane is the most common site for receptors, many are located at other sites on the neural membrane; for example, the autoreceptors on the presynaptic membrane.

Fourth, it is now clear that some neurotransmitters are not released into conventional synapses. Some neurotransmitters—in particular the neuropeptides, and to some extent the monoamines—have far-reaching effects because they are released into the extracellular fluid, the ventricles, or the bloodstream. This has led to the view that neuropeptides serve as **neuromodulators.** Unlike conventional neurotransmitters, whose function is to carry local excitatory or inhibitory messages across synapses, neuromodulators increase or decrease the sensitivity of large populations of neurons to the local effects of conventional neurotransmitters. Neuromodulators are thought to act through receptors whose activation produces gradual, long-lasting metabolic changes in their neurons via secondary messenger systems (see Chapter 3), rather than immediate brief changes in ion flow (Schwartz, 1987). Neuromodulators are thought to influence behavior by regulating emotional and motivational tone.

Agonists and Antagonists: Some Examples

The following are noteworthy examples of drugs that affect behavior by influencing neurotransmission: atropine, *d*-tubocurarine, morphine, and the benzodiazepines.

Atropine Many of the drugs that are used today in research and in medicine are extracts of plants that have long been used for medicinal and recreational purposes. For example, in the time of Hippocrates, the Greeks took extracts of the belladonna plant to treat stomach ailments and as a cosmetic. Greek women believed that its pupil-dilating effects made them more beautiful; *belladonna* means *beautiful lady*. In the 1880s, atropine was extracted from the belladonna plant and shown to be its active ingredient; and in the 1930s, it was shown to exert its effects by binding to muscarinic acetylcholine receptors and blocking the effects of acetylcholine on them (i.e., by serving as a false transmitter). The disruptive effect of high doses of atropine on memory was one of the earliest clues that Alzheimer's disease (see Chapter 5) might be caused by a disturbance of cholinergic activity in the brain.

***d*-Tubocurarine** South American Indians have long used *curare*, an extract of a certain class of woody vines, to kill their game—and occasionally their enemies. The active ingredient of curare is ***d*-tubocurarine.** Like atropine, *d*-tubocurarine is a false transmitter at cholinergic synapses, but unlike atropine, it acts at the nicotinic receptor. By binding to nicotinic receptors, *d*-tubocurarine paralyzes animals by blocking transmission at neuromuscular junctions, and this blockade eventually kills them by stopping respiration. Accordingly, when *d*-tubocurarine is used as an adjunct to anesthesia during surgery, the patient must be kept alive by a respirator.

Morphine   *Opium*, a resinous extract of the opium poppy, has long been used for both its euphoria-producing effects and its medicinal effects; it is effective in the treatment of pain, coughing, and diarrhea. In 1805, it was discovered that the main active ingredient of opium is **morphine,** named after Morpheus, the Greek god of dreams. We now know that morphine acts by stimulating receptors in the brain that are normally stimulated by a class of neuropeptides called endorphins (see Appendix VI). **Endorphin** is a general term used to refer to any morphine-like substance that occurs naturally in the brain; it is a contraction of "endogenous morphine-like substance." The two most widely studied endorphins are the **enkephalins,** two five-amino-acid peptides that are identical to one another except for one of their amino acids.

Benzodiazepines   In their attempt to create new drugs that are effective against psychological disorders, the biochemists employed by drug companies synthesize new drugs by altering the structure of chemicals that are already known to act on the brain. Then these new chemicals are turned over to the company's psychopharmacologists, who determine whether or not they are likely to have any beneficial psychological effects. An important drug that was discovered in this fashion was **chlordiazepoxide** (marketed under the name Librium). Chlordiazepoxide was shown to have *anxiolytic* (anxiety-reducing), *sedative* (sleep-inducing), and anticonvulsant effects (see Sternbach, 1983) first on animal models and then in human patients. Later, other drugs of similar structure, such as *diazepam*

To review the neurotransmitters to which you have just been introduced, fill in the blanks in the following paragraph before proceeding.

Amino acids are the neurotransmitters in the vast majority of (1) _____ -acting, _____ synapses. Four amino acids have proven to be neurotransmitters to the satisfaction of most experts: (2) _____ , (3) _____ , (4) _____ , and (5) _____ . In contrast to the amino acid neurotransmitters, the (6) _____ have slower, more diffuse effects, and they belong to one of two categories, (7) _____ or indolamines. Belonging to the former category are epinephrine, (8) _____ , and (9) _____ ; and (10) _____ is the only neurotransmitter belonging to the latter category. The neuropeptides, which are short chains of (11) _____ , are the third major class of neurotransmitters. Finally, there is (12) _____ , which is a neurotransmitter in a class by itself.

The answers to the preceding questions are (1) fast, point-to-point, (2, 3, 4, 5) glutamate, glycine, aspartate, and GABA in any order, (6) monoamines, (7) catecholamines, (8, 9) dopamine and norepinephrine in either order, (10) serotonin, (11) amino acids, and (12) acetylcholine.

(Valium), were synthesized, tested, and marketed. Chlordiazepoxide and diazepam belong to the class of drugs known as the **benzodiazepines.** The benzodiazepines appear to exert their anxiolytic effects by serving as GABA agonists. Benzodiazepines bind to the GABA receptor, but they do not exert their agonistic effect by mimicking GABA's actions. Benzodiazepine molecules do not bind to the GABA receptor at the same site at which GABA molecules bind; they bind to another part of the GABA receptor molecule, and by so doing, they increase the binding of GABA molecules to the receptor and increase GABA's inhibitory effects. In view of the anxiolytic and anticonvulsant effects of benzodiazepines, it is not surprising that benzodiazepine binding sites are particularly dense in the amygdala, a structure known to play a role in emotion and in the propagation of temporal lobe seizures.

6.4 The Chemistry and Pharmacology of Schizophrenia and Affective Disorders

In some ways, the study of mental illness and its treatment with drugs has been the biggest success story of modern neuroscience. Before the introduction of the first psychotherapeutic drugs in the mid 1950s, about 50 percent of all hospital beds in the United States were filled by people suffering from psychiatric disorders, and the numbers were increasing steadily. Soon after the first psychotherapeutic drugs were introduced, these figures began to plummet; it has been estimated that the number of people in mental hospitals in the United States today is only about 10% of what it would have been if psychotherapeutic drugs had not been discovered. Accordingly, the story of the development of psychotherapeutic drugs is more than a tale of scientific accomplishment; it is a story of the relief of untold suffering. Hundreds of thousands have been helped.

> Up until the early 1950s, a large segment of the country's schizophrenic population lived in state mental hospitals from which many of them never emerged; and because conditions in those hospitals were likely to be inferior to the conditions in bad prisons, a diagnosis of schizophrenia was, in effect, a sentence to a living death. (Snyder, 1986, pp. 68–70)

Schizophrenia and Its Neurochemical Basis

By general consensus (see the *Diagnostic and Statistical Manual of Mental Disorders-IIIR* of the American Psychiatric Association, *DSM-IIIR*), individuals with one or more of the following symptoms are classed as schizophrenic:

bizarre delusions delusions of being controlled (e.g., thought broadcasting, thought insertion); delusions of persecution (e.g., "My mother is trying to poison me" or "The communists are following me"); delusions of grandeur (e.g., "The Pope wants to meet me," or "The Boz admires my haircut").

hallucinations usually voices telling the patient what to do, commenting negatively on her or his behavior, or talking to one another

incoherent thought illogical thinking, peculiar associations between ideas, belief in supernatural forces

blunted affect failure to react with an appropriate level of emotionality to positive or negative events

odd behavior such as **catatonia** (long periods with no movement), marked impairment of personal hygiene, or talking in rhymes.

About 1% of the population is clearly schizophrenic, and about another 2 or 3% display schizophrenic symptoms that are of insufficient severity or frequency to make the diagnosis unambiguous (Snyder, 1986). Many schizophrenics display long periods of relative normality between periods of florid psychosis. It is interesting that the incidence of schizophrenia has been found to be about the same in all racial and social classes and in all parts of the world, despite wide variations in political, social, and economic climate (Strömgren, 1987).

It has long been a tradition in our society to think of mental illness as a somewhat mystical disorder, somehow separate from the physical and chemical processes of the brain; even the name *mental illness* implies that it is not part of the biological world. However, in the first half of this century, the cloak of mysticism began to be removed from mental illness by a series of studies that clearly established that schizophrenia has a genetic basis. First, it was discovered that schizophrenia runs in families. Although only about 1% of the population is diagnosed as schizophrenic, the probability of schizophrenia occurring in the close biological relatives of a schizophrenic (i.e., parents, children, or siblings) was found to be between 10 and 15% in various studies. Because these percentages were found to be about the same in children who had been adopted into healthy families as babies (e.g., Kendler & Gruenberg, 1984; Rosenthal, Wender, Kety, Welner, & Schulsinger, 1980), it was concluded that the tendency for schizophrenia to run in families was largely genetic.

Further evidence of schizophrenia's genetic basis has come from numerous studies reporting higher concordance rates for schizophrenia in identical twins than in fraternal twins (e.g., Kallman, 1946). You may recall from Chapter 6 that *monozygotic twins* (identical twins) are those with identical genes, and *dizygotic twins* (fraternal twins) are no more genetically related than any two *siblings* (brothers and sisters). If a schizophrenic is a monozygotic twin, the probability of his or her twin also being schizophrenic is about 65%, whereas if the schizophrenic is a dizygotic twin, the probability falls to the usual sibling baseline of about 15% (see Kendler, 1987). The 65% concordance rate for schizophrenia in monozygotic twins makes two important points. First, it proves that schizophrenia has a genetic basis; an individual with the same genes as a schizophrenic is 65 times more likely to become a schizophrenic than a person with no schizophrenic relatives (65% versus 1%). Second, it proves that genetics is not the entire story—if it were, the concordance rate would be 100 percent. Although it is clear that environmental factors contribute to the development of schizophrenia, it is not at all clear what these environmental factors are. Hypotheses that prenatal, natal, or childhood trauma can influence the development of schizophrenia have yet to receive unequivocal support (see Bleuler, 1978).

Evidence of schizophrenia's genetic basis has done much to counteract the tendency to think of mental illness as supernatural. It is difficult to imagine how genes, which exert their effects by controlling protein and peptide synthesis, could lead to a disorder that is not itself fundamentally biochemical. Two other important findings have made this same point. One is that numerous CAT scan and postmortem neuroanatomical studies have shown that many schizophrenics have extensive brain damage (Shelton & Weinberger, 1987). The other is that repeated large doses of **stimulants,** such as *cocaine, amphetamine, methylphenidate,* and *L-DOPA,* induce psychotic episodes that are remarkably like schizophrenia (Griffith,

Cavanaugh, Held, & Oates, 1972), and a single small dose can trigger florid schizophrenic episodes in calm schizophrenic patients (Janowsky, Huey, & Storms, 1977).

The Discovery of the First Two Antischizophrenic Drugs

The first major breakthrough in the study of the biochemistry of schizophrenia was the accidental discovery in the early 1950s of the first antischizophrenic drug, *chlorpromazine.* Chlorpromazine was first developed by a French drug company as an antihistamine, but it was judged to be ineffective and too sedating. In 1950, a French surgeon wrote to the company asking for new antihistamines to try on his patients. They sent an assortment of antihistamines including chlorpromazine. After noticing that chlorpromazine given prior to surgery had a calming effect on his patients, the surgeon enthusiastically recommended that his psychiatrist colleagues use it to calm down their psychotic patients.

Although initial efforts to calm psychotic patients with chlorpromazine were unsuccessful, it was subsequently shown that high doses continued for 2 or 3 weeks had moderate sedating effects that were useful in calming some unmanageable patients. More importantly, it was discovered that chronic exposure to high levels of chlorpromazine had an effect on schizophrenic patients that was unrelated to its sedative properties. The chlorpromazine did more than calm aroused patients; it produced a specific alleviation of their schizophrenic symptoms. Agitated schizophrenic patients were calmed by chlorpromazine, but catatonic or emotionally blunt schizophrenics were activated. Moreover, sedatives, such as **barbiturates,** proved to be no more effective than placebos in the treatment of schizophrenia. Don't get the idea that the chlorpromazine cured schizophrenia. It didn't. But in many cases, it reduced the severity of schizophrenic symptoms enough to allow chronically institutionalized patients to be discharged.

An important feature of the antischizophrenic effect of chlorpromazine—the importance of which will become more apparent in the following paragraphs—is that it is frequently associated with mild motor side effects like those of Parkinson's disease. At about the same time that the chlorpromazine regimen begins to take effect—on the schizophrenic symptoms, usually several weeks after the beginning of drug treatment—the drug often begins to elicit mild tremors, muscular rigidity, and a general decrease in voluntary movement.

If the first major breakthrough in the study of the biochemistry of schizophrenia was the discovery of the antischizophrenic effects of chlorpromazine, the second was the discovery of the antischizophrenic effects of *reserpine,* a drug that you have encountered previously in this chapter. In the early 1950s, at about the same time that the early research on chlorpromazine was going on, an American psychiatrist became interested in reports that an extract of the snakeroot plant had long been used in India for the treatment of mental illness. He gave reserpine, the active ingredient of the snakeroot plant, to his schizophrenic patients and confirmed its antischizophrenic action. Although its chemical structure is unlike that of chlorpromazine, it also produced parkinsonian side effects at antischizophrenic doses.

Reserpine is no longer used in the treatment of schizophrenia because it produces a precipitous decline in blood pressure at antischizophrenic doses. However, the discovery of its antischizophrenic effect provided an important clue to the biochemical basis of schizophrenia. The fact that the antischizophrenic effects of both chlorpromazine and reserpine were accompanied by parkinsonian side effects suggested that both their antischizophrenic effects and their parkinsonian effects might result from the same biochemical change.

The Dopamine Theory of Schizophrenia

The next major breakthrough in the study of schizophrenia came from research not on schizophrenia itself, but on Parkinson's disease. In 1960, it was reported that the normally dopamine-rich striatums of persons dying of Parkinson's disease had little dopamine (Ehringer & Hornykiewicz, 1960). This finding suggested that a disruption of dopaminergic transmission might produce Parkinson's disease, and because of the relation between Parkinson's symptoms and antischizophrenic effects, it suggested that antischizophrenic drug effects might be produced in the same way. Thus, the *dopamine theory of schizophrenia* was born—the theory that schizophrenia is caused by an excess of activity at dopaminergic synapses, and conversely that antischizophrenic drugs exert their effects by decreasing dopaminergic activity.

Lending instant support to the dopamine theory of schizophrenia were two already well-established facts. The first was that reserpine was known to be a dopamine antagonist; it depleted the brain of dopamine and other monoamines. The second was that the drugs that had been shown to trigger schizophrenic episodes (i.e., amphetamine, cocaine, methylphenidate, and L-DOPA) were known to increase the activity of dopamine and other monoamines by increasing their release and/or blocking their reuptake.

Dopamine Receptors and Antischizophrenic Drugs

In 1963, Carlsson and Lindqvist attempted to test the dopamine theory of schizophrenia by assessing the effects in rats of chlorpromazine on dopamine and its metabolites (the chemicals that are created when a substance is metabolized, or broken down). What they expected to find was that chlorpromazine, like reserpine, would deplete the brain of dopamine, but this was not what happened. The levels of both norepinephrine and dopamine were unchanged by chlorpromazine, and the levels of the metabolites of both norepinephrine and dopamine were increased. These findings, at first sight, appeared to be inconsistent with the dopamine theory of schizophrenia, but Carlsson and Lindqvist interpreted them in the following manner. They concluded that both chlorpromazine and reserpine produce antischizophrenic effects by antagonizing transmission at dopamine synapses, but that they did it in different ways—reserpine by depleting the brain of dopamine and chlorpromazine by binding to dopamine receptors. They argued that chlorpromazine is a false transmitter at dopamine synapses; that is, that it binds to dopamine receptors without activating them, and in so doing, keeps dopamine from activating them. They further postulated that the lack of activity at the postsynaptic dopamine receptor sent a feedback signal to the presynaptic cell to increase its release of dopamine and that the excess dopamine released into the synapse was quickly metabolized. This explained why the dopamine levels stayed about the same and the levels of its metabolites increased. Carlsson and Lindqvist's important findings and their interpretation of them are illustrated in Figure 6.9.

Using a technique developed in the mid 1970s, Snyder and his colleagues (Creese, Burt, & Snyder, 1976; Snyder, 1976) assessed the degree to which various antischizophrenic drugs bind to dopamine receptors. First, they added radioactively labeled dopamine to samples of dopamine-receptor-rich neural membrane obtained from the striatums of calves' brains. Then, they "washed" away the unbound dopamine molecules from the samples and measured the amount of radioactivity left in them. The amount of remaining radioactivity in each sample provided a measure of the number of dopamine receptors in it. Next, Snyder and his colleagues estimated the degree to which various drugs bind to these dopamine receptors by determining the drugs' ability to block the binding of radioactive dopamine. The rationale for their method is that drugs with a high affinity for dopamine receptors would leave fewer sites available for the dopamine. In general, they found that chlorpromazine and the other effective antischizophrenic drugs that had been developed by that time had a high affinity for dopamine receptors, whereas ineffective antischizophrenic drugs had a low affinity. There was, however, one embarrassing exception: an antischizophrenic drug called **haloperidol.** Although haloperidol is an extremely potent antischizophrenic drug, it bound to relatively few dopamine receptors. As you might imagine, Snyder and his colleagues, who are strong advocates of the dopamine theory of schizophrenia, were not exactly overjoyed with this haloperidol finding; however, subsequent research revealed an elegantly simple resolution of the inconsistency.

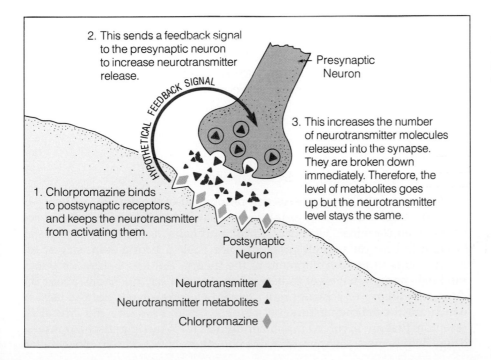

FIGURE 6.9 *The effects of chlorpromazine on the levels of dopamine and its metabolites, and an interpretation of these effects.*

The answer to the haloperidol puzzle lay in the discovery that dopamine binds to two different kinds of receptor subtypes, called D_1 and D_2 receptors. It turned out that chlorpromazine and the other antischizophrenic drugs in the same chemical class (the **phenothiazines**) all bind effectively to both D_1 and D_2 receptors, whereas haloperidol and the other antischizophrenic drugs in its chemical class (the **butyrophenones**) all bind with great potency to D_2 receptors, but not to D_1 receptors. This key finding suggested an important revision in the dopamine theory of schizophrenia. The fact that potent antischizophrenic drugs such as haloperidol selectively bound to only D_2 receptors suggested that schizophrenia is caused by hyperactivity specifically at D_2 receptors, rather than at dopamine receptors in general.

Two lines of evidence provide strong support for this D_2 modification of the dopamine theory. The first line of evidence takes advantage of the fact that there are many different antischizophrenic drugs (**neuroleptics**) in use today, which differ markedly in their potency; potent neuroleptics are those that are effective at low doses against schizophrenia. As illustrated in Figure 6.10, Snyder (1978) and his colleagues showed that the potency with which these various drugs bind to D_2 receptors predicts almost exactly their potency as antischizophrenic agents. For example, **spiroperidol,** a butyrophenone like haloperidol, was found to have the greatest affinity for D_2 receptors and to have the most potent antischizophrenic actions.

> This correlation between clinical effects of neuroleptics and their blockade of D_2 receptors is one of the more impressive examples of pharmacological analysis. It establishes the mechanism of action of neuroleptic drugs as rigorously and as firmly as that of almost any other drug in clinical medicine. (Snyder, 1986, p. 83)

Several studies have shown that radioactively labeled spiroperidol binds to dopamine-rich structures in the brains of recently deceased schizophrenics to a greater degree than it does to the same structures in control brains. Although this observation is consistent with the notion that schizophrenic symptoms result from an excess of activity at D_2 receptors, it does not provide strong support for it because there is an equally reasonable alternative (see Mackay et al., 1982; Seeman, 1980). The high levels of D_2 receptors in the brains of deceased schizophrenics could simply be a reaction to the antidopaminergic medication taken by almost all diagnosed schizophrenics.

Problems with the Dopamine Theory of Schizophrenia

The story of the development and refinement of the dopamine theory of schizophrenia is a shining example of what is possible in the neural sciences when chemical, pharmacological, and behavioral approaches are all brought to bear on a single problem—see Table 6.1 for a summary of the major events in the development of the theory. But it is a story for which the final chapters have yet to be written. Several key questions about the dopamine theory of schizophrenia remain to be resolved, not the least of which are the following three: (1) Where in the brain are the critical D_2 receptors that are involved in schizophrenia? (2) Why do antischizophrenic drugs help some schizophrenics and not others? (3) And why does it usu-

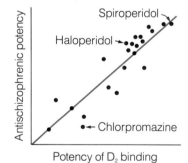

FIGURE 6.10 *The positive correlation between a neuroleptic's ability to bind to D_2 receptors and the potency of its antischizophrenic effects. Spiroperidol was the most potent antischizophrenic in this study, and it had the greatest affinity for D_2 receptors. (Adapted from Snyder, 1978.)*

Table 6.1 *The Key Events That Led to the Development and Refinement of the Dopamine Theory of Schizophrenia*

Early 1950s	The antischizophrenic effects of both chlorpromazine and reserpine were observed to be related to parkinsonian side effects.
Late 1950s	The brains of recently deceased Parkinson's patients were found to have little dopamine.
Early 1960s	It was hypothesized that schizophrenia is caused by excessive activity at dopaminergic synapses.
1960s and 70s	Various dopamine agonists were shown to induce schizophrenic symptoms.
Mid 1960s	It was discovered that chlorpromazine and other clinically effective neuroleptics were false transmitters at dopamine synapses.
Mid 1970s	The dopamine-receptor binding of phenothiazines, but not of butyrophenones, was found to be roughly correlated with their antischizophrenic potency.
Late 1970s	The binding of antischizophrenic drugs to D_2 receptors was found to be highly correlated with their antischizophrenic potency.
Currently	The D_2-receptor modification of the dopamine theory is the dominant theory of schizophrenia; schizophrenia is thought to be produced by excessive activity at D_2 receptors.

ally take weeks for the antischizophrenic effects of the neuroleptic drugs to be manifested when they block transmission at D_2 synapses almost immediately?

Tentative answers to these three questions have been offered. First, current wisdom suggests that the particular D_2 synapses involved in schizophrenia are not in the striatal terminals of the widely studied nigrostriatal dopamine pathway, which has been implicated in Parkinson's disease. It has been hypothesized that excessive D_2 activity in the **mesolimbic dopamine pathway** is the main factor in schizophrenia (Snyder, 1986). The cell bodies of this dopamine pathway lie in the midbrain (mesencephalon) next to the substantia nigra, and they project diffusely to the nucleus accumbens, the frontal cortex, and a variety of limbic structures—structures that are known to be involved in memory and emotion. Second, it has been suggested that some schizophrenics are helped more than others by antischizophrenic drugs because there are two kinds of schizophrenia (Carpenter, Heinrichs, & Alphs, 1985): one characterized by **positive schizophrenic symptoms,** such as incoherence, hallucinations, and delusions, which are assumed to be caused by increased neural activity, and one characterized by **negative schizophrenic symptoms,** such as blunt affect, catatonia, and poverty of speech, which are assumed to be caused by decreased neural activity. It has been suggested that D_2 hyperactivity produces the positive symptoms and that the negative symptoms are associated with diffuse brain damage (Crow, 1980). Accordingly, the schizophrenics with a predominance of positive symptoms benefit most from D_2 blockers. Third, it has been argued that the long delay in therapeutic effects following the onset of neuroleptic drug treatment indicates that the D_2 receptor blockade is not the specific mechanism by which schizophrenic symptoms are alleviated. Some investigators believe that the blockade of D_2 receptors triggers some slow-developing compensatory change in the brain that is the key mediator of the therapeutic effect (Sachar, 1985).

Depression:
Unipolar and Bipolar Affective Disorder

All of us have experienced depression. Depression is a normal reaction to grievous loss—the loss of a loved one, the loss of self-esteem, the loss of important personal possessions, or the loss of health. However, there are people whose tendency toward depression is out of all proportion. These people repeatedly fall into the depths of dispair, often for no apparent reason, and their depression can be so extreme that it is almost impossible for them to meet the essential requirements of their daily lives—to keep a job, to maintain social contacts, or even to maintain an acceptable level of personal hygiene. It is these people who are said to be suffering from the psychiatric disorder of **depression.** Between 5 and 10% of clinically depressed people commit suicide.

Many people who suffer from periods of recurring depression also experience periods of mania. **Mania** is at the other end of the scale of mood. During periods of mild mania, people are talkative, energetic, impulsive, positive, and very confident. In this state, they can be effective at certain jobs, and they can be great fun to be with. But when their mania becomes full-blown, it is quite a different story. After 2 or 3 hours of sleep, the florid manic often awakens in a state of unbridled enthusiasm, with an outflow of incessant chatter that careens nonstop from topic to topic. The florid manic has the world in the palm of his or her hand. No task is too difficult. No goal is unattainable. This confidence and grandiosity, coupled with high energy, distractibility, and a leap-before-you-look impulsiveness, results in a continual series of disasters. Mania typically leaves behind it a trail of unfinished projects, unpaid bills, and broken relationships.

Not all depressive patients experience periods of mania. The 60% that do not are said to suffer from **unipolar affective disorder;** the 40% that do are said to suffer from **bipolar affective disorder.** Although there is considerable variability, the periods of depression usually predominate in bipolar affective disorder; most periods of mania last a few days to a few weeks, whereas periods of depression often last for months. About 5% of men and 8% of women suffer from serious affective disorders.

Affective Disorders Have a Genetic Basis

Like schizophrenia, affective disorders have been shown to run in families. For example, about 25% of patients with unipolar affective disorder and 50% of those with bipolar affective disorder have parents with either unipolar or bipolar affective disorder. Twin studies and studies of adoptees have shown that this tendency of affective disorders to run in families is attributable to genetic factors. For example, a review of nine twin studies of bipolar affective disorder suggests a concordance rate of about 70% for identical twins and 20% for fraternal twins, whether they are reared together or apart (Winokur, 1978). Biological relatives of adoptees with bipolar affective disorder were six times more likely to commit suicide than were their adoptive relatives (Kety, 1979).

The Discovery of Antidepressant Drugs:
The Monamine Oxidase Inhibitors

Iproniazid, the first antidepressant drug, was originally developed for the treatment of tuberculosis, and as such it proved to be a dismal flop.

However, interest in the therapeutic potential of iproniazid was kindled by two findings. First, it was discovered that iproniazid left patients with tuberculosis less depressed about their disorder, although otherwise unimproved. Second, iproniazid was shown to inhibit the activity of *monoamine oxidase* (MAO), the enzyme that breaks down monoamine neurotransmitters in the cytoplasm of the neuron. As a result of these two findings, iproniazid was tested on a mixed group of psychiatric patients and found to be effective against depression. Iproniazid was first marketed as an antidepressant in 1957.

Iproniazid and the other **MAO inhibitors** proved to have several side effects; the most dangerous of these side effects is known as the **cheese effect.** Foods such as cheese, wine, and pickles contain an amine called tyramine, which is a potent elevator of blood pressure. Normally, these foods have little effect on blood pressure because tyramine is rapidly *metabolized* (broken down) in the liver by MAO. Because people taking MAO inhibitors have difficulty metabolizing tyramine, they run the risk of strokes caused by great surges in blood pressure if they consume tyramine-rich foods.

The Tricyclic Antidepressants

The **tricyclic antidepressants** are so named because of their antidepressant action and because their chemical structures all include a three-ring chain. **Imipramine,** the first tricyclic antidepressant, was initially thought to be an antischizophrenic drug. However, when its effects on a mixed sample of psychiatric patients were assessed, its antidepressant effects were immediately obvious. After several confirmations of this discovery, imipramine was marketed as an alternative to the MAO-inhibitor antidepressants.

Despite the fact that they belong to different drug classes, iproniazid (MAO inhibitor) and imipramine (tricyclic antidepressant) have remarkably similar effects. In nondepressed human subjects, neither drug has much effect, other than producing a mild degree of sedation. However, in depressed patients, both drugs produce a general alleviation of depressive symptoms, which is typically not apparent until 2 or 3 weeks after the beginning of drug therapy. In rats, neither iproniazid nor imipramine alone has much effect on behavior, but when injected in combination with reserpine, their effects are striking. Reserpine by itself produces immobility in rats; however, rats treated with a combination of reserpine and either iproniazid or imipramine become extremely active. In fact, all antidepressant drugs have the ability to produce hyperactivity when administered in combination with reserpine, and thus this is widely used as an animal model of antidepressant drug action.

The Monoamine Hypothesis of Depression

Because the behavioral effects of the tricyclic antidepressants are similar to those of the MAO inhibitors, it was thought that the tricyclics might also act on monoamine oxidase. When this turned out not to be the case, it was assumed that tricyclics must increase the release of monoamine neurotransmitters in some other way. But this did not prove to be the case either. How then do the tricyclics exert their antidepressant effect?

In the late 1950s, it was known that acetylcholinesterase terminates the action of acetylcholine in the synapse, and it was assumed that all synapses had a similar deactivation mechanism. However, over the ensuing years, each of the monoamine and amino acid neurotransmitters was shown to be deactivated, not by enzymatic degradation, but by reuptake into the presynaptic neuron. The discovery that reuptake is the primary mechanism of deactivation in monoaminergic neurons suggested that tricyclic antidepressants might function as monoamine agonists by blocking monoamine reuptake. Subsequent experiments have confirmed this hypothesis. All effective tricyclic antidepressants have been found to inhibit the reuptake of both serotonin and norepinephrine. Many tricyclic antidepressants also inhibit the reuptake of dopamine, but because some of the more effective tricyclic antidepressants have no effect at all on dopamine reuptake, it has been generally assumed that depression is not a disorder of the dopamine system. Thus was born the *monoamine theory of depression*—the theory that depression is caused by underactivity at noradrenergic and serotonergic synapses and that antidepressant drugs act by increasing noradrenergic and serotonergic effects. Consistent with this theory is the observation that many patients taking the monoamine antagonist reserpine for high blood pressure became deeply depressed and the finding that the cerebrospinal fluid of some severely depressed patients has high levels of serotonin metabolites (Åsberg, Träskman, & Thorén, 1976).

Challenges to the Monoamine Theory of Depression

Although there is considerable evidence linking serotonergic and noradrenergic effects with depression, there are a number of serious challenges still faced by the theory. The following are three of them. First, the ability of particular tricyclic antidepressants to block serotonin and norepinephrine reuptake is not highly correlated with their ability to alleviate depression. Second, although both the MAO inhibitors and the tricyclic antidepressants antagonize serotonergic and noradrenergic transmission almost immediately, therapeutic effects are usually not seen for at least 2 or 3 weeks. The answer to this problem may lie in a phenomenon called *down regulation.* In rats, it has been shown that the high levels of serotonin and norepinephrine produced by antidepressant drugs gradually lead to a reduction in the number of some noradrenergic and serotonergic receptor subtypes. Because the time course of this down regulation in rats is similar to the time course of the development of antidepressant effects in humans, it has been suggested that down regulation might be the mechanism of antidepressant drug action. The third challenge faced by the monoaminergic theory of depression is its inability to account for the remarkable therapeutic effects of lithium.

Lithium: The Wonder Metal

The discovery of the ability of **lithium,** a simple metallic ion, to block mania is yet another important pharmacological breakthrough that was made by accident. An Australian psychiatrist, John Cade, in attempting to test his theory that the urine of manic patients contains a chemical that causes mania, mixed uric acid with lithium to form a soluble injectable salt. He injected it into a group of guinea pigs, and as a control for the effects of the lithium, he injected lithium salt into another group. Because the calming effect of the lithium salt alone seemed to be as great as that of uric acid plus lithium, Cade changed his hypothesis and attributed the calming effect to the lithium, rather than to the uric acid. He then set out to confirm his conclusion in human patients. In retrospect, Cade's conclusion seems incredibly foolish. We know now that at the doses used by Cade, lithium salts produce extreme nausea. To Cade's untrained eye, his subjects' inactivity may have looked like calmness, but they weren't calm; they were ill. Be that as it may, flushed with what he thought was the success of his guinea pig experiments, Cade tried the lithium on a group of 10 manic patients, and it proved remarkably effective.

Cade reported lithium's ability to alleviate mania in 1949, but there was little reaction to his report. It was not replicated until 1954 (Schou, Juel-Nielsen, Stromberg, & Voldby, 1954), and lithium was not marketed for the treatment of mania until the mid-1960s. One reason for the relatively slow reaction to Cade's report was that Cade was not widely known; another was that few drug companies were interested in spending millions of dollars to study the therapeutic potential of a simple metallic ion, which could never be protected by a patent. A third reason was that the therapeutic potential of lithium was not fully appreciated until the late 1960s.

As the 1960s came to a close, two large-scale studies (Angst, Weis, Grof, Baastrup, & Schou, 1970; Baastrup & Schou, 1967) found lithium to be as effective against depression as it is against mania. The fact that both depression and mania are alleviated by lithium suggests that they are symptoms of the same underlying neurochemical defect. Unfortunately, this neurochemical defect has not yet been identified. Although lithium has been shown to influence the norepinephrine and serotonin in a variety of ways (Gerbino, Oleshansky, & Gershon, 1978), none has yet been directly linked to its remarkable therapeutic action.

Conclusion

In this chapter, you have learned how the study of neurotransmitters and the drugs that influence their actions has led to the development of drugs effective in the treatment of schizophrenia and disorders of affect (depression and mania). As you leave the chapter, you should be taking with you both a better appreciation for the incredible scientific and clinical accomplishments of a field of research that did not coalesce until the early 1950s and a better understanding of how scientific progress depends on the interplay between technical skill, hard work, insight, serendipity, and sheer blunder.

Science is too often described as unfolding in a systematic, sequential fashion, presided over by seemingly prescient researchers who plan every move with consummate precision, clear logic, and few false steps. In fact, this is rarely the case. One of the fascinations of the discovery process is that we often find the right answer by looking in the wrong place. The true lesson to be learned from past scientific discoveries is, "Prepare for the unexpected": be alert to chance findings, concentrate on events that strike you as peculiar, and stay hot on the trail of anything unexpected or unexplained. While these admonitions hold for all the sciences, no matter how sophisticated and well established, they are all the more paramount as guides to exploring the uncharted human mind. (Snyder, 1986, p. 119)

Food for Thought

1. How has the discussion of the recent advances in research on the neurochemistry and neuropharmacology of schizophrenia and depression changed your concept of scientific inquiry?

2. Some psychologists believe that mental illness should be treated with kindness, understanding, and insight, and not with drugs. What do you think—and more importantly, why?

ADDITIONAL READING

The following beautifully illustrated book is an excellent introduction to neurotransmitters, drugs, and mental illness:

Snyder, S. H. (1986). *Drugs and the Brain*. New York: Scientific American Books.

KEY TERMS

To help you study the material in this chapter, all of the key terms—those that have appeared in bold type—are listed and briefly defined here.

Acetylcholinesterase. The enzyme that deactivates acetylcholine in the synapse.

Agonists. Drugs that facilitate the transmission at the synapses of a particular neurotransmitter are called agonists of that neurotransmitter.

Amino acids. The molecular building blocks of proteins; amino acids are the neurotransmitters at the majority of fast-acting, point-to-point synapses in the central nervous system.

Antagonists. Drugs that inhibit transmission at the synapses of a particular neurotransmitter are called antagonists of that neurotransmitter.

Antibodies. Substances secreted by lymphocytes that bind to, and thus deactivate, specific invading protein molecules.

Atropine. A false transmitter at muscarinic synapses.

Autoreceptors. Receptors sensitive to their neuron's own neurotransmitter.

Barbiturates. A class of sedative drugs.

Benzodiazepines. A class of drugs with anxiolytic properties.

Bipolar affective disorder. A depressive condition in which the patient experiences periods of mania.

Butyrophenones. A class of antischizophrenic drugs that includes halperidol.

Catatonia. Displaying prolonged periods of total inactivity; a common symptom of some types of schizophrenia.

Catecholamines. A subgroup of monoamines that are synthesized from tyrosine.

Cheese effect. Refers to large surges in blood pressure that occur when individuals taking MAO inhibitors consume tyramine-rich foods.

Chlordiazepoxide. An anxiolytic market under the name Librium.

Chlorpromazine. The first drug widely used in the treatment of schizophrenia; its antischizophrenic action has been attributed to the fact that it binds to dopamine receptors.

Coexistence. The presence of two different neurotransmitters in the same neuron.

Collaterals. Fibers branching off from the main axon of a neuron.

***d*-Tubocurarine.** Active ingredient of curare; a false transmitter at nicotinic synapses.

Dale's principle. The assumption that each neuron releases only a single neurotransmitter.

Double-barreled micropipette. A device used for microiontophoresis.

Endorphin. A general term used to refer to any morphine-like substance that occurs naturally in the brain.

Enkephalins. Two almost identical five-amino-acid peptides that are the most widely studied endorphins.

False transmitter. A chemical that binds to a receptor and blocks the action of its intended neurotransmitter.

Haloperidol. An effective butyrophenone neuroleptic.

Histofluorescence technique. The monoamines in brain slices that have been exposed to formalin vapor glow when exposed to fluorescent light, thus revealing their location.

Indolamines. A subgroup of monoamines synthesized from tryptophan, e.g. serotonin.

Iproniazid. The first antidepressant drug.

L-DOPA. The precursor of dopamine; L-DOPA is used in the treatment of Parkinson's disease.

Lithium. A metallic ion used in the treatment of depression.

Lymphocytes. Antibody producing cells of the blood plasma.

Mania. A mental disorder in which the patient is impulsive, over-confident, highly energetic, and distractable.

Mesolimbic dopamine pathway. A dopamine pathway implicated in schizophrenia.

Microiontophoresis. A technique for measuring changes in a neuron's membrane potential in response to chemicals applied to its membrane.

Monoamine oxidase (MAO). The enzyme that breaks down monoamine neurotransmitters in the cytoplasm of the neuron.

MAO inhibitor. A drug that increases the level of monoamine neurotransmitters by inhibiting the action of monoamine oxidase.

Monoclonal antibody immunohistochemistry. A procedure for identifying the location of specific proteins by injecting labeled clones of the protein's antibody.

Morphine. The main active ingredient of opium.

Negative schizophrenic symptoms. Schizophrenic symptoms such as blunt affect, catatonia, and poverty of speech.

Neuroleptics. Antischizophrenic drugs.

Neuromodulators. Neurotransmitters whose function is to increase or decrease the sensitivity of widely distributed neurons to the local excitatory and inhibitory effects of traditional neurotransmitters.

Nicotinic receptors. Acetylcholine receptors to which nicotine binds.

Peptides. Short chains of fewer than 10 amino acids.

Phenothiazines. A group of antischizophrenic drugs that bind to both D_1 and D_2 receptors.

Polypeptides. Chains of amino acids between 10 and 100 amino acids in length.

Positive schizophrenic symptoms. Schizophrenic symptoms such as incoherence, hallucinations, and delusions.

Proteins. Chains of amino acids that comprise 100 or more amino acids.

Putative neurotransmitters. Suspected neurotransmitters.

Receptor binding autoradiography. A procedure in which a ligand is radioactively labeled and then allowed to bind to receptors to reveal their location.

Renshaw cells. Small inhibitory interneurons of the spinal gray matter.

Reserpine. A monoamine antagonist that causes monoamine neurotransmitters to leak from their vesicles.

Spectrophotofluorimetry. A procedure for estimating the concentration of monoamines in a tissue sample by measuring its fluorescence.

Spiroperidol. A potent butyrophenone neuroleptic.

Stimulants. Drugs that tend to increase the activity of CNS neurons and increase the alertness of the subject (e.g., amphetamine, cocaine, caffeine).

Tricyclic antidepressants. Drugs with an antidepressant action and a three-ring structure.

Tryptophan. The amino acid from which serotonin is synthesized.

Tyrosine. The amino acid from which the catecholamines are synthesized.

Unipolar affective disorder. A depressive condition in which the patient does not experience periods of mania.

The Nine Universally Recognized Neurotransmitters

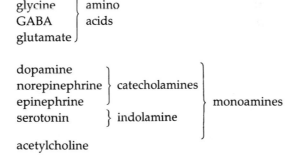

aspartate ⎫
glycine ⎪ amino
GABA ⎬ acids
glutamate ⎭

dopamine ⎫
norepinephrine ⎬ catecholamines ⎫
epinephrine ⎭ ⎬ monoamines
serotonin ⎬ indolamine ⎭

acetylcholine

7

The Visual System: From Eye to Cortex

This chapter is about the visual system. Most people think that their visual systems have evolved to respond as accurately as possible to the patterns of light entering their eyes. They, of course, recognize the obvious limitations in the visual system's accuracy, and they appreciate those curious instances, termed *visual illusions*, in which it is "tricked" into seeing things the way they aren't. But such shortcomings are generally regarded as minor imperfections in a system that responds quite faithfully to the external world. Despite its intuitive appeal, this way of thinking about the visual system is wrong. The visual system does not produce an accurate internal copy of the external world. It does much more. From the tiny, distorted, upside-down, two-dimensional retinal images projected upon the visual receptors lining the backs of our eyes, the visual system creates an accurate, richly detailed, three-dimensional perception, which is—and this is the really important part—in some respects even better than the external reality from which it was created. Regardless of what you may have heard to the contrary, "What you see is not necessarily what you get." One of my primary goals in this chapter is to help you recognize and appreciate the wonderful inherent creativity of your own visual system.

This chapter is composed of five sections. The first three sections take you on a journey

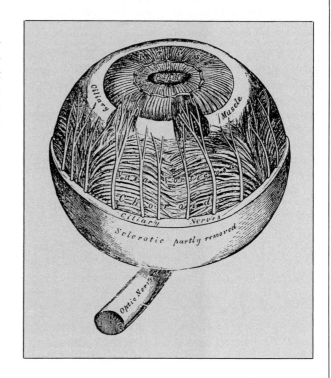

from the external visual world to the visual receptors of the retina, and from there over the major visual pathway to the primary visual cortex. The last two sections describe how the neurons of the visual system mediate the perception of two particularly important features of the visual world: edges and color.

You will see throughout this chapter how the study of the visual system involves the integration of two types of research: research that probes the visual system with sophisticated neuroanatomical, neurochemical, and neuro-physiological technology; and research that focuses on the meticulous assessment of what we see. Both approaches receive substantial coverage, but it is the second that provides you with a unique educational opportunity: the opportunity to participate as both subject and experimenter in the very phenomena that you are studying. Throughout this chapter, you are encouraged to demonstrate important visual phenomena by testing your own visual system. These demonstrations are designed to give you a taste of the excitement of scientific discovery and to illustrate the relevance of what you are learning in life outside the pages of this book.

7.1 Light Enters the Eye and Reaches the Retina

Everybody knows that cats, owls, and other nocturnal animals can see in the dark. Right? Wrong! Some animals have special adaptations that allow them to see under very dim illumination, but no animal can see in complete darkness. It is the light reflected into your eyes from the objects around you that is the basis for your ability to see them; if there is no light, there is no vision.

You may recall from high-school physics that light can be thought of in two different ways: as discrete particles of energy called *photons* traveling through space at about 300,000 kilometers (186,000 miles) per second, or as continuous oscillating waves of energy. Both theories are useful; in some ways light behaves like a particle, and in others it behaves like a wave. Physicists have learned to live with this nagging inconsistency, and we must try to do the same.

Light is sometimes defined as those waves of energy traveling through space that are between 380 and 760 nanometers (billionths of a meter) in length (see Figure 7.1). There is nothing special about this range of wavelengths except that the human visual system does not respond to wavelengths outside it. In fact, some animals can see wavelengths that we cannot. For example, rattlesnakes can see *infrared waves*, which are too long for humans to see; and as a result, they can see warm-blooded prey in what for us would be complete darkness (Newman & Hartline, 1982). Accordingly, if I were writing this book for rattlesnakes, I would be forced to suggest another, equally arbitrary, definition of light.

Wavelength and intensity are two properties of light that are of particular interest: wavelength because it plays an important role in the perception of color, and intensity because it plays a similarly important role in the perception of brightness. Because most people assume that the visual system provides a faithful representation of the stimuli entering our eyes, the

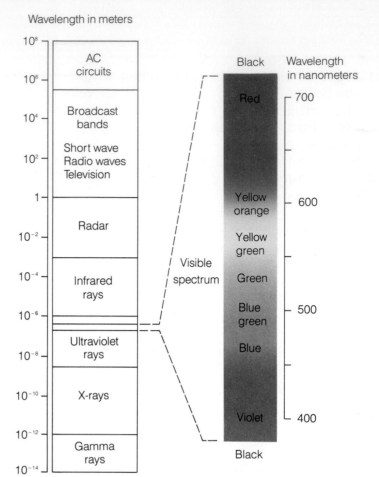

FIGURE 7.1 *The electromagnetic spectrum and the colors associated with the portion of the spectrum that is visible to humans.*

terms *wavelength* and *color* tend to be used interchangeably in everyday speech; and so do *intensity* and *brightness*. For example, we commonly refer to an intense light 700 nanometers long as being a bright red light, when in fact it is our perception of the light, not the light itself, that is bright and red. "Aha," you say, "yet another illustration of professorial nitpicking." I recognize that these distinctions may seem a trifle trivial to you at this point in the chapter, but I am confident that you will exonerate me of this nitpicking charge once you have finished the chapter.

Figure 7.2 is a drawing of a horizontal section taken through the middle of the right eye of a human. The amount of light ultimately reaching the receptors in the retinas is regulated by the donut-shaped bands of contractile tissue, the *irises*, which give our eyes their characteristic blue or brown color. Light enters the main chamber of the eye through its *pupil* (the hole in the iris). The continual adjustment of pupil size in response to changes in illumination represents a compromise between **sensitivity** (the ability to detect the presence of dimly lit objects) and **acuity** (the ability to see the details of objects). When the level of illumination is high and sensitivity is thus not important, the visual system takes advantage of the situation by constricting the pupils. When the pupils are constricted, the image falling on each retina is sharper, and there is a greater *depth of focus;* that is, a greater range of depths can be simultaneously kept in focus on the retinas.

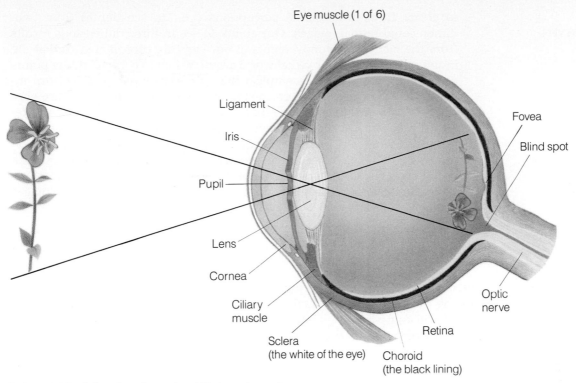

Eye muscle (1 of 6)

Ligament

Iris

Pupil

Lens

Cornea

Ciliary
muscle

Sclera
(the white of the eye)

Choroid
(the black lining)

Retina

Fovea

Blind spot

Optic
nerve

FIGURE 7.2 *A drawing of a section (slice) cut from a human eye.*

However, when the level of illumination is so low that there is insufficient light to adequately activate the receptors, the pupils dilate to let in more light.

Immediately behind each pupil is a *lens,* which focuses incoming light on the retina. When we direct our gaze at something near, the tension on the ligaments holding each lens in place is reduced by the contraction of **the ciliary muscles,** and the lens assumes its natural cylindrical shape. (Be alert here; the fact that the tension on the lens is reduced by muscle contraction is counterintuitive. See Figure 7.2.) This increases its ability to refract light and thus brings close objects into sharp focus. To focus on a distant object, the ciliary muscles relax and the lens is flattened. The process of adjusting the configuration of the lenses to bring images into focus on the retina is called **accommodation.**

No description of the eyes of vertebrates (animals with backbones) would be complete without a discussion of their most obvious feature, the fact that they—the eyes, that is—tend to come in pairs. One reason why vertebrates have two eyes, rather than say one or even three, is the fact that they have two sides. Consequently, by having one eye on each side of the head, which is by far the most common arrangement, it is possible for vertebrates to see in all, or almost all, directions without moving their heads. Clearly this is an efficient arrangement. Why then have humans and most other mammals opted for a different setup? Why are we mammals the only vertebrates with our eyes mounted side by side on the fronts of our heads? This arrangement sacrifices the ability to see behind so that we can see most of what is in front through both eyes simultaneously—an arrangement that is an important basis for our visual system's ability to create three-dimensional perceptions (i.e., to see depth) from two-dimensional retinal images. Our ability to see in three dimensions results from the fact that the movements of our eyes are coordinated so that the individual points in our visual world are projected to corresponding points on our two retinas. To accomplish this, our eyes must *converge* (turn inward), and convergence is greatest when we inspect things that are very close. But the positions of the retinal images on our two eyes cannot correspond exactly because the two eyes do not view the world from exactly the same position. It is because the difference in the position of images on the two retinas is greater for close objects than for distant objects that the visual system can use the degree of **binocular disparity** to construct one three-dimensional perception from two two-dimensional retinal images (Julesz, 1965, 1986).

Demonstration

The demonstration of binocular disparity and convergence is the first of the demonstrations that punctuate this chapter. If you compare the views from each eye (by quickly closing one eye and then the other) of objects at various distances in front of you—for example, your finger held at different distances—you will notice that the disparity between the two views is greater for closer objects. Now try the mysterious demonstration of the cocktail sausage. Face the farthest wall (or some other distant object), and bring the tips of your two pointing fingers together at arm's length in front of you—with your nails away from you, unless you prefer sausages with fingernails. Now, with both eyes open, sight through the notch between your touching fingertips, but focus on the wall. Do you see the cocktail sausage between your fingertips? Where did it come from? To prove to yourself that the sausage is a product of binocularity, make it disappear by shutting one eye.

7.2 The Retina and the Translation of Light into Neural Signals

Figure 7.3 illustrates the cellular structure of the retina. There are five different layers of cells: **receptors, horizontal cells, bipolar cells, amacrine cells,** and **retinal ganglion cells.** Notice that the function of the amacrine cells and horizontal cells appears to be specialized for *lateral communication* (i.e., for transmission across channels of sensory input). No more will be said about lateral communication here, but you will learn later in the chapter that it plays an extremely important role in vision. Notice also that the retina is inside-out in the sense that the light reaches the receptor layer only after passing through the other four layers. Then, once the receptors are activated, the neural message is passed back out through the retinal layers before reaching the retinal ganglion cells, whose axons project across the inside of the retina before exiting the eyeball. This "inside-out" arrangement is less than optimal for two reasons. One is that the incoming light is distorted by the retinal tissue through which it must pass before reaching the receptors; the other is that for the retinal ganglion cell axons to leave the eye, there must be a gap in the receptor layer. This receptorless area of the retina is called the **optic disk** or blind spot. The cross section of the central portion of the retina presented in Figure 7.4 illustrates how

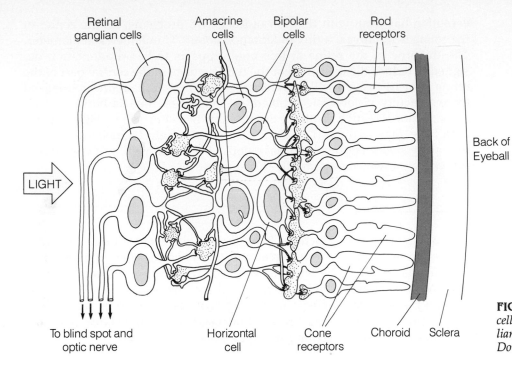

Retinal ganglian cells

Amacrine cells

Bipolar cells

Rod receptors

LIGHT

Back of Eyeball

To blind spot and optic nerve

Horizontal cell

Cone receptors

Choroid

Sclera

FIGURE 7.3 *A drawing of the cellular structure of the mammalian retina. (Adapted from Dowling, 1979.)*

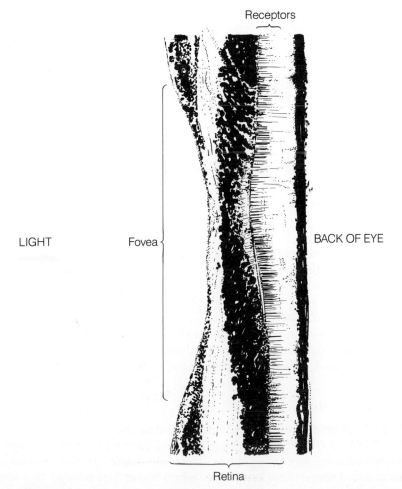

Receptors

LIGHT

Fovea

BACK OF EYE

Retina

FIGURE 7.4 *Cross section of the fovea. (Adapted from Rushton, 1962.)*

evolution has dealt with the first of these two problems. At the center of the retina is the **fovea,** a tiny indentation about .33 millimeter in diameter. The thinning of the retina at this point appears to be an adaptation designed to reduce the distortion of the retinal image in the central part of the retina, which—as you will soon learn—is the part of the retina specialized for high-acuity vision. The problem created by each eye's blind spot requires a more creative solution. Because our two sheets of visual receptors both have gaps in them (i.e., optic disks), you might be inclined to think that our visual images should have gaps in them as well. But they don't; somehow the visual system fills in the gaps.

Demonstration

First, prove to yourself that you are in fact partially blind. Close your left eye, and stare directly at the A in Figure 7.5, trying as hard as you can to not shift your gaze. While keeping the gaze of your right eye fixed on the A, hold the book at different distances from you until the dot becomes focused on your blind spot and disappears (about 20 centimeters or 8 inches). Why then is there not a black hole in your perception of the world when you look at it with one eye? You will discover the answer by holding the book at the same distance and changing the focus of your gaze to B. Suddenly the broken line becomes whole. Now switch your gaze to C. What do you see?

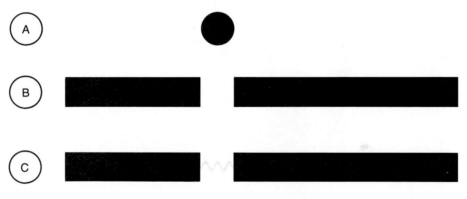

FIGURE 7.5 *Demonstration of the blind spot.*

You have just experienced **completion.** The visual system uses information provided by the receptors around the blind spot to fill in the gap in our visual field. When the visual system detects a straight bar going into one side of the blind spot and leaving the other, it fills in the missing bit for you, and what you see is a continuous straight bar regardless of what is actually there. The completion phenomenon is one of the most compelling demonstrations that the visual system does not just create a faithful copy of the external world; it creates perceptions of stimuli that are not even there.

Rod and Cone Vision

You undoubtedly noticed in Figure 7.3 that there are two different receptor types in the human retina, rod-shaped receptors called **rods** and cone-shaped receptors called **cones.** The existence of two different receptor types puzzled researchers until 1866, when it was first noticed that species active only at night tend to have rod-only retinas, that species active only in daylight tend to have cone-only retinas, and that species commonly active during both daylight and nighttime hours (e.g., humans) have both rods and cones. From these initial observations has grown the **duplexity theory** of vision: the theory that rods and cones are the receptors for two different kinds of visual systems, which are intertwined in many species (e.g., humans). The cone-driven system (i.e., the **photopic** system) takes advantage of good lighting to provide us with high-acuity (fine-detailed), colored perceptions of the world. In dim illumination, there is not enough light to reliably excite the cones, and as a result the more sensitive, rod-driven system (i.e., the **scotopic** system) takes over. However, the sensitivity of the scotopic system is not achieved without cost; the perceptions provided by the scotopic system lack both the detail and color of the photopic vision.

Strong support for the duplexity theory comes from case studies of human patients who lack either rods or cones. Individuals lacking functional rods suffer what is called *night blindness;* they have normal vision under daylight conditions, but in dim light they become functionally blind. In contrast, individuals without functional cones display *day blindness;* their perception is normal under dim illumination, but they have great difficulty seeing in daylight, and what they do see lacks color and detail.

The differences between photopic (cone) and scotopic (rod) vision stem in part from a difference in the way that the two systems are hooked up. As illustrated schematically in Figure 7.6, there is a large difference in the degree to which the output of rods and cones converges. The output of several hundred rods may ultimately converge on a single retinal ganglion cell, whereas it is not uncommon for a retinal ganglion cell to receive input from only one or two cones. As a result, the effects of dim light simultaneously stimulating many rods can summate to influence the firing of a

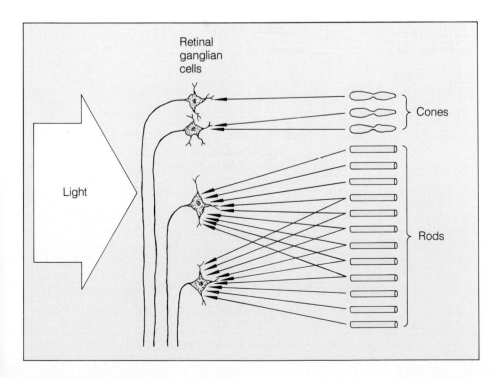

FIGURE 7.6 *A schematic representation of the convergence of rods and cones on retina ganglion cells. There is a high degree of convergence in the rod system and a low degree of convergence in the cone system.*

retinal ganglion cell onto which the output of the stimulated rods converges, whereas the effects of the same dim light applied to a sheet of cones cannot summate to the same degree, and the retinal ganglion cells may not respond to the light at all. However, the convergent scotopic system pays for its high degree of sensitivity with a low level of acuity. When a retinal ganglion cell receiving connections from several hundred rods changes its firing, the brain has no way of knowing which portion of the several hundred rods contributed to the signal. Although a more intense light is required to change the firing of a retinal ganglion cell that receives signals only from cones, when it does react there is less ambiguity about the location of the stimulus that triggered the reaction.

Rods and cones differ in their distribution on the retinas. As illustrated in Figure 7.7, there are no rods at all in the fovea, and the cones there are particularly tightly packed. At the boundaries of the foveal indentation, the proportion of cones declines markedly, but there is a corresponding increase in the number of rods, which reaches a maximum at 20° from the fovea. You may be puzzled by the fact that in the periphery of the retina, there are many more rods in the **nasal hemiretina** (the half of the retina next to the nose) than in the **temporal hemiretina** (the half next to the temples). The solution to this puzzle is as plain as the nose on your face. In fact, it is the nose on your face. Because your nose blocks the input of light onto the edges of your temporal hemiretinas, there is less need for receptors there.

Generally speaking, more intense lights appear brighter. However, wavelength also has a substantial effect on the perception of brightness.

FIGURE 7.7 *The distribution of rods and cones over the human retina. The figure illustrates the number of rods and cones per square millimeter in a horizontal slice cut through the fovea and blind spot of the left eye as a function of distance from the fovea. (Adapted from Lindsay & Norman, 1977.)*

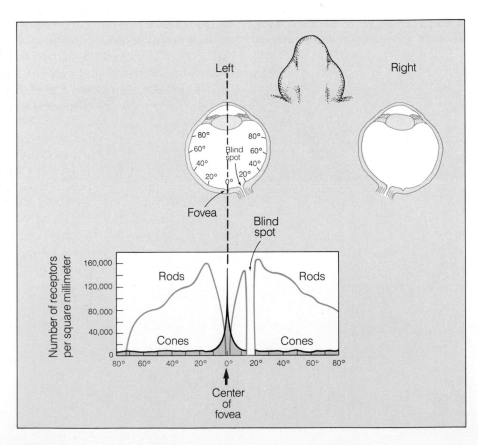

Because our visual systems are not equally sensitive to all wavelengths in the visible spectrum, lights of the same intensity, but of different wavelengths, can differ markedly in brightness. A graph of the relative brightness of lights of the same intensity presented at different wavelengths is called a *spectral sensitivity curve*. By far the most important thing to remember about spectral sensitivity curves is that humans and other animals with both rods and cones have two of them: a **photopic spectral sensitivity curve** and a **scotopic spectral sensitivity curve.** The photopic spectral sensitivity of humans is determined by having them judge the brightness of different wavelengths of light shone on the fovea, where there are only cones. The scotopic sensitivity of subjects is determined by first dark-adapting the subjects and then asking them to judge the relative brightness of different wavelengths of light shone on the periphery of the retina at an intensity too low to activate the few peripheral cones.

The scotopic and photopic spectral sensitivity curves of human subjects are plotted in Figure 7.8. Notice that under scotopic conditions, the visual system is maximally sensitive to wavelengths of about 500 nanometers, and thus a light of 560 nanometers would have to be much more intense than one at 505 nanometers to be seen as equally bright. In contrast, under photopic conditions, the visual system is maximally sensitive to wavelengths of about 560 nanometers, and thus a light at 500 nanometers would have to be much less intense than one at 560 nanometers to be seen as equally bright.

Because of the difference in scotopic and photopic spectral sensitivity, an interesting visual effect can be observed during the transition from photopic to scotopic vision. In 1985, Purkinje described the following occurrence, which has become known as the **Purkinje effect** (pronounced pur KIN gee). One evening, just before dusk, Purkinje noticed how wonderfully bright most of his yellow and red flowers appeared in relation to his blue ones. What amazed him was that just a few hours later the relative brightness of his flowers had somehow been reversed; the entire scene, when viewed at night, appeared only in shades of gray, but most of the blue flowers and much of the greenery appeared as brighter grays than did

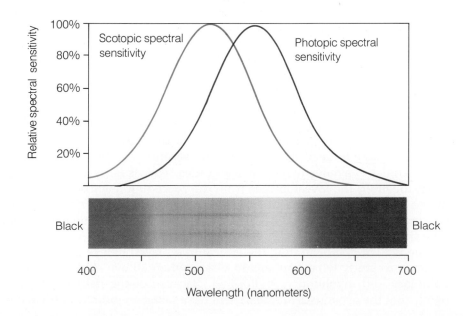

FIGURE 7.8 *Human photopic and scotopic spectral sensitivity curves. The peak of each curve has been arbitrarily set at 100%.*

the yellow and red ones. Can you explain this shift in relative brightness by referring to the photopic and scotopic special sensitivity curves in Figure 7.8?

Eye Movement

The retinal distribution of rods and cones points to an apparent paradox. If cones are in fact responsible for mediating high-acuity, color vision under photopic conditions, how can they accomplish their task when most of them are crammed into the fovea? Look around you. What you see is not a few colored details at the center of a grayish scene. You see an expansive, richly detailed, lavishly colored visual world. How can such a perception be the product of a photopic system that, for the most part, is restricted to a few degrees in the center of the visual field? This point can be illustrated by the following exercise.

=: *Demonstration* =

Close your left eye, and stare at the fixation point in Figure 7.9 with your right eye at a distance of 12 centimeters (4.75 inches). Be very careful that your gaze does not shift. What you will notice is that it is difficult to see the details of objects that are more than about 10° from the center of the fovea and that it is very difficult to perceive color at 30° or more from the center. Now just look at the page without fixing your gaze, and notice the difference that eye movement makes.

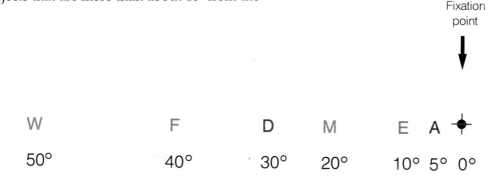

FIGURE 7.9 *The retinal distribution of high-acuity, color vision. (Adapted from Coren & Ward, 1989.)*

Eye movement has this remarkable effect because what we see at any one time is not determined just by what is projected on the retina at that particular instant (e.g., Cumming, 1978). Although we are not usually aware of it, the eye normally scans a scene by making a series of brief fixations. About three fixations occur every second, and they are connected by very quick eye movements called **saccades.** The visual system integrates (adds together) the foveal images from the preceding few fixations to produce a wide-angled, high-acuity, richly colored perception. It is because of this *temporal integration* that the world does not vanish momentarily each time that you blink.

One way of demonstrating the critical role played by eye movement in vision is to study what happens to vision when all eye movement, both voluntary and involuntary, is stopped. Because of the risks inherent in paralyzing the eye muscles, researchers have taken an indirect approach to answering this question. Rather than stopping eye movement, they have stopped the primary consequence of eye movement, the movement of the retinal image across the retina. They have accomplished this by projecting the test stimuli from a tiny projector mounted on a contact lens. Each time that the eye moves, the lens and the projector move with it, thus keeping the retinal image fixed on the same receptors, as if the eye had remained still. The effect on vision of stabilizing the retinal image is dramatic (e.g., Pritchard, 1961). After a few seconds of viewing, a simple **stabilized retinal image** disappears, leaving a featureless gray field. The movements of the eyes then increase, presumably in an attempt to bring the image back. However, such movements are futile in this situation because the stabilized retinal image simply moves with the eyes. Periodically, the stimulus pattern, or part of it, spontaneously reappears, only to disappear once again.

Why do stabilized images disappear? The answer lies in the fact that the neurons of the visual system respond to change rather than to steady input. Most neurons of the visual system respond vigorously when a stimulus is presented, moved, or terminated, but they respond only weakly to a continuous, unchanging input. Apparently, one function of eye movements is to keep the retinal image moving back and forth across the receptors, thus insuring that the receptors and the neurons to which they are connected receive a continually changing pattern of stimulation. When a retinal image is stabilized, parts of the visual system stop responding to the image, and it disappears.

Visual Transduction: The Translation of Light to Neural Signals

Transduction is a general term, which refers to the conversion of one form of energy to another; *visual transduction* refers specifically to the conversion of light to neural signals by the visual receptors. The first major advance in the study of visual transduction came in 1876 when a brilliant red *pigment* (a pigment is any substance that absorbs light) was extracted from the predominant rod retina of the frog. This pigment had a curious property. When **rhodopsin,** as the pigment became known, was exposed to continuous intense light, it was bleached (lost its color) and it lost its ability to absorb light; but when it was returned to the dark, it regained both its redness and its light-absorbing capacity.

It is now clear that the absorption and bleaching of rhodopsin by light is the first step in rod-mediated (scotopic) vision. Evidence for this view comes from demonstrations that the degree to which rhodopsin absorbs light in various situations predicts how humans see under the very same conditions. For example, it has been shown that the degree to which rhodopsin absorbs lights of different wavelengths is related to the ability of humans and other animals with rods to detect the presence of different wavelengths of light under scotopic conditions. Figure 7.10 illustrates the relation between the **absorption spectrum** of rhodopsin and the human scotopic spectral sensitivity curve. The goodness of the fit leaves little doubt that, in dim light, our sensitivity to various wavelengths is a direct consequence of rhodopsin's ability to absorb them.

Since the discovery that the bleaching action of light on rhodopsin is the basis of scotopic visual transduction, neurochemists have clarified the nature of the bleaching reaction (Wald, 1968). Rhodopsin is a compound

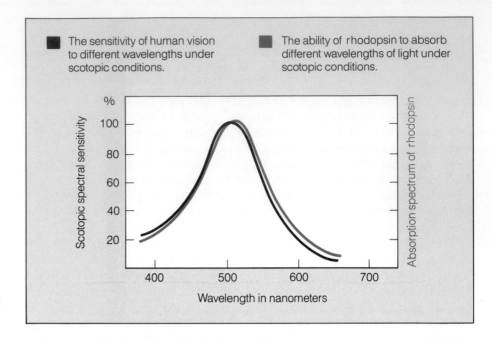

■ The sensitivity of human vision to different wavelengths under scotopic conditions.

■ The ability of rhodopsin to absorb different wavelengths of light under scotopic conditions.

FIGURE 7.10 *The absorption spectrum of rhodopsin compared with the human scotopic spectral sensitivity curve.*

made up of two molecules: *retinal* and *opsin*. As illustrated in Figure 7.11, when rods are exposed to light, the thread-like opsin molecule is released from one of its points of contact with the retinal molecule and begins to straighten out. This is the chemical change that induces a neural signal. If

FIGURE 7.11 *The response of the rhodopsin molecule to light. (Adapted from Wald, 1968.)*

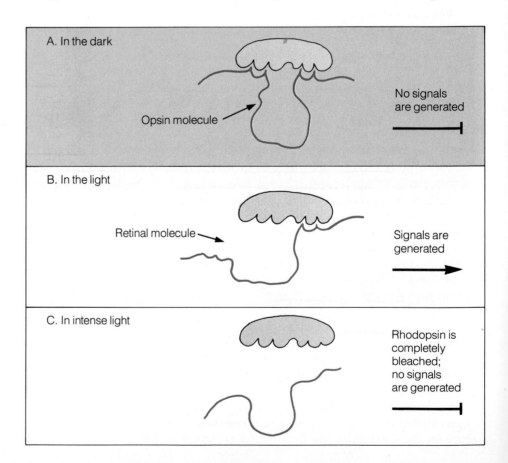

rods are exposed to intense light, the opsin and retinal separate completely, and the cells lose their capacity to absorb light and generate signals. When bleached rods are placed in the dark, the opsin and retinal assume their original configuration, and the rhodopsin regains its ability to absorb light and general signals. Because retinal is synthesized from *vitamin A*, a diet lacking vitamin A can lead to night blindness.

The reaction of unbleached rhodopsin to light stimulates the closure of sodium ion channels in rod membranes (see O'Brien, 1982). The closing of the sodium ion channels, which are normally open in the dark, hyperpolarizes the rods (Schnapf & Baylor, 1987) and reduces the amount of transmitter substance being continually released from their terminals. The chemical basis of the transduction of light by cones is not so well understood.

7.3 From Retina to the Primary Visual Cortex

Many pathways in the brain carry visual information, but by far the largest and most thoroughly studied visual pathway is the **retina-geniculate-striate pathway,** which, as its name implies, conducts signals from the retina to the **striate cortex (primary visual cortex)** via the **lateral geniculate nuclei** of the thalamus. The organization of this retina-geniculate-striate pathway is illustrated in Figure 7.12. Examine it carefully.

The main thing to notice from Figure 7.12 is that all signals produced by light in the left visual field reach the right striate cortex, either ipsilaterally via the *temporal hemiretina* of the right eye or contralaterally via the *nasal hemiretina* of the left eye—and that the opposite is true of all signals produced by light in the right visual field. Each lateral geniculate nucleus has six layers, and each layer receives input from all parts of only one retina. All of the lateral geniculate neurons projecting to the primary visual cortex end up in the lower part of cortical layer IV, thus producing a characteristic stripe or striation when viewed in cross section—hence, the name *striate cortex.*

The most important organizational principle of the retina-geniculate-striate system is that it is **retinotopic;** at each level of the system the neural inputs are organized in such a way that they map the retina. What this means is that two stimuli presented to adjacent areas of the retina excite adjacent neurons at all levels of the system. At each stage of projection, the orientation and shape of the map changes, but the two-dimensional layout of the neurons always bears a clear relation to the retina. The most important distortion of the retinotopic layout of striate cortex is the disproportionate representation of the fovea. Although the fovea is only a small part of the retina, a relatively large proportion of primary visual cortex (about 25%) is dedicated to the analysis of its input. A dramatic demonstration of the retinotopic organization of the primary visual cortex was provided by Dobelle, Mladejovsky, and Girvin (1974). They implanted an array of electrodes in the primary visual cortices of patients who were blind because of damage to their eyes. If electrical current was administered simultaneously through an array of electrodes forming a shape such as a cross on the surface of a patient's cortex, the patient reported "seeing" a glowing image of a cross.

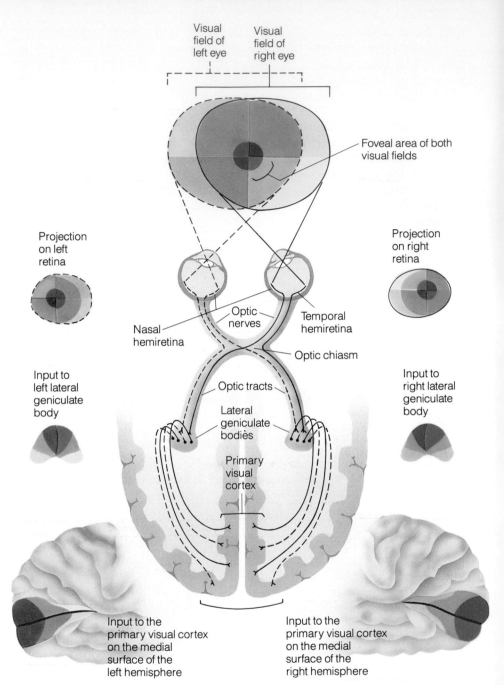

FIGURE 7.12 *The retina-geniculate-striate system: the neural projections from the retinas through the lateral geniculate nuclei to the left and right primary visual cortex (striate cortex). (Adapted from Netter, 1953.)*

Before proceeding to the last two sections of the chapter, which describe how the visual system mediates the perception of edges and color, review what you have learned so far about the visual system by filling in the following blanks.

1. Neural signals are carried from the retina to the lateral geniculate nuclei by the axons of ____ganglion____ cells.

2. The area of the retina that mediates high-acuity vision is the
fovea.

3. Cones are the receptors of the __photopic__ system.

4. The photopigment of rods is __rodopsin__.

5. The most important organizational principle of the retina-geniculate-striate system is that it is laid out __retinotopically__.

6. The retinal ganglion cells from the nasal hemiretinas decussate via the
__o.c.__.

7. Evidence that rhodopsin is the scotopic photopigment is provided by the fit between the __absorption__ spectrum of rhodopsin and the scotopic spectral sensitivity curve.

8. The high degree of __convergence__ characteristic of the scotopic system increases its sensitivity, but decreases its acuity.

9. The axons of retinal ganglion cells leave the eyeball at the optic disk or
__blind spot__.

7.4 Seeing Edges

This section of the chapter is about "seeing edges." Seeing edges does not sound like a particularly important topic, but it is. Edges are the most informative features of any visual display because they define the extent and position of the various objects in it. Given the importance of perceiving visual edges and the unrelenting pressure of natural selection, it is not surprising that the visual systems of many species are particularly good at edge perception.

Before considering the visual mechanisms underlying edge perception, it is important to appreciate exactly what a visual edge is. In a sense, a visual edge is nothing; it is simply the place where two different areas of a visual image meet. Thus, the perception of an edge is really the perception of a contrast between two adjacent areas of the visual field. This section of the chapter reviews the perception of edges (i.e., the perception of contrast) between areas that differ from one another in brightness. Color contrast is discussed in the next section.

Lateral Inhibition
and Contrast Enhancement

Carefully examine Figure 7.13. The graph just beneath the figure indicates what is there—that is, a series of homogeneous stripes of different

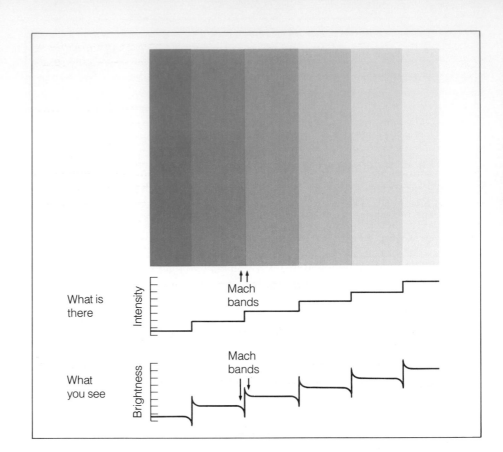

FIGURE 7.13 *Mach bands.*

intensity. But this is not exactly what you see, is it? What you see is indicated in the bottom graph. Adjacent to each edge, the brighter stripe looks brighter than it really is and the darker stripe looks darker, thus enhancing the contrast at each edge and making each edge easier to see. The nonexistent stripes of brightness and darkness running adjacent to the edges are called *Mach bands*. It is important to appreciate that **contrast enhancement** is not something that occurs just in books. Although we are normally unaware of it, every edge that we look at is highlighted for us by contrast enhancing mechanisms of our nervous systems. Thus our perceptions of edges are better than the real thing.

Demonstration

The Mach band demonstration is so compelling that you may be confused by it. You may think that the Mach bands have been created by the printers of the book, rather than by your own visual system. To prove to yourself that the Mach bands are a creation of your own visual system, conduct the following experiment. View each stripe individually by covering the adjacent ones with two pieces of paper, and you will see at once that each stripe is completely homogeneous. Now take the paper away and the Mach bands will suddenly reappear.

The classic studies of the physiological basis of contrast enhancement were conducted on the eyes of an unlikely subject: the *horseshoe crab* (e.g., Ratliff, 1972). The lateral eyes of the horseshoe crab are ideal for certain types of neurophysiological research. Unlike mammalian eyes, they are composed of very large receptors called **ommatidia,** each with its own large axon, interconnected by a simple lateral neural network called the **lateral plexus.** In order to understand the physiological basis of contrast enhancement in the horseshoe crab eye, you must first understand two simple principles. The first is that if a single ommatidium is illuminated, it fires at a rate that is proportional to the intensity of the light striking it; more intense lights produce more firing. The second is that when a receptor fires, it inhibits its neighbors via the lateral plexus—this inhibition is called **lateral inhibition** because it spreads laterally across the array of receptors, or *mutual inhibition* because neighboring receptors inhibit one another. The amount of lateral inhibition produced by a receptor is greatest when it is most intensely illuminated, and it has its greatest effect on immediate neighbors.

The neural basis of contrast enhancement can be understood in terms of the firing rates of the receptors on each side of the edge, as indicated in Figure 7.14. Notice that the receptor adjacent to the edge on the more intense side (receptor D) fires more than the other intensely illuminated receptors (A,B,C), while the receptor adjacent to the edge on the less well-illuminated side (receptor E) fires less than the other receptors on that side (F,G,H). Differences in lateral inhibition account for receptor firing. Receptors A, B, and C all fire at the same rate because they are all receiving the same high level of stimulation and the same high degree of lateral inhibition from all their highly stimulated neighbors. Receptor D fires more than do A, B, and C because it receives as much stimulation as they do, but less inhibition owing to the fact that many of its neighbors are on the dimmer

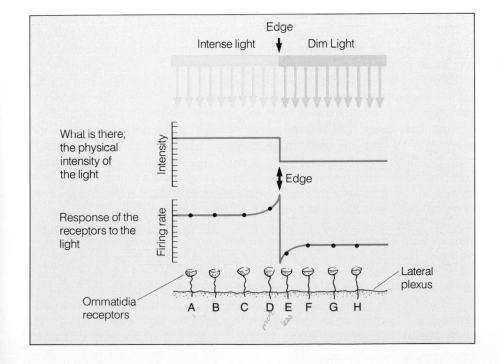

FIGURE 7.14 *How lateral inhibition produces contrast enhancement. (Adapted from Ratliff, 1972.)*

side of the edge. Remember that less intensely illuminated receptors produce less lateral inhibition. Now consider the receptors on the dimmer side. Receptors F, G, and H fire at the same rate because they are all being stimulated by the same low level of light and they are all receiving the same low level of inhibition from their neighbors. However, receptor D fires even less because it is receiving the same excitation, but more inhibition owing to the fact that many of its immediate neighbors are on the other side of the border in the more intense light. If it has not already occurred to you, this pattern of neural activity determines what you—and presumably a horseshoe crab—see when you look at such an edge (see Figure 7.13).

Receptive Fields of Visual Neurons

The Nobel-Prize-winning research of Hubel and Wiesel is the fitting climax to this discussion of edge perception; their methods have been adopted by a generation of sensory neurophysiologists. The subjects in Hubel and Wiesel's experiments are single neurons in the visual systems of cats and monkeys. First, the tip of a microelectrode is positioned near a single neuron in the visual area of interest. During testing, eye movements are blocked by *d-tubocurarine* (see Chapter 6), and the images on a screen in front of the subject are focused sharply on the retina by the experimenter using an adjustable lens. The next step in the procedure is to identify the receptive field of the neuron in question. The **receptive field** of a visual neuron is the area of the visual field within which it is possible for a visual stimulus to influence the firing of that cell. Visual system neurons tend to be continually active, and thus effective stimuli are those that either increase or decrease the baseline rate of firing. The final step in the method is to record the responses of the neuron to various stimuli within its receptive field in order to characterize the types of stimuli that most influence its activity. Then, the electrode is advanced slightly and the entire process of identifying and characterizing the receptive field properties is repeated for another neuron, and then for another, and another, and so on (see Kuffler, 1953). The general strategy involves beginning such studies near the input end of a sensory system and gradually working up through "higher" and "higher" levels of the system in an effort to understand the increasing complexity of the neural responses at each level.

Hubel and Wiesel's best known research (e.g., 1979) involves analysis of the retina-geniculate-striate system of the monkey. Given the relatively simple circuitry of the pathway from the retina to the primary visual cortex, it is not surprising that retinal ganglion cells, geniculate neurons, and **lower-layer-IV neurons** (the striate cortex neurons that receive the input from the geniculate neurons) have similar receptive fields. Most of the receptive fields of the neurons at these three levels of the retina-geniculate-striate system are round; that is, for each neuron, there is a circular area of the visual field in which a stimulus must be presented if it is to influence that cell's firing. Because there is less convergence in foveal circuits, neurons with receptive fields in the foveal area have much smaller receptive fields than do those with receptive fields in the periphery.

Most retinal ganglion cells, lateral geniculate cells, and the primary visual cortex cells in the lower region of layer IV respond in two different ways to a spot of white light that briefly appears in their receptive fields. Depending on where in the cell's receptive field the light appears, the cell might display *on firing* or *off firing;* that is, it might display an elevated firing rate while the light is on, or it might display a reduced firing rate while the light is on followed by a burst of firing when it is turned off. The receptive fields of most retinal ganglion cells, lateral geniculate cells, and lower layer IV cells fall into one of two distinct categories illustrated in Figure 7.15. **On-center cells** respond to lights shone in the central region of their fields with "on" firing and to lights shown in the periphery of their fields with inhibition followed by "off" firing when the light is turned off. **Off-center cells** display the opposite pattern, with "off" firing in response to lights in the center of their receptive fields and with "on" firing to lights in the periphery. Cells with these on-center and off-center concentric receptive fields are termed **X-type cells** (Sherman, 1985), and they are by far the most prevalent type of neuron in the retina-geniculate-striate system.

The responses of X-type cells to various patterns of illumination suggest that their function is to respond to the contrast between the level of illumination in the center of the receptive field and the level of illumination in its periphery. Figure 7.16 illustrates this point. The most effective way to influence the firing rate of an X-type cell is to maximize the contrast between the center and the periphery of its receptive field by illuminating

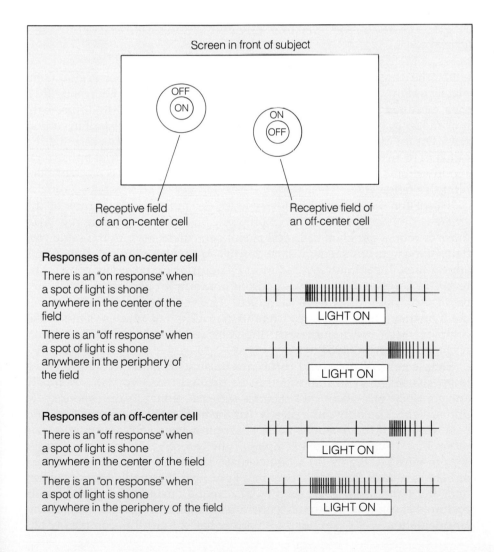

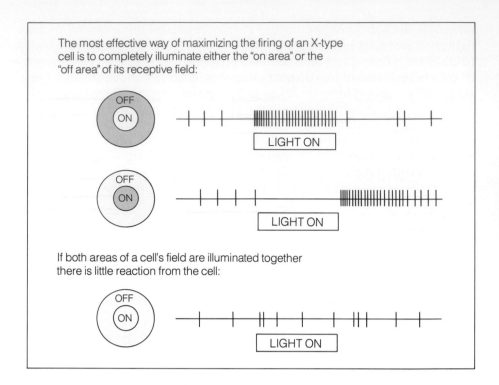

The most effective way of maximizing the firing of an X-type cell is to completely illuminate either the "on area" or the "off area" of its receptive field:

LIGHT ON

LIGHT ON

If both areas of a cell's field are illuminated together there is little reaction from the cell:

LIGHT ON

FIGURE 7.16 *Lateral inhibition in an on-center cell.*

either the center or the surround, while leaving the other region completely unilluminated. In fact, retinal ganglion cells respond only slightly if their receptive fields are diffusely illuminated; the response to diffuse light is even less in lateral geniculate cells, and it is almost nonexistent in cortical cells. On the basis of this evidence, Hubel and Wiesel suggested that the function of many neurons in the retina-geniculate-striate system is to respond to the degree of brightness contrast between the two areas of their receptive fields.

Except for the neurons in lower layer IV, most other neurons of the striate cortex have receptive field properties that are clearly different than those of retinal ganglion cells and lateral geniculate cells. In the same way that X-type neurons seem most responsive to circular edges, straight edges appear to be the stimuli favored most by neurons of the striate cortex. The receptive fields of striate cortex neurons are complex and diverse and, as a result, extremely difficult to categorize. However, it is usual to consider most of them as belonging to one of two different classes, simple and complex, each with numerous subtypes (e.g., Gilbert, 1977; Kuffler, Nicholls, & Martin, 1984).

Simple cells of the visual cortex are those with fields like those of the lower-layer-IV cells in that they can be divided into two static, mutually antagonistic "on" and "off" regions and that they are unresponsive to diffuse light. The only difference is that the borders between the "on" and "off" regions of the receptive fields of simple cortical cells are straight lines rather than circles. Several examples of the receptive fields of simple cells are presented in Figure 7.17. Notice that simple cells respond best to bars of light in a dark field, dark bars in a light field, or single edges between dark and light areas. Each simple cell responds maximally only when its preferred straight-edge stimulus is in a particular position and in a particular orientation. For example, a 45° narrow bar of light that completely fills

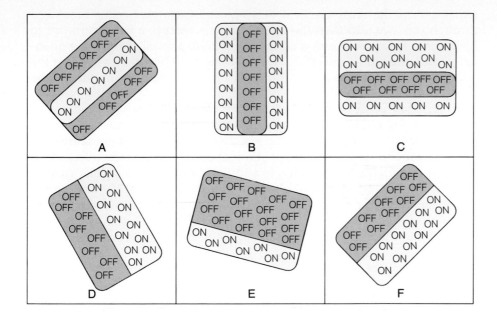

FIGURE 7.17 *Examples of visual fields of simple cortical cells.*

the "on" region of receptive field A in Figure 7.17 would produce maximal "on" firing in the cell; a weaker "on" response would occur if the bar of light were moved or rotated even slightly.

The second major class of primary visual cortex neurons are the **complex cells;** they are much more numerous than simple cells. Like simple cells, complex cells respond best to straight-line stimuli in a specific orientation, and they are unresponsive to diffuse light. However, complex cortical cells differ from simple cells in two important respects. The first is that it is not possible to divide the receptive fields of complex cells into static "on" and "off" regions. A complex cell responds to a particular straight-edge stimulus of a particular orientation regardless of its position within the receptive field of that cell. Thus, if a stimulus (e.g., a 45° bar of light) that produces "on" firing in a particular complex cell is swept across its receptive field, the cell will respond continuously to it as it moves across the field. Many complex cells display a direction preference; that is, they consistently respond more robustly to movement across their receptive field in one direction than in others. How did Hubel and Wiesel discover these "preferences" of complex cortical cells?

> We were inserting the glass slide with its black spot into the slot of the ophthalmoscope when suddenly over the audiomonitor the cell went off like a machine gun. After some fussing and fiddling we found out what was happening. The response had nothing to do with the black dot. As the glass slide was inserted its edge was casting onto the retina a faint but sharp shadow, a straight dark line on a light background. That is what the cell wanted, and it wanted it, moreover, in just one narrow range of orientations.
>
> This was unheard of (Hubel, 1982, p. 517).

The second way that complex cortical cells differ from simple cells is that many are **binocular.** Virtually all of the simple cortical cells and the neurons of the retina-geniculate-striate pathway are **monocular;** they respond to stimulation of either the right eye or the left eye, but not both. In contrast, over half the complex cortical cells respond to stimulation of either eye. If the receptive field of a binocular complex cell is measured through one eye and then the other, the two receptive fields turn out to have about the same position in the visual field, as well as the same orientation and directional selectivity. In other words, what you learn about the cell by stimulating one eye is confirmed in every respect by stimulating the other. What is more, if the appropriate stimulation is applied through both eyes simultaneously, a binocular cell usually fires more robustly than if only one eye is stimulated. However, over 50% of the binocular cells in the striate cortex of the monkey display some degree of ocular dominance; that is, they respond more robustly to stimulation of one eye than they do to the same stimulation of the other. In addition, some binocular cells fire best when the preferred stimulus is presented to both eyes at the same time, but in slightly different positions on the two retinas (e.g., Bishop, Henry, & Smith, 1971; Bishop & Pettigrew, 1986). In other words, these cells respond to retinal disparity. Presumably, they play a role in the perception of depth.

On the basis of their data, Hubel and Wiesel advanced a hierarchical model of the monkey visual cortex. In this model, the complexity of the receptive fields of neurons at progressively higher levels of the visual system is attributable to the convergence of input from the preceding, more simple level. Specifically, they proposed that neurons with cell bodies in lower layer IV converge on simple cells and that simple cells in turn converge on complex cells. Hubel and Wiesel (1979) further proposed that the primary visual cortex is divided into functionally independent columns of cells, each column being responsible for analyzing the input from one discrete area of the visual field. The main evidence for this is that if you advance an electrode vertically through the layers of visual cortex, stopping to plot the receptive fields of many cells along the way, each cell in the column has a receptive field in the same general area of the visual field. The area of the visual field covered by all of the receptive fields of cells in a given column is called the **aggregate field** of that column. If you advance an electrode nearly horizontally through the tissue, each successive cell that is encountered has a receptive field in a slightly different location. In general, cells whose fields are adjacent, but do not overlap, are 2 millimeters apart. Figure 7.18 illustrates columnar organization and the evidence for it.

Hubel and Wiesel further postulated that each functional cortical column is divided in two, with half being dominated by the right eye and half by the left eye. Input from the eyes has been found to enter lower layer IV independently in alternating patches. The best evidence of this alternating arrangement comes from a study (LeVay, Hubel, & Wiesel, 1975) in which a radioactive amino acid was injected into one eye in sufficient quantities to cross the synapses of the retina-geniculate-striate system and show up in lower layer IV of the primary visual cortex, and to a lesser degree in the layers just above and below it. The alternating patches of radioactivity and nonradioactivity clearly visible in the autoradiograph presented in Figure 7.19 indicate alternating patches of input from the two eyes. These patches of input from the two eyes then project vertically to the other columns of the primary visual cortex so that all of those neurons above or below a particular patch that display ocular dominance "prefer" the same eye.

Hubel and Wiesel also proposed that each half of a functional cortical column with the same ocular dominance is further divided into smaller columns, each with a preference for a particular straight-edge orientation.

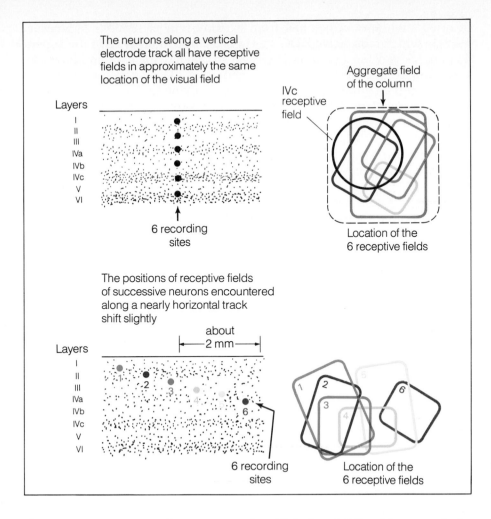

The neurons along a vertical electrode track all have receptive fields in approximately the same location of the visual field

Layers I II III IVa IVb IVc V VI

6 recording sites

IVc receptive field

Aggregate field of the column

Location of the 6 receptive fields

The positions of receptive fields of successive neurons encountered along a nearly horizontal track shift slightly

about 2 mm

Layers I II III IVa IVb IVc V VI

6 recording sites

Location of the 6 receptive fields

FIGURE 7.18 *The columnar organization of receptive field location in the primary visual cortex.*

This arrangement was first suggested to Hubel and Wiesel by a study in which they inserted a microelectrode into the primary visual cortex parallel to its layers and found that each time they advanced the electrode tip by about 25 or 50 micrometers, the orientation preference of the cells at the tip shifted by about 10 degrees. Further evidence for the existence of columns

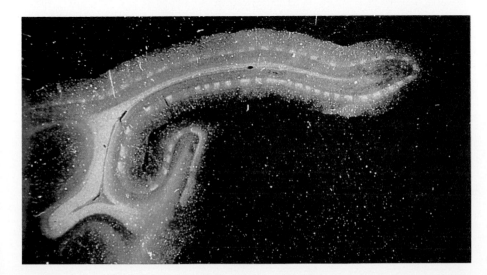

FIGURE 7.19 *The alternating input into lower layer IV of the primary visual cortex from the left and right eyes. Radioactive amino acids injected into one eye are subsequently revealed on autoradiographs of the visual cortex as patches of radioactivity alternating with patches of non-radioactivity.*

(Scientific American, September 1979)

of orientation specificity came from a study (Hubel, Wiesel, & Stryker, 1977) in which radioactive 2-DG was injected into monkeys that then spent 45 minutes viewing a pattern of vertical stripes moving back and forth. As you know from previous chapters, radioactive 2-DG is taken up by active neurons and accumulates in them, thus identifying the location of neurons that are particularly active during the test period. The autoradiograph in Figure 7.20 reveals the columns of cells in the primary visual cortex that were activated by exposure to the moving vertical stripes. Notice that the neurons in the lower portions of layer IV show no orientation specificity; these are X-type cells, which do not respond preferentially to straight-line stimuli.

Figure 7.21 summarizes the view of the systematic organization of the monkey primary visual cortex that has grown out of Hubel and Wiesel's remarkable research. See DeValois and DeValois (1980) for an alternative interpretation of Hubel and Wiesel's data.

FIGURE 7.20 *The columns of orientation specificity in the primary visual cortex of the monkey as revealed by 2-DG autoradiography.*

From "Orientation Columns in Macaque Monkey Visual Cortex Demonstrated by the 2-Deoxyglucose Autoradiographic Technique" by P. H. Wiesel, T. N. Wiesel, and M. P. Stryker. Reprinted by permission from *Nature*, Vol. 269, page 329. Copyright © 1977 by Macmillan Magazines Ltd.

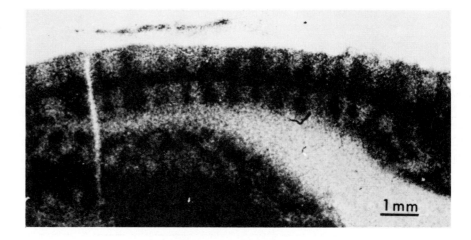

FIGURE 7.21 *Hubel and Wiesel's model of the organization of functional columns in primary visual cortex.*

A block of tissue such as this is assumed to analyze visual signals from one area of the visual field.

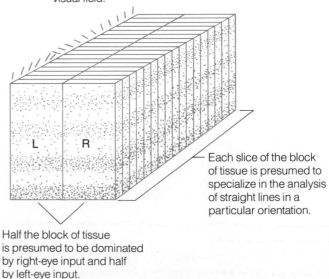

Each slice of the block of tissue is presumed to specialize in the analysis of straight lines in a particular orientation.

Half the block of tissue is presumed to be dominated by right-eye input and half by left-eye input.

7.5 Seeing Color

Color is one of the most obvious qualities of human visual experience. So far in this chapter, we have limited our discussion of vision to the so-called **achromatic colors:** black, white, and gray. Black is normally experienced when there is an absence of light; the perception of white is usually produced by an intense mixture of all wavelengths in equal proportion; and the perception of gray is produced by the same mixture at lower intensities. In this section, we deal with the perception of **chromatic colors**—colors such as blue, green, and yellow. The correct term for chromatic colors is *hues*, but in everyday language, they are referred to simply as colors; and for the sake of simplicity, I do the same here.

What is there about a visual stimulus that determines the color that we perceive? To a large degree the perception of an object's color depends on the wavelengths of light that it reflects into the eye. Figure 7.1 is an illustration of the visible spectrum demonstrating the colors associated with individual wavelengths; however, you should realize that outside the laboratory one rarely encounters objects that reflect single wavelengths. Sunlight and most sources of artificial light contain complex mixtures of most visible wavelengths. Most objects absorb the different wavelengths of light that strike them to varying degrees and reflect the rest. It is the complex mixture of wavelengths that an object reflects that influences our perception of its color.

With the development and refinement of methods for studying the responses of individual receptors and neurons in the visual system, an impressive amount has been learned in the last two or three decades about how the visual system responds to different wavelengths. However, in some ways, it is even more impressive that the basic mechanisms of color vision were derived in the last century by individuals whose research technology was limited to their own ingenuity and observational skills. Through careful observation of the perceptual abilities of their subjects, these behavioral scientists were able to infer some of the major features of the physiological basis of color vision. You have already encountered in this chapter many instances in which scientific gains have resulted from the convergence of behavioral, neurochemical, and neurophysiological research; however, the early advances in the study of the neural basis of color vision occurred long before it was possible to bring modern neurochemical and neurophysiological procedures to bear on the problem.

The **component theory** of color vision—often referred to as the *trichromatic theory*—was proposed by Young in 1802 and refined by Helmholtz in 1852. According to this theory, there are three different kinds of color receptors (cones), each with a different spectral sensitivity, and the color of a particular stimulus is presumed to be encoded by the ratio of activity in the three kinds of receptors. Young and Helmholtz derived their theory from the observation that any color of the visible spectrum could be matched by mixing together three different wavelengths of light in different proportions. This can be accomplished with any three wavelengths, provided that the color of any one of them cannot be matched by mixing the other two. The fact that three is normally the minimum number of different wavelengths necessary to match every color suggested that there were three types of receptors.

Another theory of color vision, the **opponent-process theory,** was proposed by Hering in 1878. He suggested that there are two different classes of cells in the visual system for encoding color, and another one for encoding brightness. Hering hypothesized that each of the three classes of cells encoded two complementary perceptions. One class of color-coding cells signaled red by changing its activity in one direction (e.g., hyperpolarization) and red's complementary color, green, by changing its activity in the other (e.g., hypopolarization). The other class of color-coding cells was hypothesized to signal blue and its complement, yellow, in the same opponent fashion; and the class of brightness-coding cells was hypothesized to similarly signal both black and white. **Complementary colors** are pairs of colors that produce white when combined (e.g., green light and red light).

Hering based his opponent-process theory of color vision on several behavioral observations. One was that the complementary colors blue and yellow, and red and green cannot exist together in the same color; there is no such thing as a yellowish blue or a greenish red. Another was that the afterimage produced by staring at red is green and vice versa, and the afterimage produced by staring at yellow is blue and vice versa.

⹀ Demonstration ⹀

Have you ever noticed complementary afterimages? You can see them by staring at the fixation point on the left of Figure 7.22 for 1 minute under intense illumination without moving your eyes and then quickly shifting your gaze to the fixation point on the right.

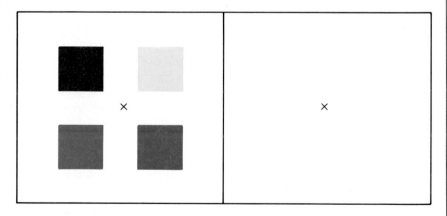

FIGURE 7.22 *Complementary afterimages.*

A somewhat misguided debate raged for many years between supporters of the component (trichromatic) and opponent theories of color vision. I say "misguided" because it was fueled more by the adversarial predispositions of the scientists involved than by the incompatibility of the two approaches. In fact, neurochemical and neurophysiological research subsequently proved that both color-coding mechanisms coexist in the same visual systems.

It was the development in the early 1960s of **microspectrophotometry,** a technique for measuring the absorption spectrum of the photopigment contained in a single cone, that allowed researchers (e.g., Dartnall, Bow-maker, & Mollon, 1983; MacNichol, 1964; Marks, Dobelle, & MacNichol, 1964; Wald, 1964) to confirm the conclusion reached by Young over a century and a half before. They found that there are indeed three different kinds of cones in the retinas of vertebrates with good color vision, and they found that each of the three has a different photopigment with its own characteristic absorption spectrum. As illustrated in Figure 7.23, some cones are maximally sensitive to short wavelengths; some are maximally sensitive to medium wavelengths; and a third class of cones is most sensitive to long wavelengths.

Although the coding of color by cones seems to operate on a purely component basis, there is evidence of opponent processing at all subsequent levels of the retina-geniculate-striate system. The first neurophysiological evidence for opponent processing of color came from an electrophysiological study of retinal neurons in the carp, a fish with excellent color vision (Svaetichin, 1956). He found neurons in the carp retina that responded in one direction (hyperpolarization or depolarization) to red-appearing wavelengths and in the other direction to green-appearing wavelengths. And he found other retinal cells that coded blue-appearing and yellow-appearing wavelengths in the same fashion.

Although it is now well established that both component and opponent processing occur in the visual systems of animals capable of perceiving color, neither can account for color constancy. **Color constancy** refers to the fact that the perceived color of an object is not a simple function of the wavelengths reflected by it. As I write this at 7:15 on a December morning, it is dark outside, and I am writing by the light of a tiny incandescent desk lamp. Later in the morning, when my students arrive, I turn on my nasty fluorescent office lights. And finally, later in the day as the sun shifts to my side of the building, I turn off my lights and work by natural light. The point of all this is that these different light sources differ substantially in the wavelengths that they contain. As a result, the wavelengths reflected by various objects in my office—my blue shirt, for example—change substantially during the course of the day. The important point is that although the wavelengths reflected by my shirt change markedly, its color does not. My shirt will be just as blue in the midmorning and in the late afternoon as it is now. Oh, there may be subtle changes in its color, but for the most part it remains the same. Color constancy is the tendency for an object to stay the same color despite major changes in the wavelengths of light reflected by it.

One of the best demonstrations of the capacity of an object's color to remain constant during major variations in the wavelengths of light reflected by it was devised by Land (1977), inventor of the Polaroid camera. Subjects viewed a pattern composed of several rectangles of different colors under two different conditions of background illumination. The wavelengths reflected by each part of the multicolored pattern were carefully measured, and the proportion of different wavelengths in the background illumination was adjusted prior to both viewings so that the wavelengths reflected by the green rectangle during the second viewing were exactly the same as those reflected by the white rectangle during the first. Amazingly, although the light entering the eye from the white rectangle during the first viewing and from the green rectangle during the second were identical, the white rectangle appeared white, and the green appeared green in both cases.

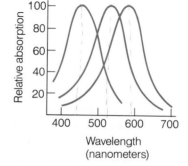

FIGURE 7.23 *The absorption spectra of the photopigments in the three classes of cones.*

Although the phenomenon of color constancy is counterintuitive, its advantage is obvious.

> Imagine the purpose of color as an aid to seeing. Color vision improves the ability to tell surfaces apart in a memorable way, so that nourishment, threats and so on can be learned and reliably recognized. Since color vision supports many more distinctions than monochromatic black-and-white vision, there is surely an advantage to seeing in color. Yet unreliable distinctions are useless. Indeed, they are a hindrance. . . . The ability to recognize things would be lessened if their color changed simply because of a change in the illumination. (Brou, Sciascia, Linden, & Lettvin, 1986, p. 87)

Clearly then, color constancy is an important aspect of color vision. How does the visual system produce constant perceptions of an object's color despite wide variations in the wavelengths that it reflects? Although this question is far from being answered, it is clear that this remarkable ability lies in the perception of contrast between adjacent areas of a visual display. Somehow the visual system compares the wavelengths of lights reflected by adjacent areas of a visual display, and from this information it estimates and discounts variations in background illumination in the perception of an object's color. Support for this notion is provided by the computer-generated visual display devised by Brou, Sciascia, Linden, and Lettvin (1986). This display is reproduced in Figure 7.24.

If the perception of color depends on the analysis of contrast between adjacent areas of the visual field, there should be neurons somewhere in the visual system that are responsive to color contrast. And there are. For example, the so-called **dual-opponent color cells** in the monkey visual cortex respond with vigorous "on" firing when the center of their circular receptive field is illuminated with one wavelength such as green and the surround is simultaneously illuminated with another wavelength such as red. And the same cells display vigorous "off" responding when the pattern of illumination is reversed; for example, red in the center and green in the surround. In essence, dual-opponent color cells respond to the contrast between the wavelengths reflected by adjacent areas of the visual field. Their responses are affected little by changes in diffuse background illumination.

Demonstration

Figure 7.24 demonstrates how color constancy breaks down in certain situations when we look at displays that lack sharply defined areas of contrast. Examine it carefully. It may surprise you to learn that the four differently colored hexagons (six-sided figures) are all emitting exactly the same wavelengths. Although you may initially have some difficulty believing this claim, you can prove that it is so by eliminating the effect of the adjacent context. Take a piece of paper and poke or cut holes in it so that only the four distinctive hexagons will be visible through it. Place the sheet of paper over the figure, and compare the four hexagons. Now do you believe me? This same figure can be used to make another point about color vision. Stare at a point in the center of the figure without moving your eyes, and in just a few seconds you will see the hexagons disappear. Apparently, eye movements play an important role in the comparison of the wavelengths reflected by different parts of the visual field and thus in the perception of color.

FIGURE 7.24 *The computer-generated display of Brou, Sciascia, Linden, and Lettvin (1986).*
(Courtesy of Jerome Y. Lettvin)

Livingstone and Hubel (1984) have found that these dual-opponent color cells are distributed in the primary visual cortex in peg-like columns that penetrate the layers of the primary visual cortex (one exception is the lower regions of layer IV), as illustrated schematically in Figure 7.25. For some reason the neurons in these peg-like columns have particularly high concentrations of **cytochrome oxidase;** thus, their distribution in the primary visual cortex can be visualized by staining slices of tissue with stains

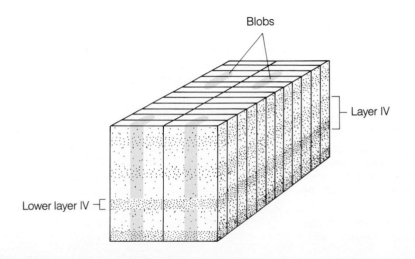

Blobs

Layer IV

Lower layer IV

FIGURE 7.25 *Hubel and Wiesel's model of cortical organization illustrating the position of the peg-like columns containing dual-opponent color cells. (Adapted from Livingstone & Hubel, 1984.)*

that have an affinity for this enzyme. When a section of striate tissue is cut parallel to the cortical layers and stained in this way, the pegs are seen as "blobs" of stain scattered over the cortex (unless the section is from lower layer IV). In fact, to the delight of instructors and students alike, the term **blobs** has stuck; it has become the accepted scientific label for peg-like, cytochrome-oxidase-rich, dual-opponent color columns.

Conclusion

This chapter began by describing the passage of light into the eye to the receptor layer of the retina. Then it followed the transmission of neural signals from the retinal receptors to the primary visual cortex via the retina-geniculate-striate system. It concluded by discussing those aspects of retina-geniculate-striate system structure and function that influence the perception of edges and color. There were two general themes. The first theme was that vision is a creative process, and numerous examples of the visual system's capacity for creativity were provided: the completion effect, contrast enhancement, and color constancy, to name a few. The second theme was that progress in neuroscience is greatest when a variety of research approaches are brought to bear on the same questions. This theme of converging operations pervades much of this book, but in no other chapter is its truth more obvious. Arguably, there is no other area of research in the neurosciences in which the convergence of neuroanatomical, neurochemical, neurophysiological, and behavioral research has led to so many important insights.

Along the way, there were many opportunities for you to demonstrate to yourself the principles of visual function under discussion. I hope that you took advantage of them and that they had the intended effect of demonstrating in a personal way the amazing abilities of your visual system and the relevance of what you were learning to your everyday life.

Food for Thought

1. In vision as in photography, one frequently has to compromise sharpness (acuity) to increase sensitivity. Discuss.

2. Why is it so important to distinguish between intensity and brightness and between wavelength and color?

3. If you mix equal proportions of red and green light, you get white light, or something close to white depending on the exact wavelengths of red and green. However, if you mix equal portions of red and green paint, you get an approximation of black paint. Explain this paradox.

ADDITIONAL READING

The best introductory readings for those interested in the biopsychology of perception are *Scientific American* articles. Their large color illustrations are without rival. The following four articles provide excellent coverage of topics discussed in this chapter.

Brou, P., Sciascia, T. R., Linden, L., & Lettvin, J. Y. (1986). The colors of things. *Scientific American, 255,* 84–91.

Hubel, D. H., & Wiesel, T. N. (1979). Brain mechanisms of vision. *Scientific American, 241,* 150–162.

Land, E. H. (1977). The retinex theory of color vision. *Scientific American, 237,* 108–128.

Ratliff, F. (1972). Contour and contrast. *Scientific American, 226,* 90–101.

To help you study the material on this chapter, all of the key terms—those that have appeared in bold type—are listed and defined here.

Absorption spectrum. A graph of the ability of a substance to absorb light of different wavelengths.

Accommodation. Focusing images on the retina by adjusting the configuration of the lenses.

Achromatic colors. Black, white, and gray.

Acuity. Ability to see detail.

Aggregate field. The area encompassing all of the receptive fields of all of the neurons in a given column of visual cortex.

Amacrine cells. A layer of retinal cells whose function is lateral communication.

Binocular. Integrating input from both eyes.

Binocular disparity. The difference between the retinal image of the same object on the two retinas.

Bipolar cell layer. The middle layer of the retina.

Blobs. Cytochrome-oxidase-rich, dual-opponent color columns.

Chromatic colors. The hues; colors such as blue, green, and yellow.

Ciliary muscles. The eye muscles that control the lens.

Color constancy. The tendency of an object to appear the same color even when the wavelengths that it reflects change.

Complementary colors. Pairs of colors that produce white when combined in equal measure; every color has a complementary color.

Completion. Using information obtained from receptors around a blind spot to create a perception of the missing portion of the retinal image.

Complex cells. Cells in the visual cortex that respond optimally to straight-edge stimuli in a certain orientation in any part of the receptive field.

Component theory (trichromatic theory). The theory that the relative amount of activity produced in three different classes of cones by a light determines its perceived color.

Cones. The visual receptors that mediate high-acuity color vision in good lighting.

Contrast enhancement. The enhancement of the perception of edges; it is thought to be mediated by lateral inhibition.

Cytochrome oxidase. An enzyme present in particularly high concentrations in the dual-opponent color cells of the visual cortex.

Dual-opponent color cells. Neurons that respond to the differences in the wavelengths reflected by adjacent areas of their receptive field.

Duplexity theory. The theory that rods and cones are the receptors for two different systems: one for scotopic conditions (rods) and one for photopic conditions (cones).

Fovea. The central indentation of the retina.

Horizontal cells. A layer of cells in the retina whose function is lateral communication.

Lateral inhibition. Inhibition of adjacent neurons or receptors in a topographic array.

Lateral plexus. The lateral neural network that interconnects the visual receptors of the horseshoe crab.

Lower-layer-IV neurons. The striate cortex neurons that receive signals from lateral geniculate neurons.

Microspectrophotometry. A technique used to measure the absorption spectrum of the photopigment contained in a single visual receptor.

Monocular. Processing input from one eye only.

Nasal hemiretina. The half of each retina next to the nose.

Off-center cells. Cells that respond to lights shone in the center of their receptive fields with "off firing" and to lights shone in the periphery of their fields with "on firing."

Ommatidia. The visual receptors of the horseshoe crab.

On-center cells. Cells that respond to lights shone in the center of their receptive fields with "on firing" and to lights shone in the periphery of their fields with "off firing."

Opponent-process theory. The theory that a receptor or neuron signals one color when it responds in one way (e.g., by increasing its firing rate) and signals its complementary color when it responds in the opposite way (e.g., by decreasing its firing rate).

Optic disk (blind spot). The area on the retina where the axons of retinal ganglion cells penetrate the retina and leave the eye.

Photopic spectral sensitivity curve. The graph of the sensitivity of cone-mediated vision to different wavelengths of light.

Photopic vision. Cone-mediated vision.

Primary visual cortex. Area of the cortex that receives direct input from the lateral geniculate nuclei.

Purkinje effect. In intense light, red and yellow wavelengths look brighter than blue or green wavelengths of equal intensity; in dim light, blue and green wavelengths look brighter than red and yellow wavelengths of equal intensity.

Receptive field. The receptive field of a visual neuron is the area of the visual field within which it is possible for the appropriate visual stimulus to influence the firing of the neuron.

Receptors. Cells that are specialized to receive chemical, mechanical, or radiant signals from the environment.

Retina-geniculate-striate pathway. The large visual pathway from the retina to the primary visual cortex (striate cortex) via the lateral geniculate nuclei of the thalamus.

Retinal ganglion cells. The layer of cells in the retina whose axons leave the eyeball.

Retinotopic. The neural inputs of the system are organized in such a way that they map the retina.

Rhodopsin. The photopigment of rods.

Rods. The visual receptors that mediate achromatic, low-acuity vision under dim light.

Saccades. The rapid movements of the eyes between fixations.

Scotopic vision. Rod-mediated vision.

Scotopic spectral sensitivity curve. The graph of the sensitivity of rod-mediated vision to different wavelengths of light.

Sensitivity. The ability to detect the presence of weak stimuli; more sensitive eyes can detect the presence of weaker lights.

Simple cells. Cells in the visual cortex that respond maximally to straight-edge stimuli in a certain position and orientation.

Stabilized retinal image. A retinal image that does not shift across the retina when the eyes move; this can be accomplished by projecting images from a contact-lens-mounted microprojector.

Striate cortex. Primary visual cortex.

Temporal hemiretina. The half of each retina next to the temple.

Transduction. A general term referring to the conversion of one type of energy to another; rods and cones transduce certain wavelengths of radiant energy into neural signals.

X-type cells. Cells with concentric on and off receptive fields.

8

Mechanisms of Perception

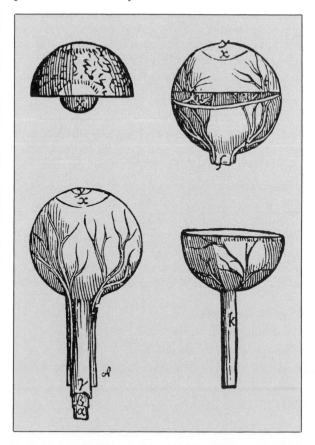

There are two chapters in this text whose primary focus is sensory. You have just finished the first (Chapter 7), and this is the second (Chapter 8). Chapter 7 is a tough act to follow because it showcases the impressive and highly successful single-unit approach to the study of vision. It describes how the analysis of the responses of individual receptors and neurons in the retina-geniculate-striate system, the major neural pathway between the eye and the cortex, has provided major insights into the neural basis of mammalian vision. To be sure, the single-unit approach has been used to good advantage in the study of other sensory systems and in the study of other parts of the visual system, but the retina-geniculate-striate system has been its most successful arena. No other major system in the mammalian brain is as well understood.

This chapter is far more general than its predecessor. Rather than focusing on one part of one sensory system, it discusses all five **exteroceptive sensory systems** (the five sensory systems that interpret stimuli from outside the body): vision, touch, hearing, olfaction (smell), and taste. It is divided into six major sections:

8.1 **Introductory Concepts**
8.2 **Cortical Mechanisms of Vision**
8.3 **Audition**
8.4 **Somatosensation: Touch and Pain**
8.5 **The Chemical Senses: Olfaction and Taste**
8.6 **Conclusion: General Principles of Sensory System Organization**

8.1 Introductory Concepts

Sensation and Perception

Psychologists frequently find it useful to divide the entire process of perceiving, in its general sense, into two distinct phases: one called "sensation" and the other called "perception." They use the word **sensation** to refer to the process of detecting the presence of simple stimuli and the word **perception** to refer to the higher order process of integrating, recognizing, and interpreting complex patterns of sensations. The need for this distinction is most apparent in neuropsychological patients suffering from severe perceptual deficits in the absence of sensory dysfunction. Dr. P.,[1] the man who mistook his wife for a hat (Sacks, 1985), is a case in point.

> Dr. P. was a musician of distinction, well-known for many years as a singer . . . and as a teacher. . . . It was obvious within a few seconds of meeting him that there was no trace of dementia [intellectual deterioration] . . . He was a man of great cultivation and charm who talked well and fluently, with imagination and humour. . . .
>
> "What seems to be the matter?" I asked him at length.
>
> "Nothing that I know of," he replied with a smile, "but people seem to think that there's something wrong with my eyes."
>
> "But *you* don't recognise any visual problems?"
>
> "No, not directly, but I occasionally make mistakes." . . .
>
> . . . It was while examining his reflexes . . . that the first bizarre experience occurred. I had taken off his left shoe and scratched the sole of his foot with a key—a frivolous-seeming but essential test of a reflex—and then, excusing myself to screw my ophthalmoscope together, left him to put on the shoe himself. To my surprise, a minute later, he had not done this.
>
> "Can I help?" I asked.
>
> "Help what? Help whom?" . . .
>
> "Your shoe," I repeated. "Perhaps you'd put it on."
>
> He continued to look downwards, though not at the shoe, with an intense but misplaced concentration. Finally his gaze settled on his foot.
>
> "That is my shoe, yes?" Did I mis-hear? Did he mis-see?
>
> "My eyes," he explained, and put his hand to his foot. "This is my shoe, no?"
>
> "No, it is not. That is your foot. *There* is your shoe."
>
> Was he joking? Was he mad? Was he blind? If this was one of his 'strange mistakes', it was the strangest mistake I had ever come across.
>
> I helped him on with his shoe (his foot), to avoid further complication. . . . I resumed my examination. His visual acuity was good: he had no difficulty seeing a pin on the floor. . . .
>
> He saw all right, but what did he see? . . .
>
> "What is this?" I asked, holding up a glove.
>
> "May I examine it?" he asked, taking it from me . . .
>
> "A continuous surface," he announced at last, "infolded on itself. It appears to have"—he hesitated—"five outpouchings, if this is the word."

---

[1] From *The Man Who Mistook His Wife for a Hat and Other Clinical Tales* (pp. 7–13) by Oliver Sacks, 1985, New York: Summit Books. Copyright © 1970, 1981, 1983, 1984, 1985 by Oliver Sacks. Reprinted by permission of Summit Books, a division of Simon & Schuster, Inc.

"Yes," I said cautiously. "You have given me a description. Now tell me what it is."

"A container of some sort?"

"Yes," I said, "and what would it contain?"

"It would contain its contents!" said Dr. P., with a laugh. "There are many possibilities. It could be a change purse, for example, for coins of five sizes. It could . . ."

. . . "Does it not look familiar? Do you think it might contain, might fit, a part of the body?"

No light of recognition dawned on his face. . . .

I must have looked aghast, but he seemed to think he had done rather well. There was a hint of a smile on his face. He also appeared to have decided the examination was over and started to look around for his hat. He reached out his hand and took hold of his wife's head, tried to lift it off, to put it on. He had apparently mistaken his wife for a hat! His wife looked as if she was used to such things.

Although the exact location of Dr. P.'s brain damage was never discovered, his case illustrates in a most compelling fashion how human brain damage can disrupt specific perceptual abilities, while apparently leaving associated capacities of sensation undisturbed.

The Classic Model of Sensory System Organization

The five exteroceptive sensory systems are thought to be similarly organized. According to the traditional model (see Merzenich & Kaas, 1980), a major pathway from each receptor organ leads to the thalamus, the collection of nuclei that sits on top of the brain stem (see Chapter 2). Each thalamic sensory relay nucleus receives input from one sensory system and relays most of its output to a circumscribed area of the neocortex, the **primary sensory cortex** for that sensory system. Much of the output of each area of primary sensory cortex is in turn transmitted to an adjacent cortical area, the **secondary sensory cortex** for that system. The ultimate destination of sensory input, according to the traditional model, is the ill-defined and poorly understood areas of cortical tissue referred to as association cortex. **Association cortex** is assumed to relate the activities of the various sensory systems, to translate sensory input into programs for motor output, and to mediate complex cognitive activities such as thinking and remembering. Figure 8.1 is a schematic diagram of this traditional model illustrated for three sensory systems.

The Hierarchical Organization of Sensory Systems

A hierarchy is a system whose members can be assigned to specific levels or ranks with respect to one another. In this chapter, you have already encountered two ways in which sensory systems are hierarchically organized. First, you learned how neuropsychologists have found it useful to regard various aspects of sensory function as falling into one of two categories, sensation or perception, which differ in their level of complexity. And then you learned how the traditional model of sensory system organization involves a flow of information from receptors into progressively higher and more complex areas of the brain. Implicit in both

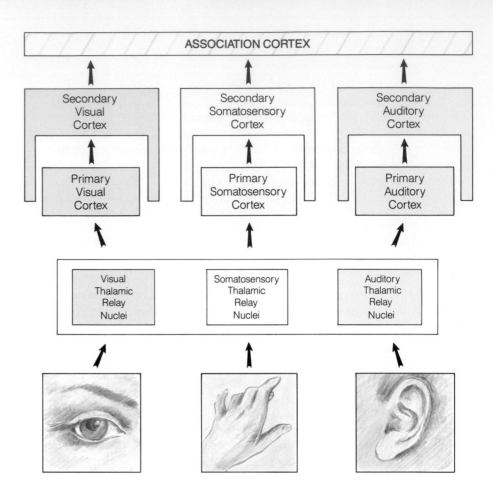

FIGURE 8.1 *The traditional model of sensory system organization.*

schemes is the idea that the two hierarchies are intimately related. It is widely held that structures at progressively "higher" levels of a sensory system play a role that is less and less sensory and more and more perceptual. The idea is that each level of the system analyzes the input from the preceding level, and in so doing, adds to the complexity of the analysis. Although it is not possible to specify a clear dividing line between sensation and perception, many adhere to the convention that sensation is subcortical and perception is cortical.

8.2 Cortical Mechanisms of Vision

The analysis of the visual system in Chapter 7 ends at the level of the primary visual (striate) cortex, but the primary visual cortex is not in any sense the ultimate destination of visual information. It is only the port of entry of visual information into the complex analytic circuitry of the cortex. Chapter 7 has delivered you to the threshold of the cortex; this section of Chapter 8 leads you across the threshold.

Neurological patients with suspected damage to the visual cortex are frequently given a test called **perimetry.** The patient's head is held motionless on a chin rest as she or he stares with one eye at a fixation point on a screen. A small dot of light is then flashed on various parts of the screen, and the patient presses a button to record when the dot is in view. Then, the entire process is repeated for the other eye. The result is a map of the visual field of each eye, which indicates any area of blindness. You may recall from Chapter 7 that we all have a blind spot in each eye.

Damage to the primary visual cortex in one hemisphere produces a **scotoma** (i.e., a damage-produced area of blindness) in the contralateral visual field (see Figure 7.12). The scotoma produced by a bullet wound to the left primary visual cortex is illustrated in Figure 8.2. Notice that the area around the center of the field of vision seems to be preferentially spared. This is a common occurrence with visual cortex damage. It is called **macular sparing**—the macula is the central part of the retina (including the fovea) that has a yellowish pigment.

Blindsight: Seeing Without Seeing

Patients who have lost all of their primary visual cortex report being totally blind—which is not surprising. It is surprising, however, that some of these *cortically blind* patients can perform visually guided tasks, such as grabbing a moving object or indicating its movement, all the while claiming to see nothing. It is this ability of cortically blind subjects to perform visually mediated tasks without conscious awareness that is known as **blindsight.** If blindsight confuses you, imagine how it confuses people who

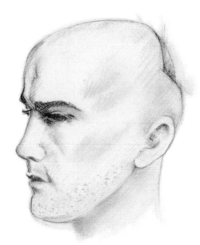

FIGURE 8.2 *The perimetric maps of a subject with a bullet wound to the left primary visual cortex. (Adapted from Teuber, Battersby, & Bender, 1960.)*

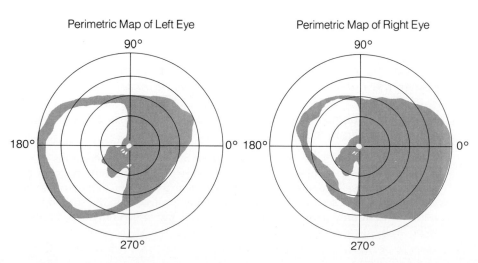

Perimetric Map of Left Eye

Perimetric Map of Right Eye

experience it. Consider, for example, the reactions to blindsight of D.B., a patient who was blind in his left visual field following surgical removal of his right occipital lobe (Weiskrantz, Warrington, Sanders, & Marhsall, 1974).

> Even though the patient had no awareness of "seeing" in his blind [left] field, evidence was obtained that (a) he could reach for visual stimuli [in his left field] with considerable accuracy; (b) could differentiate the orientation of a vertical line from a horizontal or diagonal line; (c) could differentiate the letters "X" and "O". These tasks could be performed accurately only if the stimuli were larger than a critical size. (p. 726)

> Needless to say, he was questioned repeatedly about his vision in his left half-field, and his most common response was that he saw nothing at all. . . . When he was shown his results he expressed surprise and insisted several times that he thought he was just "guessing." When he was shown a video film of his reaching and judging orientation of lines, he was openly astonished. (p. 721)

In view of the complexity of the visual system, it is not surprising that some visual capacity could survive destruction of the primary visual cortex. In this respect, most interest has been directed at a pathway that goes from each retina to the *superior colliculi* of the midbrain, then to the *pulvinar nuclei* of the thalamus, and from there directly to areas of the secondary visual cortex. One theory is that the retina-geniculate-striate system mediates pattern and color vision, whereas the **collicular-pulvinar pathway** plays a role in the detection and localization of objects in space (Schneider, 1969). Although this theory has not stood up well to experimental tests (Goodale, 1983; Mlinar & Goodale, 1984), it illustrates well the weakness of theories of vision that focus exclusively on the retina-geniculate-striate system.

Completion of Scotomas

Many patients with extensive scotomas are unaware of their deficits. One of the factors that contributes to this lack of awareness of scotomas is the phenomenon of **completion** (see Chapter 7). When some patents with scotomas look at a complex figure, part of which lies in their scotoma, they report seeing a complete figure. In some cases, this completion may depend on residual visual capacities in the scotoma; however, completion also occurs in cases in which this explanation can be ruled out. For example, some **hemianopsic** patients (patients with a scotoma covering half their field of vision) see an entire face when they focus on a person's nose, even when the side of the face in the scotoma is covered by a blank card. Consider the interesting example of completion experienced by the esteemed Karl Lashley (1941) (see Chapter 1) during a migraine attack. When experiencing a migraine attack, Lashley developed a large scotoma next to his fovea (see Figure 8.3).

> Talking with a friend I glanced just to the right of his face wherein his head disappeared. His shoulders and necktie were still visible but the vertical stripes on the wallpaper behind him seemed to extend down to the necktie. It was impossible to see this as a blank area when projected on the striped wall paper of uniformly patterned surface although any intervening object failed to be seen.

Lashley's Scotoma

What Lashley saw.

FIGURE 8.3 *The completion of a migraine-produced scotoma as described by Karl Lashley.*

Secondary and Association Cortex of the Visual System

Virtually all of the occipital lobe and large portions of the temporal and parietal lobe are involved in human vision, but the exact organization and function of these areas remains largely a matter of conjecture. The map of these areas presented in Figure 8.4 represents the current best guess, based on a few human clinical case studies and extensive research on nonhuman species (see Van Essen & Maunsell, 1983). There are two large areas of cortical tissue that are usually considered to be secondary visual cortex for two reasons: because they receive major projections from the primary visual cortex and from several other structures lower in the visual hierarchy (e.g., from the pulvinar), and because they seem to be involved in a "higher" or more abstract level of visual analysis than is the primary visual cortex. These two areas of secondary visual cortex are the **prestriate cortex,** the band of tissue in the occipital lobe that almost totally surrounds the primary visual cortex, and the **inferotemporal cortex,** the cortex of the

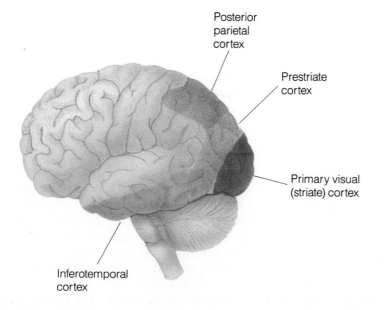

Posterior parietal cortex

Prestriate cortex

Primary visual (striate) cortex

Inferotemporal cortex

FIGURE 8.4 *The visual areas of the human neocortex.*

inferior temporal lobe. In contrast, the **posterior parietal cortex** is considered to be association cortex because, in addition to its input from primary and secondary visual cortex, it receives major input from the auditory cortex and the somatosensory cortex. It has been tentatively hypothesized that the inferotemporal cortex is generally involved in the recognition of objects and that the posterior parietal cortex is generally involved in the analysis of motion and spatial location (Ungerleider & Mishkin, 1982; Van Essen & Maunsell, 1983).

Mapping studies in laboratory primates have revealed that the inferotemporal, prestriate, and posterior parietal areas can each be subdivided into several discrete areas, each of which is a complete map of the retina and is composed of neurons that are sensitive to similar kinds of stimuli (see Cowey, 1981; Schiller, 1986). The behavioral significance of the subdivisions has yet to be determined.

Agnosia is a failure of recognition (from the Greek *gnosis* meaning *to know*) that is not attributable to sensory, verbal, or intellectual impairment (Bender & Feldman, 1972; Benson & Greenberg, 1969). Most cases of agnosia are specific to a particular sensory system; the patient cannot recognize material when it is presented through one sensory modality, but can recognize it when it is presented through another, thus ruling out a diagnosis of general intellectual or verbal impairment.

Visual agnosia is most commonly classified according to the specific category of visual material that cannot be recognized: *prosopagnosia, object agnosia,* and *color agnosia* refer to difficulty in recognizing faces, objects, and colors, respectively. **Prosopagnosia** is the most common and the most widely studied form of visual agnosia. Patients with prosopagnosia have difficulty telling one human face from another; in severe cases they cannot recognize their own face in a mirror. However, they almost never have difficulty recognizing faces as faces or in identifying individual components of a face (e.g., noses, eyes, ears). Tranel and Damasio (1985) reported the cases of two prosopagnosics who reliably displayed large electrodermal skin conductance responses (see Chapter 4) to pictures of familiar faces, despite the fact that they could not consciously recognize them. Apparently, recognition can take place in prosopagnosics at a level of the nervous system that does not involve conscious awareness.

It is believed by some that prosopagnosia results from damage to an area of the brain specifically dedicated to the recognition of faces. The primary evidence for this view is that patients who have difficulty recognizing faces have little difficulty recognizing other test objects (e.g., chair, pencil, door). Stop reading for a moment and give this line of evidence some thought. It is seriously flawed. Because prosopagnosics have no difficulty recognizing faces as faces, the fact that they can recognize chairs as chairs, pencils as pencils, and doors as doors is not particularly enlightening. The critical question is whether or not they can recognize which chair, which pencil, and which door. Two clinical cases have a bearing on this point: in one case, a farmer lost his ability to recognize particular cows when he became prosopagnosic; in the other case, a bird watcher lost his ability to distinguish between species of birds when he became prosopagnosic. These two cases demonstrate that the perceptual difficulties of at least some prosopagnosics are not restricted to faces; their problem appears to be one of distinguishing visually similar members of complex classes of visual stimuli (Damasio, Damasio, & Van Hoesen, 1982).

In a few cases, it has been possible to subject the brains of deceased

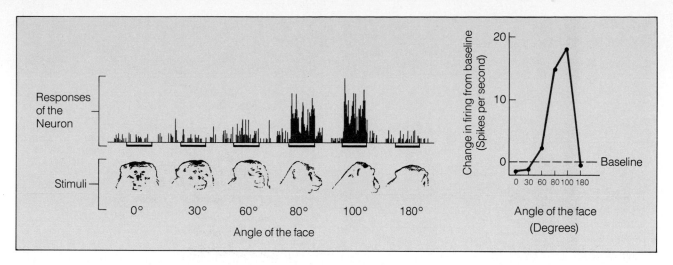

FIGURE 8.5 *The firing rate of a monkey inferotemporal neuron before, during, and after the presentation of monkey faces at different angles. The profile view (100°) was most effective in increasing the firing rate of this cell. (Adapted from Gross et al., 1985.)*

prosopagnosics to histological scrutiny (e.g., Damasio, 1985; Meadows, 1974). In most cases, bilateral damage to the inferior prestriate area and the adjoining portions of the inferotemporal cortex has been found. Consistent with this observation is the discovery of neurons that appear to react only to faces in the inferotemporal cortex of monkeys (Perrett, Rolls, & Caan, 1982; Rolls, 1985) and sheep (Kendrick & Baldwin, 1987). Figure 8.5 summarizes the responses recorded from such a neuron in the inferotemporal cortex of a monkey before, during, and after the presentation of various stimuli (Gross, Desimone, Albright, & Schwarz, 1985).

A neural circuit projecting from the primary to the prestriate cortex and on to the posterior parietal cortex appears to be involved in the analysis of spatial location (Levine, 1982; Ungerleider & Mishkin, 1982). Much of the evidence for this view comes from studies of the visuospatial abilities of monkeys with posterior parietal lesions (e.g., Milner, Ockleford, & Dewar, 1977; Petrides & Iversen, 1979; Ungerleider & Brody, 1977). Pohl (1973), for example, found that posterior parietal lesions in monkeys produced a severe deficit on a test of visuospatial ability, but did not disrupt their ability to recognize objects, whereas lesions of the inferotemporal cortex had the opposite pattern of effects. The symptoms of parietal dysfunction include misreaching in the dark and difficulties in localizing both tactile and auditory stimuli (e.g., Ridley & Ettlinger, 1975). Thus, one function of the posterior parietal cortex appears to be the location of objects in space irrespective of the sensory modality through which they are perceived.

8.3 Audition

The next time that you enter a concert hall, take note of the complex feats performed by your auditory system. Notice its amazing ability to perceive dozens of different sounds at the same time—the musicians tuning their instruments, the chatter of the audience, the rustle of clothes, the clatter of seats—and its even more amazing ability to keep all of these channels of sound separate. Notice too that any time you are so inclined, you can focus on one subset of these sounds—perhaps on an interesting conversation occurring two seats down—and block out the others. Even after the beginning of the music has driven all of its competitors from your conscious auditory experience, the whisper of your name by a friend

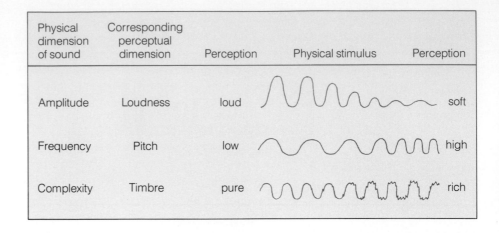

Physical dimension of sound	Corresponding perceptual dimension	Perception	Physical stimulus	Perception
Amplitude	Loudness	loud		soft
Frequency	Pitch	low		high
Complexity	Timbre	pure		rich

FIGURE 8.6 *The relation between the physical and perceptual dimensions of sound.*

seated three rows behind you immediately gains access to your consciousness. Somehow your auditory system can block from consciousness all stimuli except those of a particular kind, while unconsciously monitoring the blocked-out sounds just in case something comes up that requires attention. This adaptive capacity of our auditory systems is referred to as the **cocktail-party phenomenon** after our ability to "focus in on" specific conversations at a cocktail party, while somehow unconsciously monitoring other conversations for a piece of interesting gossip.

Sounds are vibrations of the molecules in the air. Humans can hear only those molecular vibrations between about 30 and 20,000 Hz (Herz or cycles per second). These vibrations travel through the air at over 1,100 kilometers (700 miles) per hour—the so-called sound barrier. Figure 8.6 illustrates the relation between the physical dimensions of sound and our perceptions of them. The perceived loudness, pitch, and timbre of a sound are related to the amplitude, frequency, and complexity of the vibrations, respectively. Most research is done with pure tones—that is, with sine wave stimuli—but in real life, each sound is a combination of many different sine waves, and it is the particular combination of waves that gives each sound its characteristic quality or **timbre**. Figure 8.7 illustrates the characteristic complex waveform of sounds produced by a clarinet and how such a complex sound is the sum of a variety of different sine waves.

FIGURE 8.7 *The complex sound wave produced by a clarinet and its component sine waves. (Adapted from Stereo Review, 1977.)*

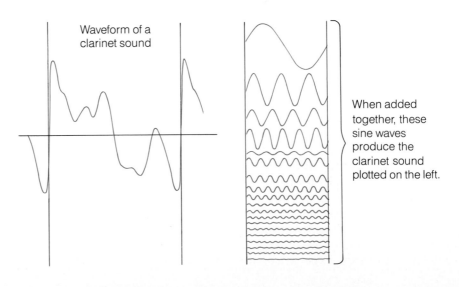

Waveform of a clarinet sound

When added together, these sine waves produce the clarinet sound plotted on the left.

Figure 8.8 illustrates how sounds make their way through the outer, middle, and inner ear and ultimately activate the auditory hair-cell receptors. Sound waves travel down the external auditory canal and cause the **tympanic membrane** (eardrum) to vibrate. These vibrations are then transferred to the three **ossicles** (small bones) of the middle ear: the **malleus** (the hammer), the **incus** (the anvil), and the **stapes** (the stirrup). The vibrations of the stapes trigger vibrations of a membrane called the **oval window,** which in turn transfers the vibrations to the fluid of the **cochlea** (from *kokhlos,* meaning *land snail*). The cochlea is a long, coiled tube with a membranous structure running down its center almost to its tip. This internal membrane contains the auditory receptor organ, the **organ of Corti.** The vibrations of the oval window travel down the fluid of the cochlea's upper duct to the tip and then back through the fluid of the lower duct to another elastic membrane, the **round window,** which dissipates the pressure

FIGURE 8.8 *Anatomy of the ear.*

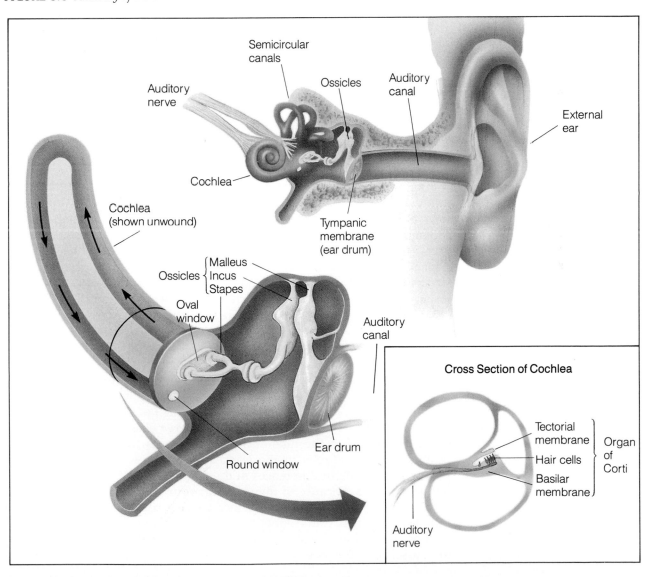

created in the cochlea by the vibrations. These waves traveling forth and back along the cochlea deform the internal membranous structure at particular spots, depending on the frequency of the vibrations. These deformations stimulate the organ of Corti contained in it. As illustrated in Figure 8.8, the organ of Corti is composed of a **basilar membrane** in which the hair-cell receptors are mounted and a **tectorial membrane,** which rests on the *hair cells*. Thus, the bending of the organ of Corti produces a shearing force on the *hair cells* (Hudspeth, 1983; Hudspeth, 1985), which causes the generation of receptor potentials that excite action potentials in the neurons of the **auditory nerve** (the eighth cranial nerve). Also illustrated in Figure 8.8 are the **semicircular canals,** which are the receptive organs of the vestibular system. The **vestibular system** carries information about the direction and intensity of head movements, and it helps us maintain our balance through its output to the motor system. The vestibular system is an **interoceptive sensory system,** in contrast to the **exteroceptive sensory systems,** which are the focus of this chapter.

The most important principle of cochlear function is that different frequencies produce maximal bending at different points along the basilar membrane; higher frequencies produce bending closer to the windows. Thus, sounds of different frequency activate different hair cells, and the signals thus created are carried out of the ear and into the brain by different neurons. The other neural structures of the auditory system are organized according to this same principle. In the same way that the organization of the visual system is **retinotopic** (each visual system structure is laid out according to a map of the retina), the auditory system is **tonotopic;** at all levels of the auditory system, the neurons composing each structure are arrayed on the basis of the frequencies to which they are responsive.

From the Ear to the Primary Auditory Cortex

There is no single major auditory pathway to the cortex comparable to the retina-geniculate-striate pathway of the visual system. Instead, there is a complex network of auditory pathways—Figure 8.9 illustrates some of them (see Irvine & Webster, 1984). Notice that signals from each ear are transmitted to both the ipsilateral and contralateral auditory cortex over several different routes. The axons of the *auditory nerve* synapse in the ipsilateral *cochlear nuclei*, from which many projections lead to the *superior olivary nuclei* (the superior olives) at the same level. The axons of the olivary neurons project via the *lateral lemniscus* tract to the *inferior colliculi*, where they synapse on neurons that project to the *medial geniculate nuclei* of the thalamus, which in turn project to the auditory cortex.

Localization of sounds in space is mediated by both the lateral and medial superior olives, but in different ways. When a sound originates to our left, it reaches the left ear first, and it is louder at the left ear than at the right ear. There are neurons in the *medial superior olives* that are sensitive to slight differences in the time of arrival of signals from the two ears. In contrast, many neurons in the *lateral superior olives* respond maximally when there are slight differences in the amplitude of the sounds received by the two ears. Because of the way that your sound localization system works, it is impossible to tell whether a sharp sound exactly equidistant from your two ears is in front of you, behind you, or above you. If you are reading with a friend, why don't you conduct a little experiment to prove to yourself that this is so.

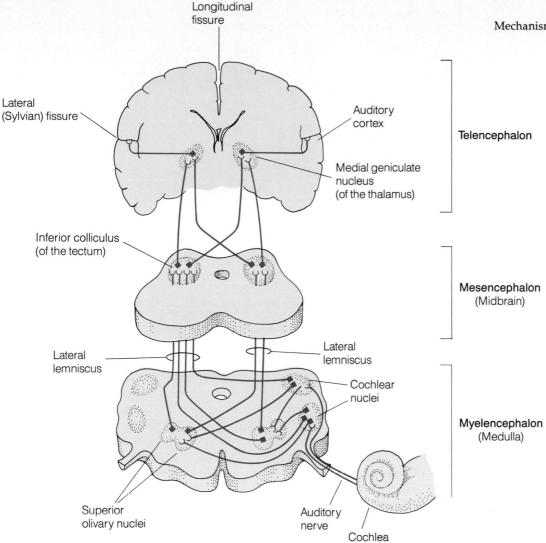

FIGURE 8.9 *The subcortical pathways of the auditory system leading from one ear.*

In humans, much of the primary auditory cortex and the adjacent areas of secondary auditory cortex are in the depths of the *lateral fissure* (see Figure 8.10)—the "armpit" of the brain. Although the auditory cortex is generally thought of as a temporal lobe structure, the various areas of secondary auditory cortex—each a separate tonotopic map—extend into the parietal cortex. Cats are widely used to study the auditory cortex because most of their auditory cortex is readily accessible on the surface of the temporal lobes. Caution must be exercised in drawing inferences about the auditory cortex of humans, a species with highly developed language abilities, from the study of a species without these abilities. In most humans, language abilities are controlled primarily from the left hemisphere, and much of the left auditory cortex appears to be specialized for speech analysis. Chapter 17 focuses on this important topic.

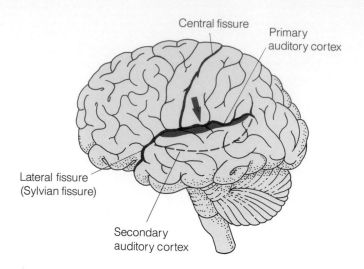

Central fissure

Primary
auditory cortex

Lateral fissure
(Sylvian fissure)

Secondary
auditory cortex

FIGURE 8.10 *Location of auditory cortex in the human brain.*

Tonotopic Organization of the Primary Auditory Cortex

In 1960, Woolsey proposed a theory of the organization of the cat's auditory cortex based on several lines of neuroanatomical and electrophysiological evidence. He proposed that the anterior (front) portions of the primary auditory cortex responded to high-frequency tones and that the more posterior portions responded to progressively lower frequencies. He also described the boundaries of the various adjacent areas of secondary auditory cortex, which he proposed were also tonotopically organized. At that time, the utility of the single-unit approach to the study of sensory systems was just being established through the efforts of Hubel and Wiesel and others studying the visual system (see Chapter 7), and soon there were several attempts to test Woolsey's theory by recording the responses of single neurons in the auditory cortex to pure tones (e.g., Evans, Ross, & Whitfield, 1965; Goldstein, Abeles, Daly, & McIntosh, 1970). Although these experiments generally confirmed the anterior-to-posterior high-to-low frequency gradient hypothesized by Woolsey, they did not support the idea that the cortex is strictly tonotopic. In various subjects, the neurons in a particular area of auditory cortex responded to a wide range of frequencies, thus suggesting that the strict tonotopic organization of the cochlea is not maintained in the cortex.

It was not until 1974 that Merzenich, Knight, and Roth were able to reconcile the apparent inconsistency between Woolsey's theory and the existing unit-recording data. Using improved procedures, Merzenich and his colleagues were able to record from many more neurons in each cat than had previously been possible. Consequently, they were able to develop tonotopic maps for individual cats, rather than combining all of the data from all of their subjects into a single map, as previous investigators had done. This approach enabled them to make two important observations. First, they found that the primary auditory cortex of each cat was strictly tonotopic (see Figure 8.11), with each cell in a given column of cortex responding best to the same frequencies. Second, they found that the exact position of the primary auditory cortex in relation to the surrounding sulci and gyri varied considerably from cat to cat. Thus, if one combined all of the data recorded from different subjects to produce a map

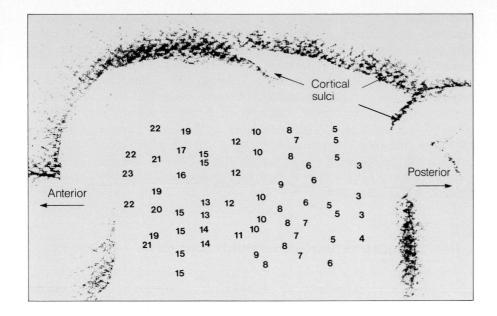

FIGURE 8.11 *The tonotopic organization of an area of cat primary auditory cortex. Each number illustrates the frequency in KHz to which the neurons at that site were most responsive. Notice the systematic anterior-to-posterior high-to-low frequency gradient. (Adapted from Merzenich et al., 1974.)*

of the average tonotopic layout, what one obtained was a "fuzzy picture" of the strictly organized tonotopic maps of individual subjects. I hope that you do not forget this lesson. Remember that although the cortices of the members of the same species seem to operate according to the same general principles, there are differences between individual members that can obscure these principles when data from different subjects are averaged.

Damage to the Human Auditory Cortex

Because the human auditory cortex is ensconced in the lateral fissure (also known as the Sylvian fissure), it is not frequently damaged, and when it is, extensive damage to surrounding tissue is inevitable. Even very large bilateral lesions of the auditory cortex do not produce deafness. The most obvious effect of human auditory cortex lesions is a deficit in the perception of temporal sequences of sounds. Patients with damage to auditory cortex have no difficulty perceiving simple auditory stimuli following cortical damage, but they do have difficulty identifying particularly brief stimuli, discriminating among sounds presented in rapid succession, and judging the temporal order of sounds presented in rapid succession. Accordingly, patients with extensive damage to their auditory cortex often complain of difficulty in perceiving rapid speech. Damage to the auditory cortex of the left hemisphere, which is the language hemisphere for most people, usually has a greater disruptive effect on auditory sequencing than does damage to the right. Cats with unilateral or bilateral lesions of the auditory cortex seem to lack the ability to localize sounds (Neff, 1977), and there is some evidence that humans with large auditory cortex lesions extending into the parietal lobe have similar difficulties, particularly when the lesions are on the right side (de Renzi, 1982).

Auditory Agnosia

Auditory agnosia refers to the impaired capacity to recognize nonverbal sounds in the absence of significant hearing loss, intellectual deterioration, or language-related difficulties. Few cases of auditory agnosia have been reported. It is difficult to estimate to what degree this paucity of cases reflects the rarity of auditory agnosia and to what degree it reflects the fact that few neurological patients ever have their complex auditory capacities systematically assessed (see Bauer & Rubens, 1985; Pirozzolo, 1978). The two most common types of auditory agnosia are amusia and agnosia for sounds. *Amusia* refers to the disruption of any of a variety of abilities involved in the recognition of music, such as the discrimination of individual tones, melodies, or rhythms; *agnosia for sounds* refers to difficulties in recognizing the meaning of nonverbal speech sounds, such as bells, bird songs, or boiling kettles (Alpert, Sparks, von Stockert, & Sax, 1972; Spreen, Benton, & Fincham, 1965).

8.4 Somatosensation: Touch and Pain

Somatosensation is a general term referring to sensations of the body. Although it is common to think of the somatosensory system as a single system, it is most appropriately viewed as three separate, but interacting, systems: (1) a system that senses various external stimuli applied to the skin; (2) a system that monitors *proprioceptive information* (information about the position of the various body parts, which comes from receptors in the muscles and joints); and (3) a system that provides general information about conditions within the body (e.g., temperature, blood pressure). The discussion deals almost exclusively with the exteroceptive touch component. Just as the touch system is only one division of the somatosensory trio, it too comprises three somewhat distinct systems (cf. Dykes, 1983): systems for perceiving mechanical stimuli (touch), thermal stimuli (hot and cold), and *nociceptive* stimuli (pain).

Cutaneous Receptors and Peripheral Pathways

There are six kinds of receptors in the skin (see Figure 8.12). **Glabrous** or hairless skin, such as that on the palms of the hands, contains four kinds of receptors. Two of these are rapidly adapting and thus respond only briefly to changes in tactile stimulation: the **Pacinian corpuscle,** the largest and

FIGURE 8.12 *A drawing of hairy and glabrous skin illustrating the six major cutaneous receptors.*

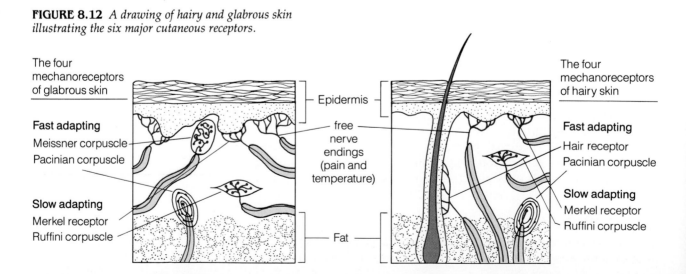

most deeply positioned cutaneous receptor, and the **Meissner corpuscle,** which is located just beneath the outermost layer of skin (the *epidermis*). In contrast, the **Merkel receptor** and the **Ruffini corpuscle** respond continuously to long, unchanging tactile stimuli. Like glabrous skin, hairy skin has Pacinian corpuscles, Ruffini corpuscles, and Merkel receptors, but instead of the rapidly adapting Meissner corpuscles, it has rapidly adapting **hair receptors** near the base of each hair.

To appreciate the functional significance of the fast and slowly adapting cutaneous receptors, consider what happens in response to a long-lasting skin indentation of constant pressure. Such a stimulus initially evokes a burst of firing in all receptors, which evokes a sensation of being touched; however, after a few hundred milliseconds, only the slowly adapting receptors remain active, and the quality of the sensation changes markedly (Martin, 1985). In fact, we are usually unaware of constant mechanical stimuli. Think for a moment about the pressure on your ankles from your socks or the feel of your wrist watch; clearly this information was being continuously sensed, but until I drew your attention to it, it did not enter your consciousness. Notice how little we can tell about objects from unchanging tactile input. Accordingly, when we try to identify objects by touch, we manipulate them in our hands so that the pattern of stimulation continually changes. The identification of objects by touch is termed **stereognosis.**

The perception of both pain and temperature changes is mediated by **free nerve endings**—the sixth and last cutaneous receptor, if you have been counting them. They are called free nerve endings because they have no specialized structures associated with the receptive portion of their membranes. Some cutaneous neurons with free nerve endings appear to signal temperature changes at low levels of activity and pain at higher levels; others are sensitive to either painful stimuli or temperature, but not both. Furthermore, different populations of temperature receptors seem responsible for signaling warming as opposed to cooling (Sinclair, 1981), and a discomforting study published in 1932 by Bazett, McGlone, Williams, and Lufkin suggested that these two classes of temperature-sensitive free nerve endings are embedded in different layers of cutaneous tissue. Carlson (1986) provides a particularly colorful description of this study.

> The investigators lifted the prepuce (foreskin) of uncircumcised males with dull fish-hooks. They applied thermal stimuli on one side of the folded skin and recorded the rate at which temperature changes were transmitted through the skin by placing small temperature sensors on the opposite side. They then correlated these observations with verbal reports of warmth and coolness. The investigators concluded that cold receptors were close to the skin and that warmth receptors were located deeper in the tissue. (This experiment shows the extremities to which scientists will go to obtain information—pun intended.) (p. 262)

The neural fibers carrying information from the somatosensory receptors gather together in the peripheral nerves and then enter the spinal cord via the dorsal roots. The area of the body innervated by the dorsal roots of a given segment of the spinal cord is called its **dermatome.** Figure 8.13 is a dermatomal map of the human body. Because there is considerable overlap between adjacent dermatomes, destruction of a single dorsal root typically produces little somatosensory loss.

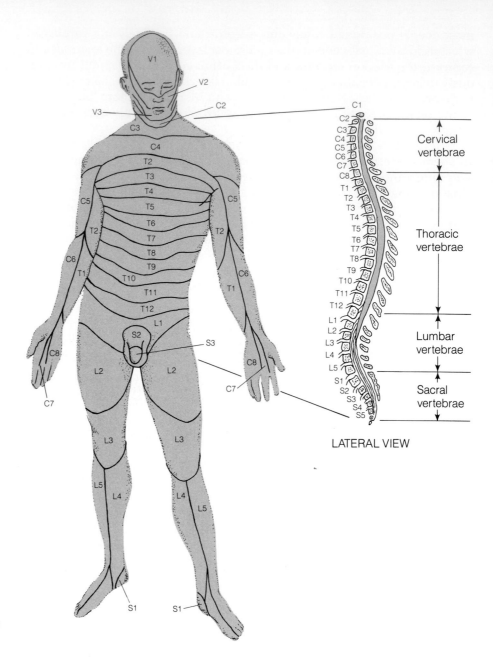

FIGURE 8.13 *Dermatomes of the human spinal segments. S, L, T, and C refer to the sacral, lumbar, thoracic, and cervical regions of the spinal cord. V1, V2, and V3 stand for the three branches of the trigeminal nerve (cranial nerve V).*

The Two Major Ascending Somatosensory Pathways

Somatosensory information ascends in the CNS over two major pathways: the dorsal-column medial-lemniscus system and the anterolateral system. The **dorsal-column medial-lemniscus system** carries information to the cortex about touch and proprioception. As illustrated in Figure 8.14, the axons of the sensory neurons that transmit information about touch and proprioception are very long. They begin at receptors in the skin, muscles, and joints, and they course through the periphery on their way to the dorsal roots and the spinal cord beyond. Then, once they have entered the spinal cord, they ascend toward the brain, forming two ipsilateral tracts in the dorsal white matter of the spinal cord, one on each side. These two ascending tracts are the **dorsal columns.** The sensory neuron axons con-

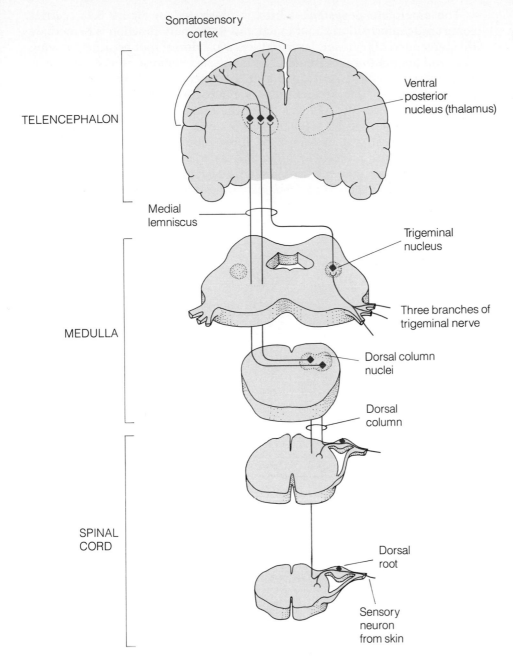

Somatosensory
cortex

TELENCEPHALON

Ventral
posterior
nucleus (thalamus)

Medial
lemniscus

Trigeminal
nucleus

MEDULLA

Three branches of
trigeminal nerve

Dorsal column
nuclei

Dorsal
column

SPINAL
CORD

Dorsal
root

Sensory
neuron
from skin

FIGURE 8.14 *A schematic diagram of the dorsal-column medial-lemniscus system.*

tinue to ascend as part of the dorsal columns until they finally terminate in the **dorsal column nuclei** of the lower brain stem (medulla); here they finally synapse on neurons whose axons *decussate* (cross over to the other side of the brain) and ascend in the **medial lemniscus** to the contralateral *ventral posterior nucleus* of the thalamus. The ventral posterior nuclei also receive input via the branches of the **trigeminal nerve,** which carry somatosensory information from the contralateral areas of the face. The neurons of the ventral posterior nucleus project to the *primary somatosensory cortex* (SI), the *secondary somatosensory cortex* (SII), and the posterior parietal cortex. Neuroscience trivia collectors will almost certainly want to add to their collection the fact that the dorsal column neurons originating in the toes are the longest neurons in the human body.

The **anterolateral system,** which is illustrated in Figure 8.15, carries some crude information about touch, but its primary function is to mediate the perception of pain and temperature. Most dorsal root neurons carrying pain and temperature information from the skin synapse almost as soon as they enter the spinal cord, in the gray matter of the dorsal horns. The axons of most of the second-order somatosensory neurons leaving the dorsal horns decussate and ascend to the brain contralaterally in the anterolateral portion of the spinal cord; however, some ascend ipsilaterally. The anterolateral system comprises three different tracts: the **spinothalamic tract,** which projects to the *ventral posterior nuclei* of the thalamus (as does the dorsal-column medial-lemniscus system); the **spinoreticular tract,** which projects to the *reticular formation* (and then to the *parafascicular* and

FIGURE 8.15 *A schematic diagram of the anterolateral system.*

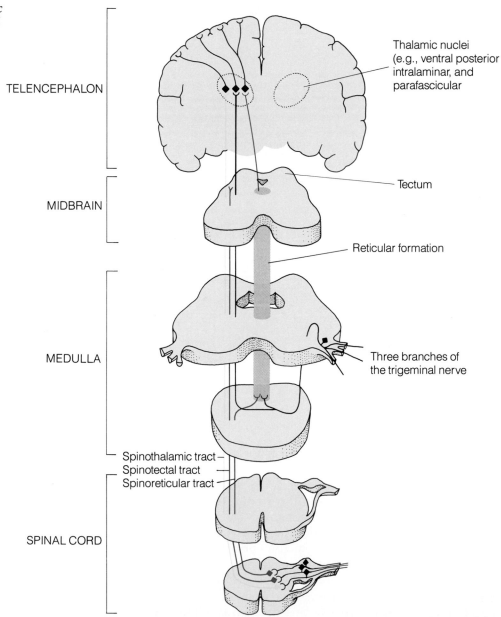

TELENCEPHALON

Thalamic nuclei (e.g., ventral posterior intralaminar, and parafascicular

MIDBRAIN

Tectum

Reticular formation

MEDULLA

Three branches of the trigeminal nerve

Spinothalamic tract
Spinotectal tract
Spinoreticular tract

SPINAL CORD

intralaminar nuclei of the thalamus); and the **spinotectal tract,** which projects to the tectum (the colliculi of the midbrain). Branches of the trigeminal nerve carry pain and temperature information from the skin of the face to the same thalamic sites. The pain and temperature information reaching the thalamus is then widely distributed to various parts of the brain, including SI, SII, and the posterior parietal cortex.

An attempt by Mark, Ervin, and Yakolev (1962) to alleviate the chronic pain of patients in the advanced stages of cancer supports the view that the different anterolateral pathways subserve different types of pain. Lesions to the ventral posterior nuclei, which receive input from both the spinothalamic tract and the dorsal-column medial-lemniscus system, produced some loss of cutaneous sensitivity to touch, to temperature change, and to sharp pain, but they had no effect on deep, chronic pain. In contrast, lesions of the parafascicular and intralaminar nuclei, which receive input via the spinoreticular tract, reduced deep chronic pain without disrupting cutaneous sensitivity.

Cortical Localization of Somatosensation

It was the neurosurgeon Wilder Penfield and his colleagues (1937) who first mapped the primary somatosensory cortex in humans (see Figure 8.16). Penfield mapped the cortices of conscious patients prior to neurosurgery by applying electrical stimulation to the cortical surface. When stimulation was applied to the *postcentral gyrus,* the patients reported somatosensory sensations in various parts of the body. When Penfield

FIGURE 8.16 *The location of human primary (SI) and secondary (SII) somatosensory cortex, and an illustration of the primary somatosensory homunculus.*

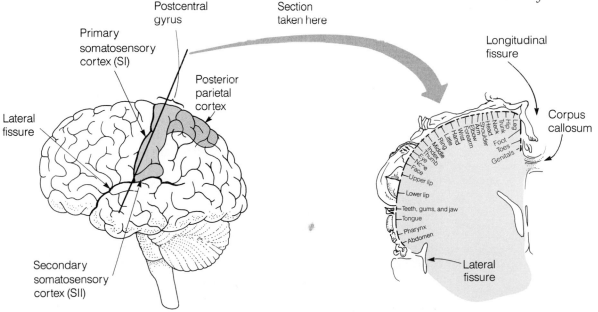

Lateral View of
Left Hemisphere

Cross Section Taken
Through Left Hemisphere
at Indicated Plane

mapped the relation between the sites of stimulation and the parts of the body in which the sensation was felt, he found that the human primary somatosensory cortex is **somatotopically** organized; that is, that different parts of the body project to different parts of the somatosensory cortex. Figure 8.16 is a schematic representation of a coronal section through the postcentral gyrus that illustrates the nature of this somatotopic map, or **somatosensory homunculus** (*homunculus* means *little man*) as it has been termed. Evidence of a second somatotopically organized area, SII, just below SI and extending into the lateral (Sylvian) fissure, was obtained in a similar manner. SII receives many of its inputs from SI (Pons, Garraghty, Friedman, & Mishkin, 1987); and in contrast to SI, whose input is largely contralateral, SII receives substantial input from both sides of the body.

You will notice from Figure 8.16 that the somatosensory homunculus is severely distorted. Just as a relatively large portion of the visual cortex receives information from the small, central (foveal) portion of the retina, which mediates high-acuity vision, the greatest proportion of somatosensory cortex is dedicated to receiving input from the parts of the body capable of making the finest tactual discriminations (e.g., hands, lips, and tongue).

Subsequently, Kaas, Nelson, Sur, and Merzenich (1981) found that the strip of primary somatosensory cortex in monkeys is not one strip at all, but four parallel strips, each with a similar, but separate, somatotopic organization. Apparently Penfield and his colleagues had not noticed that SI comprised four independent, parallel strips because they had used electrodes incapable of fine resolution. Kaas and his colleagues found that most of the neurons in a particular strip of somatosensory cortex were sensitive to the same kind of somatosensory input (e.g., deep pressure or cutaneous touch). And just like the primary visual and auditory cortices, there is evidence of columnar organization; each neuron in a particular column responded to the same stimuli and had a receptive field on the same part of the body.

Effects of Somatosensory Cortex Damage in Humans

Corkin, Milner, and Rasmussen (1970) assessed the somatosensory abilities of patients both before and after unilateral parietal excision (removal) for the relief of epilepsy. Patients with lesions involving SI displayed some loss in their ability to detect light touch, to tell whether one point or two adjacent points of their skin had been simultaneously touched, to identify the exact location of touches, and to identify objects by touch (stereognosis). All of these deficits were minor unless they involved a hand, and the deficits of most of the patients involved only the side of the body contralateral to the excision. Bilateral somatosensory dysfunction following a unilateral lesion is a sign of SII damage.

Somatosensory Agnosias

When a patient cannot recognize objects by touch, but has neither intellectual nor sensory impairments, the diagnosis is somatosensory agnosia, that is, **astereognosia.** Perhaps the most interesting form of astereognosia is **asomatognosia,** the failure to recognize parts of one's own body. An interesting case is that of "the man who fell out of bed" reported by Sacks (1985).[2]

> He had felt fine all day, and fallen asleep towards evening. When he woke up he felt fine too, until he moved in the bed. Then he found, as he put it 'someone's leg' in the bed—a *severed human leg,* a horrible thing! He was stunned, at first, with amazement and disgust. . . . [Then] he had a brainwave. . . . Obviously one of the nurses . . . had stolen into the Dissecting Room and nabbed a leg, and then slipped it under his bedclothes as a joke. . . . *When he threw it out of bed, he somehow came after it—and now it was attached to him.*
>
> 'Look at it!' he cried. . . . 'Have you ever seen such a creepy, horrible thing? . . .
>
> 'Easy!' I said. 'Be calm! Take it easy!' . . .
>
> '. . . why . . .' he asked irritably, belligerently.
>
> 'Because it's *your* leg,' I answered. 'Don't you know your own leg?' . . .
>
> . . . 'Ah Doc!' he said. 'You're fooling me! You're in cahoots with that nurse' . . .
>
> 'Listen,' I said. 'I don't think you're well. Please allow us to return you to bed. But I want to ask you one final question. If this—this thing—is *not* your left leg . . . then where is your own left leg?'
>
> Once more he became pale—so pale that I thought he was going to faint. 'I don't know,' he said. 'I have no idea. It's disappeared. It's gone. It's nowhere to be found . . .'

The Paradoxes of Pain

Pain is a unique sensory experience in the sense that it lacks clear cortical representation. No area of the cortex has been discovered that results in pain when stimulated, that responds selectively to painful stimuli, or that abolishes pain when lesioned (see Sweet, 1982). Frontal lobotomy (see Chapter 1) has been shown to reduce the emotional impact of pain, but it does not alter pain thresholds.

The value of pain is not fully appreciated by most people. To appreciate the positive aspects of pain, all one has to do is consider a case of someone born with the inability to perceive it.[3]

> The best documented of all cases of congenital insensitivity to pain is Miss C., a young Canadian girl who was a student at McGill University in Montreal. . . . The young lady was highly intelligent and seemed normal in every way except that she had never felt pain. As a child, she had bitten off the tip of her tongue while chewing food, and had suffered third-degree burns after kneeling on a radiator to look out of the window. . . . She felt no pain when parts of her body were subjected to strong electric shock, to hot water at temperatures that usually produce reports of burning pain, or to a prolonged ice-bath. Equally astonishing was the fact that she showed no changes in blood pressure, heart rate, or respiration when these stimuli were presented. Furthermore, she could not remember ever sneezing or coughing,

---

[2]From *The Man Who Mistook His Wife for a Hat and Other Clinical Tales* (pp. 53–55) by Oliver Sacks, 1985, New York: Summit Books. Copyright © 1970, 1981, 1983, 1984, 1985 by Oliver Sacks. Reprinted by permission of Summit Books, a division of Simon & Schuster, Inc.
[3]From *The Challenge of Pain* (pp. 16–17) by Ronald Melzack and Patrick D. Wall, 1982, London: Penguin Books Ltd. Copyright © Ronald Melzack and Patrick D. Wall, 1982.

the gag reflex could be elicited only with great difficulty, and corneal reflexes (to protect the eyes) were absent. A variety of other stimuli, such as inserting a stick up through the nostrils, pinching tendons, or injections of histamine under the skin—which are normally considered as forms of torture—also failed to produce pain.

Miss C. had severe medical problems. She exhibited pathological changes in her knees, hip, and spine, and underwent several orthopaedic operations. The surgeon attributed these changes to the lack of protection to joints usually given by pain sensation. She apparently failed to shift her weight when standing, to turn over in her sleep, or to avoid certain postures, which normally prevent inflammation of joints. . . .

. . . Miss C. died at the age of twenty-nine of massive infections . . . [exacerbated by] extensive skin and bone trauma.

Cases such as that of Miss C. demonstrate one paradox of pain: that pain, which seems so bad, is in fact indispensable. A second paradox of pain is that the pain of severe bodily damage, which is perhaps the most intense of all sensory experiences, can be effectively suppressed by various cognitive and emotional factors. For example, men participating in religious ceremonies swing from ropes attached to giant meat hooks in their backs without any evidence of pain (Kosambi, 1967); massive wounds suffered by soldiers in battle are often associated with little pain (Beecher, 1959); and people injured in life-threatening situations frequently feel no pain until the threat is over.

Melzack and Wall (1965) were the first to develop a theory of the neural basis of pain that could account for the ability of cognitive and emotional factors to block the perception of pain. They proposed that signals descending from the brain could activate neural gating circuits in the spinal cord that could block incoming pain signals before they even reached the brain. This **gate-control theory,** as it became known, was for many years a thorn in the side of researchers who preferred to equate pain with tissue damage and to ignore the powerful analgesic effects of cognitive and emotional factors.

Mechanisms of Descending Pain Control

An important step toward the identification of the neural basis of descending pain control was provided by Reynolds' (1969) remarkable demonstration that stimulation of several areas of the brain, particularly those in the area of gray matter just around the *cerebral aqueduct* (the duct between the third and fourth ventricles) had analgesic (pain-reducing) effects. Reynolds performed abdominal surgery on rats with no analgesia other than that provided by the stimulation of **periaqueductal gray** (PAG) area. Mayer and Liebeskind (1974) subsequently showed that PAG stimulation can reduce sensitivity to a variety of painful stimuli without diminishing sensitivity to other somatosensory input, that the analgesia produced by stimulating any one site in the PAG affects only part of the body, and that the analgesia produced by PAG stimulation can outlast the stimulation by many minutes.

A second important step toward the identification of the descending pain-control system came from the study of the analgesic effects of morphine and other opiates (see Chapters 6 and 16). Great excitement was created by the discovery that there are specialized receptor sites for opiates on neurons in many parts of the brain, including the periaqueductal gray (PAG). This discovery suggested that such substances occurred naturally in the body: Why else would there be receptors for them? The possibility that there were internally manufactured (endogenous) opiates caught the imagination of many investigators, and in the ensuing years, several different endogenous opiates—generally referred to as **endorphins**—were isolated (e.g., Hughs, Smith, Kosterlitz, Fothergill, Morgan, & Morris, 1975). This suggested that the analgesic effects of pharmaceutical opiates such as morphine may be mediated by the activation of a natural analgesia-producing system that is normally stimulated by the body's own opiates.

In their classic reviews, Basbaum and Fields (1978) and Fields and Basbaum (1984) argued that analgesia is mediated by a descending circuit involving opiate-sensitive neurons in the PAG. They proposed that the input from the PAG excited serotonergic neurons of the *raphé nuclei* (a collection of serotonergic nuclei situated in the core of the medulla), which in turn projected down the dorsal columns of the spinal cord and excited opiate-sensitive interneurons that blocked incoming pain-related transmissions in the dorsal horn. This PAG-raphé-dorsal-column analgesia circuit is summarized in Figure 8.17. Evidence for it has come from a variety of sources. For example, microinjection of opiate antagonists, such as *naloxone* or *naltrexone*, into the PAG has been found to block the analgesia produced by *systemic injection* (injection into the general circulatory system)

FIGURE 8.17 *Basbaum and Field's model of the descending analgesia circuit.*

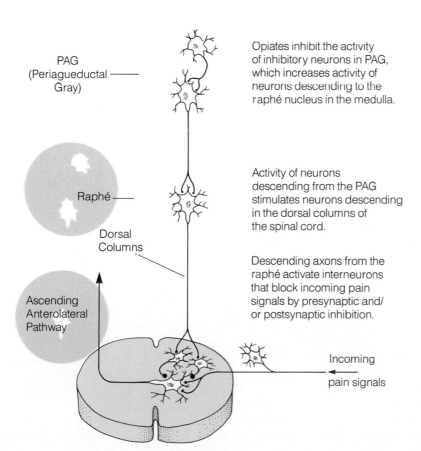

PAG
(Periaqueductal Gray)

Raphé

Dorsal Columns

Ascending Anterolateral Pathway

Opiates inhibit the activity of inhibitory neurons in PAG, which increases activity of neurons descending to the raphé nucleus in the medulla.

Activity of neurons descending from the PAG stimulates neurons descending in the dorsal columns of the spinal cord.

Descending axons from the raphé activate interneurons that block incoming pain signals by presynaptic and/ or postsynaptic inhibition.

Incoming pain signals

of morphine (Yeung & Rudy, 1978), and activation of the raphé nucleus with electrical stimulation has been shown to inhibit pain neurons in the dorsal horn of the spinal cord (Oliveras, Besson, Guilbaud, & Liebeskind, 1974). Moreover, the analgesic effects of morphine and PAG stimulation have been attenuated by lesioning the dorsal column fibers descending from the raphé, by lesioning the raphé itself, or by depleting the raphé neurons of their *serotonin* transmitter (e.g., Basbaum, Clanton, & Fields, 1976). The fact that blockade of the PAG-raphé-dorsal-column circuit does not block all analgesia (see Terman, Shavit, Lewis, Cannon, & Liebeskind, 1984) suggests that other circuits must be capable of mediating the effects of analgesic agents.

8.5 The Chemical Senses: Olfaction and Taste

Olfaction (smell) and *gustation* (taste) are referred to as the chemical senses because their primary function is to monitor the chemical content of the external environment. It is the responses of the olfactory system to molecules released into the air that determine a substance's odor; airborne molecules are detected when they are drawn by inhalation over the receptors of the *olfactory epithelia,* two tiny patches of mucous membrane in the recesses of the nasal passages. A substance's taste depends on the response of the gustatory system to those molecules in the mouth that dissolve in saliva and excite the taste receptors of the tongue and oral cavity.

When we are eating, taste and smell act in concert (McBurney, 1986; Oakley, 1986). Molecules of food excite both the taste and smell receptors and produce an integrated sensory impression termed **flavor.** Although most people understand that olfaction contributes to a food's flavor, few appreciate just how great this contribution is. As a result, some patients, initially diagnosed as **ageusic** (lacking a sense of taste) later prove to be **anosmic** (lacking a sense of smell) with normal gustatory abilities. When you weigh the relative contributions of taste and smell to flavor, you will always give olfaction its due recognition if you remember that anosmic people often have difficulty distinguishing the flavors of apples and onions.

Taste and smell have the dubious distinction of being the least understood of the exterosensory systems. One reason for this lack of knowledge is that chemical stimuli are inherently more difficult to control and administer than nonchemical stimuli, such as lights, tones, and touches. Another is that loss of the ability to taste or smell does not pose serious problems for individuals living in societies such as ours in which potential foods are screened by governmental agencies. Nevertheless, the chemical senses are of considerable interest to many. One interesting feature of the chemical senses is their phylogenetic primitiveness. Even the most simple unicellular animals have receptors that are designed to sense the presence of chemicals in the external environment. In mammals, this primitiveness is reflected by the rich connections that both the gustatory and olfactory systems make with the paleocortex (see Chapter 2). The olfactory system is the only sensory system in which signals are transmitted to the cortex (i.e., the paleocortex) before reaching the thalamus.

Interest in the chemical senses has been stimulated by the major role that they play in the social lives of many species. The members of many species release **pheromones,** chemicals that affect the behavior of their conspecifics (Brown, 1985). The study of pheromones has led to many remarkable findings—at least they are remarkable to humans, who rely primarily on visual, auditory, and somatosensory input to guide their social behavior. For example, Murphy and Schneider (1970) showed that the sexual and aggressive behavior of the golden hamster is entirely under the control of olfactory cues. They found that unfamiliar male hamsters placed in an established colony were attacked and killed by the resident males, but that unfamiliar ovulating (sexually receptive) females introduced into the colony were pursued, mounted, and impregnated. Remarkably, if the resident males were first rendered anosmic, these aggressive and sexual responses did not occur. Murphy and Schneider confirmed the olfactory basis of these aggressive and sexual behaviors in a particularly devious fashion. They swabbed a male intruder with the sex pheromone obtained from the vaginal secretions of an ovulating female hamster before placing it in a cage with other male hamsters, and the change of fragrance converted the intruder from an object of hamster assassination to an object of hamster lust.

The chemical senses participate in some interesting forms of learning. Animals that suffer from gastrointestinal upset after consuming a particular food develop a lasting aversion to its flavor (conditioned taste aversion; Chapter 4). Conversely, it has been shown that rats develop preferences for flavors that they encounter in their mother's milk (Galef & Clark, 1972; Galef & Sherry, 1973) or on the breath of conspecifics (Galef, 1989). As adults, male rats nursed by lemon-scented mothers copulate more effectively with females that smell of lemons (Fillion & Blass, 1986)—a phenomenon that has been aptly referred to as the *I-want-a-girl-just-like-the-girl-who-married-dear-old-dad phenomenon* (Diamond, 1986).

The idea that humans, like many other species, release odors that can elicit sexual advances from members of the opposite sex, has received considerable attention because of its financial and recreational potential. There have been several suggestive findings. For example: (1) The olfactory sensitivity of women is greatest when they are ovulating (e.g., Doty, Snyder, Huggins, & Lowry, 1981). (2) The menstrual cycles of women living together tend to become synchronized (McClintock, 1971). (3) Human judges—particularly women—can judge the sex of an individual on the basis of breath (Doty, Green, Ram, & Yankell, 1982) or underarm odor (Schleidt, Hold, & Attili, 1981). And (4) men can judge the stage of a woman's menstrual cycle on the basis of vaginal odor (Doty, Ford, Preti, & Huggins, 1975). However, there is no convincing evidence that any of these human odors serve as sex attractants (Doty, 1986; Engen, 1982); to put it mildly, the body odors employed in the aforementioned studies were not found attractive by many subjects.

The Olfactory System

It is not yet known what features of a molecule give it its characteristic odor. Because we can discriminate between thousands of different odors, researchers have reasonably assumed that the olfaction, like color vision (see Chapter 7), is organized according to component principles; that is, that there are a few primary receptor types and that the perception of various odors is produced by different ratios of activity in the different types. Amoore and his colleagues made the most ambitious attempt to develop such a theory (e.g., Amoore, Johnston, & Rubin, 1964). They studied over 600 odiferous substances and concluded that their perception could be explained by the combinations of activity in seven different types of receptors, each sensitive to molecules of a particular overall size and shape. The strongest support for this model came from several instances in which the odor of a newly synthesized molecule was predicted by analyzing the degree to which it would fit, like a key in a lock, into each of the seven postulated receptor configurations. However, there have proved to be so many cases in which molecules of similar size and shape produce different odors that the specifics of this theory have been largely abandoned. However, its major premise, that the olfactory system works on component principles, continues to be a rallying point for many researchers in the field.

The olfactory receptor cells are in the upper part of the nose embedded in a layer of mucus-covered tissue called the **olfactory mucosa.** They have short axons, which pass through a porous portion of the inferior skull (the **cribriform plate**) and enter the **olfactory bulbs** (the first cranial nerves). In the olfactory bulbs, they synapse on neurons that project diffusely to the *olfactory paleocortex*. From the olfactory paleocortex, one major pathway leads to the **medial dorsal nucleus** of the thalamus and then to the *primary olfactory cortex* on the inferior surface of the frontal lobes just in front of the olfactory bulbs, and another projects diffusely to various structures of the limbic system. The thalamic-neocortical projection is thought to mediate the conscious perception of odors; the limbic projection is thought to mediate the emotional component of the response to odors. Figure 8.18 is a simplified schematic representation of the olfactory system (see Scott, 1986).

FIGURE 8.18 *A schematic representation of the olfactory system.*

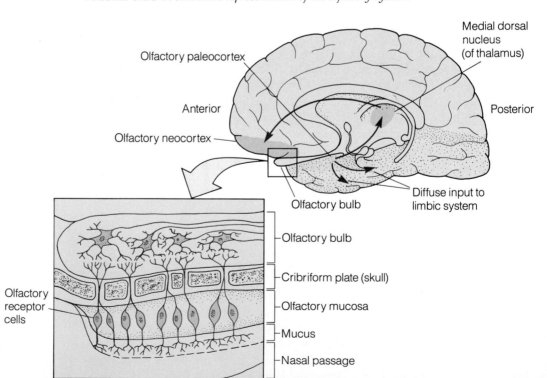

The taste receptors are found on the tongue and they line some parts of the oral cavity. Taste receptors typically occur in clusters of 50 or so called **taste buds.** On the tongue, taste buds are often arrayed about small protuberances called *papillae* (see Figure 8.19).

While component processing is still a working hypothesis in the field of olfaction research, in the field of gustation research, it has achieved the status of a proven principle. All tastes can be produced by combinations of four component qualities: sweet, sour, bitter, and salty. Taste buds on all parts of the tongue respond to all four primary tastes, but some areas of the tongue are more sensitive to some tastes than others. The front of the tongue is particularly sensitive to salty and sweet, the sides to sour, and the back to bitter.

Signals generated in taste receptors by molecules temporarily binding to them stimulate adjacent second-order neurons. The major pathways over which signals in these second-order neurons are transmitted to the cortex are illustrated in Figure 8.20. Gustatory afferents leave the mouth as part of the facial (VII), glossopharyngeal (IX), and vagus (X) cranial nerves, which carry information from the front of the tongue, back of the tongue, and back of the oral cavity, respectively. These fibers all terminate in the **gustatory nucleus** of the medulla, where they synapse on neurons that project to a portion of the **ventral posterior nucleus** of the thalamus (which also serves as a sensory relay nucleus in the somatosensory system). The axons of the ventral posterior nucleus project to the *primary gustatory cortex,* which is next to the face area of the somatosensory homunculus, and to the *secondary gustatory cortex,* which is hidden from view in the lateral fissure. The gustatory system, like the olfactory system, also projects to various parts of the limbic system. Unlike the projections of the other sensory systems, the projections of the gustatory system are primarily ipsilateral.

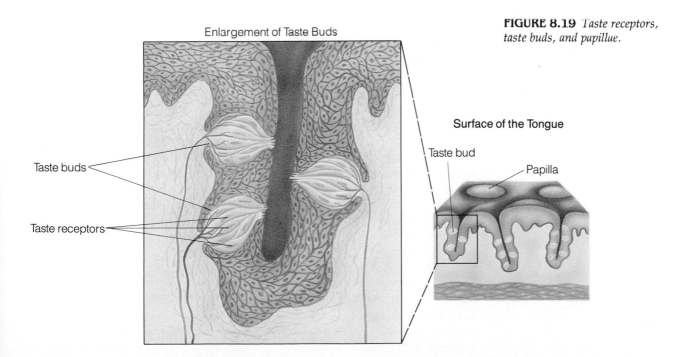

Enlargement of Taste Buds

Taste buds

Taste receptors

Surface of the Tongue

Taste bud

Papilla

FIGURE 8.19 *Taste receptors, taste buds, and papillae.*

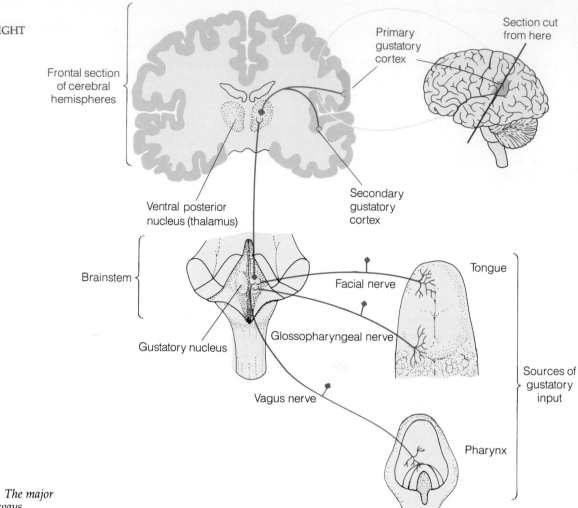

FIGURE 8.20 *The major gustatory pathways.*

Brain Damage and the Chemical Senses

The inability to smell is called **anosmia;** the inability to taste is called **ageusia.** Most cases of anosmia are caused by extensive damage to the olfactory bulbs or nerves. The most common neurological cause of anosmia is a blow to the head, such as that illustrated in Figure 8.21, which causes a displacement of the brain within the skull that shears the olfactory nerves as they pass through the holes in the cribriform plate before entering the olfactory bulb. Approximately 6% of patients hospitalized for traumatic head injuries are found to have olfactory deficits of some sort (e.g., Sumner, 1964; Zusho, 1983). In contrast, *ageusia* is extremely rare, presumably because sensory input from the mouth is carried over three separate pathways. However, **ageusia** for the anterior two-thirds of the tongue on one side is commonly observed after damage to the ear on the same side of the body. This is because the **chorda tympani,** the branch of the cranial facial nerve (VII) carrying gustatory information from the anterior two-thirds of the tongue, passes through the middle ear. One noteworthy feature of ageusia and anosmia is that they occur together in some patients. This suggests that there is some, as yet unidentified, area in the brain where

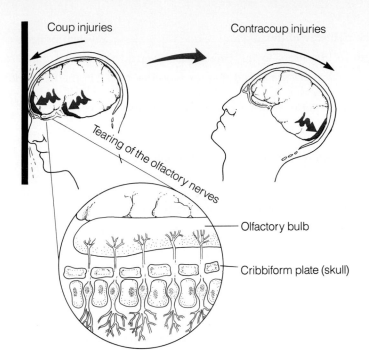

Coup injuries   Contracoup injuries

Tearing of the olfactory nerves

Olfactory bulb

Cribbiform plate (skull)

FIGURE 8.21 *Shearing of the olfactory nerves by a blow to the head. (Adapted from Costanzo and Becker, 1986.)*

taste and smell interact. Because only those patients complaining to their physicians about faulty smell and taste are likely to have these abilities tested—and then only crudely—the number of neurological patients suffering olfactory and gustatory deficits is undoubtedly much higher than current figures suggest (Costanzo & Becker, 1986).

Before proceeding to the conclusion of the chapter, review the anatomy of the various sensory systems by testing yourself with the following exercise. Complete the following sentences by inserting the name of the appropriate sensory system.

1. The collicular-pulvinar pathway is the part of the _____ system thought to play a role in the localization of pigs and other objects in space.

2. _____ cortex is tonotopically organized.

3. The dorsal-column medial-lemniscus system and the anterolateral system are components of the _____ system.

4. The ventral posterior nuclei, the intralaminar nuclei, and the parafascicular nuclei are all thalamic relay nuclei of the _____ system.

5. The periaqueductal gray and the raphé nuclei are involved in blocking the perception of _____.

6. One pathway of the _____ system projects from its receptors to the paleocortex, then to the medial dorsal nucleus of the thalamus, and then to neocortex cortex in the frontal lobe.

7. Ventral posterior nuclei are thalamic relay nuclei of both the somatosensory and _____ systems.

8. Inferotemporal cortex is an area of secondary _____ cortex.

9. Unlike the projections of all other sensory systems, the projections of the _____ system are primarily ipsilateral.

10. The inferior colliculi and medial geniculate nuclei are important structures of the _____ system.

8.6 Conclusion: General Principles of Sensory System Organization

Each sensory system is specialized to receive, encode, and interpret a different kind of sensory information. In chapters such as this, which compare several different sensory systems, these specializations inevitably come to be the focus of discussion. Nevertheless, it is important not to lose sight of the commonalities—the principles of sensory system organization that are common to more than one system. Six such general principles emerged in this chapter. They summarize its main points:

1. *Sensory systems are hierarchical systems.* In each system, there appears to be a general flow of information from "lower" to "higher" structures; and in each system the functions of "higher" structures are more perceptual and less sensory than those of "lower" structures.

2. *Sensory systems are parallel systems.* The first models of sensory system function were **serial models;** that is, they were models in which information could flow between their various components by only one route. However, it is now clear that parallel models provide a more accurate representation of sensory function. **Parallel models** are those in which information can flow between components by various routes. (See Figure 8.22.)

3. *All exteroceptive sensory systems project to the neocortex via the thalamus.* Although there are major differences between the five exteroceptive sensory systems in the routes by which their signals ascend through the various levels of the nervous system, in each of the five there is a major pathway from the thalamus to the neocortex. It is common for each sensory system to have more than one pair of thalamic relay nuclei (e.g., both the pulvinar nuclei and the lateral geniculate nuclei relay visual signals).

The following are the correct answers to the preceding questions: (1) visual, (2) auditory, (3) somatosensory, (4) somatosensory, (5) pain, (6) olfactory, (7) gustatory, (8) visual, (9) gustatory, and (10) auditory.

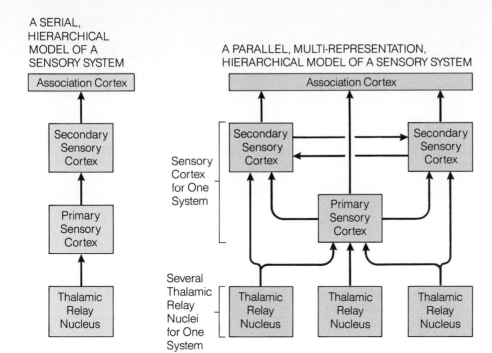

A SERIAL, HIERARCHICAL MODEL OF A SENSORY SYSTEM

A PARALLEL, MULTI-REPRESENTATION, HIERARCHICAL MODEL OF A SENSORY SYSTEM

FIGURE 8.22 *A parallel, multiple-representation, hierarchical model of sensory system organization.*

4. *Sensory cortex is organized in columns.* In all five exteroceptive sensory systems, the neurons in a given column of cortical tissue tend to be responsive to the same kinds of sensory input.

5. *The surface of the sensory cortex is systematically arrayed.* The cortex of the visual, auditory, and somatosensory systems are retinotopically, tonotopically, and somatotopically organized, respectively. The principles of gustatory and olfactory system organization have yet to be discovered. The advantage of such organization is that it facilitates interaction between adjacent channels (columns) of communication. For example, it facilitates *contrast enhancement* (see Chapter 7) between adjacent areas of the visual field, between adjacent areas of the body, and between adjacent tones.

6. *There is multiple representation of each sensory system in the cortex.* As research on sensory cortex has progressed, more sensory areas have been discovered and areas that were once thought to be a single area have been found to comprise several separate cortical maps.

Figure 8.22 completes the chapter by comparing the traditional serial, hierarchical model that began the chapter with a parallel, multiple-representation, hierarchical model that better illustrates current thinking about sensory systems.

— Food for Thought

1. In this chapter, I have tried to emphasize the similarities between various sensory systems. These similarities raise an interesting question: Would it be possible to build devices that convert sounds and sights to patterns of vibration so that the deaf and the blind could ''hear'' and ''see'' through their skin? How might one accomplish this?

ADDITIONAL READING

Those interested in the possibility of hearing and seeing through the skin (see Food for Thought) will enjoy the following two articles:

Brooks, P. L., Frost, B. J., Mason, J. L., & Gibson, D. M. (1986). Continuing evaluation of the Queen's University tactile vocoder. II: Identification of open set sentences and tracking narrative. *Journal of Rehabilitation Research and Development, 23*, 129–138.

Craig, J. C. (1977). Vibrotactile pattern perception: Extraordinary observers. *Science, 196*, 450–452.

More detailed coverage of many of the topics introduced in this chapter is provided by Chapters 23, 24, 25, 26, 31, and 32 in:

Kandel, J. H., & Schwartz, J. H. (1985). *Principles of neuroscience.* New York: Elsevier.

KEY TERMS

To help you study the material in this chapter, all of the key terms—those that have appeared in bold type—are listed and briefly defined here.

Ageusia. The inability to taste.

Agnosia. A specific inability to recognize sensory stimuli of particular classes; patients whose poor performance on recognition tests can be attributed to gross sensory, verbal, or intellectual deficits are excluded from this diagnosis.

Anosmia. Inability to smell.

Anterolateral system. The part of the somatosensory system ascending in the anterolateral area of spinal white matter; the anterolateral system transmits signals related to pain and temperature.

Asomatognosia. The failure to recognize parts of one's own body.

Association cortex. According to classical models of perception, areas of cortex that receive input from more than one sensory system.

Astereognosia. The inability to recognize objects by touch.

Auditory agnosia. Impaired capacity to recognize nonverbal sounds in the absence of significant sensory deficits, intellectual deterioration, or language-related difficulties.

Auditory nerve. The eighth cranial nerve, which carries signals from the hair cells rooted in the basilar membrane.

Basilar membrane. Part of the organ of Corti in which the hair cell receptors are embedded.

Blindsight. The ability of cortically blind subjects to perform visually mediated tasks without conscious awareness.

Chorda tympani. The branch of the cranial facial nerve (VII) that carries gustatory information from the anterior two-thirds of the tongue.

Cochlea. The long, coiled structure of the inner ear, which houses the basilar membrane and the auditory receptors.

Cocktail-party phenomenon. Our ability to monitor the contents of one conversation while consciously focusing on another.

Collicular-pulvinar pathway. A visual pathway that is thought to play a role in detection and localization of objects in space.

Completion. When a person with a scotoma views a figure that is partly in the scotoma, the visual system often "fills in" or completes the missing portion of the signal.

Dermatome. The area of the body innervated by the dorsal roots of a given segment of the spinal cord.

Dorsal column. A column of ascending somatosensory white matter in the dorsal portion of the spinal cord.

Dorsal-column medial-lemniscus system. A major pathway by which information about touch and proprioception ascends to the medulla.

Dorsal column nuclei. Medullar nuclei on which ascending dorsal-column axons synapse.

Endorphins. Endogenous (internally produced) opiates.

Exteroceptive sensory system. One of the five sensory systems that receive information about conditions outside the body (vision, touch, hearing, taste, and smell).

Flavor. The combined impression of taste and smell.

Free nerve endings. Anatomically unspecialized cutaneous receptors, which detect pain and skin temperature changes.

Gate-control theory. The theory that signals descending from the brain activate neural gating circuits in the spinal cord that block incoming pain signals.

Glabrous skin. Hairless skin.

Gustatory nucleus. A medullar nucleus on which the gustatory afferent fibers terminate.

Hair cells. The receptors of the auditory system.

Hair receptors. Receptors at the base of hair roots that respond to movements of the hair.

Hemianopsic. Patients with a scotoma covering half their field of vision.

Incus. The anvil ossicle.

Inferotemporal cortex. The cortex of the inferior temporal lobe.

Interoceptive sensory system. A sensory system that receives information about conditions inside the body (e.g., the vestibular system).

Macular sparing. Damage to the visual cortex often spares the ability to see images received by the macula (the central portion of the retina).

Malleus. The hammer ossicle.

Medial dorsal nucleus. The nucleus of the thalamus to which the neurons in the olfactory bulb project.

Medial lemniscus. The pathway of the dorsal-column medial-lemniscus system between the dorsal column nuclei and the ventral posterior nucleus of the thalamus.

Meissner corpuscle. A touch receptor located just beneath the outermost layer of glabrous skin.

Merkel receptor. A touch receptor that responds continuously to long, unchanging tactile stimuli.

Olfactory bulbs. The first cranial nerves; they are the terminals for the axons of olfactory receptor cells, and their output goes primarily to the olfactory paleocortex.

Olfactory mucosa. The membrane that lines the upper nasal passages and contains the olfactory receptor cells.

Organ of Corti. The auditory receptor organ; it comprises the basilar membrane, the hair cells, and the tectorial membrane.

Ossicles. Small bones of the middle ear.

Oval window. The cochlear membrane that transfers vibrations from the ossicles to the fluid of the cochlea.

Pacinian corpuscle. The largest and most deeply positioned cutaneous receptor.

Parallel processing. When information can flow from one component of a system to another by several routes.

Perception. The higher order process of integrating, recognizing, and interpreting complex patterns of sensations.

Periaqueductal gray (PAG). Area around the cerebral aqueduct, which contains opiate receptors; stimulation of the PAG produces analgesia in laboratory animals.

Perimetry. The method used to map scotomas.

Pheromone. A chemical that is released by one animal and affects the behavior of its conspecifics.

Posterior parietal cortex. An area of association cortex that receives input from the visual, auditory, and somatosensory systems.

Prestriate cortex. The area of secondary visual cortex that almost totally surrounds primary visual cortex.

Primary sensory cortex. The area of cortex in a sensory system that is the primary recipient of input from the thalamus.

Prosopagnosia. An inability to recognize faces that is not attributable to general sensory, verbal, or intellectual deficits.

Retinotopic. To be organized according to the spatial map of the retina.

Round window. The cochlear membrane that allows the pressure created in the fluid of the cochlea to dissipate.

Ruffini corpuscle. A touch receptor that responds continuously to long, unchanging tactile stimuli.

Scotoma. An area of blindness in the visual field.

Secondary sensory cortex. The area (or areas) of cortex in a sensory system that receives major input from the primary sensory cortex of the same system, but not from any other sensory systems.

Semicircular canals. Receptive organs of the vestibular system.

Sensation. The simple process of detecting the presence of individual stimuli.

Serial model. A model in which information flow between the components can occur by only one route.

Somatosensory homunculus. The somatosensory map constituting the primary somatosensory cortex.

Somatotopically. Organized by body region.

Spinoreticular tract. The tract of the anterolateral system that projects to the reticular formation.

Spinotectal tract. The tract of the anterolateral system that projects to the tectum.

Spinothalamic tract. The tract of the anterolateral system that projects to the ventral posterior nucleus of the thalamus.

Stapes. The stirrup ossicle.

Stereognosis. The identification of objects by touch.

Taste buds. Clusters of taste receptors.

Tectorial membrane. The cochlear membrane that rests on the hair cells.

Timbre. The quality of a sound.

Tonotopic. To be laid out according to the frequency of sound; the cochlea and the auditory cortex are tonotopic structures.

Trigeminal nerve. The cranial nerve that carries somatosensory information from the face.

Tympanic membrane. The ear drum.

Ventral posterior nucleus. A thalamic relay nucleus in both the somatosensory and gustatory systems.

Vestibular system. The sensory system that detects changes in the direction and intensity of head movements, and contributes to the maintenance of balance via its output to the motor system.

Visual agnosia. A failure to recognize visual stimuli that is not attributable to sensory, verbal, or intellectual impairment.

9

The Sensorimotor System

Yesterday, I was standing in a checkout line at the local market. I furtively scanned the headlines on the prominently displayed magazines—WOMAN GIVES BIRTH TO CAT; FLYING SAUCER LANDS IN CLEVELAND SHOPPING MALL; HOW TO LOSE 20 POUNDS IN 2 DAYS. Then, my mind began to wander, and I started to think about writing this chapter. That is when I began to watch Rhonda's movements and to wonder about the neural system that controlled them. Rhonda was the cashier—the best in the place.

I was struck by the complexity of even her most simple responses. As she deftly transferred a bag of tomatoes to the scale, there was a coordinated adjustment in almost every part of her body. In addition to her obvious finger, hand, arm, and shoulder movements, coordinated movements of her head and eyes tracked her hand to the tomatoes; and there were adjustments in the muscles of her feet, legs, trunk, and other arm, which kept her from lurching forward. The accuracy of these intricate patterns of responding suggested that they were guided by the pattern of visual, somatosensory, and vestibular changes that accompanied them—the term *sensorimotor* in the title of this chapter formally recognizes that two-way communication between sensory and motor systems is essential for effective behavior (cf. Brooks, 1986; Goodale, 1983).

As my purchases flowed through her left hand, Rhonda registered the prices with her right hand and bantered with Rick, "the bagger." I was intrigued by how little of what

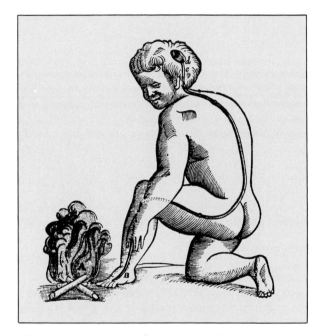

Rhonda was doing appeared to be under conscious control. She seemed to make general decisions about which items to pick up and where to put them, but she never seemed to give any thought to the exact means by which these decisions were carried out. It did not concern her that every reaching response could be made in infinite combinations of finger, wrist, elbow, shoulder, and body adjustments. Part of Rhonda's sensorimotor system—perhaps her cortex—seemed to issue conscious general commands to another part of the system, which unconsciously produced the specific patterns of muscular responses needed to carry them out. The automaticity of her performance was a far cry from the slow, effortful, considered responses that had characterized her first days at the market. Somehow experience had integrated her individual movements into smooth sequences, and it seemed to have transferred the movements' control from a mode that involved conscious effort to one that did not.

I was suddenly jarred from my contemplations by a voice. "Sir, excuse me, sir, that will be $18.65," Rhonda said, with just a hint of delight at catching me in mid-daydream. I hastily paid my bill, muttered "Thank-you," and scurried out of the market. As I write this, I am smiling both at my own embarrassment and at the thought that Rhonda has unknowingly introduced you to three principles of sensorimotor control that are themes of this chapter: (1) The sensorimotor system is hierarchically organized. (2) Motor output is guided by sensory input. (3) Practicing a response se-

quence changes the nature and the locus of its sensorimotor control.

This chapter is organized around the hierarchical model of the sensorimotor system depicted in Figure 9.1. Notice the close correspondence between the levels of the model and the sections of the chapter:

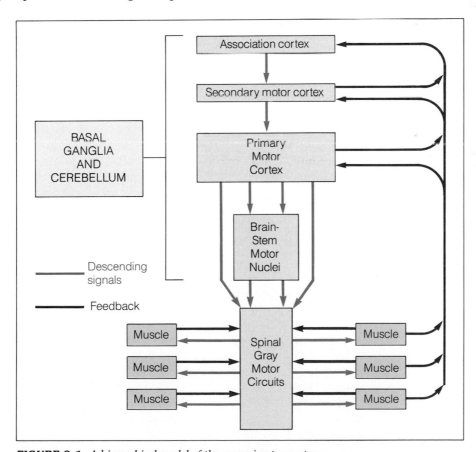

FIGURE 9.1 *A hierarchical model of the sensorimotor system.*

9.1 Three Principles of Sensorimotor Function

Before describing the neural components of the model presented in Figure 9.1, let's consider in more detail the three principles that govern its operation—the three principles already introduced by Rhonda. Remarkably, these principles are analogous to the principles that govern the operation of a large, efficient company.

The Sensorimotor System Is Hierarchically Organized

The final output of both the sensorimotor system and the executive hierarchy of a large, efficient company is directed by commands cascading down through the levels of a hierarchy from the highest level, the association cortex or president, via various routes to the lowest level, the muscles or the workers. Like the orders issued from the office of a company president, the directions that emerge from the association cortex are general goals rather than specific plans of action. Neither association cortices nor presidents routinely get involved in the details. The association cortex or the president can exert direct control over the lower levels of their respective hierarchies if they so choose—the cortex may inhibit an eye-blink reflex to enable the insertion of a contact lens and a president may personally make a delivery to an important customer—but such instances are the exception rather than the rule. The main advantage of this arrangement is that the higher levels of the hierarchy are left free to perform more complex functions.

Motor Output Is Guided by Sensory Input

Efficient companies continuously monitor the market. More importantly, they continuously monitor the profitability of their own activities, and they use this information to fine-tune them. The sensorimotor system does the same. As a behavioral sequence is initiated, the eyes, the somatosensory receptors in the skin, muscles, joints, and skin, and the organs of balance (the semicircular canals of the inner ear; see Chapter 8) all monitor its progress and feed the sensory changes produced by the movement back into sensorimotor circuits. In most instances, this **sensory feedback** plays a major role in directing the continuation of the response. The only responses that are not normally influenced by sensory feedback are brief, all-or-none, high-speed movements (i.e., *ballistic movements*), such as swatting a fly.

Motor output in the absence of just one kind of sensory feedback—the feedback carried by the somatosensory nerves of the arms—was studied both in monkeys in which the dorsal roots from the arm had been severed (Taub, 1976) and in G.O., a former darts champion who had suffered from an influenza-like infection that had destroyed the somatosensory nerves of his arms, while leaving his motor nerves intact (Rothwell, Traub, Day, Obeso, Thomas, & Marsden, 1982). In both studies, the subjects, without their usual somatosensory feedback, experienced a variety of sensorimotor problems. For example, G.O. had great difficulty performing intricate responses such as doing up his buttons or picking up coins, even under visual guidance. Other difficulties resulted from his inability to adjust his motor output in the light of unanticipated external disturbances; for example, he could not keep from spilling a cup of coffee if somebody brushed against him. However, G.O.'s greatest problem was his inability to maintain a constant level of muscle contraction.

> The result of this deficit was that even in the simplest of tasks requiring a constant motor output to the hand, G.O. would have to keep a visual check on his progress. For example, when carrying a suitcase, he would frequently glance at it to reassure himself that he had not dropped it some paces back. However, even visual feedback was of little use to him in many tasks. These tended to be those requiring a constant force output such as grasping a pen whilst writing or holding a cup. Here, visual information was insufficient for him to be able to correct any errors that were developing in the output since, after a period, he had no indication of the pressure that he was exerting on an object; all he saw was either the pen or cup slipping from his grasp. (Rothwell et al., 1982, p. 539)

Most readjustments in motor output occurring in response to sensory feedback are controlled by the lower levels of the sensorimotor hierarchy. For example, if a cup of coffee began to slip from your grasp, there would be an instantaneous increase in the strength of your grip. The point is that because the sensorimotor system does not have to transmit sensory information about the impending accident to the cortex and await for return instructions, it can respond almost instantly. In the same way, large companies run more efficiently if the clerks do not have to check with the company president each time they encounter a minor problem.

Learning Changes the Nature and Locus of Sensorimotor Control

When a company is just starting up, each individual decision is made by the company president after careful consideration. However, as the company develops, many individual actions are coordinated into sequences of prescribed procedures that are routinely carried out by junior executives. Similar changes occur during sensorimotor learning. During the initial stages of motor learning, each individual response is performed under conscious control. For example, as a beginning skier goes into a turn, each movement—the pole plant, the shift in weight from the inside edge of the downhill ski to the outside edge of the uphill ski, and then the ankle roll that transfers the weight to the inside edge—is performed individually under conscious control. However, after several years of practice, these individual responses become organized into continuous integrated sequences of action that flow smoothly and are adjusted by sensory feedback without any conscious regulation. If you think for a moment about the various sensorimotor skills that you have acquired (e.g., typing, swimming, knitting, basketball playing, dancing, piano playing), you will better appreciate that the organization of individual responses into continuous motor programs and the transfer of their control to lower levels of the nervous system characterizes most forms of sensorimotor learning.

9.2 Posterior Parietal Association Cortex

Before an effective, purposeful movement, such as picking up a cup, can be initiated, certain sensory information is required. For example, the nervous system must know the original positions of the parts of the body that are to be moved, and it must know the positions of any external objects with which the body is going to interact. The current thinking (e.g., Cheney, 1985; Ghez, 1985; Humphrey, 1979) is that the **posterior parietal cortex** is involved in the integration of such sensory information. You may recall from Chapter 8 that the posterior parietal cortex is classified as *association cortex* because it receives major input from more than one sensory system.

Three lines of evidence support the view that the posterior parietal cortex plays an important role in integrating the sensory information that is necessary for initiating voluntary responses. The first line of evidence is neuroanatomical. As indicated in Figure 9.2, the posterior parietal cortex receives input from the sensory cortices of three sensory systems involved in defining the spatial location of parts of the body and external objects: the somatosensory system, the visual system, and the auditory system. And in turn, it sends major projections to the secondary motor cortex in the frontal lobes.

The second line of evidence supporting the view that the posterior parietal cortex integrates the sensory information necessary for the initiation of voluntary movement has come from studies (e.g., Bushnell, Goldberg, & Robinson, 1981; Goldberg & Bushnell, 1981; Leinonen, Hyvärinen, Nyman, & Linnankoski, 1979; Leinonen & Nyman, 1979; Lynch, Mountcastle, Talbot, & Yin, 1977; Motter & Mountcastle, 1981) in which the activity of single neurons in the posterior parietal cortex of monkeys was recorded during the presentation of various objects to the monkeys and during the responses of the monkeys to the objects. Three types of posterior parietal neurons have been found that are of particular interest in the present context. One type of posterior parietal neuron discharges at high rates only when the subject is reaching for an object, and a second type becomes highly active only during the manual exploration of objects of interest—neither type of neuron is activated by objects in the absence of

FIGURE 9.2 *The major neural input and output of the posterior parietal cortex of humans.*

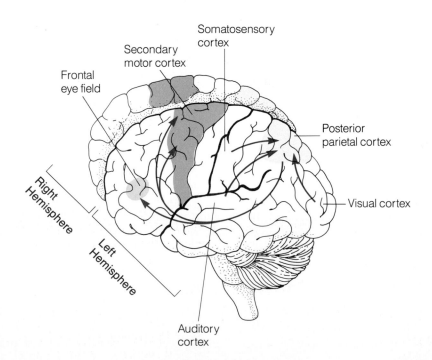

reaching or by reaching movements in the absence of objects. A third type of posterior parietal neuron seems to direct eye movements. The neurons of this type fire rapidly just before and during eye movements directed toward objects suddenly appearing in the visual field, but not during similar eye movements made in the absence of such objects. The part of the posterior parietal cortex that contains these eye-movement neurons projects to the **frontal eye fields,** which play a major role in the control of eye movement (see Figure 9.2).

The third line of evidence that suggests that the posterior parietal cortex integrates the spatial information necessary to initiate voluntary movement comes from the assessment of the behavioral deficits of patients and monkeys with unilateral damage to the posterior parietal area (e.g., Denny-Brown & Chambers, 1958; Deuel, 1977; Ettlinger & Kalsbeck, 1962). A number of specific deficits have been reported, such as difficulty in recognizing objects placed in the hand contralateral to the lesion (contralateral **astereognosia**), and inaccurate movements of the arm, hand, and fingers contralateral to the lesion. However, it is the posterior-parietal-lobe syndromes of apraxia and contralateral neglect that are the most noteworthy.

Apraxia

The first systematic descriptions of apraxia were published around the turn of the century by Leipmann. Leipmann was struck by the fact that some of his neurological patients could not perform specific hand movements when requested to do so out of context, but could spontaneously perform the very same movements with no apparent difficulty. Today the term **apraxia** is generally used to refer to any deficit of voluntary movement that is not attributable to paralysis, weakness, or some other simple motor deficit, or to deficits in comprehension or motivation (cf. Benton, 1985). Depicted in Figure 9.3 are two objective tests on which apraxic patients have extreme difficulty, the **Kimura Box Test** (Kimura, 1977) and the **Serial Arm Movements and Copying Test** (Kolb & Milner, 1981).

One of the most important features of apraxia is that although it is frequently associated with unilateral damage to the left parietal lobe, the symptoms are typically bilateral. This suggests that the left parietal lobe plays a special role in sensorimotor function that is not shared by the right parietal lobe. In contrast, lesions of the right parietal lobe disrupt constructional movements—that is, movements designed to assemble individual components of an object to form a whole. Patients with right parietal lobe lesions have difficulty completing the *block design subtest* of the Wechsler Adult Intelligence Scale (WAIS), in which blocks with patterns on them must be assembled to form a particular overall design; and they also have difficulty doing jigsaw puzzles, such as those of the WAIS *object assembly* subtest (see Chapter 4). Patients who display deficits on such tests of constructional ability are said to have **constructional apraxia.** Figure 9.4 is a drawing of a 1917 photograph of a patient with constructional apraxia.

Contralateral Neglect

One of the most intriguing effects of brain damage is a syndrome termed **contralateral neglect** (see Heilman, Watson, & Valenstein, 1985), in which there is a severe disturbance of the patient's ability to respond to visual, auditory, and somatosensory stimuli on the side of the body contralateral

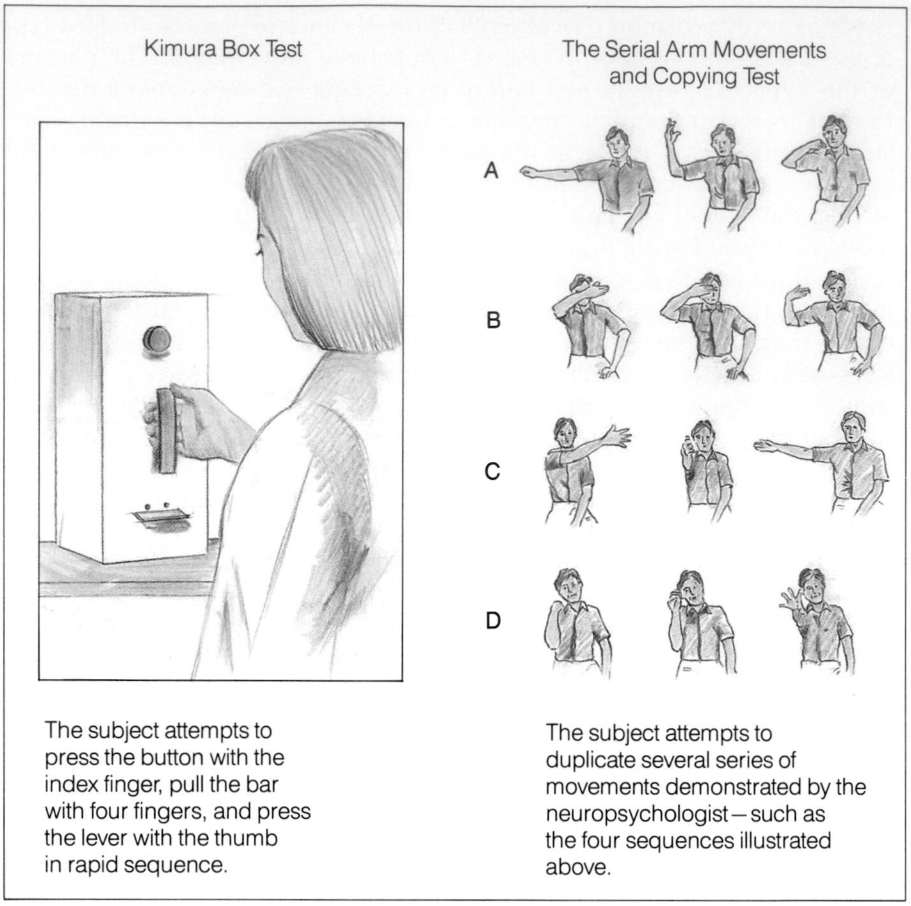

Kimura Box Test

The Serial Arm Movements
and Copying Test

A

B

C

D

The subject attempts to press the button with the index finger, pull the bar with four fingers, and press the lever with the thumb in rapid sequence.

The subject attempts to duplicate several series of movements demonstrated by the neuropsychologist—such as the four sequences illustrated above.

FIGURE 9.3 *The Kimura Box Test and the Serial Arm Movements and Copying Test. (Adapted from Kimura, 1977, and Kolb & Whishaw, 1985.)*

FIGURE 9.4 *A drawing of a photograph published in 1917 of a patient with constructional apraxia. This war veteran is clearly having difficulty duplicating the stack of blocks on his left. (Adapted from Poppelreuter, 1917.)*

to the side of the lesion. Contralateral neglect is often associated witn large lesions of the right parietal lobe (see Heilman & Watson, 1977). Typical of extreme forms of the contralateral neglect syndrome is the case of Mrs. S.,[1] an intelligent woman who suffered a massive stroke to the posterior portions of the right hemisphere.

> She has totally lost the idea of 'left', with regard to both the world and her own body. Sometimes she complains that her portions are too small, but this is because she only eats from the right half of the plate—it does not occur to her that it has a left half as well. Sometimes, she will put on lipstick, and make up the right half of her face, leaving the left half completely neglected: it is almost impossible to treat these things, because her attention cannot be drawn to them. . . .

> . . . she has worked out strategies for dealing with her [problem]. She cannot look left, directly, she cannot turn left, so what she does is turn right—and right through a circle. Thus she requested, and was given, a rotating wheelchair. And now if she cannot find something which she knows should be there, she swivels to the right, through a circle, until it comes into view. . . . If her portions seem too small, she will swivel to the right, keeping her eyes to the right, until the previously missed half now comes into view; she will eat this, or rather half of this, and feel less hungry than before. But if she is still hungry, or if she thinks on the matter, and realises that she may have perceived only half of the missing half, she will make a second rotation till the remaining quarter comes into view.

9.3 Secondary Motor Cortex

The posterior parietal association cortex is thought to contribute to the production of purposeful voluntary movement by defining the spatial coordinates that guide such behavior. However, something else is required before an effective movement can be initiated: a plan of action that specifies the sequence of muscle contractions needed to accomplish the desired end. The development of this plan appears to be carried out by two distinct areas of *secondary motor cortex* (areas of motor cortex that receive major projections from areas of association cortex and send major projections to the primary motor cortex): the **supplementary motor area** (SMA) and the **premotor cortex**. Figure 9.5 illustrates the location of these two areas and their major projections into the ipsilateral primary motor cortex. They also project to the primary motor cortex of the contralateral hemisphere via the corpus callosum.

Supplementary Motor Area

The supplementary motor area was first discovered by Penfield and his colleagues as they mapped the cortex of conscious neurosurgical patients with electrical stimulation (e.g., Penfield & Rasmussen, 1950). When Penfield stimulated an area at the top of the frontal lobes just in front of the primary motor cortex, complex movements of the body were elicited.

---

[1]From *The Man Who Mistook His Wife for a Hat and Other Clinical Tales* (pp. 73–74) by Oliver Sacks, 1985, New York: Summit Books. Copyright © 1970, 1980, 1983, 1984, 1985 by Oliver Sacks. Reprinted by permission of Summit Books, a division of Simon & Schuster.

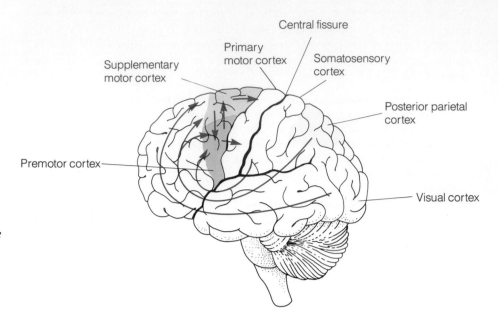

FIGURE 9.5 *The location of the supplementary motor area and premotor cortex of the human brain. Major projections from both areas terminate in the primary motor cortex.*

These movements were frequently, but not always, contralateral to the site of stimulation. He called this area of the frontal lobe, which is largely hidden from view on the medial surface of each hemisphere, the supplementary motor area. Subsequent stimulation and microelectrode recording studies of the supplementary motor area of monkeys (e.g., Brinkman & Porter, 1983; Tanji & Kurata, 1983) have confirmed Penfield's initial impression that the supplementary motor area is **somatotopically organized;** that is, they confirmed that different parts of the supplementary motor area are associated with complex movements of different parts of the body.

Support for the view that the supplementary motor area is involved in the planning of voluntary movements comes from the observation that responses of single neurons in the supplementary motor areas of monkeys frequently precede by several milliseconds the performance of the specific voluntary responses with which they are associated. Further support for this view comes from studies showing that both monkeys and humans with supplementary motor area lesions have difficulty sequencing movements properly. For example, Brinkman (1984) found that monkeys with unilateral lesions of the supplementary motor area had difficulty picking up a peanut with their contralateral hand; all of the individual reaching and grasping movements of the contralateral arm, hand, and fingers were appropriate, but they were poorly coordinated with one another. These same monkeys had particular difficulty coordinating the movements of their two hands. For example, during a test in which a morsel of food was lodged in a hole in a small horizontal piece of clear plastic, the monkeys with unilateral supplementary motor area lesions continually pushed the food through and let it drop to the floor, as illustrated in Figure 9.6. In contrast, the control monkeys obtained the food by putting one hand under the hole and pushing the food into it from above with a finger of the other hand.

The neuroanatomical connections of the supplementary motor area are consistent with the idea that it fulfills a complex integrative sensorimotor function. The supplementary motor area receives input from cortical sen-

Normal monkey getting the piece of food.

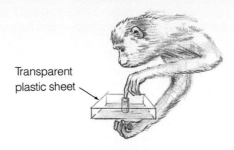

Transparent
plastic sheet

Monkey with a unilateral supplementary
motor cortex lesion losing the food.

Piece of food falling
to the ground.

FIGURE 9.6 *Illustration of the deficit in bimanual coordination produced by unilateral supplementary motor area lesions. (Adapted from Brinkman, 1984.)*

sory areas, primarily the somatosensory cortex, both directly and via the posterior parietal lobe, and it receives feedback from several subcortical motor structures. In addition to its major bilateral projections to the primary motor cortex, the supplementary motor area projects to the somatosensory cortex, the posterior parietal cortex, and to a variety of subcortical motor structures.

Premotor Cortex The premotor cortex lies anterior to the primary motor cortex and lateral to the supplementary motor area (see Figure 9.5). Its neuroanatomical organization suggests that its function is intimately related to that of the supplementary motor area. Like the supplementary motor area, the premotor cortex is somatotopically organized and projects bilaterally to the primary motor cortex and to a variety of subcortical motor structures. The premotor and supplementary motor areas are reciprocally innervated; that is, they each send neural projections to the other.

Although the supplementary motor area and premotor cortex are similarly connected to most structures, the sensory input received by the premotor cortex is primarily visual, and that of the supplementary motor area is primarily somatosensory. If a monkey is going to reach for an object that is placed in front of it, some premotor neurons respond as soon as the object appears, whereas others respond just before the reaching movement

Monkeys with a left secondary motor cortex lesion continually try to reach through the clear plastic to get the food.

Monkeys with no lesion readily learn to obtain the food beneath the plastic floor by reaching around through the hole.

FIGURE 9.7 *Monkeys with unilateral lesions of both the premotor and supplementary motor cortex could not perform this task with their contralateral arms. Instead of reaching around through the hole in the plastic floor to obtain the food, they reached directly for the food and repeatedly banged their hand on the plastic. (Adapted from Moll & Kuypers, 1977.)*

is initiated (Brinkman & Porter, 1983; Weinrich & Wise, 1982). Such anticipatory activity provides strong support for the idea that the premotor cortex has a complex motor-programming function.

Humans and monkeys with premotor damage commonly display a *grasp reflex;* each time the palm of the hand is touched, the hand immediately closes with an exaggerated grasping movement. This symptom of premotor damage indicates that the function of the premotor cortex is not restricted to complex visual-motor planning, and it also provides a good illustration of one way by which higher levels of the sensorimotor hierarchy can exert control over lower circuits. Presumably, there is a functional spinal grasp-reflex circuit in all of us, which would always be activated by palmar stimulation if it were not for the inhibitory effect of the premotor cortex. Lesions of the premotor cortex apparently remove this inhibition.

The motor-programming role played by secondary motor cortex was demonstrated by Moll and Kuypers (1977) in a study of monkeys with unilateral lesions of both premotor and supplementary motor cortex. As illustrated in Figure 9.7, the task of the monkeys was to reach through a hole in a sheet of clear plastic to obtain food on the other side of the sheet. The intact control monkeys, or the experimental monkeys using their ipsilateral arms, readily accomplished this task. However, when an experimental monkey used an arm contralateral to its lesion, it reached directly for the food and repeatedly banged its hand on the plastic sheet.

9.4 Primary Motor Cortex

The **primary motor cortex,** which is located in the *precentral gyrus* of the frontal lobe (see Figure 9.8), is strategically placed in the sensorimotor hierarchy. It is the major point of convergence of cortical sensorimotor signals, and it is the major point of departure of these signals from the cortex into lower levels of the sensorimotor system.

The Motor Homunculus

The somatotopic layout of the human motor cortex was first inferred in the mid-1800s, long before the advent of modern neuroscience. Hughlings Jackson, regarded by many as the father of neuroscience, observed that some human epileptics with discrete areas of damage to the frontal lobe had motor seizures that began in a part of the body contralateral to the lesion and systematically spread through the body from its point of origin. For example, a motor seizure that started as a tremor in the contralateral fingers might begin to involve the hand, then the wrist, then the arm, then the shoulder, and so on, until it involved much, or all, of the body. On the basis of such focal motor seizures (see Chapter 5)—frequently referred to as *Jacksonian seizures*—Jackson correctly inferred that the progression of epileptic seizures through the body reflected a disturbance spreading over a motor area in the frontal cortex that was somatotopically organized. Direct support for this inference was provided by Fritsch and Hitzig's 1870 observation that electrical stimulation of different parts of the precentral gyrus of dogs produced contractions of different contralateral muscles. In 1937, Penfield and Boldrey reported a similar finding in human patients who were stimulated during the course of neurosurgery. The somatotopic layout of the human primary motor cortex, commonly referred to as the **motor homunculus,** is illustrated in Figure 9.8. Notice that most of the primary motor cortex is dedicated to the control of parts of the body, such as the hands and mouth, that are capable of intricate movements. More

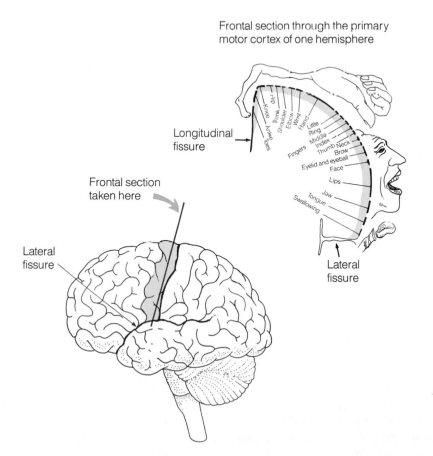

Frontal section through the primary motor cortex of one hemisphere

Longitudinal fissure

Frontal section taken here

Lateral fissure

Lateral fissure

FIGURE 9.8 *The motor homunculus: the somatotopic map of human primary motor cortex. Stimulation of sites in the primary motor cortex elicits movement in the indicated parts of the body. (Adapted from Penfield & Rasmussen, 1950.)*

recent research has revealed that in monkeys—and thus presumably in humans—there are two different areas in the primary motor cortex of each hemisphere that control the contralateral hand (see Stick & Preston, 1983).

The primary motor cortex receives indirect somatosensory, visual, and auditory input via the posterior parietal cortex, the supplementary motor area, and the premotor cortex. In addition, it receives substantial somatosensory input directly from the primary somatosensory cortex. Each site in the primary motor cortex controls the movements of a particular group of muscles and receives somatosensory information from these muscles and from the joints that they influence. But there is one notable exception to this general rule. One of the hand areas in the primary motor cortex of each hemisphere receives input from receptors in the skin rather than from receptors in the muscles and joints. Presumably this adaptation is the basis for the highly developed stereognosic abilities of your hands. Close your eyes, and explore an object with your hands. Notice how **stereognosis,** the process of identifying objects by touch, is based on a complex interplay between motor responses and the somatosensory stimulation produced by them. As a result, damage to the primary motor cortex, which eliminates a patient's ability to make independent finger movements, produces deficits in stereognosis. It also reduces the speed and force of a patient's movements.

The Cortical Blood Flow Studies

Roland and his colleagues (Roland & Larsen, 1976; Roland, Larsen, Lassen, & Skinhøj, 1980; Roland, Skinhøj, Lassen, & Larsen, 1980) measured changes in the flow of blood into different areas of the cortex of human patients as they participated in different sensorimotor activities. The rationale for their method is based on the finding that blood flow increases in those regions of the nervous system that are particularly active. To measure regional blood flow in the cortex of conscious human subjects, an inert, slightly radioactive chemical, *xenon 133,* was injected into the carotid artery, and then the accumulation of radioactivity in various parts of the ipsilateral cortex was measured with a bank of 254 *scintillation counters* placed next to the head. For each subject, regional cortical blood flow was first measured during a 45-second period of relaxation with eyes shut. Then, 20 minutes later, a second injection was administered, but this time the subject engaged in some activity during the 45-second test period. The output of each scintillation counter was fed into a computer that assessed the amount of change between the baseline resting condition and the test condition.

The major results of Roland et al.'s regional blood flow studies are summarized in Figure 9.9, which shows the pattern of regional blood flow associated with four different activities of the contralateral hand: (1) The first display shows the areas of increased blood flow in the left hemisphere during a prescribed sequence of finger movements of the right hand. There was increased blood flow in the supplementary motor area, in the hand area of the primary motor cortex, and to a lesser degree, in the primary somatosensory cortex and the frontal cortex. (2) The second display shows the increases in blood flow that occurred when the subjects remained motionless, but thought of performing the same sequence of right-hand finger movements. The increases were restricted to the supplementary motor area. (3) The third display illustrates the left-hemisphere changes

1. Areas activated by a series
   of right hand-finger movements

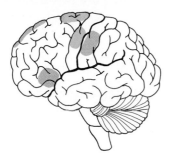

2. Areas activated by just
   thinking about performing
   a series of right-hand finger
   movements.

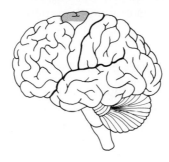

3. Areas activated by making a
   series of forceful flexions
   with one finger of right hand.

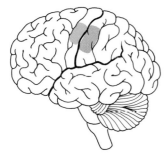

4. Areas activated by the
   performance of a finger maze
   with the right hand.

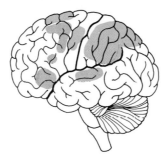

Blood flow increased more than 25%

Blood flow increased significantly,
but less than 25%

FIGURE 9.9 *The sensorimotor regions of the cortex of the human left hemisphere that display increases in blood flow during various voluntary activities associated with the right hand. (Adapted from Roland, et al., 1980.)*

associated with forceful repeated flexions of one finger of the right hand. There was an increase in blood flow of the hand areas of the primary motor and somatosensory areas. (4) The fourth display illustrates the blood flow changes associated with the performance of a *finger maze test* in which subjects moved their finger along a wire grid in response to verbal commands from the experimenter (e.g., "move two spaces to the left, move one space forward, move three spaces back," and so on). Finger-maze performance was associated with increases in the supplementary, premotor, and posterior parietal areas and in the primary motor and somatosensory areas. There was also activation of the auditory cortex and the frontal eye fields.

Roland and his colleagues concluded that the primary motor and somatosensory areas can execute a series of simple repeated movements without the contribution of other cortical areas, that the supplementary motor areas are responsible for developing and executing programs for controlling the sequencing of patterns of motor output, that the premotor areas are involved in the learning of new motor programs or in the modification of existing ones, that the parietal lobes provide sensory information to the supplementary and premotor areas, and that the supplementary and premotor areas exert most of their influence through the primary motor cortex. On this note, the chapter descends into the subcortical levels of the sensorimotor hierarchy.

9.5 Cerebellum and Basal Ganglia

The cerebellum and the basal ganglia are both important sensorimotor structures, but neither is part of the system of structures through which signals originating in the cortex descend to the sensorimotor circuits of the spinal cord. Instead, both the cerebellum and the basal ganglia interact with several different levels of the sensorimotor system, and in so doing they coordinate and modulate its activities.

Cerebellum

The complexity of the cerebellum is suggested by its structure. Although it constitutes only 10% of the mass of the brain, it contains more than half of the neurons. The cerebellum is thought to receive information about plans of action from the primary motor cortex, about descending motor signals from the brain stem motor nuclei, and about feedback from motor responses via the somatosensory and vestibular systems. By comparing these three sources of input, the cerebellum is thought to correct ongoing movements that deviate from their intended course, via its output to the brain stem motor nuclei. It is also presumed to modify central motor programs, and in so doing, to play a major role in sensorimotor learning.

The consequences of diffuse cerebellar damage are devastating. The patient loses the ability to precisely control the direction, force, velocity, and amplitude of individual movements, and to modify central motor programs so that patterns of motor output can be adapted to changing conditions. There is extreme difficulty maintaining steady postures (e.g., standing), and attempts to do so frequently lead to tremor. There are also severe disturbances in balance, gait, the articulation of speech, and the control of eye movements.

Basal Ganglia

The basal ganglia are not as large as the cerebellum, nor do they contain as many neurons, but in one sense they are more complex. Unlike the cerebellum, which is organized systematically in lobes, columns, and layers, the basal ganglia are a maze of axons, dendrites, and cell bodies with little overall pattern.

The connections of the basal ganglia suggest that, like the cerebellum, they perform a modulatory function. The basal ganglia are part of a loop that receives cortical input from various parts of the cortex and transmits it back to the motor cortex via the thalamus. They contribute no fibers to descending motor pathways.

One theory of basal ganglia function is that they play an important role in the modulation of slow movements. This theory was initially inferred from the observation of patients with Parkinson's disease (see Chapter 5), a disorder associated with degeneration of dopamine terminals in the striatum (i.e., the caudate and putamen). Parkinson's disease is character-ized by an extreme difficulty in initiating and coordinating slow, purpose-ful movements, such as walking, yet Parkinson's patients can perform simple rapid responses at normal speed. A study in monkeys supports this theory, and it supports the theory that the cerebellum plays a complemen-tary role in modulation of fast movements (DeLong & Strick, 1974). Intact monkeys were trained to push a lever rapidly in response to one light and slowly in response to another. Basal ganglia neurons were more likely to be active during slow movements, and cerebellar neurons were more likely to be active during fast movements.

Before continuing your descent into the sensorimotor circuits of the spinal cord, review the sensorimotor circuits of the cortex, cerebellum, and basal ganglia by completing the following statements.

1. Most of the direct sensory input received by the premotor area comes from the _____ system.

2. Direct sensory input to the supplementary motor area comes primar-ily from the _____ system.

3. The _____ cortex is the main point of de-parture of motor signals from the cortex.

4. Humans and monkeys with _____ cortex damage dis-play a grasp reflex.

5. The foot area of the motor homunculus is in the _____ fissure.

6. Visual, auditory, and somatosensory input converges on the _____ cortex.

7. An area of the frontal cortex called the _____ plays a major role in the control of eye movement.

8. Contralateral neglect is often associated with large lesions of the _____ lobe.

9. The secondary motor area that is largely hidden from view on the medial surface of each hemisphere is the _____ area.

10. According to the model presented in the preceding pages, the _____ cortex plays an important role in integrating the sensory information that is responsible for initi-ating voluntary responses.

11. The _____ are part of a loop that receives input from various cortical areas and transmits it back to the motor cortex via the thalamus.

12. Although the _____ constitutes only 10% of the mass of the brain, it contains more than half the neurons.

9.6 Descending Motor Pathways

Axons descending from the cortex reach the spinal cord by four different pathways. Two pathways descend in the dorsolateral portion of the spinal cord, and two descend in the ventromedial area of the spinal cord.

The Dorsolateral Corticospinal Tract and the Dorsolateral Corticorubrospinal Tract

One group of axons leaving the primary motor cortex descends along with some axons from the secondary motor cortex and the somatosensory cortex to the lower medulla, decussates in the so-called *medullary pyramids,* and then descends in the contralateral dorsolateral spinal white matter. This group of axons constitutes the **dorsolateral corticospinal tract.** Most notable among the neurons of the dorsolateral corticospinal tract are the Betz cells. **Betz cells** are extremely large neurons of the primary motor cortex, most of which have cell bodies in the finger and thumb areas of the motor homunculus and axons that synapse in the ventral horn of the spinal gray matter on the motor neurons that innervate the muscles of the fingers and thumbs. Only primates and the other few mammalian species that are capable of moving their digits independently of one another (e.g., hamsters and raccoons) have primary motor cortex neurons that synapse directly on motor neurons. Most axons of the dorsolateral corticospinal pathway synapse on small interneurons of the intermediate gray matter that, in turn, project to the motor neurons of the distal muscles (e.g., wrist, hands, fingers, and toes).

The other group of axons leaving the primary motor cortex and descending in the contralateral dorsolateral spinal white matter constitute the **dorsolateral corticorubrospinal tract,** thus named because it synapses in the red nucleus of the midbrain—*rubro* is an adjective that refers to the red nucleus. The axons of the red nucleus cells then decussate and descend through the medulla, where some of them terminate in the nuclei of those cranial nerves that control the muscles of the face. (The motor control of the face is obviously an extremely important and interesting topic, but for the sake of simplicity, it is largely ignored in this chapter.) The remaining axons of the dorsolateral corticorubrospinal tract meet up again with those of the dorsolateral corticospinal tract in the lower part of the medulla, and they descend together in the dorsolateral portion of the spinal cord. The axons of the dorsolateral corticorubrospinal tract terminate on interneurons that in turn innervate motor neurons projecting to the distal muscles of the arms and legs. The two divisions of the dorsolateral motor pathway, the direct dorsolateral corticospinal motor tract and the indirect dorsolateral corticorubrospinal tract, are illustrated schematically in Figure 9.10.

The Ventromedial Corticospinal Tract and the Ventromedial Cortico-Brainstem-Spinal Tract

Just as there are two major divisions of the dorsolateral motor pathway, one direct (the corticospinal tract) and one indirect (the corticorubrospinal tract), there are two major divisions of the ventromedial motor pathway, one direct and one indirect. The direct ventromedial pathway is the **ventromedial corticospinal tract,** and the indirect one—as you might infer from its cumbersome, but descriptive name—is the **ventromedial cortico-brainstem-spinal tract.**

The long axons of the ventromedial corticospinal tract descend ipsilaterally from the primary motor cortex directly into the ventromedial areas of the spinal white matter. As each axon of the ventromedial corticospinal

FIGURE 9.10 *The two divisions of the dorsolateral motor pathway: the dorsolateral corticospinal tract and the dorsolateral corticorubrospinal motor tract. The projections from only one hemisphere are shown.*

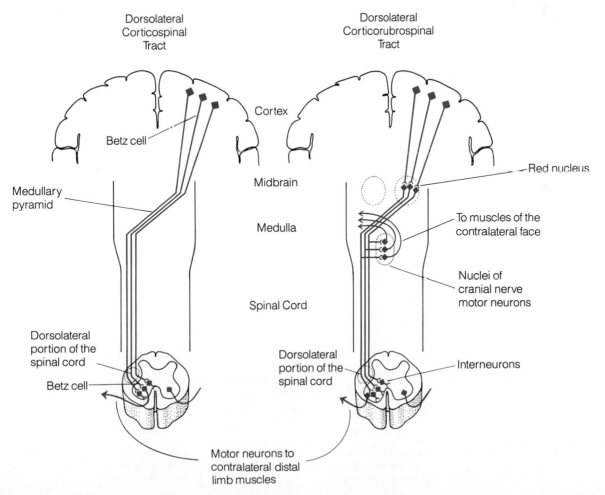

tract descends, it branches diffusely and innervates the interneuron circuits in several different spinal segments on both sides of the spinal gray matter. The less direct ventromedial cortico-brainstem-spinal tract comprises motor cortex axons that feed bilaterally into a complex network of brain stem structures. The axons of this complex brain stem motor network then descend in the ventromedial portion of the spinal cord; each side of the spinal portion of the tract carries some signals originating in the left hemisphere and some originating in the right hemisphere, and each neuron synapses on the interneurons of several different spinal cord segments.

The two divisions of the descending ventromedial pathway, the direct ventromedial corticospinal tract and the indirect ventromedial cortico-brainstem-spinal tract, are illustrated in Figure 9.11.

What brain stem structures interact with the ventromedial cortico-brain stem-spinal tract? There are four major ones: (1) the **tectum,** which receives auditory and visual information about spatial location; (2) the **vestibular nucleus,** which receives information about balance from receptors in the semicircular canals of the inner ear; (3) the **reticular formation,** which contains, among other things, motor programs for complex species-common movements such as walking, swimming, and jumping; and (4) the motor nuclei of those cranial nerves that control the muscles of the face.

FIGURE 9.11 *The two divisions of the ventromedial motor pathway: the ventromedial corticospinal tract and the ventromedial cortico-brain stem-spinal tract. The projections from only one hemisphere are shown.*

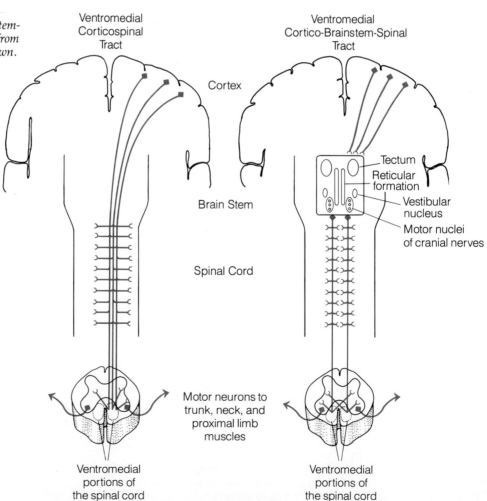

The descending dorsolateral and ventromedial pathways are similar in that each is composed of two major tracts, one whose axons descend directly to their destination in the spinal cord and another whose axons synapse in the brain stem on neurons that in turn descend to the spinal cord. However, the two dorsolateral tracts differ from the two ventromedial tracts in two major respects: (1) The two ventromedial tracts are much more diffuse; many of their axons innervate interneurons on both sides of the spinal gray matter and in several different segments, whereas the axons of the two dorsolateral tracts terminate in the contralateral half of one segment, sometimes directly on a motor neuron. (2) The motor neurons activated by the two ventromedial tracts project to the muscles of the trunk and proximal muscles of the limbs (e.g., shoulder muscles), whereas the motor neurons activated by the two dorsolateral tracts project to the distal musculature.

Because all four of the descending sensorimotor tracts originate in the cortex, they are all presumed to mediate voluntary movement; however, major differences in their routes and destinations suggest that they have different functions. This difference was first demonstrated in two experiments published by Lawrence and Kuypers in 1968. In their first experiment, Lawrence and Kuypers cut the left and right dorsolateral corticospinal tracts of their monkey subjects at the point at which they decussate in the medulla. Following surgery, these monkeys could stand, walk, and climb quite normally; however, their ability to use their limbs for activities other than walking and climbing was impaired. For example, their reaching movements were weak and poorly directed, particularly in the first few days following the surgery. Although there was a substantial improvement in their reaching over the ensuing weeks, two other deficits remained unabated. First, they never regained the ability to move their fingers independently of one another; when they picked up pieces of food, they did so by using all of their fingers as a unit, as if they were glued together. And second, they never regained the ability to release objects from their grasp; as a result, once they picked up a piece of food, they often had to root for it in their hand like a pig rooting for truffles in the ground. In view of this latter problem, it is remarkable that they had no difficulty releasing their grasp on the bars of their cage when they were climbing. This point is extremely important because it shows that the same behavior performed in different contexts can be controlled by different parts of the central nervous system.

In their second experiment, Lawrence and Kuypers (1968b) made one of two additional lesions in the monkeys from their first experiments, whose dorsolateral corticospinal tracts had already been transected. In half the monkeys, the dorsolateral corticorubrospinal tract was transected in the second experiment. Although these monkeys could stand, walk, and climb quite well after their second surgery, when they were sitting, their arms hung limply by their sides (remember that monkeys normally use their arms for standing and walking). In those few cases in which the monkeys did use an arm for reaching, they used it like one would use a rubber-handled rake—they threw it out from the shoulder to draw small objects of interest back along the floor.

The other half of Lawrence and Kuypers's monkeys had both of their ventromedial tracts transected in the second experiment. In contrast to the first group, these subjects had severe postural abnormalities. They had great difficulty walking or even sitting. If they did manage to sit or stand without clinging to the bars of their cages, the slightest disturbance, such as a loud noise, frequently made them fall. Although they had some use of their arms, the additional transection of the two ventromedial tracts eliminated their ability to control their shoulders. When they fed, they did so with elbow and whole-hand movements while their upper arms hung limply by their sides.

What do these classic experiments tell us about the roles of the various descending sensorimotor tracts in the control of movement? They suggest that the two ventromedial tracts are involved in the control of posture and whole-body movements (e.g., walking and climbing) and that they can exert control over the limb movements involved in such activities. In contrast, both dorsolateral tracts, the corticospinal tract and the corticorubrospinal tract, control the reaching movements of the limbs; this redundancy was presumably the basis of the good recovery of limb movement after the initial lesions of the corticospinal dorsolateral tract. However, only the corticospinal division of the dorsolateral system is capable of independent movements of the digits.

9.7 Sensorimotor Spinal Circuits

Muscles

Motor units are the smallest units of motor activity that can be produced by the central nervous system. Each motor unit comprises a single motor neuron and all of the individual skeletal muscle fibers that it innervates. When the motor neuron fires, all the muscle fibers of its unit contract together; hence the name, motor unit. Motor units differ appreciably in the number of muscle fibers they contain; it is those with the fewest—those of the fingers and face—that permit the highest degree of selective motor control.

A skeletal muscle comprises hundreds of thousands of thread-like muscle fibers all bound together in a tough membrane and attached to a bone by a *tendon. Acetylcholine* released by the motor neuron at the *neuromuscular junction* activates the target site on the fiber, the **motor end-plate,** and causes the fiber to contract. Accordingly, muscles can only pull; they cannot push. All of the motor neurons that innervate the fibers of a single muscle are called its **motor pool.**

Although it is an oversimplification (see Gollinick & Hodgson, 1986), skeletal muscle fibers are often considered to be of two basic types: fast and slow. *Fast muscle fibers,* as you might guess, are those that contract and relax quickly. Although they are capable of generating great force, they fatigue quickly because they are poorly vascularized, which gives them a pale color. In contrast, *slow muscle fibers,* although slower and weaker, are capable of more sustained contraction because they are more richly vascularized and hence much redder. Muscles have different proportions of fast and slow fibers depending on their function.

Many skeletal muscles belong unambiguously to one of two categories. There are **flexors,** which act to bend or flex a joint, and there are **extensors,** which act to straighten or extend it. Figure 9.12 illustrates the *biceps* and *triceps,* the flexors and extensors, respectively, of the elbow joint (see

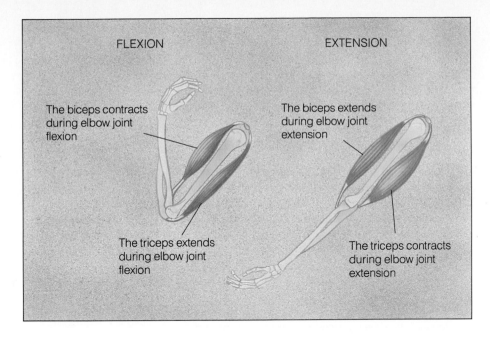

FLEXION

EXTENSION

The biceps contracts during elbow joint flexion

The biceps extends during elbow joint extension

The triceps extends during elbow joint flexion

The triceps contracts during elbow joint extension

FIGURE 9.12 *The biceps and triceps are the flexors and extensors, respectively, of the elbow joint.*

Chapter 4). Any two muscles whose contraction produces the same movement, be it flexion or extension, are said to be **synergistic,** whereas those that act in opposition, like the biceps and triceps, are said to be **antagonistic.**

To understand how muscles work, it is important to realize that muscles have elastic, rather than inflexible, cable-like properties. If you think of an increase in muscle tension as being analogous to an increase in the tension of an elastic joining two bones, you will immediately appreciate that muscle contraction can be of two types. As illustrated in Figure 9.13, excitation of a muscle can simply increase the tension that it exerts on two bones

FIGURE 9.13 *Isometric and dynamic muscular contraction.*

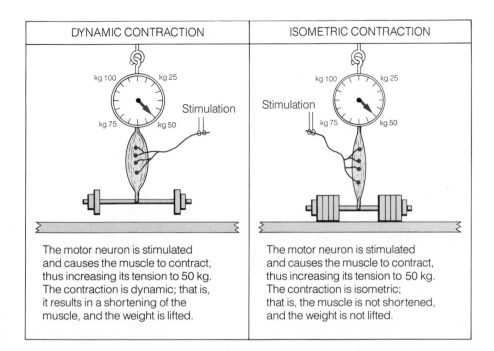

DYNAMIC CONTRACTION

ISOMETRIC CONTRACTION

kg 100   kg 25

kg 75   kg 50

Stimulation

kg 100   kg 25

Stimulation

kg 75   kg 50

The motor neuron is stimulated and causes the muscle to contract, thus increasing its tension to 50 kg. The contraction is dynamic; that is, it results in a shortening of the muscle, and the weight is lifted.

The motor neuron is stimulated and causes the muscle to contract, thus increasing its tension to 50 kg. The contraction is isometric; that is, the muscle is not shortened, and the weight is not lifted.

FIGURE 9.14 *Golgi tendon organs and muscle spindle receptors. Each tendon has many Golgi tendon organs, and each muscle has many muscle spindles. One of each is schematically represented here to illustrate the following point: Because Golgi tendon organs are hooked up in series with the muscles and muscle spindles are hooked up in parallel with muscles, Golgi tendon organs respond to muscle tension (muscle pull) and muscle spindles respond to muscle length.*

without shortening and pulling them together. This is termed an **isometric contraction.** Or the contraction can be a **dynamic contraction;** that is, it can decrease the length of the muscle, thus pulling together the bones to which it is connected. The tension in a muscle can be increased either by increasing the number of neurons in its motor pool that are firing, by increasing the firing rates of those that are active, or by a combination of the two.

The Receptor Organs of Muscles

The activity of skeletal muscles is monitored by two kinds of receptors: Golgi tendon organs and muscle spindles. **Golgi tendon organs** are embedded in the tendons, which connect each skeletal muscle to bone, and **muscle spindles** are embedded in the muscle tissue itself. Because of their different locations Golgi tendon organs and muscle spindles respond to different changes in the muscle. As illustrated in Figure 9.14, Golgi tendon

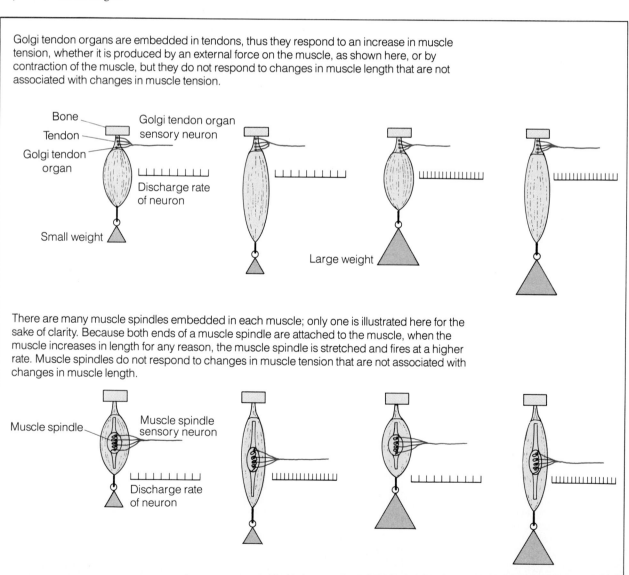

organs respond to increases in muscle tension (i.e., to the pull of the muscle on the tendon), but they are completely insensitive to changes in muscle length. In contrast, muscle spindles respond to changes in muscle length, but they do not respond to changes in muscle tension. One function of the Golgi tendon organ is to protect muscles from damage. When a great force is applied to a Golgi tendon organ, it excites inhibitory interneurons in the spinal cord that cause the muscle to relax.

Figure 9.15 is a schematic diagram of the *muscle-spindle feedback circuit*. Examine it carefully. Notice that each muscle spindle has its own threadlike muscle called an **intrafusal muscle,** which is innervated by its own motor neuron called an **intrafusal motor neuron.** Why would a receptor have its own muscle and its own motor neuron? The reason becomes apparent when you consider what would happen to a muscle spindle without intrafusal motor input. Figure 9.16A schematically represents such a hypothetical muscle spindle. Without its intrafusal motor input, a muscle spindle would fall slack each time that the skeletal muscle (also called the **extrafusal muscle**) contracted. In this slack state, the muscle spindle could not do its job, which is to respond to slight changes in extrafusal muscle length. As illustrated in Figure 9.16B, the intrafusal motor neuron solves this problem by shortening the intrafusal muscle each time that the extrafusal muscle becomes shorter, thus keeping enough tension on the middle, stretch-sensitive portion of the muscle spindle so that it remains sensitive to slight changes in the length of the extrafusal muscle.

The Stretch Reflex

When the word *reflex* is mentioned, the first thing that comes to many people's minds is an image of themselves sitting on the edge of their doctor's examination table having their knees rapped with a little rubber-headed hammer. The resulting leg extension is called the **patellar tendon reflex** (*patella* means *knee*). The patellar tendon reflex is a type of **stretch reflex,** that is, a reflex elicited by an external stretching force on a muscle.

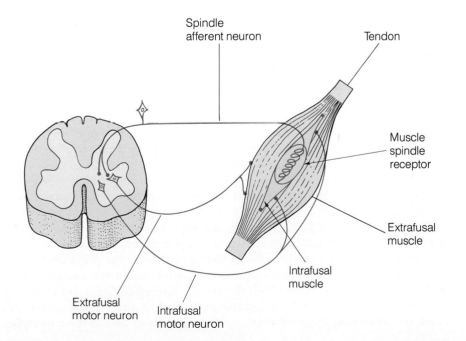

FIGURE 9.15 *The muscle-spindle feedback circuit.*

If there were no intrafusal motor neuron, the muscle spindle would fall slack when the extrafusal muscle contracted, and in this state the muscle spindle could not perform its function of responding to slight changes in extrafusal muscle length.

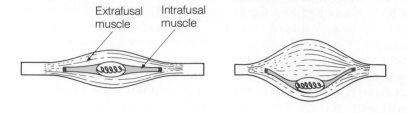

Extrafusal muscle   Intrafusal muscle

FIGURE 9.16 *The function of the intrafusal motor neuron. Represented in A is a hypothetical muscle spindle without an intrafusal motor neuron. In B, the intrafusal motor neuron adjusts the tension on the muscle spindle during changes in length of the extrafusal muscle so that it remains sensitive to slight changes in muscle length.*

To combat this problem, the intrafusal motor neuron shortens the intrafusal muscle accordingly each time that the extrafusal muscle contracts, thus maintaining the sensitivity of the muscle spindle to changes in extrafusal muscle length.

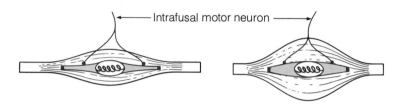

Intrafusal motor neuron

When the doctor strikes the tendon of your knee, the extensor muscle running along your thigh is stretched. This initiates the chain of events depicted in Figure 9.17. The sudden stretch of the thigh muscle stretches its muscle-spindle stretch receptors, and this in turn intiates a volley of action potentials that is carried from the stretch receptors into the spinal cord by **spindle afferent neurons** via the *dorsal root*. This volley of action potentials excites motor neurons in the ventral horn of the spinal cord, which respond by sending action potentials back to the muscle whose stretch originally excited them. The arrival of these impulses back at the starting point results in a compensatory muscle contraction, which produces a sudden leg extension.

The conditions under which the patellar tendon reflex is typically elicited in the doctor's office—that is, with the muscles of the leg completely relaxed and the stretch elicited by a sharp blow—are designed to make the reflex readily observable. However, because these conditions are so artificial, they do little to communicate the adaptive significance of the stretch reflex. In real life situations, the purpose of the stretch reflex is to keep external forces from altering the intended position of the body. When an external force, such as somebody brushing against your arm while you are holding a cup of coffee, causes an unanticipated extrafusal muscle stretch, the muscle-spindle feedback circuit produces an immediate compensatory contraction of the muscle that counteracts the force and keeps you from spilling the coffee—unless of course you have on your best clothes. The mechanism by which the stretch reflex maintains limb stability is illustrated in Figure 9.18. Examine Figures 9.17 and 9.18 carefully because the muscle-spindle feedback system illustrates two of the principles

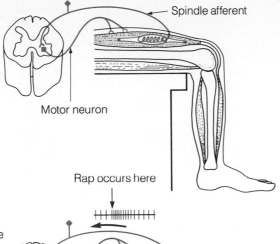

All muscles of the leg are relaxed. There is little activity in the motor neuron to the thigh muscle or in the spindle afferent from the thigh muscle.

Spindle afferent

Motor neuron

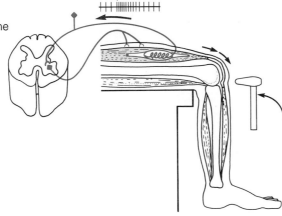

Rap occurs here

The rap on the tendon of the knee stretches the thigh muscle. This stretches the muscle spindle receptor and sends a volley of impulses along the spindle afferent.

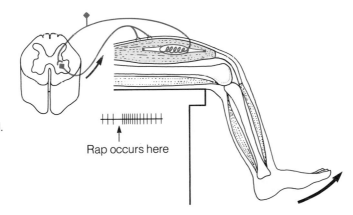

The burst of firing in the spindle afferent elicits a burst of firing in the motor neuron. This causes the thigh muscle to contract and the leg to swing forward.

Rap occurs here

FIGURE 9.17 *The elicitation of the stretch reflex. Only a single muscle spindle is depicted, but all of the muscle spindles in a muscle come into play during a stretch reflex.*

of sensorimotor system function that are the focus of this chapter: the important role played by sensory feedback in the regulation of motor output and the ability of lower circuits in the motor hierarchy to take care of "business details" without the involvement of higher levels.

The Withdrawal Reflex

We have all, at one time or another, touched something painful—a hot pot, for example—and suddenly pulled back our arm. This is the **withdrawal reflex.** Like the stretch reflex, the withdrawal reflex is *monosynaptic.* When painful stimulation is applied to the hand, the first responses are

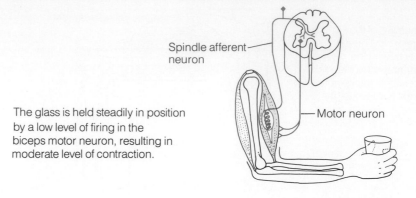

Spindle afferent neuron

Motor neuron

The glass is held steadily in position by a low level of firing in the biceps motor neuron, resulting in moderate level of contraction.

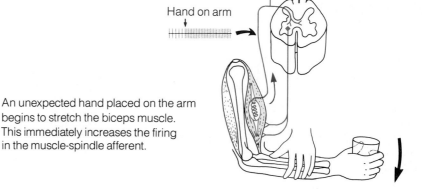

Hand on arm

An unexpected hand placed on the arm begins to stretch the biceps muscle. This immediately increases the firing in the muscle-spindle afferent.

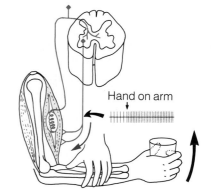

Increased firing in muscle-spindle afferent increases firing in motor neuron, which increases tension in biceps and automatically counteracts the force of the unexpected hand and keeps the arm in its original position.

Hand on arm

FIGURE 9.18 *The mainte-nance of limb position by the muscle-spindle feedback system.*

recorded in the motor neurons of the arm flexor muscles about 0.8 millisecond later, about the time that it takes a signal to cross one synapse. Can you imagine what would happen if the information about a hot pot had to be relayed to the cortex for consideration before the hand could be withdrawn?

Reciprocal Innervation

Reciprocal innervation is an important principle of spinal cord circuitry. It refers to the fact that antagonistic muscles are innervated in such a way that when one is contracted, the other relaxes to permit a smooth, unim-

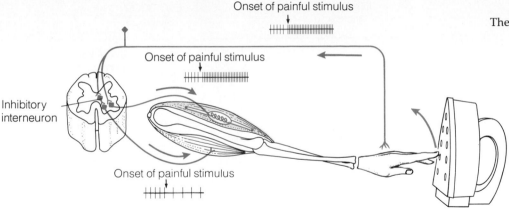

Onset of painful stimulus

Onset of painful stimulus

Inhibitory
interneuron

Onset of painful stimulus

FIGURE 9.19 *The reciprocal innervation of antagonistic muscles in the arm. During a withdrawal reflex, elbow flexors are excited, whereas extensors are inhibited.*

peded motor response. Figure 9.19 illustrates the role of reciprocal innervation in the withdrawal reflex. "Bad news" of a sudden painful event in the hand arriving in the dorsal horn of the spinal cord has two effects. The signals excite the motor neurons of the elbow flexors, and they excite an inhibitory interneuron. The excitation of the interneuron in turn inhibits the motor neurons projecting to the antagonists of the elbow flexors, the elbow extensors. Thus, a single sensory input produces a coordinated pattern of motor output; agonists and antagonists are automatically coordinated by the internal circuitry of the spinal cord.

Movements are quickest when there is simultaneous excitation of all agonists and complete inhibition of all antagonists; however, this is not the way that voluntary movement is normally produced. In practice, both agonists and antagonists are always contracted to some degree, and movements are produced by an adjustment in the level of relative **cocontraction.** Movements produced by cocontraction are smoother, and they can be stopped with precision by a slight increase in the contraction of the antagonistic muscles. Moreover, cocontraction to some extent insulates us from the effects of unexpected external forces.

Recurrent Collateral Inhibition

Like most workers, muscle fibers and the motor neurons that innervate them need an occasional break, and there are inhibitory neurons in the spinal cord that make sure that they get it. Each motor neuron branches just before it leaves the spinal cord, and this branch synapses on a small inhibitory interneuron, which synapses on the very motor neuron from which it receives its input. The inhibition produced by these local feedback circuits is called **recurrent collateral inhibition,** and the small inhibitory interneurons that mediate recurrent collateral inhibition are called the *Renshaw cells.* The consequence of recurrent collateral inhibition is that when a motor neuron fires, it produces inhibition, which makes it less likely to fire again until the inhibition has dissipated. This shifts the responsibility for the contraction of a particular muscle to other members of the muscle's motor pool. Figure 9.20 is a summary figure; it illustrates recurrent collateral inhibition and the other factors discussed in this chapter that directly influence the activity of a motor neuron, the final common motor pathway.

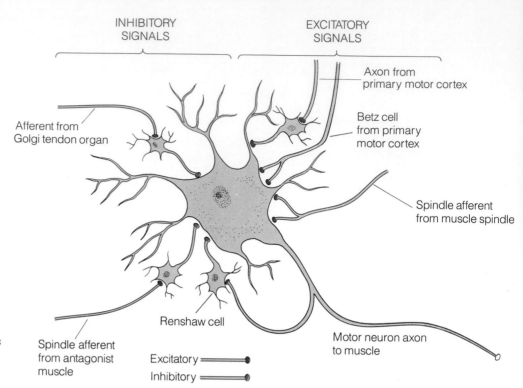

INHIBITORY
SIGNALS

EXCITATORY
SIGNALS

Axon from
primary motor cortex

Afferent from
Golgi tendon organ

Betz cell
from primary
motor cortex

Spindle afferent
from muscle spindle

Renshaw cell

Motor neuron axon
to muscle

Spindle afferent
from antagonist
muscle

Excitatory ————●

Inhibitory ————●

FIGURE 9.20 *Several signals that influence the activity of a motor neuron.*

Walking and Running: A Complex Sensorimotor Reflex

The simplicity of monosynaptic spinal reflexes, such as the stretch reflex and the withdrawal reflex, has allowed researchers—and I hope you—to gain an understanding of the kinds of circuits that mediate reflexes. However, their simplicity can be misleading—most reflexes are much more complex. Think for a moment about the complexity of the sensorimotor program needed to control an activity such as walking. Such a program must integrate visual information from the eyes, somatosensory information from the feet, knees, hips, arms, etc.; and information about balance from the semicircular canals of the inner ears to produce an integrated series of movements involving the muscles of the trunk, legs, and upper arms. The sensorimotor program for walking must also be incredibly flexible; it must be able to adjust its output immediately to changes in the slope of the terrain, to instructions from the brain to change speed, or to external forces such as a bag of groceries. Nobody has yet managed to build a robot that can come close to duplicating these feats, which we take for granted.

Grillner (1985) showed that walking is largely controlled by circuits in the spinal cord. Grillner's subjects were cats whose spinal cords had been separated from their brains by transection. He suspended the cats in a sling over a treadmill, and amazingly, when the treadmill was started so that the cats received sensory feedback like that normally accompanying walking, they began to make the complex pattern of motor movements characteristic of walking in their species.

Early in this chapter, it was pointed out that the sensorimotor system is like the hierarchy of a large, efficient company. Since then, you have learned how the executives, the supplementary motor area and premotor cortex, issue commands based on information supplied to them by the posterior parietal lobe. And you have learned how these commands are forwarded to the managing director, the primary motor cortex, for distribution over four main channels of communication, the two dorsolateral and the two ventromedial spinal motor pathways, to the metaphoric office managers of the sensorimotor hierarchy, the spinal sensorimotor circuits. Finally, in the preceding section, you learned how the spinal sensorimotor circuits direct the activities of the workers, that is, the muscles. The major role played by sensory feedback at each stage in the transmission of signals through the sensorimotor hierarchy has been emphasized throughout.

The theory on which this chapter is based is that the sensorimotor system is organized on the basis of a hierarchy of **central sensorimotor programs** (see Brooks, 1986). This theory is that the sensorimotor system does not produce activity by controlling individual muscles. In fact, only a few muscles can be individually contracted (i.e., those of the fingers and face) and even these muscles are rarely controlled in this selective fashion. The sensorimotor system is instead designed to produce functional sequences of coordinated response patterns. The central-sensorimotor-program theory suggests that all but the highest levels of the sensorimotor system have certain patterns of activity programmed into them, and that complex movements are produced by activating the appropriate combinations of these programs. Accordingly, if your association cortex decides that you might like to look at a magazine, it activates high-level programs—perhaps in motor cortex—that in turn activate lower level programs—perhaps in the brain stem—for walking, bending over, picking up, and thumbing through. These programs in turn activate specific programs in the spinal cord that control the various elements of the sequences and cause your muscles to complete the objective. Once activated, each level of the sensorimotor system is capable of operating on the basis of current sensory feedback without the direct control of higher levels. Thus, although the highest levels of our sensorimotor system retain the option of directly controlling our activities, most of the individual responses that we make are performed without direct cortical involvement, and we are barely aware of them. In much the same way, a company president who wishes to open a new branch office simply issues the command to one of her executives, and the executive responds in the usual fashion by issuing a series of commands to the appropriate people lower in the hierarchy, who in turn do the same. Each of the executives and workers of the company knows how to complete many different tasks and executes them in the appropriate fashion in the light of current conditions when instructed to do so. Good companies have mechanisms for insuring that the programs of action at different levels of the hierarchy are well coordinated and effective, and so does the sensorimotor system; this is the task of the cerebellum and basal ganglia.

How do we get our central motor programs? The results of an important experiment by Fentress (1973) indicate that some fundamental central motor programs are not learned. Fentress showed that adult mice raised from birth without forelimbs still made the patterns of shoulder movements typical of grooming in their species, and that these were well-coordinated with normal tongue, head, and eye movements. For example, they blinked each time they made the shoulder movements that would have swept their forepaws across their eyes. Fentress's study also demonstrates the importance of sensory feedback in the operation of central sensorimotor programs. The forelimbless mice, deprived of normal tongue-forepaw contact during face grooming, would often interrupt ostensible grooming sequences to lick a cage mate or even the floor.

Theories of sensorimotor learning emphasize two kinds of processes that influence central motor programs (e.g., Annett, 1985; Johnson, 1984): **response chunking** and changing the level of control. According to the response-chunking hypothesis, practice combines the central control of individual response elements into individual programs that control long sequences (or chunks) of behavior. In the novice typist, each response necessary to type a word is individually triggered and controlled, whereas in the skilled typist, sequences of letters are activated as a unit, with a marked increase in speed and continuity. An important principle of chunking is that chunks can themselves be combined into higher order chunks. For example, the responses needed to type the individual letters and digits of one's address may be chunked into longer sequences necessary to produce the individual words and numbers, and these chunks may in turn be combined so that the entire address is typed as a unit.

Shifting the level of control to lower levels of the sensorimotor system during training has two advantages. One is that it frees up the higher levels of the system to deal with more esoteric aspects of performance. For example, skilled pianists can concentrate on interpreting a piece of music because they do not have to consciously focus on pressing the right keys, and skilled secretaries can take dictation while performing other simple mental tasks (Hirst, Spelke, Reaves, Canarack, & Neisser, 1980). The other advantage is that it permits great speed because different circuits at the lower levels of the hierarchy can act simultaneously without interfering with one another. For example, the performance of a skilled typist (i.e., 120 words per minute) is possible only because the circuits responsible for activating each individual key press can become active before the preceding response has been completed (Grudin, 1983; Rummelhart & Norman, 1982).

Epilogue

Last evening I stopped off to pick up a few fresh vegetables and some fish for dinner, and I once again found myself waiting in Rhonda's line. It was the longest, but I am a creature of habit. This time I felt rather smug as I watched her. All of the reading and thinking that had gone into the preparation of this chapter had provided me with some new insights into what she was doing and how she was doing it. I wondered whether she appreciated her own finely tuned sensorimotor system as much as I. Then I hatched my plot—a little test of Rhonda's muscle-spindle feedback system. How would Rhonda's finely tuned sensorimotor system react to a bag that looked heavy, but was in fact extremely light? Next time, I would get one of those paper bags at the mushroom counter, blow it up, drop one mushroom in it, and then fold up the top so that it looked completely full. I smiled at the thought. But I wasn't the only one smiling. My daydreaming ended abruptly and the smile melted from my face as I noticed Rhonda's extended hand and her amused grin. Will I never learn?

_ Food for Thought

1. Both sensorimotor systems and large businesses are complex systems trying to survive in a competitive milieu. It is no accident that they function in similar ways. Discuss.

2. We humans tend to view cortical mechanisms as preeminent, presumably because we are the species with the largest cortices. However, one might argue from several perspectives that the lower sensorimotor circuits are more important. Discuss.

ADDITIONAL READING

For those of you interested in a more detailed introduction to the sensorimotor system, I recommend the following eight chapters:

Kandel, E., & Schwartz, J. H. (1985). _Principles of neural science_. New York: Elsevier. (Chapters 33 to 40)

The following chapters provide a neuropsychological introduction to the sensorimotor system:

Kolb, B., & Whishaw, I. Q. (1989). _Fundamentals of human neuropsychology_ (3rd ed.). New York: Freeman. (Chapters 12 & 13)

KEY TERMS

To help you study the material in this chapter, all of the key terms—those that have appeared in bold type—are listed and briefly defined here.

Antagonistic muscles. Muscles that act in opposition.

Apraxia. A loss of the ability to perform voluntary movements; apraxic patients have difficulty performing responses on request that they readily perform when they are not thinking about it.

Astereognosia. A difficulty in recognizing objects by touch that is not attributable to a simple sensory deficit or to general intellectual impairment.

Betz cells. Large neurons of the primary motor cortex that synapse directly on spinal motor neurons.

Central sensorimotor programs. Patterns of activity programmed into the sensorimotor system; complex movements are produced by activating the appropriate combinations of these programs.

Cocontraction. Under normal circumstances antagonistic muscles are both contracted to some degree.

Constructional apraxia. Inability to perform tests of construction (e.g., WAIS block designs subtest) in the absence of primary sensory deficits or general intellectual impairment.

Contralateral neglect. A disturbance of the patient's ability to respond to visual, auditory, and somatosensory stimuli on one side of the body, usually the left side of the body following damage to the right parietal lobe.

Dorsolateral corticorubrospinal tract. A descending motor tract that synapses in the red nucleus of the midbrain, decussates, and descends in the dorsolateral region of the spinal cord.

Dorsolateral corticospinal tract. The group of axons leaving the primary motor cortex, descending to the medulla, decussating in the medullary pyramids, and then descending in the contralateral dorsolateral spinal white matter.

Dynamic contraction. A contraction of a muscle that causes the muscle to shorten.

Extensors. Muscles that act to straighten or extend a joint.

Extrafusal muscle. Skeletal muscle.

Flexors. Muscles that act to bend or flex a joint.

Frontal eye fields. The areas of the frontal cortex, located just in front of the motor cortex, that play a role in the control of eye movements.

Golgi tendon organs. Receptors embedded in tendons, which are sensitive to the amount of tension in the muscle to which they are attached.

Intrafusal muscles. The muscles of the muscle spindle.

Isometric contraction. Contraction of a muscle that increases the force of its pull, but does not shorten it.

Kimura Box Test. An objective test of apraxia.

Motor end-plate. The receptive area on a muscle fiber at a neuromuscular junction.

Motor homunculus. The somatotopic map of the primary motor cortex.

Motor pool. All of the motor neurons that innervate a given muscle.

Motor units. All of the muscle fiber innervated by a single neuron.

Muscle spindles. Receptors embedded in muscle tissue, which are sensitive to muscle length.

Patellar tendon reflex. The stretch reflex elicited when the patellar tendon is struck.

Posterior parietal cortex. The cortex of the posterior parietal lobe, which is thought to receive and integrate the spatial information that guides voluntary behavior.

Primary motor cortex. The cortex of the precentral gyrus, which is the major point of departure for signals descending from the cortex into lower levels of the sensorimotor system.

Recurrent collateral inhibition. The inhibition of a neuron produced by its own activity via a collateral branch of its axon and an inhibitory interneuron; in the spinal cord, the recurrent collateral inhibition of motor neurons is mediated by Renshaw cells.

Response chunking. Practice combines the central sensorimotor programs controlling individual responses into programs that control sequences of responses (chunks of behavior).

Reticular formation. A complex network of nuclei in the core of the brain stem; among other things, it contains motor programs for complex species-common movements such as walking or swimming.

Sensory feedback. The sensory signals induced by a response that are used to guide the continuation of the response.

Serial Arm Movements and Copying Test. An objective test of apraxia.

Somatotopic. Organized according to a map of the surface of the body.

Spindle afferent neurons. Neurons that carry signals from muscle spindles into the spinal cord via the dorsal root.

Stereognosis. The process of identifying objects by touch.

Stretch reflex. A reflexive counteracting reaction to an external stretching force on a muscle.

Supplementary motor area. The area of the secondary motor cortex within and adjacent to the longitudinal fissure.

Synergistic. Producing the same joint movement.

Tectum. The division of the midbrain comprising the superior and inferior colliculi; it receives auditory and visual information about spatial location.

Ventromedial cortico-brainstem-spinal pathway. The indirect ventromedial motor pathway, which projects bilaterally to several interconnected brain stem motor structures, and then descends in the ventromedial portions of the spinal cord.

Ventromedial corticospinal pathway. The direct ventromedial motor pathway, which descends ipsilaterally from the primary motor cortex directly into the ventromedial areas of the spinal white matter.

Vestibular nucleus. The brain stem nucleus that receives information about balance from the semicircular canals.

Withdrawal reflex. The reflexive withdrawal of a limb when it comes in contact with a painful stimulus; the withdrawal reflex is monosynaptic.

10

Hormones and Sex

This chapter is about hormones and sex, a topic that holds a curious fascination for most people. Perhaps it is because we tend to hold our own sexuality in such high esteem that we are so intrigued by the fact that it depends to a large degree on the secretions of a pair of glands regarded by many as unfit topics of conversation in mixed company. Perhaps it is because we each think of our own sex as fundamental and immutable that we are fascinated by the fact that it can be altered with a snip or two and a few hormone injections. Perhaps it is the idea that our sex life might be greatly enhanced by the application of the appropriate hormones that fascinates us. For whatever reason, the topic of hormones and sex is virtually always a favorite. Some remarkable things await you in this chapter; let's go directly to them.

Hormones influence sex in two different ways: (1) by directing the development from conception to sexual maturity of the anatomical, physiological, and behavioral characteristics that distinguish one as female or male, and (2) by activating the reproduction-related behavior of sexually mature adults. The developmental and activational effects of sex hormones are dealt with separately in the second and third sections of this chapter; the first section prepares you for these topics by introducing the neuroendocrine system.

10.1 **The Neuroendocrine System**
10.2 **Hormones and Sexual Development**
10.3 **The Effects of Gonadal Hormones on Adults**

The Men-Are-Men-and-Women-Are-Women Attitude

Almost everybody brings to the topic of hormones and sex a piece of excess baggage, the men-are-men-and-women-are-women attitude —or "mamawawa." The men-are-men-and-women-are-women attitude is very seductive; it

seems so right that we are continually drawn to it without considering alternative views. Unfortunately, it is a seductive idea of the worst kind: a fundamentally wrong, seductive idea. The men-are-men-and-women-are-women attitude is the tendency to think about "femaleness" and "maleness" as discrete, mutually exclusive, complementary categories. In thinking about hormones and sex, this general attitude leads one to assume that females have female sex hormones that give them female bodies and make them do female things, and that males have male sex hormones that give them male bodies and make them do male things. Despite the fact that this men-are-men-and-women-are-women approach to hormones and sex is totally wrong, its simplicity, symmetry, and comfortable social implications continually draw us to it. Thus, this chapter grapples with it throughout.

10.1 The Neuroendocrine System

This section introduces the general principles of neuroendocrine function by focusing on the small subset of glands and hormones directly involved in sexual development and behavior. It begins with a few basic facts about hormones, glands, and reproduction; then it describes a line of research that is the basis of most of our current notions of neuroendocrine function.

Glands and Hormones

There are two types of glands: **exocrine glands,** which release substances to the outside world (e.g., sweat glands), and **endocrine glands,** which release chemicals called **hormones** into the body's general circulation. The human endocrine glands are illustrated in Figure 10.1. Hormones are also released by organs, such as the stomach, the liver, and the intestine, that are not usually considered to be part of the endocrine system; however, it is the endocrine system and in particular its sex hormones that are the focus of attention here. Once released by an endocrine gland, a hormone travels through the circulatory system until it reaches its target, the tissue on which it normally exerts its effect (e.g., the skin, an endocrine gland, sites in the nervous system).

Of particular interest to psychologists are the **neurohormones,** the hormones that interact with the nervous system. Neurohormones are like neurotransmitters in the sense that they are chemicals that influence neural activity; however, because neurohormones are released into general circulation rather than into synapses, they typically exert their effects more slowly, for a longer duration, and at greater distances from their site of release. Moreover, because there are receptors for each neurohormone in several different parts of the nervous system, the effects of neurohormones are characteristically widespread. Although it is important to appreciate these general distinctions, it is also important to realize that, as we learn more about the brain, the distinctions between hormones and neurotransmitters grow more vague. For example, it is now clear that virtually all hormones synthesized and released by endocrine glands are also synthesized and released by particular groups of neurons in the brain.

The Gonads

Central to any discussion of hormones and sex are the **gonads:** the male **testes** (pronounced TEST eez) and the female **ovaries** (see Figure 10.1). The

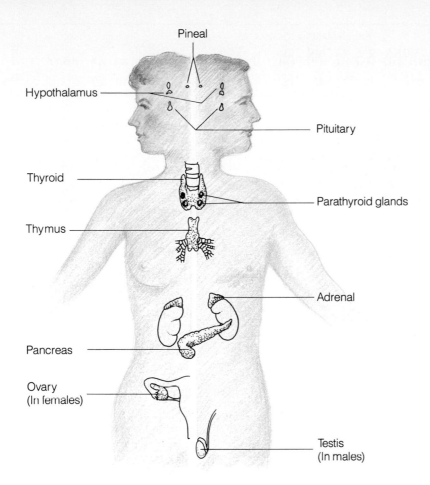

Pineal

Hypothalamus

Pituitary

Thyroid

Parathyroid glands

Thymus

Adrenal

Pancreas

Ovary
(In females)

Testis
(In males)

FIGURE 10.1 *The principal endocrine glands.*

primary function of the testes and ovaries is the production of *sperm cells* and *ova*, respectively. After **copulation** (sexual intercourse), a single sperm cell may combine with an *ovum* to form a cell called a **zygote,** which contains all of the information necessary for the growth of a complete adult organism.

With the exception of ova and sperm cells, each cell of the human body has 23 pairs of chromosomes. In contrast, the ova and sperm cells contain only half that number, one member of each of the 23 pairs. Thus, when a sperm cell fertilizes an ovum, the resulting zygote ends up with the full complement of 23 pairs of chromosomes, one of each pair from the father and one of each pair from the mother.

Of particular interest in the context of this chapter is the pair of chromosomes called the **sex chromosomes,** thus named because they contain the genetic programs that direct sexual development. The cells of females have two large x-shaped sex chromosomes, called *X chromosomes*. In males, one sex chromosome is an X chromosome, and the other is a small x-shaped chromosome called a *Y chromosome*. (There must be a good reason for calling a small x-shaped chromosome a Y chromosome, but I don't know what it is.) Consequently, the sex chromosome of every ovum is an X chromosome, whereas half the sperm cells have X chromosomes, and half have Y chromosomes (see Figure 10.2). Your gender and all its social, economic, and personal ramifications was determined by which of your

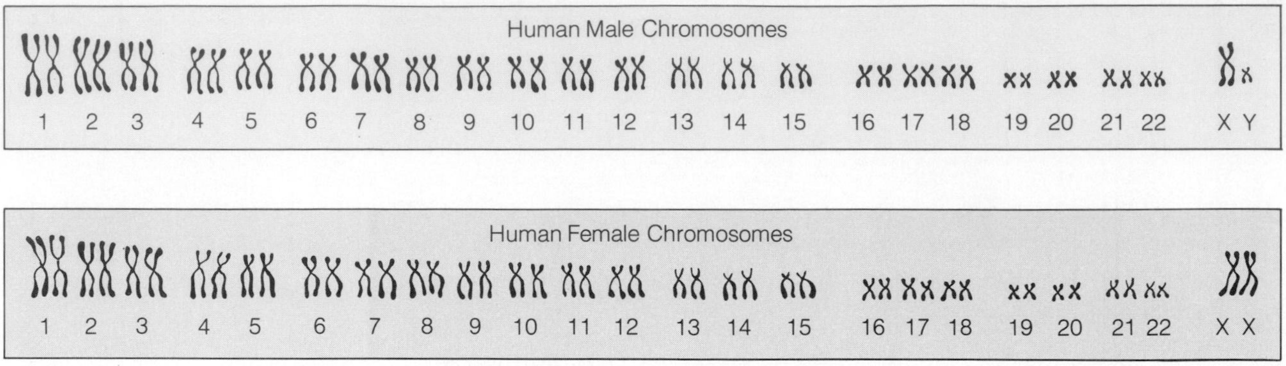

FIGURE 10.2 *The chromosomes of human females and males.*

father's sperm cells won the dash to your mother's ovum. If a sperm cell with an X sex chromosome won, you are a female; if one with a Y sex chromosome won, you are a male.

Writing this section reminded me of my grade 7 basketball team, "The Nads." The name puzzled our teacher because it was not at all like the names usually preferred by pubescent boys—names like the "Avengers," the "Marauders," and the "Vikings." Her puzzlement ended abruptly at our first game as our fans began to chant their support. You guessed it; "Go Nads, Go! Go Nads, Go!" My 14-year-old spotted-faced teammates and I considered this to be humor of the most mature and sophisticated sort. The teacher didn't.

The Gonadal Hormones

The gonads do more than create sperm and egg cells; they also produce and release hormones. Most people are surprised to learn that the testes and ovaries release the very same hormones. The two main classes of gonadal hormones are **androgens** and **estrogens; testosterone** is the most common androgen, and **estradiol** is the most common estrogen. The fact that ovaries release more estrogens than they do androgens and that testes release more androgens than they do estrogens has led to the common, but misleading, practice of referring to androgen as "the male sex hormone" and to estrogen as "the female sex hormone." This practice should be avoided because of its men-are-men-and-women-are-women implication that androgens produce maleness and that estrogens produce femaleness—they don't. The ovaries and testes also release a class of hormones called **progestins.** The most common progestin is a hormone called **progesterone,** which in females prepares the uterus and the breasts for pregnancy. Its function in males is unknown.

Sex Hormones of the Adrenal Cortex

Because the primary function of the **adrenal cortex** (the outer covering of the adrenal gland; see Figure 10.1) is the regulation of salt and glucose levels in the blood, the adrenal cortices are not generally thought of as sex glands. However, each adrenal cortex produces all of the hormones that are produced by the ovaries and testes. Most of these adrenal sex hormones are released in only small amounts, and their role in sexual development and behavior is not well understood.

The Hormones of the Pituitary

The pituitary gland is frequently referred to as the *master gland* because many of its hormones are tropic hormones. *Tropic hormones are those* whose primary function is to influence the release of hormones from other glands; *tropic* is an adjective that describes things that stimulate or change other things. For example, the **gonadotropins** are a group of pituitary tropic hormones that travel from the pituitary through the circulatory system to the gonads, where they stimulate the release of gonadal hormones.

The pituitary gland is really two glands in one, the **posterior pituitary** and the **anterior pituitary,** which fuse together during the course of embryological development. The posterior pituitary develops from a small outgrowth of hypothalamic tissue that eventually comes to dangle from the *hypothalamus* on the end of the **pituitary stalk** (see Figure 10.3). In contrast, the anterior pituitary begins as part of the same embryonic tissue that eventually develops into the roof of the mouth; during the course of development, it pinches off and migrates up to assume its position next to the posterior pituitary. It is the anterior pituitary that releases tropic hormones, and thus, it is the anterior pituitary in particular, rather than the pituitary in general, that qualifies as the master gland.

Female Gonadal Hormone Levels Are Cyclic; Male Gonadal Hormone Levels Are Steady

The major difference between the endocrine function of men and women is that in women the levels of gonadal and gonadotropic hormones go through a cycle that repeats itself every 28 days or so (see Appendix

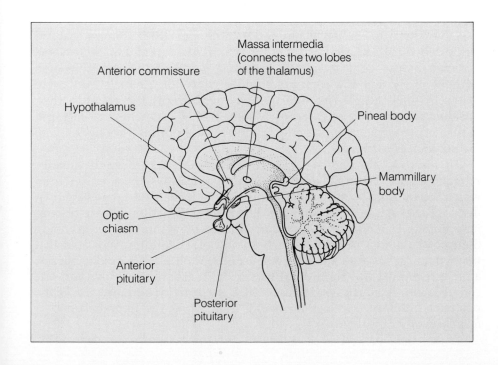

FIGURE 10.3 *A lateral view of the anterior and posterior pituitary and surrounding structures.*

VII). It is these more-or-less regular hormone fluctuations that control the female **menstrual cycle.** In contrast, human males are, from a neuroendocrine perspective, rather dull creatures; the levels of their gonadal and gonadotropic hormones change little from day to day. An interest in this fundamental difference between females and males was the stimulus for a particularly fruitful line of experiments. By the 1950s, the study of sex hormones had ascended from the loins to the pituitary, and then in the 1950s interest in the mechanisms of sex-hormone cyclicity directed the attention of researchers on upward to the brain. The ensuing study of the brain's regulation of sex-hormone cyclicity left in its wake many of our current ideas about hormonal function, two Nobel Prizes, and a general inclination for scientists to "think neuroendocrine" in situations in which "thinking endocrine" had previously been the norm. This influential line of research is the focus of the remainder of this first section of the chapter.

Because the anterior pituitary is the conductor of the endocrine orchestra, many early scientists assumed that an inherent difference between the male and female pituitary was the basis for the difference in their patterns of gonadotropic and gonadal hormone release. However, this hypothesis was discounted by a series of clever transplant studies in which female rat pituitaries were transplanted in male rats, and male rat pituitaries were transplanted in female rats (Harris & Jacobsohn, 1952). In these studies, a cycling pituitary removed from a mature female rat became a steady-state pituitary when implanted at a suitable site in a male, and a steady-state pituitary removed from a mature male began to cycle once implanted in a female. What these studies established was that anterior pituitaries are not inherently female (cyclical) or male (steady state), their patterns of hormone release are controlled by some other part of the body. The master gland seemed to have its own master. Where was it?

Neural Control of the Pituitary

The nervous system was implicated in the control of the anterior pituitary by behavioral research on female birds and other animals that are fertile only during a specific time of the year. It was found that the seasonal variation in the light-dark cycle triggered many of the fertility-related changes. If the lighting conditions under which the animals lived were reversed, for example, by transporting them across the equator, their breeding season was also reversed (Marshall, 1937). Somehow visual input to the nervous system was controlling the release of tropic hormones from the anterior pituitary.

The search for the particular neural structure that controlled the anterior pituitary turned, naturally enough, to the *hypothalamus,* the structure from which the pituitary is suspended. This shift in focus paid immediate dividends. For example, it was quickly demonstrated that the release of pituitary hormones could be triggered or blocked by stimulating or lesioning the hypothalamus, respectively. These and other findings indicated that the hypothalamus does indeed regulate anterior pituitary hormone release; all that remained was to find out how it did it. There was, however, one complication. As illustrated in Figure 10.4, the anterior pituitary, unlike the posterior pituitary, receives no neural input from the hypothalamus or from any other structure.

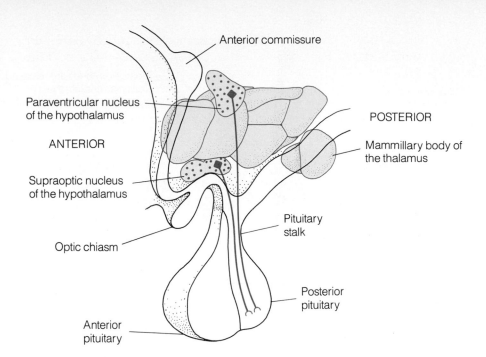

FIGURE 10.4 *The neural connections between the hypothalamus and the pituitary. The anterior pituitary has no neural connections.*

Control of the Anterior and Posterior Pituitary by the Hypothalamus

There are two different mechanisms by which the hypothalamus controls the pituitary: one for the posterior pituitary and one for the anterior pituitary. The two major hormones of the posterior pituitary, **vasopressin** and **oxytocin,** are manufactured in the cell bodies of neurons in the **paraventricular nuclei** and **supraoptic nuclei** of the hypothalamus (see Figure 10.4). They are then transported down the axons of these neurons to their terminals in the posterior pituitary and are stored there until the arrival of action potentials causes them to be secreted into the bloodstream. Neurons specialized for the release of hormones into general circulation are called **neurosecretory cells.** In women, oxytocin stimulates contractions of the uterus and the ejection of milk during suckling; its functions in men are unknown. Vasopressin facilitates the reabsorption of water by the kidneys in both sexes.

The neural control of the neuron-free anterior pituitary was more difficult to explain. Harris (1955) suggested that the release of hormones from the anterior pituitary was itself regulated by hormones released from the hypothalamus. Two findings provided early support for this idea. One was the discovery of a vascular network, the **hypothalamopituitary portal system,** that seemed well suited to the task of carrying hormones from the hypothalamus to the anterior pituitary. As illustrated in Figure 10.5, a network of hypothalamic capillaries feeds a bundle of portal veins that carries blood down the pituitary stalk into another network of capillaries in the anterior pituitary; *portal* is a general term that refers to any vein connecting one capillary network with another. The other line of evidence

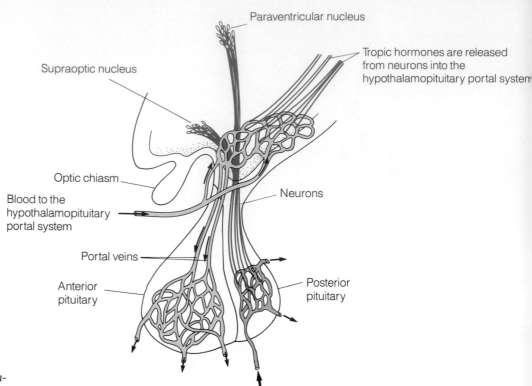

Paraventricular nucleus

Tropic hormones are released
from neurons into the
hypothalamopituitary portal system

Supraoptic nucleus

Optic chiasm

Neurons

Blood to the
hypothalamopituitary
portal system

Portal veins

Anterior
pituitary

Posterior
pituitary

FIGURE 10.5 *The hypothalamopituitary portal system.*

supporting the notion that hypothalamic hormones control the anterior
pituitary was the finding that cutting the portal veins of the pituitary stalk
disrupts the release of anterior pituitary hormones until the damaged veins
regenerate (Harris, 1955).

The Isolation and
Synthesis of Hypothalamic Hormones

It was suggested that each anterior pituitary hormone might be controlled by its own hypothalamic hormone. The putative (hypothesized)
hypothalamic hormones that were thought to exert their influence by
stimulating the release of an anterior pituitary hormone were referred to as
releasing factors; those thought to exert control by inhibiting the release of
an anterior pituitary hormone were referred to as **inhibitory factors.** Efforts to isolate these putative hypothalamic releasing and inhibitory factors
led to a major breakthrough in 1969. Guilleman and his colleagues isolated
thyrotropin-releasing hormone from the hypothalami of sheep, and
Schally and his colleagues isolated the same hormone from the hypothalami of pigs. Thyrotropin-releasing hormone triggers the release of **thyrotropin** from the anterior pituitary, which in turn stimulates the release of
hormones from the *thyroid gland.* It is difficult to appreciate the effort that
went into the initial isolation of thyrotropin-releasing hormone. Releasing
and inhibiting factors exist in such small quantities that a mountain of
hypothalamic tissue is required to extract even minute quantities. For example, Schally (1978) reported that the work of his group required over one
million pig hypothalami. And where did Schally get such a quantity of pig
hypothalami? From Oscar Mayer & Company—where else?

Why would two research teams dedicate over a decade of their lives just to accumulate a pitifully small quantity of thyrotropin-releasing hormone? The reason was that it enabled both Guilleman and Schally to determine thyrotropin-releasing hormone's chemical composition and then to develop methods of synthesizing larger quantities for research and clinical use. For their efforts in isolating, characterizing, and synthesizing thyrotropin-releasing hormone, Guilleman and Schally were each awarded a Nobel Prize in 1977.

You may have noticed a change in terminology during the preceding discussion: from "releasing factors" to **releasing hormones.** This shift reflects the usual practice of referring to a hormone as a "factor" or "substance" until it has been isolated and its chemical structure identified.

Gonadotropin-Releasing Hormone

Within the context of a chapter about hormones and sex, Schally and Guilleman's isolation and synthesis of thyrotropin-releasing hormone, a nonsex hormone, is important because it provided the ultimate confirmation that hypothalamic releasing hormones controlled the release of hormones from the anterior pituitary and because it provided the major impetus for the isolation and synthesis of **gonadotropin-releasing hormone** by Schally and his group in 1970. Gonadotropin-releasing hormone stimulates the release of both of the anterior pituitary's gonadotropins, **follicle stimulating hormone** (FSH) and **luteinizing hormone** (LH) (Schally, Kastin, & Arimura, 1971).

Feedback in the Neuroendocrine System

The hypothalamus controls the pituitary, and the pituitary in turn controls its target glands, but neuroendocrine regulation is not a one-way street. The hormones released by the target glands often feed back on the very organs that originally triggered their release: the pituitary, the hypothalamus, and related sites in the brain (see McEwen, Davis, Parsons, & Pfaff, 1979). Most of this feedback is negative. In general, the function of **negative feedback** is the maintenance of stability—increases produce compensatory decreases, and decreases produce compensatory increases. In the neuroendocrine system, the function of negative feedback is the maintenance of stable levels of circulating hormones; accordingly, high gonadal hormone levels in the blood often have effects on the hypothalamus and pituitary that decrease gonadal activity, and low levels often have effects that increase gonadal activity. Although negative feedback is much more common, there are also **positive feedback** effects in the neuroendocrine system; in some instances increases in the levels of a circulating hormone produce further increases and decreases produce further decreases. For example, just before **ovulation** (the release of a mature ovum from the package of cells, or **follicle,** in which it develops), injection of a small dose of estradiol produces an increase, rather than the usual decrease, in the release of estradiol from the ovary, by stimulating the release of gonadotropin-releasing hormone from the hypothalamus and by increasing the sensitivity of the anterior pituitary to the gonadotropin-releasing hormone that reaches it (e.g., Arimura & Schally, 1971; Castro-Vazquez & McCann, 1975; Martin, Tyrey, Everett, & Fellows, 1974). It has been suggested that a shift from the usual negative feedback mode to a positive feedback mode may be the key factor in producing the surge in the levels of progesterone and estradiol in the blood of females that is responsible for triggering ovulation (see Appendix VII for details of the hormone fluctuations that occur during the **menstrual cycles** of human females). A similar mechanism has been proposed to account for the surge of gonadal hormones that occurs in both males and females during puberty.

Pulsatile Hormone Release

In the last decade, evidence has accumulated that virtually all hormones are released from endocrine glands in pulses (Karsch, 1987). It is now clear that hormones do not continuously seep from endocrine glands into the bloodstream; they are discharged several times per day in large surges, which typically last no more than a few minutes each. Accordingly, hormone levels in the blood are regulated by changes in the frequency and duration of the hormone pulses (Reame, Sauder, Kelch, & Marshall, 1984). The direct consequence of **pulsatile hormone release** is that there are often large minute-to-minute fluctuations in the levels of circulating hormones in a given subject (e.g., Koolhaas, Schuurman, & Wiepkema, 1980). Accordingly, when the pattern of male gonadal hormone release is referred to as steady, it means that there are no systematic changes in circulating gonadal hormone levels from day to day, not that the levels never vary.

A Summary Model
of Gonadal Endocrine Regulation

Pictured in Figure 10.6 is a summary model of the regulation of gonadal hormones. According to this model, the brain controls the release of gonadotropin-releasing hormone from the hypothalamus into the hypothalamopituitary portal system, which carries it to the anterior pituitary. In the anterior pituitary, the gonadotropin-releasing hormone stimulates the release of gonadotropins, which are carried by the circulatory system to the gonads. In response to the gonadotropins, the gonads release androgens, estrogens, and progestins, which feed back onto the pituitary and hypothalamus to regulate subsequent gonadal hormone release. Armed with this general perspective of neuroendocrine function, you are ready to consider how hormones influence sexual development (Section 10.2) and adult sexual behavior (Section 10.3).

10.2 Hormones and Sexual Development

You have undoubtedly noticed that humans are *dimorphic*, that they come in two standard models: female and male. This section describes how hormones control the development of those physical characteristics that identify us as male or female. The last part of this section is special because it focuses on three cases of exceptional sexual development. There is another reason for focusing on these three cases other than the fact that they are extraordinarily interesting; this reason is expressed concisely by the widely misunderstood proverb, "the exception proves the rule." Most people think that the proverb means that the exception "proves" the rule in the sense that it establishes its truth, but this is clearly wrong—the truth of a rule is challenged, not confirmed, by exceptions to it. The word *proof*

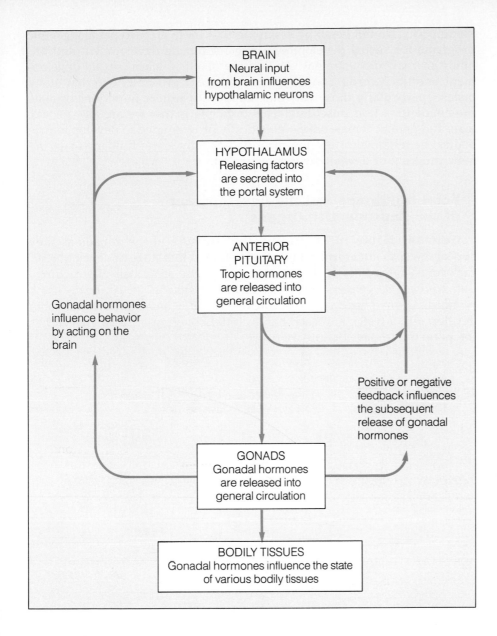

FIGURE 10.6 *Summary model of the regulation of gonadal hormones.*

comes from the Latin *probare*, which means *to test*—as in "proving ground" or "printers proof"—and this is the sense in which it is used in the proverb (Gould, 1980). Accordingly, this seemingly nonsensical proverb actually capsulizes a very important principle of scientific inquiry: It makes the point that it is the explanation of exceptional cases that provides the major challenge for any theory. Thus, the explanation of the three exceptional cases that cap off this section provides a major test for the theory of normal sexual development that evolves in the preceding parts of the section.

Sexual differentiation in mammals begins at fertilization with the production of two kinds of zygotes: one with an XX (female) pair of sex chromosomes and one with an XY (male) pair. It is the genetic information on these sex chromosomes that normally determines whether development will occur along female or male lines. But be cautious here; do not fall into the seductive embrace of the men-are-men-and-women-are-women assumption. Do not begin by assuming that there are two parallel genetic programs for sexual development: one for female development and another for male development. As you are about to learn, sexual development unfolds according to an entirely different principle, one that many males—particularly those who still stubbornly adhere to notions of male pre-eminence—find unsettling. This principle is that we are all—genetic male and genetic female alike—genetically programmed to develop female bodies; genetic males develop male bodies only if the fundamentally female program of development is overruled.

Fetal Hormones and the Development of the Reproductive Organs

Gonads   Figure 10.7 represents the structure of the gonads as they appear 6 weeks after fertilization. Notice that at this stage of development, each fetus, regardless of its genetic sex, has the same pair of structures, called *primordial gonads—primordial* means *existing at the beginning*. Each primordial gonad has an internal core or *medulla,* which has the potential to develop into a testis, and each has an outer covering or *cortex,* which has the potential to develop into an ovary.

FIGURE 10.7 *The development of a testis and an ovary from the medulla and cortex, respectively, of the primordial structure present 6 weeks after fertilization.*

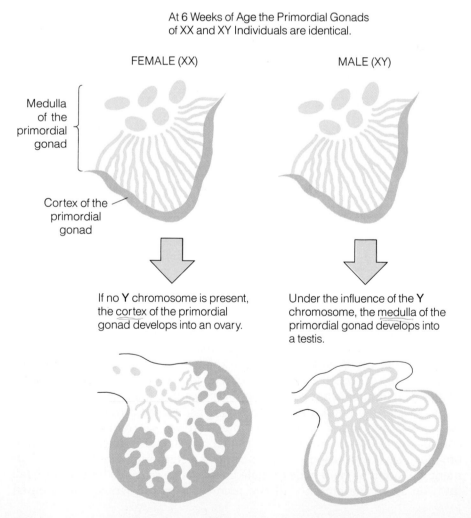

At 6 Weeks of Age the Primordial Gonads of XX and XY Individuals are identical.

FEMALE (XX)   MALE (XY)

Medulla of the primordial gonad

Cortex of the primordial gonad

If no **Y** chromosome is present, the cortex of the primordial gonad develops into an ovary.

Under the influence of the **Y** chromosome, the medulla of the primordial gonad develops into a testis.

Six weeks after conception, the Y chromosome of the male triggers the manufacture of a protein called **H-Y antigen,** and this hormone causes the medulla of each primordial gonad to grow and to develop into a testis. There is no female counterpart of H-Y antigen (Haseltine & Ohno, 1981); the critical event in the development of ovaries is the absence of H-Y antigen, not the presence of a female antigen. In the absence of H-Y antigen, the cortical cells of the primordial gonads develop into ovaries (Jost, 1972). Accordingly, if H-Y antigen is injected into a genetic female fetus at the critical stage of development, the result is a genetic female with testes; or if drugs that block the H-Y antigen are injected at the appropriate time into a male fetus, the result is a genetic male with ovaries. Such "mixed-gender" cases expose in a dramatic fashion the basic incorrectness of "mamawawa" thinking (Crews, 1988).

Internal Reproductive Ducts   Six weeks after fertilization, both males and females have two complete sets of reproductive ducts. They have a male **Wolffian system,** which has the capacity to develop into the male reproductive ducts (e.g., the *seminal vesicles,* which hold the *seminal fluid* in which the sperm cells are ejaculated, and the *vas deferens,* through which the sperm cells travel to the seminal vesicles). And they have a female **Müllerian system,** which has the capacity to develop into the female ducts (e.g., the *uterus,* the upper part of the *vagina,* and the *fallopian tubes,* which carry ova from the ovaries to the uterus, where they can be fertilized). In the third month of male fetal development, the testes secrete androgens—primarily testosterone—and **Müllerian-inhibiting substance.** The androgens stimulate the development of the Wolffian system (see Figure 10.8), and the Müllerian-inhibiting substance causes the Müllerian system to degenerate and the testes to descend into the **scrotum** (Wilson, George, & Griffin, 1981). Because it is the testicular androgens and not the sex chromosomes that trigger Wolffian development, genetic females injected with androgens during the appropriate fetal period develop male reproductive ducts along with their female ones (Jost, 1972).

The differentiation of the internal ducts of the female reproductive system (see Figure 10.8) is not under the control of ovarian hormones; the ovaries are almost completely inactive during fetal development. The development of the Müllerian system and the degeneration of the Wolffian system occurs naturally in all fetuses not exposed to androgen during the critical fetal period. Accordingly, normal intact female fetuses, ovariectomized female fetuses, and orchidectomized male fetuses all develop female reproductive ducts (Jost, 1972). **Ovariectomy** refers specifically to the removal of the ovaries, and **orchidectomy** refers specifically to the removal of the testes (*orchis* is Greek for *testicle*). **Gonadectomy** and **castration** both refer generally to removal of gonads, either ovaries or testes.

External Reproductive Organs   There is a basic difference between the differentiation of the external reproductive organs and the differentiation of the internal reproductive organs (i.e., the gonads and reproductive ducts). As you have just read, every normal fetus develops separate precursors for the male (medulla) and female (cortex) gonads and for the male (Wolffian system) and female (Müllerian system) reproductive ducts; then only one set, male or female, normally develops. In contrast, the male and female external **genitals** (reproductive organs) both develop from the very same precursor. This *bipotential precursor* and its subsequent differentiation is illustrated in Figure 10.9.

In the second month of pregnancy, the bipotential precursor of the external reproductive organs consists of four parts: the glans, the urethral folds, the lateral bodies, and the labioscrotal swellings. Then it begins to differentiate. The *glans* grows into the head of the *penis* in the male or the **clitoris** in the female; the *urethral folds* fuse in the male or enlarge to become the *labia minora* in the female; the *lateral bodies* form the shaft of the penis in the male or the hood of the clitoris in the female; and the *labioscrotal swellings* form the *scrotum* in the male or the *labia majora* in the female.

Like the development of the internal reproductive ducts, the development of the external genitals is controlled by the presence or absence of androgens. If androgen is present at the appropriate stage of fetal development, male external genitals develop from the bipotential precursor; if androgen is not present, the development of the external genitals proceeds along female lines.

FIGURE 10.8 *A schematic representation of the development of the internal ducts of the male and female reproductive systems.*

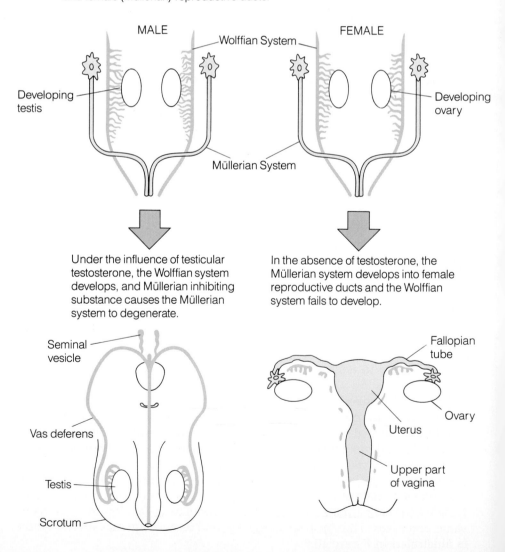

At 6 weeks, all human fetuses have the antecedents of both male (Wolffian) and female (Müllerian) reproductive ducts.

MALE — Wolffian System — FEMALE

Developing testis — Developing ovary

Müllerian System

Under the influence of testicular testosterone, the Wolffian system develops, and Müllerian inhibiting substance causes the Müllerian system to degenerate.

In the absence of testosterone, the Müllerian system develops into female reproductive ducts and the Wolffian system fails to develop.

Seminal vesicle

Vas deferens

Testis

Scrotum

Fallopian tube

Ovary

Uterus

Upper part of vagina

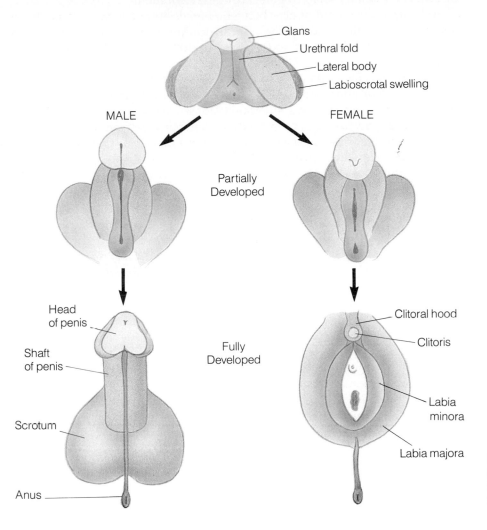

Undifferentiated male and female external sex organs 6 weeks after conception

Glans
Urethral fold
Lateral body
Labioscrotal swelling

MALE

FEMALE

Partially Developed

Head of penis
Shaft of penis
Scrotum
Anus

Fully Developed

Clitoral hood
Clitoris
Labia minora
Labia majora

FIGURE 10.9 *The development of the male and female external reproductive organs from the same bipotential precursor.*

Gonadal Hormones and the Differentiation of the Brain

Although female and male brains are basically the same, several neuroanatomical and functional differences between them have been identified. Because experiments on the sexual differentiation of the human brain are usually impractical for a variety of technical and ethical reasons, most of the evidence for sexual dimorphism of the brain comes from the study of other species. Rats, in particular, have proven to be convenient subjects for the study of hormones and brain development, primarily because they are born just 22 days after conception. At 22 days of age, the period during which androgen can influence genital development of rats is largely over, but the period during which androgen can influence brain development has yet to begin. Accordingly, it is possible to study the effects of hormones on brain development unconfounded by changes in genital development by manipulating the hormone levels of rats shortly after their birth. Current evidence suggests that the sexual differentiation of the brain, like the sexual differentiation of the internal reproductive ducts and external reproductive organs, is directed by the presence (male) or absence (female) of androgen during development.

Although several differences between female and male brains have been shown to be influenced by the administration of androgens during the *perinatal* (around birth) period (see Ehrhardt & Meyer-Bahlburg, 1981; Gorski, 1985; MacLusky & Naftolin, 1981), most research on sex differences in the brain has focused on the hypothalamus and its role in controlling the cyclic release of gonadotropins from the anterior pituitary in females and their steady release in males. Pfeiffer (1936) studied the effects of gonadectomy and gonad transplants in *neonatal* (newborn) rats on the cyclicity of their gonadotropin release as adults. He found that castrating rats of either sex shortly after their birth resulted in adults that displayed the female cyclic pattern of gonadotropin release. Transplantation of testes into gonadectomized or intact male or female neonatal rats resulted in adults that displayed the steady male pattern of gonadotropin release; however, transplantation of ovaries had no effect. He concluded that the female cyclic pattern of gonadotropin release develops in adulthood unless the preprogrammed female cyclicity is overridden by androgens present during the critical period of perinatal development (see also Harris & Levine, 1965).

Because nobody knew in 1936 that the pituitary was passively controlled by the hypothalamus, Pfeiffer assumed that the presence or absence of testicular hormones in neonatal rats influenced the development of the pituitary. However, once it was discovered that gonadotropin release was regulated by the hypothalamus, research on the sexual dimorphism of gonadotropin release shifted its focus to the hypothalamus and the rest of the brain. Several lines of research (see Gorski, 1985; McEwen, 1981) pointed to the **preoptic area** of the hypothalamus as the area that controls gonadotropin release; the name *preoptic* comes from its position just in front of the *optic chiasm* (see Figure 10.5).

Several neuroanatomical differences between female and male brains have been reported (e.g., Greenough, Carter, Steerman, & DeVoogd, 1977; Raisman & Field, 1971); one such difference is illustrated in Figure 10.10. Shown in Figure 10.10 are two comparable Nissl-stained coronal brain sections through the preoptic area, one cut from the brain of an adult female rat and one from an adult male rat. A comparison of the two sections readily reveals that the **sexually dimorphic nuclei** of the male are much larger. The reason for this difference appears to be that males, but not females, are exposed to androgens perinatally (Gorski, 1980). Castrating day-old, but not 4-day-old, male rats significantly reduced the volume of their sexually dimorphic nuclei as adults, whereas injecting neonatal (newborn) female rats with testosterone significantly increased the size of theirs (Figure 10.11). Swaab and Fliers (1985) found that the human male sexually dimorphic nucleus is 2.5 times larger than its female counterpart. Because the function of the sexually dimorphic nucleus is unknown, the significance of the sex difference in its size is unclear.

All gonadal and adrenal sex hormones are **steroid** compounds. This means that they are all derived from *cholesterol,* a fatty organic compound. Because the steroid hormones have similar structures, they are readily converted from one to the other. For example, the addition of a simple benzene ring to a testosterone molecule changes it to estradiol—a process called *aromatization.* It has been hypothesized that aromatization is a critical

Male

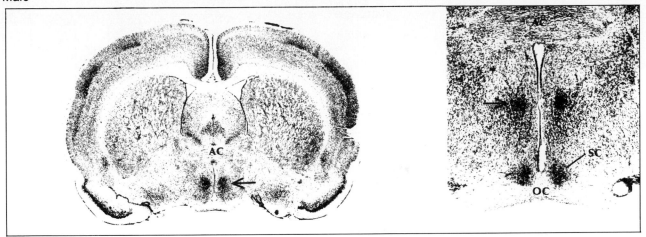

Female

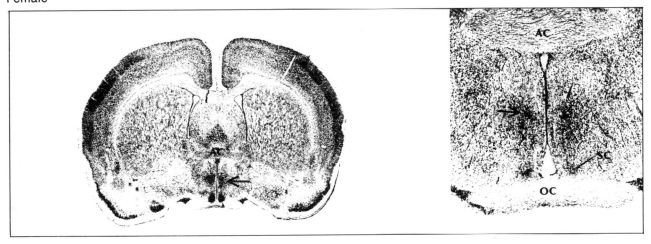

FIGURE 10.10 *Nissl-stained coronal sections through the preoptic area of the male and female rat hypothalamus. Note that the sexually dimorphic nuclei (indicated by the arrows) are bigger in the male.*

step in the masculinization of the brain. This **aromatization hypothesis** is that perinatal testosterone does not directly masculinize the brain, and that the brain is masculinized from estradiol aromatized from perinatal testosterone. Although the idea that estradiol—the alleged female hormone—masculinizes the brain is counterintuitive, there are four lines of evidence that this is the case for the male rat: (1) the enzyme necessary for aromatization of testosterone is present in the neonatal rat (Selmanoff, Brodkin, Weiner, & Siiteri, 1977); (2) neonatal injections of estradiol can masculinize the rat brain (Gorski, 1971); (3) **dihydrotestosterone,** an androgen that cannot be converted to estrogen, has no masculinizing effect on the rat brain (Whalen & Rezek, 1974); and (4) agents that block the aromatization of testosterone (McEwen, Lieberburg, Chaptal, & Krey, 1977) or block estrogen receptors (Booth, 1977) interfere with the masculinizing effects of testosterone on the rat brain.

The idea that the masculinization of the brain depends on the aromatization of testosterone to estradiol raises a problem: How do female fetuses keep from being masculinized by their mother's estrogen circulating through the fetal blood supply (Ojeda, Kalra, & McCann, 1975)? Alpha fetoprotein provides the answer. **Alpha fetoprotein** is a protein present in

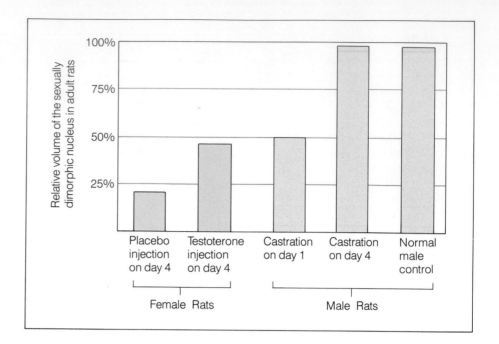

FIGURE 10.11 *The effects of neonatal testosterone exposure on the size of the sexually dimorphic nuclei in mature genetic male and female rats. (Adapted from Gorski, 1980.)*

the blood of neonatal rats (Plapinger, McEwen, & Clemens, 1973) that deactivates circulating estradiol by binding to it. Although alpha fetoprotein solves one problem, it creates another: How does estradiol masculinize the brain of the male fetus in the presence of the deactivating effects of alpha fetoprotein? The *blood-brain barrier* provides the answer to this question. Because testosterone is immune to alpha fetoprotein, it can travel unaffected from the testes to the brain, where it enters cells and is converted there to estradiol. The estradiol is not broken down in the brain because alpha fetoprotein does not readily penetrate the blood-brain barrier. Although the evidence that aromatization plays an important role in the masculinization of the rat brain is quite strong, ethical constraints preclude the conduct of direct experimental tests of the aromatization hypothesis in humans.

Fetal Hormones and Behavioral Development

In view of the fact that prenatal hormones influence the development of the brain, it should come as no surprise to you that they also influence the development of behavior. Most of the research on hormones and behavioral development has focused on the role of prenatal hormones in the development of sexually dimorphic copulatory behaviors in male and female laboratory animals (Feder, 1981, 1984).

Phoenix, Goy, Gerall, and Young (1959) were among the first to systematically demonstrate that the prenatal injection of testosterone can both **masculinize** and **defeminize** a genetic female's adult copulatory behavior. First, they injected pregnant guinea pigs with testosterone. Then, when the litters were born, they ovariectomized the female offspring. Finally, when these ovariectomized female guinea pigs reached maturity, they injected them with testosterone and assessed their copulatory behavior. Phoenix and his colleagues found that the females exposed prenatally to testosterone displayed much more male-like mounting behavior in re-sponse to testosterone injections in adulthood than did adult females not exposed prenatally to testosterone. And when as adults they were injected with progesterone and estradiol and mounted by males, they displayed less **lordosis,** the intromission-facilitating arched-back posture of female receptivity. Grady, Phoenix, and Young (1965) performed the complementary study on male rats and found that the lack of early exposure of male rats to androgens had both **feminizing** and **demasculinizing** effects on their copulatory behavior as adults. Male rats castrated shortly after birth failed to display the normal male copulatory pattern of mounting, **intromission** (penis insertion), and **ejaculation** (ejecting sperm) when they were treated with testosterone and given access to a sexually receptive female; and when they were injected with estrogen and progesterone as adults, they exhibited more lordosis than did uncastrated controls. The aromatization of perinatal testosterone to estradiol seems to be important for both the defeminization and the masculinization of rodent copulatory behavior (Goy & McEwen, 1980; Shapiro, Levine, & Adler, 1980).

The preceding findings on the sexual differentiation of rat copulation can be misleading unless they are considered within a broader context. Three points require consideration. First, feminizing and demasculinizing effects do not always go together; nor do defeminizing and masculinizing effects. That is, hormone treatments can enhance female behavior without disturbing male behavior and vice versa. Second, there are major differences between species in both the degree to which, and the ways in which, hormones influence the sexual differentiation of copulation. In general, the differentiation of copulatory behavior in humans and other primates is much less influenced by hormones and much more influenced by social factors than it is in rats (e.g., Goy, 1978). In contrast to its effects in rats, exposure of female primates to androgens does not defeminize their female copulatory behavior (Baum, 1979); however, it does masculinize it. Third, there is much more to the sexual differentiation of behavior than the differentiation of copulation. Unfortunately, most of the research on the effects of hormones on behavioral development has focused on the copulatory act itself and has largely ignored the complex preparatory, search, and (**proceptive**) solicitation behaviors that precede copulation (see Chapter 4), as well as the other gender-related behaviors that are not directly related to reproduction. Although they have not received much study, the following effects of perinatal androgen on development of noncopulatory behaviors have been reported: it disrupts the proceptive hopping, darting, and ear wiggling of receptive female rats (Fadem & Barfield, 1981); it increases the aggressiveness of female mice (Edwards, 1969); it disrupts the maternal behavior of female rats (Ichikawa & Fujii, 1982); and it increases rough social play in female monkeys (Goy, 1970) and rats (Meaney & Stewart, 1981).

Puberty: Hormones and the Development of Secondary Sex Characteristics

During childhood, levels of circulating sex hormones are low, the reproductive organs remain in an immature state, and the overall appearance of males and females differs little. This period of developmental quiescence ends abruptly with the onset of puberty. **Puberty** is the transitional period between childhood and adulthood during which fertility is achieved, the adolescent growth spurt occurs, and the secondary sex characteristics develop. **Secondary sex characteristics** are those features of male and female bodies, other than the reproductive organs, that characterize sexual maturity. The bodily changes associated with puberty are illustrated in Figure 10.12—you are undoubtedly familiar with at least half of them. In North America and Western Europe, puberty typically begins at about 11 years of age in girls and at about 12 in boys (Marshall & Tanner, 1969). Believe it or not, there has been a 4-year acceleration in puberty onset over the last century and a half in the countries of Western Europe and North America—presumably because of the general improvement in health, nutrition, and socioeconomic conditions.

Puberty is associated with an increase in the release of hormones by the anterior pituitary. The increase in the release of **growth hormone**, which is the only anterior pituitary hormone that does not have an endocrine gland as its primary target, acts directly on bone and muscle tissue to produce the pubertal growth spurt. Increases in gonadotropic and **adrenocorticotropic hormone** release cause the gonads and adrenal cortex to increase their release of gonadal and adrenal hormones, which in turn initiate the maturation of the genitals and the development of secondary sex characteristics.

The general principle guiding normal pubertal sexual maturation is a simple one. In pubertal males, androgen levels are higher than estrogen

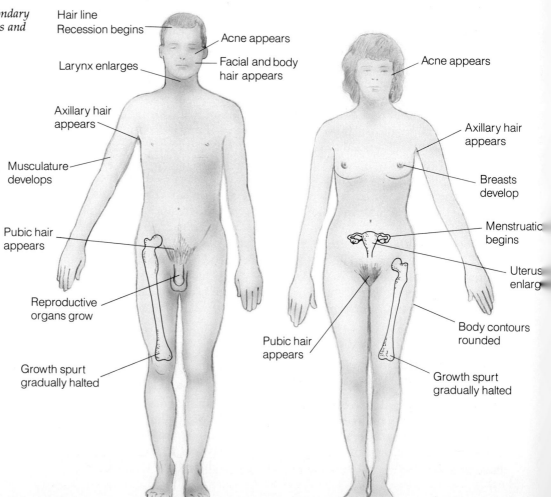

FIGURE 10.12 *The secondary sex characteristics of males and females.*

Hair line
Recession begins
Acne appears
Larynx enlarges
Facial and body hair appears
Axillary hair appears
Musculature develops
Pubic hair appears
Reproductive organs grow
Growth spurt gradually halted

Acne appears
Axillary hair appears
Breasts develop
Menstruation begins
Uterus enlarges
Pubic hair appears
Body contours rounded
Growth spurt gradually halted

levels, and masculinization is the result; in pubertal females, estrogen predominates, and the result is feminization. Individuals castrated prior to puberty do not become sexually mature unless they receive replacement injections of androgen or estrogen. But even here, in its only sphere of relevance, the men-are-men-and-women-are-women approach to hormones and sex stumbles badly. You see, **androstenedione,** an androgen released primarily by the adrenal cortices, is normally responsible for the growth of pubic and **axillary hair** (underarm hair) in females. It is hard to take seriously the practice of referring to androgens as "the male hormone" when one of their group is responsible for the development of the female pattern of pubic hair growth. The female pattern is an inverted pyramid; the male pattern is a pyramid—see Figure 10.12.

Before proceeding to a consideration of three cases of abnormal human sexual development, review the basics of normal development by completing the following exercise.

1. Six weeks after conception, the Y chromosome of the human male triggers the production of ___H-Y antigen___.

2. In the absence of H-Y antigen, the cortical cells of the primordial gonads develop into ___ovaries___.

3. In the third month of male fetal development, the testes secrete testosterone and ___Müllerian inhibiting___ substance.

4. The hormonal factor that triggers the development of the human Müllerian system is the lack of ___androgen___ around the third month of fetal development.

5. The scrotum and the ___labia majora___ develop from the same bipotential precursor.

6. The female pattern of cyclic ___gonadotropic___ release from the anterior pituitary develops in adulthood unless androgens are present in the body during the perinatal period.

7. The sexually dimorphic nuclei of the ___preoptic___ area are larger in male rats and humans than in female rats and humans.

8. It has been hypothesized that perinatal testosterone must first be changed to estrogen before it can masculinize the male rat brain. This is called the ___aromatization___ hypothesis.

9. ___androstenedione___ is normally responsible for pubic and axillary hair growth in human females during puberty.

Three Cases of Exceptional Human Sexual Development

So far in Section 10.2, you have learned the rules according to which hormones influence sexual development. In this part of Section 10.2, these exceptions are offered to "prove" (i.e., to test) these rules.

Case 1: The Case of Anne S.

Anne S., an attractive 26-year-old female, sought treatment for two sex-related disorders: lack of menstruation and pain during sexual intercourse (Jones & Park, 1971). She sought help because she and her husband of 4 years had been trying without success to have children, and she correctly surmised that her lack of a menstrual cycle was part of the problem. A physical examination revealed that Anne was a healthy young woman. Her only readily apparent peculiarity was the sparseness and fineness of her pubic and axillary hair. Examination of the external genitals revealed no abnormalities; however, there were some problems with her internal genitals: her vagina was only 4 centimeters long and her uterus was also underdeveloped.

At the start of this chapter, I said that you would encounter some amazing things, and the diagnosis of Anne's case certainly qualifies as one of them. Anne's doctors concluded that she was a man. No, this is not a misprint; they concluded that Anne, the attractive young housewife, was in fact Anne, the happily married man. Three lines of evidence supported this diagnosis. First, analysis of some cells scraped from the inside of Anne's mouth revealed that they were of the normal male XY type. Second, a tiny incision in Anne's abdomen, which enabled Anne's physicians to look inside, revealed a pair of internalized testes, but no ovaries. Finally, hormone tests revealed that Anne's hormone levels were those of a male.

Anne suffers from a disorder called the **androgenic insensitivity syndrome;** all of her symptoms stem from the fact that her body lacks androgen receptors. During development, Anne's testes released normal amounts of androgen for a male, but her body could not respond to them in the absence of androgen receptors, and her development thus proceeded as if no androgens had been released. Her external genitals, her brain, and her behavior developed along preprogrammed female lines during fetal development without the effects of androgen to override the female program. Anne did not develop normal internal female reproductive ducts because, like other genetic males, her testes released Müllerian inhibiting substance. At puberty, Anne's testes released enough estrogens to feminize the body in the absence of the counteracting effects of androgens; however, without androgen receptors, adrenal androstenedione could not stimulate the growth of pubic and axillary hair.

Money and Ehrhardt (1972) studied the psychosexual development of 10 androgen insensitive patients and concluded that the placidity of their childhood play, their goals, their fantasies, their sexual behavior, and their maternal tendencies—several had adopted children—all "conformed to the idealized stereotype of what constitutes femininity in our culture" (p. 112). However, it is not clear what part of this normal female psychosexual development is attributable to their androgen insensitivity, and what part is attributable to their experience of being raised as a female.

An interesting issue of medical ethics is raised by the androgenic insensitivity syndrome. Many people believe that physicians should always disclose all relevant findings to their patients. If you were Anne's physician, would you tell her that she is a man? Would you tell her husband? Anne's vagina was surgically enlarged, she was counseled to consider adoption, and, as far as I know, she is still happily married and unaware of her genetic sex.

The **adrenogenital syndrome** is a disorder characterized by a decrease in the release of the hormone *cortisol* from the adrenal cortices, which results in the production of high levels of adrenal androgens. This has little effect on the development of males other than accelerating the onset of their puberty, but it has major effects on the development of genetic females. Females suffering from the adrenogenital syndrome are usually born with an enlarged clitoris and partially fused labia, as illustrated in Figure 10.13. Their internal ducts are usually normal because the abnormally abundant adrenal androgens are released too late to stimulate the development of the Wolffian system. If identified at birth, the abnormalities of the external genitals are surgically corrected, and cortisol is administered to reduce the levels of circulating adrenal androgens to normal. These early-treated cases frequently begin to menstruate later than normal, but otherwise they grow up to be physically normal, and they thus provide an excellent opportunity to study the effects of fetal androgen exposure on psychosexual development.

Cortisone-treated adrenogenital teenage girls have been reported to display a high degree of "tomboyishness" and a lack of interest in maternity (e.g., Ehrhardt, Epstein, & Money, 1968). Many prefer boys' clothes, play mainly with boys, and show little interest in handling babies. They also tend to display a general lack of enthusiasm for the prospect of having children, and they tend to daydream about future careers rather than motherhood. It is important not to lose sight of the fact that many healthy teenage girls in this culture display the same propensities—and why not? Accordingly, the behavior of treated adrenogenital females, although perhaps tending toward the masculine, is well within the range that is considered normal by the current standards of our culture. The most interesting questions about the development of females with adrenogenital syndrome concern the development of their romantic and sexual preferences. Although they seem to lag behind normal females in dating and marriage—perhaps because of the delayed onset of their menstrual cycle—their sexual interests appear to remain largely heterosexual, although one study has reported a slight tendency toward bisexuality (Ehrhardt & Meyer-Bahlburg, 1981). Unfortunately, there is no way of telling whether this slight tendency toward tomboyishness and bisexuality is a direct effect of early androgen exposure or a secondary reaction of the patient and of others to the physical masculinization. There is no evidence that perinatal androgen exposure directly increases the tendency of genetic females to engage in sexual activities with other females.

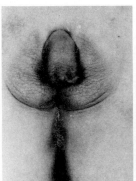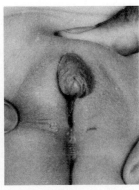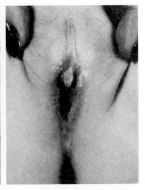

FIGURE 10.13 *Genetic female babies with the adrenogenital syndrome display varying degrees of clitoral enlargement and labial fusion. The case on the right has been surgically treated.*
Courtesy of John Money, Ph.D. First published in: JH Med. Journal, 122: 160–167, 1968.

Prior to the development in 1950 of cortisone therapy for the adrenogenital syndrome, many cases were simply diagnosed as hermaphroditism and left untreated. Strictly speaking, the term **hermaphrodite** refers to organisms with fully developed male and female reproductive organs; however, in the human clinical literature, it is used to refer to individuals born with reproductive organs that are not unambiguously either male or female. One of the problems faced by untreated adrenogenital genetic females is that there is no way of telling whether the estrogen released by the ovaries or the androgen released by the adrenals will predominate at puberty. Thus, an individual who has been raised as a male might be feminized at puberty, or one raised as a female might be masculinized.

One such case was referred to specialists (Money & Ehrhardt, 1972) for treatment at the age of 12. Although her external genitals were somewhat ambiguous, they were clearly more female than male, and as a result, she had been raised as a female without incident until puberty. Needless to say, the sudden masculinization that occurred at puberty was the subject of great distress both to her and to her parents and that is why treatment was sought. Treatment involved surgical enlargement of her vaginal opening, removal of her large clitoris, and the initiation of cortisone therapy, which suppressed androgen release and allowed her ovarian estrogens to feminize her body.

> She became an attractively good-looking young woman. Narrow hips and mildly short stature remained unchanged, as the *epiphyses* [the ends of bones, where bone growth takes place] of the bones had already fused under the influence of precocious masculinization. These two signs alone remained as reminders of the past, except for a small amount of coarse facial hair, requiring removal by electrolysis. The voice was husky, but so used as to be not mistaken as masculine. . . . The capacity for orgasm was not lost. The proof came fifteen years later, upon establishment of a sexual relationship and marriage. (p. 157)

As you might well imagine, not all cases of adrenogenital syndrome left untreated until puberty have such a satisfactory resolution.

Case 3: Sex Reassignment of a Twin with Ablatio Penis

One of the most famous cases in the literature on sexual development is that of a male identical twin whose penis was accidentally destroyed—a disorder termed **ablatio penis**—during circumcision at the age of 7 months. Because there was no satisfactory way of surgically replacing the lost penis, a widely respected expert in such matters, John Money, recommended that the boy be castrated, that an artificial vagina be created, that the boy be raised as a girl, and that estrogen be administered at puberty to feminize the body. After a great deal of consideration and anguish, the parents followed Money's advice.

Money's (1975) report of this case has had a great influence on current thinking about sexual development. It has been seen by some as the ultimate test of the *nature-nurture controversy* with regard to the development of sexual identity and behavior. It pitted the masculinizing effects of male genes and male hormones against the effects of being reared as a female. And the availability of a genetically identical control subject, the twin brother, made the case all the more interesting. According to Money, the outcome of this bizarre case comes down strongly on the side of the *social-learning theory* of sexual identity. Money reported in 1975, when the patient was 12, that "she" had developed as a normal female, thus confirming his prediction that being raised as a girl would override the masculinizing effects of male genes and early androgens. Because it is such an interesting case, Money's description of it has been featured in many textbooks of psychology, medicine, sociology, and women's studies, as well as in many television, magazine, and newspaper stories, each time carrying with it the message that the sexual identity and behavior of men and women is largely a matter of upbringing. However, there is reason to question the rosy picture painted by Money.

In 1980, a British news team preparing a report on the case discovered that several psychiatrists had examined the patient in 1976 when she was 13 and had reached a conclusion that conflicted with that of Money. Their conclusion was that the patient was having significant psychological problems, including considerable ambivalence toward the female role. She refused to draw pictures of females, she aspired to occupations that are commonly regarded as masculine (e.g, auto mechanic), and her masculine gait was the object of scorn from classmates, who referred to her as "cave woman." Clearly, things were not as cut-and-dried as Money's report, published the year before, had made them out to be.

> It is scientifically regrettable that so much of a theoretical and philosophical superstructure has been built on the supposed results of a single, uncontrolled and unconfirmed case. It is further regrettable that we here in the United States had to depend for a clinical follow-up by a British investigative journalist team for a case originally and so prominently reported in the American literature. The issues raised by this case are too important to be settled by the media. For scientific and medical reasons, a full updated scientific report on both twins is called for and hopefully will be forthcoming from the team presently associated with this case. . . . It is further hoped that this particular case will be resolved to the best interest of the particular twin and family involved. The twin should be allowed to truly express any desired sexual identity with familial, social, and medical support. (Diamond, 1982, pp. 184–185)

These three case studies: (1) Ann S., the married woman who was an androgen-insensitive genetic male; (2) the untreated adrenogenital female, who at age 12 was masculinized by her own androgens; and (3) the identical twin boy who suffered ablatio penis and was raised as a girl complete this section on hormones and sexual development. Does current theory pass the test of these three exceptions? I think so. Current theories of hormones and sexual development greatly increase the understanding of each of these three cases, and they provide an effective basis for prescribing treatment. However, it is important to recognize that current theories do better with respect to gonads, reproductive organs, and secondary sex characteristics than they do with respect to brain and behavior. For example, we still do not know why some individuals develop into persons who feel that they are trapped inside a body of the wrong sex or why others become sexually and romantically attracted to members of the same sex (Money, 1987). Because each of the three patients is male in some respects and female in others, together they strike at the heart of the men-are-men-and-women-are-women assumption.

10.3 The Effects of Gonadal Hormones on Adults

Once an individual reaches sexual maturity, gonadal hormones begin to play a role in activating the reproductive machinery. Such activational effects of hormones are the focus of this, the third and final section of the chapter. This section has three parts. The first deals with the role of hormones in activating the reproduction-related behavior of men. The second deals with the role of hormones in activating the reproduction-related behavior of women. And the third deals with the use of anabolic steroids by athletes.

Male Reproduction-Related Behavior and Testosterone

The important role played by gonadal hormones in activation of male sexual behavior is clearly demonstrated by the asexualizing effects of castration. One of the most extensive case studies of male orchidectomy was that of Bremer (1959), who reviewed the cases of 157 men legally castrated in Norway. Many of these men had been jailed for sex-related offenses and requested castration "to bring their sexual urges under control"; others were psychiatric cases whose castration was requested by their guardian and sanctioned by a panel of "experts." Two significant generalizations can be drawn from Bremer's study. The first is that the castration of adult males virtually always leads to a reduction in sexual interest and behavior; the second is that the rate and degree of the loss is extremely variable. According to Bremer, about half the cases became completely asexual within a few weeks of the operation; others quickly lost their ability to achieve an erection, but continued to experience some sexual interest and pleasure; and a few continued to achieve erection and copulate successfully, although somewhat less enthusiastically, for the duration of the study. Adrenal androgens may play some role in the maintenance of sexual activity in castrated men, but there is no direct support for this idea (Davidson, Kwan, & Greenleaf, 1982). Bremer also reported that of the 102 sex offenders in his study who were castrated between 1935 and 1949, only three were reconvicted of sex offenses during that time. Accordingly, Bremer recommended castration as a treatment of last resort for male sex offenders. Castrated men typically experience a reduction of hair on the trunk, extremities, and face; the deposition of fat on the hips and chest; a softening of the skin; and a reduction in strength.

Orchidectomy, in one fell swoop—or, to put it more precisely, in two fell swoops—removes a pair of glands that normally release a variety of hormones. Because testosterone is the major hormone released by the testes, it was assumed that the symptoms of orchidectomy in adult males result from the loss of testosterone, rather than from the loss of some other testicular hormone or from some nonhormonal consequence of the surgery. The therapeutic effects of testosterone **replacement injections** have confirmed this assumption.

The very first case report of the effects of testosterone replacement therapy was that of a 38-year-old World War I veteran, who was castrated in 1918 at the age of 19 by a shell fragment that removed his testes but left his penis undamaged.

> His body was soft; it was as if he had almost no muscles at all; his hips had grown wider and his shoulders seemed narrower than when he was a soldier. He had very little drive. . . .
>
> Just the same this veteran had married, in 1924, and you'd wonder why, because the doctors had told him he would surely be **impotent** [unable to get an erection]. . . . He confessed that he made some attempts at sexual intercourse "for his wife's satisfaction" but he confessed that he had been unable to satisfy her at all. . . .
>
> Dr. Foss began injecting it [testosterone] into the feeble muscles of the castrated man in good stiff doses [I assume that no pun was intended]. . . .
>
> After the fifth injection, erections were rapid and prolonged. . . . But that wasn't all. During twelve weeks of treatment he had gained eighteen pounds, and all his clothes had become too small. Originally, he wore

fourteen-and-a-half inch collars. Now fifteen-and-a-half were too tight. . . . testosterone had resurrected a broken man to a manhood he had lost forever. (de Kruif, 1945, pp. 97–100)

Since Dr. Foss's first clinical trial, testosterone has breathed sexuality into the lives of many castrated males. Testosterone reliably remasculinizes the body and behavior of men with testicular disorders, and it initiates pubertal development in men who failed to mature sexually because their testicular dysfunction preceded puberty (Davidson, Camarga, & Smith, 1979; Skakkebaek, Bancroft, Davidson, & Warner, 1980). However, testosterone does not eliminate the **sterility** (inability to reproduce) of castrated men.

The fact that testosterone is necessary for male sexual behavior has led many to incorrectly assume that the level of a man's sexuality is a function of the amount of testosterone that he has in his blood, and thus, that a man's sex drive can be readily increased or decreased by manipulating his testosterone levels. However, attempts to correlate sex drive with the level of testosterone in healthy men and to influence sex drive by injecting testosterone or drugs that increase or decrease its level or its effect have met with little success. It seems that each male has far more testosterone than is required to activate the neural circuits underlying his sexual behavior (Damassa, Smith, Tennent, & Davidson, 1977; Salmimies, Kockott, Pirke, Vogt, & Schill, 1982), and that having more than this minimum is of no particular advantage when it comes to sexual behavior (Brown, Moonti, & Corriveau, 1978; Kraemer, Becker, Brodie, Doering, Moos, & Hamburg, 1976; Raboch & Starka, 1973). An experiment by Grunt and Young (1952) clearly illustrates this point. First, Grunt and Young rated the sexual behavior of each of the male guinea pigs in their experiment. Then, on the basis of the ratings, Grunt and Young divided the male guinea pigs into three experimental groups: low, medium, and high sex drive. Following castration, the sexual behavior of all of the guinea pigs fell to negligible levels within a few weeks (see Figure 10.14), but it recovered soon after the

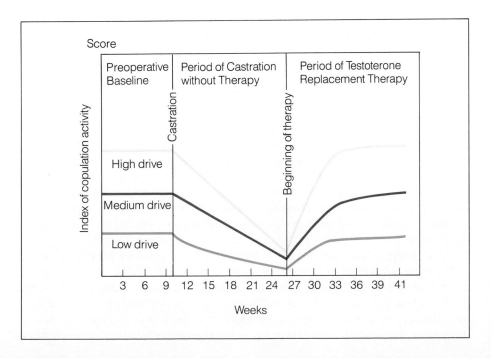

FIGURE 10.14 *The sexual behavior of male rats with low, medium, and high sex drive is disrupted by castration and returned to its original level by very large replacement injections of testosterone. (Adapted from Grunt & Young, 1952.)*

initiation of a series of testosterone replacement injections. The important point is that although each subject received the same, very large replacement injections of testosterone, the injections simply returned each to its own previous level of copulatory activity. Apparently, with respect to the effects of testosterone on sexual behavior, more is not necessarily better.

Dihydrotestosterone, a nonaromatizable androgen, failed to reactivate the copulatory behavior of castrated male rats in several studies (MacLusky & Naftolin, 1981). This led to the hypothesis that the activational effects of testosterone on male sexual behavior are produced by estrogen aromatized from the testosterone. However, dihydrotestosterone has been shown to be effective in activating sexual behavior in castrated guinea pigs and rhesus monkeys, and preliminary reports suggest that it can do the same in castrated men (Davidson, Kwan, Greenleaf, 1982; Gooren, 1982).

Gonadal Hormones and Female Reproduction-Related Behavior

Sexually mature female rats and guinea pigs display 4-day cycles of gonadal hormone release. There is a gradual increase in the secretion of estrogen by the developing follicle in the 2 days prior to ovulation, followed by a sudden surge in progesterone as the egg is released. These sequential surges of estrogen and progesterone initiate **estrus** a period of 12 to 18 hours during which the female is: (1) fertile, (2) *receptive* (likely to assume the *lordosis* posture when mounted), (3) *proceptive* (likely to engage in behaviors that serve to attract the male), and (4) sexually attractive (smelling of chemicals that attract males). The close relation between the cycle of hormone release and the **estrous cycle** (i.e., the cycle of sexual receptivity) in female rats and guinea pigs and many other mammalian species suggests that female sexual behavior in these species is under strict hormonal control. The effects of ovariectomy and replacement injections confirm this conclusion. Unlike the gradual and unpredictable decline in male sexual behavior after orchidectomy, ovariectomy produces a rapid decline of proceptive and receptive behavior in females. Ovariectomized rats and guinea pigs can be quickly brought into a state of estrus by an injection of estrogen, followed a day and a half later by an injection of progesterone.

Women are not at all like female rats and guinea pigs when it comes to the hormonal control of their sexual behavior. The sexual motivation and behavior of women does not go through regular changes associated with their menstrual cycles (see Sanders & Bancroft, 1982), and ovariectomy has surprisingly little effect (e.g., Gath, Cooper, & Day, 1981; Martin, Roberts, & Clayton, 1980). Ovariectomy does decrease the vaginal lubrication of women, which can interfere with intercourse if a commercial lubricant is not used, but there is typically little or no associated decline in their sexual interest (Dennerstein & Burrows, 1982) or in the feminine appearance of their bodies. Estrogen replacement therapy replenishes the vaginal lubrication.

One interpretation of these findings is that hormones play little or no role in the activation of sexual behavior in human females. Another interpretation is that the sexual behavior of human females is under hormonal control, but that the key hormone is androgen, not estrogen. According to this theory enough androgen is released from the human adrenal glands to maintain the sexual motivation of women even after their ovaries have been removed. The major support for this theory comes from a study in which ovariectomy plus adrenalectomy, but not ovariectomy alone, abolished sexual desire and responsiveness in female cancer patients (Waxenberg, Drellich, & Sutherland, 1959). Adrenalectomized and ovariectomized adult female monkeys are rendered receptive by androgens, but not by estrogens (Herbert, 1977).

Hormones and Sexual Preference

Before leaving the topic of the activational effects of sex hormones, one point requires emphasis: Although hormones are necessary to maintain the sexual behavior of adults, they do not influence its direction. For example, castration reduces the amount of sexual activity of **heterosexuals** (those sexually attracted to members of the other sex), **homosexuals** (those sexually attracted to members of their own sex), and **bisexuals** (those sexually attracted to members of both sexes), but it does not redirect it. And replacement injections simply serve to reactivate the behaviors that were there prior to castration. Current wisdom (e.g., Money, 1987) suggests that the neural circuitry underlying a person's sexual preference is established by a complex interplay between perinatal hormones and experience as a child, and that the function of adult hormones is to simply maintain the activity of these circuits, once they have been established. Although it is a topic of great concern and interest to many, the factors that influence whether a person will develop into a homosexual, a heterosexual, or a bisexual have been difficult to identify because scientists cannot ethically manipulate variables in human subjects that might disrupt the natural course of their sexual development. Unfortunately, this question cannot be studied in laboratory species because nobody has yet provided convincing evidence of homosexuality or bisexuality in nonhumans. The members of many species occasionally direct sexual behavior at conspecifics of their own sex—for example, female rats frequently mount other female rats—but, unlike human homosexuals and bisexuals, when they are given a choice, they virtually always opt for reproductive activities with a member of the opposite sex.

Anabolic Steroids and Athletes

Anabolic steroids are steroid drugs that were derived from the testosterone molecule in an effort to develop drugs with powerful *anabolic*, or growth-promoting, effects. Testosterone itself is not very useful as an anabolic drug because it is broken down very rapidly after injection and because its anabolic effects are often accompanied by undesirable masculinizing side effects. Although chemists have successfully synthesized a number of highly potent and long-acting anabolic steroids, they have not been able to synthesize one that does not produce serious side effects. We are currently in the midst of an epidemic of anabolic steroid abuse. Many athletes and body builders are illicitly using appallingly large doses of anabolic steroids to increase their muscularity and strength.

Do anabolic steroids really increase the muscularity and the strength of the athletes that use them? Initially, the athletes said "yes," and the scientists said "no," but it is the athletes who have been proven correct. The early scientific studies, although well designed, involved doses of steroids much smaller than those used by training athletes because of the concern of the experimenters for the welfare of their subjects. On the basis of these early studies, it was concluded that anabolic steroids are of little or no benefit. However, more recent studies, in which larger doses of anabolic steroids have been administered to training athletes for longer periods of time, have proven their efficacy (see Haupt & Rovere, 1984). In fact, many athletes believe that it is impossible to compete at the highest levels of some sports without an anabolic-steroid boost. It is difficult indeed to ignore the testimonials of steroid users such as the gentleman pictured in Figure 10.15. It is unfortunate that many in the medical community are still clinging self-righteously to the view that steroids do not increase muscle bulk and strength, or improve athletic performance. The resulting loss of credibility has led many users to assume that warnings about the dangers of steroid use are also unreliable.

So far all of the published experiments assessing the effects of anabolic steroids on muscularity and strength have been performed on males. This is not because steroids do not increase the muscularity and strength of females. In fact, the increase is probably even greater in females. The problem is that anabolic steroids have such marked side effects in females that administering them to females, even for research purposes, is frowned on in most countries. However, these side effects have not prevented female athletes from using anabolic steroids.

> The most popular story of the 1976 Montreal Olympics involved the success of East German women swimmers. When asked why so many of their women had deep voices, an East German coach replied, "We have come here to swim, not sing." (*New York Times*, quoted in Goldman, 1984, p. 19)
>
> Now when Renate Vogel Heinrich looks at pictures of herself, during her competitive years, she says, "I get sick. We never really noticed what we looked like, because swimmers were always kept together. It didn't hit me until an old friend said, "Wow Renate, you speak like a man, and you've got unbelievably broad shoulders . . ." Renate managed to flee from a training environment where anabolic steroids were handed to her like morning orange juice. (Goldman, 1984, p. 52)

Although athletes use steroids for their anabolic effects, it is their sex-

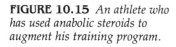

FIGURE 10.15 *An athlete who has used anabolic steroids to augment his training program.*

Carl Iwasaki/*Sports Illustrated*.

related side effects that are of primary relevance here. It has proven extremely difficult to document these side effects because most athletes who use anabolic steroids will not admit it for fear of being disqualified from competition. Nevertheless, there is general agreement (Goldman, 1984; Haupt & Rovere, 1984; Wilson & Griffin, 1980) that men and women taking high doses of anabolic steroids risk the following sex-related symptoms. In men, the negative feedback from high levels of anabolic steroids reduces gonadotropin release, and this in turn can lead to a reduction in androgen release by the testes, *testicular atrophy* (wasting away of the testes from disuse), and sterility. *Gynecomastia* (i.e., breast growth in men) can occur in men using anabolic steroids, presumably as the result of their conversion to estrogen. In women, anabolic steroids can produce *amenorrhea* (cessation of menstruation), sterility, *hirsutism* (the excessive growth of body hair), growth of the clitoris, development of a masculine body shape, baldness, and deepening and coarsening of the voice.

Both men and women using anabolic steroids can suffer muscle spasms, muscle pains, blood in the urine, acne, general swelling from the retention of water, bleeding of the tongue, nausea, vomiting, and a variety of psychotic behaviors, including fits of depression and anger (Pope & Katz, 1987). Oral anabolic steroids reportedly produce blood-filled cysts in the liver and cancerous liver tumors.

Cases in which healthy young men and women are suddenly exposed to very high levels of testosterone-like substances make two important points about hormones and sex. The first is that testosterone-like substances do not produce increases in the sexual motivation and behavior of people with hormone levels in the normal range. Testosterone-like substances can breathe sexuality back into the lives of castrated men and perhaps into the lives of castrated and adrenalectomized women, but they do not "improve" the sex lives of adults with normal levels of circulating testosterone. The second is that the effects of sex hormones on the structure of the human body are not restricted to critical prenatal and pubertal periods. High doses of anabolic steroids can masculinize the bodies of men and women long after their physical development is complete. Although there are periods in one's life when hormones (or other agents or experiences) can have a particularly great effect on certain aspects of development, they can also influence development when administered in high doses outside these periods.

Conclusion

The primary purpose of this chapter was to describe the role of hormones in sexual development and behavior. But there were also two important subthemes: (1) that exceptional cases play a particularly important role in testing scientific theory and (2) that the men-are-men-and-women-are-women attitude is a misleading perspective from which to consider sexual matters. If you now appreciate why exceptional cases have been so important in the study of hormones and sex, you have learned a fundamental principle that has relevance to all fields of scientific inquiry. If you now are better able to resist the seductive appeal of the men-are-men-and-women-are-women attitude, you are leaving this chapter a more tolerant and understanding person than when you began it. I hope that you now have an abiding appreciation of the fact that maleness and femaleness are slight, multidimensional, and at times ambiguous, variations of one another.

Food for Thought _____

1. Over the last century and half, the onset of puberty has changed from 15 or 16 to 11 or 12, but there has been no corresponding acceleration in psychological and intellectual development. Precocious puberty is like a loaded gun in the hand of a child. Discuss.

2. Do you think that sex-change operations should be permitted? Why?

3. What should be done about the current epidemic of anabolic steroid abuse? Would you make the same recommendation if a safe anabolic steroid were developed? If a drug were developed that would dramatically improve your memory, would you take it?

ADDITIONAL READING

The following book contains lavishly illustrated, introductory articles on many major topics of neuroendocrine research written by top researchers in their respective fields:

Krieger, D. T., & Hughes, J. C. (1980). *Neuroendocrinology*. Sunderland, Massachusetts: Sinauer.

The following article by Money is a review of clinical cases of abnormal sexual development and what they tell us about the factors that influence the development of sexual identity and sexual preference.

Money, J. (1987). Sin, sickness, or status? Homosexual gender identity and psychoneuroendocrinology. *American Psychologist, 42,* 384–399.

KEY TERMS

To help you study the material in this chapter, all of the key terms—those that have appeared in bold type—are listed and briefly defined here.

Ablatio penis. Accidental destruction of the penis.

Adrenal cortices. The outer coverings of the adrenal glands, which regulate salt and glucose levels in the blood and secrete gonadal hormones.

Adrenocorticotropic hormone. The anterior pituitary hormone that causes the adrenal cortex to release its hormones.

Adrenogenital syndrome. A disorder characterized by a decrease in the release of the hormone cortisol from the adrenal cortices, which results in the production of high levels of adrenal androgens and masculinizes the bodies of genetic females.

Alpha fetoprotein. A protein present in the blood of neonatal rats that deactivates circulating estradiol by binding to it.

Anabolic steroids. A group of steroid drugs that are derived from the testosterone molecule and have powerful anabolic or growth-promoting effects.

Androgens. One class of gonadal hormones; testosterone is the major androgen.

Androstenedione. The androgen that triggers the growth of pubic and axillary hair in pubertal human females.

Anterior pituitary. The part of the pituitary gland that releases tropic hormones.

Aromatization hypothesis. The hypothesis that it is estrogen aromatized from perinatal testosterone that masculinizes the brain of genetic males.

Axillary hair. Underarm hair.

Bisexual. Individuals who are sexually attracted to members of both sexes.

Castration. The surgical removal of the gonads (testes or ovaries).

Clitoris. The female analogue of the head of the male penis.

Copulation. Sexual intercourse.

Defeminizing. Suppressing or disrupting female characteristics.

Demasculinizing. Suppressing or disrupting male characteristics.

Dihydrotestosterone. An androgen that cannot be converted to estrogen (i.e., that cannot be aromatized).

Ejaculation. Ejection of sperm.

Endocrine glands. The glands that release hormones into the general circulation of the body.

Estradiol. The most common estrogen.

Estrogens. A major class of gonadal hormones; estradiol is the major estrogen.

Estrous cycle. A cycle of sexual receptivity and non-receptivity displayed by many female mammals; female rats and guinea pigs have estrous cycles of about 4 days; human females do not have estrous cycles.

Estrus. The portion of the estrous cycle characterized by fertility and sexual receptivity.

Exocrine glands. The glands that secrete chemicals to the external world.

Fallopian tubes. Female ducts through which ova pass from the ovaries to the uterus.

Feminizing. Enhancing or producing female characteristics.

Follicle. The package of cells within which each ovum begins its development in the ovary.

Follicle stimulating hormone (FSH). The gonadotropic hormone that stimulates development of ovarian follicles.

Genitals. The reproductive organs.

Gonadectomy. The surgical removal of the gonads (testes or ovaries).

Gonadotropin-releasing hormone. The hypothalamic releasing hormone that controls the release of the two gonadotropic hormones.

Gonadotropins. The two pituitary tropic hormones (i.e., follicle stimulating hormone and luteinizing hormone) that stimulate the release of gonadal hormones.

Gonads. The testes and ovaries.

Growth hormone. An anterior pituitary hormone that acts directly on bone and muscle tissue to produce the pubertal growth spurt.

H-Y antigen. The protein that stimulates the cells of the medullary portion of the primordial gonads to proliferate and develop into testes.

Hermaphrodite. Strictly speaking, an organism with fully developed male and female reproductive organs; or more loosely speaking, an individual with reproductive organs that are not unambiguously either male or female.

Heterosexual. An individual who is sexually attracted to members of the opposite bodily sex.

Homosexual. An individual who is sexually attracted to members of the same bodily sex.

Hormones. Chemicals released by the endocrine system into general circulation.

Hypothalamopituitary portal system. A vascular network that carries hormones from the hypothalamus to the anterior pituitary.

Impotent. Males unable to achieve a penile erection.

Inhibitory factors. Hypothalamic hormones thought to regulate anterior pituitary hormones by inhibiting their release.

Intromission. Insertion of the penis into the vagina.

Lordosis. The intromission-facilitating, arched-back, tail-to-the-side posture of female rodent receptivity.

Luteinizing hormone (LH). One of the gonadotropic hormones; one of its functions is to cause the developing ovum to be released from its follicle.

Masculinizing. Enhancing or producing male characteristics.

Menstrual cycle. The hormone-regulated cycle in women of follicle growth, egg release, uterus lining build-up, and menstruation.

Müllerian-inhibiting substance. The substance released during male development that causes the precursors of the female reproductive ducts to degenerate.

Müllerian system. The embryonic precursors of the female reproductive ducts.

Negative feedback. A signal from the change of a measure in one direction that results in a compensatory change in the other direction; for example, an increase in the release of gonadal hormones often reduces their subsequent release.

Neurohormones. Hormones that interact with the nervous system.

Neurosecretory cells. Neurons specialized for the release of hormones into general circulation.

Orchidectomy. The removal of the testes.

Ova. The egg cells produced by the female ovary (singular: *ovum*).

Ovariectomy. The removal of the ovaries.

Ovaries. The female gonads.

Ovulation. The release of the ovum from the follicle in which it develops; ovulation signals the beginning of the fertile period of the menstrual cycle.

Oxytocin. One of the two major hormones released by the posterior pituitary; in females, it stimulates contractions of the uterus and the ejection of milk during suckling.

Paraventricular nucleus. One nucleus of the hypothalamus in which the hormones of the posterior pituitary are synthesized.

Pituitary stalk. The structure connecting the hypothalamus and the pituitary.

Positive feedback. A signal from the change of a measure in one direction that causes a further change in the same direction.

Posterior pituitary. The part of the pituitary gland that contains the terminals of hypothalamic neurons.

Preoptic area. One area of the hypothalamus that is thought to play a key role in the control of gonadotropin release from the anterior pituitary.

Proceptive. Engaging in behaviors that serve to attract the sexual advances of the other sex.

Progesterone. A progestin that prepares the uterus and breasts for pregnancy.

Progestins. A class of gonadal hormones; progesterone is the major progestin.

Puberty. The transitional period between childhood and adulthood during which fertility is achieved, the adolescent growth spurt occurs, and the secondary sex characteristics develop.

Pulsatile hormone release. Virtually all hormones are released from endocrine glands in large pulses or surges, which typically occur several times a day and last for several minutes each.

Releasing factors. Suspected (putative) releasing hormones; releasing hormones are called releasing factors until they have been isolated from hypothalamic tissue.

Releasing hormones. Chemicals synthesized in the hypothalamus that stimulate the release of hormones from the anterior pituitary.

Replacement injection. The injection of a hormone whose natural release has been curtailed by the removal of the gland that normally releases it.

Scrotum. The sac that holds the male testes.

Secondary sex characteristics. Structural features, other than the reproductive organs, that distinguish men from women.

Seminal vesicles. The small sacs containing the seminal fluid in which the sperm cells are ejaculated.

Sex chromosomes. The pair of chromosomes (XX or XY) that contains the genetic information that directs sexual development.

Sexually dimorphic nuclei. Two nuclei in the preoptic area that are larger in males than in females.

Sterility. The inability to reproduce.

Steroid. A class of related hormones derived from cholesterol, including all gonadal and adrenal sex hormones.

Supraoptic nucleus. A nucleus of the hypothalamus in which the hormones of the posterior pituitary are synthesized.

Testes. Male gonads.

Testosterone. The most common androgen.

Thyrotropin. An anterior pituitary hormone that stimulates the release of hormones from the thyroid gland.

Thyrotropin-releasing hormone. A hypothalamic hormone that stimulates the release of thyrotropin from the anterior pituitary; the first releasing hormone to be isolated.

Vas deferens. The part of the male reproductive duct system that carries sperm cells from the testes to the seminal vesicles.

Vasopressin. One of the two major hormones of the posterior pituitary; it facilitates reabsorption of water by the kidneys.

Wolffian system. The embryonic male reproductive duct system.

Zygote. The cell formed from the fusion of a sperm cell and an ovum; it contains all the information necessary for the growth of a complete adult organism.

11

The Biopsychology
of Eating

This chapter is about the biopsychology of eating. In order to appreciate the basics of eating, it is useful to consider the body without its protuberances, that is, as a simple living tube with a hole at each end. In order to supply itself with sources of energy and other nutrients, the tube puts materials containing them into one of its holes—typically the one with teeth—and passes them down its internal canal so that the nutrients can be absorbed through specialized membranes lining its inner surface; then the leftovers are jettisoned from the other end. Although this is not a particularly appetizing description of eating, it does serve to illustrate the frequently misunderstood point that, strictly speaking, food has not been consumed until it has been broken down and absorbed from the **gastrointestinal tract.** This act of breaking down food and absorbing it is commonly referred to as **digestion.** The gastrointestinal tract and the process of digestion are illustrated in Figure 11.1.

Eating has long been a major subject of biopsychological research. This chapter begins in the early part of this century with the first influential experiments on the biopsychology of eating, and it traces the evolution of the field to the present. The historical approach provides a particularly revealing perspective of the biopsychology of eating, and it also illustrates some of the fundamentals of scientific inquiry as well. There are three sections, each dealing with a different era of research on the biopsychology

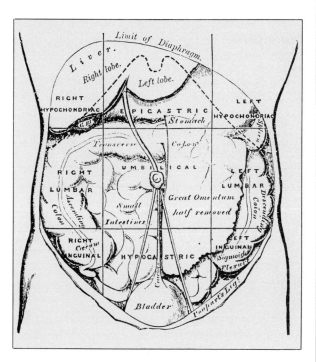

of eating; however, the discussion of current theories and data in Section 11.3 is the focus of this chapter:

11.1 **Peripheral Mechanisms: The Early Years of Research on Eating**

11.2 **The Dual-Center Set-Point Model of the 1950s and 60s**

11.3 **The Modern Era of Research on Eating**

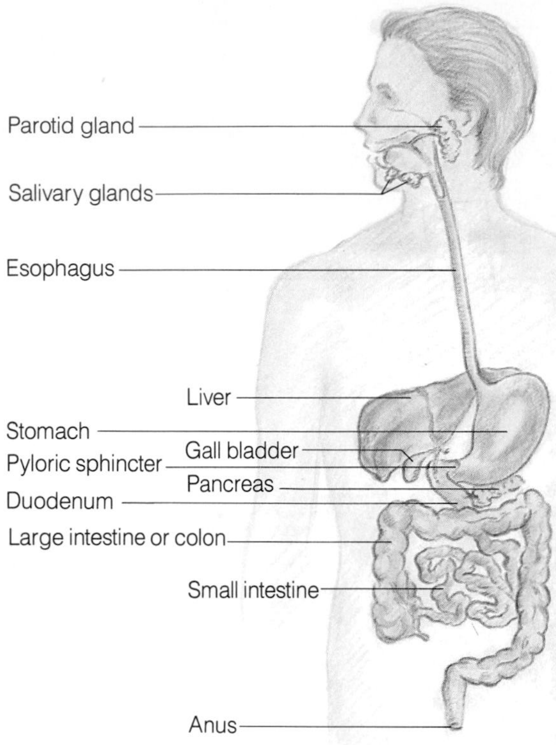

1. Chewing breaks up the food and mixes it with saliva.
2. Saliva lubricates the food and begins the process of digestion.
3. Swallowing moves the food down the esophagus to the stomach.
4. The primary function of the stomach is to serve as a storage reservoir. The hydrochloric acid in the stomach breaks the food down into small particles, and pepsin begins the process of breaking down protein molecules to amino acids.
5. The stomach gradually empties its contents through the pyloric sphincter into the duodenum, the upper portion of the intestine, where most of the absorption of nutrients takes place.
6. Digestive enzymes in the duodenum, many of them from the gall bladder and pancreas, break down protein molecules to amino acids and starch and complex sugar molecules to simple sugars. Simple sugars and amino acids readily pass through the duodenum wall into the bloodstream and are carried to the liver.
7. Fats are emulsified (broken into droplets) by bile, which is manufactured in the liver and stored in the gall bladder until it is released into the duodenum. Emulsified fat cannot pass through the duodenum wall and is carried by small ducts in the duodenum wall into the lymphatic system.
8. The large intestine reabsorbs water and electrolytes from the waste, and the remainder is ejected from the anus.

Labels on figure: Parotid gland, Salivary glands, Esophagus, Liver, Stomach, Pyloric sphincter, Gall bladder, Pancreas, Duodenum, Large intestine or colon, Small intestine, Anus

FIGURE 11.1 *The gastrointestinal tract and the process of digestion.*

This chapter has the air of a detective novel. You are provided with the clues (i.e., the data) gathered by scientist detectives, and you are implicitly challenged to come up with solutions before they are revealed to you. Before beginning Section 11.1, try the following puzzle. It illustrates a major theme of the chapter: that unintentional, unrecognized assumptions frequently block the way to otherwise obvious solutions.

"It's been a tough day," Slade thought to himself as he held down the brim of his hat with one hand and clutched the collar of his trench coat with the other to protect himself from the biting wind. The star witness had skipped town, and now Boris was on the streets once again, armed and looking for him. It's a good thing that Stella, the chief's secretary, had offered him her couch for a few days—just until things blew over.

As he turned the corner, Slade saw the lights come on in Stella's second-story apartment. Then Stella appeared at the window. Slade sensed immediately that something was wrong. Stella's face was taut and distorted, and the open window exposed her unprotected body and the flapping curtains to the full force of the gale. "Damn that Boris," he cursed to himself as he raced up the stairs.

He moved cautiously down the hall toward the sound of Stella's muffled sobs. Then he paused, drew his revolver, and burst into the apartment. Stella turned, and with a look of terror on her face, she fainted into Slade's arms. Then Slade saw the problem; there on the floor by the window lay the body of Freddie the Finn. As Slade examined the body—Freddie's, not Stella's—he noticed the tell-tale signs: the pieces of broken glass scattered around the body, the water on the carpet, and the end table laying on its side beneath the window.

"One of the easiest cases I ever solved," Slade thought, as he attempted to rouse Stella, "a clear case of accidental death by asphyxiation."

Your challenge is to figure out the details of Freddie's death from these clues. The solution to this puzzle and its relation to the biopsychology of eating are discussed later in the chapter.

11.1 Peripheral Mechanisms: The Early Years of Research on Eating

The Stomach

The search for the physiological basis of eating began in earnest in the early 1900s; it initially focused on the stomach. The procedure developed by Cannon and Washburn in 1912 for studying stomach contractions is illustrated in Figure 11.2. It was a perfect collaboration; Cannon had the ideas, and Washburn had the ability to swallow a balloon. First, Washburn swallowed an empty balloon tied to the end of a thin tube. Then, Cannon pumped some air into the balloon and connected the end of the tube to a water-filled glass U-tube so that Washburn's stomach contractions produced an increase in the level of the water at the other end of the U-tube. As hypothesized, Washburn reported a "pang" of hunger each time that a large stomach contraction was recorded.

Cannon and Washburn's results were soon confirmed by a case study of a patient with a tube implanted through his stomach wall just above the navel. The patient had accidentally swallowed some acid, which caused the walls of his *esophagus* to fuse shut. The tube was implanted to provide the patient with a means of feeding himself; however, it also provided a

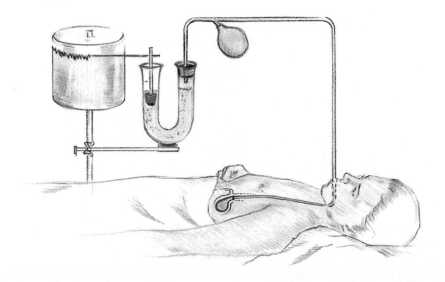

FIGURE 11.2 *The system developed by Cannon and Washburn in 1912 for measuring stomach contractions.*

window through which the activities of his stomach could be observed Carlson (1912). When there was food in the patient's stomach, small rhythmic contractions, subsequently termed **peristaltic contractions,** mixed the food and moved it along the digestive tract. In contrast, when the stomach was empty, there were large contractions that were associated with the patient's reports of hunger. Recordings of these peristaltic and hunger-related stomach contractions are illustrated in Figure 11.3.

Early reports that large stomach contractions are associated with hunger were complemented by reports suggesting that the stomach also plays a role in satiety. For example, in one influential study (Adolph, 1947), non-nutritive roughage was added to the diet of rats to reduce its **nutritive density** (calories per unit of volume). When the nutritive density of the diet was reduced slightly, the rats initially consumed the same volume of food that they had consumed before the diet was changed, but eventually they learned to increase their volume of intake enough to maintain their caloric intake at its usual level. However, when the nutritive density was reduced by 50% or more, their increases in consumption were not sufficient to maintain their body weights. This experiment made three points. First, it showed that rats learn on the basis of past experience with a diet to consume a certain volume of it; second, it showed that rats have mechanisms for detecting and adapting to changes in the caloric value of their diet; and third, it suggested that the stomach distension has an inhibitory effect on caloric intake.

The theory that the stomach plays the major role in hunger and satiety was tempered by two early observations. First, cutting the neural connections between the gastrointestinal tract and the brain had little effect on the food intake of experimental animals or human patients (Bash, 1939; Morgan & Morgan, 1940). Second, humans whose stomachs had been surgically removed and their esophaguses "hooked up" directly to their **duodenums** (see Figure 11.1) continued to report feelings of hunger and satiety, and they maintained their normal body weights by eating more meals of smaller size (MacDonald, Ingelfinger, & Belding, 1947; Wangensteen & Carlson, 1930).

The Mouth

Next, the attention of researchers turned to the mouth. Because the mouth is the first part of the gastrointestinal tract to receive chemical information about food, it seemed a likely site for a regulatory mechanism. One

FIGURE 11.3 *Peristaltic and hunger-related stomach contractions. (Adapted from Carlson, 1912.)*

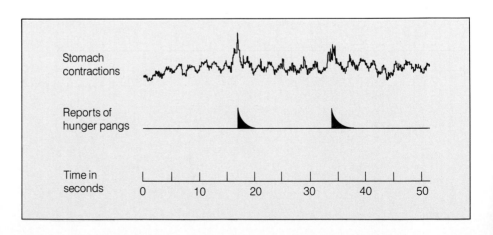

method developed for studying the role of oral factors in feeding was to cut the esophagus of an experimental animal and bring the cut end to the surface of the body so that when food was swallowed, it went down the esophagus and out the neck (see Figure 11.4). **Sham eating**—as this method was termed—permitted the study of oral factors in eating in the absence of other physiological signals normally associated with food intake. The first postsurgery meals of esophagotomized subjects proved to be larger than their usual meals; and within a few hours, many esophagotomized subjects were sham eating almost continuously (Janowitz & Grossman, 1949). This showed that meal termination is not controlled entirely by learning associated with the taste, texture, and volume of previous meals.

Epstein and Teitelbaum (1962) conducted an experiment that was in a sense complementary to the sham-eating experiments; it was an experiment in which oral cues were omitted and the other physiological cues were left intact. It seemed to prove that oral cues contributed little to the regulation of food intake. (I will get back to the "seemed to" part of the sentence later in the chapter.) The set-up for conducting this experiment is illustrated in Figure 11.5. A fine tube was fed through the top of the rat's scalp, forward beneath the skin to its nose, and then back down its *pharynx* (i.e., its throat) into its stomach. This **nasopharyngeal gastric fistula** was fixed in place by skull screws covered in dental acrylic (see Chapter 4). The tube was then connected to a liquid food pump so that each time the rat pressed the lever in a Skinner box, a small amount of liquid diet was pumped into the subject's stomach. This procedure is known as **intragastric feeding.** Remarkably, the rats in Epstein and Teitelbaum's study learned to press the lever to self-administer approximately the same quantity of the diet each day, and when the nutritive density of the diet was reduced by diluting it with water, they responded by increasing their lever pressing enough to maintain their usual level of daily caloric intake. This suggested that eating was almost entirely regulated by some nonoral mechanism sensitive to the caloric value of the food.

Although Epstein and Teitelbaum's influential intragastic feeding experiment suggested that food intake could be regulated in the absence of cues from the mouth, many other early studies demonstrated the importance of

FIGURE 11.4 *Sham eating.*

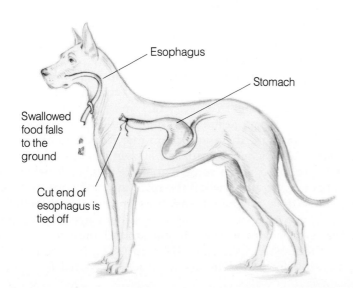

Esophagus

Stomach

Swallowed
food falls
to the
ground

Cut end of
esophagus is
tied off

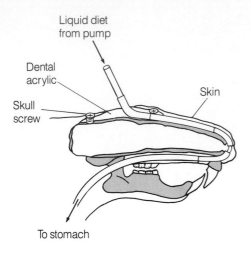

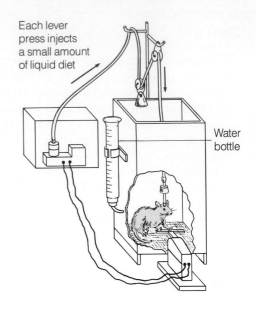

FIGURE 11.5 *A nasopharyngeal gastric fistula and the equipment used to allow a rat to inject liquid food into its own stomach. (Adapted from Epstein & Teitelbaum, 1962.)*

oral cues. One interesting example is a case study of a man named Tom (Wolf & Wolff, 1947), who, at the age of nine, tried to sneak a drink of what he thought was beer. It was in fact scalding hot clam chowder, which severely burnt his esophagus and necessitated the implantation of a fistula through the wall of his stomach so that he could feed himself. Although Tom was able to maintain his body weight by intragastric feeding, he found that food consumed in this fashion did not satisfy his hunger. Eventually, Tom solved this problem by chewing his food and then spitting it down his tube. There was, however, one exception to this procedure. After taking a taste or two of beer, he simply poured the remainder directly into his stomach.

Interpreting the Early Studies

The interpretation of early studies of gastric and oral regulatory feeding mechanisms was guided by two influential assumptions. The first was the **dual-center assumption.** Because humans and other animals often eat in bursts with reasonably well-defined starting and stopping points, it was widely assumed that feeding is controlled by two separate motivational centers in the brain: a hunger center, which initiates the bursts of eating, and a satiety center, which terminates them. The second assumption was the **set-point assumption,** the assumption that feeding is one component of a classic set-point, negative-feedback system. It was widely assumed that hunger is produced when some signal or signals fall below their hypothetical set points, and that when the resulting food consumption raises the signals above their set points, satiety is produced and feeding stops. You may recognize at once that this is a system just like the one that regulates the temperature in your home around the set point that you select on the thermostat. Ever since Bernard (1878) had pointed out that set-point, negative-feedback circuits were ideally suited for maintaining homeostasis (i.e., the stability of an organism's internal environment), such circuits had dominated thinking about homeostasis. In fact—and this is the important part—such set-point circuits started to be implicitly equated with homeostasis: Evidence that a system was homeostatic began to be accepted as evidence of set-point regulation. Other options—and there are other options, as you will see later in the chapter—were never seriously considered.

From the perspective provided by these two assumptions, most authors in the 1930s and 40s concluded that the primary *hunger signals* in humans and laboratory animals are contractions of the stomach, which are triggered when the amount of food in the stomach and/or the amount of fat in the body are below their set points. Three different *satiety signals* were postulated: (1) an oral signal—animals were thought to chew and swallow certain volumes of food on the basis of past experience; (2) an energy signal—animals were thought to monitor their energy intake and stop eating once their energy set point was reached; and (3) a gastric signal—signals from the stretch receptors in the stomach wall were thought to override the other factors when further eating would exceed the capacity of the stomach.

Arguably, the most important conclusion of the early era of feeding research was that eating is regulated by multiple, redundant mechanisms. The early studies showed that a variety of gastric, oral, and caloric factors contribute to the regulation of food intake, but they also showed that no single factor is essential. Such multiple-mechanism, redundant regulation is biologically advantageous, but it is extremely difficult to sort out experimentally. The task of identifying the physiological bases of eating was going to be far more complex than first anticipated.

11.2 The Dual-Center Set-Point Model of the 1950s and 60s

In the 1950s and 60s, researchers discovered the factors that appeared to be regulated by the presumed set-point feeding system, and they located the dual centers in the brain that appeared to be involved in this regulation. In so doing, they brought a topic that had been studied primarily by gastrointestinal physiologists into the mainstream of biopsychological inquiry. (Did the word *appeared* catch your eye in the first sentence? It is a forewarning that the feeding theories of the 50s and 60s, although viewed at the time as ultimate solutions, later proved to be seriously flawed. Try to anticipate some of the flaws as I describe the theories. And don't forget the case of Freddie the Finn; have you solved it yet?)

The Glucostatic Theory

The early research on feeding had clearly established that signals arising from the gut could influence hunger and satiety, but the fact that feeding was not disrupted by severing the neural connections between the gut and the brain suggested that information about conditions in the gut must be communicated to the brain via the body's other route of internal communication: the circulatory system. It suggested that some product of a meal was absorbed from the gastrointestinal tract into the bloodstream and carried to the brain, where it produced satiety by providing feedback about the increasing energy supply of the body. There were three obvious possibilities—the three different sources of energy that we derive from food: (1) **lipids** (fats), (2) **amino acids** (the breakdown products of proteins), and (3) **glucose,** a simple sugar, which is the breakdown product of more complex **carbohydrates** (starches and sugars). The **glucostatic theory** of feeding was proposed by several individuals in the late 1940s and early 1950s. They proposed that the primary stimulus for hunger is a decrease in the level of blood glucose below its set point, and that the primary stimulus for satiety is an increase in the level of blood glucose above its set point. It made sense that the main purpose of eating should be to maintain the blood glucose set point because glucose is the body's, and in particular, the brain's, primary fuel. The term *glucostat* was intended to emphasize the similarity between the hypothesized feeding mechanism and that of a thermostat.

The glucostatic theory of Mayer (1955) was particularly influential because it dealt with a serious problem associated with earlier versions of the theory. Mayer postulated that it was glucose utilization, rather than the blood glucose level per se, that was regulated by feeding. Under normal circumstances this distinction is of little consequence; because glucose is the preferred fuel of the body and brain, there is normally a high correlation between blood glucose levels and the level of glucose utilization. The reason for postulating that glucose utilization, rather than the blood-glucose level per se, provides the critical signal for the regulation of food intake was that it could account for those few instances in which high blood glucose levels are associated with **hyperphagia** (overeating). For example, Mayer argued that people with **diabetes mellitus** overeat despite very high levels of blood glucose because their pancreases do not produce sufficient quantities of the hormone **insulin,** which is needed for glucose to enter most cells of the body and to be utilized by them. Mayer suggested that glucose utilization is monitored by cells, termed **glucoreceptors,** that compare the levels of glucose entering the brain and the levels of glucose leaving it, and that this information is used to stimulate or inhibit feeding in order to maintain glucose utilization around a prescribed utilization set point.

The glucostatic theory received a major boost from the results of a brilliantly conceived series of experiments that appeared to identify the location in the brain of the critical glucoreceptors. Mayer and Marshall (e.g., Marshall, Barrnett, & Mayer, 1955; Mayer & Marshall, 1956) reasoned that they could determine the location of glucoreceptors in the brains of mice by injecting **gold thioglucose** into them. They assumed that the glucose in the compound would bind preferentially to the glucoreceptors, wherever they might be, and that the tissue in the area would be destroyed by the gold, which is a *neurotoxin* (nervous system poison). Remarkably, the mice injected with gold thioglucose began to eat huge quantities of food, and as a result they soon became extremely obese, which was consistent with the notion that there had been damage to a system involved in satiety. Subsequent histological examination of their brains revealed damage in the general area of the *ventromedial hypothalamus* (VMH)—see Figure 11.6.

The Lipostatic Theory

The **lipostatic theory** is a second theory of feeding that rose to prominence in the 1950s and 60s. It is based on the observation that the level of body fat (i.e., body lipids) appears to be kept at a relatively constant level in most individuals; under most conditions, changes in the body weights of adults reflect changes in the amount of body fat because the weight of other tissues normally remains reasonably constant. According to this theory (e.g., Kennedy, 1953), every person has a set point for body fat, presumably established by genetic and perinatal factors, and deviations from this set point produce compensatory adjustments in the level of eating. The most frequently cited support for this theory is the failure of short-term diet programs to produce long-term reductions in weight; as soon as patients stop "dieting," they tend to regain the weight that they have just lost.

The lipostatic and glucostatic theories are complementary, not mutually exclusive. The glucostatic theory was explicity designed to account for the short-term regulation of feeding; thus, it can readily account for meal initiation and termination, but not for the tendency of animals to quickly regain lost weight after an extended period of deprivation. In contrast, the lipostatic theory was expressly proposed to account for long-term regulation. Accordingly, the dominant view of the 1950s and 60s was that eating is strictly regulated by the interaction between two set-point systems: a short-term glucostatic system and a long-term lipostatic system.

The Hypothalamic Feeding Centers

It had been known for well over a century that tumors in the general area of the hypothalamus can produce *hyperphagia* (overeating) and obesity in human subjects. However, it was not until the development of stereotaxic surgery (see Chapter 4) in the late 1930s that experimenters were able to accurately position lesioning electrodes at specific hypothalamic sites to identify with more precision the areas of the hypothalamus responsible for these changes. The research that followed (see Stellar, 1954) seemed to suggest that signals that influenced feeding behavior were received and integrated by two different regions of the hypothalamus: a **ventromedial hypothalamus** (VMH) satiety center and a **lateral hypothalamus** (LH) feeding center (see Figure 11.6).

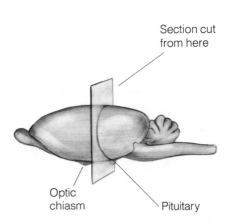

Section cut from here

Optic chiasm

Pituitary

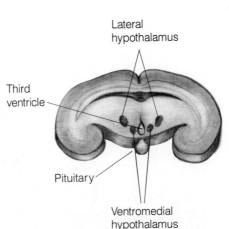

Frontal Section Through the Rat Brain

Lateral hypothalamus

Third ventricle

Pituitary

Ventromedial hypothalamus

FIGURE 11.6 *The location in the rat brain of the ventromedial hypothalamus and the lateral hypothalamus.*

The VMH Satiety Center   It was known as early as 1940 that large bilateral lesions in the ventromedial region of the rat hypothalamus produce hyperphagia and extreme obesity (Hetherington & Ranson, 1940). Although the ventromedial nucleus (VMN) was only one of several hypothalamic structures disrupted by such lesions, it was generally assumed that the hyperphagia and obesity resulted from VMN damage. The graphs in Figure 11.7 compare the weight gain and food intake of an adult rat with bilateral VMH lesions to those of an adult control rat.

The VMH hyperphagia syndrome has two different phases (e.g., Brobeck, Tepperman, & Long, 1943). The first phase is the **dynamic phase,** which usually begins soon after the subject regains consciousness after the operation. It is characterized by several weeks of grossly excessive eating and rapid weight gain. As the rat approaches its asymptotic (maximal) weight, consumption gradually declines to a level that is just sufficient to maintain a stable level of obesity. This period of stability is called the **static phase.** The most important feature of the static phase is that the animal "defends" its new body weight. If a rat in the static phase is deprived of food until it has lost a substantial amount of weight, it will temporarily increase its intake until the lost weight is regained; and if it is made to gain even more weight by forced feeding, it will temporarily reduce its intake until the excess is lost.

The phenomenon of VMH hyperphagia has been interpreted in terms of both the glucostatic and lipostatic theories. The glucostatic interpretation of VMH hyperphagia is that VMH lesions produce hyperphagia by destroying most of the glucoreceptors presumed to reside there, thereby

FIGURE 11.7 *Postoperative hyperphagia and obesity in a rat with bilateral VMH lesions compared to the food intake and weight of a control rat. (Adapted from Teitelbaum, 1961.)*

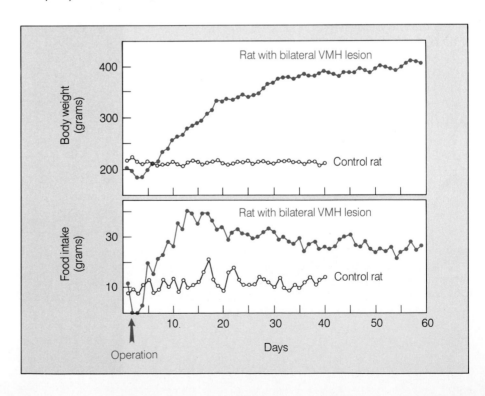

attenuating the satiety-producing effects of feeding (Brobeck, 1955; Miller, Bailey, & Stevenson, 1950). This interpretation is consistent with the observation that most of the increased food intake of rats with VMH lesions is attributable to the fact that they eat more per meal, rather than more meals (Teitelbaum & Campbell, 1958). The lipostatic interpretation of VMH hyperphagia is that VMH lesions somehow increase the set point for body fat (Hoebel & Teitelbaum, 1961). In support of this latter view, Keesey and Powley (1975) showed that VMH lesions produce less hyperphagia in rats made obese prior to the lesions.

Paradoxically, despite their prodigious levels of consumption, VMH-lesioned rats seem less hungry than unlesioned controls in other respects. Although VMH-lesioned rats eat much more than do intact rats when palatable food is readily available, they are less willing to work for it (Teitelbaum, 1957) or to consume it if it is unpalatable (Miller, Bailey, & Stevenson, 1950). Weingarten, Chang, and Jarvie (1983) have shown that the finickiness of VMH rats is a consequence of their obesity and not a primary effect of their lesion; VMH rats are no less likely to consume quinine-adulterated food than are unlesioned rats of equivalent obesity.

The LH Feeding Center   In 1951, Anand and Brobeck reported that bilateral lesions to the lateral hypothalamus (LH) produced **aphagia** (a complete cessation of eating); even rats first made hyperphagic by VMH lesions were rendered aphagic by the addition of LH lesions. They concluded that the lateral region of the hypothalamus contained a feeding center. Teitelbaum and Epstein (1962) subsequently discovered two important features of the syndrome produced in rats by LH lesions. First, they found that the aphagia was always accompanied by **adipsia** (a complete cessation of drinking). Second, they found that the lesioned rats would partially recover from both the aphagia and the adipsia if they were kept alive by tube feeding; after several days, they would begin to eat wet, palatable foods, such as chocolate chip cookies soaked in milk, and eventually they could maintain themselves on the standard laboratory fare of dry food pellets and water.

Many studies have shown that electrical stimulation of the LH can elicit feeding (e.g., Miller, 1957, 1960). However, to put this finding in perspective, it is important to keep two related findings in mind. The first is that feeding is not the only behavior that can be elicited by electrical stimulation of the LH: drinking, gnawing, temperature changes, sexual activity, and many other responses can be reliably elicited by LH stimulation in the appropriate environmental contexts. The second is that feeding can be elicited by the electrical stimulation of areas of the brain other than the LH—primarily other parts of the hypothalamus, amygdala, hippocampus, thalamus, and frontal cortex (e.g., Robinson, 1964). Accordingly, the term "hunger center" is a misnomer both in the sense that the LH is not the only structure involved in the production of eating and in the sense that eating is not the only motivated behavior influenced by the LH.

One issue that received considerable attention in the 50s and 60s was the question of whether or not the eating produced by LH stimulation is motivated by hunger. Do LH-stimulated subjects eat because they are hungry or because the current simply elicits a series of eating responses in the absence of any motivation to engage in them? The discovery that LH stimulation causes satiated rats to run a maze or press a lever to obtain food (e.g., Coons, Levak, & Miller, 1965) suggested that the current was making them hungry rather than simply eliciting eating movements.

The Dual-Center Set-Point Model

The model in Figure 11.8 characterizes the explanations of the physiological basis of feeding offered by most of the texts covering the topic in the 1950s and 60s. Although the contributions of factors other than blood glucose and body fat were briefly acknowledged, the basic system was thought to be a set-point negative-feedback circuit in which hypothalamic hunger (LH) and satiety (VMH) centers received signals about deviations from set points of blood glucose and body fat and produced the appropriate compensatory motivational changes. In effect, the model was the embodiment of the dual-mechanism and set-point assumptions, with a healthy helping of hypothalamus thrown in for good measure. The impact of the dual-center set-point theory was extraordinary. When it was at the height of its influence, it was served up to wave after wave of students as if the evidence for it were unassailable. There was a sense that it had answered the basic questions about the regulation of feeding and that only the details remained to be resolved.

The two-decade reign of the dual-center set-point theory of feeding was a period of transition. The dual-center set-point theory was both the culmination of the first 50 years of feeding research and the beginning of the modern era. The dual-center set-point theory integrated the relevant assumptions and theories of the first 50 years of research on the biopsychology of feeding into one theory, and that theory has served ever since as the primary target of attack for research in the field. There is nothing special about the intellectual hammering that the theory has taken. The purpose of all theories is to serve as targets of attack, so that their weaknesses can be exposed and used as the bases for improved theories, which in their turn are challenged.

FIGURE 11.8 *The dual-center set-point model of feeding, which was presented as the physiological basis of feeding by most texts in the 1950s and 60s, by many in the 1970s, and by a few in the 1980s.*

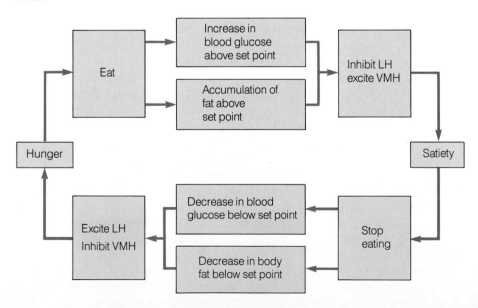

Before entering the modern era of research on feeding, complete the following exercise, which recapitulates the findings of the early years. And while you're at it, why don't you give the puzzle of Freddie the Finn one more try, if you haven't already solved it.

1. The primary function of the ___stomach___ is to serve as a storage reservoir for undigested food.

2. Most of the absorption of nutrients into the body takes place through the wall of the ___duodenum___ or upper intestine.

3. Stomach contractions are correlated with reports of ___hunger___.

4. Rats maintained in laboratory cages with access to only a single food increase their consumption of it when its ___nutrient___ density is reduced.

5. The phenomenon of ___sham___ eating demonstrates that oral signals by themselves are incapable of producing satiety.

6. Feeding by pressing a lever that causes a liquid diet to be pumped through a nasopharyngeal gastric fistula is called ___intragastric___ feeding.

7. Arguably, the most important conclusion of the early era of research on eating was that eating is regulated by multiple, ___redundant___, mechanisms.

8. Mayer argued that people with diabetes mellitus overeat because their bodies are unable to ___utilize___ glucose.

9. Gold thioglucose injected into mice created large lesions in the general area of the ventromedial hypothalamus and rendered them ___hyperphagic___ and obese.

10. Large bilateral lesions of the lateral hypothalamus made rats ___aphagic___ and adipsic.

11. During the ___static___ phase, the weight of a rat with large bilateral VMH lesions remains relatively constant.

11.3 The Modern Era of Research on Eating

What amazes many people about the dual-center set-point theory is the way that it has survived in the face of serious criticism. It dominated the field for the 20 years between 1950 and 1970, and even today it is still presented in a few texts as the current theory of eating. I believe that one reason for its staying power is that the set-point assumption is so ingrained in most people's thinking about feeding that they do not see alternative solutions. This reference to obstructive assumptions brings us full circle, back to the case of Freddie the Finn. Earlier in the chapter, you left Freddie lying in a pool of water and broken glass on the floor of Stella's apartment, and you were warned about the hazards of hasty assumptions. If you didn't make the usual mistake of assuming that Freddie was a human from Finland, you likely had little difficulty figuring out that Freddie was Stella's pet fish whose bowl had been knocked to the floor by the wind blowing through her open window. However, if you did unwittingly wander into the logical trap that I set for you, the experience will have left you with a better appreciation of how easy it is to make an incorrect assumption without realizing that you have made any assumption at all, and of how difficult it is to solve a problem once this has happened. You should now be better able to appreciate the accomplishments of modern biopsychologists who, with great insight, have recognized the implicit assumptions of the 50s and 60s and conducted innovative studies to expose them.

Because the first half century of research on the biopsychology of feeding was dominated by the assumption that eating was strictly regulated by deviations from internal set points, eating was typically studied in situations in which there were no external influences. For example, as you have seen, most of the key early studies examined the effects of various gastrointestinal or hypothalamic manipulations on the eating behavior of rats living in isolation with access to only one diet: commercial lab chow and water. Since the early 1970s, there has been an increase in the number of studies focusing on the effects on eating of external factors such as the palatability of the food, the social context, and certain learning situations. These studies have clearly established that external factors have powerful effects on what, when, and how much humans and laboratory animals eat. The idea that eating is controlled solely by deviations from internal set points is humbled by a piece of pecan pie with whipped cream. The recent studies of external factors and eating have emphasized the need for a new biopsychological model of eating—one that integrates both internal and external influences. The chapter culminates with the description of such a model.

The Influence of Palatability on Eating

Imagine your favorite food. Perhaps it is a succulent morsel of lobster meat covered with melted garlic butter, a piece of chocolate cheesecake, or a simple plate of sizzling home-made french fries. Are you starting to feel a bit hungry? If the home-made french fries—my personal weakness—were sitting in front of you right now, wouldn't you reach out and have one, or maybe the whole plateful? Have you not on occasion felt discomfort after a large main course, only to proceed to "polish off" a substantial dessert? The usual answers to these questions lead unavoidably to the conclusion that an important factor in most human eating is the anticipated pleasurable effects of the food. And the same is true for the laboratory rat. The overwhelming effects of palatability on the eating behavior of rats can be readily demonstrated simply by modifying the palatability of the standard rat lab chow without changing its nutritive value. The addition of a small amount of *saccharin*, which increases the sweetness of the chow without adding calories, produces a substantial increase in both consumption and body weight. The addition of bitter-tasting *quinine* has the opposite effects.

The Effects of Variety on Palatability: Sensory-Specific Satiety

There is an old country-and-western song in which the male singer tries to justify his infidelity by crooning metaphorically that when you eat steak every day, the occasional plate of beans can taste mighty fine. Although this creative attempt to placate his mate meets with little success, it does acknowledge the important effects of variety on palatability. Even a commonly preferred taste, such as that of steak, becomes less palatable if it is continually experienced, and thus other tastes, such as that of beans, may be temporarily preferable. Barbara and Edmund Rolls and their colleagues have studied this phenomenon and termed it **sensory-specific satiety**. In one study (Rolls, Rolls, Rowe, & Sweeney, 1981), human subjects were asked to rate the palatability of eight different foods, and then they ate a meal of one of them. After the meal, they were asked to rate the palatability of the eight foods once again, and it was found that their rating of the food that they had just eaten had declined substantially more than had their ratings of the other seven foods. Moreover, when the subjects were offered an unexpected second course, they consumed most of it unless it was the same as the first. Some foods produce greater sensory-specific satiety than other foods; the sensory-specific satiety produced in humans by the consumption of foods rich in fats and proteins can last for weeks, whereas foods such as rice, bread, potatoes, sweets, and green salads can be eaten almost every day with only a slight decline in their palatability (Lepkovsky, 1977).

The phenomenon of sensory-specific satiety has two important consequences. First, it encourages the consumption of a varied diet. If there were no sensory-specific satiety, an animal would tend to eat its preferred food and nothing else, and the result could be life-threatening malnutrition. Second, sensory-specific satiety encourages those animals that have access to a variety of foods to eat a greater amount than those that do not; an animal that has eaten "its fill" of one food tends to begin eating again if it is offered a different one. This encourages animals to take full advantage of times of abundance, which are all too rare in nature.

The effect of variety on feeding is most evident in animals, such as laboratory rats, that normally have access to only a single, nutritionally complete food. The effect of offering a laboratory rat a varied diet of highly palatable foods—commonly referred to as a **cafeteria diet**—is dramatic. For example, adult rats offered bread and chocolate in addition to their usual laboratory diet increased their intake of calories an average of 84%, and after 120 days they had increased their body weights an average of 49% (Rogers & Blundell, 1980). The spectacular effects of cafeteria diets on consumption and body weight clearly run counter to the idea that eating is rigidly controlled by internal energy deficits. If you consider for a moment that almost all of us in this society are exposed each day to cafeteria diets, you will better understand why obesity is such a problem. Our eating system did not evolve under access to a virtually limitless variety of food, and it thus has difficulty adapting to it.

Re-examination of the Glucostatic Theory

Although the glucostatic theory of feeding has been subjected to severe criticism (e.g., Friedman & Stricker, 1976; Russek, 1975, 1981), it still has many adherents (e.g., Le Magnen, 1981). Two general arguments can be mounted against the notion that the initiation and termination of meals are controlled, respectively, by decreases and increases in blood glucose levels. The first is the evidence, which you have just seen, that external incentives exert substantial control over eating. The second is that the metabolic processes of the body are geared to keep blood glucose levels and glucose utilization by the brain relatively constant, even during severe fluctuations in food intake and energy output. It does not seem likely that a signal that is itself maintained at a relatively constant level could bear the primary responsibility for the regulation of feeding.

Figure 11.9 illustrates how the relative constancy of blood glucose levels is maintained during the three phases of metabolism associated with a meal (see Woods, Taborsky, & Porte, 1986): (1) the **cephalic phase,** which

FIGURE 11.9 *The regulation of energy sources in the body.*

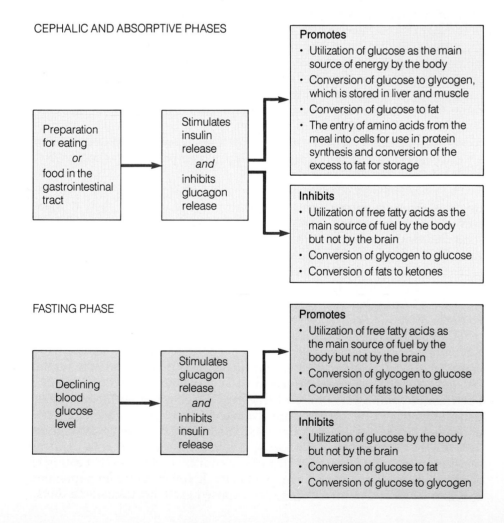

CEPHALIC AND ABSORPTIVE PHASES

Preparation for eating *or* food in the gastrointestinal tract → Stimulates insulin release *and* inhibits glucagon release

Promotes
• Utilization of glucose as the main source of energy by the body
• Conversion of glucose to glycogen, which is stored in liver and muscle
• Conversion of glucose to fat
• The entry of amino acids from the meal into cells for use in protein synthesis and conversion of the excess to fat for storage

Inhibits
• Utilization of free fatty acids as the main source of fuel by the body but not by the brain
• Conversion of glycogen to glucose
• Conversion of fats to ketones

FASTING PHASE

Declining blood glucose level → Stimulates glucagon release *and* inhibits insulin release

Promotes
• Utilization of free fatty acids as the main source of fuel by the body but not by the brain
• Conversion of glycogen to glucose
• Conversion of fats to ketones

Inhibits
• Utilization of glucose by the body but not by the brain
• Conversion of glucose to fat
• Conversion of glucose to glycogen

covers the brief period between the sight, odor, and taste of food and the beginning of its absorption into the bloodstream from the intestine, (2) the **absorptive phase,** which covers the period of time during which the energy absorbed into the bloodstream from the meal is meeting all of the body's energy needs, and (3) the **fasting phase,** which covers the period from the completion of the absorptive phase to the preparation for the next meal. Metabolism is primarily under the control of two pancreatic hormones: insulin and glucagon. **Insulin** is released during the cephalic and absorptive phases, and it promotes the utilization of glucose by the body, as well as its conversion to glycogen and fat. **Glycogen,** which is stored in liver and muscle, and fat, which is stored beneath the skin in the adipose layer, are the primary forms in which the body stores energy. Insulin thus keeps blood glucose levels from increasing markedly during the absorptive phase, when there are substantial amounts of glucose entering the blood from the meal, and it promotes the storage of the excess energy. In contrast, **glucagon,** which is released during the fasting phase, keeps the blood levels of glucose from declining precipitously during the fasting phase by promoting the conversion of glycogen to glucose. During the fasting phase, the tissues of the body cannot use glucose as a source of energy because without insulin glucose cannot enter their cells. At this time, the body receives its energy from **free fatty acids** released from fat. However, the brain continues to use glucose during the fasting phase because, unlike other cells of the body, most of the cells of the central nervous system do not need insulin for glucose to enter them. The extent to which the body will go to maintain the relative constancy of blood glucose levels is demonstrated during starvation. At such times, the body attempts to keep the blood glucose levels from falling by breaking down its own tissues and converting the released amino acids to glucose, a process called **gluconeogenesis.** During starvation, the brain can get a portion of its energy from **ketones,** a breakdown product of fat.

What evidence is there in favor of glucostatic theories? Support comes from the observation (Le Magnen, 1981) that there is often a slight—less than 6%—decrease in the blood glucose levels of rats before they start to eat a meal. This line of evidence has two weaknesses. One is that decreases in blood glucose levels do not always precede eating (Strubbe & Steffens, 1971). The other is summed up by the admonition presented in Chapter 1: Correlation does not imply causation. The fact that slight glucose reductions precede meals does not mean that they cause meals; in fact, it has been argued that the decline in blood glucose preceding a meal may be a response elicited by the intention to start eating, not the other way around (de Castro, 1981; Friedman, 1981; Rowland, 1981; Sclafani, 1981; Stricker, 1981). In response to this second criticism, Campfield, Brandon, and Smith (1985) have provided evidence that premeal declines in blood glucose may play a causal role in initiating meals, rather than being just correlated with meal initiation. By infusing glucose into the blood of rats at the first sign of a decrease in blood glucose, they were able to delay the onset of meals.

Also offered in support of the glucostatic theory of feeding is the widely reported finding that insulin injections both reduce blood glucose levels and increase eating. The problem with this line of reasoning is that insulin injections must reduce blood glucose levels by about 50% in order to initiate feeding (Rowland, 1981), a level of reduction never seen under free-feeding conditions. Moreover, infusions of metabolic fuels other than glucose can block insulin-induced eating without attenuating the decline in blood glucose (Stricker, Rowland, Saller, & Friedman, 1977). Overall, the research on glucose deficits suggests that the feeding system is designed to prevent large glucose deficits, not to react to them; but on those rare occasions when large glucose deficits do occur, they are a powerful motivating force. Whether the circuits that mediate glucose-deficit-induced feeding are in the hypothalamus, in the liver, or in both is still a matter of serious debate, and it is still not clear whether these circuits are specifically sensitive to glucose or whether they respond to energy levels in general.

What about the other side of the coin: Do glucose injections suppress feeding? The results of experiments designed to answer this question have been mixed. Although there have been some positive findings, a number of investigators have failed to observe the predicted suppressive effects on feeding of glucose injections into the hypothalamus, the liver, or into general circulation. Some of the confusion might stem from differences in the rate of blood glucose infusion. Geiselman (1987) has argued that rapid, but not gradual, increases in blood glucose might trigger excessive insulin release that might ultimately reduce blood glucose levels by negative feedback.

Regulation of Body Fat: Regulatory Effect of Energy Expenditure

A serious shortcoming of the dual-center set-point theory is that it is based on the premise that the regulation of the body's energy resources occurs entirely at the intake end of the system (Keesey & Powley, 1986). However, there is strong evidence that the body responds to shortages and excesses of energy resources by regulating how efficiently it uses the energy at its disposal. This point is clearly made by the progressively declining effectiveness of both weight-loss and weight-gain programs (Garrow, 1974). Initially, low-calorie and high-calorie diets produce substantial weight loss and weight gain, respectively, but the rate of weight change diminishes with each successive week of the diet—most dieters are all too familiar with this disappointing trend. If a dieter adheres strictly to his or her diet for a sufficiently long time, eventually an equilibrium will be reached, and no further weight losses or gains will occur (see Figure 11.10).

Why does the rate of weight gain on high-calorie diets and of weight loss on low-calorie diets decline progressively? The evidence suggests that animals with little or no body fat are "energy misers"; they make efficient use of all of the energy that they consume. In contrast, animals with more fat tend to use energy less efficiently. In fact, it has been shown that as animals gain weight, they tend to waste more and more of the energy that they consume by generating excess heat. The effect of this **diet-induced thermogenesis** is to counteract further weight gain. Rothwell and Stock (1979, 1982) have shown that the resting energy expenditure of a group of rats made obese by a cafeteria diet was 45% greater than that of a group of control rats, and that they had more than twice the control level of **brown adipose tissue.** Brown adipose tissue has been shown to be the main nonmuscular site of heat generation in the body (Trayhurn & James, 1981).

What signal makes us likely to increase our food intake when our fat reserves are particularly low and to decrease it when they are particularly high? What provides the information to the brain about the level of body fat? The fact that **basal blood insulin levels** (the blood levels of insulin after

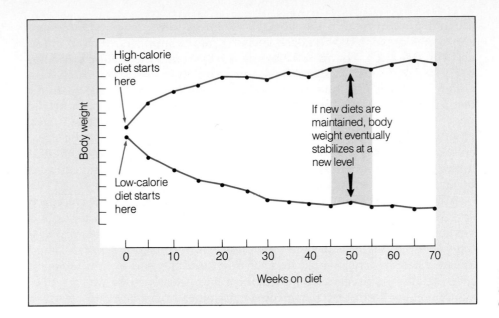

FIGURE 11.10 *The effect on body weight of switching to either a low- or high-calorie diet.*

an overnight fast) are higher in fat people suggested that blood insulin levels might signal this crucial information to the brain. However, this hypothesis was rejected because levels of blood insulin fluctuate markedly during the day in response to all sorts of events such as exercise, stress, and eating. How could widely fluctuating levels of blood insulin provide the brain with accurate information about its relatively stable reserves of body fat (Panksepp, 1975)? A resolution was suggested by Woods and Porte (1977). They found that insulin from general circulation penetrates the cerebrospinal fluid at a very slow rate, and thus, that the level of insulin in cerebrospinal fluid does not reflect the moment to moment fluctuations in the level of insulin in the blood. Accordingly, they suggested that it is the levels of insulin in cerebrospinal fluid that provide the brain with information about levels of fat in the body. In support of this hypothesis was the discovery of specific insulin binding sites in the hypothalamus and other parts of the brain (Baskin, et al., 1983; Porte & Woods, 1981) and the observation that insulin infused into the lateral ventricles of baboons for 2 to 3 weeks produced a dose-dependent decline of food intake and weight (Woods, Lotter, McKay, & Porte, 1979). At the highest dose, food intake was reduced by close to 75% without altering blood insulin or blood glucose levels.

Role of the Gastrointestinal Tract in Satiety

The study of the regulation of feeding began in the early part of this century with a series of studies on the role of the stomach, but interest in gastrointestinal factors in feeding declined in the 50s and 60s when notions of hypothalamic feeding centers reigned supreme. However, several subsequent findings have rekindled interest in the role of the gastrointestinal tract in satiety. For example, the discovery that the injection of small amounts of food into the duodenum terminates sham feeding (Gibbs, Maddison, & Rolls, 1981; Liebling, Eisner, Gibbs, & Smith, 1975) suggested the existence of a duodenal satiety mechanism, and the discovery that the accumulation of food in the stomach produces satiety even when its absorption is prevented by a noose devise (Kraly & Smith, 1978) or an inflatable cuff (Deutsch, Young, & Kalogeris, 1978) around the **pyloric sphinctor** suggested that satiety signals also emanate from the stomach. It was widely assumed that the satiety-producing effects of food in the gastrointestinal tract were mediated by neural signals carried to the brain by the *vagus;* however, food in the stomach was found to inhibit food intake even in *vagotomized* rats (Kraly & Gibbs, 1980). This suggested that the presence of food in the gastrointestinal tract leads to release of some chemical in the blood that serves as a satiety signal. This hypothesis was confirmed by an interesting experiment by Koopmans (1981).

As illustrated in Figure 11.11, Koopmans transplanted an extra stomach and length of intestine in several rats and joined the major arteries and veins attached to the implants to the recipient rats' own circulatory systems. Despite the fact that the transplant had no functional nerves, food injected into the transplanted stomach decreased the eating of the recipient rat in relation to its volume and caloric value. Clearly there was a satiety signal coming from the transplanted gastrointestinal tract, and clearly it was being transmitted to the brain through the blood rather than through the nervous system. Koopmans concluded that the satiety signal was a hormone released by the transplanted gastrointestinal tract rather than the absorbed constituents of the meal because food injected into the implanted stomach inhibited the feeding behavior of the recipient even when the food

FIGURE 11.11 *Koopmans (1981) implanted an extra stomach and length of small intestine in each subject. Food injected into the extra stomach decreased eating in proportion to its volume and caloric value. (Adapted from Carlson, 1986.)*

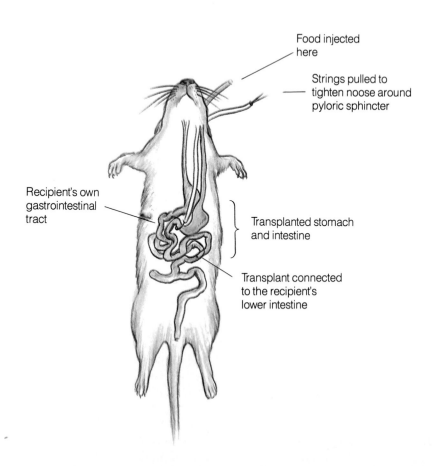

Food injected here

Strings pulled to tighten noose around pyloric sphincter

Recipient's own gastrointestinal tract

Transplanted stomach and intestine

Transplant connected to the recipient's lower intestine

was trapped in the implanted stomach by a noose around the pyloric sphincter so that it could not be absorbed into the bloodstream from the duodenum.

It is widely believed that one or more of the peptide hormones released by the gastrointestinal tract serves as a satiety signal. In fact, injections of three different peptide hormones—*cholecystokinin* (CCK), *bombesin*, and *somatostatin*—have been shown to inhibit feeding in a variety of situations (see Halmi, Ackerman, Gibbs, & Smith, 1987). Of these three putative gastrointestinal peptide satiety hormones, **cholecystokinin** has been the most widely studied. Because CCK does not appear to readily penetrate the blood-brain barrier, it has been assumed to produce satiety by acting peripherally. McHugh and Moran (1985) have suggested that CCK released from the duodenal wall produces satiety by inhibiting stomach emptying. In this model, which is illustrated in Figure 11.12, CCK is released in proportion to the number of calories in the duodenum, and it activates receptors in the pyloric sphincter that cause it to close.

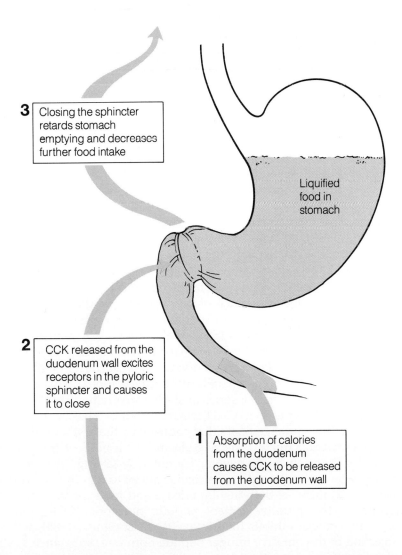

FIGURE 11.12 *The model proposed by McHugh and Moran to account for the ability of cholecystokinin to inhibit eating.*

3 Closing the sphincter retards stomach emptying and decreases further food intake

Liquified food in stomach

2 CCK released from the duodenum wall excites receptors in the pyloric sphincter and causes it to close

1 Absorption of calories from the duodenum causes CCK to be released from the duodenum wall

Hypothalamic Regulation of Eating: A Re-evaluation

You have already learned that bilateral lesions of the ventromedial hypothalamus (VMH) have two striking effects; they produce both hyperphagia and obesity. The traditional interpretation of these effects has been that the VMH is a satiety center. However, today this view has few adherents; there is overwhelming evidence that the primary role of the hypothalamus is the regulation of metabolism rather than the direct regulation of feeding. Why then do VMH-lesioned animals overeat and become obese? The initial interpretation was that the obesity of VMH animals is caused by their overeating; however, recent evidence suggests that the converse is true. It suggests that their tendency to become obese causes them to overeat. This second way of thinking about the relation between eating and obesity of VMH rats is counterintuitive, so proceed cautiously.

The current view is that the primary effect of VMH lesions is to increase the body's tendency to produce fat (**lipogenesis**) and to decrease its tendency to release fats into the bloodstream (**lipolysis**)—perhaps as the result of the increases in insulin release observed following the lesion (e.g., Powley, Opsahl, Cox, & Weingarten, 1980). The idea is that because the calories of VMH-lesioned rats are converted to fat at such a high rate, the rats must keep eating to insure that they have enough calories in their blood to meet their immediate energy requirements. The rats with VMH lesions are like misers who run to the bank each time they make a bit of money and deposit most of it in a savings account from which withdrawals cannot be made—they continually have to be earning more spending money. The following observations have provided convincing support for this interpretation of VMH hyperphagia: (1) Insulin levels in the blood are elevated after VMH lesions, even when the rats have not yet been allowed to overeat, and the degree of this **hyperinsulinemia** displayed by each rat is a good predictor of its subsequent weight gain when it is given free access to food (Hustvedt & Løvø, 1972). (2) Rats with VMH lesions accumulate more fat than do controls, even when they eat the same amount of food (Han, Feng, & Kuo, 1972; Slaunwhite, Goldman, & Bernardis, 1972). (3) During the day, when normal rats sleep and derive their energy from fat stores, VMH rats get some of their energy from gluconeogenesis, which is normally observed only in starving animals (Holm, Hustvedt, & Løvø, 1973). (4) Cutting the branch of the vagus nerve that transmits signals from the brain to the pancreas eliminates the hyperphagia and obesity produced by VMH lesions in rats (Sawchenko, Eng, Gold, Simson, 1977).

It has long been assumed that large bilateral VMH lesions produce obesity and hyperphagia by damaging the ventromedial nuclei (VMN); however, Gold and his colleagues (Gold, 1973; Gold, Jones, Sawchenko, & Kapatos, 1977) have shown in a series of studies involving tiny stereotaxically positioned knife cuts that VMH lesions produce obesity and hyperphagia because they damage fibers that course past the VMN on their way to the **paraventricular nuclei.** Discrete electrolytic lesions of the paraventricular nuclei themselves (Leibowitz, Hammer, & Chang, 1981) or knife cuts to the tracts leaving the paraventricular nuclei to join the vagus (Gold & Simson, 1982) increase both insulin release and food consumption. Microinjection of the putative satiety peptide hormone, CCK, into the paraventricular nuclei inhibits food intake (Faris & Olney, 1985), whereas microinjection of the putative hunger peptide hormone, **substance Y,** stimulates feeding (Gray & Morley, 1986).

The role of the LH in feeding is still not well understood. One complication is that the behavioral effects of LH lesions are very general. Large bilateral lesions of the LH produce general motor disturbances and a general lack of responsiveness to sensory input, of which food and drink are but two examples. A second complication is that the LH is a relatively large, complex, and ill-defined area with many small nuclei and several major nuclei and a number of major tracts coursing through and around it. A third complication is that the aphagia associated with the LH syndrome differs markedly from subject to subject, perhaps as a result of different lesion placements; for example, some aphagic rats develop serious gastric ulcers, while others do not (Schallert, Whishaw, & Flannigan, 1977).

Learning and Eating

The modern era of feeding research has been characterized by an increasing awareness of the major role played by learning in determining when we eat, what we eat, how much we eat, and even how the food that we eat is digested and metabolized. The conception of the feeding system has changed from that of an immutable system that maintains glucose and fat levels at predetermined set points, to that of a flexible system that operates within certain general guidelines, but is "fine-tuned" by experience. The following are some of the findings that have contributed to the evolution of this new concept.

Learning and the Cephalic Phase of Digestion   The digestive and metabolic events that are elicited by the sight, odor, or taste of food are referred to as *cephalic-phase responses*. Salivation, gastric secretions (e.g., Moore & Motoki, 1979), and insulin secretions (e.g., Lucas, Bellisle, & Di Maio, 1987) are the most frequently studied cephalic-phase responses. Pavlov (1927) was the first to show that a cephalic-phase response, namely salivation, can be conditioned. He argued that the sight and/or smell of food elicits salivation because these stimuli have previously been paired with food consumption. In support of this view, he reported that the sight or smell of milk elicited copious salivation in puppies raised on a milk diet, but not in those raised on solid foods. He also showed in his classic experiments that a tone acquired the ability to elicit salivation if it was paired several times with food. Whether insulin release can be influenced by similar forms of learning is still a matter of debate (see Woods, Vasselli, Kaestner, Szakmary, Milburn, & Vitiello, 1977); however, Berthoud, Bereiter, Trimble, Siegel, & Jeanrenaud, 1981 found that rats had elevated blood levels of insulin during the time of day when they were usually fed.

Learning and Meal Initiation   Weingarten (1983, 1984) has shown that learning can influence the initiation of a meal. During the conditioning phase of one of his experiments, Weingarten presented a 4.5-minute buzzer-and-light conditional stimulus to rats before each of their meals. Each meal, which consisted of a small amount of a highly palatable liquid diet, was presented during the last half minute of the conditional stimulus. The rats received six such meals per day at irregular intervals, and at the midpoint between each meal, a pure tone was sounded. This conditioning procedure was continued for 11 consecutive days. Throughout the ensuing test phase of the experiment, the palatable liquid diet was continuously available in the rats' home cages. Despite the fact that the subjects were never deprived during test phase, each time that the buzzer and light were presented, the rats started to eat. In contrast, eating in response to the pure tone was rare. Weingarten's research suggests that we do not become hungry at meal time because we are experiencing an energy deficit—few of us in this society begin meals in need of energy. We usually become hungry because of the presence of external cues (such as time of day) that have previously predicted a meal.

Learning What to Eat There are many objects in the environment; some are edible and some are not. How do humans and other mammals know what to eat? Part of the answer is that they are born with preferences for sweet and salty tastes, which are usually associated in nature with health-promoting foods, and with aversions for bitter tastes, which in nature are usually associated with toxins. However, superimposed on these inherited preferences and aversions are learned preferences and aversions. Flavors followed by illness become aversive (conditioned taste aversion, Chapter 4), whereas flavors followed by an improved state of affairs, such as an infusion of calories, come to be preferred (Arbour & Wilkie, 1988; Bolles, Hayward, & Crandall, 1981; Capaldi, Campbell, Sheffer, & Bradford, 1987; Mehiel & Bolles, 1988). Rats also learn to prefer flavors that they experience in mother's milk (Galef & Sherry, 1973) and those that they smell on the breaths of conspecifics (Galef, 1989).

The food that we eat not only supplies us with energy, but it also supplies us with essential vitamins and minerals. How do animals select a diet that provides all of the vitamins and minerals that they need? To answer this question, researchers have studied how dietary deficiencies influence diet selection. Two patterns of results have emerged: one for sodium deficiency and the other for deficiencies in other essential vitamins and minerals. When an animal is deficient in sodium, it develops an immediate and compelling preference for the taste of sodium salt. This is clearly not a learning effect because sodium-deprived rats also develop a preference for *lithium chloride,* which tastes the same as *sodium chloride* (table salt), but is toxic (Nachman, 1963). In contrast, animals do not have an innate capacity to prefer the tastes of other specific nutrients that they require; in fact, they cannot taste most of them in their diets at their usual concentrations. Instead, animals maintained on a diet deficient in an essential vitamin or mineral other than sodium seem to develop an aversion to this diet, and thus are encouraged to eat different foods until they find one that alleviates their deficiency.

If rats, and presumably we humans, are so good at learning to eat healthy diets, why are dietary deficiencies so common in societies such as ours in which many healthy foods are readily available? One reason is that, in order to maximize profits, manufacturers sell foods with the tastes that we prefer, but with most of the essential nutrients extracted from them; even rats prefer chocolate chip cookies to nutritionally complete rat chow. The second reason is illustrated by the classic study of Harris, Clay, Hargreaves, and Ward (1933). When thiamine-deficient rats were offered two new diets, one with **thiamine** (vitamin B_1) and one without, within days almost all of them were eating the complete diet and avoiding the deficient one. However, when they were offered 10 new diets, only one of which contained the badly needed thiamine, very few developed a preference for the right diet. The number of different substances consumed each day by most people in industrialized societies is immense, and such variety makes it very difficult for our bodies to use their natural ability to learn which foods are beneficial and which are not.

Incentive Theories of Eating

Several authors have suggested a new way of thinking about the biopsychology of eating (e.g., Bindra, 1978; Bolles, 1980; Booth, 1981; Collier, 1980; Rolls, 1981; Toates, 1981; Wirtshafter & Davis, 1977; Wyrwicka, 1969). They have argued that humans and other animals are normally not driven to eat by internal energy deficits; they are drawn to eat by the anticipated pleasure-producing effects of food, that is, by the food's **incentive properties.** This new way of thinking about eating does not deny the importance of internal regulatory factors. In fact, it suggests how internal regulatory factors exert their effects. According to the incentive theories, both internal and external factors influence eating in the same way, by changing the incentive value of available foods (see Cabanac, 1971). You have already learned in this chapter about a variety of factors that can change a food's incentive value. For example, the incentive value of a particular food is reduced if its consumption is followed by gastrointestinal upset or if a large amount of that food has recently been consumed; in contrast, a full stomach reduces the incentive value of all foods. On the other side of the coin, experiencing the health-promoting effects of a food increases the incentive value of that particular food, whereas deprivation or expecting a meal tend to increase the incentive value of all palatable foods. If you have difficulty appreciating these incentive notions, compare in your mind the incentive value that a turkey sandwich would have if it were offered to you after 3 days without food as opposed to 5 minutes after your last mouthful of a traditional Christmas dinner.

Since the proposal of incentive theories of eating, the interaction between the energy levels of the body and the incentive properties of food has become an important area of research. For example, Booth (1981) asked subjects to rate the momentary pleasure produced by the flavor, the smell, the sight, or just the thought of various foods at different times after consuming a high-calorie, high-carbohydrate liquid diet. There was strong evidence of an immediate sensory-specific decrease in palatability; as soon as the drink was consumed, foods of the same or similar flavor were judged to be much less palatable. This was followed by a general decrease in the palatability of all substances about 30 minutes later. Thus, it appears that signals from taste receptors produce an immediate decline in the incentive value of similar tastes, and some signal associated with the increased energy supply from a meal produces a general decrease in the incentive properties of all foods.

Incentive theories of eating receive strong support from Rolls and Rolls's (1982) discovery of neurons in the LH that respond to the incentive properties of food, rather than to food itself. When monkeys were repeatedly allowed to eat one palatable food, the response of the LH neurons to it declined, although their response to other palatable foods did not. Furthermore, neurons that responded to the sight of food would come to respond to a neutral stimulus that reliably predicted the presentation of food (see Figure 11.13). The repeated presentation of a palatable food (e.g., a

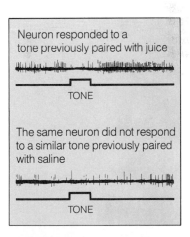

Neuron responded to a tone previously paired with juice

TONE

The same neuron did not respond to a similar tone previously paired with saline

TONE

FIGURE 11.13 *The response of a neuron in the vicinity of the lateral hypothalamus to a tone that had been associated with the presentation of fruit juice (top trace) or saline (bottom trace). (Adapted from Rolls, Sanghera, & Roper-Hall, 1979.)*

banana) to a monkey without allowing the monkey to eat it eventually rendered that item incapable of producing its usual neural response (Mora, Rolls, & Burton, 1976).

The influential study of intragastric feeding by Teitelbaum and Epstein (1962) mentioned earlier in the chapter seems to contradict the notion that internal states influence eating by changing the incentive value of food. Teitelbaum and Epstein reported that rats would maintain their usual body weights without experiencing the gustatory and olfactory properties of food by pressing a lever to inject calorically appropriate amounts of food directly into their stomachs through a nasopharyngeal gastric fistula. Several authors have failed to replicate these findings; for example, Nicolaidis and Roland (1977) found that rats maintained on intragastric feeding lost a great deal of weight. Holman (1968) showed that oral stimulation from the chilled liquid diet as it was pumped down the nasopharyngeal cannula was an unrecognized, but critical, factor in Teitelbaum and Epstein's results. Holman found that rats would not reliably lever press to inject solutions maintained at body temperature down nasopharyngeal cannulas and that they would not lever press to inject any solution directly through the stomach wall in the absence of concomitant oral stimulation. Holman concluded that intragastric injections do not reinforce lever pressing directly, but that they do so by influencing the incentive properties of the oral stimuli associated with them. Recall Tom, the beer-loving patient with the fused esophagus, who was satisfied by food poured into his stomach only if he tasted it first (see also Jordan, 1969). Also consistent with Holman's conclusion is Nicolaidis and Roland's finding that rats do not maintain their normal body weight when they must feed themselves by pressing a lever for intravenous infusions of nutrients.

The Leaky-Barrel Model:
Set Points versus Settling Points

Since the beginning of the study of the physiological basis of eating early in this century, many researchers have been searching the nervous system for a certain kind of eating circuit: one that involves independent satiety and hunger mechanisms that are sensitive to deviations from one or more hypothetical set points. Although such a model accounts for the homeostasis (stability) of the body's energy resources, it has two major shortcomings. The first is that it is unnecessarily complex; homeostasis can be explained without having to postulate set points, deviation detectors, or hunger and satiety centers. The second is that it cannot account for numerous instances in which feeding behavior is clearly not homeostatic. An unprepossessing alternative to the dual-center set-point model is presented in Figure 11.14. I call it the **leaky-barrel model** of homeostatic regulation. Let's see how well it can account for the maintenance of the body's fat reserves.

The leaky-barrel model is an analogy. (1) The amount of water entering the hose is analogous to the amount of food available to the subject; (2) the weight of the barrel on the hose is analogous to the strength of the satiety signal; (3) the water pressure at the nozzle is analogous to the incentive value of the available food; (4) the amount of water entering the barrel is analogous to the amount of consumed energy; (5) the water level in the barrel is analogous to the level of body fat; and (6) the amount of water leaking from the barrel is analogous to the amount of energy being expended. The essence of the leaky-barrel model is that the level of fat in the body, like the level of water in a barrel, rather than being regulated around a predetermined set point, is regulated around a natural **settling point,** the point at which various factors that influence its level achieve an equilibrium (see Booth, Fuller, & Lewis, 1981). This model always achieves an equilibrium because it is a negative-feedback model: Factors that decrease fat levels always produce reactions that increase them, and vice versa. Familiarize yourself with the operation of the model; see how it reacts to various changes. What you should notice is that this kind of settling-point model accounts admirably for many of the findings described in this chapter. Let's see how well the leaky-barrel model accounts for the three findings commonly offered in support of set-point models.

Finding 1: Total body fat—usually inferred from body weight—remains relatively constant in many adult animals, and therefore it must be regulated around a set point. Rebuttal 1: Constant body weight does not require, or even imply, a set point. Consider the leaky-barrel model. As water from the tap begins to fill the barrel, the weight of the water in the barrel increases. This increases the amount of water leaking out of the barrel and decreases the amount of water entering the barrel by increasing the pressure of the barrel on the hose. Eventually this system settles into an equilibrium where the water level stays constant, but because this level is neither predetermined nor actively defended, it is more appropriately referred to as a **settling point** (Wirtshafter & Davis, 1977) than a set point. A neuron's resting potential is another well-known biological settling point (see Chapter 3).

Finding 2: If a subject's intake of food is reduced, metabolic changes occur that counteract the effects of the reduction, and weight loss is limited. The opposite occurs when the subject overeats. Therefore, there must be a set point for body fat that is actively defended. Rebuttal 2: The leaky-barrel model lacks a set point and yet responds in exactly the same way. When water intake is reduced, the water level in the barrel begins to drop, but the drop is counteracted by a

FIGURE 11.14 *The leaky-barrel model of body weight (body-fat) regulation.*

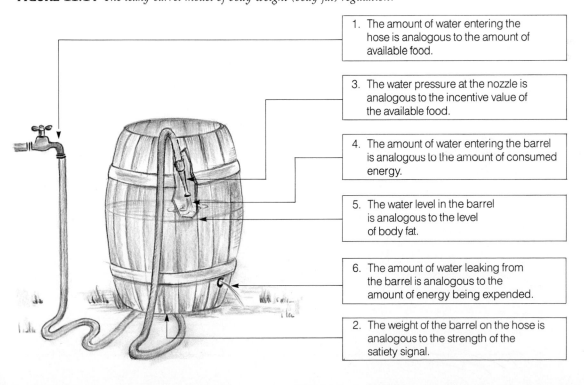

1. The amount of water entering the hose is analogous to the amount of available food.

3. The water pressure at the nozzle is analogous to the incentive value of the available food.

4. The amount of water entering the barrel is analogous to the amount of consumed energy.

5. The water level in the barrel is analogous to the level of body fat.

6. The amount of water leaking from the barrel is analogous to the amount of energy being expended.

2. The weight of the barrel on the hose is analogous to the strength of the satiety signal.

decrease in leakage attributable to the falling water pressure in the barrel. Eventually, a new settling point is achieved, but the reduction in water level is not as great as one might expect because of the offsetting changes. The opposite happens when water inflow is increased.

Finding 3: After an individual has lost a substantial amount of weight, either by dieting, exercise, or even by **lipectomy,** the surgical removal of fat (Faust, Johnson, & Hirsch, 1977), there is a tendency for the original weight to be regained once the subject returns to his or her previous eating-and-energy-related lifestyle. Surely the fact that the lost weight is regained proves that there is an actively defended set point. Rebuttal 3: Again, these results can be accounted for without having to postulate the existence of a set point. Reducing the water level in the leaky-barrel model—whether by temporarily decreasing input (dieting), by temporarily increasing output (exercising), or by scooping out some of the water (lipectomy)—produces only a temporary drop in the settling point. When the original conditions are reinstated, the water level inexorably drifts back to the original settling point. The course of the typical weight-reduction diet is illustrated and interpreted in Figure 11.15.

The leaky-barrel model has two advantages over the traditional set-point model. You have just seen one of them; the leaky-barrel model readily accounts for the three findings commonly offered in support of the set-point model, and it does it without having to postulate the existence of a set-point mechanism for which there is no direct evidence. The second advantage is that, unlike the set-point model, the leaky-barrel model can explain those instances when a person's weight does stabilize at a new level. The essence of the leaky-barrel model is that body weight stabilizes at a point where the various factors that influence inflow and outflow are in equilibrium. Because this settling point is not actively defended, it will drift to a new settling point any time there is a long-term change in one of the factors that influence the availability of food, its incentive value, or the output of energy.

FIGURE 11.15 *The four stages of a temporary weight-loss program.*

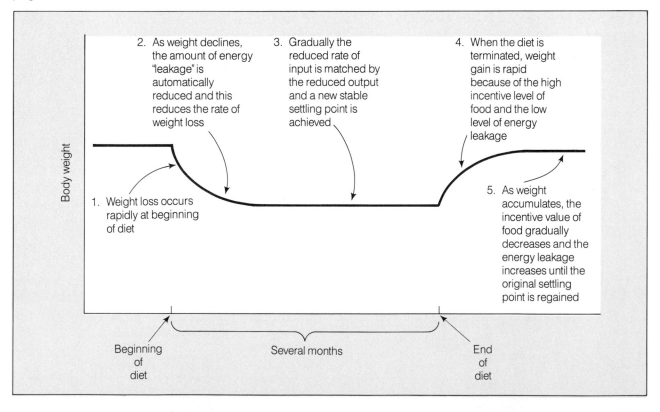

This chapter began on a somewhat unconventional note—with the mystery of Freddie the Finn—and I would like to return to it to make two concluding points about the progress of research on the biopsychology of eating—one about the path eating research has taken and one about where it is likely to go. In the 50s and 60s, the research on feeding was dominated by assumptions that in retrospect appear to have been misguided. Although these assumptions created the impression that major breakthroughs were about to be achieved, they ultimately led up a series of blind alleys, as did the misguided assumption of Freddie the Finn's humanity. In the 70s and 80s, these assumptions were recognized and challenged, and thus, there is reason for optimism as a new era of feeding research begins.

Food for Thought

1. Set-point theories suggest that attempts at permanent weight loss are a waste of time. What do settling-point models such as the leaky-barrel model suggest?

2. When saccharin is added to a rat's chow, its weight increases and gradually stabilizes at a new higher level. How do settling-point and set-point models explain this?

3. Most of the dietary problems that people in our society face occur because the conditions under which we live are different from those in which our "eating systems" evolved. Discuss.

ADDITIONAL READING

The following articles provide particularly readable accounts of specific areas of feeding research.

Bolles, R. C. (1980). Some functionalist thoughts about regulation. In F. M. Toates & T. R. Halliday (Eds.), *Analysis of motivated processes* (pp. 62–75). New York: Academic Press.

Brown, P. J., & Konner, M. (1987). An anthropological perspective on obesity. *Annals of the New York Academy of Sciences, 499,* 29–46.

Halmi, K. A., Ackerman, S., Gibbs, J., & Smith, G. (1987). Basic biological overview of the eating disorders. In H. Y. Meltzer (Ed.), *Psychopharmacology: The third generation of progress* (pp. 1255–1266). New York: Raven Press.

Keesey, R. E., & Powley, T. L. (1986). The regulation of body weight. *Annual Review of Psychology, 37,* 109–133.

Polivy, J., & Herman, C. P. (1985). Dieting and binging: A causal analysis. *American Psychologist, 40,* 193–201.

Powley, T. L., Opsahl, C. A., Cox, J. E., & Weingarten, H. P. (1980). Role of the hypothalamus in energy homeostasis. In P. J. Morgane & J. Panksepp (Eds.), *Behavioral studies of the hypothalamus* (pp. 211–298). New York: Marcel Dekker.

Scalfani, A. (1980). Dietary obesity. In A. J. Stunkard (Ed.), *Obesity* (pp. 167–181). Philadelphia: W. B. Saunders.

Weingarten, H. P. (1985). Stimulus control of eating: Implications for a two-factor theory of hunger. *Appetite, 6,* 387–401.

Woods, S. C., Taborsky, G. J., & Porte, D. (1986). Central nervous system control of nutrient homeostasis. In F. E. Bloom (Ed.), *Handbook of physiology: Nervous system IV* (pp. 365–411). Bethesda, MD: American Physiological Society.

KEY TERMS

To help you study the material in this chapter, all of the key terms—those that have appeared in bold type—are listed and briefly defined here.

Absorptive phase. The metabolic phase during which the body is operating on the energy from a recently consumed meal and is storing the excess as body fat and glycogen.

Adipsia. Complete cessation of drinking.

Amino acids. The breakdown products of protein.

Aphagia. Complete cessation of eating.

Basal blood insulin levels. The blood levels of insulin after an overnight fast.

Brown adipose tissue. The main nonmuscular site of heat generation in the body.

Cafeteria diet. A diet offered to experimental animals that is composed of a wide variety of palatable foods.

Carbohydrates. Sugars and starches.

Cephalic phase. The metabolic phase during which the body prepares for food that is about to be absorbed; it is initiated by the presence of food in the gastrointestinal tract, or by the sight or smell of palatable food.

Cholecystokinin (CCK). A peptide that is released by the gastrointestinal tract and is thought to signal satiety.

Diabetes mellitus. A disorder in which the pancreas does not produce sufficient insulin, thus preventing blood glucose from entering cells of the body.

Diet-induced thermogenesis. The increased heat production of obese subjects.

Digestion. The process by which food is broken down and absorbed through the lining of the gastrointestinal tract.

Dual-center assumption. The idea that feeding is controlled by two different centers: a hunger center, which initiates bouts of eating, and a satiety center, which terminates them.

Duodenum. The upper portion of the intestine through which most of the glucose and amino acids are absorbed into the bloodstream.

Dynamic phase. The first phase of the hyperphagia syndrome induced by VMH lesions, which is characterized by grossly excessive eating and weight gain.

Fasting phase. The metabolic phase that begins when energy from the preceding meal is no longer sufficient to meet the needs of the body; during this phase, energy is extracted from fat and glycogen stores.

Free fatty acids. Released from fat, they are the main source of the body's energy during the fasting phase.

Gastrointestinal tract. The tube that extends from the mouth to the anus.

Glucagon. A pancreatic hormone that promotes the conversion of glycogen to glucose and the utilization of fat by the body.

Gluconeogenesis. The process by which glucose is synthesized from the breakdown products of the body's own tissue; this normally occurs only during starvation.

Glucoreceptors. Cells that are thought to detect glucose levels in the body.

Glucose. A simple sugar, which is the breakdown product of more complex sugars and starches (carbohydrates); the body's, and in particular the brain's, main source of energy.

Glucostatic theory. The theory that blood glucose level or blood glucose utilization is the main regulatory factor in controlling daily food intake.

Glycogen. One of the forms in which energy is stored in the body, primarily in the liver.

Gold thioglucose. A neurotoxin, which is thought to bind to glucoreceptors.

Homeostasis. The stability of an organism's internal environment.

Hyperinsulinemia. A condition in which too much insulin is released into the blood.

Hyperphagia. Overeating.

Incentive properties. The incentive properties of a food are the pleasurable effects anticipated from eating it.

Insulin. A pancreatic hormone that facilitates the entry of glucose into cells and the conversion of glucose to fat and glycogen.

Intragastric feeding. When an animal feeds itself by pressing a lever that causes food to be pumped directly into its stomach.

Ketones. The breakdown products of fat, which can be used as a source of energy for the brain when glucose is in short supply.

Lateral hypothalamus (LH). An area of the hypothalamus once thought to be the feeding center.

Leaky-barrel model. A settling-point model of body-fat regulation; an alternative to traditional set-point models.

Lipectomy. The surgical removal of body fat.

Lipids. Fats.

Lipogenesis. The production of body fat.

Lipolysis. The breakdown of body fat.

Lipostatic theory. The theory that eating is controlled by deviations from a hypothetical body-fat set point.

Nasopharyngeal gastric fistula. A tube that runs under the scalp down a nostril and into the stomach and allows food to be pumped directly into the stomach.

Nutritive density. Calories per unit volume of food.

Pancreas. The gland that regulates metabolism by producing insulin and glucagon.

Paraventricular nuclei. Hypothalamic nuclei; it is now thought that the hyperphagia and obesity caused by large VMH lesions result from damage to the paraventricular nuclei or their connections.

Peristaltic contractions. Small rhythmic contractions that move food along the digestive tract.

Pyloric sphincter. The ring of muscles that can contract to close the opening from the stomach to the duodenum.

Sensory-specific satiety. When a particular food is consumed, more satiety is produced for foods of the same taste than for other foods.

Set-point assumption. The idea that feeding is controlled by deviations from hypothetical bodily set points, in the same way that the operation of a home heating system is controlled by deviations from the thermostat set point.

Settling point. The point at which various factors that influence the level of some regulated function achieve an equilibrium.

Sham eating. The animal chews and swallows food, which leaves the body through an esophageal fistula.

Static phase. The second phase of the VMH hyperphagia syndrome during which the animal regulates its body weight at a greatly elevated level.

Substance Y. A putative hunger peptide hormone.

Thiamine. Vitamin B_1.

Ventromedial hypothalamus (VMH). The area of the hypothalamus that was once thought to be the satiety center.

12

Motivation: Drinking, Aggression, and Temperature Regulation

This is the third in a series of chapters on motivational topics. If you have been reading the chapters in sequence, you will have just read about the biopsychology of sex and eating in Chapters 10 and 11. In this chapter, you will encounter three more motivational topics, one in each of its three sections:

12.1 **Drinking**
12.2 **Aggression**
12.3 **Temperature Regulation**

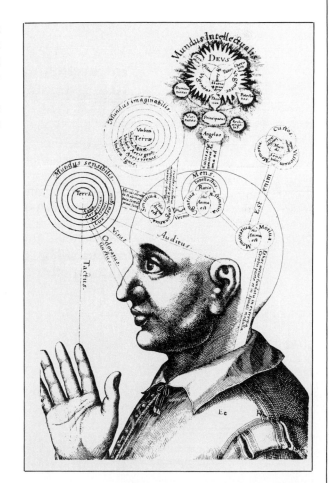

12.1 Drinking

The Dry-Mouth Theory of Thirst

Many people subjectively identify a dry mouth as the primary stimulus for thirst, and through the centuries many scholars have supported this notion. There is no question that having a dry mouth is correlated with bodily fluid deficiency, and there is no question that under some circumstances a dry mouth can motivate drinking; however, experiments in which dry mouth has been dissociated from the other consequences of fluid deficiency have proven that dry mouth is not the primary factor in thirst. For example, producing chronic dry mouth by removing the *salivary glands* does not substantially increase water intake unless subjects are fed dry food or maintained in a very hot environment (e.g., Epstein, Spector, Samman, & Goldblum, 1964). Conversely, blocking the sensation of dry mouth with local anesthetics or neural transection does not decrease water intake (Grossman, 1967). The most convincing evidence against the dry-mouth theory of thirst comes from studies of **sham drinking.** In sham drinking experiments, the water that a subject drinks flows down its esophagus and then out of its body through a fistula before it can be absorbed (see Figure 12.1). Despite their lack of a dry mouth, subjects with an internal water deficit sham drink almost continuously (Maddison, Wood, Rolls, Rolls, & Gibbs, 1980).

Intracellular and Extracellular Fluid Compartments

Evidence that dry mouth is not a major factor in drinking focused efforts to understand the biopsychology of drinking on other, more central, aspects of fluid regulation. With respect to the regulation of fluid levels, the body can be thought of as two separate fluid-filled compartments: an *intracellular compartment* and an *extracellular compartment*. As depicted in Figure 12.2, about two-thirds of the body's water is inside cells, and about one-third is outside. The water found in the extracellular compartment is found in the **interstitial fluid** (the fluid in which the cells are bathed), the blood, and the cerebrospinal fluid (CSF).

Normally the fluids in the intracellular and extracellular body-fluid compartments are of equal concentration; that is, they are **isotonic** with one another. In other words, the proportion of the intracellular fluid that is composed of *solutes* (substances dissolved in a fluid) is the same as the

FIGURE 12.1 *Animals with open esophageal, gastric, or duodenal fistulas sham drink almost continuously despite the lack of a dry mouth.*

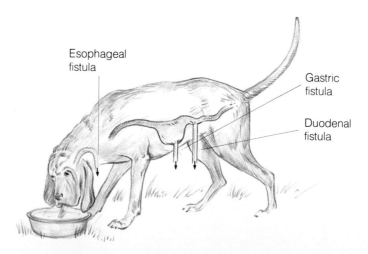

Esophageal
fistula

Gastric
fistula

Duodenal
fistula

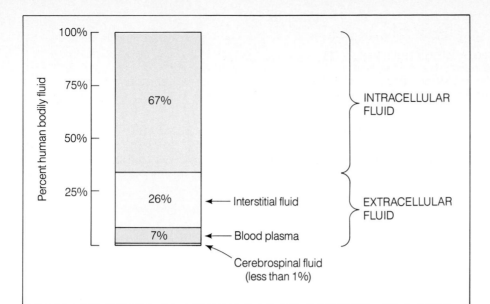

FIGURE 12.2 *The amount of fluid normally present in the various compartments of the human body.*

proportion of the extracellular fluid that is composed of solutes. In this isotonic state there is no tendency for the water inside cells to be drawn out of cells, or for water in the interstitial fluid to be drawn into cells. However, if the fluid in one of the compartments is made more concentrated than the other (by adding solutes to it or by removing water from it), the more concentrated fluid draws water from the less concentrated fluid through the cell membranes until their isotonicity is reestablished. Conversely, if the concentration of the solution in one of the compartments is decreased (by adding water to it or by removing solutes from it), water is drawn from it into the other compartment. The pressure that draws water from less-concentrated **(hypotonic)** solutions through semipermeable membranes into more-concentrated **(hypertonic)** solutions is called **osmotic pressure** (see Figure 12.3).

It is important for our survival that the levels of intracellular and extracellular fluid be precisely regulated. Accordingly, much of the research on the biopsychology of drinking has focused on drinking in response to deficits in the volume of intracellular and extracellular fluids, and it is the focus of the first part of this section on drinking.

Deprivation-Induced Drinking

There appear to be two different physiological systems that mediate deprivation-induced drinking: one that is sensitive to reductions in intracellular fluid volume **(cellular dehydration)** and one that is sensitive to reductions in blood volume.

Cellular Dehydration and Thirst

As the bartenders who supply free salted nuts well know, salt (sodium chloride) makes one thirsty. The thirst produced by salty food is caused by cellular dehydration. Because salt does not readily pass into cells, it accumulates in the extracellular fluid, making it hypertonic and drawing

Isotonicity

In subjects who have not been water deprived, there is normally about twice as much intracellular fluid as there is extracellular fluid. Also, the intracellular and extracellular fluid are normally isotonic—they have the same concentration (i.e., the same proportion of solutes dissolved in them). As a result of the isotonicity, there is normally little osmotic pressure drawing water either in or out of cells.

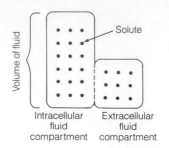

Deviations from Isotonicity

There are four different ways in which the concentration of the fluid in a body-fluid compartment can be changed: solutes can be added to it or taken away from it or water can be added to it or taken away from it.

When differences between the concentrations of intracellular and extracellular fluids occur, osmotic pressures are created that draw water through cell membranes.

Adding solutes to the extracellular space makes the extracellular fluid hypertonic, and water is drawn out of cells until isotonicity is reestablished.	Taking solutes from the extracellular space makes the extracellular fluid hypotonic, and water is drawn into cells until isotonicity is reestablished.	Adding water to the extracellular space makes the extracellular fluid hypotonic, and water is drawn into cells until isotonicity is reestablished.	Taking water from the extracellular space makes the extracellular fluid hypertonic, and water is drawn out of cells until isotonicity is reestablished.

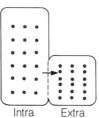 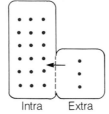 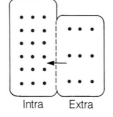 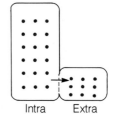

FIGURE 12.3 *Illustration of isotonicity, hypertonicity, and hypotonicity.*

water from cells into the interstitial fluid without substantially influencing blood volume. Cellular dehydration is usually induced in experimental animals, not by offering them salted nuts, but by injecting them with hypertonic solutions of salt or other solutes that do not readily pass through cell membranes (see Fitzsimons, 1972; Gilman, 1937). Cellular dehydration can also be produced simply by depriving subjects of water, but because water deprivation also reduces the volume of water in the extracellular compartment, researchers interested specifically in the role of cellular dehydration in drinking usually study drinking in response to the injection of hypertonic solutions.

Most of the research on cellular dehydration has been aimed at locating the cells in the body that are responsible for detecting it. The cells that detect cellular dehydration are called **osmoreceptors** (Gilman, 1937; Rolls & Rolls, 1982).

Evidence that there are osmoreceptors in the brain that play a role in drinking comes from studies in which hypertonic solutions have been injected into the *carotid arteries* (arteries of the neck, which carry blood to the brain) of nondeprived animals. For example, in one study solutions of sodium chloride were bilaterally infused through the carotid arteries of nondeprived dogs at concentrations that increased cerebral osmolarity without having a significant effect on the osmolarity of the body as a whole (Wood, Rolls, & Ramsay, 1977). Figure 12.4 shows that the infusions substantially increased the dogs' water consumption during a subsequent 5-minute test and that the amount of water consumed during the test was a function of the concentration of the infused solution.

Four lines of evidence suggest that cerebral osmoreceptors that encourage drinking are in the *lateral hypothalamus* and the *lateral preoptic area* of the hypothalamus: First, minute quantities of slightly hypertonic saline injected bilaterally into various sites in the lateral preoptic area and lateral hypothalamus (see Figure 12.5) have been shown to elicit drinking in rats (Blass & Epstein, 1971; Peck & Blass, 1975) and rabbits (Peck & Novin, 1971). Second, control injections of hypertonic sucrose solutions into the same sites were as effective as the sodium chloride injections in inducing drinking, whereas hypertonic urea injections were completely ineffective. Sucrose, like sodium chloride, does not readily enter cells, and thus it draws water out of them, whereas urea readily enters cells, and thus it has no dehydrating effect. Third, drinking elicited by an injection of sodium chloride into the *peritoneum* (abdominal cavity) is temporarily suppressed by the bilateral infusion of small amounts of water directly into sites in the lateral preoptic area (Blass & Epstein, 1971). And fourth, the firing of neurons in the lateral hypothalamus and lateral preoptic area increases in proportion to the hypertonicity of solutions of sodium chloride or sucrose injected into the carotid artery (Malmo & Malmo, 1979; Figure 12.6).

In addition to increasing water consumption, hypothalamic osmoreceptors also control the release of **antidiuretic hormone** (ADH), also known as vasopressin, from the posterior pituitary (see Chapter 10). Antidiuretic hormone conserves bodily fluids by decreasing the volume of urine produced by the kidneys. The hypothalamic osmoreceptors that control ADH release do not appear to be the same ones that control drinking. Intracerebral injections of hypertonic solutions that induce drinking do not always induce ADH release, and vice versa. Other osmoreceptors that regulate

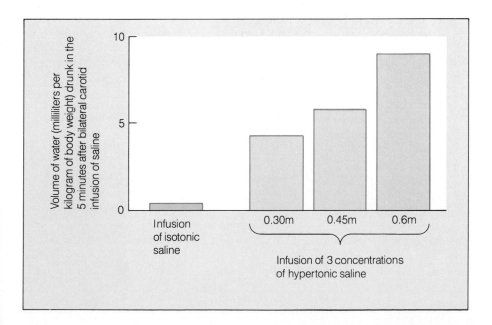

FIGURE 12.4 *Nondeprived dogs begin to drink when hypertonic sodium chloride solutions are infused through the carotid arteries of the neck—the greater the concentration of the solutions, the more they drink.*
These results suggest that there are osmoreceptors in the brain that influence thirst. (Adapted from Rolls & Rolls, 1982.)

Lateral views of the rat brain illustrating the location of the lateral preoptic area and the lateral hypothalamus

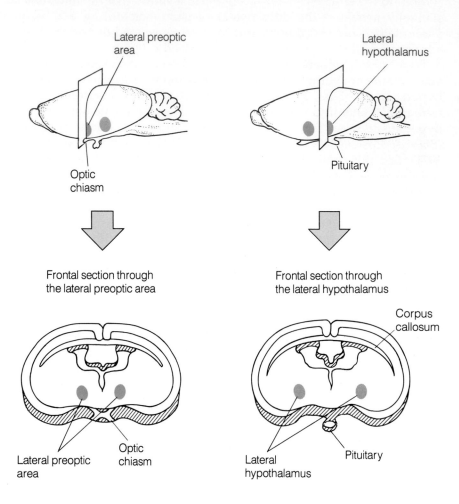

FIGURE 12.5 *The lateral preoptic area and the lateral hypothalamus are sites into which microinjections of hypertonic solutions elicit drinking in rats.*

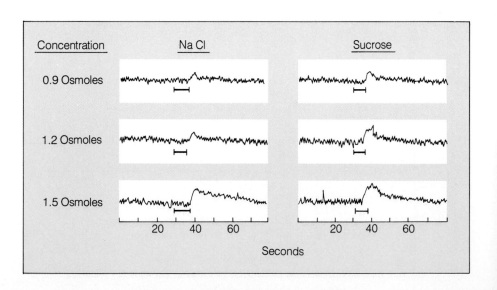

FIGURE 12.6 *The increases in the integrated multiple unit activity of rat lateral preoptic area neurons in response to hypertonic sucrose or sodium chloride injections into the carotid artery. Notice the similarity of the response to the two solutions and the fact that more concentrated solutions produce a greater increase in cell firing. (Adapted from Malmo & Malmo, 1979.)*

ADH release are distributed throughout the stomach, the **hepatic-portal system** (the branch of the circulatory system that carries water and other nutrients from the stomach and duodenum to the liver), and other parts of the gut. Whether or not these gut osmoreceptors also play a role in the regulation of drinking has not yet been clearly established—some say "yes" (Kozlowski & Drzewiecki, 1973; Kraly, Gibbs, & Smith, 1975), and some say "no" (Wood, Rolls, & Ramsay, 1977).

The Effects of Reduction in Blood Volume on Thirst

A reduction in blood volume is called **hypovolemia.** Hypovolemia is produced in experiments in one of two ways. One method is to withdraw blood from the subjects; the other is to inject a colloid substance into the peritoneal cavity. **Colloids** are glue-like substances with molecules much too large to pass through cell membranes. Thus, colloids injected into the peritoneum stay there, and like sponges, they draw blood plasma out of the circulatory system into the peritoneum and hold it there. Neither bleeding nor colloid injections change the osmolarity of the extracellular fluid; thus they reduce blood volume without producing cellular dehydration.

Reduction in the volume of blood plasma is detected by **baroreceptors** (blood pressure receptors) in the wall of the heart and by **blood-flow receptors** in the kidneys, and the activity of these two kinds of receptors initiates a series of compensatory reactions. The decreased firing of the baroreceptors in the heart triggers the release of ADH from the posterior pituitary, which in turn increases water conservation by causing the kidneys to reabsorb more water from the urine. Both the ADH and the increased activity of the blood-flow receptors in the kidneys cause the kidneys to release **renin.** Renin causes the formation of the peptide hormone **angiotensin II,** and the angiotensin II in turn produces a compensatory increase in blood pressure by constricting the peripheral blood vessels and triggering the release of aldosterone from the adrenal cortices. **Aldosterone** causes the kidneys to reabsorb much of the sodium that would otherwise have been lost in the urine. Because sodium accounts for 95% of the osmolarity of blood plasma, the maintenance of high levels of sodium in the blood is critical for the prevention of further decreases in blood volume; the higher the concentration of the blood, the more water it will retain. These physiological reactions to hypovolemia are summarized in Figure 12.7.

In addition to increasing the conservation of bodily fluids, a reduction in blood volume induces drinking (Fitzsimons, 1961). The search for the mechanisms mediating this **hypovolemic drinking,** as it has been termed, has focused directly on the baroreceptors in the heart and the blood-flow receptors in the kidneys. Evidence suggests that both play a role (see Figure 12.8). For example, Fitzsimons (1972) implicated the *renal* (pertaining to the kidneys) blood-flow receptors by showing that partially tying off the renal arteries of rats to reduce renal blood flow causes them to drink. And Stricker (1973) implicated the cardiac baroreceptors in hypovolemic drinking by showing that injections of colloid into the peritoneal cavity of **nephrectomized** rats (i.e., rats whose kidneys have been removed) caused them to drink. This implicated the cardiac baroreceptors because hypovolemic drinking in kidneyless rats cannot possibly be mediated by receptors in the kidneys.

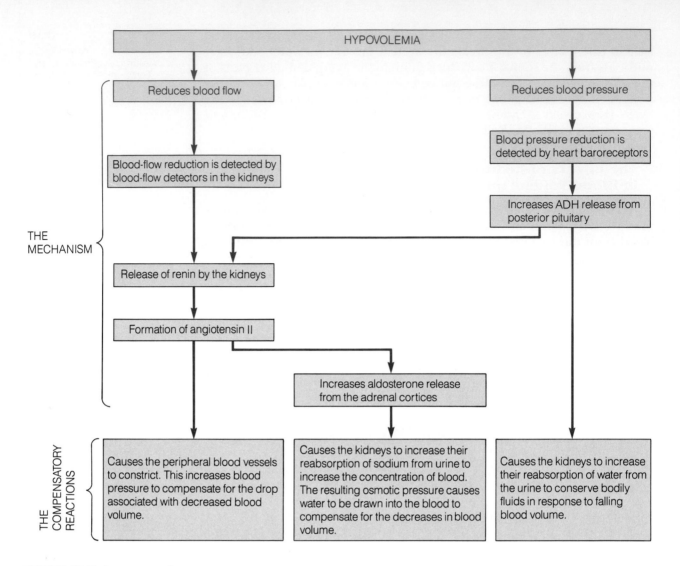

FIGURE 12.7 *A summary of the compensatory physiological reactions to hypovolemia.*

The Role of Angiotensin II in Hypovolemic Drinking

The fact that the intraperitoneal injection of kidney extracts causes rats to drink suggested that the kidneys produce a **dipsogen,** a substance that induces drinking. This dipsogen has proven to be angiotensin II. In species after species (e.g., cat, rat, monkey, goat, chicken, possum, iguana), intravenous infusion of angiotensin II has been found to increase drinking without influencing other motivated behaviors (e.g., Fitzsimons & Simons, 1969).

Much of the research on the dipsogenic effect of angiotensin II has been directed at discovering its site of action in the brain. Two early clues focused attention on the **subfornical organ** (SFO), a midline structure on the dorsal surface of the third ventricle, just between the openings from the two lateral ventricles (see Figure 12.9). The first clue was that the subfornical organ is one of only a small number of sites in the brain that are not protected by the *blood-brain barrier* (see Chapter 2). The second clue was that intraventricular infusions of angiotensin II proved to be particularly

Evidence That Cardiac Baroreceptors Are Involved In Hypovolemic Drinking

Reducing blood flow to the kidney by partially tying off the renal arteries increased drinking. This indicates that kidney blood-flow detectors can mediate hypovolemic drinking (Fitzsimons, 1972).

Evidence That Renal Blood-Flow Receptors Are Involved In Hypovolemic Drinking

Hypovolemia produced by a colloid injection caused nephrectomized rats to drink. Because hypovolemic drinking in rats without kidneys cannot possibly be mediated by renal blood-flow receptors, cardiac baroreceptors were implicated (Stricker, 1973).

FIGURE 12.8 *Evidence that both cardiac baroreceptors and kidney blood-flow detectors mediate hypovolemic drinking.*

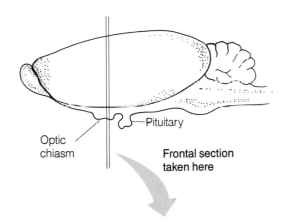

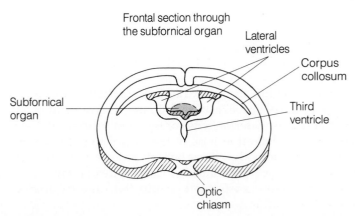

FIGURE 12.9 *The location of the subfornical organ in the rat in relation to the cerebral ventricles. It is on the midline dorsal surface of the third ventricle between the openings to the two lateral ventricles.*

effective in inducing drinking. The following four findings subsequently confirmed the hypothesis that the subfornical organ is the site of the angiotensin II receptors that mediate hypovolemic drinking: (1) Microinjections of angiotensin II into the subfornical organ reliably elicit drinking (e.g., Simpson, Epstein, & Camardo, 1978). (2) **Saralasin,** a blocker of angiotensin II receptors, blocks the dipsogenic action of intraventricular injections of angiotensin II (Fitzsimons, Epstein, & Johnson, 1978). (3) Destruction of the subfornical organ abolishes the drinking induced by intravenous injection of angiotensin II (Simpson et al., 1978). (4) Neurons in the subfornical organ display dose-dependent increases in firing in response to microinjections of angiotensin II (Phillips & Felix, 1976).

The kidney is not the body's only source of angiotensin II; it is also synthesized by the brain. The finding that lesions of the subfornical organ permanently block the ability of blood-borne angiotensin II to promote drinking suggests that the subfornical organ is the primary mediator of the dipsogenic effect of any angiotensin II that is released by the kidney into general circulation. However, the fact that lesions of the subfornical organ do not permanently block drinking induced by intraventricular injection of angiotensin II (e.g., Buggy, Fisher, Hoffman, Johnson, & Phillips, 1975) suggests that brain-produced angiotensin II or its metabolites can activate receptors in the brain that are normally insulated from general circulation by the blood-brain barrier (Epstein, 1987).

Drinking Produced by Naturally Occurring Water Deficits

As you have just learned in the preceding two subsections, the dipsogenic effects of intracellular and extracellular dehydration are often studied independently of one another. However, because water deprivation simultaneously reduces the water in both the intracellular and extracellular fluid compartments, the key to understanding the drinking that results from naturally occurring water shortages lies in understanding the interaction of the deficits in the two compartments. Rolls and her colleagues (e.g., Ramsay, Rolls, & Wood, 1977; Rolls, Wood, & Rolls, 1980) have studied the relative effects on drinking of intracellular and extracellular fluid deficits after overnight water deprivation. They injected their water-deprived subjects (rats, dogs, and monkeys) with either water or isotonic saline. The water, because it was hypotonic, was quickly taken up by the dehydrated cells, and thus it eliminated the intracellular deficit without substantially influencing the extracellular deficit. Conversely, the saline, because it was isotonic, was not taken up by cells to any significant degree, and thus it eliminated the extracellular deficit without substantially influencing the intracellular deficit. They found that the elimination of the intracellular deficit reduced the drinking of their water-deprived subjects by about 75% and that the elimination of the extracellular deficit reduced drinking by about 15% (Rolls & Rolls, 1982). Where do the systems that detect intracellular and extracellular water deficits converge to produce thirst and drinking? Because large bilateral lesions of the lateral hypothalamus eliminate drinking in response to both cellular dehydration and hypovolemia, "these tissues remain the favored candidates for the zone of convergence of thirst afferents and for their transformation into the urge to drink" (Epstein, 1982, p. 197).

So far, we have focused on the physiological systems that mediate drinking in response to fluid deficits; however, drinking often occurs in the absence of such deficits. We often drink to enjoy the pleasurable effects of the flavor of our beverages, to adjust our body temperature, to eliminate the discomfort of a dry mouth, to prevent anticipated fluid deficits, or to experience the pharmacological effects of the drugs in some of our favorite drinks (e.g., coffee, beer, and wine). As a result, most humans regularly drink far more than is required for the maintenance of their fluid balance. Rather than relying on the capacity of their kidneys to maintain fluid balance by conserving water, lavish amounts are regularly consumed and then abundantly excreted as dilute urine. As a result, few of us ever face substantial fluid deficits (Rolls & Rolls, 1982). Drinking in the absence of fluid deficits is called **spontaneous drinking.**

Flavor   The effects of flavor on drinking can be readily demonstrated by simply adding a bit of saccharin to the water of nondeprived rats. Their water intake skyrockets (Rolls, Wood, & Stevens, 1978). Conversely, there is a substantial decrease in fluid consumption if the palatability of a rat's water supply is reduced by adding a small amount of quinine to it. When rats were maintained for 60 days with quinine-adulterated water as their only source of fluid, their fluid intake decreased substantially, but there were no signs of ill health (Nicolaidis & Rowland, 1975). It seems that, like humans, rats with easy access to water or other palatable fluids drink far more than they need.

Variety   Drinking a large quantity of a particular beverage temporarily decreases its *incentive value* (see Chapter 11). This principle is demonstrated by Figure 12.10, which illustrates a phenomenon known as the **saccharin**

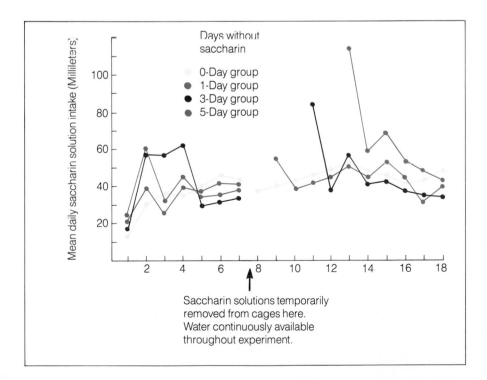

FIGURE 12.10 *The saccharin elation effect. Four different groups of rats had continuous access to water and to a saccharin solution for 8 days. Then, they were deprived of the saccharin solution for 0, 1, 3, or 5 days, but they continued to have free access to the water. Longer periods of saccharin deprivation produced greater increases in saccharin drinking when the saccharin was returned. (Adapted from Pinel & Rovner, 1977.)*

elation effect. Rats living with continuous access to water and a saccharin solution consume large amounts of the saccharin solution, but they consume even more of it after the saccharin solution has been withdrawn for several days (e.g., Pinel & Rovner, 1977). A similar elation effect has been demonstrated with weak solutions of quinine and alcohol (Pinel & Huang, 1976; Sinclair, 1972).

As a result of the decline of the incentive value associated with the continual consumption of a particular flavor, much more is drunk when subjects have access to a great variety of beverages than when they have access to only a few. For example, Rolls and Wood (cited in Rolls, Wood, & Rolls, 1980) offered nondeprived rats access to water for 1 hour, to water with an artificial flavor added to it for 1 hour, or to water with a different artificial flavor added to it every 15 minutes during the hour. As illustrated in Figure 12.11, the addition of one flavor to the water increased intake by 88%, whereas the availability of four sequential flavors increased intake by 182%. Grossly excessive fluid consumption is referred to as **polydipsia.**

Learning   Humans readily learn to drink to prevent anticipated water deficits; for example, joggers learn to take a drink before starting out on a hot day. Other animals display a similar form of learning. For example, Weisinger (1975) repeatedly paired the odor of menthol with a subcutaneous injection of formalin, which induces temporary hypovolemia, and found that after several pairings the odor by itself would elicit excessive drinking. A similar point was made in a different way in a study by Fitzsimons and LeMagnen (1969). They studied the increased water consumption of rats forced to shift from a high-carbohydrate to a high-protein diet; the latter diet absorbs much more water from the body into the intestine than does the former diet. Initially, the increased drinking occurred long after the protein meal was consumed, presumably in response to the hypovolemia that it created. But eventually the copious drinking occurred with, rather than after, each meal. Apparently, the rats learned to adjust their water intake to prevent the protein-produced dehydration.

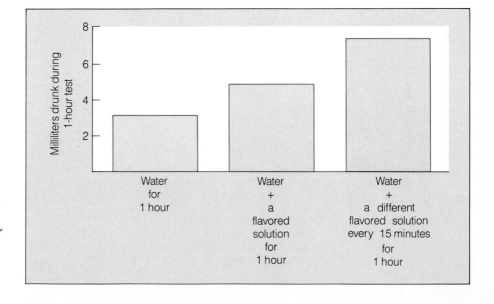

FIGURE 12.11 *The effects of variety on the fluid intake of nondeprived rats during a 60-minute test. The rats in one group drank water for the 60 minutes; the rats in another group drank water with a flavor added; and the rats in the third group were presented with water of a different flavor every 15 minutes during the test. (Adapted from Rolls, Wood, & Rolls, 1980.)*

So far in this section, deprivation-induced and spontaneous drinking have been discussed, but nothing has been said about the factors that terminate drinking. If drinking were an enterprise designed to maintain body fluids at their homeostatic level, then a return to homeostasis should be the cue that eliminates thirst and terminates drinking. There are two serious problems with this idea. The first is that the elimination of water deficits could not possibly be responsible for terminating drinking initiated in the absence of any water deficits. The second is that even when drinking is triggered by water deprivation, it usually stops before much fluid has been absorbed from the intestine.

Research on the termination of drinking has suggested that the amount that we consume is not rigorously regulated; we seem to be designed to drink when palatable fluids are readily available and to regulate internal fluid levels by passing off the excess in the form of dilute urine. Although there are several factors that tend to reduce drinking in certain situations, none, with the exception of extreme stomach distension, appears to be particularly potent. This strong bias toward excessive drinking is evident in the previously discussed polydipsia of laboratory animals with access to a variety of palatable solutions. Polydipsia also occurs during tests in which animals without a fluid deficit are given a small piece of food every minute or so (Falk, 1964). In the intervals, they drink huge volumes of water— about 10 times more than they would if the food were given all at once during the test. This excessive drinking is called **schedule-induced polydipsia.**

12.2 Aggression

Aggression has undoubtedly played an important role in the evolution of our species, but there are few who would not agree that modern human society would be better off without it. Interpersonal aggression in its various forms produces emotional and physical damage to the individuals involved, and the consequences of all-out aggression between modern industrialized nations are too horrible to even contemplate.

Types of Aggression

Aggression occurs in many different situations, and it takes many different forms. Most biopsychologists agree that different categories of aggressive behavior are controlled by different neural and hormonal substrates. Consequently, a variety of different schemes for classifying aggressive behavior have been proposed (see Blanchard & Blanchard, 1984). The following three-category classification scheme was devised by Albert and his colleagues (e.g., Albert & Chew, 1980; Albert & Walsh, 1984) to explain effects of brain lesions and hormone manipulations on the aggressive behavior of rats. According to this scheme, the three major categories of aggressive behavior are:

1. *Defensive aggression.* Defensive aggression refers to attacks that occur in direct response to perceived threat. In the rat, defensive aggression is most frequently assessed by scoring the responses of the rat to being touched or picked up by the experimenter. Rats that have not previously

been handled, or those that have been handled but have received brain lesions that increase defensive aggression, typically respond to the touch of an experimenter by jumping, shrieking, and biting. They often roll over and assume an "on-back defensive position" from which they can kick, scratch, or bite and readily protect their most vulnerable area—their backs. Similar defensive behavior is observed in rats attacked by other rats.

2. *Predatory aggression.* Predatory aggression refers to the stalking and killing of members of another species for the purpose of eating them. Rats in the wild prey on a variety of small animals including frogs, which they kill by delivering a lethal bite to the back of the neck.

3. *Social aggression.* Social aggression is unprovoked aggression directed at a conspecific for the purpose of establishing, altering, or maintaining a social hierarchy. In rats, it is most commonly observed among males that live in colonies with females. The social aggression of male rats is commonly assessed by introducing a small unfamiliar male into their colony or by pairing them off in a series of "fights" for pieces of food.

The complex dance of social aggression and defensive aggression in the rat has been nicely characterized by Blanchard and Blanchard[1]:

> The attack of an experienced **alpha male** [the dominant male in the colony] on a stranger in his colony is very stereotyped and usually quite intense. The alpha approaches the stranger and sniffs at its perianal area. . . . If the intruder is an adult male, the alpha's sniff leads to piloerection. . . .
>
> Shortly after piloerecting, the alpha male usually bites the intruder, and the intruder runs away. The alpha chases after it, and after one or two additional bites, the intruder stops running and turns to face its attacker. It rears up on its hind legs, using its forelimbs to push off the alpha. . . . However, rather than standing nose to nose with the **"boxing"** intruder, the attacking rat abruptly moves to a lateral orientation, with the long axis of its body perpendicular to the front of the defending rat. . . . It moves sideways toward the intruder, crowding and sometimes pushing it off balance. If the defending rat stands solid against this **"lateral attack"** movement, the alpha may make a quick lunge forward and around the defender's body to bite at its back. In response to such a lunge, the defender usually pivots on its hindfeet, in the same direction as the attacker is moving, continuing its frontal orientation to the attacker. If the defending rat moves quickly enough, no bite will be made.
>
> However, after a number of instances of the lateral attack, and especially if the attacker has succeeded in biting the intruder, the stranger rat may roll backward slowly from the boxing position, to lie on its back. The attacker then takes up a position on top of the supine animal, digging with its forepaws at the intruder's sides. If the attacker can turn the other animal over, or expose some portion of its back . . . it bites. In response to these efforts, the defender usually moves in the direction of the attacker's head, rolling slightly on its back to continue to orient its ventrum [front] toward the alpha, and continuing to push off with both forelimbs and hindlimbs. Although all four legs and abdomen of the defending rat are exposed, the attacker does not bite them. This sequence of bites, flight, chasing, boxing, lateral attack, lying on the back, and standing on top is repeated . . . until the stranger rat is removed. (pp. 8–9)

---

[1] From "Affect and aggression: An animal model applied to human behavior" by D.C. Blanchard and R.J. Blanchard in *Advances in the Study of Aggression, Volume 1*, 1984, edited by D.C. Blanchard and R.J. Blanchard. San Diego: Academic Press. Copyright 1984 by Academic Press. Reprinted by permission.

Figure 12.12 is a schematic horizontal cross section of the six brain structures that have been frequently implicated in the modulation of defensive aggression, predatory aggression, and social aggression in rats and other laboratory species. These six structures are (1) the lateral septum, (2) the raphé nuclei, (3) the medial accumbens, (4) the medial hypothalamus, (5) the lateral hypothalamus, and (6) the amygdala. Other brain structures have been implicated in aggression, but these are the six whose roles in aggression have been studied most extensively (see Albert & Walsh, 1984).

Brain Lesions and Aggression

Large bilateral lesions to each of the six brain structures illustrated in Figure 12.12 have similar effects on defensive aggression and predatory aggression. Lesions of the lateral septum, medial accumbens, medial hypothalamus, or raphé nuclei increase both defensive aggression (e.g., Brady & Nauta, 1955; Malsbury, Kow, & Pfaff, 1977) and predatory aggression (e.g., Albert, Walsh, Siemens, & Louie, 1986; Marques, Malsbury, & Daood, 1979; Penot, Vergnes, Mack, & Kempf, 1978) in most laboratory species, whereas lesions of the lateral hypothalamus and the amygdala commonly decrease both (e.g., Shipley & Kolb, 1977; Woods, 1956). However, despite the fact that large bilateral lesions of the aforementioned six structures have the same general effects on both defensive and predatory aggression, there is reason to believe that these two kinds of aggression are independently regulated. In a key series of studies, Albert and Wong (1978a, 1978b) assessed the effects of small temporary lesions produced by

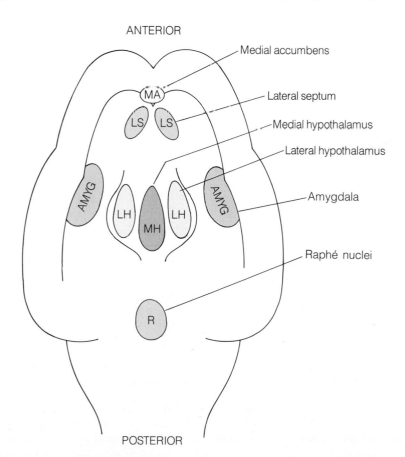

ANTERIOR

Medial accumbens

Lateral septum

Medial hypothalamus

Lateral hypothalamus

Amygdala

Raphé nuclei

POSTERIOR

FIGURE 12.12 *A schematic horizontal cross section of six of the areas of the rat brain that seem to be involved in defensive aggression, predatory aggression, and social aggression.*

microinjections of a local anesthetic to various parts of the septum and medial hypothalamus. They found that many of the lesions had selective effects; some lesions affected predatory aggression without affecting defensive aggression, whereas others affected defensive aggression without affecting predatory aggression. Thus, in the rat at least, it seems that the neural substrates of defensive aggression and predatory aggression are intertwined but separate.

The pattern of lesion effects on social aggression is quite different from the pattern of lesion effects on defensive and predatory aggression. Rather than producing increases, lesions of the lateral septum, medial accumbens, medial hypothalamus, and raphé nuclei usually decrease social aggression in male animals (e.g., Albert, Dyson, & Walsh, 1987; Blanchard, Blanchard, & Takahashi, 1977). The effects of brain lesions on defensive, predatory, and social aggression are summarized in Table 12.1.

Unlike defensive and predatory aggression, in many species social aggression is displayed almost exclusively by males and is dependent on the gonadal hormone **testosterone.** Following castration, alpha males lose their dominant position in their colony to other males (e.g., Albert, Walsh, Gorzalka, Siemens, & Louie, 1986; Debold & Miczek, 1984), but soon regain it if they are given testosterone replacement injections.

One interesting form of aggression that is difficult to categorize in terms of Albert's three-category system is **maternal aggression,** the aggressive behavior directed by mothers at conspecifics (Svare, 1977) or members of other species that approach the nest site. Although maternal aggression appears to serve a defensive function, it looks more like social aggression (Albert, Walsh, Zalys, & Dyson, 1987), and lesions of the septum do not intensify it as they do other forms of defensive aggression (Flannelly, Kemble, Blanchard, & Blanchard, 1986). In addition to maternal aggression, rat mothers display a variety of other complex defensive behaviors designed to protect their pups from risk. For example, if a dangerous object is placed near the nest site, rat mothers bury the object and move both their pups and their nests to a safer location (Pinel & Mana, 1989). See Figure 12.13.

The Effects of Brain Damage on Human Aggression

Although the evidence regarding the effects of brain lesions on human aggression is meager, it is of course of special interest. The evidence comes from those few case studies (e.g., Reeves & Plum, 1969; Zeman & King, 1958) in which patients who have uncharacteristically become extremely aggressive have later been found to have a localized tumor. For example, in one case, a mild-mannered, well-liked, middle-aged lawyer, who was later shown to have a tumor in the medial hypothalamus, began to display uncharacteristic outbursts of aggressive behavior that were shocking to all who knew him. The most trivial event could trigger such an outburst, and more than one good friend had to flee in order to avoid harm (Alpers, 1937).

Temporal-Lobe Epilepsy and Aggression

Reports that *temporal-lobe epileptics* (see Chapter 5) are hyperaggressive have been widely accepted because they are consistent with the suggestion from lesion studies that the amygdala, a major temporal-lobe structure,

Table 12.1 *The typical effects of lesions of the lateral septum, medial accumbens, medial hypothalamus, raphé nuclei, amygdala, and lateral hypothalamus on defensive, predatory, and social aggression in various species (Based on Albert & Walsh, 1984).*

	EFFECT ON DEFENSIVE AGGRESSION	EFFECT ON PREDATORY AGGRESSION	EFFECT ON SOCIAL AGGRESSION
Lateral Septum	+	+	−
Medial Accumbens	+	+	−
Medial Hypothalamus	+	+	−
Raphé Nuclei	+	+	−
Amygdala	−	−	unclear
Lateral Hypothalamus	−	−	unclear

plays a role in promoting aggressive behavior. However, several studies have failed to observe any relation between temporal-lobe epilepsy and aggression. Pinel, Treit, and Rovner (1972) attempted to circumvent the problems involved in studying aggression in human temporal-lobe epileptics by using the *kindled seizure animal model* (see Chapter 5). Kindled epileptic foci were established in rats in one of two temporal-lobe structures—the amygdala or the hippocampus—or in the caudate nucleus by briefly (for 1 second) stimulating the target site about 15 times per week for 8 weeks. At first there was no response to the stimulations, but by the end of the 8 weeks, each stimulation elicited a generalized clonic convulsion in each rat. As indicated in Figure 12.14, only the groups kindled in one of the two temporal-lobe structures displayed statistically significant increases in defensive aggression. However, despite the high degree of control provided by the kindling model, the effects of temporal-lobe foci on aggressive

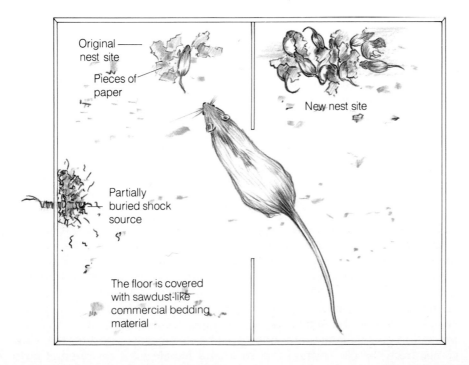

FIGURE 12.13 *A rat mother shocked by a wire-wrapped dowel inserted into her nest chamber, carried her pups to the safety of an adjoining chamber, buried the shock source, dismantled the original nest, and built a new nest in the adjoining chamber from the salvaged material. Here she is fetching her last remaining pup to transport it to the new nest. (From Pinel & Mana, 1989.)*

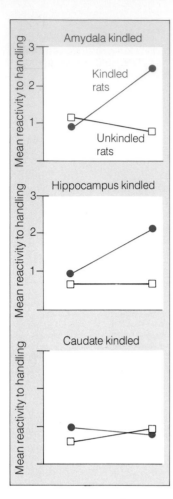

FIGURE 12.14 *Defensive aggression of rats kindled in the caudate, the amygdala, or the hippocampus. Only rats with epileptic foci in the two temporal lobe structures (the amygdala or hippocampus) displayed high levels of defensive aggression. (Adapted from Pinel et al., 1977.)*

behavior were variable. The high mean defensive aggression scores displayed by the temporal-lobe groups reflected the fact that a few of the 20 subjects in each of these two groups became extremely aggressive; most remained unchanged. This pattern of results may explain why attempts to document the existence of hyperaggressiveness in human epileptics have yielded such inconsistent results.

Psychosurgery for the Control of Aggression

Simple solutions to complex problems should always be treated with skepticism; they are appealing, but they rarely work. A case in point is the idea that **psychosurgery** (the destruction of a part of the brain for the purpose of changing behavior) provides an effective solution to the problem of human violence. The advocates of this view (e.g., Mark & Ervin, 1970) argue that violent people have excessive activity in the structures of the brain that produce violent behavior and that their violence should be controlled by destroying these structures. The amygdala is the most commonly advocated target of such psychosurgery. Those who advocate *amygdalectomy* as a treatment for aggression support their recommendation by pointing out that bilateral amygdalectomy has been shown to significantly reduce the aggression of laboratory animals. This is true, but not particularly relevant. True, amygdalectomy often reduces the average level of aggressive behavior in a group of experimental animals, but there are many individual animals that show no decrease—too many to warrant using amygdalectomy to treat human aggression. Another problem with the evidence used to justify amygdala psychosurgery is that it focuses on one kind of aggression test at the exclusion of others. The advocates of human amygdalectomy commonly cite the observation that amygdalectomized laboratory animals are easier to handle, but they rarely acknowledge studies in which free-ranging animals have been captured, amygdalectomized, and then returned to their natural habitat. In such a study by Kling (1972), amygdalectomized monkeys were found to be incapable of responding appropriately to a variety of social signals. This did have the effect of reducing their aggressive behavior in some situations, but it had other important consequences as well. Frequently, when approached by other monkeys in a nonthreatening way, amygdalectomized monkeys often fled or cowered. Conversely, they would sometimes fail to respond submissively when approached by a dominant troop member, and they would take a severe beating as a result. The consequence of this social ineptitude was isolation from the troop and death from starvation or predation—hardly a strong basis for adopting amygdalectomy as a form of therapy for human aggression.

Testosterone and Aggression

The fact that social aggression in many species occurs more commonly among males than among females is usually explained with reference to the organizational and activational effects of testosterone (e.g., Edwards, 1969). The brief period of testosterone release that occurs around birth in genetic males is thought to organize their nervous systems along masculine lines and hence to create the potential for male patterns of aggressive behavior to be activated by the high testosterone levels that are present in genetic males after puberty. The strongest support for this view comes from the observation that male and female mice castrated at birth display high levels of intraspecific fighting in response to testosterone injections in adulthood only if they receive organizing testosterone injections as neonates. The most striking demonstration of the activational role of testosterone in adult male social aggression is the sudden decrease in intramale fighting that is observed following castration in various species of rodents and *ungulates* (animals with hooves).

Attempts to demonstrate organizational and activational effects of testosterone on the aggressive behavior of humans and other primates have been inconsistent (Meyer-Bahlburg, 1981). This inconsistency is often taken as evidence that testosterone plays a less prominent role in organizing and activating the aggressive behavior of male primates (Dixson, 1980; Meyer-Bahlburg, 1981) than it does in other species. Alternatively, the inconsistency of findings in humans may in part reflect differences in the type of aggression under investigation rather than differences between species. Most studies of the effects of testosterone on the aggressive behavior of humans have focused on forms of aggression quite different from the intermale fighting that has been shown to be influenced by testosterone in rodents and ungulates. Measures of aggression used in the studies of human aggression include the frequency of violent crimes, the scores on paper-and-pencil tests of aggression, and the aggressiveness of athletic play.

Brain Stimulation and Aggression

The effects of brain stimulation on aggression have generally confirmed the findings of the lesion studies. For example, stimulation studies have confirmed that the lateral hypothalamus is an important structure for the elicitation of attack; lateral hypothalamic stimulation has been shown to elicit predatory aggression (Egger & Flynn, 1963; King & Hoebel, 1968; Woodworth, 1971), social aggression (Kruk, Van der Laan, Meelis, Phillips, Mos, & Van der Poel, 1984; Panksepp, 1971), and defensive aggression (Albert, Nanji, Brayley, & Madryga, 1979), but the exact lateral hypothalamic sites at which these three forms of aggression can be elicited seem to be different (Albert et al., 1979). Moreover, stimulation of the amygdala, another structure presumed on the basis of lesion studies to facilitate aggression, has been shown to elicit mouse killing in rats (Vergnes & Karli, 1969). In contrast, stimulation of the septum, a structure that has been shown by lesion studies to have an inhibitory effect on defensive aggression, inhibits the hyperaggressiveness induced in rats by medial hypothalamic lesions (Brayley & Albert, 1977).

Robinson, Alexander, and Bowne (1969) reported a particularly interesting case of stimulation-induced aggression. They reported that stimulation to the anterior hypothalamus of a small rhesus monkey did not cause the monkey to respond aggressively either to the experimenter or to inanimate objects. However, when the subject was put in a cage with a female monkey and a large dominant male, it vigorously attacked the male—but never the female—each time that it was stimulated. Of course, the dominant male responded to the attack from the subordinate in the expected manner, by viciously counterattacking. Nevertheless, each time that the subject was stimulated, it launched another vigorous attack until eventually the large male began to assume the submissive role. The important point of this demonstration is that although the stimulation reliably elicited social aggression, it did not increase the tendency to attack other targets.

One problem in interpreting stimulation-induced aggression in experimental animals is that it is difficult to rule out the possibility that the stimulation is simply painful or that it is eliciting the aggressive response in the absence of aggressive affect (e.g., Kruk, Meelis, Van der Poel, & Mos, 1981). However, studies of the effects of brain stimulation in humans suggest that brain stimulation can produce subjective feelings of aggression. For example, note the following transcript of a patient's response to amygdala stimulation (King, 1961).

Amygdala stimulation at 5 milliamperes (mA):

Interviewer: How do you feel now?

Subject: I feel like I want to get up from this chair. Please don't let me do it! Don't do this to me. I don't want to be mean.

Interviewer: Feel like you want to hit me?

Subject: Yeah. I just want to hit something. I want to get something and just tear it up. Take it so I won't. (Hands her scarf to the interviewer; he hands her a stack of paper, which she tears to shreds.) I don't like to feel like this!

Current reduced to 4 mA:

Subject: I know it's silly, what I'm doing.

Interviewer: Now, feel better?

Subject: A little bit.

Interviewer: Can you tell me a little bit more about how you were feeling a moment ago?

Subject: I wanted to get up from this chair and run. I wanted to hit something; tear up something—anything. Not you, just anything. I just wanted to get up and tear. I had no control of myself.

Current increased to 5 mA again:

Subject: Don't let me hit you!

Interviewer: How do you feel now?

Subject: I think I feel better like this. I get it out of my system. I don't have those other thoughts when I'm like this. . . . Take my blood pressure, I say! Quit holding me! I'm getting up! You'd better get somebody else if you want to hold me! I'm going to hit you! (p. 485)

12.3 Temperature Regulation

All species of multicellular animals can function effectively only within a narrow range of temperatures. The simplest way for an animal to meet this thermal requirement is to live in a place where temperatures are always in its required range, but such thermally stable habitats are rare. Most habitable parts of the earth's surface undergo regular **circadian** (about every 24 hours) cycles of temperature, and these are superimposed on seasonal cycles and irregular changes produced by local weather conditions. Because most surface-dwelling species live in thermally fluctuating climates, the maintenance of a stable body temperature is a major motivating force in their lives.

Maintaining a nearly constant body temperature is extraordinarily important for humans and other species with well-developed brains (i.e., species of mammals and birds). The reason is that during the course of evolution there has been a trade-off; as nervous systems have become more and more complex, they have become less and less capable of functioning effectively in extreme temperatures. In humans, for example, the range of temperatures at which the brain functions effectively is so small that it is commonly referred to as a point—37°C (98.6°F)—rather than a range. However, the core temperature of the body tends to cycle each day between about 36.5°C to 37.5°C in healthy males kept inactive at a constant room temperature (Figure 12.15). In females this circadian (daily) temperature cycle is superimposed on a monthly rhythm that has its peak after ovulation (see Chapter 10)—postovulation rectal temperatures are about 0.5°C greater than preovulation temperatures. If the core temperature shifts from 37°C by as little as 2.5°C in either direction, the unmatched analytic ability and creativity of the human brain gives way to confusion and poor judgment. It should be noted, however, that temperature increases are far more dangerous than temperature decreases—we live just a few degrees below our death points (see Lipton, 1987).

Why do all living forms function within only a relatively narrow range of temperatures, and why is this range more narrow for more complex species? The answers to these questions can be derived from the fact that temperature influences the rate of all biochemical reactions. At a given temperature, some reactions may occur at a high rate, others may occur slowly, and still others may not occur at all. This means that organisms whose activities involve the coordinated activity of many different biochemical reactions can function effectively only within the range of temperatures at which their various interrelated chemical reactions occur at rates that are in harmony with one another. Thus, as the complexity of an organism's functions increases (i.e., as they involve a greater variety of biochemical reactions), the range of temperatures at which they will be in harmony tends to shrink.

FIGURE 12.15 *The circadian cycle of rectal temperatures observed in a healthy human male confined to bed. (Adapted from Hardy, 1980.)*

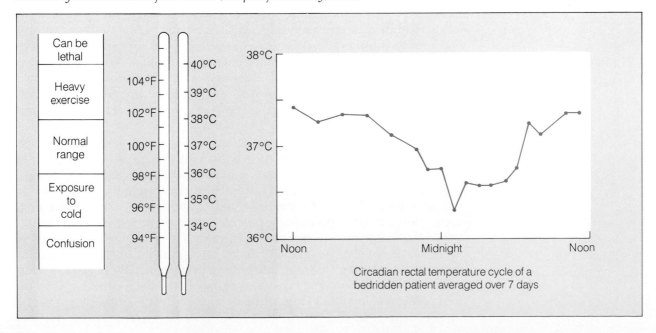

Circadian rectal temperature cycle of a
bedridden patient averaged over 7 days

Homoiotherms and Poikilotherms

With respect to temperature regulation, animals are commonly divided into two major categories. Mammals and birds are classed as **homoiotherms** (warm-blooded animals) because they maintain their body core at a relatively constant temperature, even when the temperature of their environment fluctuates. Other species do this less well and are classed as **poikilotherms** (cold-blooded animals). Let's begin with the poikilotherms because they are more simple.

Poikilotherms Many people believe that cold-blooded animals cannot regulate their body temperature. This is not quite right. The characteristic that defines cold-bloodedness is not the inability to regulate body temperature; it is the inability to reflexively regulate body temperature. Only the most simple poikilotherms do not regulate their body temperatures at all; to survive, they must live in thermally stable environments such as oceans or the bodies of homoiotherms, or they must have the capacity to lie dormant when the temperature of their environment becomes unsuitable. In contrast, more complex poikilotherms—such as fish, reptiles, and amphibians—do regulate their body temperatures, although not reflexively. Their most common thermoregulatory response is simply to move to cooler surroundings when they are too hot and to warmer ones when they are too cold. For example, fish frequently respond to the heat of day by moving to deeper water, and desert lizards burrow deeply into the sand during both the hottest parts of the day and the coolest parts of the night. Figure 12.16 summarizes the results of a laboratory demonstration of this mode of temperature regulation. A lizard was placed in a test apparatus with two compartments, one maintained at 45°C and the other at 15°C. In this situation, the lizard kept its rectal temperature between 28°C and 38°C by changing compartments about every 30 minutes (Hammel, Caldwell, & Abrams, 1967).

Social insects are poikilotherms with very interesting modes of temperature regulation. For example, rather than leaving their hive when it gets too hot or too cold, worker bees stay to participate in a living central heating and air conditioning system, which maintains the hive and the larvae within a degree or two of 35°C (Lindauer, 1961). When the hive becomes too cold, workers become more active and thus generate considerable heat through their combined muscular exertion. When it becomes too hot, the worker bees spread dilute nectar on the combs, which contain the larvae, and then they cause it to evaporate by fanning it with their wings. If you doubt the potent cooling action of evaporation, lick your wrist and blow on it.

Poikilothermic temperature regulation has one very serious shortcoming: Poikilotherms are slaves to their body temperature. When their bodies get too hot or too cold, they must interrupt what they are doing to take remedial action. Accordingly, in order that thermoregulatory behaviors do not completely dominate other essential activities (e.g., eating, sleeping, copulation, avoiding predation), poikilotherms are restricted to habitats in which the temperature changes are slight, or at least to ones in which there are enclaves of thermal stability (e.g., subterranean burrows). Furthermore, poikilotherms are incapable of long periods of activity even in thermally stable environments because they have no reflexive mechanisms for dissipating the heat that is generated.

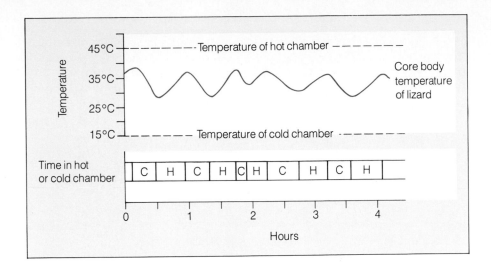

FIGURE 12.16 *A lizard maintained its temperature between 28°C and 38°C by moving back and forth between the two chambers of its test apparatus, one maintained at 15°C and one at 45°C. (Adapted from Hammel, Caldwell, & Abrams, 1967.)*

Homoiotherms Like poikilotherms, homoiotherms (mammals and birds) respond to extremes of body temperature by taking overt action; however, as you might expect, the overt regulatory responses of homoiotherms are more complex and varied than those of the more primitive poikilotherms. For example, in response to a drop in temperature, humans jump up and down, put on jackets, have hot drinks, or, if they are lucky enough to be in the right situation with the right person, they snuggle. Humans are not the only species to engage in thermoregulatory snuggling. For example, infant rats quickly lose body heat if placed by themselves in a cold environment because they are hairless and lack a functional internal thermoregulatory system. However, if a litter of infant rats is placed in a cold environment, each rat maintains a near normal temperature by snuggling its brothers and sisters (Alberts, 1978). As the ones on the top of the pile cool off, they burrow into the warm center of the pile, while their warmer siblings drift up through the pile and cool down.

Homoiotherms readily learn to perform arbitrary operant responses to control their temperature. Rats placed in a cold environment will press a lever to obtain heat from a heat lamp (Weiss & Laties, 1961), and those placed in a hot environment will press a lever to obtain a cooling spray of water (Epstein & Milestone, 1968). Furthermore, they often perform thermoregulatory responses in anticipation of temperature change, rather than as a result of it. For example, humans buy heaters, carry jackets on evening strolls, and plan winter vacations in tropical climates.

We are not always aware of our own voluntary thermoregulatory activities. The next time that you are in a classroom that is either too hot or too cold, study the postures of the people around you. Although it may never have crossed their minds that the amount of body heat lost to the air is a function of the proportion of their body surface that is exposed to it, their postures suggest that at some level they understand this principle well. See Figure 12.17.

In contrast to poikilotherms, homoiotherms have a second line of defense against temperature fluctuations. In addition to their extensive repertoire of overt, voluntary thermoregulatory behaviors, homoiotherms have an arsenal of internal reflexive responses that automatically counteract deviations from optimal body temperature. These reflexive thermoregulatory responses fall naturally into two different categories: those that cool

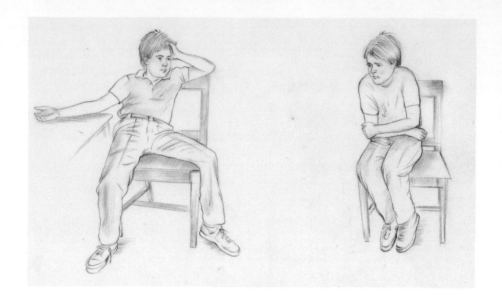

FIGURE 12.17 *The postures naturally assumed by people exposed to warm or cold environments influence heat loss to the air. Heat is conserved in cold environments by postures that minimize the area of the body surface exposed to the air, and the opposite is true in hot environments.*

the body when it is warm and those that warm it when it is cool. We humans have three major reflexive cooling responses: (1) increased respiration (panting), which increases heat loss through the lungs; (2) increased perspiration, which increases evaporation-produced heat loss; and (3) dilation of the peripheral blood vessels *(vasodilation)*, which increases the amount of blood near the surface of the body and thus increases the loss of heat from the blood to the air. We also have three reflexive warming responses: (1) shivering, which generates heat in the muscles; (2) peripheral *vasoconstriction,* which reduces heat loss from the blood by shunting it to the core of the body; and (3) the release of **thyroxine** from the thyroid gland, which accelerates heat production by increasing the general metabolic rate.

You have undoubtedly noticed that the hairs on your body stand up when you get cold—a response called **piloerection.** This response to cold seems to be the vestige of a heat-conservation response inherited from some fur-bearing prehistoric ancestor. Piloerection is one of the most effective thermoregulatory responses available to fur-bearing mammals, and birds have a feather equivalent. Piloerection greatly increases the insulating properties of a coat of fur by increasing the thickness of the layer of dead air that it traps around the body. We humans achieve the same end by putting on a sweater.

The Neural Control of Thermoregulation

The neural system maintaining the homeostasis of body temperature is thought to be a set-point negative-feedback system that operates much like the climate control system of a modern building. *Thermodetectors* in various parts of the body are assumed to transmit their signals to a thermoregulatory center (the thermostat), which compares them to the set points for these areas and triggers responses that counteract deviations from them (Hardy, 1980). For example, if the body core is above its 37°C set point, thermoregulatory responses are elicited that reduce the core temperature, whereas if the temperature of the core is below 37°C, responses are elicited that increase it.

In order to establish that a particular area of the nervous system contains thermodetectors, it is not enough to find neurons in the area that change their firing rate when they are heated or cooled. All neurons do this. It is necessary to demonstrate that heating or cooling the suspected thermo-receptors results in a compensatory thermoregulatory response. Receptors that meet this criterion have been identified in the skin (Nadel, Bullard, & Stolwijk, 1971), the gut (Rawson, Quick, & Coughlin, 1969), the spinal cord (Thauer, 1970), and in the **POAH** (the preoptic and anterior hypo-thalamus). The POAH seems to be a particularly important area for the reception of temperature information because, in addition to containing its own thermoreceptors, it receives information from thermoreceptors situated in other parts of the body.

Figure 12.18 illustrates the effects of heating the POAH or the spinal cord on the respiration rate of a rabbit and on the firing rate of one POAH neuron (Guieu & Hardy, 1970). Notice that each time either the POAH or the spinal cord was heated above the rabbit's normal core temperature of 38°C, there was an increase in both cell firing and respiration rate. Cooling below 38°C had no effect on either the firing of this cell or respiration. The

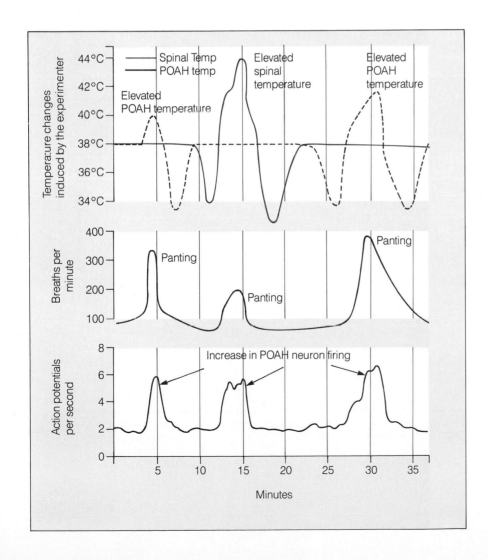

FIGURE 12.18 *The effects of heating the preoptic and anterior hypothalamus (POAH) or the spinal cord on the respiration rate of a rabbit and on the firing rate of one neuron in its POAH. Heating of either area above 38°C increased both cell firing and respiration, but cooling either area below 38°C had no effect on either cell firing or respiration. (Adapted from Guieu & Hardy, 1970)*

fact that many neurons in the POAH do not increase their firing rate in response to heating until the usual core temperature is exceeded is presumably the physiological basis of the rabbit's temperature set point.

Heating or cooling of the POAH can influence the behavioral regulation of body temperature (Adair, Casby, & Stolwijk, 1970). In one study, monkeys were trained to regulate the ambient temperature of their test chambers by pulling a chain which controlled the influx of hot (50°C) and cold (10°C) air; each time they pulled the chain, it changed the temperature of the air being blown into the test chamber from 10°C to 50°C, or vice versa. Once they learned the task, all monkeys tested under control conditions pulled the chain in such a way that temperature of the test chamber was almost always within a degree or two of 35°C. Figure 12.19 illustrates how heating or cooling the POAH by implanted temperature probes affected the selection of ambient temperatures by one monkey. Each time the POAH was heated, the monkey selected a cooler environment, and each time it was cooled, the monkey selected a warmer environment.

Some theories of temperature regulation specify the POAH as the site of the **thermostat,** the hypothetical neural circuit that receives temperature-related signals, compares them to a set point, and initiates the appropriate thermoregulatory responses. Evidence for this view comes from the observation that animals with large POAH lesions frequently do not survive in hot or cold environments that are readily tolerated by intact controls.

FIGURE 12.19 *Effect of heating and cooling the POAH of a monkey on its selection of ambient temperatures. Heating the POAH caused the monkey to select a cooler ambient temperature, and cooling it caused the monkey to select a warmer temperature. (Adapted from Adair et al., 1970)*

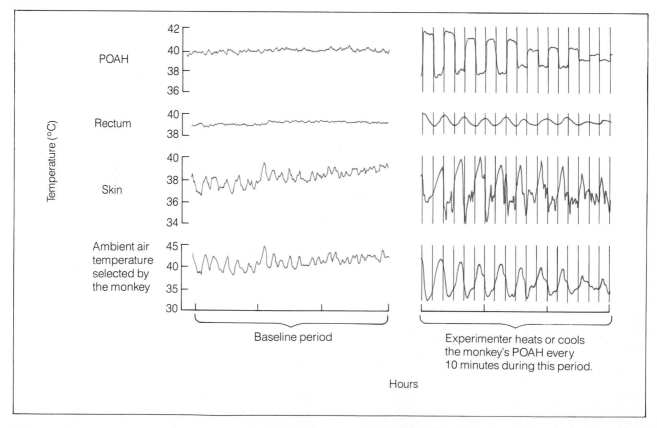

However, systematic analysis of the effects of POAH lesions on various thermoregulatory responses has supported an alternative view. The observation that even very large POAH lesions affect only some thermoregulatory responses argues strongly for a multiple-thermostat model. In rats, for example, POAH lesions disrupt both shivering (Satinoff, Valentino, & Teitelbaum, 1976) in response to cold and sprawling (lying down with legs splayed) in response to heat (Roberts & Martin, 1977), but they do not disrupt cold-induced vasoconstriction (Satinoff et al., 1976) or the ability to regulate body temperature by lever pressing for warmth or cold (Carlisle, 1969; Lipton, 1968). Satinoff (1982) argues that most thermoregulatory responses originally served other adaptive functions, and still do, but that during the course of evolution one by one they came under the influence of temperature detectors in various parts of the body. For example, panting originally evolved as a response to respiratory deficits, but now it can also be elicited by a high body temperature. If the thermoregulatory system did indeed evolve in this piecemeal fashion, it seems unlikely that there would now be a single central thermostat to control all thermoregulatory responses.

Fever and Hypothermia

This section of the chapter on temperature regulation concludes with the discussion of two deviations from thermal homeostasis: fever and hypothermia.

Fever   Fever is an elevation of body temperature associated with infection or injury. Fever speeds up the general metabolic rate of the body, and in so doing, increases the rate of bodily repair and the capacity of the immune system to combat infection. **Pyrogenic** (fever-inducing) infections or injuries do not act directly on the thermoregulatory system. Instead, they cause the patient's own tissues to release a factor, which has yet to be completely characterized, but is generally referred to as **endogenous pyrogen.** Endogenous pyrogen then travels through the blood to the central nervous system, where it acts to induce the fever. It does this by increasing the body's set point. The thermoregulatory system continues to function normally, except that it begins to defend a body temperature from 1 to 4°C higher than normal.

Although the severity and duration of a fever depend on its cause, most fevers follow a similar course, which you have likely experienced. First is the **chill phase,** during which patients act and feel as if they are cold. Despite having an increasingly high body temperature, they shiver violently, they assume the characteristic hunched-over arms-tight-to-the-chest posture of heat conservation, and they often wrap themselves in a cocoon of blankets. The point at which the body temperature stops rising marks the end of the chill phase and the beginning of the plateau phase. The **plateau phase** is the phase during which the *febrile* (pertaining to fever) temperature is actively defended by the body's thermoregulatory system; increases or decreases from this level are counteracted in the usual way by compensatory thermoregulatory reactions. One of the major symptoms of the plateau phase is uncomfortably hot and dry skin. The third and last phase of a fever is the **defervescence phase,** during which the set point returns to normal, and the body rids itself of the extra heat that it has been storing. Defervescence is commonly associated with profuse sweating.

The correlation between sweating and the decline of fever is the basis for the common view that sweating promotes recovery from fever. Generations of loving parents—including my own—have prescribed warmth in the form of hot drinks, chicken soup, hot-water bottles, and extra blankets "to sweat their childrens' fevers out of them." Admirable intentions aside, this common fallacy provides yet another illustration of the incorrect causal interpretation of correlational data (see Chapter 1). Sweating does not promote recovery; recovery promotes sweating. In fact, further increasing the body temperature of a patient who has a high fever can be hazardous.

Attempts to discover the site of action of endogenous pyrogen initially focused on the POAH. Microinjection of endogenous pyrogen into the POAH was found to induce fever in a variety of laboratory species (e.g., Cooper, Cranston, & Honour, 1967; Rosendorff & Mooney, 1971), and microinjection of an **antipyretic**—such as **salicylate,** a constituent of aspirin—into the POAH was shown to reduce fever. However, the POAH is not the only site capable of mediating the pyrogenic effects of endogenous pyrogen; intraventricular injections of endogenous pyrogen induce fever even in animals whose POAH has been completely destroyed (e.g., Andersson, Gale, Hokfelt, & Larsson, 1965; Lipton & Trzcinka, 1976; Veale & Cooper, 1975).

Hypothermia   **Hypothermia** is arbitrarily defined in humans as a condition in which the core temperature of the body falls below 35°C. It is a major cause of death in boating accidents, in mountaineering and polar expeditions, and in aged people living in cold climates in homes with no central heating. Table 12.2 lists the symptoms associated with various levels of hypothermia. It illustrates two important points. The first is that manifestations of cerebral dysfunction (i.e., apathy, amnesia, confusion, poor judgment, and hallucinations) are among the earliest overt signs of hypothermia as the temperature of the body core drops. As a result, the idiosyncratic behavior of people under dangerously frigid conditions often increases the hazardousness of the situation. The second point is that humans can recover from core temperatures below 27°C, although they appear to be dead at such temperatures, with no detectable heart beat, respiration, or EEG (e.g., Niazi & Lewis, 1958). The only certain sign of death in hypothermia is failure to recover when warmed (Lloyd, 1986).

Considerable experience in the treatment of hypothermia was gained during World War II. After the war, research began on the possibility of using hypothermia as a surgical tool (e.g., Bigelow, Lindsay, Harrison, Gordon, & Greenwood, 1950). Because hypothermic tissues and organs use so little oxygen, it was reasoned that cooled patients would be better capable of withstanding an interruption of their blood supply. In fact, at a core temperature of 28°C, it proved possible to safely stop a person's heart for 10 minutes, thus making the first open-heart operations possible. Today, it is not necessary to cool patients during open-heart surgery because their blood flow is not interrupted; it is maintained by a pump that *oxygenates* the blood. However, it is usual to cool down patients during open-heart surgery as a precautionary measure; this is accomplished by cooling their blood.

Table 12.2 *The symptoms of various levels of hypothermia (Adapted from Harnett, Pruitt, & Sias, 1983). As the temperature of the body core declines, the following symptoms are observed.*

37°C	· normal core temperature
36°C	· increased metabolic rate to generate heat
34°–35°C	· shivering maximal at this temperature · blood shunted to body core to prevent further heat loss
31°–33°C	· most shivering ceases · pupils dilate · patients become apathetic and confused and display poor judgment · hallucinations and amnesia may be experienced · blood pressure decreases · decline in metabolic rate
27°–30°C	· loss of consciousness · heart beat slows and becomes irregular · increased muscular rigidity · slow respiration
26°–27°C	· no voluntary movement, and reflexes cannot be elicited · victims seem dead to untrained observers
21°–24°C	· severe danger of death
20°C	· heart sounds become inaudible
17°C	· cortical EEG flattens
9°C	· lowest recorded core temperature from which a human has recovered
4°C	· lowest recorded core temperature from which a monkey has recovered
−7°C	· lowest recorded core temperature from which rats and hamsters have recovered

Conclusion

Discussed in this chapter were the physiological systems that control three classes of motivated behavior: drinking, aggression, and temperature regulation. The following three paragraphs summarize these sections.

Two different physiological systems recognize water deficits: one that is sensitive to cellular dehydration and one that is sensitive to hypovolemia. Although osmoreceptors, which detect cellular dehydration, are distributed throughout the body, it is those in the lateral preoptic area and the lateral hypothalamus that appear to play the major role in the control of drinking. Drinking in response to hypovolemia is triggered by baroreceptors (blood pressure receptors) in the heart and blood-flow receptors in the kidneys. Both the baroreceptors and blood-flow receptors cause renin to be released from the kidney, which causes the formation of angiotensin II in the blood. Angiotensin II stimulates drinking by activating cells in the subfornical organ on the ceiling of the third ventricle. Although most of the research on the physiology of drinking has focused on the mechanisms of deprivation-induced drinking, most of the drinking of humans and other organisms with ready access to water occurs in the absence of water deficits.

Aggressive behavior appears to be under the control of at least three separate but intertwined neural systems: one for defensive aggression, one for predatory aggression, and one for social aggression. The septum, the medial accumbens, the medial hypothalamus, and the raphé nuclei appear to inhibit both defensive and predatory aggression, whereas the lateral hypothalamus and the amygdala seem to facilitate both. In contrast, the septum, the medial accumbens, the medial hypothalamus, and the raphé nuclei appear to facilitate social aggression. The role of the amygdala and lateral hypothalamus in social aggression is not clear. Unlike defensive and predatory aggression, social aggression is more common in males than in females, and it has been shown to depend on the presence of testosterone. Our current understanding of the biopsychology of aggression suggests that attempts to control human aggression by psychosurgery are ill-advised.

There are two kinds of temperature-regulation systems. Poikilotherms have only one of them; they can regulate their body temperatures only by making overt behavioral responses. In contrast, homoiotherms have both; in addition to their ability to regulate their body temperature by changing their overt behavior, they have a repertoire of reflexive thermoregulatory responses such as panting, sweating, and shivering. Thermodetectors distributed in various parts of the body relay temperature information to "thermostats," which analyze it and trigger thermoregulatory responses that maintain the core temperature around a set point—37°C for humans. The preoptic and anterior hypothalamus (POAH) appears to be a particularly important component of the thermoregulatory system; it contains its own thermoreceptors and it also receives information from some thermoreceptors in other parts of the body. Fever and hypothermia are two deviations from thermal homeostasis that are of great interest to medical science.

Food for Thought

1. How would you recognize hypothermia in yourself or someone else? How would you deal with the situation?
2. When did you last take a drink? What did you drink and why do you think you drank it? What does your own pattern of fluid intake tell you about the kinds of physiological systems that regulate drinking?
3. How do defensive, predatory, and social aggression differ in the rat? Do they differ in humans? How?

ADDITIONAL READING

The following three references provide excellent coverage of the three motivational topics of this chapter: aggression, temperature regulation, and drinking, respectively.

Blanchard, D. C., & Blanchard, R. J. (1984). *Advances in the study of aggression, Volume 1.* Orlando, Florida: Academic Press.

Crawshaw, L. I., Moffitt, B. P., Lemons, D. E., & Downey, J. A. (1981). The evolutionary development of vertebrate thermoregulation. *American Scientist*, September-October, 543–549.

Rolls, B. J., & Rolls, E. T. (1982). *Thirst.* Cambridge: Cambridge University Press.

KEY TERMS

To help you study the material in this chapter, all of the key terms—those that have appeared in bold type—are listed and briefly defined here.

Aldosterone. The hormone that is released from the adrenal cortices in response to angiotensin II; aldosterone causes the kidneys to reabsorb much of the sodium that would otherwise be lost in the urine.

Alpha male. The dominant male animal in a colony.

Angiotensin II. A peptide hormone that is synthesized in the blood in response to renin release; it produces a compensatory increase in blood pressure by constricting the peripheral blood vessels, by triggering the release of aldosterone from the adrenal cortices, and perhaps by stimulating thirst.

Antidiuretic hormone (ADH). A hormone released from the posterior pituitary that encourages the conservation of bodily fluids by decreasing the volume of urine produced by the kidneys.

Antipyretic. An agent that works against fever.

Baroreceptors. Blood pressure receptors.

Blood-flow receptors. Receptors that monitor the volume of blood flowing through the kidneys.

Boxing. When a rat rears up on its hind legs and uses its forelegs to fend off an attacker.

Cellular dehydration. Reduction in intracellular fluid volume.

Chill phase. The first phase of a fever in which patients act and feel as if they are cold despite their normal body temperature.

Circadian cycles. Daily cycles of physiological activity.

Colloids. Glue-like substances with molecules too large to pass through cell membranes.

Defensive aggression. Attacks that occur in response to perceived threats.

Defervescence phase. The final phase of a fever, in which the set point returns to normal.

Deprivation-induced drinking. The drinking that occurs in response to fluid deficits.

Dipsogen. A substance that induces drinking.

Endogenous pyrogen. Fever-inducing substances produced by the body.

Fever. An elevation of body temperature associated with infection or injury.

Hepatic-portal system. The branch of the cardiovascular system that carries water and other nutrients absorbed from the gastrointestinal tract to the liver.

Homoiotherms. Warm-blooded animals.

Hypertonic. More concentrated than some reference solution.

Hypothermia. A condition in which the temperature of the human body falls below 35°C.

Hypotonic. Less concentrated than some reference solution.

Hypovolemia. Decreased blood volume.

Hypovolemic drinking. Drinking induced by decreased blood volume.

Interstitial fluid. The fluid surrounding the cells of multicellular organisms.

Isotonic. Two solutions are said to be isotonic if they contain the same concentration of solutes.

Lateral attack. A pattern of attack employed by dominant male rats against other male rats; the dominant male moves sideways into its opponent.

Maternal aggression. The aggressive behavior directed by mothers at conspecifics or members of other species that approach the nest site.

Nephrectomized. Organisms in which the kidneys have been removed.

Osmoreceptors. Receptors sensitive to dehydration.

Osmotic pressure. The pressure that draws water from a hypotonic solution to a hypertonic solution.

Piloerection. When the hairs on one's body stand up.

Plateau phase. The phase of a fever in which the body's elevated temperature is actively defended.

POAH. The preoptic and anterior hypothalamus; a site that contains thermoreceptors and receives information from thermoreceptors in other parts of the body.

Poikilotherms. Animals with no system to reflexively control body temperature.

Polydipsia. Grossly excessive fluid consumption.

Predatory aggression. The stalking and killing of members of another species for the purpose of eating them.

Psychosurgery. Destruction of a part of the brain for the purpose of therapeutically changing behavior.

Pyrogen. Fever-inducing substance.

Renin. A hormone that is released from the kidneys in response to increasing ADH levels or decreasing signals from cardiac baroreceptors; renin stimulates the synthesis of the peptide hormone angiotensin II.

Saccharin elation effect. Nondeprived animals that normally have continuous access to a saccharin solution prefer it to water even more than usual following a period during which it was not available.

Salicylate. An antipyretic constituent of Aspirin.

Saralasin. A blocker of angiotensin II receptors.

Schedule-induced polydipsia. An animal receiving a pellet of food every minute or so consumes huge volumes of water between pellets.

Sham drinking. Drinking that occurs in animals with esophageal, gastric, or duodenal fistulas; the water drunk by such an animal flows out through its fistula before it can be absorbed from the gastrointestinal tract into the bloodstream.

Social aggression. Unprovoked aggression directed at a conspecific for the purpose of establishing, altering, or maintaining a social hierarchy.

Spontaneous drinking. Drinking in the absence of fluid deficits.

Subfornical organ (SFO). The midline structure on the dorsal surface of the third ventricle that is thought to be the site of the angiotensin II receptors that mediate the dipsogenic effects of angiotensin II.

Testosterone. The gonadal hormone on which the expression of social aggression depends.

Thyroxine. A hormone released from the thyroid gland that accelerates heat production by increasing general metabolic rate.

13

Sleep, Dreaming, and Circadian Rhythms

Most of us have a fondness for eating, drinking, and sex, the three highly esteemed motivated behaviors discussed in Chapters 10, 11, and 12. But the amount of time devoted to these three behaviors by even the most amorous gourmands pales in comparison to the amount of time that he or she spends sleeping—most of us will sleep for well over 175,000 hours in our lifetimes. This extraordinary commitment of time implies that sleep fufills a critical biological function. But what is it? And what about dreaming; why do we spend so much time dreaming? And why do we tend to get sleepy at about the same time every day, regardless of how much work we have done? Answers to these questions await you in this chapter.

Almost every time that I give a lecture about sleep, somebody asks, "How much sleep do we need?" and each time, I provide the same unsatisfying answer. I explain that there are two fundamentally different answers to this question, but that neither has emerged a clear winner. One answer stresses the presumed health-promoting and recuperative powers of sleep and suggests that people need as much sleep as they can comfortably get. The other answer is that many of us sleep much more than we need to and are consequently sleeping our lives away. Just think how your life could change if you slept 5 hours per night instead of 8. You would have an extra 21 waking hours each week, a mind-boggling 10,952 hours each decade.

As I prepared to write this chapter, I began to think of some of the personal implications of the idea that we get more sleep than we need. That is when I decided to do something a bit unconventional. While I write this chapter, I am going to be your subject in a sleep-reduction experiment. I am going to try to get no more than 5 hours of sleep per night—11:00 P.M. to 4:00 A.M.—until this chapter is written. As I begin, I am excited by the prospect of having more time to write, but a little worried that this extra time might be obtained at a personal cost that is too dear.

It is the next day now—4:50 Saturday morning to be exact—and I am just beginning to write. There was a party last night, and I didn't make it to bed by 11:00, but considering that I slept for only 3 hours and 35 minutes, I feel quite good. I wonder what I will feel like later in the day? In any case, I will report my experiences to you at the end of the chapter. This chapter comprises the following 10 sections:

Miss M. . . . is a busy lady who finds her ration of twenty-three hours of wakefulness still insufficient for her needs. Even though she is now retired she is still busy in the community, helping sick friends whenever requested. She is an active painter and has recently finished a biography of William Morris, the British writer and designer. Although she becomes tired physically, when she needs to sit down to rest her legs, she does not ever report feeling sleepy. During the night she sits on her bed . . . reading, writing, crocheting or painting. At about 2:00 A.M. she falls asleep without any preceding drowsiness often while still holding a book in her hands. When she wakes about an hour later, she feels as wide awake as ever. It would be wrong to say that she woke refreshed because she did not complain of tiredness in the first place.

To test her claim we invited her along to the laboratory. She came willingly but on the first evening we hit our first snag. She announced that she did not sleep at all if she had interesting things to do, and by her reckoning a visit to a university sleep laboratory counted as very interesting. Moreover, for the first time in years, she had someone to talk to for the whole of the night. So we talked.

In the morning we broke into shifts so that some could sleep while at least one person stayed with her and entertained her during the next day. The second night was a repeat performance of the first night. . . . Things had not gone according to plan. So far we were very impressed by her cheerful response to two nights of sleep deprivation, but we had very little by way of hard data to show others.

In the end we prevailed upon her to allow us to apply EEG electrodes and to leave her sitting comfortably on the bed in the bedroom. She had promised that she would co-operate by not resisting sleep although she claimed not to be especially tired. . . . At approximately 1:30 A.M., the EEG record showed the first signs of sleep even though . . . she was still sitting with the book in her hands. . . .

The only substantial difference between her sleep and what we might have expected from any other seventy-year-old lady was that it was of short duration. . . . [After 99 minutes], she had no further interest in sleep and asked to be allowed to leave the bedroom so that she could join our company again (Meddis, 1977, pp. 42–44).

The Three Standard Psychophysiological Measures of Sleep

It was first observed in the 1930s that there are major changes in the human EEG during the course of a night's sleep (Loomis, Harvey, & Hobart, 1936). Although the EEG waves accompanying sleep are generally large and slow, there are periods throughout the night that are dominated by low-voltage, fast waves similar to those seen in waking subjects. In 1953, Aserinsky and Kleitman discovered that **rapid eye movements** (REMs) occur under the closed eyelids of sleeping subjects during these periods of low-voltage, fast EEG activity. And in 1962, Berger and Oswald discovered that there is also a loss of electromyographic activity in the neck muscles during these same sleep periods. Subsequently, the **electroencephalogram** (EEG), the **electro-oculogram** (EOG), and the neck **electromyogram** (EMG) became the three standard psychophysiological bases for defining stages of sleep (Rechtschaffen & Kales, 1968). Figure 13.1 depicts how EEG, EOG, and EMG activity are recorded during a sleep experiment. If being a subject in a sleep experiment looks like an easy way to earn a little extra cash, it is.

Although the physical discomfort created by the recording leads is minimal, a subject's first night in the sleep laboratory is often fitful. That is why it is the usual practice to have a subject sleep several nights in the laboratory before beginning to study his or her sleep patterns. The disturbance of sleep observed during the first night in a sleep laboratory is called the **first-night phenomenon.** It is well known to markers of introductory psychology examinations because of the creative definitions of it offered by students who forget that it is a sleep-related, rather than a sex-related, phenomenon.

The Five Stages of Sleep EEG

The EEG of a subject during a typical night's sleep is commonly divided into four separate classes: stage 1, stage 2, stage 3, and stage 4. Examples of these four stages of sleep EEG are presented in Figure 13.2. After a subject shuts her or his eyes and prepares to go to sleep, **alpha waves** (8 to 12 Hz) begin to punctuate the low-amplitude, high-frequency EEG of active wakefulness. Then, as the subject falls asleep, there is a sudden transition to a period of stage 1 sleep EEG. Stage 1 sleep EEG is a low-amplitude high-frequency signal that is similar to, but slower than, that of active wakefulness. Then, as the subject continues to sleep, there is a progressive increase in the amplitude of the EEG waves and a slowing of their frequency, which is customarily divided into three stages: 2, 3, and 4. The primary distinguishing feature of stage 2 sleep EEG, in addition to the fact that it has a slightly higher amplitude and lower frequency than stage 1, is the fact that it is punctuated by two characteristic wave forms: **K complexes,** which are composed of a single large negative wave (upward deflection) followed by a single large positive wave (downward deflection), and **sleep spindles,** which are 1-to-2-second waxing and waning bursts of 12-to-14-Hz waves. Stage 3 sleep EEG is defined by the occasional presence of **delta waves,** the largest and slowest EEG waves, with a frequency of 1 to

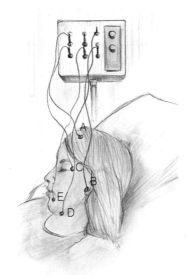

Electrodes

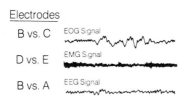

B vs. C	EOG Signal
D vs. E	EMG Signal
B vs. A	EEG Signal

FIGURE 13.1 *A subject participating in a sleep experiment.*

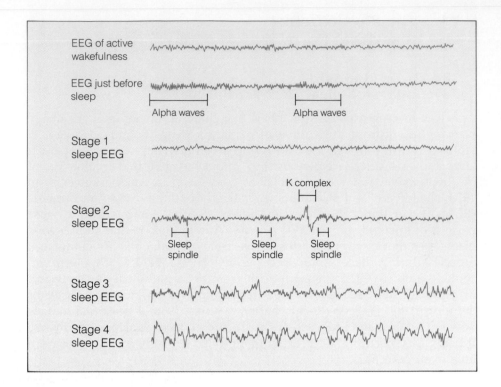

FIGURE 13.2 *Waking EEG, presleep EEG, and the four stages of sleep EEG. Each trace is 30 seconds long.*

2 per second. The defining feature of stage 4 EEG is the predominance of delta waves. After spending some time in stage 4, sleeping subjects retreat back through the stages of sleep EEG to stage 1. However, when they return to stage 1, things are not at all the same as they were the first time through. Although the first period of stage 1 EEG recorded during a night's sleep (**initial stage 1 EEG**) is not accompanied by any noteworthy electromyographic or electro-oculographic events, subsequent periods of stage 1 sleep EEG (**emergent stage 1 EEG**) are all accompanied by REMs and by a loss of tone in the muscles of the body core.

After the first cycle of sleep EEG—from initial stage 1 to stage 4 and back to emergent stage 1—the rest of the night is spent like a pendulum, going back and forth through the stages. Figure 13.3 illustrates the cycles of a typical night's sleep and the close relation between emergent stage 1 sleep, REMs, and the lack of tone in the core muscles. Notice that each cycle tends to be about 90 minutes long and that as the night progresses, more and more time is spent in emergent stage 1 sleep, and less and less time is spent in the other stages, particularly in stage 4. Notice also that there are brief periods during the night when the subject is awake; these periods of wakefulness are usually not remembered in the morning.

Let's pause here to get some sleep-stage terms straight before proceeding with more substantive matters. Emergent stage 1 sleep is often called **paradoxical sleep** because the EEG signals and autonomic nervous system changes associated with it are similar to those of wakefulness, and stages 3 and 4 are sometimes lumped together and called **delta sleep** after the delta waves that characterize them. Although the term **deep sleep** is commonly used in the scientific literature on sleep, I am going to refrain from using it here because of its ambiguity. Some researchers refer to stage 4 sleep as deep sleep (e.g., Jouvet, 1967) because stage 4 sleep is characterized by the

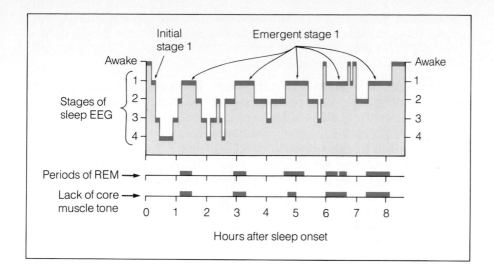

FIGURE 13.3 *The stages of EEG during a typical night's sleep and their relation to periods of REM and lack of tone in core muscles.*

largest and slowest EEG waves; other researchers refer to emergent stage 1 sleep as deep sleep because it is emergent stage 1 sleep during which the muscles are most relaxed and from which it is most difficult to awaken experimental animals. (Note that although it has proven most difficult to awaken laboratory animals from emergent stage 1 sleep, the results of comparable studies in humans have been mixed; see Cohen, 1979.) In this chapter, I will adopt the common practice of referring to that stage of sleep characterized by rapid eye movements, loss of core muscle tone, and low-amplitude high-frequency EEG as **REM sleep.** The term **slow-wave sleep** (SWS) will be used to refer generally to stages 2, 3, and 4.

REMs, loss of core muscle tone, and low-amplitude high-frequency EEG are not the only physiological correlates of human REM sleep. The neural activity, blood flow, and oxygen consumption of the brain increase to close-to-waking levels during REM sleep, and there is an increase in blood pressure, in respiration rates, and in the irregularity of the heart beat. The muscles of the extremities often twitch noticeably despite the complete relaxation of the muscles of the body core. Also, there is virtually always a penile or clitoral erection of some degree during REM sleep.

13.2 REM Sleep and Dreaming

Kleitman's laboratory was an exciting place following the discovery of REM sleep there in 1953. Kleitman and his colleagues were driven by the fascinating implication of their discovery. With the exception of the loss of muscle tone in the core muscles, all of the other measures suggested that REM sleep episodes were emotion-charged. Could REM sleep be the physiological correlate of dreaming? Could REM sleep provide researchers with a window into the subjective inner world of dreams? They began by waking a few subjects in the middle of REM episodes and asking them if they had been dreaming. The results were remarkable.

The vivid recall that could be elicited in the middle of the night when a subject was awakened while his eyes were moving rapidly was nothing short of miraculous. It [seemed to open] . . . an exciting new world to the subjects whose only previous dream memories had been the vague morning-after recall. Now, instead of perhaps some fleeting glimpse into the dream world each night, the subjects could be tuned into the middle of as many as ten or twelve dreams every night. (Dement, 1978, p. 37)

The results of a controlled comparison between REM and nonREM (NREM) awakenings were published in 1957 (Dement & Kleitman): 80% of the awakenings from REM sleep, but only 7% of the awakenings from NREM sleep, led to dream recall. The phenomenon of dreaming, which for centuries had been the subject of wild speculation, was finally rendered accessible to scientific investigation. The following anecdote related by Dement communicates some of the excitement felt by those involved in the discovery.

I decided to be a subject primarily out of envy; having listened with amazement and awe as many subjects recounted their dreams, I wished to enjoy the experience myself. . . . On the first night I felt like an actor preparing for a performance as I sat in front of the mirror donning my "makeup" of electrodes. I will never forget this "opening night." . . .

A hastily trained medical student . . . was monitoring the EEG and supervising my arousals. I went to sleep prepared for an exciting night and woke up with a certain urgency. . . . I searched my mind . . . I could remember nothing. . . . So I went back to sleep and was suddenly aware of being wrenched from the void once again. This time I could remember nothing except a very, very vague feeling of a name or a person. Disappointed but sleepy, I dozed off again.

The next time I was jolted awake—still unable to recall anything—I began to worry. Why didn't I remember a dream? I had expected to dazzle the medical student with my brilliant recall! After a fourth and fifth awakening with exactly the same results, I was really upset. What in the world was wrong? I began to doubt the whole REM-dreaming hypothesis. . . .

The experience had left me exhausted and extremely puzzled, and I was anxious to look at the polygraphic record of my miserable night. Upon examining the record I discovered, to my utter delight and relief, that the medical student had been mistakenly arousing me in NREM [stage 2 sleep]. Not once had I awakened during a REM period.

The next night, with additional instruction . . . the medical student hit the REM periods right on the button, and vivid recall flooded my mind with each awakening. (Dement, 1978, pp. 38–39)

Testing Common Beliefs about Dreaming

The high correlation between REM sleep and dream recall provided an opportunity to test some common beliefs about dreaming. The following are six such beliefs that have been subjected to empirical tests.

1. Many people believe that external stimuli sensed while they are dreaming become incorporated into their dreams. Dement and Wolpert (1958) sprayed water on sleeping subjects after they had been in REM sleep for a few minutes, and a few moments after the spray, each subject was awakened. In 14 of 33 cases, the water was incorporated into the dream report. The following narrative was reported by a subject who had been dreaming that he was acting in a play.

I was walking behind the leading lady when she suddenly collapsed and water was dripping on her. I ran over to her and water was dripping on my back and head. The roof was leaking. . . . I looked up and there was a hole in the roof. I dragged her over to the side of the stage and began pulling the curtains. Then I woke up. (Dement & Wolpert, 1958, p. 550)

2. Some people believe that dreams last only an instant, but research suggests that dreams run on "real time." In one study (Dement & Kleitman, 1957), subjects were awakened 5 or 15 minutes after the beginning of a REM episode and asked to decide on the basis of the duration of the events in their dreams whether they had been dreaming for 5 or 15 minutes. They were correct in 92 of 111 cases.

3. It is commonly believed that some people do not dream. However, people who claim that they do not dream have been found to have just as much REM sleep as "normal dreamers." Moreover, those claiming to be nondreamers report dreams when awakened in the sleep laboratory during REM episodes (Goodenough, Shapiro, Holden, & Steinschriber, 1959), although they do so far less frequently than do normal dreamers.

4. Many assume that penile erections are indicative of dreams with sexual content. However, penile erections occur during REM periods even in male infants; in adult males, penile erections are no more complete during dreams with frank sexual content than during those without it (Karacan, Goodenough, Shapiro, & Starker, 1966).

5. Most people believe that sleep talking and sleep walking (**somnambulism**) reflect the acting out of dreams. This is not so; sleep talking and somnambulism occur least frequently during dreaming, when core muscles tend to be totally relaxed, and most frequently during stage 4 sleep.

6. Many people accept Freud's theory that dreams are simply extensions of the stressful or sexual events of the previous day, but there is little experimental support for this idea. Neither a particularly violent western film (Foulkes & Rechtschaffen, 1964) nor a documentary showing sexually explicit aboriginal initiations (Goodenough, Witkin, Koulack, & Cohen, 1975) were incorporated into the dream reports of subjects who viewed them just before bedtime.

13.3 Why Do We Sleep?
Recuperative and Circadian Theories

We humans have a tendency toward self-aggrandizement; we tend to think that most of what we do has a special, higher order function. For example, it has been suggested that human sleep helps reprogram our complex computer-like brains, or that it permits some kind of emotional release to maintain our mental health. This is why many people are surprised to learn that virtually all mammals and birds sleep and that their sleep is much like ours; it is characterized by high-amplitude, low-frequency EEG waves punctuated by periods of low-amplitude, high-frequency activity. Even fish, reptiles, amphibians, and insects go through periods of inactivity and unresponsiveness akin to human sleep.

The fact that sleep is so common in the animal kingdom suggests that it serves a critical function, but there is no consensus on what this critical function is. There are two general theoretical approaches to the function of sleep: *recuperation theories* and *circadian theories*. The essence of the recuperation theories is that being awake disrupts the homeostasis of the body in some way and that sleep is required to restore it. In contrast, the circadian theories argue that sleep is not a response to internal imbalance. According to the circadian theories, a neural mechanism has evolved to encourage animals to sleep during those times of the day when they do not usually engage in activities necessary for their survival. For example, prehistoric humans in their natural environment clearly had enough time to get their eating, drinking, and reproducing out of the way during the daytime, and their strong motivation to sleep at night may have evolved to conserve their energy resources and to make them less susceptible to mishap (e.g., predation) in the dark. The circadian theory views sleep as an instinct somewhat akin to the instinct to engage in sexual activity. In essence, recuperation theories view sleep as a nightly repairman who fixes damage produced by wakefulness, while the circadian theories regard sleep as a strict parent who demands inactivity because it keeps us out of trouble. Choosing between the recuperation and circadian approaches to sleep is the logical first step in the search for the physiological basis of sleep. Is the sleep system run by a biological clock that produces compelling urges to sleep at certain times of the day to conserve energy and protect us from mishap or is it a homeostatic system whose function is to correct some adverse consequence of staying awake?

One of the major challenges faced by both the circadian and recuperation theories of sleep is to explain the vast differences among species in the amount of sleep that they get. Table 13.1 illustrates the number of hours of sleep per day of various mammals. Why do giant sloths typically sleep 20 hours per day while horses sleep only about 2 hours?

The next two sections of this chapter deal with two topics—circadian sleep cycles and sleep deprivation—that have a direct bearing on the question of whether sleep is fundamentally circadian or recuperative.

Table 13.1 *The number of hours of sleep per day characteristic of various mammalian species.*

HOURS OF SLEEP PER DAY	MAMMALIAN SPECIES
20	giant sloth
19	opossum, brown bat
18	giant armadillo
17	owl monkey, nine-banded armadillo
16	Arctic ground squirrel
15	tree shrew
14	cat, golden hamster
13	mouse, rat, gray wolf, ground squirrel
12	Arctic fox, chinchilla, gorilla, raccoon
11	mountain beaver
10	jaguar, vervet monkey, hedgehog
9	rhesus monkey, chimpanzee, baboon, red fox
8	human, rabbit, guinea pig, pig
6	gray seal, gray hyrax, Brazilian tapir
5	tree hyrax, rock hyrax
3	cow, goat, elephant, donkey, sheep
2	roe deer, horse

13.4 Circadian Sleep Cycles

The world in which we live cycles continually from light to dark and back again once every 24 hours, and most surface-dwelling animals have adapted to this regular change in their environment by developing a variety of so-called **circadian rhythms**—*circadian* means **diurnal** or lasting about 1 day. For example, most species display a regular circadian sleep-wake cycle. Humans and most other animals take advantage of the light afforded during the day to take care of their biological needs, and then they sleep for a major proportion of the night, whereas **nocturnal animals,** such as rats, sleep for much of the day and stay awake at night. Although the so-called sleep-wake cycle is the most obvious circadian rhythm, "it is virtually impossible to find a physiological, biochemical, or behavioral process in animals which does not display some measure of circadian rhythmicity" (Groos, 1983, p. 19). Each day our bodies adjust themselves in a variety of ways to meet the demands of the two environments in which we live: light and dark.

Free-Running Circadian Sleep-Wake Cycles

The existence of regular sleep-wake cycles does not by itself provide evidence for an internal sleep-timing mechanism. Sleep and wakefulness might simply be controlled by environmental cues, such as sunset and sunrise or regularly scheduled meals. For this reason, investigators have been particularly interested in the sleep-wake cycles of humans and experimental animals living under constant conditions in underground caves or sound-proof, windowless laboratories. The usual finding is that under conditions in which there are absolutely no temporal cues, humans and other animals continue to maintain all of their circadian rhythms. These circadian rhythms in constant environments are said to be **free-running,** and their duration is called the **free-running period.** Free-running periods have three important features: they vary in length from subject to subject within a given species, they are of relatively constant duration within a given subject, and they are usually longer than 24 hours—about 25 hours in most humans. It seems that we all have an internal *biological clock* that habitually runs a little slow unless it is *entrained* by time-related cues in the environment. Environmental cues that can entrain circadian rhythms (e.g., sunrise and sunset) are called **zeitgebers** (pronounced "ZITE gay bers"), a German word meaning *time givers*. Perhaps the most remarkable characteristic of free-running circadian cycles is that they do not have to be learned. Even rats that are born and raised in an unchanging laboratory environment (i.e., in continual light or in continual darkness) display regular free-running sleep-wake cycles of about 25 hours (Richter, 1971).

A typical free-running circadian sleep-wake cycle of a man living under constant conditions is illustrated in Figure 13.4 (Wever, 1979). Notice the regularity of his cycle; without any external cue, he fell asleep approximately every 25.3 hours for an entire month. The fact that such regularity is maintained despite day-to-day variations in physical and mental activity provides strong support for the dominance of circadian factors over recuperative factors in the regulation of sleep. Figure 13.5 provides an extreme illustration of this point; a full 24 hours of sleep deprivation on day 24 had little effect on the subsequent free-running circadian sleep-wake cycle.

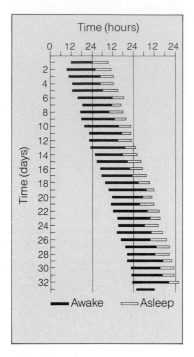

FIGURE 13.4 *A typical free-running 25.3-hour circadian sleep-wake cycle. Each day the subject went to sleep approximately 1.3 hours later than he did the day before; that is, his free-running period was 25.3 hours. (Adapted from Wever, 1979, p. 30.)*

The relation between the length of a period of sleep and the length of the preceding period of wakefulness has been assessed in several studies, and the usual finding is that the correlation is negative, even when the cycle is free running. What this means is that on those occasions when a subject stays awake longer than usual, the following sleep tends to be shorter (Wever, 1979). We appear to be programmed to go through a sleep-wake cycle of a specific length; hence, the longer one is awake during a particular cycle, the less time there is for sleep. This is exactly the opposite of what the recuperative theory of sleep predicts: It predicts that longer periods of wakefulness should produce greater deviations from homeostasis and thus should be followed by longer periods of sleep.

Under natural living conditions in which there are a variety of external cues as to the time of day, the circadian cycles displayed by various bodily functions are all exactly 24 hours. Most subjects tend to sleep during the falling phase of the circadian body-temperature cycle and to awaken during the rising phase, suggesting that the sleep-wake and body-temperature cycles may be causally related. However, when subjects are housed in constant environments, the sleep-wake cycle and the body-temperature cycle often break away from one another. This phenomenon is called **internal desynchronization**. For example, in one case the free-running sleep-wake and body-temperature periods of a human subject were both 25.7 hours for 14 days; then when there was, for some unknown reason, an increase in the free-running period of the sleep-wake cycle to 33.4 hours, while the free-running period of body temperature changed to 25.1 hours. The phenomenon of internal desynchronization has prompted the hypothesis that there is more than one circadian timing mechanism.

Jet Lag and Shift Work

Modern industrialized societies are faced with two different types of problems associated with the disruption of circadian rhythmicity. One is **jet lag**, a case in which the zeitgebers that control the phases of various circadian rhythms are accelerated during eastern flights or decelerated during western flights. The other is *shift work,* a case in which the zeitgebers stay the same, but workers are forced to adjust their natural sleep-wake cycles in order to meet the demands of changing work schedules. Both of these circadian changes produce disturbances in the duration and patterning of sleep, reports of fatigue and general malaise, and deficits on a variety of objective tests of physical and cognitive function. These disturbances can last for many days; for example, it typically takes about 10 days to completely adjust to a Tokyo-to-Boston flight—a phase advance of 10.5

FIGURE 13.5 *The effect of 24 hours of sleep deprivation on the free-running activity-rest circadian rhythm of a rat. Black bars indicate periods of activity; thus, long blank spaces are generally indicative of sleep. On day 24, the rat was totally deprived of sleep, yet the timing of its 25.3-hour free-running circadian rest-activity cycle was unaffected. (Adapted from Borbély, 1982.)*

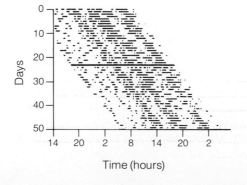

Time (hours)

hours. It is usually more difficult to adapt to *phase advances* (accelerations of circadian rhythms) than to *phase delays* (decelerations of circadian rhythms); that is, it is usually more difficult to adjust to eastern flights and to changes in shift work that call for earlier rising.

Adapting to the cycle-disrupting effects of a jet flight or a new work schedule can be an uncomfortable process. Wouldn't it be nice if we could somehow reset our internal clocks to eliminate these disruptive effects just as we reset our watches before a trip? Two approaches hold such promise. Exposure to a pulse of intense light (Daan & Lewy, 1984) or to a *benzo-diazepine* (Turek & Losee-Olson, 1986) can advance or delay free-running sleep-wake cycles depending on the phase of the cycle during which they are administered. A benzo-diazaphine injection or an intense light, both of which promote sleep in rats, advance their cycle when administered shortly before a regular sleep period and delay when administered shortly after.

13.5 Effects of Sleep Deprivation

Recuperation and circadian theories of sleep make different predictions about the effects of sleep deprivation. Because the recuperation theory is based on the premise that sleep is a response to the accumulation of some debilitating effect of wakefulness, it predicts the following: (1) that long periods of wakefulness will produce physiological and behavioral disturbances, (2) that these disturbances will grow steadily worse as the deprivation continues, and (3) that after the period of deprivation has ended, much of the missed sleep will be regained. In contrast, the circadian theory predicts (1) that there will be no debilitating effects of sleep deprivation other than those that can be attributed to an increase in the tendency to fall asleep, (2) that the increase in the desire to sleep produced by deprivation will be greatest during the phases of the circadian cycle when the subjects normally sleep, and (3) that there will be little or no compensation for the loss of sleep once the period of deprivation has ended. Think about these six predictions for a moment. On which side do you think the scientific evidence falls? Because most people tend to think of sleep as a recuperative process, you may be surprised to learn that the bulk of the evidence from sleep-deprivation studies confirms the predictions of the circadian theory. For example, consider Kleitman's (1963) description of one of the earliest sleep-deprivation studies, which he conducted in 1922, and Dement's (1978) descripion of the widely publicized case of Randy Gardner.

> While there were differences in the many subjective experiences of the sleep-evading persons, there were several features common to most. . . . during the first night the subject did not feel very tired or sleepy. He could read or study or do laboratory work, without much attention from the watcher, but usually felt an attack of drowsiness between 3 A.M. and 6 A.M. . . . Next morning the subject felt well, except for a slight malaise which always appeared on sitting down and resting for any length of time. However, if he occupied himself with his ordinary daily tasks, he was likely to forget having spent a sleepless night. During the second night . . . reading or study was next to impossible because sitting quietly was conducive to even greater sleepiness. As during the first night, there came a 2–3-hour period in the early hours of the morning when the desire for sleep was almost overpowering. . . . Later in the morning the sleepiness diminished once more, and the subject could perform routine laboratory work, as usual. It was not safe for him to sit down, however, without danger of falling asleep, particularly if he attended lectures. . . .

The third night resembled the second, and the fourth day was like the third. . . . At the end of that time the individual was as sleepy as he was likely to be. Those who continued to stay awake experienced the wavelike increase and decrease in sleepiness with the greatest drowsiness at about the same time every night. (Kleitman, 1963, pp. 220–221)

As part of a 1965 science fair project, Randy Gardner and two classmates, who were entrusted with keeping him awake, planned to break the then world-record of 260 hours of consecutive wakefulness. After about 80 hours of deprivation, Dement read about the project in the newspaper, and seeing an opportunity to collect some important data, joined the team, much to the comfort of Randy's worried parents. Randy proved to be a friendly and cooperative subject, although he did complain vigorously when his team would not permit him to close his eyes for more than a few seconds at a time. However, in no sense could Randy's behavior be considered abnormal or disturbed. Near the end of his vigil, Randy held a press conference attended by reporters and television crews from all over the United States, and he conducted himself impeccably. When asked how he had managed to stay awake for 11 days, he replied politely, "It's just mind over matter." Randy went to sleep exactly 264 hours and 12 minutes after his alarm clock had awakened him 11 days before. And how long did he sleep? Only 14 hours the first night, and thereafter he returned to his usual 8-hour schedule. Although it may seem amazing that Randy did not have to sleep longer to "catch up" on his lost sleep once his goal was achieved, the lack of substantial recovery sleep is typical of such cases. Mrs. Maureen Weston has supplanted Randy Gardner in the Guinness Book of World Records. During a rocking-chair marathon in 1977, Mrs. Weston kept rocking for 449 hours (18 days, 17 hours)—an impressive bit of "rocking around the clock." By the way, my own modest program of sleep-reduction is now in its tenth day.

Many studies have been conducted for the purpose of documenting the debilitating physiological effects of long-term wakefulness predicted by the recuperation theory of sleep. In view of the variety of physiological, motor, and cognitive tests that have been employed in these studies, their results have been remarkably consistent. Karadžić (1973), after reviewing the studies of the physiological effects of sleep deprivation (including studies of heart rate, respiration rate, blood pressure, skin conductance, body temperature, body weight, EMG, EEG, and evoked responses), reached the following conclusion: "There is little evidence that sleep deprivation, for periods even exceeding 200 hours, produces any marked physiological alterations" (p. 173), a conclusion echoed by Horne (1982) and Martin (1986).

One might expect that the complex cognitive abilities of human subjects might be particularly sensitive to disruption by sleep deprivation; however, this has not been found to be the case. For example, subjects deprived of sleep for one night displayed no deficits whatsoever on a battery of abstract reasoning, spatial relations, logical reasoning, and comprehension tests written under demanding time constraints (Percival, Horne, & Tilley, 1983). Paradoxically, it is the boringly easy tests of mental ability—particularly those requiring long periods of continuous attentiveness—that are most likely to be disrupted by sleep deprivation (Meddis, 1977; Webb, 1968; Wilkinson, 1965). This has led to the hypothesis that many of the behavioral deficits associated with sleep deprivation result from the subject's inability to stay awake. After 2 or 3 days of sleep deprivation, it

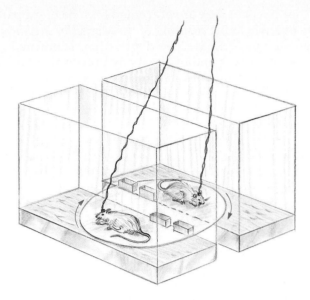

FIGURE 13.6 *The carousel apparatus is used to deprive one rat of sleep while its yoked control is exposed to the same number and pattern of disk rotations. The disk on which both rats rest rotates every time the experimental rat has a sleep EEG. (Adapted from Rechtschaffen, Gilliland, Bergmann, & Winter, 1983.)*

becomes very difficult to keep subjects from having microsleeps during the performance of sedentary boring tasks. **Microsleeps** are brief periods (usually 2 or 3 seconds long) of sleep EEG during which the eyelids droop and the subjects become less responsive to external stimuli, even though they remain sitting or even standing.

Studies using a **carousel apparatus** (see Figure 13.6) to deprive rats of sleep suggest that sleep deprivation may not be as inconsequential as the research on human subjects suggests. Two rats, an experimental rat and its yoked control, are placed in separate chambers of the apparatus. Each time that the EEG activity of the experimental rat indicates that it is sleeping, the disk, which serves as the floor of both chambers, starts to slowly rotate and the sleeping experimental rat gets shoved off the disk into a shallow pool of water on the other half of each chamber. The yoked control is exposed to exactly the same pattern of disk rotations, but if it is not sleeping, it can easily avoid getting dunked by walking in the direction opposite to the direction of disk rotation. In one study using the carousel apparatus (Rechtschaffen, Gilliland, Bergmann, & Winter, 1983), the experimental rats died after several days, while the yoked control animals stayed reasonably healthy. Although this finding seems to prove that sleep deprivation can be lethal, the fact that human subjects have been sleep deprived for similar periods of time without dire consequences argues for caution in interpreting this finding. It may be that repeatedly being plunged into water while sleeping kills the experimental rats not because it keeps them from sleeping, but because it is extremely stressful and physically damaging. This latter interpretation is certainly consistent with the variety of pathological symptoms revealed in some of the experimental rats by postmortem examination: swollen adrenal glands, collapsed lungs, fluid in the lungs, gastric ulcers, internal bleeding, skin lesions, scrotal damage, swollen limbs, and enlarged bladders.

Selective Sleep Deprivation

Researchers have attempted to determine the specific functions of the different stages of sleep by conducting studies in which subjects can sleep as much as they like, but they are prevented from having a particular stage of sleep. The overwhelming majority of these *selective sleep-deprivation studies* have been studies of REM-sleep deprivation, stimulated by a general fascination with dreaming and by the many provocative theories concerning its function. These theories fall into three general categories (Webb, 1973): (1) those that hypothesize that REM sleep is necessary for the maintenance of an individual's mental health, (2) those that hypothesize that REM sleep is necessary for the maintenance of normal levels of motivation, and (3) those that hypothesize that REM sleep is necessary for the processing of memories. Accordingly, the explicit purpose of most REM-deprivation studies has been to document the particular personality, motivational, or memorial disturbances predicted by the experimenter's favored theory.

REM-sleep deprivation has two consistent effects (see Figure 13.7). The first is that with each successive night of REM deprivation, there is a greater tendency for subjects to initiate REM sequences. Thus, as REM deprivation proceeds, subjects have to be awakened more and more frequently to keep them from accumulating significant amounts of REM-sleep time. For example, during the first night of REM deprivation in one experiment (Webb & Agnew, 1967), the subjects had to be awakened 17 times to

FIGURE 13.7 *The two consistent effects of REM-sleep deprivation.*

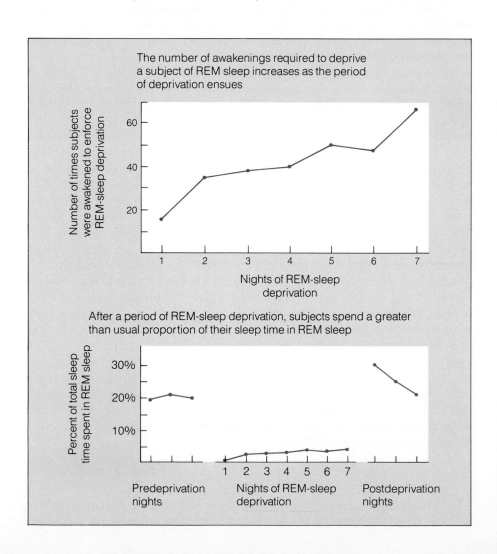

keep them from having extended periods of REM sleep, but during the seventh night of deprivation, they had to be awakened 67 times. The second consistent result of REM deprivation is that subjects have more than their usual amount of REM sleep for the first two or three nights after REM deprivation has been curtailed. In contrast to these two consistent observations, early claims (Dement, 1960) that REM-sleep deprivation leads to personality, motivational, and memorial disturbances have not received strong support. The most convincing evidence that REM-sleep deprivation is not severely debilitating comes from the study of patients taking *tricyclic antidepressant drugs*. Because tricyclic antidepressants selectively block REM sleep, patients regularly taking large doses get little or no REM sleep for months at a time, and yet they experience no serious side effects.

Interim Report It is an appropriate point, here at the end of the section on sleep deprivation, for me to file a brief progress report. It has now been 2 weeks since I began my 5-hours-per-night sleep schedule. Generally, things are going well. My progress on this chapter has been faster than usual. I am not having any difficulty getting up on time or in getting my work done, but I am finding that it takes a major effort to stay awake in the evening. If I try to read the newspaper or watch a bit of television after 10:30, I experience many microsleep attacks. Luckily, there are those around me who delight in the opportunity to make sure that these transgressions last no more than a few seconds.

13.6 Recuperation and Circadian Models Combined

If you began the chapter thinking of sleep as a recuperative process, as most people do, you were probably surprised to learn that sleep is closely regulated by circadian factors and that sleep deprivation appears to have relatively few adverse effects. However, it is important not to overreact to this evidence. Although recuperative factors may be somewhat less important in controlling sleep than you first thought, and circadian factors somewhat more important, it is not necessarily an all-or-none issue; recuperation and circadian models are not mutually exclusive. In fact, Borbély (1984) has proposed a model of sleep that integrates the effects of both circadian and sleep-deprivation factors. This two-process model is illustrated in Figure 13.8. The postulated circadian sleep-promoting factor is illustrated in the top trace of the figure. This factor is assumed to take the form of a sine wave with minimum at about 4:00 P.M. and a maximum at about 4:00 A.M. The postulated sleep-promoting effects of wakefulness are illustrated in the middle trace for a subject who slept on the first night between 11:00 P.M. and 6:00 A.M. and then missed the next two nights' sleep. The bottom trace illustrates how the effects of the circadian and wakefulness factors hypothetically combine to influence the subject's sleepiness.

If sleep is influenced by the duration of the preceding period of wakefulness, why has sleep deprivation had so little effect on subsequent sleep times in most studies? The answer seems to be that it is slow-wave EEG in particular, rather than sleep in general, that plays the major recuperative role following sleep deprivation (Horne, 1983b). Several lines of

Sleepiness produced by the postulated circadian factor over 3 days

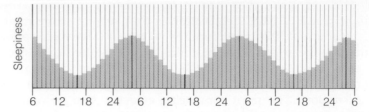

Sleepiness produced by the postulated wakefulness factor for a subject who sleeps one night and then misses two nights of sleep

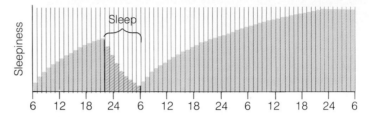

The sleepiness experienced by the above subject is the sum of the effects of both circadian and wakefulness factors

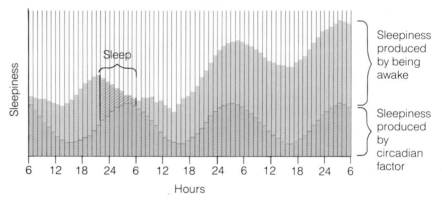

FIGURE 13.8 *A model of how circadian factors and the duration of wakefulness interact to determine the propensity to sleep. (Adapted from Borbély, 1984.)*

evidence support this view: (1) Although subjects regain only a small proportion of the total lost sleep after a period of sleep deprivation, they regain most of their lost stage 4 sleep (e.g., Borbély, Baumann, Brandeis, Strauch, & Lehmann, 1981; Horne, 1976). (2) Subjects asked to decrease their sleep time do so by reducing stage 1 and stage 2 sleep, but the amount of stage 3 and stage 4 sleep remains the same as before (Mullaney, Johnson, Naitoh, Friedman, & Globus, 1977; Webb & Agnew, 1975). (3) Short sleepers normally get as much stage 3 and stage 4 sleep as do long sleepers (e.g., Jones & Oswald, 1966; Webb & Agnew, 1970). (4) If subjects are asked to take an extra nap in the morning after a full night's sleep, it contains little stage 3 or stage 4 sleep, and it does not reduce the duration of the following night's sleep (e.g., Åkerstedt & Gilberg, 1981; Hume & Mills, 1977; Karacan, Williams, Finley, & Hursch, 1970). (5) After sleep deprivation, the EEG of both humans (Borbély, 1981) and rats (Mistlberger, Bergmann, & Rechtschaffen, 1987) is characterized by substantially higher proportions of slow waves.

Research on the physiological and neurochemical bases of sleep is discussed in the next section of the chapter. Because it is the most complex section of the chapter, before you proceed, complete the following exercise to consolidate what you have learned so far in this chapter.

1. The three most commonly studied psychophysiological correlates of sleep are EEG, EMG, and ___EOG___ .

2. ___initial___ stage 1 EEG is accompanied by neither REM nor loss of muscle tone.

3. Stage 4 sleep EEG is distinguished by a predominance of ___delta___ waves.

4. Environmental cues that can entrain circadian rhythms are called ___zeitgebor___ or time givers.

5. In contrast to the prediction of the recuperative model of sleep, when a subject stays awake longer than usual, the following period of sleep tends to be ___shorter___ even under free-running conditions.

6. The most convincing evidence that REM-sleep deprivation is not debilitating comes from the study of patients taking ___tricyclic antidepressants___ .

7. After a lengthy period of sleep deprivation, a subject's first night of sleep is only slightly longer than usual, but it contains a much higher proportion of ___delta___ waves.

8. ___Stage 3 & 4___ sleep in particular, rather than sleep in general, appears to play the major recuperative role.

13.7 The Physiological and Neurochemical Bases of Sleep

The first influential theory of the physiology of sleep was proposed by Bremer in 1936. He hypothesized that sleep is caused by a lack of sensory input to the brain. To test his hypothesis, he severed the brain stems of cats between their *inferior colliculi* and *superior colliculi* in order to disconnect their forebrains from ascending sensory input (see Figure 13.9)—this surgical preparation is called a **cerveau isolé preparation** (pronounced "ser-voe ees-o-lay"; literally *isolated forebrain*). As you might well imagine, cerveau

Evidence for Bremer's 1937 Passive
Sensory Theory of Sleep

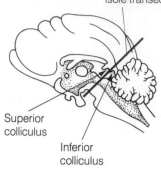

Level of cerveau
isolé transection

Cats with a midcollicular
transection (cerveau isolé
preparation) displayed a
continuous sleep (slow-wave)
EEG, Bremer concluded that
sleep occurs when there is
no sensory input to the
cortex from the caudal
brain stem.

Superior
colliculus

Inferior
colliculus

Evidence for Moruzzi and Magoun's Active
Reticular-Activating-System Theory of Sleep

Lesions at the midcollicular
level that damaged the reticular
formation core but left the
sensory fibers intact, produced a
continuous sleep (slow-wave)
cortical EEG.

Electrical stimulation of
reticular formation
desynchronized the cortical
EEG and awakened sleeping cats.

Cats with a transection of
the caudal brain stem (encéphale
isolé preparation) displayed
normal sleep-wake cycles of
cortical EEG. This suggested
that a wakefulness-producing
area was between the levels
of the cerveau and encéphale
isolé transections.

Reticular
formation

FIGURE 13.9 *Evidence for
the passive sensory theory of
sleep and for the active reticular-
activating-system theory.*

isolé preparations are not too useful for the study of behavior because the subjects are paralyzed below the level of the transection, but they can be used to assess neurophysiological responses of the forebrain in the absence of ascending influences. In line with his hypothesis, Bremer found that the cortical EEG of the isolated cat forebrains was indicative of almost continuous slow-wave sleep. Only when strong visual or olfactory stimuli were presented (the cerveau isolé has intact visual and olfactory input) could the continuous high-amplitude, slow-wave activity be **desynchronized** (i.e., changed to low-amplitude, high-frequency activity), but this arousing effect barely outlasted the stimuli. Bremer's theory is classed as a *passive theory of sleep* because it postulated no mechanism of active sleep regulation; it viewed sleep as a passive consequence of a decline in sensory input.

The Reticular-Activating-System Theory of Sleep

Bremer's passive sensory theory of sleep regulation was gradually replaced by the theory that sleep is actively regulated by an arousal mechanism in the *reticular formation*—by a **reticular activating system.** Three findings contributed to the wide acceptance of this reticular-activating-system theory of sleep (see Figure 13.9). The first finding came from the study of the **encéphale isolé preparation** (pronounced awn-say-fell ees-o-lay), an experimental preparation in which the brain is disconnected from the rest of the nervous system by a transection of the caudal brain stem. Despite cutting most of the same sensory fibers as the cerveau isolé transection, the encéphale isolé transection did not disrupt the normal cycle of sleep EEG and wakefulness EEG (Bremer, 1937). This suggested that a mechanism for maintaining wakefulness was located somewhere in the brain stem between the two transections. The second finding was that partial transections at the cerveau isolé level disrupted normal sleep-wake cycles of cortical EEG only when they severed the reticular-activating-system core of the brain stem; when they were restricted to more lateral areas, which contain the ascending sensory tracts, they had little effect on the cortical EEG (Lindsey, Bowden, & Magoun, 1949). The third finding was that electrical stimulation of the reticular formation of sleeping cats awakened them and produced a lengthy period of EEG desynchronization (Moruzzi & Magoun, 1949). On the basis of these three findings, Moruzzi and Magoun (1949) proposed that low levels of activity in the reticular formation produce sleep and that high levels produce wakefulness.

Three Important Discoveries about the Neural Basis of Sleep

The wave of research stimulated by the reticular-activating-system theory led to several important discoveries; the following three are particularly noteworthy (see Steriade & Hobson, 1976).

Sleep Is Not a State of Neural Quiescence   Because the body is relatively inactive during sleep, it had long been assumed that sleep is a state of general neural quiescence. Single unit recording studies revealed that this is not the case. Many neurons in the brain are less active during slow-wave sleep than they are during relaxed wakefulness, but the reduction in discharge rate rarely exceeds 10%—a far cry from the total inactivity assumed by the scions of the early sleep literature. Moreover, during REM sleep, many neurons become even more active than they are during relaxed wakefulness.

There Are Sleep-Promoting Circuits in the Brain   The reticular-activating-system concept implied that sleep occurred as a consequence of low levels of activity in circuits whose primary role was the maintenance of wakefulness. This view was changed by two observations: that the stimulation of certain brain sites can induce sleep and that discrete bilateral lesions can disrupt it. Both of these findings suggest that sleep is not simply a consequence of low levels of activity in a wakefulness-promoting structure; they suggest that there are structures in the brain whose function is the promotion of sleep. One such sleep-promoting structure appears to be in the caudal brain stem (medulla). Anesthetizing (Magni,

Moruzzi, Rossi, & Zanchetti, 1957) or cooling (Berlucchi, Maffei, Moruzzi, & Strata, 1964) the caudal brain stem caused sleeping cats to awaken immediately.

The Various Correlates of Sleep Are Dissociable Most neurophysiological theories of sleep have treated REM sleep and slow-wave sleep (SWS) as if each was a unitary entity. However, evidence has accumulated that the physiological changes that go together to define REM sleep sometimes break apart and go their separate ways—and the same is true of the changes that define SWS. For example, during REM-sleep deprivation, penile erections, which normally occur during REM sleep, begin to occur during SWS. And during total sleep deprivation, slow waves, which normally occur only during SWS, begin to occur during wakefulness. This suggests that REM sleep, SWS, and wakefulness are not each controlled by a single mechanism; each state seems to result from the interaction of a variety of mechanisms, which are capable under certain conditions of operating independently of one another.

The classic example of the dissociation between the behavioral and EEG indices of SWS is the study of Feldman and Waller (1962), who compared the effects of lesions to the cat midbrain reticular formation with those of lesions to the adjacent posterior hypothalamus. The hypothalamic lesions produced behavioral sleep that persisted even when the cats' desynchronized cortical EEG suggested that they were awake. In contrast, the midbrain reticular formation lesions produced a high-amplitude slow-wave cortical EEG that persisted even when the cats were fully alert (see Vanderwolf & Robinson, 1981).

The Structures of the Brain
Implicated in Sleep and Dreaming

In keeping with the notion that sleep is regulated by a number of different interacting systems, many areas of the brain have been identified that seem to play some role in it. The following are four such areas: the raphé nuclei, the basal forebrain region, the REM sleep circuits in the caudal brain stem, and the suprachiasmatic nuclei.

Raphé Nuclei Interest generated by the early evidence of a sleep-promoting area in the medulla focused attention on the **raphé** (pronounced "ra-fay") **nuclei,** a cluster of serotonin-producing nuclei running in a thin strip down the midline of the caudal reticular formation (see Figure 13.10). Lesions destroying 80 to 90% of the raphé nuclei in cats produced complete insomnia for 3 or 4 days, which was followed by a partial recovery that never exceeded more than 2.5 hours of sleep per day, all of which was SWS (Jouvet & Renault, 1966). Cats normally sleep about 14.5 hours per day, which is one reason why they are favored as subjects in sleep experiments.

Supporting the theory that the raphé nuclei promote sleep is the observation that a single injection of **parachlorophenylalanine** (PCPA), which temporarily blocks the synthesis of serotonin, produces temporary insomnia in cats (Mouret, Bobillier, & Jouvet, 1968). However, when PCPA is injected every day, both REM sleep and SWS eventually recover to about 80% of their total levels, despite the fact that serotonin levels remain very low (Dement, Mitler, & Henriksen, 1972). Thus, although the raphé nuclei and the serotonin that they release appear to play a role in sleep, neither appear to be necessary for it.

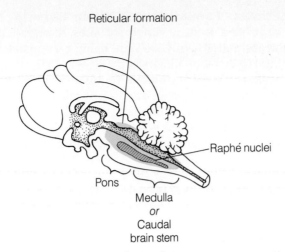

Reticular formation

Raphé nuclei

Pons

Medulla
or
Caudal
brain stem

FIGURE 13.10 *The location of the raphé nuclei.*

Basal Forebrain Region Although much of the research on the physiology of sleep has focused on the reticular formation in general and the raphé nuclei in particular, there is also good evidence that an area of the forebrain just in front of the hypothalamus is also involved. This ill-defined area, which includes the preoptic area, is generally referred to as the **basal forebrain region.** As can be seen in Figure 13.11, bilateral lesions of this area in cats produce a substantial reduction of daily sleep time that is maximal 2 weeks after the lesion and recovers somewhat thereafter (McGinty & Sterman, 1968). Electrical stimulation of the basal forebrain produces cortical EEG synchrony (Sterman & Clemente, 1962a), drowsiness, and sometimes sleep (Sterman & Clemente, 1962b).

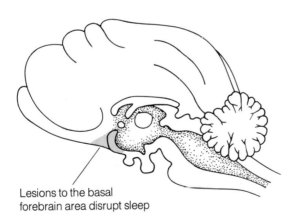

Lesions to the basal
forebrain area disrupt sleep

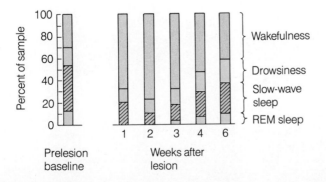

FIGURE 13.11 *The effects of basal forebrain lesions on the sleep of cats. (Adapted from McGinty & Sterman, 1968.)*

Caudal Reticular Formation REM-Sleep Circuits REM sleep appears to be controlled from a variety of sites scattered throughout the caudal reticular formation, with each site being responsible for controlling one of the major indices of REM sleep (Siegel, 1983; Vertes, 1983). The approximate location of these putative regulatory centers is illustrated by Figure 13.12, which is based on an analysis of relevant stimulation, lesion, and recording studies. The main challenge now facing those that study the physiological basis of REM sleep is to determine how and why the activity of these respective structures becomes coordinated in intact animals during normal REM cycles.

The Suprachiasmatic Nuclei and Circadian Sleep-Wake Cycles
The fact that circadian sleep-wake cycles persist in the absence of circadian signals from the environment suggests that the physiological systems regulating sleep must be controlled by some internal timing mechanism. The first major breakthrough in the search for the location of this internal **biological clock** was Richter's (1967) discovery that large medial hypothalamic lesions disrupt circadian cycles of eating, drinking, and activity in rats without disrupting the responses themselves. Next, the **suprachiasmatic nuclei** (SCN) were identified as the specific medial hypothalamic structures involved in the control of circadian cycles of adrenal hormone release (Moore & Eichler, 1972), drinking, and activity (Stephan & Zucker, 1972) in rats. This discovery of an SCN circadian timing mechanism created great interest in the SCN, and SCN lesions were subsequently shown to disrupt all kinds of rodent biological rhythms, including the sleep-wake cycle (see Ibuka, Inouye, & Kawamura, 1977; Rusak, 1979; Rusak &

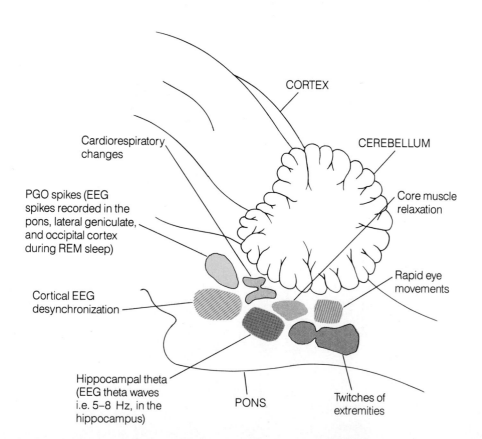

FIGURE 13.12 *A schematic sagittal section taken about 3 millimeters from the midline of the brain stem of the cat. Illustrated are the areas that seem to control various indices of REM sleep. (Adapted from Vertes, 1983)*

Zucker, 1979). The amount of time spent sleeping is not reduced by bilateral SCN lesions (e.g., Coindet, Chouvet, & Mouret, 1975; Stephan & Nunez, 1977), but its circadian periodicity is. Under certain conditions, SCN lesions can abolish some circadian rhythms but not others (e.g., Boulos & Terman, 1980); this suggests that there may be more than one circadian timing mechanism in the brain.

Further support for the conclusion that the SCN contain a circadian timing mechanism comes from the observation that the SCN display circadian cycles of electrical, metabolic, and biochemical activity (e.g., Moore, 1982), and that they do so even when they have been surgically isolated from the rest of the brain by circular knife cuts (Groos & Hendricks, 1982; Inouye & Kawamura, 1982). Figure 13.13 shows that the SCN of rats take up less radioactive 2-deoxyglucose during the night than they do during the day, when the rats normally sleep (Schwartz & Gainer, 1977). Furthermore, electrical stimulation of the SCN has been shown to produce phase shifts in free-running rhythms (Rusak & Groos, 1982; Zatz & Herkenham, 1981).

How does the 24-hour light-dark cycle entrain the sleep-wake cycle and other circadian rhythms? To answer this question, researchers began at the obvious starting points—the eyes. They tried to identify and track the specific neurons that left the eyes and carried information about light and dark to the biological clock. The fact that cutting the *optic nerves* as they left the eyes of rats eliminated the ability of the light-dark cycle to influence circadian rhythms suggested that they were on the right track. However, when the *optic tracts* were cut at the point where they left the *optic chiasm,* the ability of the light-dark cycle to entrain circadian rhythms was not lost. As illustrated in Figure 13.14, these two findings together suggested that the critical axons were branching off from the optic nerve in the vicinity of the optic chiasm and projecting to circuits responsible for entraining circadian rhythms. This inference prompted a more careful examination of the projections of the optic nerve, and the result was the discovery of two small bundles of visual neurons that left the optic chiasm and projected to the adjacent hypothalamus (Hendrickson, Wagoner, & Cowan, 1972; Moore & Lenn, 1972). And where do you think that the two **retinohypothalamic tracts** terminate? If you guessed the SCN, you are correct. Although we now know how signals from visual zeitgebers reach the SCN, it is still not clear how the SCN control the sleep-producing mechanisms of the reticular formation and basal forebrain (Groos, 1984).

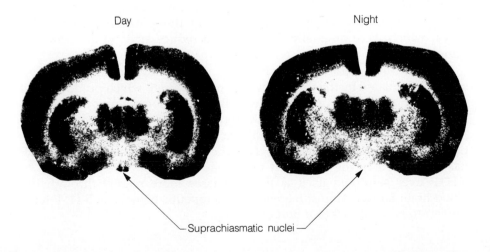

Day   Night

Suprachiasmatic nuclei

FIGURE 13.13 *Autoradiographs illustrating the increased uptake of radioactive 2-deoxyglucose by the rat SCN during the day (from Schwartz & Gainer, 1977)*

(Dr. William Schwartz, published in SCIENCE, Vol. 197, pages 1089–91, September 9, 1977. Copyright 1977 by the AAAS.)

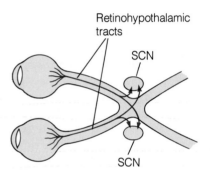

Transection of the optic nerves eliminated the ability of light-dark cycles to entrain circadian rhythms

Transection of the optic tracts did not eliminate the ability of light-dark cycles to entrain circadian rhythms

Optic chiasm

To thalamus and visual cortex

Optic nerve

Optic tract

To thalamus and visual cortex

This suggested that the visual neurons critical for entraining circadian rhythms branched off from the major visual pathways in the area of the optic chiasm and projected to the circuits responsible for controlling circadian rhythms. The retinohypothalamic tracts were subsequently found to terminate in the suprachiasmatic nuclei.

Retinohypothalamic tracts

SCN

SCN

FIGURE 13.14 *The discovery of the retinohypothalamic tracts. Neurons from each retina project to both the ipsilateral and contralateral suprachiasmatic nuclei (SCN).*

13.8 Hypnotic and Antihypnotic Drugs

Hypnotics

For many years, **barbiturates** were commonly prescribed as **hypnotic drugs** (sleep-promoting drugs); however, because of their dangerous side effects, they are no longer recommended for this purpose. **Benzodiazepines,** which were originally developed to reduce anxiety, are now the clinical hypnotics of choice.

Interest in the possibility of using serotonergic drugs as clinical hypnotics was stimulated by the theory that the raphé nuclei, which produce most of the brain's serotonin, promote sleep. Because insomnia produced in cats (Pujol, Buguet, Froment, Jones, & Jouvet, 1971) and rats (Laguzzi & Adrien, 1980) by the serotonin antagonist, PCPA, is reversed by an injection of **5-hydroxytryptophan** (5-HTP), the precursor of serotonin, 5-HTP has been tried in the treatment of human insomnia. The advantage of 5-HTP over serotonin itself is that it passes more readily through the blood-brain barrier. Unfortunately, the therapeutic benefits of 5-HTP have proven to be marginal (see Borbély, 1983).

Many **antihypnotic drugs** (sleep-reducing drugs) increase the activity of the *catecholamine neurotransmitters* (Hartmann, 1978). Drugs such as amphetamine, cocaine, and the widely prescribed tricyclic antidepressants, increase the activity of catecholamines (norepinephrine, epinephrine, and dopamine) by increasing their release and/or blocking their re-uptake from the synapse. Stimulants can totally suppress REM sleep, even at doses that have little effect on total sleep time.

Endogenous Sleep Factors In the last decade, there has been a revival of the old idea that sleep-inducing chemicals are created in the body (e.g., Drucker-Colin, Aguilar-Roblero, & Arankowsky-Sandoval, 1985; Krueger, 1985; Ursin, 1984). These putative sleep-inducing chemicals are usually referred to as the **endogenous sleep factors. Factor S** and **delta sleep-inducing peptide** (DSIP) illustrate the two approaches that have been used to collect endogenous sleep factors: factor S was initially collected from sleep-deprived animals, whereas DSIP was initially gathered from sleeping animals.

The first step in identifying factor S was the demonstration that the cerebrospinal fluid (CSF) extracted from sleep-deprived goats would increase SWS in rats when slowly infused into their cerebral ventricles (Pappenheimer, Koski, Fencl, Karnovsky, & Krueger, 1975). This initial observation began the long process of separating the cerebrospinal fluid from sleep-deprived animals into various fractions and testing them to see which were active. Eventually, Krueger, Pappenheimer, and Karnovsky (1982) managed to isolate factor S, to identify its chemical structure, and to create active synthetic analogues. The finding that microinjection of factor S into the basal forebrain or the hypothalamus has hypnotic effects (Garcia-Arraras & Pappenheimer, 1983) suggests that these are its sites of action.

The effects of delta sleep-inducing peptide (DSIP) were first demonstrated using a **parabiotic preparation,** a preparation in which two subjects share one physiological system. Monnier, et al. (1975) connected the circulatory systems of two rabbits and found that when the *intralaminar thalamic nuclei* (see Appendix III) of one was stimulated at a frequency that elicited cortical slow waves, both rabbits tended to fall asleep. This suggested that an endogenous sleep factor was being released into the blood of the stimulated rabbit and was affecting both it and its partner. DSIP was subsequently isolated from the blood of stimulated rabbits, its structure characterized, and methods for synthesizing it developed. Intraventricular or intravenous injections of DSIP promote sleep in a variety of species (e.g., Scherschlicht, 1983; Schneider-Helmert, 1985; Schoenenberger & Graf, 1985).

13.9 Sleep Disorders

Sleep disorders are often **iatrogenic** (physician created). The classic example of an iatrogenic sleep disorder is the insomnia caused by hypnotic drugs—the very drugs prescribed for its treatment. At first, the hypnotic drugs are effective in increasing sleep, but soon the patient is trapped into a rising spiral of drug use, as *tolerance* to the drug develops (see Chapter 16) and more and more drug is required to produce its original hypnotic effect.

Soon the patient cannot stop taking the drug without running the risk of experiencing *withdrawal symptoms* (see Chapter 16), which unfortunately feature insomnia as the primary symptom. The following case study vividly illustrates this problem.

> Mr. B. was studying for a civil service exam, the outcome of which would affect his entire future. He was terribly worried about the test and found it difficult to get to sleep at night. Feeling that the sleep loss was affecting his ability to study, he consulted his physician for the express purpose of getting "something to make me sleep." His doctor prescribed a moderate dose of barbiturate at bedtime, and Mr. B. found that this medication was very effective . . . for the first several nights. After about a week, he began having trouble sleeping again and decided to take two sleeping pills each night. Twice more the cycle was repeated, until on the night before the exam he was taking four times as many pills as his doctor had prescribed. The next night, with the pressure off, Mr. B. took no medication. He had tremendous difficulty falling asleep, and when he did, his sleep was terribly disrupted. . . . Mr. B. now decided that he had a serious case of insomnia, and returned to his sleeping pill habit. By the time he consulted our clinic several years later, he was taking approximately 1,000 mg sodium amytal every night, and his sleep was more disturbed than ever. . . . Patients may go on for years and years—from one sleeping pill to another—never realizing that their troubles are caused by the pills. (Dement, 1978, p. 80)

Sleep apnea is another common cause of insomnia. **Sleep apnea** is a condition in which interruptions in breathing punctuate each night's sleep. Spasms of the throat muscles block air intake as many as 500 times per night (see Coleman, 1986). Each time, the patient awakens, begins to breathe again, and drifts back to sleep. Sleep apnea usually leads to a sense of having slept very poorly, and thus it is usually diagnosed as **insomnia** (a disorder of initiating and maintaining sleep). However, some patients with sleep apnea are diagnosed as having **hypersomnia** (a disorder of excessive sleep or sleepiness) because they are totally unaware of their multiple awakenings and complain of excessive sleepiness during the day. It has been suggested that sleep apnea may be a causal factor in cases of **sudden infant death syndrome** (SIDS).

Two other causes of insomnia are usually lumped together because they both involve the legs: nocturnal myoclonus and restless legs. **Nocturnal myoclonus** is a periodic twitching of the body during sleep, primarily of the legs. Most patients suffering from this disorder are unaware of the nature of their problem, and they generally complain of poor sleep and day-time sleepiness. In contrast, people with **restless legs** are all too aware of their problem. They complain of a hard-to-describe tension or uneasiness in their legs that keeps them from falling asleep. Benzodiazepines are often prescribed in cases of nocturnal myoclonus and restless legs because of their *anxiolytic* (antianxiety), muscle relaxant, and anticonvulsant properties; however, they are rarely effective.

Many insomniacs get much more sleep than they think. In one large study, insomniacs claimed to take an average of 1 hour to fall asleep and to sleep an average of only 4.5 hours per night, but when they were tested in a sleep laboratory, they were found to have an average sleep latency of only 15 minutes and an average nightly sleep duration of 6.5 hours. It used to be common medical practice to assume that people who claimed to suffer from insomnia but slept more than 6.5 hours per night were neurotic. However, this practice stopped when some of those diagnosed as neurotic *pseudoinsomniacs* were subsequently found to be suffering from sleep apnea, nocturnal myoclonus, or other sleep-disturbing problems. In insomnia, the problem is not necessarily the lack of sleep; it is the lack of undisturbed sleep.

Narcolepsy is a disorder of hypersomnia characterized by repeated, brief (10-to-15-minute) daytime sleep attacks. Although narcoleptics typically sleep an hour or two per day more than average, it is the inappropriateness of their sleep episodes that is most telling. Most of us occasionally fall asleep on the beach, in front of the television, or in the most *soporific* (sleep-promoting) of all daytime sleep sites, the large, dimly lit lecture theatre. But narcoleptics fall asleep in the middle of a conversation, while eating, while engaging in sexual activities, or even while scuba diving. Cataplexy is a common symptom of narcolepsy. **Cataplexy** is a sudden loss of muscle tone that is sometimes triggered by an emotional event. In its mild form, it may simply require that the patient sit down for a few seconds; in its extreme form the patient drops to the ground as if shot and remains there for a minute or two, all the while remaining fully conscious. The fact that narcoleptics, unlike normal subjects, go directly into REM sleep when they go to sleep (Rechtschaffen, Wolpert, Dement, Mitchell, & Fisher, 1963) has led to the view that narcolepsy is a disorder in which REM-sleep phenomena encroach on wakefulness. According to this view, an attack of cataplexy occurs when the lack of core muscle tonus that normally occurs during REM sleep occurs during wakefulness. The hypersomnia of narcolepsy is usually treated with stimulants administered in the morning, whereas the cataplexy is treated with tricyclic antidepressants administered in the evening.

13.10 Conclusion: The Effects of Sleep Reduction

I began this chapter 4 weeks ago with both zeal and trepidation. I was fascinated by the idea that I could wring 2 or 3 extra hours of living out of each day by sleeping less, and I hoped that adhering to a sleep-reduction program while writing about sleep would create a feeling for the subject that I could pass on to you. On the other hand, I was more than a little concerned about the negative effect that losing 3 hours of sleep per night might have on me.

The research on the subject of sleep reduction—albeit limited—suggested that my objective was not unreasonable. There have been only two systematic studies of long-term sleep reduction. In one (Webb & Agnew, 1974), a group of 16 subjects slept for only 5.5 hours per night for 60 days, with the only detectable deficit on an extensive battery of mood, medical, and performance tests being a slight deficit on a test of auditory vigilance. In the other (Friedman, Globus, Huntley, Mullaney, Naitoh, & Johnson, 1977; Mullaney, Johnson, Naitoh, Friedman, & Globus, 1977), 8 subjects reduced their nightly sleep by 30 minutes every 2 weeks until they reached 6.5 hours per night, then by 30 minutes every 3 weeks until they reached 5 hours, and then by 30 minutes every 4 weeks thereafter. After a subject indicated that he or she did not want to reduce his or her sleep further, he or she slept for 1 month at the shortest duration of nightly sleep that was achieved, then for 2 months at the shortest duration plus 30 minutes. Finally, each subject slept each night for 1 year for however long he or she preferred. The minimum duration of nightly sleep achieved during the experiment was 5.5 hours for two subjects, 5.0 hours for four subjects, and an impressive 4.5 hours for two subjects. In each of the subjects, a reduction in sleep time was associated with an increase in sleep efficiency: with a decrease in the amount of time that it took the subjects to fall asleep after going to bed, a decrease in the number of night-time awakenings, and an increase in the proportion of stage 4 sleep. After the subjects had reduced their sleep to 6 hours per night, they began to experience daytime sleepiness, and this became a problem as sleep time was further reduced. Nevertheless, there were no deficits on any of the mood, medical, and performance tests given to the subjects throughout the experiment. The most encouraging result was the observation that during the 1-year follow-up, all subjects slept less than they had previously—between 7 and 18 hours less each week—with no excessive sleepiness.

Rather than using the gradual step-wise reduction method of Friedman and his colleagues, I jumped into my 5-hours-per-night sleep schedule with both feet. However, this proved to be less difficult than you might think. I took advantage of a trip to the East Coast from my home on the West Coast to reset my circadian clock. When I was in the East, I got up at 7:00 A.M. each morning, which is 4:00 A.M. here on the West Coast, and I just kept on the same schedule when I got home. I decided to add my extra waking hours to the beginning of my day rather than to the end so that there would be no temptation to waste them; there are not too many distractions around this university at 5:00 A.M.

Figure 13.15 is a record of my sleep times for the 4-week period that it took me to write a first draft of this chapter. I didn't quite meet my goal of

FIGURE 13.15 *Sleep record of J.P.J.P. during a 4-week sleep-reduction program.*

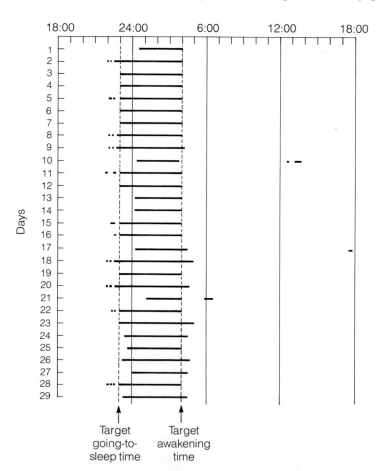

sleeping less than 5 hours every night, but I didn't miss by much—the overall mean was 5.05 hours per night. Notice that in the last week, there was a tendency for my circadian clock to run a bit slow; I began sleeping in until 4:30 A.M. and staying up until 11:30 P.M. What were the positives and negatives of the experience? The main positive was the time to do things that was created—having an extra 21 hours a week was wonderful. Furthermore, because my daily routine was out of synchrony with everybody else's, I spent little time sitting in rush-hour traffic or waiting in line. The only negative of the experience was sleepiness. It was no problem during the day, when I was active. However, staying awake during that last hour before I went to bed—an hour during which I usually engaged in sedentary activities, such as reading the newspaper and watching the news on television—was at times a real problem. This is when I became personally familiar with the phenomenon of microsleep, and it was then that I required some assistance in order to stay awake. Going to bed and falling asleep each night became a fleeting but wonderful experience.

I began this chapter with a question, "How much sleep do we need?" And I gave you my best professorial, it-could-be-this-it-could-be-that answer. However, that was a month ago. Now, after experiencing sleep reduction first hand, I am less inclined toward wishy-washiness, at least on the topic of sleep. Two lines of evidence suggest that the answer is about 5½ hours for most people. First, most committed subjects can reduce their sleep to about 5½ hours per night without great difficulty or adverse consequences. Second, the quality of a night's sleep declines precipitously after the first 5½ hours; there is little slow-wave sleep after this point (see Figure 13.3). Why then do most of us sleep 8 to 10 hours each night? The reason may be that, as an incentive, sleep ranks up there with the big three consummatory behaviors of Chapters 10, 11, and 12. When food, drink, and sex are freely available, most of us partake of more than is required for survival. It seems that the same is true of sleep.

Food for Thought

1. Do you think that your life could be improved by changing when or how long you sleep each day? In what ways? What negative effects do you think such changes might have on you?

2. Some people like to stay up late, some people like to get up early, others like to do both, and still others like to do neither. Design a sleep-reduction program that is tailored to your own biology and life style and that is consistent with the research literature on sleep deprivation. Design a program that would produce the greatest benefits for you with the least discomfort.

3. How has reading about sleep research changed your views about sleep? Give three specific examples.

ADDITIONAL READING

There are several interesting introductions to the topic of sleep; the following three are my favorites:

Dement, W. C. (1978). *Some must watch while some must sleep.* New York: W. W. Norton.

Hartman, E. L. (1973). *The functions of sleep.* Westford, MA: Murray Printing Company.

Meddis, R. (1977). *The sleep instinct.* London: Henley and Boston.

To help you study the material in this chapter, all of the key terms—those that have appeared in bold type—are listed and briefly defined here.

Alpha waves. 8-to-12 Hz rhythmic EEG waves; they commonly punctuate the EEG of human subjects just before they fall asleep.

Antihypnotic drugs. Sleep-reducing drugs.

Barbiturates. A class of hypnotic drugs that are rarely used to treat insomnia because of their dangerous side effects.

Basal forebrain region. The area of the forebrain just in front of the hypothalamus.

Benzodiazepines. A class of anxiolytic drugs.

Biological clock. An internal timing mechanism capable of timing physiological events independently of temporal cues in the environment.

Carousel apparatus. An apparatus used to study the effects of sleep deprivation in laboratory rats.

Cataplexy. A disorder characterized by sudden losses of muscle tone; it is often seen in cases of narcolepsy.

Cerveau isolé preparation. An experimental preparation in which the forebrain is disconnected from the rest of the brain by a midcollicular transection.

Circadian rhythms. Diurnal (daily) cycles of bodily function.

Deep sleep. Used by some researchers to refer to stage 4 sleep and by others to refer to REM sleep.

Delta sleep. That portion of sleep punctuated by delta waves; i.e., stages 3 and 4.

Delta sleep-inducing peptide (DSIP). A putative endogenous sleep factor.

Delta waves. The largest, slowest EEG waves.

Desynchronized EEG. Low-amplitude, high-frequency EEG.

Diurnal. Daily.

Electroencephalogram (EEG). A gross measure of the electrical activity of the brain; commonly recorded from the scalp of human subjects.

Electromyogram (EMG). A measure of the electrical activity of muscles.

Electro-oculogram (EOG). A measure of eye movement.

Emergent stage 1 EEG. The first period of stage 1 EEG (low-voltage, fast activity) during a night's sleep is called initial stage 1; the subsequent periods of stage 1 EEG are called emergent stage 1.

Encéphale isolé preparation. An experimental preparation in which the brain is separated from the rest of the nervous system by a transection of the caudal brain stem.

Endogenous sleep factors. Sleep-inducing chemicals produced in the body.

Factor S. A putative endogenous sleep factor.

First-night phenomenon. The sleep disturbances experienced during the first few nights that a subject sleeps in a laboratory.

Free-running period. The duration of one cycle of a free-running rhythm.

Free-running rhythms. Circadian rhythms that do not depend on environmental cues to keep them running on a regular schedule.

5-Hydroxytryptophan (5-HTP). The precursor of serotonin.

Hypersomnia. A disorder characterized by excessive sleep or sleepiness.

Hypnotic drugs. Sleep-promoting drugs.

Iatrogenic disorder. A physician-created disorder.

Initial stage 1 EEG. The period of stage 1 EEG that occurs at the onset of sleep; unlike other periods of stage 1 EEG, it is not associated with dreaming.

Insomnia. A disorder of initiating and maintaining sleep.

Internal desynchronization. When the free-running circadian cycles of two different processes begin to cycle on different schedules.

Jet lag. When zeitgebers that control the phases of various circadian rhythms are accelerated during eastern flights or decelerated during western flights.

K complexes. The large biphasic EEG waves that are characteristic of stage 2 sleep EEG.

Microsleeps. Brief periods of sleep EEG that are commonly observed in sleep-deprived subjects while they remain sitting or standing; the eyelids droop and there is a decrease in responsiveness to external stimuli.

Narcolepsy. A disorder of hypersomnia characterized by repeated, brief daytime sleep attacks.

Nocturnal animals. Animals that stay awake during the night and sleep during the day.

Nocturnal myoclonus. Periodic sleep-disrupting twitching of the legs during sleep.

Parabiotic preparation. A physiological preparation in which two subjects share one physiological system.

Parachlorophenylalanine (PCPA). A chemical that temporarily blocks the synthesis of serotonin, thus producing a temporary insomnia.

Paradoxical sleep. Emergent stage 1 sleep; so called because the EEG signals and ANS changes associated with it are paradoxically similar to those of wakefulness.

Raphé nuclei. A cluster of serotonin-producing nuclei running in a thin strip down the midline of the caudal reticular formation.

Rapid eye movement sleep (REM sleep). The stage of sleep characterized by rapid eye movements, loss of core muscle tone, and low-amplitude high-frequency EEG.

Restless legs. Insomnia caused by a tension or uneasiness in the legs that keeps people from falling asleep.

Reticular activating system. The reticular formation is commonly referred to as the reticular activating system because it contains circuits that maintain wakefulness.

Retinohypothalamic tracts. Tracts running from the retinas to the suprachiasmatic nuclei of the hypothalamus.

Sleep apnea. A condition in which sleep is repeatedly disturbed by momentary interruptions in breathing.

Sleep spindles. 1-to-2-second bursts of 12-to-15-Hz EEG waves characteristic of stage 2 sleep.

Slow-wave sleep (SWS). Sleep stages 2, 3, and 4.

Somnambulism. Sleep walking.

Sudden infant death syndrome (SIDS). When an infant dies during sleep for no apparent reason; thought to be related to sleep apnea.

Suprachiasmatic nuclei (SCN). Nuclei of the hypothalamus that control the circadian cycles of various bodily functions.

Zeitgebers. Environmental cues, such as the light-dark cycle, that entrain circadian rhythms.

Memory and Amnesia

Ironically, the person who has contributed more than any other to our understanding of the neuropsychology of memory is not a neuropsychologist. In fact, although he has collaborated on dozens of studies of memory, he has no formal training in memory research whatsoever and not a single degree to his name. He is H.M., a man who in 1953 at the age of 27 underwent bilateral removal of the medial portions of his temporal lobes for the treatment of a severe case of epilepsy. Just as the Rosetta Stone has provided archaeologists with important clues to the meaning of Egyptian hieroglyphics, H.M.'s postsurgical memory deficits have been instrumental in the achievement of our current understanding of the neuropsychological bases of human memory.

Much of the first section of this chapter (Section 14.1) deals with H.M. It deals with the impact of his memory problems on his everyday life, the results of the 35-year program of objective testing that has followed his operation, and the implications of his case for current theories of memory. Subsequent sections of the chapter describe the amnesias associated with Korsakoff's syndrome (Section 14.2), with Alzheimer's disease (Section 14.3), and with nonpenetrating brain injuries (Section 14.4). Section 14.5 focuses on the use of animal models to study the neural bases of amnesia, and Section 14.6 discusses several theoretical issues that are the focus of current memory research. The chapter ends with Section 14.7 and the ironic case of R.M., a biopsychologist who recently suffered a severe blow to the head and thus had an opportunity to observe his own amnesia. The following are this chapter's seven sections.

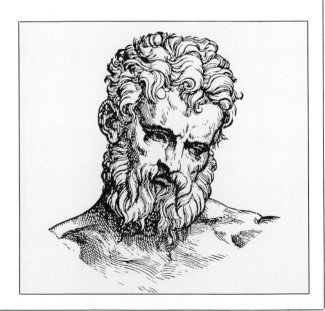

14.1 The Amnesic Effects
of Bilateral Medial Temporal Lobectomy
and the Unfortunate Case of H.M.

397
Memory and
Amnesia

Early Theories of Memory Storage

In order to understand the impact of H.M.'s case, it is important to appreciate the state of the field in the mid 1950s, when the first reports of H.M.'s case began to appear. At that time, the study of the neural bases of memory was strongly influenced by two ideas. First, the field of memory research was reeling from Lashley's fruitless search for the location of the **engram,** the change in the brain responsible for storing a memory. Lashley, the most influential physiological psychologist of the day, had spent 35 years training rats, cats, and monkeys to perform complex learning tasks and then cutting, destroying, or removing specific parts of their brains in a vain attempt to erase the memory of their training. For example, in one series of studies, rats received lesions of various sizes to different parts of the cerebral cortex after they learned a maze task to a criterion of 10 consecutive correct trials. Ten days later, they were trained again to the same criterion in order to test their memory for the task. Lashley found that only very large cortical lesions disrupted retention and, more importantly, that the particular site of the lesion was of no major consequence. Cortical lesions of equal size produced similar effects regardless of where they were placed. On the basis of these findings, Lashley concluded that memories for complex tasks are stored diffusely throughout the neocortex (the **principle of mass action**) and that all parts of the neocortex play an equal role in their storage (the **principle of equipotentiality**). Although Lashley conceded that certain areas of the neocortex may play a more important role than other areas in the storage of certain memories—for example, the visual cortex may play a more important role in the storage of the memories of learned visual discriminations—he argued that memories were stored diffusely and equally throughout these functional areas. The impact of Lashley's work was to discourage theories of memory that assigned specific memorial processes to specific parts of the brain.

The second idea about the physiological bases of memory that was prevalent in the mid 1950s was the theory that there are two different memory storage mechanisms: a short-term mechanism and a long-term mechanism. Research from several sources had suggested that a memory is temporarily retained in short-term storage while the physiological changes underlying long-term storage are taking place. Accordingly, in order to remember a new phone number, we hold it in the short-term storage mode by actively thinking about it until its continued presence in the short-term mode eventually produces the changes underlying its long-term storage. The transfer of a memory from short-term to long-term storage was termed **consolidation.** According to the most influential version of this theory (Hebb, 1949), the memory for a particular event is stored in the short-term mode by *reverberating neural activity* (neural activity that goes around and around in closed-loop neural circuits; see Figure 14.1) in the specific neural circuit excited by the event. This reverberatory activity was thought to produce structural changes in the synapses of that circuit that would facilitate the later occurrence of the same pattern of activity. This structural synaptic facilitation was believed to be the basis of long-term storage (see Figure 14.1). The major prediction of this two-stage theory of memory

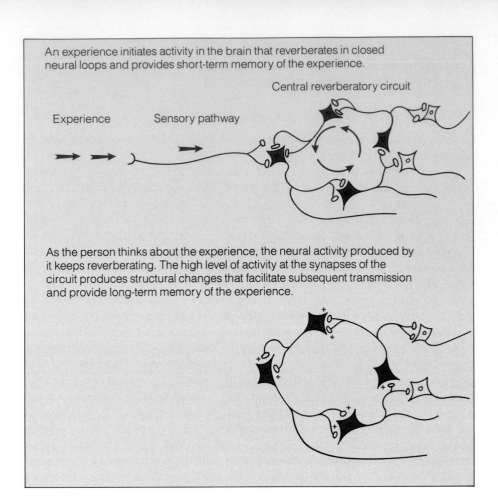

An experience initiates activity in the brain that reverberates in closed neural loops and provides short-term memory of the experience.

Central reverberatory circuit

Experience   Sensory pathway

As the person thinks about the experience, the neural activity produced by it keeps reverberating. The high level of activity at the synapses of the circuit produces structural changes that facilitate subsequent transmission and provide long-term memory of the experience.

FIGURE 14.1 *An illustration of Hebb's 1949 theory of how short-term memories are consolidated into long-term memories.*

storage is that experiences that are not held in short-term storage for a sufficient period of time by conscious consideration will not become integrated into the store of long-term memories. The classic example of this prediction is the complete loss of recall experienced by people when they are distracted just after they have looked up a new phone number.

Bilateral Medial Temporal Lobectomy

During the 11 years preceding his surgery, H.M. suffered an average of one generalized convulsive attack each week and many partial convulsions each day, despite massive doses of anticonvulsant medication. Electroencephalography suggested that H.M.'s convulsive attacks arose from foci in the medial portions of both his left and right temporal lobes. Because the removal of one medial temporal lobe had proven to be an effective treatment without serious side effects in patients with evidence of a unilateral temporal lobe focus (see Van Buren, Ajmone-Marsan, Mutsuga, & Sadowski, 1975), the decision was made to perform a **bilateral medial temporal lobectomy** on H.M. This operation (see Figure 14.2) had been performed on only a few previous occasions; it has never been performed again. By the way, the term **lobectomy** refers to an operation in which a lobe of the brain, or a major part of one, is removed; the term **lobotomy** (as in prefrontal lobotomy; see Chapter 1) refers to an operation in which a lobe of the brain, or a major part of one, is separated from the rest of the brain by a large cut, but is not removed.

In one sense, H.M.'s bilateral medial temporal lobectomy was an unqualified success. The incidence of his generalized convulsions was reduced from one per week to one every 2 or 3 years, and minor attacks occurred only once or twice a day, despite a substantial reduction in the level of his anticonvulsant medication. Furthermore, H.M. entered surgery a reasonably well-balanced, stable individual with normal perceptual abilities and superior intelligence, and he left it in the same condition.

> H.M.'s memory defect is not accompanied by any general intellectual loss. In 1953, shortly before his operation, he obtained an intelligence quotient of 104 on Form I of the Wechsler-Bellevue Intelligence Scale; the verbal quotient was 101 and the performance quotient 106. When tested again in 1955, two years after the operation, he achieved a full-scale quotient of 112, with a verbal quotient of 107 and a performance quotient of 114. This postoperative improvement may well have been due to a reduction in the frequency of his minor attacks, which preoperatively had been observed to occur as often as 12 times during a single two-hour testing session. Seven years later, in 1962, he showed further improvement; when tested with Form II of the Wechsler Intelligence Scale, his full-scale I.Q. was 118, the verbal and performance quotients being 109 and 125, respectively. (Milner, Corkin, & Teuber, 1968, pp. 218–219)

H.M.'s Postsurgical Memory Deficits

In assessing the amnesic effects of brain surgery, it is usual to administer two fundamentally different kinds of tests: tests of the patient's ability to

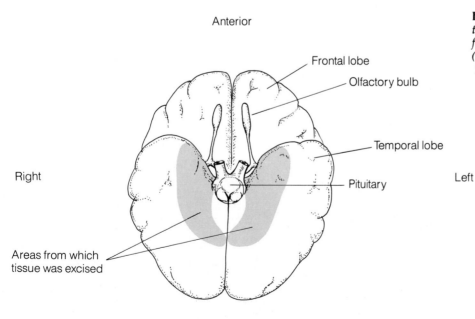

Anterior

Frontal lobe

Olfactory bulb

Temporal lobe

Right

Pituitary

Left

Areas from which
tissue was excised

Posterior

FIGURE 14.2 *The portion of the medial temporal lobes removed from the brain of H.M. (Adapted from Scoville & Milner, 1957.)*

remember things learned before the surgery and tests of the patient's ability to remember things learned after the surgery. Deficits on the former category of tests lead to a diagnosis of **retrograde** (backward-acting) **amnesia;** those on the latter category of tests lead to a diagnosis of **anterograde** (forward-acting) **amnesia.** Like his intellectual abilities, H.M.'s memory for events predating his surgery remains largely intact. He has a mild retrograde amnesia for only those events occurring in the year or two before surgery; his memory for more remote events (e.g., the events of his childhood, for example) seems entirely normal. H.M.'s big problem is a devastating anterograde amnesia. In a nutshell, H.M.'s problem is that he cannot form new long-term memories. His ability to hold items in short-term storage is well within the normal range—he has a **digit span** (see Chapter 4) of 6 digits (Wickelgren, 1968); however, once he stops thinking about something that has just happened to him, it is lost forever from his memory. In effect, H.M. became suspended in time on that day in 1953 when he regained his health, but lost his future. Consider the following descriptions of H.M.'s personal life.

> As far as we can tell, this man has retained little if anything of events subsequent to the operation, although his I.Q. rating is actually slightly higher than before. Ten months before I examined him, his family had moved from their old house to a new one a few blocks away on the same street. He still had not learned the new address (though remembering the old one perfectly), nor could he be trusted to find his way home alone. He did not know where objects in constant use were kept, and his mother stated that he would read the same magazines over and over again without finding their contents familiar. . . . forgetting occurred the instant the patient's focus of attention shifted . . . (Milner, 1965, pp. 104–105)

> During three of the nights at the Clinical Research Center, the patient rang for the night nurse, asking her, with many apologies, if she would tell him where he was and how he came to be there. He clearly realized that he was in a hospital but seemed unable to reconstruct any of the events of the previous day. On another occasion he remarked "Every day is alone in itself, whatever enjoyment I've had, and whatever sorrow I've had." Our own impression is that many events fade for him long before the day is over. He often volunteers stereotyped descriptions of his own state, by saying that it is "like waking from a dream." His experience seems to be that of a person who is just becoming aware of his surroundings without fully comprehending the situation, because he does not remember what went before. . . .
>
> He still fails to recognize people who are close neighbours or family friends but who got to know him only after the operation. When questioned, he tries to use accent as a clue to a person's place of origin and weather as a clue to the time of year. Although he gives his date of birth unhesitatingly and accurately, he always underestimates his own age and can only make wild guesses as to the date. . . . [Having aged since his surgery, he does not recognize a current photograph of himself.]

> After his father's death, H.M. was given protected employment in a state rehabilitation centre, where he spends week-days participating in rather monotonous work, programmed for severely retarded patients. A typical task is the mounting of cigarette-lighters on cardboard frames for display. It is characteristic that he cannot give us any description of his place of work, the nature of his job, or the route along which he is driven each day, to and from the centre. (Milner, Corkin, & Teuber, 1968, pp. 216–217)

The Formal Assessment of H.M.'s Anterograde Amnesia

In this subsection, H.M.'s performance on six standardized neuro-psychological tests of memory is described. His performance on the first three tests illustrates his anterograde memory deficit; his performance on the last three tests illustrates an aspect of his anterograde memory that has survived.

Digit Span +1 Test   H.M. was asked to repeat 5 digits read to him at 1-second intervals. He got all 5 correct, thus on the next trial the same 5 digits were presented in the same sequence, with 1 digit added to the end of the sequence. The same 6-digit sequence was presented several times until he got it right, and then another digit was added to the end of it, and so on. After 25 trials of this **digit span +1 test,** H.M. had still not success-fully repeated more than 7 digits—only 1 more than his normal digit span. Normal subjects can usually expand their digit spans to about 18 digits after 25 such digit-span +1 trials (Drachman & Arbit, 1966).

Block-Tapping Memory-Span Test   Milner (1971) demonstrated that H.M.'s anterograde amnesia was not restricted to verbal material by assessing his performance on a nonverbal analogue of the digit-span test, the **block-tapping memory-span test.** An array of nine blocks was spread out on a board in front of H.M., and he was asked to watch the neuro-psychologist touch a sequence of them and then to repeat the same se-quence of touches. H.M.'s block-tapping span was normal, but, unlike normal subjects, he could not learn to touch a sequence of one greater than his immediate block-tapping span even when the same sequence was re-peated 12 times. Because H.M. has amnesia for information presented in every sensory modality, he is said to have **global amnesia.**

Verbal and Nonverbal Matching-to-Sample Tests   In a **matching-to-sample test,** the subject is presented with a sample item, and then after a delay, an array of test items is presented from which the subject must select the one that matches (i.e., is the same as) the sample. Sidman, Stoddard, and Mohr (1968) tested H.M. with verbal and nonverbal forms of this test. In each, the sample was presented briefly on the center panel of a 3 × 3 matrix of panels (see Figure 14.3); then after various delays, the test items were simultaneously presented on the other eight panels. H.M.'s task was to indicate by pressing the appropriate panel which of the eight test items matched the sample. When the stimuli were verbal (i.e., se-quences of three consonants), H.M. had no difficulty even at the longest retention intervals (40 seconds). In contrast, when the stimuli were non-verbal (i.e., different shapes of ellipses), H.M. could not perform at reten-tion intervals of more than 5 seconds. In contrast, a control group of school children made almost no errors on either the verbal or nonverbal versions of the test. Sidman and his colleagues concluded that the verbal matching-to-sample performance of H.M. was superior to his performance on the nonverbal version of the test because letters but not ellipses can be actively rehearsed—we have no words for different ellipses that would allow us to rehearse them during a retention interval.

Mirror-Drawing Test   The first indication that H.M.'s anterograde amnesia did not apply equally to all kinds of long-term memories came

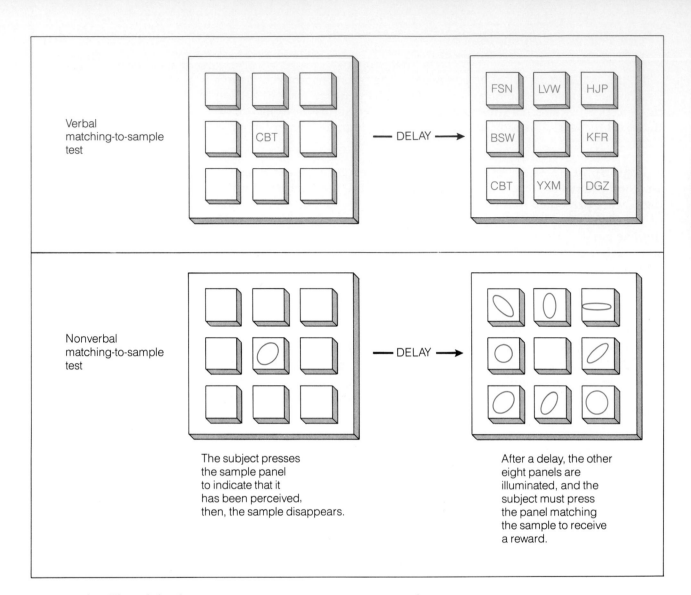

Verbal matching-to-sample test

CBT

— DELAY →

FSN LVW HJP

BSW   KFR

CBT YXM DGZ

Nonverbal matching-to-sample test

— DELAY →

The subject presses the sample panel to indicate that it has been perceived, then, the sample disappears.

After a delay, the other eight panels are illuminated, and the subject must press the panel matching the sample to receive a reward.

FIGURE 14.3 *The verbal and nonverbal matching-to-sample tests given to H.M. by Sidman, Stoddard, and Mohr (1968). H.M. performed errorlessly on the verbal form of the test up to the longest, 40-second, retention interval, but he could not perform the nonverbal form at intervals of greater than 5 seconds.*

from the results of a **mirror-drawing test** conducted by Milner (1965). As indicated in Figure 14.4, H.M.'s task was to draw a line within the boundaries of a star-shaped target by watching his hand in a mirror. H.M. was asked to trace the star 10 times on each of 3 consecutive days, and the number of times that he went outside the boundaries on each trial was recorded. As can be seen in Figure 14.5, H.M.'s performance improved over the 3 days, thus indicating good retention of the task. However, when questioned at the beginning of each daily test session, he insisted that he had never seen the task before.

Rotary-Pursuit Test In the **rotary-pursuit test,** the subject tries to keep the tip of a stylus in contact with a target rotating on a revolving turntable (see Figure 14.6). Corkin (1968) found that H.M.'s performance of the rotary-pursuit task improved significantly over nine daily practice sessions, despite the fact that he never recalled practicing the task or even seeing the pursuit rotor. He retained this improved performance over a 7-day retention interval.

FIGURE 14.4 *The mirror-drawing test.*

Incomplete-Pictures Test   The **incomplete-pictures test** employs 5 sets of 20 fragmented drawings. Each set contains drawings of the same objects, but they differ in their degree of sketchiness. As illustrated in Figure 14.7, set 1 contains the most fragmented drawings, and set 5 the complete drawings (Gollin, 1960). The subject is first shown all 20 of the most sketchy cards (i.e., set 1) and asked to identify them. Then the unrecognized items in set 2 are presented in the same fashion, but in a different order. If necessary, the presentation is repeated with the unidentified items in sets 3, 4, and finally 5 until all 20 items have been identified. Figure 14.8 illustrates the initial performance of H.M. on this test and his performance on the same test administered unexpectedly 1 hour later. Clearly, there were substantial savings on the test, even though H.M. did not recall performing the task 1 hour earlier (Milner, Corkin, & Teuber, 1968).

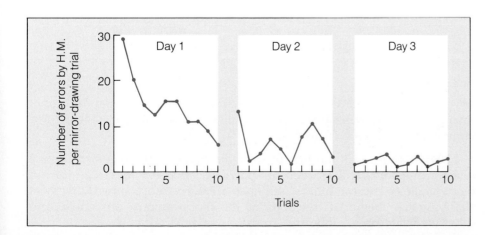

FIGURE 14.5 *Retention of the mirror-drawing task by H.M. (Adapted from Milner, 1965)*

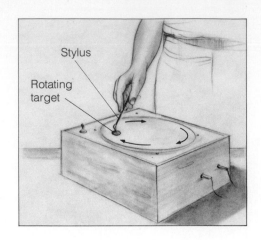

FIGURE 14.6 *The rotary-pursuit task. The subject tries to keep the stylus in contact with the rotating target.*

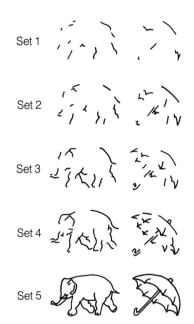

FIGURE 14.7 *The five sets of two of the drawings from the incomplete-pictures test. (Adapted from Gollin, 1960.)*

Other Cases of Bilateral Medial Temporal Lobectomy

It is always risky to base general theories on a single case. However, there is good evidence that H.M.'s case is not idiosyncratic. For example, Milner (1965) reported three cases in which surgical removal of one medial temporal lobe produced grave memory deficits similar to, but less severe than, H.M.'s. Because unilateral medial temporal lobectomy normally produces only slight deficits, Milner suggested that these three patients may have had preexisting damage to the contralateral medial temporal lobe. One of them (P.B.) died of unrelated causes 15 years after surgery, and the discovery of extensive hippocampal atrophy contralateral to his surgical lesion confirmed Milner's suggestion. Another relevant case was that of a 47-year-old male physician who underwent bilateral medial temporal lobectomy prior to H.M., but was not extensively studied because he displayed a variety of psychotic symptoms both before and after surgery.

> This man did not know that he had had a brain operation and did not recall anything of the hospital in which he had spent six months postoperatively. He had no knowledge of his present surroundings, yet could give minute details of his early life and medical training. He still had an I.Q. rating of 122. . . . At the examiner's request he drew a dog and an elephant [see Figure 14.9]. When shown these drawings again a mere half-hour later, he did not find them familiar and had no idea who had drawn them. Moreover, he called the dog a "deer" and rejected any suggestion that it might be a dog. (Milner, 1965, pp. 103–104)

The Influence of H.M.'s Case on the Search for the Neural Basis of Memory

I began this chapter by asserting that H.M. has contributed more than any other person to our current understanding of the neuropsychology of memory. The following are six important ideas about memory that are, to a large degree, a legacy of his case:

1. H.M.'s case was the first to strongly implicate the medial temporal lobes in memory, and as such, it spawned a massive research effort in biopsychology and the other disciplines of neuroscience aimed directly at clarifying the memorial functions of the hippocampus, amygdala, and other medial temporal lobe structures.

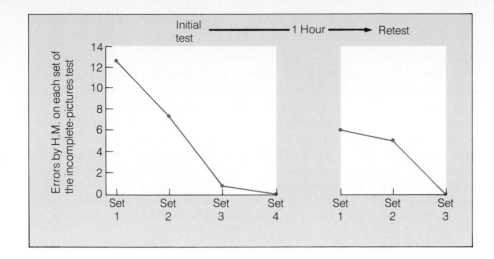

FIGURE 14.8 *H.M.'s initial performance on the incomplete-pictures test and his savings on the same test administered unexpectedly 1 hour later. (Adapted from Milner, Corkin, & Teuber, 1968.)*

2. H.M.'s case seriously challenged the view that memorial functions are diffusely and equivalently distributed throughout the brain. Because lesions of comparable size in other parts of the forebrain do not have similar effects, it is perfectly clear that some part of the medial temporal lobes plays an important role in memory not shared by other areas. In making this general point, H.M.'s case renewed efforts to relate particular brain structures to particular memorial processes.

3. H.M.'s case provided support for the view that there are physiologically distinct modes of storage for short-term and long-term memory. The fact that bilateral medial temporal lobectomy abolishes the ability to form certain kinds of long-term memories without significantly disrupting performance on tests of short-term memory is among the strongest evidence for this dual-system hypothesis.

4. The studies of H.M.'s case were among the first to show that an amnesic subject might claim no recollection of a previous experience, while at the same time demonstrating memory for it by improved test performance—recall H.M.'s savings without conscious recollection on the mirror-drawing test, the incomplete-pictures test, and the rotary-pursuit test. Tests on which memories are expressed by conscious declaration have been labeled tests of **explicit memory** (i.e., recall and recognition tests); tests on which memories are expressed by improved test performance have been termed tests of **implicit memory** (see Graf & Schacter, 1985, 1987).

5. H.M.'s case suggested that the medial temporal lobes play an important role in memory consolidation. H.M.'s capacity to store short-term

FIGURE 14.9 *Drawings of a dog and an elephant made by a 47-year-old physician following bilateral medial temporal lobectomy. He did not recognize them as his 30 minutes later. (Redrawn from Milner, 1965.)*

memories remained intact, as did his capacity to store most long-term memories formed before his operation. His problem is transferring short-term explicit memories to long-term storage.

6. The 2-year time span covered by H.M.'s mild retrograde amnesia challenged notions of memory consolidation that were popular in the 50s and 60s. It was assumed in the 50s and 60s that consolidation reflects a transfer of a memory from short-term storage by reverberating neural activity to long-term storage by structural synaptic changes, and it was further assumed that this transfer takes place in minutes, at which point the memory is as resistant to disruption as it is going to get. The fact that H.M.'s memory for events occurring in the 2 years prior to his surgery was more susceptible to disruption than his memory for more remote events suggests that the resistance of memories to disruption continues to increase for years after acquisition.

Damage to Which Structure of the Medial Temporal Lobes Causes Medial-Temporal-Lobe Amnesia?

Bilateral medial temporal lobectomy damages several major structures; however, the amnesic effects of bilateral medial temporal lobectomy have usually been attributed to hippocampal damage. In their original description of the effects of the bilateral temporal lobe surgery, Scoville and Milner (1957) reported that there seemed to be a correlation between the extent of hippocampal removal in different subjects and the degree of memory impairment. Despite the wide acceptance of this hippocampal interpretation of medial-temporal-lobe amnesia, the issue is far from settled. Two alternative hypotheses have been proposed. One alternative hypothesis is that **temporal stem** damage is the critical factor in medial-temporal-lobe amnesia. The temporal stem is a fiber bundle lying just above the hippocampus. Most of the axons from the temporal cortex funnel through it on their way to other parts of the brain. The second alternative hypothesis is that damage to both the amygdala and the hippocampus is necessary for the production of substantial memory deficits. Because all of the patients with hippocampal damage who were included in Scoville and Milner's original analysis also had extensive temporal stem and amygdala damage, both of these alternative hypotheses warrant careful consideration.

The case of R.B. is relevant to this issue (Zola-Morgan, Squire, Amaral, 1986). At the age of 52, R.B. suffered brain damage from **ischemia** (an interruption of the blood supply to an area, which results in cell death) during cardiac-bypass surgery, and he experienced amnesia thereafter. Although R.B.'s amnesia was not as severe as H.M.'s, it was comparable in many respects. R.B. died in 1983 of a heart attack, and a detailed postmortem examination of his brain was carried out with the permission of his family. The only damage that was discovered was to one area (the **CA1 subfield**) of one layer (the **pyramidal cell layer**) of both the left and right hippocampus (CA is the abbreviation for *cornu ammonis*, another name for hippocampus). See Figure 14.10. Although the fact that R.B.'s brain damage was restricted to the hippocampus does not exclude the possibility that damage to the amygdala or temporal stem contributes to the amnesic effects of medial temporal lobectomy, it suggests that hippocampal damage by itself can produce amnesia. There is more about this issue later in the chapter.

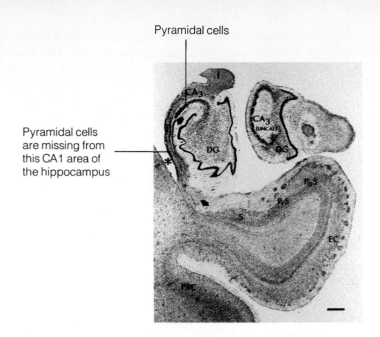

Pyramidal cells

Pyramidal cells
are missing from
this CA1 area of
the hippocampus

FIGURE 14.10 *A Nissl-
stained cross section through the
hippocampus of R.B. reveals
selective damage to the pyramidal cell layer of the CA1
subfield. Notice that the CA1
region of R.B.'s pyramidal cell
layer is the only region of the
layer that lacks cell bodies.
(From Squire, 1987.)*

14.2 The Amnesia of Korsakoff's Syndrome

Although the study of H.M., R.B., and the other amnesic patients with
bilateral medial temporal lobe damage has been extremely informative,
patients with Korsakoff's syndrome have served as subjects in the vast
majority of studies of human amnesia. **Korsakoff's syndrome** is a disease
that develops in individuals who chronically consume alcohol. In its advanced stages, it is characterized by a variety of sensory and motor problems, extreme confusion, striking personality changes, and a risk of death
from liver, gastrointestinal, or heart disorders. Postmortem neuroanatomical examination typically reveals extensive peripheral nerve damage, lesions to the *diencephalon* (the thalamus and hypothalamus), and diffuse
damage to a variety of other brain structures, most notably the neocortex
and cerebellum.

The major difference between the amnesia associated with Korsakoff's
syndrome and that associated with bilateral temporal lobectomy is that
Korsakoff patients typically suffer from a severe retrograde amnesia in
addition to their anterograde deficits. Unlike patients with bilateral medial
temporal lobe damage, Korsakoff patients have extreme difficulty recalling
events that occurred many years prior to their hospitalization. For example, in a study conducted in the early 1970s (Marslen-Wilson & Teuber,
1975), Korsakoff patients proved to be worse than H.M. at recognizing the
faces of individuals famous in the 1930s and 1940s.

In general, the memory of Korsakoff patients for recent events is disrupted more than their memory for remote events. There are two possible
interpretations for this finding. The usual interpretation is that the brain
damage associated with Korsakoff's syndrome produces a long gradient of
retrograde amnesia. The problem with this interpretation arises from the
fact that Korsakoff's syndrome has an insidious, rather than a sudden,
onset. Because there is no well-defined point of onset, it is not clear to what
extent memory deficits for events prior to diagnosis reflect the retrograde

disruption of existing long-term memories or the gradually worsening anterograde blockage of the formation of new ones. Squire (1982) has suggested that Korsakoff patients have cognitive difficulties that equally impede the recall of all past experiences and that their particular difficulty in recalling events occurring in the months and years immediately before their hospitalization reflects the progressive development of anterograde amnesia.

Does Midline Diencephalic Damage Cause the Amnesia Observed in Korsakoff Patients?

Because the brain damage associated with Korsakoff's syndrome is so diffuse, it has not been easy to identify the portion of it that is specifically responsible for the amnesia. The first hypothesis, which was based on several small postmortem studies, was that damage to the **mammillary bodies** of the hypothalamus was responsible for the memory deficits of Korsakoff patients. However, a large-scale postmortem study by Victor, Adams, and Collins (1971) subsequently revealed several severe cases of Korsakoff's amnesia with no mammillary body damage, but none was found that did not have damage to the **mediodorsal nuclei** of the thalamus. Independent support for the mediodorsal-nucleus-damage interpretation of Korsakoff amnesia comes from the observation that otherwise healthy patients with relatively localized **infarctions** (areas of cell death produced by ischemia) in the area of the mediodorsal nuclei often suffer from amnesia (e.g., Graff-Radford, Damasio, Yamada, Eslinger, & Damasio, 1985; von Cramon, Hebel, & Schuri, 1985; Winocur, Oxbury, Roberts, Agnetti, & Davis, 1984). However, there is some evidence that amnesia occasionally occurs in Korsakoff patients in the absence of mediodorsal nuclei damage (Brion & Mikol, 1978).

The Case of N.A.

With respect to the study of amnesia, N.A. is to the diencephalon as H.M. is to the medial temporal lobes. After a year of junior college, N.A. joined the air force and served as a radar technician until his accident in December of 1960. On that fateful day,

> N.A. was assembling a model airplane in his barracks room. His roommate had removed a miniature fencing foil from the wall and was making thrusts behind N.A.'s chair. N.A. turned suddenly and was stabbed through the right nostril. The foil penetrated the **cribriform plate** [the thin bone around the base of the brain], taking an upward course to the left into the forebrain. (Squire, 1987, p. 177)

> The examiners . . . noted that at first he seemed to be unable to recall any significant personal, national or international events for the two years preceding the accident, but this extensive retrograde amnesia appeared to shrink. . . . Two-and-a-half years after the accident, the retrograde amnesia was said to involve a span of perhaps two weeks immediately preceding the injury, but the exact extent of this retrograde loss was (and remains) impossible to determine. . . .
> During . . . convalescence (for the first six to eight months after the accident), the patient's recall of day-to-day events was described as extremely poor, but "occasionally some items sprang forth uncontrollably; he suddenly

recalled something he seemed to have no business recalling." His physicians thus gained the impression that his memory was patchy: he appeared to have difficulty in calling up at will many things that at other times emerged spontaneously. . . .

Since his injury, he has been unable to return to any gainful employment, although his memory has continued to improve, albeit slowly. (Teuber, Milner, & Vaughan, 1968, pp. 268–269)

N.A. received a CAT scan test (see Chapter 4) in the late 1970s (Squire & Moore, 1979). What makes N.A.'s case particularly important is that the scan revealed a small lesion in the left mediodorsal nucleus of the thalamus, the nucleus implicated in the amnesia of Korsakoff patients. Damage to other neural structures along the path of the foil was not identifiable by the CAT scan. This observation adds support to the view that the mediodorsal area of the thalamus is part of a system underlying memory.

The Contribution of Prefrontal Damage to Korsakoff Amnesia

In addition to their medial thalamic lesions, Korsakoff patients commonly have diffuse damage to the prefrontal cortex. Investigators have used two strategies to determine how this prefrontal damage contributes to the amnesia of Korsakoff patients. They have compared the memorial deficits of Korsakoff patients with those of patients with prefrontal damage, and they have compared the memorial deficits of Korsakoff patients with those of N.A., who has the thalamic damage, but lacks the prefrontal damage alone. The use of these two strategies has led to the view that two features of Korsakoff amnesia are attributable to prefrontal damage: failure to release from proactive interference and amnesia for temporal order. **Proactive interference** refers to the interfering effects of performing one task on the performance of a subsequent one. For example, subjects exhibit a gradual decline in their ability to learn and recall successive lists of words of the same category, for example, lists of animal names, due to the accumulating proactive interference from learning preceding lists. However, when a list of words from a different category, for example, a list of vegetables, is inserted in the series, normal subjects and N.A. display an improvement in their ability to recall these novel items (Squire, 1982). Such a release from proactive interference does not occur in Korsakoff patients (Cermak, Uhly, & Reale, 1980) or in patients with localized prefrontal damage (Moscovitch, 1982). This suggests that the inability of Korsakoff's patients to release from proactive interference is associated with their diffuse prefrontal damage.

Another memory deficit that is common in Korsakoff patients and in patients with prefrontal lobe damage (Milner, 1974), but has not been observed in N.A. is a deficit in *memory for temporal sequence* (see Squire, Nadel, & Slater, 1981). In one study (Squire, 1982), N.A., a group of Korsakoff patients, and a group of control subjects received a test of memory for temporal order, which had previously been shown to be sensitive to prefrontal damage. The subjects read 12 unrelated sentences, and then waited 3 minutes and read another 12. Later, their ability to recognize the sentences and to recall whether they had appeared in the first or second list was assessed. Like the Korsakoff patients, N.A. had difficulty recognizing the sentences, but unlike the Korsakoff patients, N.A. had no more difficulty than did the control subjects in specifying whether those sentences that he recognized were from the first or second list. This suggests that the prefrontal lobes are involved in memory for temporal sequence.

14.3 The Amnesia of Alzheimer's Disease

You learned about Alzheimer's disease in Chapter 5, but let me refresh your memory. Alzheimer's disease is the most common cause of *dementia* (general intellectual deterioration) in old people; it is estimated that close to 5% of all people over 65 suffer from the disorder. At autopsy, the brains of Alzheimer's patients are characterized by **neurofibrils** (thread-like structures in the neural cytoplasm), **amyloid plaques** (tangles of degenerating neural fibers interspersed with abnormal protein, called amyloid), and neuronal degeneration, particularly in the frontal and temporal neocortex, hippocampus, and basal forebrain.

One of the first signs of Alzheimer's disease is a deterioration of memory. An individual in the early stages of Alzheimer's disease begins to have more than the usual difficulty remembering recently learned information, such as names, appointments, words, and phone numbers. In its advanced stages, Alzheimer's disease is characterized by severe intellectual deterioration of all kinds, including an almost total loss of memory. At this stage, the patient is totally confused, requires constant supervision, and may fail to remember even the most basic information, such as the face of a son or daughter.

Many clinical investigators have studied the brains of deceased Alzheimer's patients in the hope of identifying the neural basis of the disorder; of particular scientific value are the brains of Alzheimer's patients who die before brain deterioration becomes extreme. Interest in this line of research has been stimulated by the possibility that it might provide some insights into the neural basis of memory and amnesia. Several studies have suggested that there is a massive reduction in cholinergic activity in the brains of Alzheimer's patients; there is less acetylcholine, less *choline acetyltransferase* (the enzyme that stimulates the synthesis of acetylcholine), and less *acetylcholinesterase* (the enzyme that breaks down acetylcholine in the synapse) in the hippocampus and neocortex (see Coyle, Price, & DeLong, 1983; Marchbanks, 1982). However, there is no reduction in the density of cholinergic receptors in these structures (see Bartus, Dean, Beer, & Lippa, 1982), which suggests that the degenerative changes occur selectively to the cholinergic neurons terminating in the neocortex and hippocampus, rather than to the postsynaptic neurons on which they terminate.

Many of the cholinergic axons terminating in the neocortex and hippocampus originate in cell bodies located in the basal forebrain just in front of the hypothalamus. In particular, many of the cell bodies of cholinergic neurons projecting to the neocortex and hippocampus originate in a cluster of basal forebrain nuclei that includes the *nucleus basalis of Meynert*, the *diagonal band of Broca*, and the *medial septal nucleus*. The involvement of cholinergic forebrain projections in Alzheimer's disease has been confirmed by the discovery that Alzheimer's disease is virtually always associated with massive cell loss in this area. For example, Whitehouse, Price, Struble, Clark, Coyle, and DeLong (1982) found that there were 79%

fewer neurons in the nucleus basalis of Meynert of deceased Alzheimer's victims than in the brains of deceased age-matched control patients.

Although cholinergic neurons are not the only ones attacked by Alzheimer's disease (see Coyle, 1987), the largest and most reliable deficits have been observed in this system. As a result, efforts have been made to treat Alzheimer's disease with cholinergic agonists, such as *choline*, the precursor of acetylcholine, in the same way the L-DOPA, the precursor of dopamine, has been successfully used to treat Parkinson's disease (see Chapter 6). Unfortunately, choline and other cholinergic agonists have not been able to forestall the inexorable progression of Alzheimer's disease.

The association between Alzheimer's disease and the degeneration of cholinergic neurons has led researchers to explore the involvement of cholinergic mechanisms in memory. The major support for this idea has come from the finding that cholinergic antagonists disrupt memory. For example, the drug *scopolamine*, which blocks cholinergic receptors of the *muscarinic* subtype (see Chapter 6), has been shown to disrupt the recent memory of healthy young adults (Drachman & Leavitt, 1974; Sitaram, Weingartner, & Gillin, 1978). There have also been some reports that cholinergic agonists are **nootropics** (memory-improving agents; pronounced no oh TROP iks), but these claims are best viewed with caution at the present time.

Another approach to the study of cholinergic systems and memory has been to assess the effects of bilateral lesions of the nucleus basalis of Meynert on the behavior of experimental animals. Fibiger, Murray, and Phillips (1983) made such lesions in rats and then assessed their ability to learn a 16-arm radial maze (see Chapter 4). Each day the same 8 arms of the maze were baited with food, while the other 8 arms always remained empty. The control rats soon learned to visit only the 8 food-baited arms without visiting an arm twice on the same day. In contrast, the rats with lesions solved only part of the problem; they readily learned to visit only the 8 food-baited arms, but they often revisited an arm that they had recently stripped of its booty. This suggests that cholinergic circuits might be involved in memory for the temporal order of events. The rats with lesions remembered that they had been rewarded for visiting particular arms, but they did not seem to remember when they had previously visited them. Injections of *physostigmine*, a cholinergic agonist, eliminated this lesion-induced deficit.

14.4 The Amnesia after Closed-Head Injury

Blows to the head that do not penetrate the skull (i.e., closed-head injuries) are by far the most common causes of amnesia. Amnesia so produced is referred to as **posttraumatic amnesia** (PTA). Posttraumatic amnesia is usually composed of both retrograde and anterograde memory deficits.

Following a blow to the head of sufficient intensity to produce amnesia, there is a period of coma, which usually lasts a few seconds or minutes, but can in more extreme cases last for weeks. Once the victim regains consciousness, he or she typically displays considerable confusion. For example, it is not uncommon for an individual who has had the details of the accident carefully explained to her or him to ask for the very same information a few seconds later.

Victims of a closed-head injury are not usually referred to a neuropsychologist for testing until several days after the blow to the head, if they are referred at all. At this point, the general confusion has usually subsided, unless the blow was particularly severe. Testing usually reveals that the patient has a permanent retrograde amnesia for the events that led up to the accident and a permanent anterograde amnesia for the events that followed it. The anterograde memory deficits following a closed-head injury are often quite puzzling to the friends and relatives who visit the victim in the hospital soon after the accident. Although the patient may seem perfectly lucid at the time, she or he often has no recollection of the visit the next day.

Figure 14.11 summarizes the effects of closed-head injury on memory. Although there is great variability in such cases, the figure illustrates the fact that the duration of the period of anterograde amnesia is typically much longer than the duration of the coma, which is in turn usually longer than the period of permanent retrograde amnesia. More severe blows to the head tend to produce longer comas, longer periods of anterograde amnesia, and longer periods of retrograde amnesia (Levin, Papanicolaou, & Eisenberg, 1984). Not illustrated in Figure 14.11 are the so-called islands of memory that are a common, but poorly understood, feature of many cases of amnesia. **Islands of memory** are memories for isolated events that occurred during periods that have otherwise been totally forgotten.

Because **electroconvulsive shock** (ECS) has amnesic effects similar to those produced by a blow to the head, its use in the treatment of depression has provided a unique opportunity to study posttraumatic amnesia. The advantage of ECS over accidental closed-head injury in the study of posttraumatic amnesia is that ECS is a scheduled and precisely administered treatment. Prior to an ECS, patients are injected with a tranquilizer and a muscle relaxant to prevent muscle and bone damage from the resulting grand mal convulsion; some patients are also anesthetized. The convulsion itself is elicited by passing a very large alternating current across the brain through large plate electrodes clamped to the surface of the skull—usually one on each side of the brain. *Electroconvulsive therapy* (ECT) usually involves a series of ECSs, for example, three per week for 3 weeks.

Electroconvulsive Shock and Gradients of Retrograde Amnesia

In the 1950s and 1960s, electroconvulsive shock was of particular interest to researchers studying memory and amnesia because it seemed to provide the ideal method for testing the popular theory that memory consolidation

FIGURE 14.11 *The retrograde and anterograde amnesia produced by a closed-head injury.*

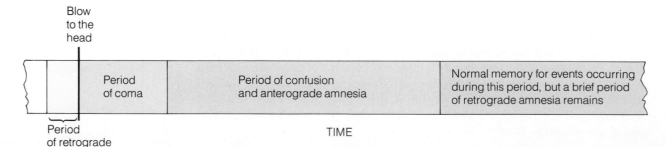

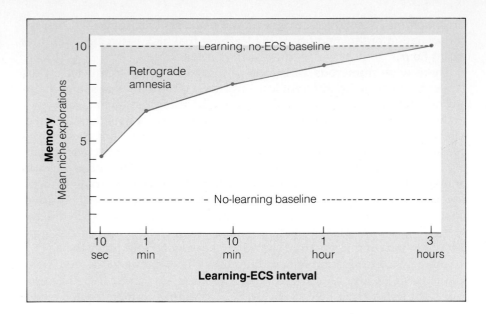

FIGURE 14.12 *Retention of one-trial appetitive learning by no-ECS control rats and by groups of rats receiving ECS at various intervals after the learning trial. (Adapted from Pinel, 1969.)*

reflects the transfer of memory by reverberatory neural activity from short-term storage to long-term structural storage (Hebb, 1949). The idea was that the ECS would erase from storage any memories that had not already been converted to structural synaptic changes, but that it would leave the structural changes themselves unaffected. In other words, it was assumed that the duration of the period of retrograde amnesia prior to an electroconvulsive shock would provide a means of estimating the amount of time that it takes for memory consolidation to be completed. For example, if a subject remembered events that occurred 5 minutes before an ECS, but had some difficulty remembering those that occurred 4 minutes before, it would suggest that consolidation takes between 4 and 5 minutes.

In one such study (Pinel, 1969), rats that were maintained on a schedule of water deprivation were placed for 10 minutes on each of 5 consecutive days in a test box with a small niche, just large enough for a rat to poke its head into. By the fifth of these habituation sessions, most rats explored the niche only 1 or 2 times per session. On the sixth day, there was a water spout in the niche, and each rat was allowed to drink for 15 seconds after it discovered the spout. This was the learning trial. Then 10 seconds, 1 minute, 10 minutes, 1 hour, or 3 hours later each rat received a single ECS. The electrodes were attached to the subjects in a separate control group, but these rats received no ECS. The next day the retention of all subjects was assessed by recording how many times each explored the niche in the test box when the water spout was no longer present. The no-ECS control rats explored the empty niche an average of 10 times during the 10-minute test session, thus suggesting that they remembered well their discovery of water the previous day. As indicated in Figure 14.12, the rats that had received ECS 1 hour or 3 hours after the learning trial also explored the niche about 10 times, which indicated that they remembered the learning trial as well as did the control rats. In contrast, the rats that received the ECS 10 seconds, 1 minute, or 10 minutes after the learning trial explored the empty niche significantly less on the test day. This suggested that the consolidation of the memory of the learning trial took between 10 minutes and 1 hour.

There were numerous variations of this experiment conducted in the 1950s and 1960s, with different learning tasks, different species, and different numbers and intensities of ECSs. Initially, there was some consistency in the findings; most seemed to suggest a rather brief consolidation time of a few minutes or less (e.g., Chorover & Schiller, 1965). But then things became complicated. It was reasonable to think of the neural activity resulting from an experience reverberating through the brain for a few seconds or even a few minutes, but reports of ECS gradients of retrograde amnesia covering hours, days, and even weeks began to appear (e.g., Squire & Spanis, 1984). Whatever the ECS gradients were measuring, it did not seem to be the transfer of memory storage from short-term reverberatory activity to long-term structural change. It was a good idea to try to use ECS to estimate consolidation times, but things just didn't work out. Long gradients of ECS-produced retrograde amnesia suggested that the resistance of memories to disruption by ECS continues to increase for a very long time after learning, if not indefinitely.

The long-term progressive increase in the resistance of memories to disruption has been most clearly demonstrated by studies of the retrograde amnesia of patients following ECT. For example, Squire and his colleagues (e.g., Squire & Cohen, 1979; Squire, Slater, & Chace, 1975) measured the memory of their subjects for television shows that played for only one season in different years prior to the ECT. They tested each subject twice on different forms of the test, once before they received a series of five ECSs and once 1 hour after. The difference between the before and after scores served as an objective estimate of the memory loss for the events of each year. Figure 14.13 illustrates that five ECSs disrupted retention of events occurring in the 2 years prior to treatment, but not of earlier events.

FIGURE 14.13 *A series of five ECSs produced retrograde amnesia for television shows playing for one season between 1 and 3 years before ECT, but not for one-season shows playing in earlier years. (Adapted from Squire et al., 1975.)*

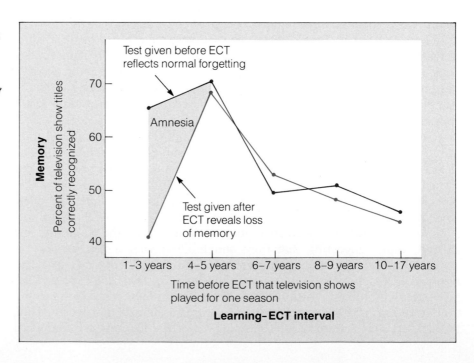

The chapter now moves from the amnesia associated with human brain damage to a consideration of the animal models used to study brain-damage-produced amnesia. Before you make this transition, review the basics of human amnesia by completing the following exercise.

1. The theoretical transfer of a memory from a short-term storage mode to a long-term storage mode is termed __Consolidation__.

2. H.M.'s anterograde amnesia appears to result from an inability to form __long__-term memories of the type needed to successfully perform tests of __explicit__ memory.

3. The rotary-pursuit test, the incomplete-pictures test, and the mirror-drawing test are all tests of __implicit__ memory.

4. In the initial reports of H.M.'s case, his amnesia was attributed to __hippocampal__ damage.

5. Support for the view that hippocampal damage can by itself cause amnesia comes from the study of R.B., a subject who suffered __ischemia__-produced damage to the pyramidal cells of the CA1 hippocampal subfield.

6. The current view is that damage to the __prefrontal__ cortex and to the __mediodorsal__ nuclei of the thalamus is responsible for the memory deficits of people with Korsakoff's disease.

7. N.A. had damage to the __mediodorsal__ nucleus of the thalamus.

8. Patients with Korsakoff's disease and patients with __prefrontal__ cortex damage have difficulty remembering the temporal order of events and they fail to display a release from proactive interference.

9. Alzheimer's disease is associated with degenerative changes to __cholinergic__ neurons.

10. In animal experiments, posttraumatic amnesia is often induced with __electroconvulsive shock__.

11. Because gradients of retrograde amnesia are extremely variable in their duration, it is clear that they cannot be used as a basis for estimating the duration of memory __consolidation__, at least not as conceived of in Hebb's theory.

14.5 Animal Models of Brain-Damage-Produced Amnesia

As you have already seen, the in-depth investigation of the memory deficits of a small group of brain-damaged patients has contributed much to our understanding of the neural bases of memory and amnesia. The group is small because only those few patients, such as H.M., R.B., and N.A., who have circumscribed lesions and specific memory impairments with little intellectual deterioration are sources of readily interpretable data. As valuable as the study of amnesic patients has proven to be, it has also proven to have major limitations. Many important questions about the neural bases of memory and amnesia require controlled multi-subject experiments for their resolution. For example, in order to determine the effects of damage to various brain structures on memory with reasonable certainty, it is necessary to make discrete lesions in different structures in the brains of large groups of subjects, and to control with great precision what and when the subjects learn and how and when their retention is tested. Because such studies are clearly not feasible in human subjects, there has been considerable effort to develop useful animal models of brain-damage-produced amnesia to complement the study of human cases.

One particularly promising animal model of human amnesia has been developed in the macaque monkey. Before I describe it I want to emphasize the obvious: Macaque monkeys are not human and thus the results of their study must be applied to humans with caution. This point was made by Mishkin and Appenzeller (1987).

> Our route to understanding human memory is an indirect one, with unavoidable drawbacks. The macaque brain is about one-fourth the size of the brain of the chimpanzee, the nearest relative of human beings, and the chimpanzee brain in turn is only about one-fourth the size of the human brain. With the increase in size has come greater complexity. The structures we study in the macaque all have counterparts in the human brain, but their functions may well have diverged in the course of evolution. The unique human capacity for language, in particular, and the cerebral specializations it has brought set limits to the comparative approach. Yet basic neural systems are likely to be common to monkeys and human beings . . . (p. 80).

For these reasons, it is clear that the study of animal models of amnesia can never by itself provide unequivocal answers to questions about human amnesia. The power of animal models lies in their convergence with human case studies. Because the animal-model and human case-study approaches each compensate for the specific shortcomings of the other, together they can provide convincing answers to questions that neither can answer satisfactorily by itself.

The task that has been used most successfully to assess memorial deficits in the monkey model of amnesia is the **nonrecurring-items delayed nonmatching-to-sample task.** A monkey with a brain lesion is presented with a distinctive object (the sample), such as a baseball, under which it finds a simian (pertaining to monkeys) delicacy such as banana pellet. Then, after a delay, the monkey is presented with two test objects: the original sample object and a new one. To perform correctly on this test, the monkey must remember the sample and select the other object to receive the food concealed beneath it. New test objects (i.e., nonrecurring items) are used on each trial. The performance of a correct trial is illustrated in

The monkey moves sample to obtain food from the well beneath it.

A screen is lowered in front of the monkey during the delay period.

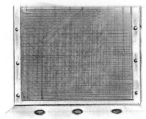

The monkey is confronted with the sample object and a nonsample object.

The monkey must remember the sample and select the other object to obtain food.

FIGURE 14.14 *The correct performance of a delayed non-matching-to-sample trial. (Adapted from Mishkin & Appenzeller, 1987.)*

Figure 14.14. When the delay between the presentation of the sample object is a few minutes or less, normal monkeys trained on the nonrecurring-items delayed nonmatching-to-sample test perform almost perfectly.

Medial-Temporal-Lobe Amnesia in Monkeys

As described earlier, there have been three neuroanatomical hypotheses concerning the basis of medial-temporal-lobe amnesia. The original hypothesis of Scoville and Milner (1957) is that hippocampal damage is the critical factor. Mishkin (1978) later suggested that combined hippocampal and amygdaloid damage is necessary for the syndrome, and Horel (1978) suggested that the damage to the temporal stem, the fiber bundle adjacent to the hippocampus and amygdala, is the critical factor.

Although the issue is far from settled, study of the effects of lesions in the monkey model seems to have ruled out the temporal-stem interpretation (see Figure 14.15). Monkeys with bilateral transections of the temporal stem displayed no deficits on the nonrecurring-items delayed nonmatching-to-sample test, whereas those with combined hippocampal and amygdaloid lesions were severely impaired (Zola-Morgan, Squire, & Mishkin,

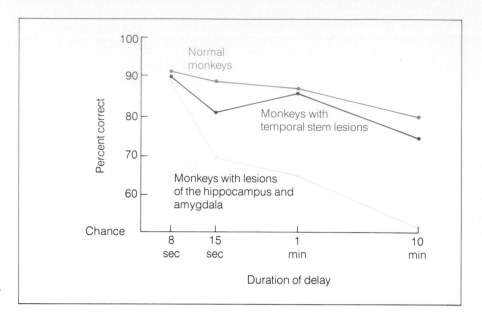

FIGURE 14.15 *The effects of bilateral temporal stem lesions and of combined bilateral hippocampal and amygdaloid lesions on nonrecurring-items delayed nonmatching-to-sample in monkeys. (Adapted from Zola-Morgan, Squire, & Mishkin, 1982.)*

1982). The fact that the memory deficit of monkeys with combined hippocampal and amygdaloid lesions is also exhibited on a tactual version of the test (Mishkin, 1978), and the fact that it is exacerbated by distracting stimuli during the delay (Zola-Morgan & Squire, 1985) both argue that the deficit is similar to that of human medial-temporal-lobe amnesia.

Three experiments have pitted the hippocampus interpretation of medial-temporal-lobe amnesia against the hippocampus-plus-amygdala interpretation, but unfortunately each has led to a different conclusion. In each of the three studies, the effect of bilateral hippocampal lesions on the nonrecurring-items delayed nonmatching-to-sample performance of monkeys was compared with the effect of combined bilateral lesions of the hippocampus and amygdala. One experiment supported the hippocampus interpretation by showing that the deficits produced by combined lesions of the hippocampus and amygdala were no more severe than those produced by hippocampus lesions alone (Mahut, Moss, & Zola-Morgan, 1981). Another experiment supported the hippocampus-plus-amygdala interpretation by showing that combined hippocampus-amygdala lesions produced severe deficits, whereas those produced by damage to either structure alone were minimal (Mishkin, 1978). And the third experiment suggested a compromise position by showing that hippocampal lesions by themselves are capable of producing amnesia, but that the amnesia is more severe if the amygdalas are also damaged (Squire & Zola-Morgan, 1985). The contribution of damage to the overlying cortical structures, which is inevitable during hippocampal and amygdalar excision, has yet to be systematically determined.

Do monkeys with large, bilateral medial-temporal-lobe lesions display retrograde memory deficits similar to those of H.M.? The answer seems to be yes. In one study (Salmon, Zola-Morgan, & Squire, 1987), monkeys learned five different object discrimination tasks at five different times in the 8 months prior to bilateral medial temporal lobectomy, which included the hippocampus, amygdala, and overlying cortex. The surgery disrupted memory for all five discriminations. Thus, in monkeys, as in humans, bilateral medial temporal lobectomy produces a severe retrograde amnesia that extends back several months or more.

As an important step in establishing the comparability of the effects of bilateral medial temporal lobectomy in monkeys and humans, Zola-Morgan and Squire (1984) demonstrated that, like H.M., lesioned monkeys have no difficulty learning or retaining motor-skill tasks. They tested the memories of the lesioned monkeys for two such tasks: the **lifesaver motor-skill task,** in which monkeys learn to obtain a lifesaver-shaped candy by quickly threading it along a metal rod and around a bend (see Figure 14.16), and the **barrier motor-skill task,** in which monkeys learn to obtain a fragile bread stick by manipulating it around a system of barriers. Monkeys with medial-temporal-lobe lesions learned and retained these two tasks as well as did control monkeys.

Diencephalic Amnesia in Monkeys

Aggleton and Mishkin (1983) were the first to demonstrate that non-recurring-items delayed nonmatching-to-sample task is sensitive to diencephalic damage in monkeys. They found that large lesions to the medial area of the thalamus produced severe deficits in the performance of this task. The subsequent finding that discrete lesions of the mediodorsal nuclei produce substantial deficits in nonrecurring-items delayed non-matching-to-sample performance (Zola-Morgan & Squire, 1985), but that mammillary body lesions do not (Aggleton & Mishkin, 1983), supports the widely held view that mediodorsal nucleus damage is an important, if not critical, factor in Korsakoff amnesia.

Memory Deficits in Monkeys with Prefrontal Cortex Damage

Because the prefrontal cortex contains no primary sensory or motor areas, it has long been assumed to be involved in complex cognitive functions, and studies of human clinical cases with prefrontal damage have borne this out. For example, you may recall from earlier in this chapter that Korsakoff patients and other patients with prefrontal damage often have difficulty remembering the temporal order of events. Monkeys with pre-

FIGURE 14.16 *A monkey performing the lifesaver motor-skill task. (Adapted from Zola-Morgan, 1984)*

frontal lesions display a pattern of performance deficits that suggests that they have a similar problem. Although monkeys with prefrontal lesions have no deficits on the nonrecurring-item delayed nonmatching-to-sample test (Bachevalier & Mishkin, 1986; Kowalska, Bachevalier, & Mishkin, 1984), they have difficulty performing similar tasks that require them to remember temporal order (Mishkin & Manning, 1978). For example, they have difficulty performing a **recurring-items delayed matching-to-sample task.** In this task the monkeys are presented on each trial with a sample, which is one of the same two items that they see on each trial. Then, after a delay they are presented with both items, and they must pick the sample to get a reward. Because the same two items are presented on each trial, the monkeys must remember which one of the two they have seen most recently and choose it.

Monkeys with prefrontal lesions also have difficulty performing the **delayed-alternation task** (Mishkin, 1957), which also involves memory for the temporal order of previous events. In this task, the position of the reward alternates between the two test objects from trial to trial. Thus, in order to receive a pellet, the monkey must remember where the pellet was on the preceding trial and select the other object.

The Performance of Human Amnesics on Memory Tests Designed for Monkeys

You have just read about how the deficits of monkeys with medial-temporal-lobe or diencephalic lesions on the nonrecurring-items delayed nonmatching-to-sample task have been used as a model to study the neural bases of human amnesia. The fact that the results of these monkey studies have generally been in accord with the results of human clinical case studies has supported the general validity of this model. Squire, Zola-Morgan, and Chen (1988) have completed the circle by testing human amnesics on the nonrecurring-items delayed nonmatching-to-sample task and on several other tests that have been used to assess memory in monkeys. The group of human amnesics, which included five patients with Korsakoff's syndrome and three who had suffered a stroke, displayed deficits similar to those displayed by monkeys with medial-temporal-lobe or diencephalic lesions. A similar study of human amnesics was conducted by Aggleton, Nicol, Huston, & Fairbairn (1988) and a similar conclusion reached. These studies would appear to remove all doubts about the usefulness of the monkey-model approach to the study of human amnesia.

Development of a Rat Model of Brain-Damage-Produced Amnesia

Although the nonrecurring-items delayed nonmatching-to-sample monkey model of brain-damage-produced amnesia has already contributed greatly to the study of the neural bases of amnesia, it has its limitations. The main one is that for ethical and financial reasons large-scale experiments with monkeys are impractical; most experiments with monkeys involve only a few subjects. Clearly, a comparable rat model would greatly increase the possibilities for conducting the large multiple-group studies required to answer many of the questions in the field. But can a rat perform the nonrecurring-items delayed nonmatching-to-sample task? The answer is "yes" (Aggleton, 1985; Rothblat & Hayes, 1987). The most promising of the nonrecurring-items delayed nonmatching-to-sample paradigms that

The sample object is placed over one food cup at one end. An object identical to the sample object and a novel object are placed over the two food cups at the other end.

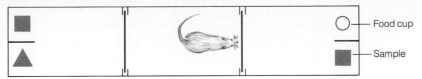

When the sliding door is raised exposing the sample, a trained food-deprived rat runs down to it and pushes it aside. Then a piece of food is deposited by a food-delivery mechanism into the exposed food cup.

The sample object is immediately removed by the experimenter, and the rat remains in the same end of the Mumby box until the prescribed delay period is over (e.g., for 1 minute).

Then, the other sliding door is raised to expose the two objects at the other end. Trained rats, remembering their previous encounter with the sample, run to the novel object, push it aside, and food is delivered to the exposed food cup. The sliding door at the other end is lowered behind the rat.

The rat then runs to the center of the Mumby box, and the sliding door is closed behind it. Then new objects are arranged for the next trial. One advantage of the Mumby-box paradigm is that the rats do not have to be handled either during or between trials.

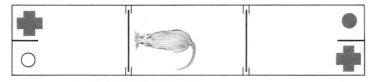

FIGURE 14.17 *The Mumby-box paradigm; nonrecurring-items delayed nonmatching-to-sample in rats.*

have been developed for rats is the **Mumby-box paradigm** (Mumby, Pinel, & Wood, 1989; Pinel & Mumby, 1989), which is illustrated in Figure 14.17. Amazingly, the performance of rats in the *Mumby box* is comparable to the performance of monkeys in the conventional nonrecurring-items delayed nonmatching-to-sample paradigm (see Figure 14.18). Preliminary results suggest that conjoint hippocampal and amygdalar lesions (Mumby, Pinel, & Wood, 1989) and ischemia-induced CA1 lesions (Wood, Mumby, Pinel, & Phillips, 1989) produce performance deficits in the Mumby-box paradigm similar to those observed in humans and monkeys.

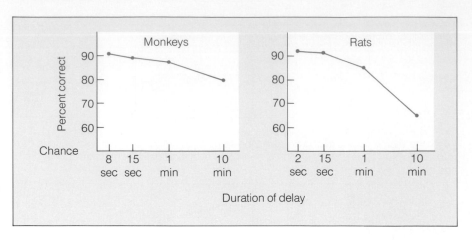

FIGURE 14.18 *A comparison of the performance of rats (Mumby, Pinel, & Wood, 1989) and the performance of monkeys (Zola-Morgan, Squire, & Mishkin, 1982) on the nonrecurring-items delayed nonmatching-to-sample task.*

14.6 Current Theoretical Issues in the Study of Memory and Amnesia

To bring the data already reviewed in this chapter into sharper focus, the remainder of the chapter dwells on four central theoretical issues: (1) Where are memories stored? (2) Are there different systems for explicit and implicit memory? (3) Does amnesia result from a defect in encoding, storage, or retrieval? and (4) Are the amnesias associated with medial-temporal-lobe and diencephalic damage distinct from one another?

Where Are Memories Stored?

Lashley's ground-breaking research on the neural basis of complex memories focused attention on the question of whether memories are stored diffusely throughout the brain or localized at particular sites. It now seems that the answer lies somewhere between these two extremes. Memory storage appears to be diffuse in the sense that no single center exists for the storage of all memories and in the sense that several parts of the brain appear to participate in the storage of the memory for any single experience, but it appears to be localized in the sense that there are specific areas of the brain that appear to be involved in memory storage.

The current consensus (see Mishkin & Appenzeller, 1987; Squire, 1987) is that memories of particular events are likely stored in the very sensory areas of the cortex that are involved in their initial analysis. The strongest support for this view comes from the study of the memorial functions of inferotemporal cortex. **Inferotemporal cortex,** you may recall from Chapter 8, is the site of the most complex level of processing in the visual system. Mishkin (1982) found that monkeys trained to criterion on the nonrecurring-items delayed nonmatching-to-sample task could not relearn the task after bilateral lesions of the inferotemporal cortex. After 1,500 trials, they did manage to improve their performance from 50% to 85% correct when the delay was only 10 seconds, thus indicating that they could perceive the difference between the test objects and learn the principle of the task; however, they could not perform the task at intervals greater than 1 minute.

Analogous lines of evidence have been used to implicate other areas of sensory cortex in memory storage. For example, it has been suggested that the **posterior parietal cortex** stores information about spatial location (Ungerleider & Mishkin, 1982) and that the **secondary somatosensory area** stores tactile pattern information (Mishkin, 1979).

Are There Different Systems for Explicit and Implicit Memory?

The memory of amnesic patients has traditionally been assessed by tests that require the conscious retrieval of information about past events (i.e., by *recall* or *recognition tests*). However, since the discovery that amnesic patients can display savings on certain memory tests in the absence of conscious recall or recognition, there has been a growing interest in such tests (Schacter, 1987).

On what kinds of tests do amnesic patients display implicit memory; that is, on what kinds of tests do they display savings in the absence of recall or recognition? H.M. was found to have implicit memory for various sensory-motor tasks, and subsequent research revealed that many amnesic patients retain sensory-motor skills without consciously remembering the training sessions that produced them. Since these early observations, amnesic patients have demonstrated implicit memory on three additional kinds of tests: tests of perceptual learning, classical conditioning, and priming. In a study of perceptual learning, amnesic patients who had been trained to read the mirror images of words retained the ability over a 3-month retention interval, although they often failed to recall the training sessions (Cohen & Squire, 1980). In a study of classical conditioning (Weiskrantz & Warrington, 1979), two amnesic patients learned a conditioned eyeblink response and retained it over 24 hours, despite the fact that just minutes after their training was completed, they had no conscious recollection of it. Most of the recent research on implicit memory in amnesic subjects has employed a task called **repetition priming.** A list of words is presented, and then later, the subjects are presented with fragments of the words that were in the list (e.g., __SS_SS_ _). Then they are asked to complete the fragments with the first words that come to mind. Despite the fact that they display no recall or recognition for the words on the list, they are often able to correctly complete the word fragments (e.g., ASSASSIN).

The current consensus is that implicit and explicit tests of memory tap two intrinsically different systems of memory storage. Supporting this view are two different kinds of evidence. First, a number of studies have shown that certain experimental manipulations can influence performance on implicit tests of memory without influencing performance on explicit tests and vice versa (see Graf & Schacter, 1985, 1987). Second, some amnesic subjects whose performance on explicit tests of memory is pitiful perform as well as normals on tests of implicit memory (Graf, Squire, & Mandler, 1984). Although several different theories have been proposed to account for the fact that many amnesics do not have deficits on implicit tests of memory, the most influential has been that popularized by Squire and his colleagues (e.g., Squire, 1987). They contend that there are two different memory storage systems in the brain, one for what they call **declarative memories** and one for what they call **procedural memories,** and that it is only the system for storing declarative memories that is disturbed in most amnesics. Squire describes these two systems in the following manner.

Declarative memory is explicit and accessible to conscious awareness, and it includes the facts, episodes, lists, and routes of everyday life. It can be declared, that is, brought to mind verbally as a proposition or nonverbally as an image. It includes both **episodic memory** (specific time-and-place events) as well as **semantic memory** (facts and general information gathered in the course of specific experiences). Declarative memory depends on the integrity of the neural systems damaged in amnesia as well as on the particular neural systems that store the information being learned.

In contrast, procedural memory is implicit, and it is accessible only through performance, by engaging in the skills or operations in which the knowledge is embedded. . . . In priming, preexisting representations are activated, and the information that is acquired is implicit and has other characteristics of procedural knowledge. (Squire, 1986, p. 1614)

Does Amnesia Reflect a Deficit in Encoding, Storage, or Retrieval?

Like the storage of information in a computer, the storage of information in memory is commonly considered to comprise three separate stages: (1) the information is encoded and entered, (2) it is stored, and (3) it is retrieved (see Jacoby, 1984). In terms of this model, amnesia might reflect a malfunction at any one of these three stages, or at any combination of them.

Because retrograde amnesia is by definition amnesia for events that precede the amnesia-producing brain disturbance, it cannot be the result of an encoding problem. There are two patterns of retrograde amnesia, one commonly attributed to a disruption of storage and one commonly attributed to a disruption of retrieval. The temporally graded form of retrograde amnesia—that is, the form of retrograde amnesia that preferentially disturbs recent memories and leaves more remote memories undisturbed—is commonly assumed to reflect a disturbance in the consolidation of memories during storage. As you have already learned, consolidation was at one time thought to be a relatively brief postencoding process that translated labile short-term memories into more stable long-term memories; however, the fact that some gradients of retrograde amnesia extend back for years suggests that consolidation is a very long-term process.

Retrograde amnesia that is not temporally graded is usually thought to reflect a deficiency in retrieval. Amnesics who have difficulty in recalling remote as well as recent events are assumed to have difficulty engaging in the complex cognitive activities involved in searching memory and retrieving the required piece of information. Memory retrieval is a very complex process, which involves much more than simply calling up stored representations of previous events. We usually think of our own memories as being accurate representations of real events, but they are not; they are complex *reconstructions*. Numerous experiments have shown that we remember only a few details of any event, and from these we reconstruct our memory of the event by filling in the gaps with best guesses of what was likely to have happened given the circumstances. The remembered details and best guesses meld inseparably together to form the memory.

The fact that most of our memories are best guesses rather than accurate representations complicates the interpretation of eyewitness testimony. Consider the results of the following classic experiment of Loftus and Palmer, 1974.

Students watched a film of a traffic accident. One group was asked, "About how fast were the cars going when they hit each other?" Another group was asked, "About how fast were the cars going when they smashed into each other?" The "hit" group estimated 34 miles an hour; the "smashed into" group estimated 41 miles an hour. When asked whether they remembered seeing broken glass—actually, the film showed no broken glass—only 14 percent of the hit group remembered broken glass, but 32 percent of the "smashed into" group remembered broken glass. (Kalat, 1985, p. 218)

Most efforts to characterize anterograde amnesia have focused on the anterograde amnesia of Korsakoff patients. Although the situation is far from clear, there appears to be growing support for the view that the anterograde amnesia of Korsakoff patients reflects a general cognitive deficit that affects encoding as well as retrieval. The theory is that the well-documented tendency of Korsakoff patients to rigidly focus on superficial aspects of their environment and to adhere to particular lines of thought to the exclusion of others makes it difficult for them at the time of encoding to establish the rich network of associations that facilitates subsequent recall. The same superficiality and rigidity makes it difficult for them at the time of retrieval to scan and evaluate various associations needed to reactivate and reconstruct the memory (e.g., Jacoby, 1983; Winocur, Kinsbourne, & Moscovitch, 1981).

Are the Amnesias Associated with Medial-Temporal-Lobe Damage and Diencephalic Damage Distinct from One Another?

There are two different views of the neural basis of amnesia. One is that all cases of amnesia are qualitatively the same. According to this view, differences between different cases of amnesia are either simply a matter of degree, or they reflect the effects of damage to parts of the brain not directly involved in the amnesia. The other view is that different parts of the brain involved in memory play different roles, and hence that damage to different parts of the memory system produce qualitatively different forms of amnesia. The debate over whether amnesia is best viewed as a unitary disorder or as a group of distinct memory disorders has focused on the differences between medial-temporal-lobe amnesia and diencephalic amnesia.

Although early analyses emphasized the similarity of medial-temporal-lobe amnesia and diencephalic amnesia, several recent studies have been aimed at showing that they are fundamentally different. One current hypothesis is that medial-temporal-lobe amnesia is a storage disorder and is thus associated with rapid forgetting, whereas diencephalic amnesia is an encoding and retrieval disorder and is thus associated with a normal rate of forgetting. The two attempts to provide experimental confirmation of this hypothesis used the same general procedure. In both experiments, an effort was made to insure that all groups began with equivalent memory for the test material by allowing amnesic patients more time than the normal subjects to learn the test material. It is possible to compare forgetting rates only if retention is equal to begin with. One of the experiments compared normal humans, H.M., and a sample of Korsakoff patients (Huppert & Piercy, 1978, 1979); the other compared normal monkeys,

monkeys with combined hippocampus and amygdala lesions, and monkeys with mediodorsal nucleus lesions (Zola-Morgan & Squire, 1982). The results of both studies suggest that medial-temporal-lobe damage accelerates forgetting and that diencephalic damage does not. When the diencephalic amnesics were given enough time to learn the test material, their forgetting curve was not substantially different from that of normal control subjects.

The conclusion that the medial temporal lobes and the diencephalon are not part of a single memorial system has received further support from the finding that destruction of the *fornix*, a major pathway between them, does not seem to have amnesic effects in either humans (Squire & Moore, 1979) or monkeys (Zola-Morgan, Dabrowska, Moss, & Mahut, 1983).

14.7 Conclusion: The Ironic Case of R.M.

This chapter began with the case of H.M., and you learned how the in-depth study of this one case and of a few other less well-known cases of medial-temporal-lobe amnesia (e.g., R.B.) has led to our current theories of the role of the medial temporal lobes in memory. Next was a discussion of Korsakoff's syndrome and of the memory deficits produced in Korsakoff patients by their diencephalic and prefrontal damage. The role of cholinergic dysfunction in the amnesia of Alzheimer's disease was described next, followed by an explanation of how gradients of retrograde amnesia produced by accidental closed-head injuries and electroconvulsive shock have been used to estimate the time course of consolidation. Finally, you learned how the development of the nonrecurring-items delayed nonmatching-to-sample model of amnesia in monkeys has provided a means of investigating brain-damage-produced amnesia in controlled experiments.

In the introduction, I said that this chapter would end on an ironic note with the case of R.M., and so it shall. The case of R.M. differs from the other cases of amnesia described in this chapter in two ways: first, the case has not been previously reported, and second, R.M. is himself a biopsychologist, an expert in circadian rhythms who was cited in the last chapter. R.M. fell on his head while skiing, and when he regained consciousness, he was suffering from both retrograde and anterograde amnesia. For several hours, he could recall little of his previous life: he could not remember if he was married, he could not remember where he lived, and he could not remember where he worked. Also, many of the things that happened to him in the hours after his accident were immediately forgotten as soon as his attention was diverted from them. In essence, his was a classic case of posttraumatic amnesia. Like H.M., he was trapped in the present with only a cloudy past and seemingly no future. The irony of the situation was that during these few hours, when R.M. could recall few of the events of his own life, his thoughts repeatedly drifted back to thoughts of one person—a person that he remembered hearing about somewhere in his muddled past. Through the cloud he remembered H.M., his fellow prisoner of the present, and he wondered if the same fate lay in store for him.

R.M. is now fully recovered and looks back on what he can recall of his experience with bemusement and puzzlement and with a certain feeling of empathy for H.M. R.M. received a reprieve, but his experience left him with a better appreciation for the situation of those, like H.M., who are serving life sentences. For the amusement of my fellow biopsychologists, I have coined a term for R.M.'s experience: *hypermetaamnesia*, the loss of memory of everything except H.M.

Food for Thought

1. The study of the anatomy of memory has come a long way since H.M.'s misfortune. What kind of research on this topic do you think will prove to be most important in the next decade?

2. What are the advantages and shortcomings of animal models of amnesia?

3. Using examples from your own experience, compare implicit and explicit memory.

ADDITIONAL READING

The following two sources provide excellent readable reviews of much of the material in this chapter.

Mishkin, M., & Appenzeller, T. (1987). The anatomy of memory. *Scientific American, 256,* 80–89.

Squire, L. R. (1987). *Memory and the brain.* New York: Oxford University Press.

KEY TERMS

To help you study the material in this chapter, all of the key terms—those that have appeared in bold type—are listed and briefly defined here.

Amyloid plaques. Tangles of degenerating neural fibers found in the brains of patients with Alzheimer's disease.

Anterograde amnesia. Loss of memory for events occurring after the amnesia-inducing event.

Barrier motor-skill task. A task in which monkeys learn to obtain a fragile bread stick by manipulating it around a system of barriers.

Bilateral medial temporal lobectomy. The removal of the medial portions of both temporal lobes, including the amygdalas and hippocampuses; H.M.'s operation.

Block-tapping memory-span test. A nonverbal equivalent of the digit-span test.

CA1 subfield. An area of the hippocampus; R.B.'s ischemic brain damage was restricted to the pyramidal cell layer of this area.

Consolidation. The hypothetical process by which a memory is transferred from a short-term mode of storage to a long-term mode of storage.

Declarative memory. Memory for which there is conscious awareness; a memory that can be declared (i.e., stated).

Delayed-alternation task. The subject must choose between the same two items on each trial, and the correct choice is the item that was wrong on the previous trial.

Digit span. The standard measure of verbal short-term memory.

Digit span +1 test. Each time the subject correctly repeats a sequence of digits, the next test item is the same sequence with an additional digit added to the end of it.

Electroconvulsive shock (ECS). A massive electric shock to the head that induces a convulsion.

Engram. The hypothetical change in the brain responsible for the storage of a memory.

Episodic memory. Memory for specific events.

Explicit memory. Memories that result from the deliberate effort to remember; memory expressed on tests of recall or recognition.

Global amnesia. Amnesia for information in all sensory modalities.

Implicit memory. Memory that results in improved performance without conscious recall or recognition.

Incomplete-pictures test. A test of memory involving the improved ability to identify fragmented figures that have been previously observed.

Infarction. Area of cell death produced by an interruption of blood supply.

Inferotemporal cortex. A site of complex visual processing.

Ischemia. Shortage in blood supply to an area that results in the death of cells.

Islands of memory. Memories for isolated events that occurred during periods that have otherwise been totally forgotten.

Korsakoff's syndrome. A memory disorder that develops in individuals who chronically consume alcohol; the memory deficits appear to result from a combination of diencephalic and prefrontal damage.

Lifesaver motor-skill task. A task in which monkeys learn to obtain a lifesaver-shaped piece of candy by threading it along a metal rod and around a bend.

Lobectomy. An operation in which a lobe, or a major part of one, is removed from the brain.

Lobotomy. An operation in which a lobe, or a major part of one, is separated from the brain by a large cut, but is not removed.

Mammillary bodies. A pair of hypothalamic nuclei; damage to these nuclei was originally thought to produce the memory deficits associated with Korsakoff's syndrome.

Matching-to-sample test. A sample stimulus is momentarily presented, followed by a delay, and then the subject must identify the sample stimulus from a group of test stimuli.

Mediodorsal nuclei. Damage to these thalamic nuclei is thought to be responsible for some of the memory deficits associated with Korsakoff's syndrome.

Mirror-drawing test. A test in which the subject traces a star while watching her or his hand in a mirror.

Mumby-box paradigm. A variation of the nonrecurring-items delayed nonmatching-to-sample paradigm developed for rats.

Neurofibrils. Thread-like structures in the neural cytoplasm of patients with Alzheimer's disease.

Nonrecurring-items delayed nonmatching-to-sample task. A task in which the subject is presented with an unfamiliar sample object and then, after a delay, is presented with a choice between the same object and another unfamiliar object; the correct choice is the non-sample object.

Nootropics. Memory-improving agents; choline has been hypothesized to be a nootropic.

Posterior parietal cortex. An area of cortex thought to store information about spatial location.

Posttraumatic amnesia (PTA). Amnesia produced by closed-head injuries, which typically includes both retrograde and anterograde memory deficits.

Principle of equipotentiality. The idea that all parts of the neocortex play an equal role in the storage of memories for complex tasks.

Principle of mass action. The idea that memories for complex tasks are stored diffusely throughout the neocortex.

Proactive interference. The interfering effects of performing one task on performance of a subsequent one.

Procedural memory. Memory that is revealed by improved performance without conscious recall; also referred to as implicit memory.

Pyramidal cell layer. A major layer of cell bodies in the hippocampus.

Recurring-items delayed matching-to-sample task. A sample object that the subject has seen on each previous trial is presented, then after a delay it and the other object seen on previous trials is presented; the subject must choose the sample; monkeys with prefrontal lesions have difficulty performing this task.

Repetition priming. A test of implicit memory in which a list of words is presented; later, fragments of the original words are presented and the subject is asked to complete the fragments.

Retrograde amnesia. Backward-acting memory deficit; loss of memory for information learned before the amnesia-inducing event.

Rotary pursuit test. A test in which the subject tries to keep the end of a stylus in contact with a target rotating on a turntable.

Secondary somatosensory area. An area of cortex thought to store tactile memories.

Semantic memory. A memory for facts and general information gathered in the course of specific experiences.

Temporal stem. A fiber bundle lying just above the hippocampus; damage to the temporal stem has been hypothesized to be responsible for medial-temporal-lobe amnesia.

15

Neuroplasticity: Development, Learning, and Neurotransplantation

Most of us tend to think of the nervous system as a three-dimensional array of neural elements "wired" together in a massive network of circuits. The sheer magnitude and complexity of this wiring-diagram concept of the nervous system, with its billions upon billions of synaptic connections, is undeniably staggering, but it nevertheless sells the nervous system short by failing to capture one of its most important features. The nervous system is not a static network of interconnected elements as is implied by the wiring-diagram model. It is a plastic, living organ, which grows and changes continuously in response to the interaction between its genetic programs and its environment. These neuroplastic processes are the subject of this chapter.

This chapter has three major sections, each of which deals with a different aspect of neuroplasticity. Section 15.1 is about neural development; it describes how the billions of specialized neurons that compose the nervous system are created, and how they travel to the appropriate location of the body and establish appropriate synaptic contacts. Section 15.2 is about the ways in which the nervous system changes in response to experience; in particular, it describes the search for the neural changes that underlie learning. Section 15.3 deals with the reaction of

neurons to damage; it discusses neural degeneration, regeneration, and the exciting new field of neurotransplantation. The following are the three major sections of this chapter:

15.1 **Neural Development**
15.2 **Neuroplasticity in Simple Neural Systems: The Cellular Bases of Learning**
15.3 **Neural Degeneration, Regeneration, and Neurotransplantation**

The Simple-Systems Approach

This chapter features an approach to the study of the neural basis of behavior called the **simple-systems approach.** In this chapter, you will encounter numerous studies that at first appear to be strange fodder for students of biopsychology. You will read about studies of fish, chicks, frogs, salamanders, and snails. Why have researchers interested in neuroplasticity dedicated their lives to the study of such an odd assortment of creatures? The answer in one word is "simplicity." There is a great advantage in studying the relation between neural plasticity and behavior by focusing on neural circuits that are complex enough to mediate behavioral change, but simple enough to be analyzed neuron by neuron and synapse by synapse.

15.1 Neural Development

In the beginning there is a *zygote*, a single cell formed by the amalgamation of an ovum and a sperm. The zygote divides to form two daughter cells (Why aren't they ever called son cells?), and these two divide to form four, and these four divide to form eight, and so on . . . until a mature organism is produced. Of course, there must be more to it than this; if there were not, each of us would have ended up like a bowl of rice pudding—an amorphous mass of homogeneous cells. To save us from this fate, three things other than cell multiplication must happen. First, the cells must *differentiate;* they must develop specialized structural, biochemical, and physiological properties—some must become muscle cells, some must become multipolar neurons, some must become glial cells, and so on. Second, each type of cell must make its way to an appropriate site in the body and align itself with the cells around it to form the various organs of the body. Third, they must establish the connections or functional relations with other cells that are necessary for them to function properly. Section 15.1 describes how neurons accomplish these three things.

Three weeks after conception, the tissue that is destined to develop into the human nervous system becomes recognizable as the **neural plate,** a small patch of ectodermal tissue (**ectoderm** is the outermost layer of cells) on the dorsal surface of the developing embryo. As illustrated in Figure 15.1, the neural plate gradually begins to fold, thus forming the so-called *neural groove,* and ultimately, when the edges of the groove fuse, the **neural tube.** The inside of the neural tube eventually becomes the *spinal canal* and the *ventricles.* By the end of the fourth week, the brain becomes visible as a swelling at one end of the tube. During the transformation of the neural plate into the neural tube, the number of cells destined to develop into the nervous system remains relatively constant, at about 125,000; however, once the tube has formed, they *proliferate* (increase in number) rapidly. By 40 days of age, three swellings in the neural tube are clearly apparent, and these ultimately develop into *forebrain, midbrain,* and *hindbrain* structures (see Figures 2.18 and 2.19).

This section of the chapter is divided into five subsections, which correspond to the five phases of neurodevelopment: (1) induction of the neural plate, (2) neural proliferation, (3) migration and aggregation, (4) axon growth and the formation of synapses, and (5) neuron death and synapse rearrangement.

Induction of the Neural Plate

Prior to the development of the neural plate, the cells of the dorsal ectoderm are **totipotential**—that is, they all have the potential to develop into any type of body cell—but with the development of the neural plate, they lose their totipotency. For example, before the induction of the neural plate, if the part of the ectoderm that would normally have developed into the forebrain is transplanted in the area of the embryo that normally develops into hair, the transplanted tissue develops into hair. However, if the same transplantation test is performed after the induction of the neural plate, the transplanted tissue from the forebrain area of the neural plate develops into forebrain tissue regardless of where it is implanted.

The neural plate seems to develop under the direction of chemical signals from the underlying **mesoderm layer.** Tissue taken from the dorsal

Dorsal surface
of embryo

Cross section of dorsal
ectoderm of embryo

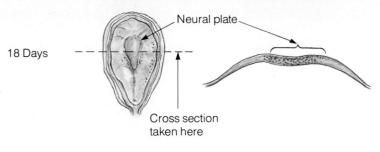

18 Days

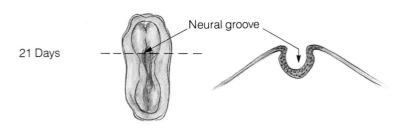

21 Days

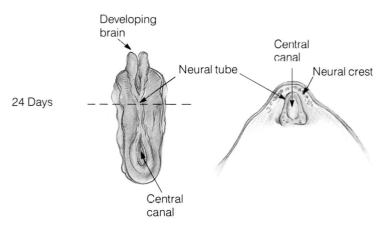

24 Days

FIGURE 15.1 *How the neural plate develops into the neural tube during the third and fourth weeks of human embryologic development. (Adapted from Cowan, 1979.)*

mesoderm of one embryo and implanted beneath the ventral ectoderm (which normally does not develop into nervous tissue) of another, induces the development of an extra neural plate on the ventral surface of the host. One of the most fanciful demonstrations of **induction** is one that may require the abandonment of the expression, "as scarce as hen's teeth." Believe it or not, Kollar and Fisher (1980) induced teeth to grow from the ectodermal cells of chick embryos. First, from a mouse embryo, they cut a tiny piece of mesoderm from under the portion of the ectoderm that would normally have developed into the mouse's mouth. Then, they implanted this mesoderm next to the ectoderm of a chick embryo, and low and behold, the overlying cells of the chick ectoderm developed into teeth.

Neural Proliferation

Once the lips of the invaginated neural plate have fused to create the neural tube, the cells of the tube begin to rapidly increase in number.

However, proliferation does not occur simultaneously or equally in all parts of the tube. In each species, the cells in different parts of the neural tube proliferate in a characteristic sequence that is responsible for the pattern of swelling and folding that gives each brain its species-characteristic shape.

Most cell division in the neural tube occurs in a layer called the **ventricular zone,** which is adjacent to the *ventricle* (the fluid-filled center of the tube). Figure 15.2 illustrates the division cycle of one neural-tube cell. Each dividing cell sends out two tentacle-like processes, one to the ventricular surface of the tube and one to its outer surface. Using these processes, the cell pulls itself away from the ventricular surface into the center of the ventricular zone. This is where the DNA of the cell is doubled in preparation for cell division. Then, the cell moves back to the ventricular surface and divides. After division, the two daughter cells either divide again or migrate to another part of the tube.

Migration and Aggregation

Migration During the period of **migration,** a temporary network of glial cells, called **radial glial cells** (see Figure 15.3), is apparent in the developing neural tube. Migrating neurons appear to move along these radial glial cells to their destinations (Rakic, Stensas, Sayre, & Sidman, 1974). As the cells of the neural tube begin to proliferate, most migrate away from the ventricular zone and form a progressively thickening layer of cells called the *intermediate zone* (see Figure 15.3). After the intermediate zone is well established, some of the cells being produced in the ventricular zone migrate to form a layer between the ventricular and intermediate zones. The cells that migrate to this so-called *subventricular zone* are destined to be either glial cells or interneurons. Other newly created forebrain cells begin to migrate through these layers to establish a layer of cells called the *cortical plate*, which eventually develops into the layers of the cerebral cortex. Because the cells of the deepest of the six layers of cortex arrive at their destination first, the cells of progressively higher layers must migrate through them; this is referred to as the **inside-out pattern of cortical development** (Rakic, 1974). When the migration of cells away from the ventricular zone is complete, the cells remaining there develop into *ependymal cells,*

FIGURE 15.2 *The typical cell-division cycle of a neural tube cell. (Adapted from Cowan, 1979.)*

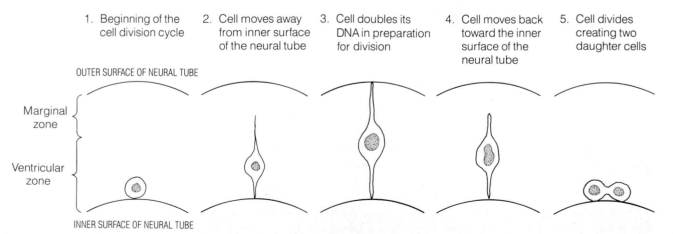

1. Beginning of the cell division cycle
2. Cell moves away from inner surface of the neural tube
3. Cell doubles its DNA in preparation for division
4. Cell moves back toward the inner surface of the neural tube
5. Cell divides creating two daughter cells

OUTER SURFACE OF NEURAL TUBE

Marginal zone

Ventricular zone

INNER SURFACE OF NEURAL TUBE

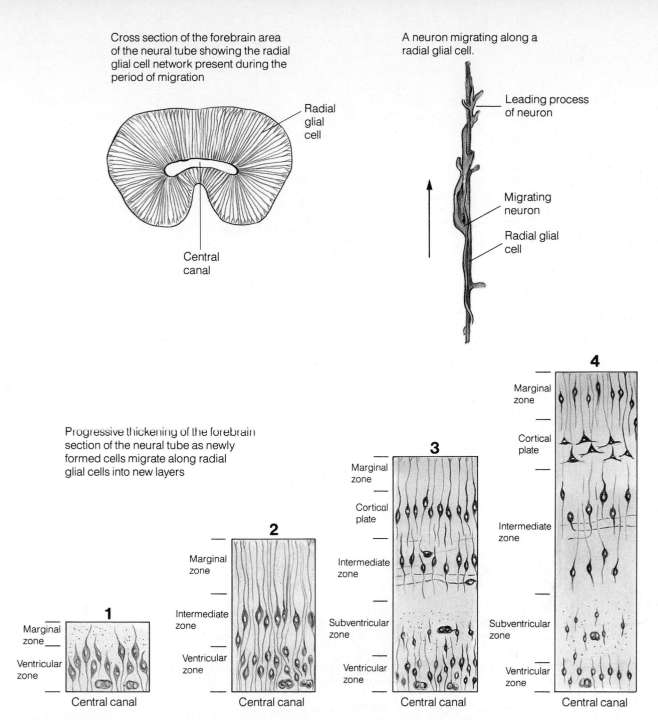

Cross section of the forebrain area of the neural tube showing the radial glial cell network present during the period of migration

Radial glial cell

Central canal

A neuron migrating along a radial glial cell.

Leading process of neuron

Migrating neuron

Radial glial cell

Progressive thickening of the forebrain section of the neural tube as newly formed cells migrate along radial glial cells into new layers

1

Marginal zone

Ventricular zone

Central canal

2

Marginal zone

Intermediate zone

Ventricular zone

Central canal

3

Marginal zone

Cortical plate

Intermediate zone

Subventricular zone

Ventricular zone

Central canal

4

Marginal zone

Cortical plate

Intermediate zone

Subventricular zone

Ventricular zone

Central canal

FIGURE 15.3 *New cells are created by cell division in the ventricular zone of the developing neural tube; then, they migrate out of the ventricular zone to create new layers of cells. Shown here is the expansion of the forebrain area of the tube.*

which form the lining of the ventricles of the brain and central canal of the spinal cord.

The **neural crest** is a structure that is situated just dorsal to and to both sides of the neural tube (see Figure 15.1). It is formed from cells that break off from the neural tube. There is a great interest in the migration of neural crest cells because they develop into the neurons and glia of the peripheral nervous system, and thus must migrate over great distances. Interestingly, it appears to be the media through which they travel, rather than the information contained within the cells themselves, that directs them to their destination. If cells are transplanted from one part of the neural crest to another, they adopt the route characteristic of their new location (Le Douarin, 1982). The **differential adhesion hypothesis** is that neural crest cells migrate through tissue by following pathways to which they tend to adhere.

Aggregation   Once developing neurons make their way to the general area in which they will function in the adult nervous system, they must align themselves in precise relation to the other cells that have migrated there so that the various gross structures of the nervous system are formed. This process is called **aggregation.** Aggregation is thought to be mediated by molecules called **neural cell adhesion molecules,** which are located on the surface of the neurons and recognize other neurons of the same type and adhere to them in specific orientations (Hoffman & Edelman, 1983; Rutishauser, Acheson, Hall, Mann, & Sunshine, 1988).

Axon Growth and the Formation of Synapses

Once neurons have migrated to their appropriate position, axons and dendrites grow from them to other cells. Intuitively, one would expect that these neural projections would be established in a very precise, species-characteristic manner; it is hard to imagine how the nervous system could work if its parts were not wired up according to a prescribed plan. In fact, accurate and stereotyped patterns of axonal growth have been demonstrated in a variety of systems. For example, the point-to-point mapping of retinal ganglion cells onto the surface of the optic tectum in frogs, salamanders, and other lower invertebrates has been well documented (e.g., Gaze, 1974; Jacobson & Hunt, 1973), as have the specific patterns of outgrowth of motor neurons to various muscles in chicks (e.g., Landmesser, 1978). Particularly convincing evidence of the accuracy with which axons can grow has come from studies in which the same distinctive neuron is labeled with horseradish peroxidase in several different embryos of the same species. Using this method, particular neurons in developing insect nervous systems (e.g., Bastiani, Doe, Helfand, & Goodman, 1985) and developing fish spinal cords (Kuwada, 1986) have been shown to grow by complex, highly stereotyped routes to particular target cells.

At each growing tip of an axon or dendrite is an amoeba-like structure called a **growth cone** (see Figure 15.4), which extends and retracts finger-like cytoplasmic extensions called *filopodia.* Three hypotheses have been proposed to explain how growth cones find their way to their appropriate destination: the chemoaffinity hypothesis, the blueprint hypothesis, and the topographic-gradient hypothesis.

Chemoaffinity Hypothesis   In 1943, Roger Sperry conducted a marvelous series of experiments. In one key study, Sperry cut the optic nerves of frogs, rotated their eyeballs 180°, and waited for the **retinal ganglion cells,** which compose the optic nerve, to *regenerate* (regrow)—frogs, unlike mammals, have retinal ganglion cells that are capable of regeneration. Once regeneration was complete, Sperry used a convenient behavioral test to assess the frogs' visual capacities. As illustrated in Figure 15.5, when a

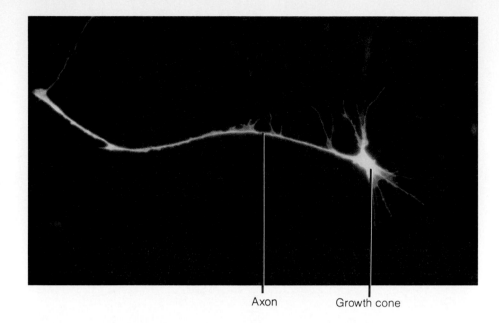

Axon   Growth cone

FIGURE 15.4 *A growth cone.*

lure was dangled behind the frogs, they struck forward, thus indicating that their visual world, like their eyes, had been rotated 180°. Frogs whose eyes had been rotated, but whose optic nerves had not been cut, responded in exactly the same way. This was strong evidence that each retinal neuron had grown back to the same part of the **optic tectum** (the main destination of retinal ganglion cells in lower vertebrates) on which it had originally synapsed. A subsequent neuroanatomical study confirmed this conclusion (Attardi & Sperry, 1963).

Sperry's classic studies of regeneration in the optic nerve were the basis of his **chemoaffinity hypothesis** of axonal development (Sperry, 1963). He hypothesized that each postsynaptic surface in the nervous system bears a specific chemical label, and that each growing axon is attracted by the label of its postsynaptic target during the process of axon growth and synapse formation. The chemoaffinity hypothesis receives general support from the discovery of several chemicals that have the capacity to attract growing axons. The most well known of these is **nerve growth factor** (NGF), which has the ability to attract the growing axons of sympathetic nervous system neurons. Levi-Montalcini (1952, 1975) discovered that injections of nerve growth factor into the brains of neonatal rats cause the axons of sympathetic neurons to grow into the spinal cord (which they normally never do) and from there into the brain.

The chemoaffinity hypothesis accounts for some aspects of axon growth, but it cannot explain why targets transplanted to novel positions become incorrectly innervated. For example, when Whitelaw and Holly-day (1983) implanted an extra thigh segment in the legs of developing chick embryos so that the sequence was thigh, thigh, calf, foot instead of the normal thigh, calf, foot, the second thigh segment became innervated by axons that normally would have innervated the calf.

Blueprint Hypothesis Although the chemoaffinity hypothesis explains how an axon can grow to its correct destination, it does not explain how it can follow the very same route in every member of the species. This

When an insect is dangled in front of a normal frog, the frog strikes at it accurately with its tongue.

When the eye is rotated 180° without cutting the optic nerve, the frog misdirects its strikes by 180°.

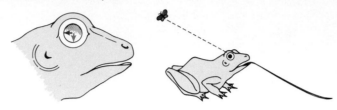

When the optic nerve is cut and the eye rotated by 180°, at first the frog is blind, but once the optic nerve has regenerated the frog misdirects its strikes by 180°.

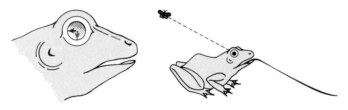

This suggests that the cut axons of the optic nerve grew back out to their original synaptic targets in the optic tectum.

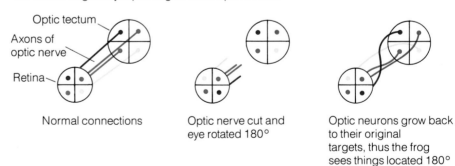

Optic tectum

Axons of optic nerve

Retina

Normal connections

Optic nerve cut and eye rotated 180°

Optic neurons grow back to their original targets, thus the frog sees things located 180° from their actual position

FIGURE 15.5 *Sperry's classic study of eye rotation and regeneration.*

shortcoming led to the proposal of the **blueprint hypothesis** (Singer, Nordlander, & Egar, 1979). According to the blueprint hypothesis, the undeveloped nervous system contains various chemical and/or mechanical trails (blueprints) that growing axons follow to their destinations. **Pioneer growth cones,** the first growth cones to grow into a particular area of the developing nervous system, are presumed to follow the correct trail by interacting with the cells along the route (Bentley & Keshishian, 1982). Later growth cones seem to just follow the routes blazed by the pioneers. The tendency of growing axons to grow along the same path established by preceding axons is called **fasciculation.** When pioneer axons in the fish spinal cord were destroyed with a laser, subsequent axons did not reach their usual destinations (Kuwada, 1986).

The blueprint hypothesis cannot account for the fact that some axons are capable of growing to their targets when their starting points have been shifted. For example, when Lance-Jones and Landmesser (1980) cut a small portion of the spinal cord from a chick embryo, inverted it, and implanted it back into the same embryo, the axons grew out to their original target muscles despite the fact that they started from a new position (see Figure 15.6).

The pathways normally followed by the motor neuron axons growing out from the spinal cord of a chick embryo to two target muscles.

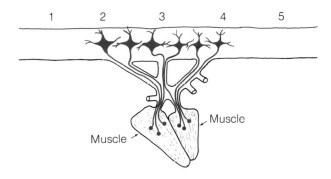

Muscle

Muscle

Before the motor neuron axons grew to their target muscles, Lance-Jones and Landmesser cut out a section from a developing chick spinal cord and reversed it.

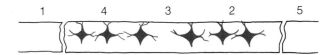

Although the cell bodies of the motor neurons were now in an abnormal position, they grew out to their appropriate muscle.

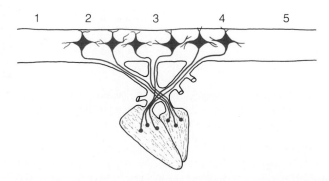

FIGURE 15.6 *An illustration of the study of Lance-Jones and Landmesser (1980). A section of spinal cord was cut from a chick embryo, inverted, and reimplanted. The motor neuron axons grew out to their original target muscles, despite the inversion. (Adapted from Hopkins & Brown, 1984.)*

Topographic-Gradient Hypothesis Much of the axonal growth in complex nervous systems involves growth from one topographic array of neurons to another. The neurons on one array project to another, maintaining the same topographic relation that they had on the first; for example, the topographic map of the retina (see Figure 15.7) is maintained on the optic tectum by the systematic distribution of the synapses of retinal ganglion cell axons. Prior to the last 10 or 15 years, it was widely believed that the integrity of such topographical relations was maintained by point-to-point chemoaffinity. Although such a rigid plan may prevail in invertebrates and in some simple vertebrate systems, research on the vertebrate visual system—the very system that spawned the chemoaffinity hypothesis—has led to the less restrictive **topographic-gradient hypothesis** (Easter, Purves, Rakic, & Spitzer, 1985). According to this hypothesis, axons grow out from one sheet of cell bodies, such as the retina, to their target structure, which is another sheet of target cells, such as the optic tectum. Once there, they arrange their synaptic terminals according to the relative position of their cell bodies on the original sheet (e.g., the retina), as defined by their relative position on two intersecting right-angle gradients; for example, their relative position on an up-down gradient and on a left-right gradient.

There are three kinds of studies supporting the topographic-gradient hypothesis. In the first (e.g., Gaze & Sharma, 1970; Yoon, 1971), the optic nerves of mature frogs were cut and their pattern of regeneration was

FIGURE 15.7 *The regeneration of the optic nerve of the frog after portions of either the retina or the optic tectum have been destroyed.*

Axons normally grow out from the frog retina to fill up the available space on the optic tectum in an orderly fashion. This was initially taken as evidence for the idea that there was accurate point-to-point growth (i.e., for the chemoaffinity theory).

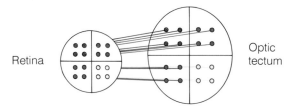

However, the following two observations challenged the point-to-point (i.e. chemoaffinity) interpretation.

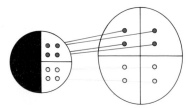

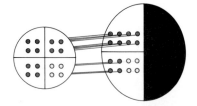

A. When half the retina was destroyed and the optic nerve cut, the remaining retinal ganglion cells regenerated their axonal projections systematically over the entire tectum.

B. When half the optic tectum was destroyed and the optic nerve cut, the axons of the retinal ganglion cells grew back out in an orderly fashion to the remaining tectum.

assessed after parts of either the retina or the optic tectum had been destroyed. In both cases, axons did not grow out to their original points of connection as predicted by the chemoaffinity or blueprint hypotheses; they grew out to fill the available space in an orderly fashion. Axons from the remaining portion of a lesioned retina spread out in an orderly fashion to fill all of the available space. Conversely, axons from an intact retina growing to a lesioned tectum "squeezed in" so that the retina was completely mapped on the remaining portion of the tectum. These results are illustrated schematically in Figure 15.7.

In the second kind of study supporting the topographic-gradient hypothesis, the connectivity between the retina and optic tectum was determined at different stages of development. It was found that the synaptic connections between eyes and tectums are established long before either reaches full size. As both the eyes and the optic tectums grow, the synaptic connections that were initially formed by retinal ganglion cells on the optic tectum gradually shift to other tectal neurons so that the retina is always faithfully mapped onto the tectum, regardless of their relative sizes during development (Gaze, Keating, Ostberg, & Chung, 1979; Reh & Constantine-Paton, 1984).

The third and most compelling kind of support for the topographic-gradient hypothesis comes from the studies of Jacobson (1968). When he rotated the eyes of frog embryos 180° at an early stage in their development, the axons grew out from the eye to the tectum in the normal pattern (see Figure 15.8); for example, the new top of the retina (the former bottom) grew to the area of the tectum that normally receives inputs from the top. In contrast, when frog eyes were rotated 180° just 20 hours later in their development, the eventual projections of the retina were reversed in both their front-back and top-bottom dimensions (see Figure 15.8). The key result, as far as the topographic-gradient hypothesis is concerned, occurred in frog embryos whose eyes were rotated 180°, at an intervening stage. The eventual retinal projections of frog embryos whose eyes were rotated at this stage were normal in the up-down dimension, but inverted in the front-back dimension (see Figure 15.8). Thus, the growth of the retinal projections is guided by two intersecting gradients that are established at different stages of development.

Neuron Death and Synapse Rearrangement

Neural development seems to operate on the principle of survival of the fittest: More neurons and synapses are produced than are required, they compete for limited resources, and only the fittest survive. Three findings suggest that neurons die because of their failure to compete successfully for some limited life-preserving factor received from their targets, which is believed to be nerve growth factor for some neurons. First, the implantation of extra target sites decreases neuron death. For example, Hollyday and Hamburger (1976) grafted an extra limb on one side of a chick embryo, thus providing motor neurons on that side with a greater target area, and fewer motor neurons on that side died. Second, destroying some of the neurons growing into an area before the period of cell death increases the target sites available to the remaining neurons and increases the survival rate (e.g., Pilar, Landmesser, & Burstein, 1980). And third, increasing the number of axons that initially innervate a target decreases the proportion

The results of Jacobson suggest that the retinal ganglion cell axons grow to targets on the optic tectum that are defined by positions on two intersecting gradients (up-down and back-front). Control frogs did not have their eyes rotated 180°, whereas experimental frogs had their eyes rotated 180° at one of three different stages of development.

Control frogs display a normal pattern of axon growth from the retina to the optic tectum.

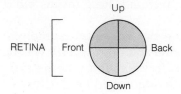

RETINA

Up

Front · Back

Down

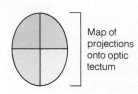

Map of projections onto optic tectum

Early rotation of eye by 180° does not affect the pattern of projections to the retina; the retinal ganglion cells grow to the destinations that are normal for their new position.

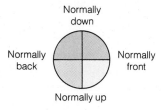

Normally down

Normally back · Normally front

Normally up

Late rotation of the eye by 180° reverses the projections in both the up-down and back-front dimensions; by this stage the destination of each axon appears to have been determined and each grows into its prescribed destination regardless of the rotation.

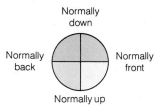

Normally down

Normally back · Normally front

Normally up

Rotation of the eye by 180° at an intermediate stage reverses the projections in the front-back dimension but not in the up-down dimension; by this stage the destination of each axon appears to have been determined in terms of the front-back gradient, but not in terms of the up-down gradient.

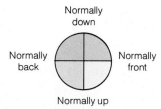

Normally down

Normally back · Normally front

Normally up

FIGURE 15.8 *A schematic representation of the effects of eye rotation on the growth of the axons from the eye to the optic tectum at different stages of the frog's development. These results suggest that the retinal projections are guided by two gradients that are established at different stages of development.*

that survive. One purpose of neuron death may simply be to match the number of innervating neurons with the receptive capacity of the targets. However, the fact that neurons establishing incorrect connections are particularly vulnerable to neuron death suggests that cell death also increases the overall accuracy of neural connections (Lamb, 1984).

During the period of neuron death, many synaptic contacts disappear, but there are also many new ones being formed. Thus, during this period, there is a rearrangement of synaptic contacts, rather than a simple reduction in their number. Most developing axons initially establish a few synaptic contacts with each of many different postsynaptic cells, but after rearrangement, each axon is typically left with many synapses on each of a smaller number of cells. This general principle of synapse rearrangement is illustrated in Figure 15.9.

One particularly noteworthy example of synapse rearrangement occurs in *layer IV of the primary visual cortex* (see Chapter 7). In the newborn monkey and cat (and presumably human), input into layer IV from the left and right eyes is intermingled. However, during the course of development, the input from the two eyes becomes segregated into alternating stripes that are about 0.5 millimeter wide. Thus, if a radioactive substance is injected into one eye of an adult animal and layer IV is later examined, well-defined columns of radioactivity are readily apparent (LeVay, Stryker, & Shatz, 1978)—see Figure 7.19.

Diffuse pattern of synaptic contact characteristic of early stages of development

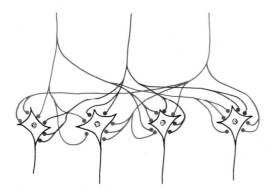

More focused pattern of synaptic contact present after synapse rearrangement

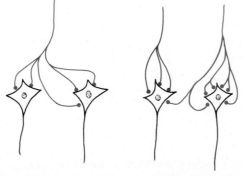

FIGURE 15.9 *During neuron death and synapse rearrangement, the synaptic contacts of each axon become focused on a small number of cells.*

Effects of Experience on Neural Development

Neural circuits must be used in order for them to develop normally. For example, the primary visual cortices of animals reared in the dark have been found to have fewer synapses (e.g., Cragg, 1975) and fewer dendritic spines (e.g., Valverde, 1971); dark-reared animals have deficits in depth (e.g., Walk & Walters, 1973) and pattern (e.g., Tees, 1968; Tees & Cartwright, 1972) perception as adults. The competitive nature of synapse formation is illustrated by the fact that the disruptive effects of early deprivation of one eye on the development of the visual circuits associated with that eye are greater if the other eye is not also deprived. After one eye has been deprived of input early in life, there is both a marked reduction in the number of cortical neurons that can be activated by stimulation of that eye and an increase in the number of cortical neurons that can be activated by stimulation of the nondeprived eye. Hubel, Wiesel, and LeVay (1977) have shown that the stripes of input to layer IV of the primary visual cortex are much wider from the nondeprived eye than from the deprived eye.

Another approach that demonstrates the effects of experience on neural development has been to compare the brains of rats raised in isolation in barren laboratory cages to those of rats raised in large colony cages with access to a variety of complex toys. The cortices of the rats raised in the complex environments have been shown to be thicker (Bennett, Diamond, Krech, & Rosenzweig, 1964), with greater dendritic development (Greenough & Volkmar, 1973), and with more synapses per neuron (Turner & Greenough, 1983).

In order to provide yourself with an overview of neural development before proceeding to Section 15.2, fill in the blanks in the following chronological list of the major stages in the development of the nervous system:

1. Induction of the neural _____

2. Formation of the neural tube

3. Neural _____

4. Neural _____

5. Neural aggregation

6. Growth of _____

7. Formation of _____

8. Neuron _____ and synapse _____

The following are the answers to the preceding questions: (1) plate, (3) proliferation, (4) migration, (6) neural processes (axons and dendrites), (7) synapses, and (8) death; rearrangement.

15.2 Neuroplasticity in Simple Neural Systems: The Cellular Bases of Learning

Up to this point, the chapter has concentrated on the initial development of the nervous system. This section focuses on the plasticity of the adult nervous system; in particular, it examines those neural changes that are presumed to be the bases of learning. If it has not already occurred to you, the neural changes that underlie learning are intimately related to those that underlie memory. In fact, the study of learning and the study of memory are inextricably related. The study of learning focuses on the changes produced in the brain by various experiences, whereas the study of memory focuses on how these changes are maintained. Learning is impossible without memory, and memory is impossible without learning.

Interest in the neural bases of learning and memory has spawned many different lines of research. For example, the preceding chapter describes how studies of amnesia in humans and laboratory primates has contributed greatly to our understanding of memorial processes. In this section, an entirely different approach is highlighted. It focuses on the research of biopsychologists and other neuroscientists who have tried to understand learning and memory at the single-cell level through the study of simple forms of learning by simple neural circuits. Three highly successful examples of this approach are highlighted: (1) nonassociative and associative learning in the gill-withdrawal-reflex circuit of Aplysia, (2) long-term potentiation in the mammalian hippocampus, and (3) learning in the nictitating-membrane circuit of the rabbit.

Nonassociative and Associative Learning in the Gill-Withdrawal-Reflex Circuit of Aplysia

The *Aplysia* is a simple marine snail that spends its life oozing along the ocean floor eating seaweed and avoiding predation by tasting as bad as it looks (see Figure 15.10). The Aplysia *siphon* is a small fleshy spout that is used to expel seawater and waste. When the siphon is touched, it and the adjoining gill are reflexively drawn up under its protective *mantle*. This response to touch is the Aplysia *gill-withdrawal reflex*. The neural circuit mediating the gill-withdrawal reflex is relatively simple. There are 24 sensory neurons in the skin of the siphon that synapse on 6 motor neurons that are responsible for retracting the siphon and gill. The sensory neurons also activate interneurons that in turn synapse on the motor neurons. This circuit is illustrated schematically in Figure 15.11.

FIGURE 15.10 *An Aplysia.*

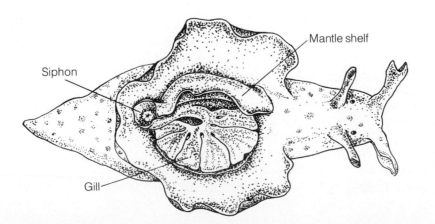

Mantle shelf

Siphon

Gill

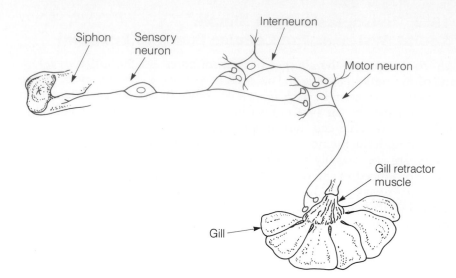

FIGURE 15.11 *A schematic illustration of the neural circuit that mediates the Aplysia gill-withdrawal reflex.*

Nonassociative Learning in Aplysia Nonassociative learning refers to a change in behavior that results from the repeated experience of a single stimulus or of two or more different stimuli that are not spatially or temporally related. The three most commonly studied forms of nonassociative learning are habituation, sensitization, and dishabituation. **Habituation** is the decrease in the strength of the behavioral reaction to a stimulus that occurs when that stimulus is repeatedly presented. For example, if the Aplysia siphon is touched repeatedly at relatively brief intervals (e.g., once every 30 seconds), the gill-withdrawal reflex becomes habituated; that is, it becomes less and less vigorous. Similar habituation of withdrawal reflexes can be demonstrated in most species, including humans. Habituation of the Aplysia gill-withdrawal reflex lasts 2 or 3 hours following a single habituation session involving 10 stimuli; several such sessions can produce habituation that lasts for weeks (Carew, Pinsker, & Kandel, 1972).

The first clue to the identity of the neural mechanism underlying habituation of the Aplysia gill-withdrawal reflex came from a study in which the responses of the gill motor neurons were recorded during habituation to repeated touches of the siphon produced by a precisely regulated jet of water (Castellucci, Pinsker, Kupfermann, & Kandel, 1970). As the intensity of the gill-withdrawal reflex declined, there was an associated decline in the number of action potentials elicited in the gill motor neurons by each touch. Because the responsiveness of the motor neurons to the neurotransmitter released by the sensory neurons did not decline during habituation (Castellucci & Kandel, 1974), it was concluded that the progressive decline in the number of motor neuron action potentials elicited by each siphon touch during the course of habituation resulted from a progressive decline in the amount of neurotransmitter being released from the sensory neurons onto the postsynaptic membranes of the motor neurons.

What causes the siphon sensory neurons to release progressively less neurotransmitter in response to each successive touch of the siphon during the course of habituation? There are only two possibilities. One possibility is that less neurotransmitter is released from the siphon sensory neurons during the course of habituation because progressively fewer action potentials are elicited in them by each successive touch. The only other possibility is that the number of action potentials elicited in the siphon sensory neurons by repeated siphon touches does not decline, but that the amount of neurotransmitter released in response to each action potential does. Tests of these two hypotheses ruled out the first hypothesis (Castellucci & Kandel, 1974).

Once it became clear that the habituation of the Aplysia gill-withdrawal reflex resulted from a decrease in the amount of neurotransmitter released from siphon sensory neurons in response to each of their own action potentials, researchers began the search for the mechanism underlying this decrease. The search focused on *calcium ion influx* because it is the inflow of calcium ions into the terminal buttons that permits synaptic vesicles to fuse with the presynaptic membrane and release their contents into the synapse. It was soon established that the decrease in neurotransmitter release underlying habituation of the gill-withdrawal reflex results from a decrease in the number of calcium ions entering the terminal buttons of the siphon sensory neurons in response to each of their own action potentials (Klein & Kandel, 1978; Klein, Shapiro, & Kandel, 1980).

The following theory of habituation of the Aplysia gill-withdrawal reflex has emerged from this line of research (see Figure 15.12). With repeated elicitation of the gill-withdrawal reflex, each siphon stimulation continues to fully activate the sensory neurons, sending the same full barrage of action potentials down their axons. However, because fewer calcium ions enter the synaptic terminals in response to each successive barrage of action potentials, less and less neurotransmitter is released from the sensory neurons into the synapses, fewer and fewer action potentials are elicited in the motor neurons, and the contraction of the gill muscle in response to each siphon stimulation grows less and less strong (see Hawkins, 1983; Kandel, 1985; Quinn, 1984).

Sensitization is the general increase in an animal's responsiveness to stimuli following a noxious stimulus. For example, the gill-withdrawal reflex elicited by touching an Aplysia's siphon is increased in intensity for several minutes following the administration of a single severe shock to its tail (Carew, Castellucci, & Kandel, 1971). The sensitization of the Aplysia gill-withdrawal reflex can last for weeks following a series of tail shocks administered over several days (Pinsker, Hening, Carew, & Kandel, 1973). In direct contrast to the mechanism of habituation, sensitization was shown to result from an increase in the amount of neurotransmitter released by the siphon sensory neurons in response to their own action potentials (Castellucci & Kandel, 1976).

How does tail shock cause the siphon sensory neurons to increase their release of neurotransmitter onto the gill motor neurons? The answer is by **presynaptic facilitation.** Sensory fibers from the Aplysia tail synapse on facilitatory interneurons that in turn synapse on the buttons of siphon sensory neurons (Bailey, Hawkins, & Chen, 1983; Hawkins, Castellucci, & Kandel, 1981). Via these axoaxonic synapses, the barrage of activity elicited in the interneurons by the tail shock changes the siphon sensory neuron buttons so that each action potential arriving there from the siphon results in a greater influx of calcium ions and a greater release of neurotransmitter onto the motor neurons (Figure 15.13).

Bailey and Chen (1983, 1988) showed that long-term habituation and sensitization can induce structural changes in the synaptic terminals of the siphon sensory neurons. They labeled the siphon sensory neurons of three groups of Aplysia with horseradish peroxidase and examined their synaptic terminals by electron microscopy. Relative to the sensory neurons of control Aplysia, those of the habituated subjects had fewer active zones of transmitter release, smaller active zones, and fewer synaptic vesicles. In contrast, the sensory neurons of the sensitized Aplysia had more active zones, larger active zones, and more synaptic vesicles than did the controls. Because such structural changes cannot occur rapidly enough to

FIGURE 15.12 *Mechanisms thought to underlie habituation and sensitization of the Aplysia gill-withdrawal reflex.*

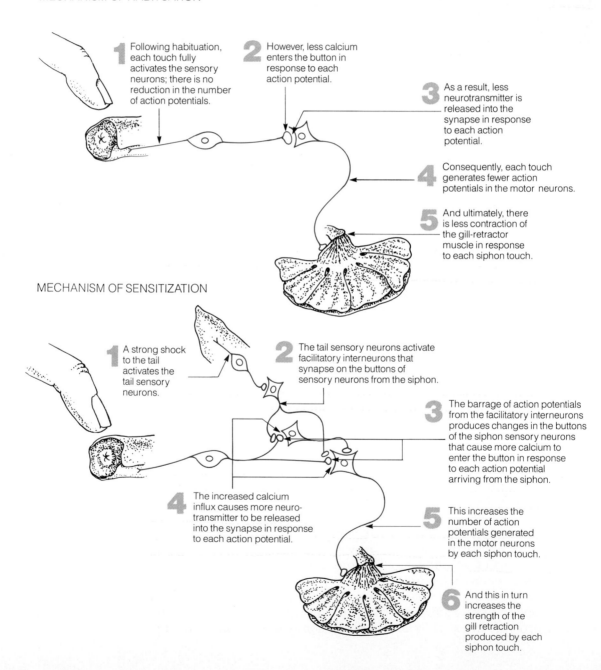

MECHANISM OF HABITUATION

1 Following habituation, each touch fully activates the sensory neurons; there is no reduction in the number of action potentials.

2 However, less calcium enters the button in response to each action potential.

3 As a result, less neurotransmitter is released into the synapse in response to each action potential.

4 Consequently, each touch generates fewer action potentials in the motor neurons.

5 And ultimately, there is less contraction of the gill-retractor muscle in response to each siphon touch.

MECHANISM OF SENSITIZATION

1 A strong shock to the tail activates the tail sensory neurons.

2 The tail sensory neurons activate facilitatory interneurons that synapse on the buttons of sensory neurons from the siphon.

3 The barrage of action potentials from the facilitatory interneurons produces changes in the buttons of the siphon sensory neurons that cause more calcium to enter the button in response to each action potential arriving from the siphon.

4 The increased calcium influx causes more neurotransmitter to be released into the synapse in response to each action potential.

5 This increases the number of action potentials generated in the motor neurons by each siphon touch.

6 And this in turn increases the strength of the gill retraction produced by each siphon touch.

account for short-term retention of sensitization and habituation, the relation between the mechanisms of short-term and long-term storage need to be examined (Byrne, 1987).

Dishabituation is a phenomenon very much like sensitization. Like sensitization, dishabituation is an increase in the strength of a reflex (e.g., the Aplysia gill-withdrawal reflex) following an unassociated noxious stimulus (e.g., a tail shock). But unlike sensitization, dishabituation refers specifically to the ability of an unassociated noxious stimulus to release a reflex from habituation. In view of the similarity between sensitization and dishabituation, it has been assumed that they are mediated by the same mechanism (e.g., Carew, Castellucci, & Kandel, 1971; Groves & Thompson, 1970). However, several lines of evidence suggest that this is not the case (e.g., Hochner, Klein, Schacher, & Kandel, 1986). For example, Rankin and Carew (1987, 1988) tested the assumption that the mechanisms of sensitization and dishabituation are the same by assessing the ability of tail shock to produce sensitization and disinhibition in juvenile Aplysia of different ages. Rankin and Carew found that dishabituation mechanisms were functional as soon as gill and siphon development was complete, but that the Aplysia did not display sensitization until they were much older. This finding suggests that the mechanisms underlying sensitization are different, and it illustrates the ability of the developmental approach to provide important insights into the neural basis of learning and memory (see Rankin, Nolen, Marcus, Stopfer, & Carew, 1988).

Associative Learning in Aplysia   Aplysia are capable of several different kinds of associative learning (Carew & Sahley, 1986); however, it is the **Pavlovian conditioning** of the gill-withdrawal reflex that is best understood. In Pavlovian conditioning, the subject learns an association between a *conditional stimulus* and an *unconditional stimulus* (see Chapter 4). If a light touch of the siphon (the conditional stimulus) is paired with a strong shock to the tail (the unconditional stimulus) every few minutes for several trials, the light touch by itself begins to elicit a robust gill-withdrawal response similar to that induced by the tail shock. The associative nature of this effect is shown by the fact that the increase in the intensity of the reflex is not nearly so great if the two stimuli are presented in an unpaired fashion (Carew, Walters, & Kandel, 1981)—unpaired presentations produce sensitization, but no conditioning. The conditional response is typically retained for several days after 20 or so conditioning trials.

The Aplysia gill-withdrawal reflex has also been shown to be capable of **discriminated Pavlovian conditioning** (Carew, Hawkins, & Kandel, 1983). In the discriminated version of the paradigm (illustrated in Figure 15.13), two conditional stimuli are administered, mild stimulation to the mantle and mild stimulation to the siphon, each of which elicits a weak gill-withdrawal response. During training, one of these stimuli (called the CS^+) is always paired with the unconditional stimulus, a severe tail shock, and the other conditional stimulus (called the CS^-) is not. At the end of training, the CS^+ elicits a strong withdrawal reaction, whereas the CS^- elicits only a weak reaction, as a result of the nonassociative effects of the tail shock. Optimal conditioning occurs when the CS^+ precedes the unconditional stimulus by 0.5 second, and it doesn't occur at all when the CS^+ follows the unconditional stimulus.

Pavlovian conditioning of the gill-withdrawal reflex can be thought of as a special case of sensitization. In effect, it is a demonstration that tail shock

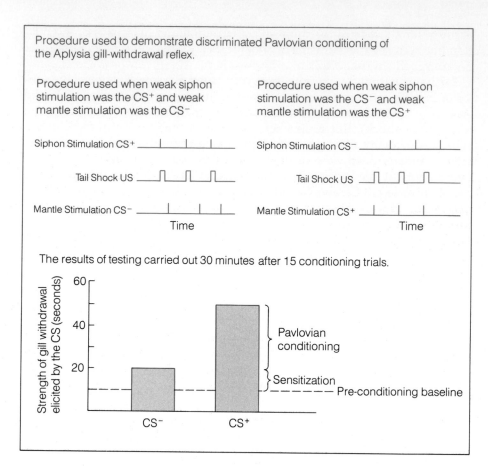

FIGURE 15.13 *The discriminated Pavlovian conditioning of the Aplysia gill-withdrawal reflex. (Adapted from Carew, Hawkins, & Kandel, 1983.)*

has the greatest sensitizing effect on reflexes elicited by those stimuli that are administered just prior to the shock. This relation between sensitization and Pavlovian conditioning is reflected in the model that has been proposed to explain it (see Figure 15.14). Like sensitization, Pavlovian conditioning of the gill-withdrawal reflex is assumed to be mediated by the action of tail-shock-activated interneurons on the sensory neurons that normally activate the reflex. However, unlike sensitization, Pavlovian conditioning depends on the temporal relation between the activation of the interneuron by tail shock and the sensory neuron by the CS$^+$. The greatest increase in the release of neurotransmitter from the CS$^+$ sensory neurons is produced following trials in which they are in the act of firing at the time when input reaches their terminals from the tail-shock activated interneurons (see Hawkins, Abrams, Carew, & Kandel, 1983; Hawkins, Clark, & Kandel, 1987).

Long-Term Potentiation in the Mammalian Hippocampus

Not all attempts to identify the cellular changes associated with memory have focused on learning in simple organisms. A slightly different strategy has been to study the plasticity of simple circuits that are components of complex nervous systems. One noteworthy example of this approach is the study of long-term potentiation (Bliss & Gardner-Medwin, 1973; Bliss &

Lømo, 1973; Lømo, 1966). **Long-term potentiation** (LTP) refers to the observation that in some neural circuits, a few seconds of intense high-frequency electrical stimulation to presynaptic fibers can produce a lasting increase in the response of the postsynaptic neurons to subsequent low-level stimulation of the same presynaptic fibers. This potentiation can last for many minutes after a single stimulation or for many days after multiple stimulations (Racine & deJonge, 1988; Racine, Milgram, & Hafner, 1983). Long-term potentiation has been most frequently studied in the hippocampus of rabbits and rats, where it is often produced by stimulating the **perforant path,** which is a major input into the hippocampus, and recording a multiple-unit response from the **granule-cell layer** of the hippocampal *dentate gyrus,* which receives this input. Long-term potentiation can be studied in freely moving animals or in a **hippocampal-slice preparation** (i.e., in slices of hippocampal tissue that have been cut from a living brain and maintained alive for many hours in a saline bath). Figure 15.15 illustrates the conduct of a typical long-term potentiation experiment.

FIGURE 15.14 *The model that has been proposed to explain discriminated Pavlovian conditioning of the gill-withdrawal reflex. (Adapted from Kandel, 1985.)*

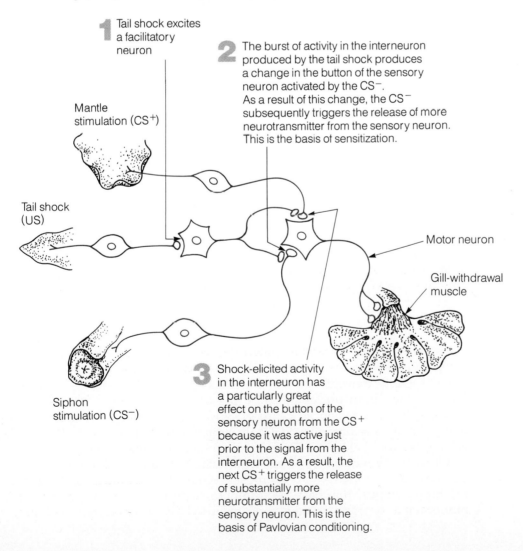

1 Tail shock excites a facilitatory neuron

2 The burst of activity in the interneuron produced by the tail shock produces a change in the button of the sensory neuron activated by the CS⁻.
As a result of this change, the CS⁻ subsequently triggers the release of more neurotransmitter from the sensory neuron. This is the basis of sensitization.

Mantle stimulation (CS⁺)

Tail shock (US)

Motor neuron

Gill-withdrawal muscle

Siphon stimulation (CS⁻)

3 Shock-elicited activity in the interneuron has a particularly great effect on the button of the sensory neuron from the CS⁺ because it was active just prior to the signal from the interneuron. As a result, the next CS⁺ triggers the release of substantially more neurotransmitter from the sensory neuron. This is the basis of Pavlovian conditioning.

A slice of hippocampal tissue displaying the major circuitry

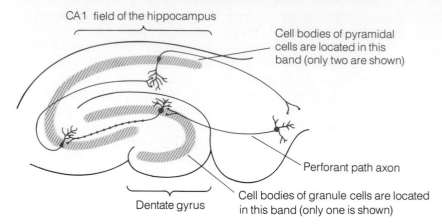

CA1 field of the hippocampus

Cell bodies of pyramidal cells are located in this band (only two are shown)

Perforant path axon

Cell bodies of granule cells are located in this band (only one is shown)

Dentate gyrus

Long-term potentiation induced at the synapse between perforant path neurons and the granule cells of the dentate gyrus

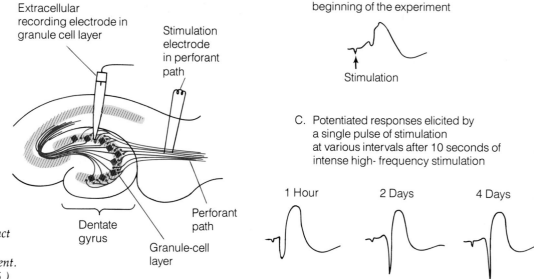

A. Experimental set-up

Extracellular recording electrode in granule cell layer

Stimulation electrode in perforant path

Dentate gyrus

Granule-cell layer

Perforant path

B. The response to a single pulse of stimulation at the beginning of the experiment

Stimulation

C. Potentiated responses elicited by a single pulse of stimulation at various intervals after 10 seconds of intense high- frequency stimulation

1 Hour   2 Days   4 Days

FIGURE 15.15 *The conduct of a typical long-term potentiation (LTP) experiment. (Adapted from Teyler, 1986.)*

The reason why researchers interested in the cellular basis of memory are so interested in the phenomenon of LTP is that the long-term facilitation of synaptic transmission that underlies LTP is similar to the facilitation that has long been presumed to be the basis of memory storage (e.g., Hebb, 1949). Teyler and DiScenna (1984) listed five lines of indirect evidence that the mechanisms of LTP are similar to those of memory: (1) LTP is long lasting; (2) although LTP is usually induced by high-intensity stimulation, it can be induced by levels of stimulation that mimic natural neural neuronal activity; (3) LTP occurs most prominently in structures, such as the hippocampus, that have been implicated in memory; (4) changes in hippocampal synaptic transmission similar to LTP have been reported following behavioral conditioning; and (5) there are parallels between the effects of drugs on memory and their effects on LTP (Brown, Chapman, Kairiss, & Keenan, 1988; Skelton, Scarth, Wilkie, Miller, & Phillips, 1987). These lines of indirect evidence do not prove that the neural changes underlying LTP are involved in memory, but they suggest that the study of LTP may indicate the kinds of neural changes that store memories.

Perhaps the most important discovery about LTP—from the psychological perspective, at least—is that it is amenable to associative conditioning. For example, Kelso and Brown (1986) implanted four electrodes in a hippocampal slice preparation: three stimulation electrodes in fibers projecting into the CA1 area and one recording electrode in the CA1 area itself (*CA* is the abbreviation for *cornu ammonis,* another name for *hippocampus*). Next, stimulation intensities at each stimulation electrode were set so that stimulation through two of them (termed W_1 and W_2) was too weak to induce LTP, whereas stimulation through the third (S) was strong enough to induce LTP. As illustrated in Figure 15.16, Kelso and Brown found that after pairing stimulation through one of the "weak electrodes" (conditional stimulus) with stimulation through the "strong electrode" (unconditional stimulus) five times, stimulation through the same weak electrode, but not through the other weak electrode, elicited a potentiated multiple-unit response at the recording electrode.

Although the exact mechanism of LTP in the hippocampus is still unknown, there is strong evidence implicating a particular glutamate receptor subtype; **glutamate** is thought to be the main excitatory neurotransmitter of the hippocampus, and perhaps in the entire brain. This critical glutamate receptor subtype is the **NMDA receptor,** so-called because it, but not other glutamate receptors, is activated by *N-methyl-D-aspartate,* an analogue of glutamate. Antagonists of the NMDA receptor block the development of LTP, but do not impair synaptic transmission or prevent the expression of LTP that has already been induced (e.g., Collingridge & Bliss, 1987; Cotman, Monoghan, & Ganong, 1988). Because the binding of glutamate to the NMDA receptor in the presence of a large voltage across the receptive membrane permits the entry of calcium ions into the postsynaptic neurons, the influx of calcium through channels associated with activated NMDA receptors is thought to be the critical event in the induction of LTP (e.g., Baudry & Lynch, 1987). And how does an influx of calcium ions through activated NMDA receptors potentiate the responses of the postsynaptic neuron to subsequent input from the same synapses? The answer may lie in the discovery that hippocampal LTP is associated with a rapid increase in the number of hippocampal synapses (Chang & Greenough, 1984) and in the number of hippocampal glutamate receptors (Lynch, Halpain, & Baudry, 1982), but several other mechanisms have been proposed.

Learning and Memory in the Nictitating-Membrane Circuit of the Rabbit

Perhaps the best understood vertebrate circuit capable of associative learning and memory at the behavioral level is the circuit that mediates the Pavlovian conditioning of the *nictitating-membrane response* in rabbits. Most studies of this circuit have employed the conditioning procedure of Gormezano (1972). On each trial, a tone (the conditional stimulus) is turned on, and then 250 milliseconds later, a puff of air to the eye (the unconditional stimulus) is presented. The tone and the air puff terminate simultaneously. At first the rabbit does not respond to the tone, but when the air puff is administered, an inner eyelid called the **nictitating membrane** slides over the eye to protect it. With repeated trials, the nictitating-membrane response begins to be elicited by the tone, before the puff of air is administered, thus indicating that the circuit controlling the response has learned and retained the association between the tone conditional stimulus and the puff unconditional stimulus.

FIGURE 15.16 *The experiment of Kelso and Brown (1986): associative conditioning of long-term potentiation.*

Position of stimulation and recording electrodes in the CA1 field of a hippocampal slice in Kelso and Brown's experiment.

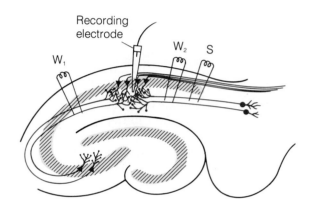

W_1 First weak-stimulation electrode

W_2 Second weak-stimulation electrode

S   Strong-stimulation electrode

When stimulation through one of the weak-stimulation electrodes was followed by stimulation through the strong-stimulation electrode for several trials, stimulation through that weak electrode (CS+) but not the other (CS−) elicited a potentiated response.

A. After W_1 served as the CS+ and W_2 as the CS−, W_1 elicited a potentiated response

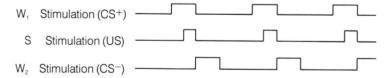

W_1 Stimulation (CS+)

S   Stimulation (US)

W_2 Stimulation (CS−)

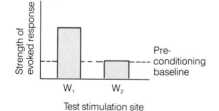

B. After W_2 served as the CS+ and W_1 as the CS−, W_2 elicited a potentiated response

W_1 Stimulation (CS−)

S   Stimulation (US)

W_2 Stimulation (CS+)

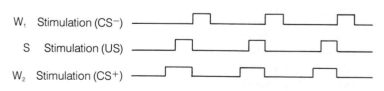

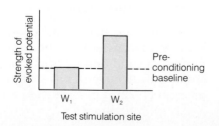

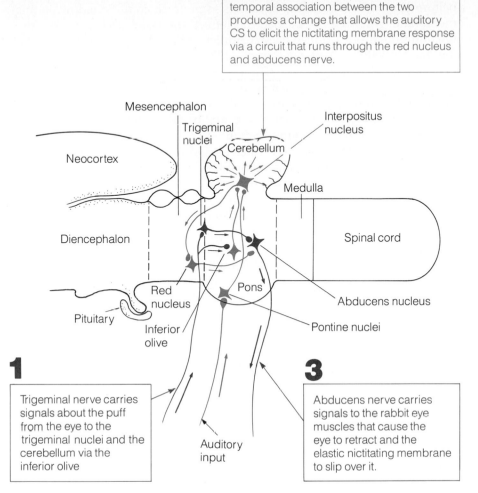

2 The cerebellum receives information about the auditory CS and the puff US. The temporal association between the two produces a change that allows the auditory CS to elicit the nictitating membrane response via a circuit that runs through the red nucleus and abducens nerve.

Mesencephalon

Trigeminal nuclei

Interpositus nucleus

Cerebellum

Neocortex

Medulla

Diencephalon

Spinal cord

Red nucleus

Pons

Pituitary

Abducens nucleus

Inferior olive

Pontine nuclei

1 Trigeminal nerve carries signals about the puff from the eye to the trigeminal nuclei and the cerebellum via the inferior olive

Auditory input

3 Abducens nerve carries signals to the rabbit eye muscles that cause the eye to retract and the elastic nictitating membrane to slip over it.

FIGURE 15.17 *The circuit that has been hypothesized to mediate the Pavlovian conditioning of the rabbit nictitating-membrane response to an auditory conditional stimulus.*

The circuit mediating the nictitating-membrane reflex is a simple one (see Figure 15.17). The puff of air activates receptors in the skin around the eye, and a volley of action potentials is transmitted down a branch of the **trigeminal nerve** (fifth cranial nerve) to the *trigeminal nuclei* of the brain stem. The neurons of the trigeminal nuclei in turn excite motor neurons in the adjacent *abducens nucleus*, which project as a branch of the **abducens nerve** (the sixth cranial nerve) to muscles that pull the eye back into the socket, thus causing the elastic nictitating membrane to slip over it.

The question that challenges those interested in the neural bases of learning is, "What change occurs in this hindbrain circuit during Pavlovian conditioning to permit the nictitating-membrane reflex to be driven by an auditory conditional stimulus?" Although it is not yet known what this change is, it is now clear where it is taking place. An important clue was provided by the demonstration that eye-blink conditioning in cats does not require the forebrain or midbrain. Norman, Buchwald, and Villablanca (1977) showed that the hindbrain of a cat can learn and retain a conditioned eye-blink response to an auditory conditional stimulus after it has been surgically separated from the rest of the brain. This finding focused the search for the mechanism of nictitating-membrane conditioning on the hindbrain, and this focus soon led to the cerebellum. Lesions of the cerebellum eliminated the ability of rabbits to perform conditioned nictitating-membrane responses, but had no effect on their ability to perform unconditioned ones (Lincoln, McCormick, & Thompson, 1982; Yeo, Hardiman, Glickstein, & Steele-Russell, 1982). In a subsequent series of experiments, McCormick and Thompson (1984) showed that electrical stimulation of the **interpositus nucleus** of the cerebellum produces nictitating-membrane responses, that a unilateral lesion restricted to the interpositus nucleus eliminates the ability of rabbits to perform conditioned nictitating-membrane responses only in the ipsilateral eye, and that neurons in the interpositus nucleus and in the cerebellar cortex begin to respond to the auditory conditional stimulus as conditioning of the nictitating-membrane response proceeds.

Thompson (1986) has suggested that signals elicited by puffs of air to the eye reach the cerebellum via the *inferior olive* and that auditory signals elicited by the auditory conditional stimuli reach the cerebellum via the *pontine nuclei*. He further suggests that changes in cerebellar neurons produced by the pairing of auditory stimuli and puffs to the eye allow the conditional auditory stimuli to activate the nictitating-membrane response through a circuit that adjusts the nictitating-membrane circuit by its output to the motor neurons of the eye retractor muscle through a circuit that passes through the *red nucleus*. A simplified version of this hypothetical circuit is illustrated in Figure 15.17.

By this point in the chapter, you are probably beginning to appreciate that the topic of neuroplasticity is not only one of the most productive and interesting areas of neuroscientific research, but it is also one of the most technical. Accordingly, I recommend that you pause here to consolidate what you have learned in Section 15.2 by completing the following sentences.

1. _habituation_, _sensitization_, and dishabituation are examples of nonassociative learning.

2. _Habituation_ of the Aplysia gill-withdrawal reflex is associated with a decrease in the amount of neurotransmitter released from siphon sensory neurons in response to each siphon sensory neuron action potential.

3. _Sensitization_ of the Aplysia gill-withdrawal reflex is mediated by presynaptic facilitation acting on the buttons of siphon sensory neurons so that each of their action potentials results in the release of more neurotransmitter.

4. _dishabituation_ is a phenomenon very much like sensitization, but developmental studies suggest that their mechanisms are different.

5. In effect, _____Pavlovian_____ conditioning of the gill-withdrawal reflex is a demonstration that the tail shock unconditional stimulus has the greatest sensitizing effect on reflexes elicited by stimuli that have occurred just prior to the shock (i.e., by reflexes elicited by conditional stimuli).

6. The two major layers of cell bodies in the hippocampus are the _____pyramidal_____-cell layer of the hippocampus proper and the _____granule_____-cell layer of the dentate gyrus.

7. _____Long-term potentiation_____ refers to the observation that a few seconds of intense, high-frequency electrical stimulation to pre-synaptic fibers can produce a lasting increase in the responses produced in the postsynaptic neurons by low-level stimulation to the same presynaptic site.

8. _____Long-term potentiation_____ is of great interest to research-ers interested in memory because the long-term facilitation of synaptic transmission has long been thought to be the mechanism of memory storage.

9. There is strong evidence implicating _____MNOA_____ glutamate receptors in LTP.

10. The nictitating-membrane reflex of a rabbit is mediated by a circuit that involves sensory neurons in the skin around the eye that project via a branch of the _____Trigeminal_____ nerve to the trigeminal nu-clei, neurons in the trigeminal nuclei that project to the abducens nu-cleus, and neurons in the _____abducens_____ nucleus that project via the abducens nerve to the muscles that retract the eye.

11. The _____interpositus_____ nucleus of the cerebellum is thought to play an important role in the Pavlovian conditioning of the nictitating-membrane reflex.

The following are the correct answers to the preceding questions: (1) Habituation; sensitization (or vice versa), (2) Habituation, (3) Sensitization, (4) Dishabituation, (5) Pavlovian, (6) pyramidal; granule, (7) Long-term potentiation, (8) Long-term potentiation, (9) NMDA, (10) trigeminal; abducens, (11) interpositus.

15.3 Neural Degeneration, Neural Regeneration, and Neurotransplantation

The third and last section of this chapter is about neuronal damage. More specifically, it is about two responses to neuronal damage—*degeneration* and *regeneration*—and about attempts to treat neuronal damage by *neurotransplantation*.

Neural Degeneration

After a multipolar neuron is **axotomized** (i.e., after its axon is severed), two kinds of neural degeneration (i.e., neural deterioration) occur: degeneration of the **distal segment,** the segment between the cut and the synaptic terminals, and degeneration of the **proximal segment,** the segment between the cut and the cell body. Degeneration of the distal segment is commonly referred to as **anterograde degeneration,** and degeneration of the proximal segment is called **retrograde degeneration** (see Figure 15.18). Anterograde degeneration occurs quickly because the cut separates the distal segment of the axon from the cell body, which is the metabolic center of the neuron. Within a day, the distal portion becomes swollen, and by the fifth day it breaks into fragments. In the proximal portion of the neuron, the first reaction to the cut is the degeneration of the portion of axon adjacent to the cut, usually back to the first *node of Ranvier* (the first gap between adjacent segments of the myelin sheath) or sometimes to the

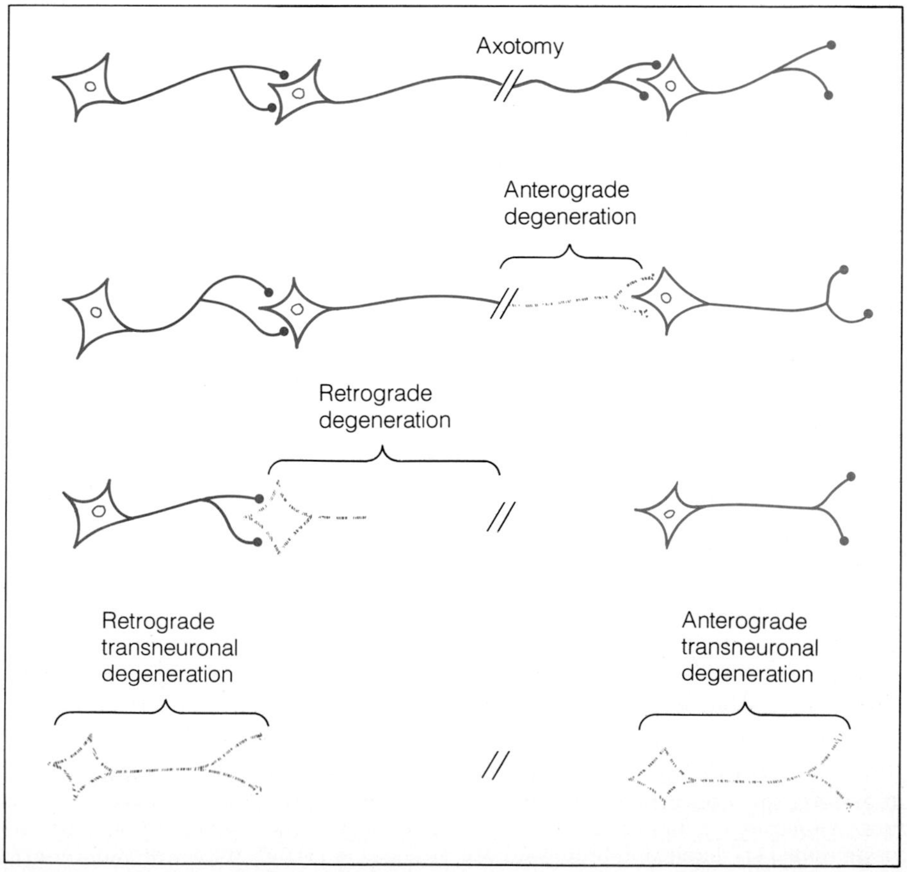

FIGURE 15.18 *Neuronal and transneuronal degeneration following axotomy.*

first point at which there is a major *collateral branch* leaving the axon. Within 2 or 3 days, major changes in the cell body also become apparent. These cell body changes are of one of two types: degenerative or regenerative. Early degenerative changes in the cell body of an axotomized neuron (e.g., decrease in the size) suggest that it will ultimately die. Early regenerative changes (e.g., increase in size) indicate that the cell body is involved in a massive synthesis of the proteins needed to replace the degenerated portions of the axon. But regeneration does not guarantee long-term survival of a damaged neuron. If a regenerating axon does not manage to make synaptic contact with an appropriate target, it will eventually die.

If the cut axon is in the CNS, specialized glial cells, primarily **astroglia** (see Chapter 2), proliferate and absorb the debris. This reaction is termed **phagocytosis,** and astroglia are thus referred to as **phagocytes.** Astrocytes are particularly fibrous cells, and thus their accumulation at sites of damage in the CNS forms scar tissue. In the PNS, the neural debris is absorbed by **Schwann cells,** the cells that compose the myelin sheaths of peripheral axons.

Transneuronal Degeneration   Degeneration is not necessarily limited to the damaged neurons; it can be *transneuronal*. In some cases, the neurons on which a degenerating neuron synapses degenerate **(anterograde transneuronal degeneration);** and in some cases, the neurons that synapse on a damaged neuron degenerate **(retrograde transneuronal degeneration).** Neurons two or three synapses away from the site of damage can be adversely affected. Figure 15.18 is a schematic illustration of the various kinds of neuronal and **transneuronal degeneration.**

Neural Regeneration

Neural regeneration (i.e., regrowth of damaged neurons) does not proceed as successfully in mammals and other higher vertebrates as it does in most invertebrates and lower vertebrates. For some reason, the capacity for accurate axon growth, which is possessed by higher vertebrates during their original development, is lost once they reach maturity. Regeneration is virtually nonexistent in the central nervous systems of adult mammals, and regeneration in the peripheral nervous systems of mammals is at best a hit-and-miss affair.

Regrowth from the proximal stump of a damaged mammalian peripheral nerve begins a day or two after the damage. If the nerve has been damaged but the Schwann-cell myelin sheaths have remained intact, the regenerating axons grow out in their original sheaths to their original targets at a rate of a few millimeters per day. However, if the nerve has been completely severed and the cut ends separated, the regrowth is not nearly so accurate because regenerating axon tips often grow into incorrect sheaths, and they are guided by them to incorrect destinations. This is why it often requires great effort for victims of peripheral nerve damage to relearn to use affected limbs.

If the cut ends of a mammalian peripheral nerve become widely separated, or if a lengthy section of the nerve is damaged, there may be no meaningful regeneration at all. Regenerating axon tips that do not encounter the Schwann-cell myelin sheaths of the distal portion usually grow in a tangled mass around the proximal stump and ultimately die. In contrast, the regenerating axons of lower vertebrates often reach their original targets whether or not they manage to grow into remnant Schwann-cell sheaths. The accuracy of regeneration in lower vertebrates is like a carrot dangling in front of the noses of the women and men of medical neuroscience. If the factors that promote accurate regeneration in lower vertebrates can be identified and applied to humans, it might prove possible to promote recovery from brain damage. (In writing this paragraph, I discovered a particularly difficult tongue-twister: "Schwann-cell sheaths." Try repeating it quickly.)

Healthy axons sometimes respond to the degeneration of adjacent axons by developing collateral sprouts that innervate synaptic sites abandoned by the degenerating axons (e.g., Cotman, Nieto-Sampedro, & Harris, 1981; Tsukahara, 1981). **Collateral sprouting** is illustrated in Figure 15.19. Notice that collateral sprouts may originate from the axon terminals or from a node of Ranvier. Although it is tempting to assume that collateral sprouting contributes to the recovery that sometimes follows brain damage, there is no direct evidence for this hypothesis (Finger & Almi, 1985).

Collateral sprouting was at first assumed to be triggered by substances released by the degenerating axons, but several lines of evidence suggest that it is triggered by some factor released from the target tissue. For example, collateral sprouting can be induced in motor neurons in the absence of degeneration simply by rendering the target muscle inactive (e.g., Brown & Ironton, 1977), and the collateral sprouting observed in motor axons following damage to adjacent axons can be blocked by electrically stimulating the target muscle (Ironton, Brown, & Holland, 1978).

Neurotransplantation in the Brain and Spinal Cord

My introduction to the concept of brain transplantation came at an early age. Perhaps you were introduced to it in the same way. A scenario that is repeated in many television cartoons is one in which a mad scientist places a helmet with a bundle of wires coming from it on the head of one animal subject and a similar helmet on the head of another subject of a different species. Then he throws a massive switch. There are some sparks, a puff of

FIGURE 15.19 *Collateral sprouting after neuron damage.*

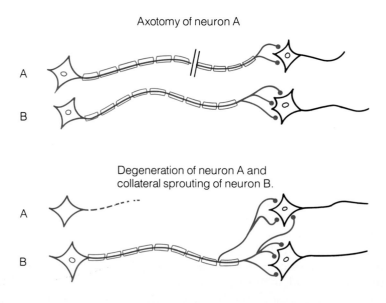

Axotomy of neuron A

A

B

Degeneration of neuron A and collateral sprouting of neuron B.

A

B

smoke, and voilà, the brains of the two subjects are switched. This is good for a few laughs but the highlight of the cartoon comes when the scientist accidentally gets one of the helmets on his own head and his brain ends up in the body of a chicken, and vice versa. It is ironic that this childhood fantasy is now one of the most exciting lines of research in neuroscience. Real-life neurotransplants are not performed by the simple pull of a switch, and they involve only portions of the nervous system, but they are no less amazing.

In 1971, the modern era of neurotransplantation began with a study that provided conclusive evidence of the survival of transplanted neural tissue in the brain of a host. First, radioactively labeled thymidine was injected into the brains of 7-day-old donor rats, where it was incorporated into the DNA of their neurons. Then, slabs of labeled cerebellum were removed from them and transplanted in similar sites in the brains of host rats of the same age. Two weeks later, autoradiographs of slides taken from the host cerebellum indicated that many of the transplanted neurons had survived (Das & Altman, 1971). Subsequent research has shown that rejection of CNS transplants between members of the same species is rare, particularly if the tissue is taken from neonatal donors (Das, Hallas, & Das, 1980) and/or implanted in neonatal hosts (Hallas, Oblinger, & Das, 1980). The optimal sites for neurotransplants are those that are highly vascularized and have sufficient growth space (Brundin & Björklund, 1987; Fine, 1986). A piece of tissue dissected from a donor can be implanted in some existing cavity such as the wall of a ventricle, it can be implanted in a cavity that has been surgically created in advance, or the donor tissue can be broken up into individual cells and then injected into the host brain.

Does transplanted embryonic brain tissue develop as it would have had it been left in the donor, or is its development determined more by its site of implantation in the host? The experimental evidence supports the first alternative. In one series of studies, embryonic precursors of visual cortex (Jaeger & Lund, 1981) or retina (McLoon & Lund, 1980) were transplanted into the *superior colliculi* (optic tectums) of neonatal rats, and the result was the development of normal appearing cortical and retinal tissue, respectively.

Do neural fibers grow from the host's nervous system into a neural implant, and is the pattern of projections normal? The answer to the first question is "Yes," and the answer to the second is, "It depends." If the implant is placed in the host at the same site that it occupied in the donor, it seems to become normally innervated. For example, superior colliculus tissue implanted in rats at a site created in the superior colliculus became innervated by axons from both the retina and visual cortex (Lund & Harvey, 1981). However, visual cortex tissue implanted into a similar superior colliculus site became innervated by fibers from several structures that do not normally innervate the visual cortex or the superior colliculus (e.g., Jaeger & Lund, 1981).

Studies of the establishment of connections in the other direction, that is, from the implant to surrounding tissue, seem to tell a similar story: An implant will develop a reasonably normal pattern of projections only if it is implanted at a suitable site. For example, when embryonic retinal precursors were implanted in neonatal rats in structures such as the cortex or cerebellum, which do not normally receive retinal inputs, the implants survived, but no fibers grew to other structures. However, when retinal implants were positioned next to the superior colliculus, a structure to which it normally projects, a reasonably normal pattern of axonal projections from the implant developed (McLoon & Lund, 1980). Interestingly, there were more projections from the retinal transplant if the eye contralateral to the implant was first removed, thus reducing competition for synaptic sites. Similarly, the *locus coeruleus* (a noradrenergic brain stem nucleus, which innervates the hippocampus and several other forebrain structures; pronounced LOW-kus se-RULE-ee-us) transplanted into the hippocampus of adult rats established its normal pattern of projections into the hippocampus only if the host's own locus coeruleus had first been lesioned (Björkland, Segal, & Stenevi, 1979).

Raisman, Morris, and Zhou (1987) took advantage of the highly regular arrangement of cell bodies and connections in the hippocampus to study the ability of tiny hippocampal transplants to establish normal connections. Figure 15.20 is a photograph of a slice taken through a granule cell implant that was first labeled with *horseradish peroxidase* (see Chapter 2). Notice how precisely the axons grew out to their normal targets.

Neurotransplantation research has been motivated by the idea that it might prove possible to develop transplantation procedures for the treatment of human brain damage. Two different approaches to this goal have

FIGURE 15.20 *The axonal terminations of embryonic rat granule cells labeled with horseradish peroxidase and implanted in an adult hippocampus.*

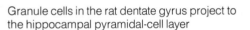

Granule cells in the rat dentate gyrus project to the hippocampal pyramidal-cell layer

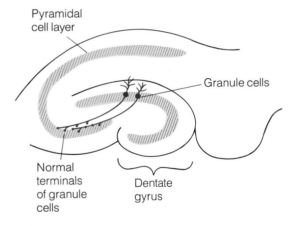

Pyramidal cell layer

Granule cells

Normal terminals of granule cells

Dentate gyrus

Granule cells were removed from a rat embryo, labelled with horseradish peroxidase, and implanted in the hippocampus of an adult rat whose natural granule-cell projections had been destroyed. Notice how precisely projections from the implant have grown out to their normal target.

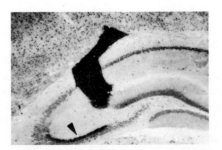

been taken. The first has been to develop implant procedures that might promote the regeneration of the patient's own damaged tissue. The second has been to implant replacement parts, that is, to replace damaged neural tissue with healthy tissue of the same type. Each of these approaches is considered in turn.

Promotion of Regeneration in the Central Nervous System

Efforts to promote regeneration in the mammalian central nervous system have focused on the question of why PNS neurons regenerate and CNS neurons do not (see Freed, Medinaceli, & Wyatt, 1985). One simple hypothesis is that CNS and PNS neurons are intrinsically different and that CNS neurons do not have the capacity to regenerate. Evidence against this hypothesis has come from studies in which CNS neurons implanted in the PNS have regenerated, and PNS neurons implanted in the CNS have not. Furthermore, peripheral sensory neurons regenerate normally until they reach the spinal cord, at which point their regeneration comes to an abrupt halt. These findings suggest that there is something about the environment of the CNS that impedes regeneration. What could that something be? Two possibilities have been widely entertained. One is that the astroglia scar tissue that forms at areas of damage in the CNS, but not in the PNS, is the major impediment; however, attempts to promote regeneration by removing the scar tissue from CNS lesions have not been successful. The other possibility is that, unlike Schwann cells, **oligodendroglia,** which myelinate CNS axons, do not provide a physical substrate through which regenerating axons can grow (see Keynes, 1987).

Aguayo (1987) and his colleagues have conducted two noteworthy studies based on the premise that CNS axons will regenerate if provided with a Schwann-cell "pipeline." In the first of these, David and Aguayo (1981) dissected 35-millimeter segments of peripheral nerve from donor rats and grafted one end of each segment to the brain stem and the other to the spinal cord of host rats. Both the brain stem and spinal cord were damaged at the grafting sites. Several months later, histological examination revealed that axons from cell bodies at both ends of the graft had grown into the graft, along it, and out the other end back into the CNS. However, once the growing axon tips reentered the CNS, they stopped growing. In the second study, Bray, Vidal-Sanz, and Aguayo (1987) employed a similar procedure for promoting neural regeneration in the brain (see Figure 15.21). First, they cut the optic nerves of several rats and grafted a 4-centimeter length of peripheral nerve to each of the proximal stumps. The other end of the transplant was brought outside the skull and tied off. Two months later, the tied-off end of the transplant was untied. In half the cases, the untied end was injected with horseradish peroxidase, which revealed that axons from approximately 12,000 retinal ganglion cells had regenerated into the transplant. In the other half of the cases, the untied end of the transplant was grafted to one of the superior colliculi. Two months later, histological examination indicated that many retinal ganglion cells had regenerated through the Schwann-cell bridge into the superior colliculus. The next step in this line of research will be to determine whether or not such regeneration enables the rats to see.

The optic nerve of a rat was cut, and a segment of peripheral nerve excised from another rat was grafted to the proximal stump. The other end of the graft was brought outside the body and tied off. Two months later the axons of many retinal ganglion cells had regenerated into the graft.

In some rats, the other end of the graft was implanted in the superior colliculus. Subsequent injections of horseradish peroxidase into the eye revealed that the axons of many retinal ganglion cells had grown through the graft and into the superior colliculus.

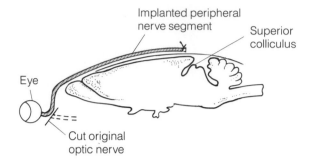

Implanted peripheral nerve segment

Superior colliculus

Eye

Cut original optic nerve

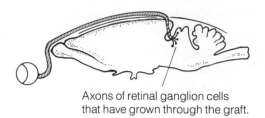

Axons of retinal ganglion cells that have grown through the graft.

FIGURE 15.21 *Illustration of the transplantation study of Bray, Vidal-Sanz, and Aguayo (1987).*

The Transplantation of Neural Replacement Parts in the Brain

The second experimental approach to the treatment of brain damage by transplantation has been to replace damaged tissue with healthy tissue obtained from other sources. This approach has been used on several fronts, but the most progress has been made in the treatment of Parkinson's disease. You may recall from Chapter 5 that the symptoms of Parkinson's disease (e.g., rigidity, tremor at rest, and lack of spontaneous movement) seem to result from the degeneration of a population of dopamine-releasing neurons that projects from the *substantia nigra* to the *striatum* via the *nigrostriatal bundle*.

The first demonstration that transplanted neural tissue can improve the behavior of a brain-damaged mammal came from a study of the *6-hydroxydopamine model* of dopamine function (see Chapter 4). First, the neurotoxin 6-hydroxydopamine was injected directly into one substantia nigra of each of a group of rats. The resulting destruction of dopaminergic neurons in the area produced a severe postural asymmetry and caused the rats to circle toward the side of the lesion each time they walked. Dopamine-releasing substantia nigra precursor cells obtained from rat embryos were then implanted in the ventricular wall next to the lesion. These implants reduced the circling behavior of the lesioned rats even though only a few axons from the implant grew into the striatum (Perlow, Freed, Hoffer, Seiger, Olson, & Wyatt, 1979). In a subsequent study (Björkland & Stenevi, 1979), substantia nigra precursor cells were implanted in rats with unilateral 6-hydroxydopamine lesions in a prepared cavity adjacent to the striatum. Numerous axons from the implant subsequently grew into the striatum, and the degree of innervation in various rats was related to the degree of their behavioral improvement. The behavioral improvement following nigral implants in rats with unilateral 6-hydroxydopamine lesions lasts for at least 6 months (Freed, Perlow, Karoum, Seiger, Olson, Hoffer, & Wyatt, 1980), but the circling can be fully reinstated by subsequent surgical removal of the graft (Björkland, Dunnett, Stenevi, Lewis, & Iversen, 1980).

Bilateral transplantation of fetal substantia nigra cells has also proven successful in alleviating the parkinsonian symptoms induced in monkeys by intramuscular injections of MPTP (Sladek, Redmond, Collier, Haber, Elsworth, Deutch, & Roth, 1987). (You may remember from Chapter 5 that MPTP was discovered in 1982 when a group of young drug addicts developed Parkinson's disease after they self-administered a synthetic opiate that had been incorrectly manufactured and contained the MPTP toxin.) Fetal substantia nigra transplants survived in the MPTP-treated monkeys, they innervated adjacent striatal tissue, they released dopamine, and most importantly, they alleviated the severe poverty of movement, tremor, and rigidity produced by the MPTP. The fact that the degree of improvement observed in each monkey was related to the degree to which dopaminergic axons from the graft invaded the striatum suggested that the innervation of the striatum by the implant was the critical factor in their recovery.

Despite the success of this line of research, it is unlikely that human fetal implants will ever be widely used in the treatment of Parkinson's disease because of the ethical barriers against the acquisition of donor tissue from human fetuses. A more practical procedure involves the transplantation of a portion of the patient's own *adrenal medulla,* which is a good source of dopamine, next to the striatum. Despite the fact that the beneficial effects of adrenal medulla **autotransplants** were found to be both modest and temporary in rats with 6-hydroxydopamine lesions (e.g., Strömberg, Herrera-Marschitz, Ungerstedt, Ebendal, & Olson, 1985), this procedure was subsequently tried on people with Parkinson's disease. Some clinical investigators claim that this method has little or no therapeutic benefit (Backlund, Granberg, Hamberger, Sedvall, Seiger, & Olson, 1985), whereas others have heralded it as a major breakthrough in the treatment of Parkinson's disease (Madrazo, Drucker-Colin, Diaz, Martínez-Mata, Torres, Becerril, 1987). Despite the controversy, this operation is currently being performed at dozens of hospitals around the world.

"Any competent neurosurgical team can perform this operation," notes John Sladek of the University of Rochester Medical Center. "But there is no question in my mind that people are rushing ahead too quickly. I can understand why there is so much excitement about the prospects of being involved in this endeavor. But, with laboratory experimentation still at a very early and uncertain stage, the rush to the clinic begins to look premature." For instance, more humans have now undergone the adrenal implant procedure in the clinic than monkeys have experimentally in the laboratory. . . . Many of the neurosurgeons apparently felt, "it works, so let's get on with it." By contrast, many of the research neuroscientists were more cautious, saying, "it's not clear what's going on here, so let's get some more information." (*Science, 237,* 1987, p. 245)

Conclusion

In this chapter, you have learned about various aspects of neuroplasticity. You have learned about the changes in the nervous system that occur during development (Section 15.1); about the changes in simple neural circuits that may be the basis of learning (Section 15.2); and about neural regeneration, degeneration, and transplantation (Section 15.3). Section 15.3 began with the image of a cartoon scientist running about clucking like a chicken, and the chapter ends on a similar, but less frivolous, note. It ends with the experiment of Balaban, Teillet, and LeDouarin (1988), who removed the segment of the neural tube of a chicken fetus that would have normally developed into the mesencephalon and diencephalon, and in its place implanted tissue from the corresponding area of a Japanese quail neural tube. A few days after the five chicks in this condition hatched, Balaban and his colleagues performed a spectrographic analysis of their crowing sounds. All five of the chicks made abnormal crowing sounds, and three of them made sounds unmistakably like those of a Japanese quail. Transplantation of other segments of the neural tube did not have this effect. With this experiment, the cross-species transfer of behavior by neuronal transplantation has left the realm of childhood fantasy. The possibilities of this procedure boggle the imagination.

___ **Food for Thought** _____

1. Neurotransplants are now being used in the treatment of Parkinson's disease. Can you think of some other potential applications of this procedure?
2. Do you think it will ever be possible to transplant memories? How might such an experiment be conducted?
3. How has this chapter changed your concept of the brain?

ADDITIONAL READING

Two excellent books on neurodevelopment are

Hopkins, W. G., & Brown, M. C. (1984). *Development of nerve cells and their connections.* Cambridge: Cambridge University Press.

Purves, D., & Lichtman, J. W. (1985). *Principles of neural development.* Sunderland, Massachusetts: Sinauer.

Research on the cellular basis of learning is reviewed in

Byrne, J. H. (1987). Cellular analysis of associative learning. *Physiological Reviews, 67,* 329–437.

A good introduction to the topic of neurotransplantation is provided by

Fine, A. (1986). Transplantation in the central nervous system. *Scientific American, 255,* 52–58B.

KEY TERMS

To help you study the material in this chapter, all of the key terms—those that have appeared in bold type—are listed and briefly defined here.

Abducens nerve. The sixth cranial nerve; in the rabbit, it includes axons innervating the eye retractor muscle.

Aggregation. The alignment of cells during development to form the various organs of the body.

Anterograde degeneration. The degeneration of the distal segment of a cut axon.

Anterograde transneuronal degeneration. The degeneration of a neuron caused by damage to neurons that synapse on it.

Astroglia. Specialized glial cells that absorb debris at sites of neuronal damage in the CNS.

Autotransplantation. Transplanting a body part to a different location in the same body.

Axotomy. Severing an axon.

Blueprint hypothesis. The hypothesis that the undeveloped nervous system contains various chemical and/or mechanical trails that growing axons follow to their destinations.

Chemoaffinity hypothesis. The hypothesis that each postsynaptic surface in the nervous system bears a specific chemical label to which a particular axon is attracted during development.

Collateral sprouting. When processes grow out of the axons of healthy cells to synapse on sites abandoned by adjacent degenerating axons.

Differential adhesion hypothesis. The hypothesis that neural crest cells migrate through tissue by following pathways to which they tend to adhere.

Discriminated Pavlovian conditioning. When a conditional stimulus that has been paired with the unconditional stimulus elicits a conditional response, but a conditional stimulus that has not been paired with the unconditional stimulus does not.

Dishabituation. When a stimulus releases a response from habituation.

Distal segment. The segment of a cut axon between the cut and the synaptic terminals.

Ectoderm. The outermost layer of cells in the developing embryo.

Fasciculation. The tendency of growing axons to grow along the paths followed by previous axons.

Glutamate. The main excitatory neurotransmitter of the hippocampus, and perhaps the brain.

Granule-cell layer. A layer of cell bodies in the dentate gyrus of the hippocampus.

Growth cone. The structure at the growing tip of an axon or dendrite, which is thought to guide its growth.

Habituation. The decrease in the strength of the behavioral reaction to a repeatedly presented stimulus.

Hippocampal-slice preparation. Slices of hippocampal tissue that have been cut from a living brain and maintained alive in a saline bath so that their circuitry can be studied.

Induction. When a cell's environment influences its course of development; the mesoderm seems to induce changes in the adjacent neural plate.

Inside-out pattern of cortical development. The deepest layers of the cortex are formed first; thus, cells migrating to the outer layers must pass through the deepest layers.

Interpositus nucleus. A nucleus in the cerebellum that is thought to play a role in the Pavlovian conditioning of the nictitating-membrane reflex.

Long-term potentiation (LTP). After a few seconds of intense high-frequency electrical stimulation to presynaptic fibers, the response of the postsynaptic neurons to low-intensity stimulation of the presynaptic fibers is increased; LTP can last for several days.

Mesoderm layer. The layer beneath the ectoderm in the developing fetus.

Migration. The movement of cells from their site of creation in the ventricular zone of the neural tube to their ultimate location in the mature nervous system.

Nerve growth factor (NGF). A chemical that has the ability to attract the growing axons of the sympathetic nervous system.

Neural cell adhesion molecules. The molecules on the surface of the neural cells that are thought to mediate aggregation.

Neural crest. The structure formed above and to the sides of the neural tube, which develops into the peripheral nervous system.

Neural plate. A small patch of embryonic ectodermal tissue from which the neural groove, the neural tube, and ultimately the mature nervous system develops.

Neural tube. The tube formed in the embryo when the edges of the neural groove fuse; the neural tube develops into the central nervous system.

Nictitating membrane. The inner eyelid of animals such as rabbits.

N-methyl-D-aspartate (NMDA) receptor. A glutamate receptor subtype that is thought to play a critical role in LTP.

Nonassociative learning. A change in behavior that results from the repeated experience of a single stimulus or of two or more stimuli that are not temporally or spatially related.

Oligodendroglia. Glial cells that myelinate CNS neurons.

Optic tectum. In lower vertebrates, the main destination of visual neurons—rather than the visual cortex.

Pavlovian conditioning. A procedure in which a conditional stimulus comes to elicit a conditional response as the result of its being paired with an unconditional stimulus.

Perforant path. A major input into the hippocampus; perforant path axons synapse on neurons in the granule-cell layer.

Phagocytes. Cells, such as astroglia, that absorb dead or foreign material.

Phagocytosis. The act of absorbing cellular debris.

Pioneer growth cones. The first growth cones to grow into a particular area of the developing nervous system.

Presynaptic facilitation. The cellular mechanism thought to underlie sensitization and Pavlovian conditioning.

Proximal segment. The segment of a cut axon between the cut and the cell body.

Radial glial cells. Glial cells found in the neural tube only during the period of neural migration; they form a matrix along which developing neurons migrate.

Retinal ganglion cells. The cells that compose the optic nerve.

Retrograde degeneration. Degeneration of the proximal segment.

Retrograde transneuronal degeneration. When a neuron degenerates as the result of damage to neurons on which it synapses.

Schwann cells. The cells that compose the myelin sheaths of peripheral nervous system axons.

Sensitization. The increase in an animal's responsiveness to stimuli following a noxious stimulus.

Simple-systems approach. Attempting to find the neural basis of complex processes such as learning and memory by studying them in simple neural systems.

Topographic-gradient hypothesis. The hypothesis that neuronal growth is guided by relative position on intersecting gradients, rather than by a point-to-point coding of neural connections.

Totipotential. Cells that have the potential to develop into any type of body cell are said to be totipotential.

Transneuronal degeneration. Degeneration of a neuron that is caused by damage to other neurons in the same neural circuit.

Trigeminal nerve. The fifth cranial nerve; it includes sensory fibers carrying touch information from receptors in the skin around the eye.

Ventricular zone. The zone adjacent to the ventricle in the developing neural tube.

16

Drug Abuse and Reward Circuits in the Brain

Psychoactive drugs are drugs that influence subjective experience and behavior by acting on the nervous system. In the preceding chapters, you have repeatedly encountered psychoactive drugs functioning at their best, in the study of the nervous system and in the treatment of its disorders. This chapter, with its focus on drug abuse, provides a perspective of the more sinister side of psychoactive drugs.

There are three main sections in this chapter. Section 16.1 introduces you to some basic pharmacological principles and concepts. Section 16.2 discusses five commonly abused drugs (tobacco, alcohol, marijuana, cocaine, and heroin), and Section 16.3 describes a circuit in the brain that is thought to be involved in drug addiction. A concluding case study of one remarkable addict, Sigmund Freud, ties the three sections together and provides closing food for thought.

16.1 The Basic Principles of Drug Action

16.2 Five Commonly Abused Drugs

16.3 Biopsychological Theories of Addiction and Reward Circuits in the Brain

While reading this chapter, it is important for you to keep from being misled by the legal and social status of the drugs under discussion. Most laws governing drug abuse in various parts of the world were enacted in the last century or in the early part of this one, long before

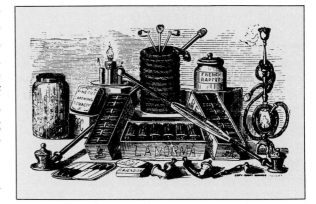

there was any scientific research on the topic. Many people do not appreciate this fact, and they equate drug legality with drug safety. This point was recently made to me in a particularly ironic fashion.

I was invited to address a convention of high school teachers on the topic of drug abuse. When I arrived at the convention center to give my talk, I was escorted to a special suite, where I was encouraged to join the executive committee in a round of drug taking—the drug was a special high-proof single-malt whiskey. Later, the irony of the situation had its full impact. As I stepped to the podium under the influence of a psychoactive drug (i.e., the whiskey), I looked out through the haze of cigarette smoke at an audience of educators, who had invited me to speak to them because they were concerned about the unhealthy impact of drugs on their students. The welcoming applause gradually gave way to the melodic tinkling of ice cubes in liquor glasses, and I began.

16.1 The Basic Principles of Drug Action

Drug Administration and Absorption

Drugs are most commonly administered in one of four ways: by oral ingestion; by injection; by inhalation; or by absorption through the mucous membranes of the nose, mouth, or rectum. The route of administration is an important determinant of the effects of a drug because it influences the rate at which and the degree to which it reaches its sites of action.

Ingestion The oral route is the preferred route of administration for many drugs. Once they are swallowed, they dissolve in the fluids of the stomach and are carried by them to the intestine, where they are absorbed into the bloodstream. Those drugs that are not readily absorbed from the digestive tract or are broken down into inactive metabolites before they can be absorbed must be taken by some other route. The two main advantages of the oral route over other routes are its ease and relative safety. Its main disadvantage is its unpredictability; absorption from the digestive tract into the bloodstream can be greatly influenced by difficult-to-gauge factors such as the amount and type of food in the stomach. Drugs, such as alcohol, that readily pass through the stomach wall take effect soon after ingestion because they do not have to be carried to the intestine to be absorbed.

Injection Drug injection is common in medical practice because the effects of injected drugs are large, rapid, and predictable. Drug injections are typically made into the fatty tissue just beneath the skin [**subcutaneously** (SC)], into large muscles [**intramuscularly** (IM)], or directly into veins at points where they run just beneath the skin [**intravenously** (IV)]. Many addicts prefer the intravenous route because the bloodstream delivers most of an intravenously injected drug directly to the brain. However, the speed and directness of the intravenous route are mixed blessings; after an intravenous injection, there is little or no opportunity to counteract the effects of an overdose, an impurity, or an allergic reaction. Furthermore, many addicts develop scar tissue, infections, and collapsed veins at the few sites on their bodies where there are large superficial veins.

Inhalation Some drugs can be quickly absorbed into the bloodstream through the rich network of capillaries in the lungs. Many anesthetics are commonly administered by *inhalation*, as are tobacco and marijuana. The two main shortcomings of this route are that it is difficult to precisely regulate the dose of inhaled drugs, and many inhaled substances damage the lungs.

Absorption through Mucous Membranes Some drugs can be administered through the mucous membranes of the nose, mouth, and rectum. Cocaine, for example, is commonly self-administered through the nasal membranes (i.e., snorted)—but not without damaging them.

Penetration of the Central Nervous System by Drugs

Once a drug enters the bloodstream, it readily enters the circulatory system of the central nervous system. Fortunately, a protective filter, the *blood-brain barrier,* makes it difficult for many potentially dangerous blood-borne chemicals to pass from the circulatory system of the CNS into the CNS per se (see Chapters 2 and 4).

Mechanisms of Drug Action

Psychoactive drugs influence the nervous system in many ways (see Koob & Bloom, 1988). Some, such as alcohol and many of the general anesthetics, act diffusely on neural membranes throughout the CNS. Others act in a less general way: by binding to particular synaptic receptors; by influencing the synthesis, transport, release, or deactivation of particular neurotransmitters; or by influencing the chain of chemical reactions elicited in postsynaptic neurons by the activation of their synaptic receptors (see Chapters 3 and 6). Although some drugs are much more selective in their actions than others, the lesson taught by decades of psychopharmacological research is that no psychoactive drug has effects that are entirely selective. At doses high enough to produce psychological changes, all psychoactive drugs influence CNS activity in a variety of ways.

Drug Metabolism and Elimination

The actions of most drugs are terminated when enzymes synthesized by the liver stimulate their conversion to nonactive forms, a process referred to as **drug metabolism.** In most cases, these metabolic changes eliminate a drug's ability to pass through lipid membranes so that it can no longer penetrate the blood-brain barrier. Some drugs are temporarily deactivated by being bound to fat deposits or to large proteins in the blood. Although such binding reduces the drug effect in the short term, it often increases it in the long term as the bound drug is gradually released back into circulation. Small amounts of some psychoactive drugs are eliminated from the body in sweat, feces, breath, and mother's milk before they can be metabolized.

Drug Tolerance

Drug tolerance is a state of decreased sensitivity to a drug that develops as a result of exposure to it. Drug tolerance can be demonstrated in two ways: by showing that a given dose of the drug has less effect than it had before exposure to it, or by showing that it takes more of the drug to produce the same effect. In essence, what this means is that tolerance is a shift in the *dose-response curve* (a graph of the magnitude of the effect of different doses of the drug) to the right (see Figure 16.1).

There are three important points to remember about the specificity of drug tolerance. The first is that exposure to one drug can produce tolerance to other drugs that act by the same mechanism. This is known as **cross tolerance.** The second is that tolerance often develops to some effects of a drug and not to others. Failure to understand this second point can have tragic consequences for people who think that because they have become tolerant to some effects of a drug (e.g., to the nauseating effects of alcohol or tobacco), they are tolerant to all of them. The third is that drug tolerance is not a unitary phenomenon in the sense that there is a single basic mechanism underlying all examples of it. When a drug is administered at active doses, many kinds of adaptive changes can occur to reduce the effect of the drug. It is usual to refer to tolerance that results from a reduction in

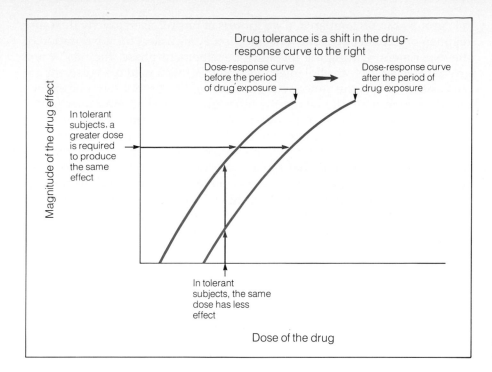

Drug tolerance is a shift in the drug-
response curve to the right

Dose-response curve
before the period
of drug exposure

Dose-response curve
after the period of
drug exposure

In tolerant
subjects, a
greater dose
is required
to produce
the same
effect

Magnitude of the drug effect

In tolerant
subjects, the same
dose has less
effect

Dose of the drug

FIGURE 16.1 *Drug tolerance is a shift in the dose-response curve to the right as the result of exposure to the drug.*

the amount of drug getting to its sites of action as **metabolic tolerance.** Drug tolerance resulting from a reduction in the reactivity of the target sites to the drug is called **functional tolerance.** Tolerance to psychoactive drugs is primarily functional.

Several different kinds of neural adaptations have been shown to contribute to the development of functional tolerance to psychoactive drugs. For example, exposure to a drug can reduce the degree to which that drug subsequently binds to receptors on neural membranes; it can produce chemical changes in neurons that reduce the impact of the drug's binding to receptors; and it can produce changes in the structure of neural membranes that diminish the drug's effect. All of these changes are caused by direct exposure of the neurons to the drug, and they are often studied by neurochemists in experiments in which tissue cultures are exposed to measured concentrations of the drug in strictly controlled chemical environments. However, psychopharmacologists have shown that some of the changes that contribute to the development of tolerance to psychoactive drugs are learned, and thus cannot be studied *in vitro* (i.e., outside of the living organism). This point has been emphasized by two important lines of research on tolerance: by one line that has focused on what subjects do while they are under the influence of a psychoactive drug, and by one line that has focused on the environments in which the drug effects are experienced.

Those studies of drug tolerance that have focused on the behavior of subjects during drug exposure have often employed the **before-and-after design** (Chen, 1968). In before-and-after experiments, two groups of subjects receive the same series of drug injections and the same series of tests, but the subjects in one group receive an injection before each test, while those in the other group receive an injection after each test. At the end of the experiment, all subjects receive the same dose of the drug followed by a test so that the degree to which the drug disrupts test performance in the two groups can be compared. Two groups of rats received exactly the same regimen of alcohol injections, one injection every 2 days for the duration of the experiment. During the tolerance-development phase, the rats in one group received each alcohol injection 1 hour before a mild convulsive brain stimulation so that the anticonvulsant effect of the alcohol could be experienced on each trial. The rats in the other group received their injections 1 hour after each convulsive stimulation so that the anticonvulsant effect could not be repeatedly experienced. At the end of the experiment, all of the subjects received a test injection of alcohol, followed 1 hour later by a convulsive stimulation so that the amount of tolerance to the anticonvulsant effect of alcohol could be compared in the two groups. As illustrated in Figure 16.2, the rats that received alcohol on each trial before a convulsive stimulation became tolerant to alcohol's anticonvulsant effect, whereas those that received the same injections and stimulations but in the reverse order did not. This same pattern of findings has been reported in many other experiments involving different drugs and different drug effects (e.g., Demellweek & Goudie, 1983; Pinel, Kim, Paul, & Mana, 1989; Poulos & Hinson, 1984; Traynor, Schlapfer, & Barondes, 1980; Wenger, Tiffany, Bombadier, Nicholls, & Woods, 1981)—perhaps the most provocative of these is an experiment in which tolerance to the disruptive effects of alcohol on male sexual behavior developed fully in male rats only if they were allowed to engage in sexual activity after each injection (Pinel, Pfaus, & Christensen, 1988). Together, these various effects—which are generally referred to as *contingent drug tolerance* (Carlton & Wolgin, 1971)—suggest that many forms of tolerance are adaptations to the repeated experience of the drug effect (e.g., the anticonvulsant effect of alcohol), rather than to exposure to the drug per se. The major strength of this **drug-effect theory of tolerance** is that it explains how tolerance can develop to one effect of a drug, while at the very same time in the same subject not develop to other effects of a drug.

The second important line of research to demonstrate the major role of learning in drug tolerance has focused on the environment in which the drug effects are experienced. For example, in one study (Crowell, Hinson, & Siegel, 1981), two groups of rats received 20 alcohol and 20 saline injections in an alternating sequence, one injection every other day. The only difference between the two groups was that the rats in one group received all 20 alcohol injections in a distinctive test room and the 20 saline injections in their colony room, while the rats in the other group received the alcohol in the colony room and the saline in the distinctive test room. Then, the tolerance of all rats to the **hypothermic** (temperature-reducing) effects of alcohol was assessed in both environments. As illustrated in Figure 16.3, tolerance was observed only when the rats were injected in the environment that had previously been paired with alcohol administration. This *situational specificity of drug tolerance* has been demonstrated in many other experiments involving a variety of drugs (e.g., Le, Poulos, & Cappell, 1979; Mansfield & Cunningham, 1980; Siegel, 1978).

The numerous demonstrations of the situational specificity of drug tolerance led Siegel and his colleagues to propose that addicts may be particularly susceptible to the lethal effects of a drug *overdose* when the drug is administered in a new context. Their hypothesis is that addicts become tolerant when they repeatedly self-administer their drug in the same environments, and as a result, they begin taking larger and larger doses to counteract the diminution of drug effects. Then, when the addict adminis-

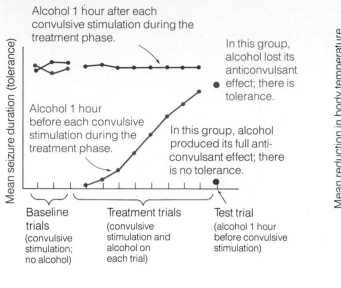

Alcohol 1 hour after each convulsive stimulation during the treatment phase.

In this group, alcohol lost its anticonvulsant effect; there is tolerance.

Alcohol 1 hour before each convulsive stimulation during the treatment phase.

In this group, alcohol produced its full anticonvulsant effect; there is no tolerance.

Baseline trials (convulsive stimulation; no alcohol)

Treatment trials (convulsive stimulation and alcohol on each trial)

Test trial (alcohol 1 hour before convulsive stimulation)

Trials every 2 days

FIGURE 16.2 *Tolerance to the anticonvulsant effect of alcohol depends on the repeated experience of the anticonvulsant effect. The rats that received alcohol (1.5 g/kg) on each trial before a convulsive stimulation became tolerant to its anticonvulsant effect; those that received the same injections after a convulsive stimulation on each trial did not become tolerant. (Adapted from Pinel, Mana, & Kim, 1989.)*

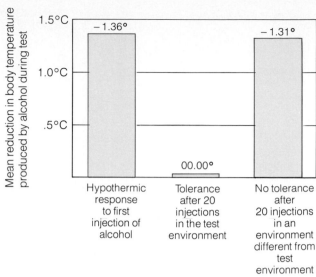

FIGURE 16.3 *The situational specificity of tolerance to the hypothermic effects of alcohol. (Adapted from Crowell et al., 1981.)*

ters her or his usual massive dose in an unusual situation, tolerance effects are not present to counteract the effects of the drug, and there is a greater risk of death from overdose in a new context. In support of this hypothesis, Siegel, Hinson, Krank, and McCully (1982) found that 96% of a group of heroin-tolerant rats died following a high dose of heroin administered in a novel environment, but only 64% died following the same dose administered in their usual injection environment. (Heroin kills by suppressing respiration.)

Of the several noteworthy theories that have been proposed to account for the situational specificity of drug tolerance (see Baker & Tiffany, 1985; Eikelboom & Stewart, 1982; Paletta & Wagner, 1986), Siegel's theory has been the most influential. Siegel views each incidence of drug administration as a Pavlovian conditioning trial (see Chapter 4) in which various environmental stimuli that regularly predict the administration of the drug (e.g., pubs, washrooms, needles, other addicts) are conditional stimuli, and the drug effects are unconditional stimuli. The central assumption of the theory is that, unlike most conventional forms of Pavlovian conditioning, conditional stimuli that predict drug administration come to elicit conditional responses opposite to the unconditional effects of the drug. Siegel has termed these hypothetical opposing conditional responses **conditioned compensatory responses**. The theory is that as the stimuli that repeatedly predict the effects of a drug come to elicit greater and greater conditioned compensatory responses, they increasingly counteract the unconditional effects of the drug and produce situationally specific tolerance. A schematic illustration of Siegel's conditioned compensatory response theory is presented in Figure 16.4.

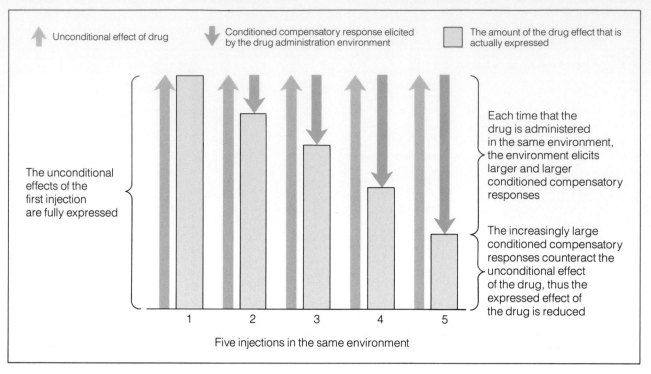

Legend at top of figure:

↑ Unconditional effect of drug   ↓ Conditioned compensatory response elicited by the drug administration environment   ▢ The amount of the drug effect that is actually expressed

The unconditional effects of the first injection are fully expressed

Each time that the drug is administered in the same environment, the environment elicits larger and larger conditioned compensatory responses

The increasingly large conditioned compensatory responses counteract the unconditional effect of the drug, thus the expressed effect of the drug is reduced

1   2   3   4   5

Five injections in the same environment

FIGURE 16.4 *A schematic illustration of the conditioned compensatory response interpretation of the situational specificity of drug tolerance.*

Drug Withdrawal and Physical Dependence

After substantial amounts of a drug have been in the body for a long time (e.g., several days), its sudden elimination can trigger an illness called a **withdrawal syndrome.** The nature and severity of the withdrawal symptoms depend on the particular drug in question, on the duration and degree of the preceding drug exposure, and on the speed with which the drug is eliminated from the body. Withdrawal symptoms are generally assumed to be produced by some of the same functional changes that underlie drug tolerance. It is assumed that the presence of the drug produces compensatory changes in the nervous system that offset the drug effects and produce tolerance. Then, when the drug is eliminated from the body, these compensatory changes, without the drug to offset them, manifest themselves as withdrawal symptoms. As a result, withdrawal effects are usually opposite to the initial effects of the drug; for example, the withdrawal of sleeping pills often produces insomnia (see Chapter 13), and the withdrawal of anticonvulsants often triggers convulsions. Individuals who suffer withdrawal reactions when they stop taking a drug are said to be **physically dependent** on that drug.

Addiction, Physical Dependence, and Psychological Dependence

Not all drug users are addicts. Addicts are those drug users who continue to use drugs despite the drugs' adverse effects on their health and social life, and despite their repeated efforts to stop. The greatest source of misconception about drug addiction comes from the tendency of some experts and most lay people to equate it with physical dependence. The addict is seen as a person who is helplessly trapped on a merry-go-round of drug taking, withdrawal symptoms, and further drug taking to combat the withdrawal symptoms. While appealing in its simplicity, this conception of drug addiction is wrong. Although addicts sometimes take drugs to alleviate their withdrawal symptoms, this is usually not the primary motivating factor in their addiction. If it were, addicts could be easily cured of their addiction simply by hospitalizing them for a few days, until their withdrawal symptoms have subsided. This treatment approach has proven to be almost totally ineffective; most addicts quickly renew their drug taking even after months or years of enforced abstinence. This is an important issue; we will return to it later in this chapter.

16.2 Five Commonly Abused Drugs

This section is about five commonly abused drugs: tobacco, alcohol, marijuana, cocaine, and heroin.

Tobacco

Next to caffeine, tobacco is the most widely used psychoactive drug in our society. When a cigarette is smoked, **nicotine,** the major psychoactive ingredient of tobacco, and numerous other chemicals, including *carbon monoxide,* are absorbed through the lungs. Because considerable tolerance develops to some of the immediate adverse effects of tobacco, the effects of smoking a cigarette on nonsmokers and smokers can be quite different. Nonsmokers often respond to a few puffs of a cigarette with various combinations of nausea, vomiting, coughing, sweating, abdominal cramps, dizziness, flushing, and diarrhea. In contrast, smokers report that they are more relaxed, more alert, and less hungry after a cigarette.

There is no question that heavy smokers are drug addicts in every sense of the word (Jones, 1987). The compulsive drug craving, which is the major defining feature of addiction, is readily apparent in any heavy smoker who has run out of cigarettes or who is forced by circumstance to refrain from smoking for several hours. Furthermore, heavy smokers who stop smoking experience a variety of withdrawal effects such as depression, anxiety, restlessness, irritability, constipation, and difficulties in sleeping and concentrating.

The consequences of long-term tobacco use are alarming. **Smokers' syndrome** is characterized by chest pain, labored breathing, wheezing, coughing, and a heightened susceptibility to infections of the respiratory tract. Chronic smokers are highly susceptible to a variety of potentially lethal lung disorders including pneumonia, *bronchitis* (chronic inflammation of the bronchioles of the lungs), *emphysema* (loss of elasticity of the lung from chronic irritation), and lung cancer. Although the increased risk of lung cancer receives the greatest publicity, smoking also increases the risk of cancer of the larynx (voice box), mouth, esophagus, kidneys, pancreas, bladder, and stomach. Smokers also run a great risk of developing a variety of cardiovascular diseases, which may culminate in heart attack or stroke.

Sufferers from **Buerger's disease** provide a startling illustration of the addictive power of nicotine. Buerger's disease is a condition in which the blood vessels, especially those supplying the legs, are constricted whenever nicotine enters the bloodstream.

If a patient with this condition continues to smoke, gangrene may eventually set in. First a few toes may have to be amputated, then the foot at the ankle, then the leg at the knee, and ultimately at the hip. Somewhere along this gruesome progression gangrene may also attack the other leg. Patients are strongly advised that if they will only stop smoking, it is virtually certain that the otherwise inexorable march of gangrene up the legs will be curbed. Yet surgeons report that it is not at all uncommon to find a patient with Buerger's disease vigorously puffing away in his hospital bed following a second or third amputation operation. (Brecher, 1972, pp. 215–216)

The adverse effects of tobacco smoke are unfortunately not restricted to those who smoke. There is now strong evidence that individuals who live or work with smokers are more likely to develop heart disease and cancer than those who don't. Even the unborn are vulnerable; smoking during pregnancy increases the likelihood of miscarriage, stillbirth, and early death of the child. The levels of nicotine in the blood of a breast-fed infant are frequently as great as those in the blood of the mother.

Alcohol

Ethyl alcohol is a psychoactive drug, which readily invades all parts of the body because of its lipid solubility and small molecular size. Most of its psychological effects are attributable to the fact that it depresses neural firing—hence it belongs to the class of drugs called **depressants.** At low doses, it produces a general feeling of well-being and relaxation. At moderate doses, the drinker experiences various degrees of cognitive, perceptual, verbal, and motor impairment, as well as a loss of control that can lead to a variety of socially unacceptable actions. High doses result in unconsciousness, and if blood levels reach 0.5%, there is a risk of death from respiratory depression. The tell-tale red flush of alcohol intoxication is produced by the dilation of blood vessels in the skin; this increases the amount of heat that is lost from the blood to the air and leads to a decrease in body temperature. Alcohol is a **diuretic;** that is, it increases the production of urine by the kidney.

Alcohol, like many addictive drugs, produces both tolerance and physical dependence. The livers of heavy drinkers metabolize alcohol more quickly than do the livers of nondrinkers, but this increase in metabolic efficiency contributes only slightly to overall alcohol tolerance—most alcohol tolerance is functional. Alcohol withdrawal often produces a mild syndrome of headache, nausea, vomiting, and tremulousness euphemistically referred to as a *hangover* (Pinel & Mucha, 1980), but in its severe form, the alcohol withdrawal syndrome is life-threatening and comprises three distinguishable phases. The first phase begins about 5 or 6 hours after the cessation of a long bout of heavy drinking and is characterized by severe tremors, agitation, headache, nausea, vomiting, abdominal cramps, profuse sweating, and sometimes hallucinations. The defining feature of the second phase, which typically occurs between 15 and 30 hours after cessation of drinking, is convulsive activity, which is frequently *grand mal* (see Chapter 5). The third phase, which usually begins a day or two after the cessation of drinking and lasts for 3 or 4 days, is called **delirium tremens** (the DTs). The DTs are characterized by disturbing hallucinations, bizarre delusions, agitation, confusion, *hyperthermia* (high temperature), and *tachycardia* (rapid heartbeat). The convulsions and the DTs produced by alcohol withdrawal are often lethal.

Alcohol attacks almost every tissue in the body. Chronic alcohol consumption produces extensive brain damage and an associated disorder known as **Korsakoff's syndrome** (see Chapter 14), which is characterized by severe memory loss, sensory and motor dysfunction, and severe *dementia* (intellectual deterioration). It also causes extensive scarring or **cirrhosis** of the liver, which is the major cause of death among heavy alcohol users. It erodes the muscles of the heart and thus increases the risk of heart attack. It irritates the lining of the digestive tract, and in so doing increases the risk of oral and liver cancer, stomach ulcers, *pancreatitis* (inflammation of the pancreas), and *gastritis* (inflammation of the stomach). And not to be forgotten is the carnage that it produces on our highways.

Like nicotine, alcohol readily penetrates the placental membrane and affects the fetus. The result is that the offspring of mothers who consume substantial quantities of alcohol during their pregnancy frequently suffer from a disorder known as **fetal alcohol syndrome** (see Mattson, Barron, & Riley, 1988). The FAS child suffers from some or all of the following symptoms: mental retardation, poor coordination, poor muscle tone, low birth weight, retarded growth, and various physical deformities.

Marijuana

Marijuana is the name commonly given to the dried leaves and flowers of the common hemp plant **(Cannabis sativa).** The usual mode of consumption is to smoke these leaves in a *joint* (a cigarette of marijuana) or pipe, but it is also effective when ingested orally if first baked into an oil-rich substrate, such as a chocolate brownie, to promote absorption from the gastrointestinal tract. The psychoactive effects of marijuana are largely attributable to a constituent called delta-9-tetrahydrocannabinol **(delta-9-THC);** however, marijuana contains over 80 *cannabinoids* (chemicals of the same chemical class as delta-9-THC), which may also be psychoactive (see Kephalas, Kiburis, Michael, Miras, & Papadakis, 1976). Most of the cannabinoids are found in a sticky resin covering the leaves and flowers of the plant, which can be extracted and dried to form a dark cork-like material called **hashish.** The hashish can be further processed into an extremely potent product called *hash oil.*

Written records of marijuana use go back 6,000 years in China, where its stem was used to make rope, its seeds were used as a grain, and its leaves and flowers were used for their psychoactive and medicinal effects. One story of ancient cannabis use, whose misrepresentation has had a major impact on modern attitudes toward the drug, involved a Muslim sect headed by one Hashishin-i-Sabbah, a fanatic who tried to purge the Muslim religion of false prophets by having his followers assassinate them. Hashishin reportedly rewarded his successful assassins with a psychoactive drug, which was likely opium (Grinspoon, 1977), but the story spread that it was hashish. Both the words "assassin" and "hashish" were derived from his name.

Cannabis cultivation spread from the Middle East into Western Europe; however, in Europe, it was grown primarily for the manufacture of rope, and its psychoactive properties were largely forgotten. During the period of European imperialism, rope was in high demand for sailing vessels, and in 1611 the American colonies responded to this demand by growing cannabis as a cash crop—George Washington was one of the more notable cannabis growers. The practice of smoking the leaves of the cannabis plant and the word "marijuana" itself seem to have been introduced to the United States in the early part of this century by Mexican laborers, and its use gradually became popular among certain subgroups, such as the poor in city ghettos and jazz musicians. In 1926, an article appeared in a New Orleans newspaper exposing the "menace of marijuana," and soon similar stories were appearing in newspapers all over the United States under titles such as "the evil weed," "the killer drug," and "marijuana madness." The population was told that marijuana turned normal people into violent, drug-crazed criminals who rapidly become addicted to heroin. The old story of Hashishin was revived in a revised form, which had Hashishin giving hashish to his followers, not as a reward for a job well done, but to transform them into killers. The result was the enactment of many laws against the drug. In many states, marijuana was legally classified as a **narcotic** (a legal term generally used to refer to opiates) and punishment was dealt out accordingly. (The structure of marijuana and its physiological and behavioral effects bear no resemblance to those of the other narcotics; thus, legally classifying marijuana as a narcotic was like passing a law that black is green.)

The popularization of marijuana smoking among the middle and upper classes in the 1960s stimulated a massive program of research that has lasted a quarter of a century, yet there is still considerable confusion about marijuana among the general population. One of the difficulties in characterizing the effects of marijuana is that they are subtle, difficult to measure, and greatly influenced by the social situation.

> At low, usual "social" doses, the intoxicated individual may experience an increased sense of well-being: initial restlessness and hilarity followed by a dreamy, carefree state of relaxation; alteration of sensory perceptions including expansion of space and time; and a more vivid sense of touch, sight, smell, taste, and sound; a feeling of hunger, especially a craving for sweets; and subtle changes in thought formation and expression. To an unknowing observer, an individual in this state of consciousness would not appear noticeably different. (National Commission on Marijuana and Drug Abuse, 1972, p. 68)

At unusually high oral doses equivalent to several rapidly smoked joints, the preceding symptoms are intensified and other symptoms may appear. Short-term memory is likely to be impaired, and the ability to carry out tasks involving multiple steps to reach a specific goal declines. Speech often becomes slightly slurred, and meaningful conversation becomes difficult. A sense of unreality, emotional intensification, sensory distortion, slight motor impairment, and general silliness are also common. However, even after very high doses, an unexpected knock at the door can often bring about the return of a reasonable semblance of normal behavior. In the light of such effects, the earlier claims that marijuana would trigger a wave of violent crimes in the youth of America seem absurd. It is difficult to imagine how anybody could believe that the red-eyed, gluttonous, sleepy, giggling products of common social doses of marijuana would be more likely to commit violent criminal acts. In fact, there is evidence that marijuana actually curbs aggressive behavior (Tinklenberg, 1974). There is one effect of marijuana that warrants special mention because of its serious consequences. Marijuana-intoxicated drivers can stop as quickly as normal drivers, but they are not always so quick to notice the things for which they should stop (Moskowitz, Hulbert, & McGlothlin, 1976).

What are the hazards of long-term marijuana use? The main risk appears to be lung damage. Those who regularly smoke marijuana tend to have deficits in respiratory function (e.g., Tilles, Goldenheim, Johnson, Mendelson, Mello, & Hales, 1986), and they are more likely to develop a chronic cough, bronchitis, and asthma (Abramson, 1974). Some authors list four other adverse effects of regular marijuana use; however, in each case, the evidence is either indirect, inconsistent, or incomplete (see Mendelson, 1987). First, there have been reports that chronic marijuana smoking lowers the plasma *testosterone* levels of males (e.g., Kolodny, Masters, Kolodner, & Toro, 1974), but the reported reductions have been too slight to influence sexual behavior, and several studies have failed to confirm them. Second, there has been some suggestion that marijuana can adversely influence the *immune system*, but it has yet to be demonstrated that marijuana smokers are generally more susceptible to infection than are comparable marijuana nonsmokers. Third, because *tachycardia* (rapid heart rate) is one of the most reliable effects of marijuana, there has been some concern that chronic marijuana consumption might cause cardiovascular problems, but again there is no direct evidence for this hypothesis. Fourth, many people have hypothesized that the relaxation produced by marijuana could reach pathological proportions and produce what is generally referred to as **amotivational syndrome.** Although the evidence that marijuana use causes a significant amotivational syndrome is far from strong— no significant difference was found between the grade point averages of marijuana smokers and nonsmokers in a study of 2,000 college students— it seems unlikely that heavy users would not experience some decline in productivity.

The addiction potential of marijuana is low. Most people who use marijuana do so only occasionally, and most who use it as youths curtail their use in their 30s and 40s. Tolerance can develop to marijuana during periods of sustained use (Babor, Mendelson, Greenberg, & Kuehnle, 1975), and withdrawal symptoms (e.g., nausea, diarrhea, sweating, chills, tremor, restlessness, sleep disturbance) can occur, but only in contrived laboratory situations in which massive oral doses are regularly administered.

Some of the effects of marijuana have been shown to be of clinical benefit (see Cohen & Stillman, 1976). The most notable example is marijuana's ability to block the nausea of cancer patients undergoing chemotherapy—*Nabilone*, a synthetic cannabis analogue, is now sometimes prescribed with chemotherapy (Lemberger & Rowe, 1975). Marijuana has also been shown to block seizures (Corcoran, McCaughran, & Wada, 1973), to dilate the bronchioles of asthmatics, and to decrease the severity of *glaucoma* (i.e., a disorder characterized by an increase in the pressure of the fluid inside the eye), but it is not normally prescribed for these purposes.

Cocaine

Cocaine is prepared from the leaf of the coca bush, which is found primarily in Peru and Bolivia. A crude extract called *coca paste* is usually made directly from the leaves; then **cocaine hydrochloride,** the nefarious odorless white power, is extracted from the paste. Cocaine hydrochloride is sometimes converted by abusers to its free-base form and smoked in a pipe. **Crack** is an impure free-base product that is widely used because it is relatively inexpensive.

Cocaine hydrochloride is an effective local anesthetic, and it was once widely prescribed as such until it was supplanted by synthetic analogues such as *procaine* and *lidocaine*. It is not, however, cocaine's anesthetic actions that are of interest to its users. People eat, smoke, snort, or inject cocaine in its various forms in order to experience its psychological effects.

Users report being swept by a wave of well-being; they feel self-confident, alert, energetic, friendly, outgoing, fidgety, and talkative; and they have less desire for food and sleep. These effects are similar to those produced by **amphetamine,** another widely abused stimulant. **Stimulant drugs** are those such as caffeine, nicotine, amphetamine, and cocaine, whose primary effect is to increase neural activity. Coca-Cola is a commercial stimulant preparation consumed by many people around the world. Today, its stimulant action is attributable to caffeine, but when it was first introduced, "the pause that refreshes" purportedly packed a real wallop in the form of small amounts of cocaine.

Like alcohol, cocaine is frequently consumed in *binges*. Cocaine addicts tend to go on so-called **cocaine sprees,** in which extremely high levels of intake are maintained for periods of a day or two. During a cocaine spree, users become increasingly tolerant to the euphoria-producing effects of cocaine. Accordingly, larger and larger doses are often administered to maintain the initial level of euphoria. The spree usually ends when the cocaine is gone or when it begins to have serious toxic effects. During these binges, extremely high blood levels of cocaine are achieved, and sleeplessness, tremors, nausea, and psychotic behavior often occur. The syndrome of psychotic behavior observed during cocaine sprees is called **cocaine psychosis.** It is similar to, and has often been mistakenly diagnosed as, schizophrenia. Although cocaine is extremely addictive, there are typically no obvious withdrawal effects after abrupt termination of a cocaine spree other than a general feeling of lethargy and depression. During cocaine sprees, there is a risk of seizures, loss of consciousness, and death from respiratory arrest or stroke. Although tolerance develops to most effects of cocaine, repeated cocaine exposure makes subjects even more sensitive to its convulsive effects (Stripling & Ellinwood, 1976)—this is called **reverse tolerance.** Fatalities from cocaine overdose are most likely following IV injection; cocaine snorting damages the nasal membranes; and cocaine smoking damages the lungs.

The Opiates: Heroin and Morphine

Opium, the sap that exudes from the seeds of the opium poppy, has several psychoactive ingredients, most notably **morphine** and its weaker relative, **codeine.** These drugs, their stronger and more notorious relative **heroin,** and other drugs that have similar structures or effects are commonly referred to as the **opiates.** The opiates have a Jekyll-and-Hyde problem of major proportions. On their Dr. Jekyll side, opiates are unmatched as **analgesics** (painkillers), and they are also extremely effective in the treatment of severe cases of cough or diarrhea. But unfortunately, the kindly Dr. Jekyll always brings with him the evil Mr. Hyde, the risk of addiction.

Archeological evidence suggests that the practice of eating opium became popular in the Middle East sometime before 4,000 B.C., and then it spread throughout Africa, Europe, and Asia (see Berridge & Edwards, 1981; Latimer & Goldberg, 1981). Three historic events fanned the flame of opiate addiction. First, in 1644, the Emperor of China banned tobacco smoking, and many Chinese tobacco smokers tried smoking opium and liked it. Because smoking opium has a greater effect on the brain than does eating it, many more people became addicted to opium as the practice of opium smoking slowly spread to other countries. Second, morphine, the most potent constituent of opium, was isolated from opium in 1803, and in the 1830s it became available commercially. Third, the hypodermic needle was invented in 1856, and soon injured soldiers (e.g., those of the American Civil War) were introduced to morphine through a needle; during this era morphine addiction was known as *soldiers' disease.*

Most people are surprised to learn that until the late 1800s, opium was legally available and consumed in great quantity in many parts of the world, including Europe and North America. For example, in 1870, opiates were available in cakes, candies, and wines, as well as in a variety of over-the-counter medicinal offerings. Opium potions such as *laudanum* (a very popular mixture of opium and alcohol), *Godfrey's Cordial,* and *Dalby's Carminative* were very popular. (The word *carminative* should win first prize for making a sow's ear at least sound like a silk purse—a carminative is a drug that expels gas from the digestive tract, thus reducing stomach cramps and flatulence. *Flatulence* is the obvious pick for second prize.) There were even over-the-counter opium potions just for baby: potions such as *Mrs. Winslow's Soothing Syrup* and the aptly labeled *Street's Infant Quietness* were popular in many households. Although pure morphine could not be purchased without a prescription at this time, it was so frequently prescribed by physicians for so many different maladies that morphine addiction was very common among those who could afford doctors.

The **Harrison Narcotics Act,** passed in 1914, made it illegal to sell or use opium, morphine, or cocaine in the United States. However, the Act did not mention heroin. Heroin had been synthesized in 1870 by adding two acetyl groups to the morphine molecule, which greatly increased its ability to penetrate the blood-brain barrier. In 1898, heroin was marketed by the Bayer Drug Company; it was freely available without prescription, and was widely advertised as a super aspirin. Tests showed that heroin was a more potent analgesic than morphine and that it was less likely to induce nausea and vomiting. Moreover, the Bayer Company, on the basis of flimsy evidence, claimed that heroin was not addictive; this is why it was not covered by the Harrison Narcotics Act. The consequence of this omission was that opiate addicts in the United States, forbidden by law to use opium or morphine, turned to the readily available and much more potent heroin, and the flames of addiction were further fanned. In 1924, the U.S. Congress made it illegal for anybody to possess, sell, or use heroin. Unfortunately, the laws enacted to stamp out opiate addiction in the United States have been far from an unequivocal success: an estimated 2,000,000 Americans currently use heroin, and organized crime flourishes on the proceeds.

The effect of opiates most valued by opiate addicts is the *rush* that follows intravenous injection. The *heroin rush* is a wave of intense, abdominal, orgasmic pleasure that evolves into a state of serene, drowsy euphoria. Many opiate users, drawn by these pleasurable effects, begin to use the drug more and more frequently. Then, once they reach a point where they keep themselves drugged much of the time, tolerance and physical dependence develop and contribute to the problem. Opiate tolerance encourages addicts to progress to higher doses, to more potent drugs (e.g., heroin), and to more direct routes of administration (e.g., IV injection); and physical dependence adds to the already high motivation to take the drug.

The direct health hazards of opiate addiction are surprisingly minor. The main risks are constipation, pupil constriction, menstrual irregularity, and reduced libido (sex drive). Many opiate addicts have taken large, prescribed doses of pure heroin or morphine for years with no serious ill effects.

> An individual tolerant to and dependent upon an opiate who is socially or financially capable of obtaining an adequate supply of good quality drug, sterile syringes and needles, and other paraphernalia may maintain his or her proper social and occupational functions, remain in fairly good health, and suffer little serious incapacitation as a result of the dependence (Julien, 1981, p. 117).

> One such individual was Dr. William Stewart Halsted, one of the founders of Johns Hopkins Medical School and one of the most brilliant surgeons of his day. . . . known as "the father of modern surgery." And yet, during his career he was addicted to morphine, a fact that he was able to keep secret from all but his closest friends. In fact, the only time his habit caused him any trouble was when he was attempting to reduce his dosage . . . (McKim, 1986, p. 197).

The classic heroin withdrawal syndrome usually begins 6 to 12 hours after the last dose of heroin. The first withdrawal sign is typically an increase in restlessness; the addict begins to pace and fidget. Watering eyes, running nose, yawning, and sweating are also common during the early stages of heroin withdrawal. Then the addict often falls into a fitful sleep called the *yen*, which typically lasts for several hours. After the sleep is over, the original symptoms may be joined in extreme cases by chills, shivering, profuse sweating, goose-flesh, nausea, vomiting, diarrhea, cramps, pains, dilated pupils, tremor, and muscle spasms. The goose-flesh skin and leg spasms of the opiate withdrawal syndrome are the basis for the expressions "going cold turkey" and "kicking the habit." The symptoms are typically most severe in the second or third days after the last injection, and by the seventh day they have all but disappeared. The symptoms of opiate withdrawal are not trivial, but their severity has been widely exaggerated. Opiate withdrawal is about as serious as a bad case of the flu—a far cry from the convulsions, delirium, and risk of death associated with alcohol withdrawal.

> Opiate withdrawal is probably one of the most misunderstood aspects of drug use. This is largely because of the image of withdrawal that has been portrayed in the movies and popular literature for many years. . . . Few addicts . . . take enough drug to cause the . . . severe withdrawal symptoms that are shown in the movies. Even in its most severe form, however, opiate withdrawal is not as dangerous or terrifying as withdrawal from **barbiturates** or alcohol. (McKim, 1986, p. 199)

Because opiates create relatively few direct health problems for those addicts with an affordable source of pure drug, the main risks of opiate addiction are indirect. They are risks that arise out of the battle between the relentless addictive power of opiates and the attempts of governments to eradicate them by making them illegal. The opiate addicts who cannot give up their habits—treatment programs report success rates of only 10%—are caught in the middle. Because most opiate addicts must purchase their morphine and heroin from illicit dealers at greatly inflated prices, those who are not wealthy become trapped in a life of poverty and petty crime. They are poor, they are undernourished, they receive poor medical care, they are often driven to prostitution, and they run great risk of contracting infections from unsterile needles. Moreover, they never know for sure

what they are injecting: some street drugs are poorly processed, and virtually all have been *cut* (stretched by adding some similar-appearing substance to it) to some unknown degree. The exact number of heroin-related
deaths is impossible to determine, but their number is substantial, and it is
likely to increase in the next few years as the number of drug-related cases
of AIDS goes up. What makes these deaths particularly tragic is that many
of them seem to be caused by the very laws designed to prevent them.

The British have taken a different approach to opiate addiction, one that
treats the addict as a patient suffering from a relatively incurable disease,
rather than as a law breaker. The **British system** is based on the assumption that much of the harm done by street opiates stems from the fact that
they are illegal, impure, and expensive. In Britain, opiate addicts are provided with their drugs free of charge by medical prescription. As a result,
most addicts remain healthy and live productive, crime-free lives. As a
byproduct, this approach has reduced drug-related crime, and it has produced a modest decrease in the number of new users. Treating addiction as
a medical problem rather than as a crime seems to have reduced the
glamour of drugs in Britain—"sickness is generally less attractive than sin"
(Bewley, 1974, p. 160).

Section 16.2: Conclusions

Normally, at the end of a major section, I would supply you with a brief
summary of the major conclusions; however, in this case, I am asking you
to interpret this section for yourself by completing the following exercises.

Exercise 1: List the major direct health hazards of the following five drugs. Omit indirect hazards resulting from the drugs' legal or social status.

Tobacco	Alcohol	Marijuana	Cocaine	Heroin
1. _____	1. _____	1. _____	1. _____	1. _____
2. _____	2. _____	2. _____	2. _____	2. _____
3. _____	3. _____	3. _____	3. _____	3. _____
4. _____	4. _____	4. _____	4. _____	4. _____
5. _____	5. _____	5. _____	5. _____	5. _____
6. _____	6. _____	6. _____	6. _____	6. _____

Exercise 2: On the basis of comparisons among your five lists, rate the five drugs in terms of the overall dangerousness of their direct health hazards.

Most Hazardous   1. _____

                                2. _____

                                3. _____

                                4. _____

Least Hazardous   5. _____

Completing these exercises will provide you with your own personal interpretation of the main points of Section 16.2. It should also provide you with some disturbing insights. You should be disturbed by the adverse effects that tobacco, alcohol, marijuana, cocaine, and heroin have on the millions of people who use them—particularly if you, your friends, or your family are among the users. You should be disturbed by the dangerous misinformation that is fed to us by the popular press, entertainment industry, and public officials. And you should be disturbed by the fact that many of our current laws related to drug abuse were enacted at a time when there was little or no scientific information about drugs. What do you think should be done about the situation?

16.3 Biopsychological Theories of Addiction and Reward Circuits in the Brain

So far in this chapter, you have been introduced to some basic psychopharmacological concepts (Section 16.1) and to five commonly abused drugs (Section 16.2). This, the third and final section of the chapter focuses on a theory of addiction that links it to activity in a particular circuit in the brain: the mesotelencephalic dopamine pathway.

Physical-Dependence Theories of Addiction

Early attempts to explain the phenomenon of drug addiction attributed it to physical dependence. According to the **physical-dependence theory of addiction,** physical dependence traps addicts in a vicious circle of drug taking and withdrawal symptoms. The idea was that drug users whose intake had reached a level sufficient to induce physical dependence were driven by their withdrawal symptoms to self-administer the drug each time they attempted to curtail their intake.

Early drug-addiction treatment programs were based on the physical-dependence theory of addiction. They attempted to break the vicious circle of drug taking by gradually withdrawing drugs from addicts in a hospital environment—gradual withdrawal produces less severe withdrawal symptoms than does sudden withdrawal. Unfortunately, once discharged, almost all of the **detoxified addicts** (addicts who have none of the drug to which they are addicted in their body and are no longer experiencing withdrawal symptoms) returned to their former drug-taking habits. The failure of this approach to treatment is not surprising for two reasons. First, some highly addictive drugs, such as cocaine, do not produce severe withdrawal distress. Second, the pattern of drug taking routinely displayed by many addicts involves an alternating cycle of binges and detoxification (Mello & Mendelson, 1972). There are a variety of reasons for this pattern of drug use; for example, some addicts adopt it because weekend binges are compatible with their work schedule, others adopt it because they do not have enough money to use drugs continuously, and still others have it forced on them because their binges often land them in jail. In some ways, the most pitiful of the addicted intermittent drug users are those who keep trying to quit, but each time are drawn back to drug use. The point is that whether detoxification is by choice or necessity, it does not stop an addict from renewing his or her drug-taking habit.

Modern physical-dependence theories of drug addiction attempt to account for the fact that addicts frequently relapse after lengthy drug-free periods by postulating that withdrawal symptoms can be conditioned (e.g., Ludwig & Wikler, 1974; O'Brien, Ternes, Grabowski, & Ehrman, 1981; Wikler, 1980). According to this theory, when addicts who have remained drug-free for a considerable period of time return to a situation in which they have previously experienced the drug, conditioned withdrawal effects opposite to the effects of the drug (Siegel's hypothesized conditioned compensatory responses) are elicited. These conditioned withdrawal effects are presumed to result in a powerful craving for the drug to counteract them. Although there is good evidence that conditioned withdrawal effects can occur in some situations (see Siegel, 1983), the theory that *relapse* is motivated by an attempt to counteract them encounters two major problems (see Eikelboom & Stewart, 1982; Zelman, Tiffany, & Baker, 1985). One is that many of the effects elicited by environments that have previously been associated with drug administration are similar to those of the drug rather than being antagonistic to them (Stewart & Eikelboom, 1987). The second is that experimental animals and addicts often display a preference for drug-predictive cues, even when no drug is forthcoming (e.g., Bozarth & Wise, 1981; Mucha, Van der Kooy, O'Shaughnessy, & Bucenieks, 1982; White, Sklar, & Amit, 1977). For example, some detoxified heroin addicts called *needle freaks* derive pleasure from sticking an empty needle into themselves (Levine, 1974; O'Brien, Chaddock, Woody, & Greenstein, 1974). It seems unlikely that relapse could be motivated by an attempt to suppress conditioned drug effects that are either similar to the effects of the drug or pleasurable.

Positive-Incentive Models of Addiction

The failure of physical-dependence theories to fully account for the major aspects of addiction has lent support to the theory that the primary reason that most addicts take drugs is not to escape or avoid the unpleasant consequences of withdrawal or conditioned withdrawal, but rather to obtain the drugs' pleasurable effects. This **positive-incentive theory of addiction** acknowledges that addicts may sometimes self-administer drugs to suppress withdrawal symptoms or to escape from other unpleasant aspects of their existence, but they hold that the primary factor in most cases of addiction is the craving for the positive-incentive (pleasure-producing) properties of the drugs (McAuliffe et al., 1986; Stewart, de Wit, & Eikelboom, 1984). Strong anecdotal support for this view comes from the addicts themselves:

> I'm just trying to get high as much as possible. I would have to spend $25 a day on heroin to avoid withdrawal, but I actually use about $50 worth. If I could get more money, I would spend it all on drugs. All I want is to get loaded. I just really like shooting dope. I don't have any use for sex; I'd rather shoot dope. I like to shoot dope better than anything else in the world. I have to steal something every day to get my dope.

With the increasing acceptance of the theory that the primary factor in drug addiction is the pleasure-producing effect of drugs, attempts to understand the neural basis of addiction turned to the study of **intracranial self-stimulation** (ICS), a phenomenon discovered by Olds and Milner in 1954. They were the first to report that animals will repeatedly press a lever to administer brief bursts of electrical stimulation through implanted electrodes to sites in their own brains. Olds and Milner argued that the brain circuits that support this intracranial self-stimulation behavior are those that normally mediate the pleasurable effects of rewarding stimuli, such as food, water, sex, and presumably addictive drugs.

The discovery of intracranial self-stimulation provided researchers with a technique for studying the neural basis of pleasure, and with increasing acceptance of the idea that pleasure is the primary motivating factor in drug addiction, the study of intracranial self-stimulation began to have a major impact on ideas about the neural basis of addiction. Many researchers now believe that the neural circuits that mediate intracranial self-stimulation are the very ones that mediate the rewarding effects of addictive drugs. Accordingly, this chapter digresses for a few pages to describe the fundamentals of intracranial self-stimulation before linking them to the topic of drug addiction.

The Intracranial-Self-Stimulation Phenomenon

Early studies of intracranial self-stimulation were based on the assumption that it is a unitary phenomenon; that is, they were based on the assumption that the fundamental properties of intracranial self-stimulation are the same regardless of the site of stimulation. Because the particular site of stimulation was assumed to be of little consequence, most early studies involved septal or lateral hypothalamic stimulation because the rates of self-stimulation from these sites are spectacularly high—rats typically press a lever thousands of times per hour for stimulation of these sites, stopping only after they have become exhausted. Illustrated in Figure 16.5 is a rat lever pressing for electrical brain stimulation.

Early studies of intracranial self-stimulation suggested that lever pressing for brain stimulation was fundamentally different from lever pressing for natural reinforcers such as food or water. For example, despite their extremely high response rates, many rats stopped pressing the self-stimulation lever almost immediately when the current-delivery mechanism was shut off. This finding was puzzling because high rates of operant responding are generally assumed to indicate that the reinforcer is particularly pleasurable, whereas rapid rates of *extinction* are usually assumed to indicate that it is not. Would you stop pressing a lever that had been delivering hundred-dollar bills the first few times that a press did not produce one? A related observation was that experienced self-stimulating rats often did not recommence lever pressing when they were returned to the apparatus after being briefly removed from it. In such cases, the rats had to be **primed** by a few free stimulations to get them going. The experimenter simply pressed the lever a couple of times, and the hesitant rat immediately began to self-stimulate at a high rate once again.

These differences between lever pressing for rewarding lateral hypothalamic or septal stimulation and lever pressing for food or water seemed to discredit Olds' and Milner's original theory that intracranial self-stimulation involves the activation of natural reward circuits in the brain. Accordingly, many of the investigators who studied self-stimulation in the 1950s and 60s viewed it as some kind of artifact—albeit a particularly

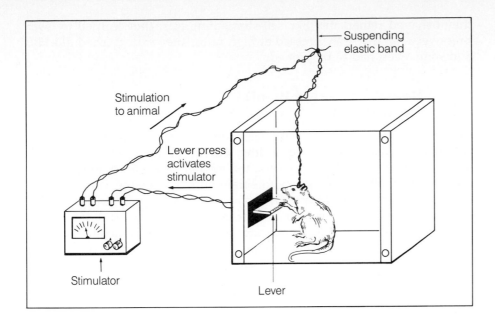

Suspending
elastic band

Stimulation
to animal

Lever press
activates
stimulator

Stimulator

Lever

FIGURE 16.5 *A rat pressing a lever for rewarding brain stimulation.*

interesting one. However, since then, the pendulum of opinion has swung back to its original position, and the current consensus seems to be that the circuits mediating intracranial self-stimulation phenomena are natural reward circuits.

The return to the natural-reward-circuit view of intracranial self-stimulation was based on four kinds of evidence. First, brain stimulation through electrodes that mediate self-stimulation often elicits natural motivated behaviors such as eating, drinking, maternal behavior, and copulation in the presence of the appropriate goal objects. This evidence led Glickman and Schiff (1967) to suggest that the activation of circuits that produce species-typical motivated behaviors is the physiological basis of reward. Second, increasing levels of natural motivation (for example, by food or water deprivation, by hormone injections, or by the presence of prey objects) often increases self-stimulation rates (e.g., Caggiula, 1970). Third, lever pressing for stimulation at some brain sites (other than the lateral hypothalamus and septum on which the early studies focused) is often quite similar to lever pressing for natural rewards (i.e., acquisition is slow, response rates are low, extinction is slow, and priming is not necessary). And fourth, it became clear that subtle differences between the situations in which rewarding brain stimulation and natural rewards were usually studied contribute to the impression that their rewarding effects are qualitatively different. For example, comparisons between lever pressing for food and lever pressing for brain stimulation are usually confounded by the fact that subjects pressing for brain stimulation are nondeprived and by the fact that the lever press delivers the reward directly and immediately. In contrast, in studies of lever pressing for natural rewards, subjects are deprived and they press a lever for a food pellet or drop of water that they then must approach and consume to experience rewarding effects. In a clever experiment, Panksepp and Trowill (1967) eliminated these confounds and found that some of the major differences between lever pressing for food and lever pressing for brain stimulation disappeared. When nondeprived rats lever pressed to inject a small quantity of chocolate milk directly into their mouths through an intraoral tube, they behaved remarkably like self-stimulating rats; they learned to lever press very rapidly, they pressed at high rates, they extinguished quickly, and some even had to be primed.

The Medial Forebrain Bundle and Intracranial Self-Stimulation

A theory that resulted from the early research on intracranial self-stimulation was that the rewarding effects of brain stimulation are mediated by a single neural system: the **medial forebrain bundle** or MFB (Olds & Olds, 1963). The medial forebrain bundle is a large, complex bundle of fibers that courses directly through the lateral hypothalamus and innervates the septum, as well as a variety of other structures. It includes both ascending and descending axons, as well as numerous interneurons. Three lines of evidence argued against the notion that activation of the medial forebrain bundle is the critical event underlying the reinforcing effects of brain stimulation. First, rats and many other vertebrates from fish (Boyd & Gardiner, 1962) to humans (Bishop, Elder, & Heath, 1963) were found to lever press for stimulation to a variety of brain structures (see Figure 16.6), many of which have no direct connection to the medial forebrain bundle. Second, extensive lesions of the medial forebrain bundle

FIGURE 16.6 *The major intracranial self-stimulation sites in the rat brain. (Adapted from Phillips & Fibiger, 1989.)*

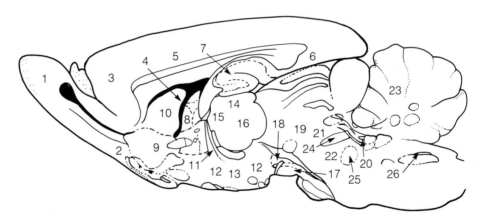

TELENCEPHALON
1. Olfactory Bulb
2. Prepyriform Cortex
3. Prefrontal Cortex
4. Subfornical organ
5. Cingulate Cortex
6. Entorhinal Cortex
7. Hippocampus
8. Septum
9. Nucleus Accumbens
10. Striatum

DIENCEPHALON
11. Fornix
12. Lateral Hypothalamus
13. Ventromedial Hypothalamus
14. Mediodorsal Nucleus of Thalamus
15. Nucleus Paratenialis of Thalamus
16. Central Nucleus of Thalamus

MESENCEPHALON
17. Substantia Nigra
18. Ventral Tegmental Area
19. Periaqueductal Grey
20. Mesencephalic Nucleus of Trigeminal Nerve
21. Dorsal Raphé
22. Median Raphé

METENCEPHALON
23. Cerebellum
24. Superior Cerebellar Peduncle
25. Motor Nucleus of Trigeminal Nerve

MYELENCEPHALON
26. Nucleus Tractus Solitarius

STRUCTURES NOT SHOWN
Globus Pallidus
Amygdala
Habenula

were found to have little effect on septal self-stimulation (Valenstein & Campbell, 1966). And third, 2-deoxyglucose studies (see Chapter 4) indicated that although rewarding brain stimulation to the medial forebrain bundle activates the bundle (Gallistel, Gomita, Yadin, & Campbell, 1985), rewarding brain stimulation applied to other sites does not (e.g., medial prefrontal cortex; Yadin, Guarini, & Gallistel, 1983). Notice that these three lines of evidence do not prove that the medial forebrain bundle does not mediate the rewarding effects of stimulation to some brain sites; they simply prove that the medial forebrain bundle does not mediate all intracranial self-stimulation. In fact, one component of the medial forebrain bundle, the mesotelencephalic dopamine system, has been strongly implicated in intracranial self-stimulation at several sites, and as you are about to see, in drug addiction.

The Mesotelencephalic Dopamine System

The **mesotelencephalic dopamine system** refers to the ascending projections of dopamine-releasing neurons from the mesencephalon (midbrain) into various regions of the telencephalon (see Chapter 2). It courses through the area of the lateral hypothalamus as part of the medial forebrain bundle. As indicated in Figure 16.7, the neurons that compose the mesotelencephalic dopamine system have their cell bodies in two different midbrain nuclei, the **substantia nigra** and the more medial **ventral tegmental area,** and their axons project to a variety of telencephalic sites, including specific regions of prefrontal neocortex and limbic cortex, the nucleus accumbens (a nucleus adjacent to the septum), the olfactory tubercle, the amygdala, the septum, and the striatum. It was originally thought that all of the dopamine neurons in the substantia nigra project to the striatum and that all of those arising in the ventral tegmental area project to limbic and cortical structures. However, recent research has revealed a considerable

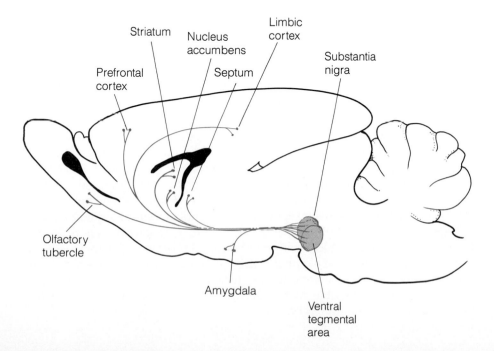

FIGURE 16.7 *The mesotelencephalic dopamine system.*

intermingling of these projections, and the original distinction between the so-called *nigrostriatal pathway* and the *mesocortical limbic pathway* has become blurred (Björkland & Lindvall, 1986). Because the role of the mesotelencephalic dopamine system in intracranial self-stimulation and drug self-administration is the focus of the following two subsections, you might find it useful to carefully review Figure 16.7 before proceeding.

The Mesotelencephalic Dopamine System and Intracranial Self-Stimulation

Although it is generally acknowledged that animals stimulate their brains for a variety of rewarding effects and that these different effects are likely mediated by different neural systems, some researchers believe that the mesotelencephalic dopamine system plays a particularly important role in the rewarding effects of brain stimulation (e.g., Bozarth, 1987; Phillips & Fibiger, 1989; Porrino, 1987; Wise & Bozarth, 1984). Four kinds of experiments have supported this view: (1) mapping experiments, (2) dopamine-turnover experiments, (3) 2-deoxyglucose experiments, and (4) unilateral brain lesion experiments.

Mapping Experiments After Routtenberg and Malsbury (1969) established that rats will lever press for mesencephalic stimulation, Crow (1972) carefully mapped the area and found that the positive mesencephalic self-stimulation sites were in the substantia nigra or ventral tegmental area. Subsequently, Corbett and Wise (1980) conducted a study in which movable electrodes were used to identify positive and negative intracranial self-stimulation sites along the track of each electrode. Then, the brains were sectioned along the electrode track and subjected to fluorescence histochemistry (see Chapter 2) to identify the precise location of dopamine-containing cell bodies. Corbett and Wise found that the current thresholds for self-stimulation were lower and response rates were higher in the areas of the substantia nigra and ventral tegmental area in which the dopaminergic neurons were most dense. The research of Shizgal and his colleagues (e.g., Bielajew & Schizgal, 1986; Shizgal & Murray, 1989) suggests that the mesotelencephalic dopamine system may also mediate the rewarding effects of stimulation to sites other than the substantia nigra and ventral tegmental area. They showed, for example, that rewarding stimulation of the lateral hypothalamus activates nondopaminergic neurons that descend to the ventral tegmental area.

Dopamine-Metabolism Experiments An increase in the release of dopamine in an area can be inferred from an increase in the ratio between 3, 4 dihydroxyphenylacetic acid (mercifully abbreviated **DOPAC**), one of dopamine's major metabolites, and dopamine. Increases in the DOPAC/dopamine ratio in various terminals of the mesotelencephalic dopamine system have been reported after bouts of ventral tegmental area (Fibiger, Le Piane, Jakubovic, & Phillips, 1987) or lateral hypothalamic (Garrigues & Cazala, 1983) self-stimulation. Moreover, the increases in dopamine metabolism associated with self-stimulation were seen only at dopamine terminals ipsilateral to the stimulation site, thus indicating that they were not attributable to the general increases in motor activity involved in self-stimulation behavior.

2-Deoxyglucose Experiments   Porrino and her colleagues (Porrino, 1987; Porrino, Esposito, Seeger, Crane, Pert, & Sokoloff, 1984) have used the 2-deoxyglucose technique to study the patterns of increased neural activity produced by self-stimulation of the ventral tegmental area and the substantia nigra. There were some differences in the patterns of activity associated with self-stimulation at the two sites, but in both cases high levels of 2-deoxyglucose accumulated in the prefrontal cortex, nucleus accumbens, septum, and mediodorsal thalamus, thus suggesting that activity in these terminals of the mesotelencephalic dopamine system mediates the rewarding effects of mesencephalic stimulation.

Lesion Experiments   Convincing evidence that the mesotelencephalic dopamine system can mediate brain-stimulation reward comes from studies in which the system has been destroyed unilaterally by injections of **6-hydroxydopamine** (6-OHDA; see Chapter 6). For example, Fibiger, Le Piane, Jakubovic, and Phillips (1987) recently showed that 6-OHDA lesions ipsilateral to a stimulation electrode in the ventral tegmental area reduced self-stimulation, whereas contralateral lesions did not. The fact that contralateral lesions produced no deficit suggests that general motor deficits produced by the lesions did not contribute to the decline in self-stimulation rate.

The Mesotelencephalic Dopamine System and the Rewarding Effects of Addictive Drugs

The animal model that best approximates human drug addiction is the **drug self-administration paradigm** (see Yokel, 1987). Laboratory rats and primates readily learn to press a lever to inject the drugs to which humans become addicted. Once they have learned to self-administer a drug in this fashion, their drug-taking behavior often mimics many of the features of the corresponding human addiction. For those researchers interested in the neural basis of addiction, drug self-administration studies in which the lever press injects minute quantities of the drug directly into particular brain sites have proven particularly enlightening (see Bozarth, 1987; Koob, Vaccarino, Amalric, & Bloom, 1987); however, only the neural substrates of opiate and stimulant self-administration have been extensively investigated in this fashion (Wise, 1987).

Neural Substrates of Opiate Reward   To test whether the reinforcing properties of opiates are mediated by their action on central opiate receptors or on peripheral opiate receptors, Koob, Pettit, Ettenberg, and Bloom (1984) administered one of two opiate antagonists (see Chapter 6) to rats self-administering intravenous injections of heroin at a stable rate. One opiate antagonist was **naloxone,** which readily penetrates the blood-brain barrier and enters the CNS; the other was a derivative of naloxone, which does not. They found that the injections of the naloxone at low doses produced a temporary increase in the self-administration of heroin, whereas injections of the derivative had no effect, even at a dose 200 times greater than the effective dose of naloxone. These findings suggest that the reinforcing effects of opiates are mediated by their effects within the CNS, rather than in the PNS. (At first glance, the finding that an opiate antagonist increases opiate self-administration might seem counterintuitive. The idea is that because naloxone counteracts the effects of heroin, the rats increase the amount that they self-administer so that they can obtain the level of effect that they prefer—just as addicts take larger doses of weaker drugs.)

Two lines of evidence suggest that the rewarding effects of opiates can be mediated by the mesotelencephalic dopamine system. The first is that rats lever press for microinjections of opiates into either the ventral tegmental area (e.g., Bozarth & Wise, 1982; Phillips & LePiane, 1980) or the nucleus accumbens (e.g., Goeders, Lane, & Smith, 1984). The second comes from studies of **conditioned place preference** (Carr, Fibiger, & Phillips, 1989; Van der Kooy, 1987). Normally, if opiates are administered to rats in a distinctive chamber of a two- or three-chamber test apparatus, they subsequently prefer to stay in the opiate-paired compartment during subsequent tests in which no drugs are administered. However, when large doses of dopamine antagonists are administered with the opiates, such preferences do not develop (e.g., Phillips, Spyraki, & Fibiger, 1982). The main advantage of the place-preference paradigm is that the subjects are tested in the absence of drugs, which means that a measure of the incentive value of a drug can be obtained that is unconfounded by other effects that the drugs might have on behavior.

Neural Substrates of Stimulant Reward Both cocaine and amphetamine increase transmission at both dopaminergic and noradrenergic synapses, cocaine by blocking reuptake of dopamine and norepinephrine from synapses and amphetamine by both blocking their reuptake and increasing their release. However, current evidence suggests that the rewarding effects of cocaine and amphetamine are attributable specifically to their dopaminergic effects (e.g., Wise & Bozarth, 1987). Dopamine antagonists, but not norepinephrine antagonists, have been shown to block the rewarding effects of various intravenous stimulants (e.g., Risner & Jones, 1980) in rats and the euphoria-producing effects of amphetamine in humans (Gunne, Änggård, & Jönsson, 1972).

The involvement of the mesotelencephalic dopamine system in stimulant-produced reward has been established by studies showing that dopamine-depleting lesions of either the ventral tegmental area (Roberts & Koob, 1982) or the nucleus accumbens (Roberts, Corcoran, & Fibiger, 1977; Roberts, Koob, Klonoff, & Fibiger, 1980)—but not the other terminal structures of the mesotelencephalic dopamine system (Roberts & Zito, 1987)—disrupt intravenous self-administration of amphetamine or dopamine. Furthermore, rats have also been shown to lever press for microinjections of amphetamine to the nucleus accumbens (Hoebel, Monaco, Hernandez, Aulisi, Stanley, & Lenard, 1983).

Conclusion

In Section 16.1, you were introduced to basic pharmacological concepts and phenomena; recent psychopharmacological studies demonstrating the situational specificity and response contingency of drug tolerance were highlighted. Section 16.2 discussed five commonly abused drugs: tobacco, alcohol, marijuana, cocaine, and heroin. By summarizing current scientific knowledge about these five drugs within a historical and legal context, Section 16.2 stressed the great gaps that often exist between common belief, legal status, and scientific findings. Finally, Section 16.3 argued that the pleasure-producing effects of drugs, rather than their ability to suppress withdrawal symptoms, is the primary factor in addiction. Recent studies of rewarding brain stimulation and drug self-administration suggest that the mesotelencephalic dopamine system may mediate the pleasure-producing effects of some addictive drugs.

To illustrate in a more personal way some of the things that you have learned about addiction, this chapter concludes with a series of quotes describing the interactions of one drug addict with two different drugs of abuse: cocaine and tobacco. The addict is Sigmund Freud, a man of very special significance to psychology. Freud's battles with these two drugs have some sobering implications. The following excerpts are from a report written in 1972 by Edward Brecher.

> The chief ingredient in coca leaves, the alkaloid cocaine, was isolated in pure form in 1844. Little use was made of it in Europe, however, until 1883, when a German army physician . . . issued it to Bavarian soldiers during their autumn maneuvers. . . .
>
> Among those who read [the] . . . account with fascination was a poverty-stricken twenty-eight-year-old Viennese neurologist, Dr. Sigmund Freud. . . . "I have been reading about cocaine, the essential ingredient of coca leaves, which some Indian tribes chew to enable them to resist privations and hardships," Freud wrote his fiancée, Martha Bernays, on April 21, 1884. "I am procuring some myself and will try it. . . ."
>
> In addition to taking cocaine himself, Freud offered some to his friend and associate, Dr. Ernst von Fleischl-Marxow, who was suffering from an exceedingly painful disease of the nervous system, and who was addicted to morphine. . . .
>
> Freud even sent some of his precious cocaine to Martha. . . . "he pressed it on his friends and colleagues, both for themselves and their patients; he gave it to his sisters. In short, looked at from the vantage point of present knowledge, he was rapidly becoming a public menace." (pp. 272–273)

Freud's famous essay "Song of Praise" to cocaine was published in July 1884. In this article, Freud wrote in such glowing terms about his own personal experiences with cocaine that he created a wave of interest in the drug. But within a year, there was a critical reaction to Freud's premature advocacy.

> In July 1885, a German authority on morphine addiction named Erlenmeyer launched the first of a series of attacks on cocaine as an addicting drug. In January 1886 Freud's friend Obersteiner, who had first favored cocaine, reported that it produced severe mental disturbances [later called cocaine psychosis]. . . . Other attacks soon followed; and Freud was subjected to "grave reproaches." Freud continued to praise cocaine as late as July 1887. . . . But soon thereafter he discontinued all use of it both personally and professionally. Despite the fact that he had been taking cocaine periodically over a three-year span, he appears to have had no difficulty in stopping. (p. 274)

Some 9 years later in 1894, when Freud was 38, his physician and close friend ordered him to stop smoking because it was causing a heart arrhythmia. Freud was a heavy smoker; he smoked approximately 20 cigars per day.

> Freud did stop for a time . . . but his subsequent depression and other withdrawal symptoms proved unbearable. . . .
>
> Within seven weeks, Freud was smoking again.

On a later occasion, Freud stopped smoking for fourteen very long months. . . .

More than fifteen years later, at the age of fifty-five, Freud was still smoking twenty cigars a day—and still struggling against his addiction. [In a letter written at the time, he commented on the sudden intolerance of his heart for tobacco.]

Four years later he wrote . . . that his passion for smoking hindered his analytic studies. Yet he kept on smoking.

In February 1923, at the age of sixty-seven, Freud noted sores on his right palate and jaw that failed to heal. They were cancers. An operation was performed—the first of thirty-three operations for cancer of the jaw and oral cavity which he endured during the sixteen remaining years of his life. "I am still out of work and cannot swallow," he wrote shortly after his first operation. "Smoking is accused as the etiology [i.e., cause] of this tissue rebellion." Yet he continued to smoke.

In addition to his series of cancers . . . Freud now suffered attacks of "tobacco angina" [i.e., heart pains] whenever he smoked. . . . Yet he continued to smoke.

At seventy-three, Freud was ordered to retire to a sanitarium for his heart condition. He made an immediate recovery [because he stopped smoking] . . . for twenty-three days. Then he started smoking one cigar a day. Then two. Then three or four. . . .

In 1936, at the age of seventy-nine . . . Freud had more heart trouble . . . His jaw had by then been entirely removed and an artificial jaw substituted; he was in almost constant pain; often he could not speak and sometimes he could not chew or swallow. Yet at the age of eighty-one, Freud was still smoking what . . ., his close friend at this period, calls, "an endless series of cigars."

Freud died of cancer in 1939. . . . (pp. 214–215)

__ Food for Thought

1. There are many misconceptions about drug abuse. Describe three. What do you think are the reasons for these misconceptions?

2. A man who had been a heroin user for many years was found dead of an overdose at a holiday resort. He appeared to have been in good health, and no foul play was suspected. What factors might have led to his death?

3. If you had an opportunity to redraft the current legislation related to drug abuse in the light of what you have learned in this chapter, what changes would you make? Why?

ADDITIONAL READING

There are a number of interesting paperbacks that provide interesting introductions to the topic of drug abuse. The following two are my favorites:

Julien, R. M. (1981). *A primer of drug action.* San Francisco: Freeman.

McKim, W. A. (1986). *Drugs and behavior.* Englewood Cliffs, New Jersey: Prentice-Hall.

A recent collection of articles on the topic of reward circuits and their relation to drug abuse is:

Liebman, J. M., & Cooper, S. J. (Eds.). (1989). *The neuropharmacological basis of reward.* Oxford: Clarendon Press.

To help you study the material in this chapter, all of the key terms—those that have appeared in bold type—are listed and briefly defined here.

Amotivational syndrome. Chronic lack of motivation produced by drug use; marijuana is thought by some people to produce amotivational syndrome.

Amphetamine. A stimulant drug that blocks the reuptake of dopamine and norepinephrine and increases their release.

Analgesic. Pain-killing.

Barbiturates. A class of depressant drugs; the barbiturate withdrawal syndrome is similar to the alcohol withdrawal syndrome.

Before-and-after design. An experimental design used to demonstrate contingent drug tolerance; the experimental group receives the drug before each of a series of behavioral tests, while the control group receives the drug after each test.

British system. A system of treating drug addicts that is based on the idea that drug addicts are sick individuals rather than criminals; drugs are given to addicts by prescription.

Buerger's disease. A nicotine-produced disease in which blood flow to the legs is restricted, ultimately resulting in gangrene and amputation.

Cannabis sativa. The common hemp plant; the source of marijuana.

Cirrhosis. Scarring; cirrhosis of the liver is caused by alcohol.

Cocaine hydrochloride. A strong stimulant and analgesic extracted from coca paste.

Cocaine psychosis. Psychotic behavior observed during a cocaine spree; it is similar in many respects to schizophrenia.

Cocaine sprees. Binges of cocaine use.

Codeine. A weak psychoactive ingredient in opium.

Conditioned compensatory responses. Responses elicited by stimuli that are regularly associated with drug taking; they are opposite to the effects of the drug, and they are thought to contribute to tolerance development.

Conditioned-place-preference test. A test which assesses the animal's preference for environments in which it has previously experienced drug effects.

Crack. The free-base form of cocaine.

Cross tolerance. When exposure to one drug creates tolerance to another drug.

Delirium tremens (DTs). A phase of the alcohol withdrawal syndrome characterized by hallucinations, delusions, and extremely agitated behavior.

Delta-9-THC. The main psychoactive ingredient of marijuana.

Depressants. A class of drugs that depress neural activity and behavior (e.g., alcohol and barbiturates).

Detoxified addicts. Addicts who have none of the drug to which they are addicted in their body and who are no longer experiencing withdrawal symptoms.

Diuretic. A drug that increases the production of urine.

DOPAC. A major metabolite of dopamine.

Drug-effect theory of tolerance. A theory of tolerance based on the idea that the animal must experience the effect of the drug to become tolerant to that effect.

Drug metabolism. The conversion of a drug from its active form to a nonactive form.

Drug self-administration paradigm. Laboratory animals repeatedly press a lever to inject an addictive drug into themselves.

Drug tolerance. A state of decreased sensitivity to a drug that develops as a result of exposure to the drug; a shift in the dose-response curve to the right.

Ethyl alcohol. The alcohol commonly consumed by humans.

Fetal alcohol syndrome (FAS). A syndrome produced by prenatal exposure to alcohol; characterized by mental retardation, low birth weight, and a variety of other physical abnormalities.

Functional tolerance. Tolerance resulting from a reduction in the reactivity of the nervous system to the drug.

Harrison Narcotics Act. Passed in 1914, this Act made it illegal to sell or use opium, morphine, or cocaine.

Hashish. The processed resin of Cannabis.

Heroin. A powerful semisynthetic opiate.

6-Hydroxydopamine (6-OHDA). A neurotoxin that selectively destroys neurons that release dopamine or norepinephrine.

Hypothermic. Temperature-reducing.

Intracranial self-stimulation (ICS). An animal will repeatedly press a bar to receive electrical stimulation to certain sites in its brain.

Intramuscularly (IM). Injection into muscle.

Intravenously (IV). Injection into a vein.

Korsakoff's syndrome. The severe memory loss and dementia commonly associated with alcohol addiction.

Medial forebrain bundle (MFB). A neural pathway that courses through the lateral hypothalamus and innervates the septum and other forebrain structures; it was once thought to mediate the effects of all rewarding brain stimulation.

Mesotelencephalic dopamine system. The ascending projections of dopamine-releasing neurons from the substantia nigra and ventral tegmental area of the mesencephalon (midbrain) into various regions of the telencephalon.

Metabolic tolerance. Tolerance that results from a reduction in the amount of drug getting to its sites of action.

Morphine. The major active ingredient in opium.

Naloxone. An opiate antagonist that readily penetrates the blood-brain barrier.

Narcotic. A legal classification of certain drugs, mostly opiates.

Nicotine. The major psychoactive ingredient of tobacco.

Opiates. Morphine, codeine, heroin, and other chemicals with similar structures or effects.

Opium. The sap that exudes from the opium poppy; it contains many psychoactive ingredients, including morphine and codeine.

Physical-dependence theory of addiction. The theory that the main factor motivating drug addicts to take drugs is the prevention or termination of withdrawal symptoms.

Physically dependent. Individuals who suffer from withdrawal symptoms when they stop taking a drug are said to be physically dependent on that drug.

Positive-incentive theory of addiction. The theory that the primary factor in most cases of addiction is a craving for the pleasure-producing effects of drugs.

Priming. Inducing a rat to resume self-stimulation by providing it with a few "free" stimulations.

Psychoactive drugs. Drugs that influence subjective experience and behavior by acting on the nervous system.

Psychological dependence. Compulsive drug-taking that occurs in the absence of physical dependence.

Reverse tolerance. A condition of heightened sensitivity to a drug effect resulting from previous exposure to the drug.

Smoker's syndrome. The chest pain, labored breathing, wheezing, coughing, and heightened susceptibility to infections of the respiratory tract commonly observed in smokers.

Stimulant drugs. Drugs that increase neural and behavioral activity; for example, caffeine, nicotine, amphetamine, and cocaine.

Subcutaneously (SC). Injection under the skin.

Substantia nigra. A midbrain nucleus that includes the cell bodies of some of the neurons in the mesotelencephalic dopamine system.

Tachycardia. Increased heart rate.

Ventral tegmental area. A midbrain nucleus that includes the cell bodies of some of the neurons in the mesotelencephalic dopamine system.

Withdrawal syndrome. The illness brought on by the elimination from the body of a drug to which the subject has become physically dependent.

17

Lateralization, Language, and the Split Brain

With the exception of a few midline orifices, we have two of almost everything—one on the left and one on the right. Even the brain, which most people view as the unitary indivisible basis of self, reflects this general principle of bilateral duplication. In its upper reaches, the brain comprises two structures, the left and right cerebral hemispheres, which are completely separate except for the **cerebral commissures,** which connect them. The fundamental duality of the human forebrain and the location of the cerebral commissures is illustrated in Figure 17.1.

Section 17.1 of this chapter is about the discovery that the two hemispheres, although comparable in general appearance, differ markedly in function—a topic commonly referred to as **lateralization of function.** The different abilities of the two hemispheres are most evident in patients in whom the cerebral commissures have been severed so that the two hemispheres function independently. The study of these **commissurotomized (split-brain)** patients is the subject of Section 17.2. Section 17.3 focuses on language, the most lateralized of all human cognitive functions, and in particular on the localization of language circuits in the cortex of the left hemisphere. The following are the three sections of this chapter.

17.1 Lateralization of Function
17.2 Studying Lateralization of Function in Split-Brain Patients
17.3 The Cortical Localization of Language

Research showing that the two hemispheres have different abilities and are capable of functioning independently challenges the concept that we have of ourselves as unitary beings. Thus, the discussion of lateralization, language, and the split-brain is a fittingly high note on which to end the text. I hope that you both enjoy it.

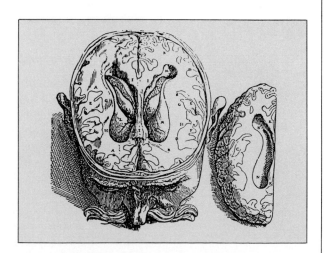

495

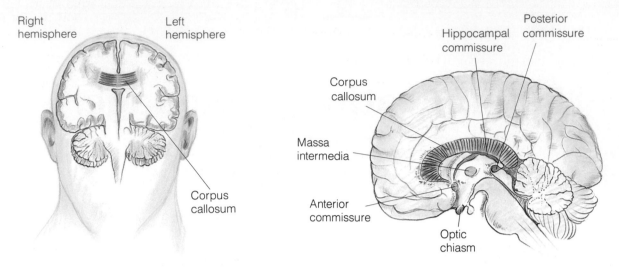

Frontal section of the human brain illustrating the fundamental duality of the human forebrain

Right hemisphere

Left hemisphere

Corpus callosum

Midsagittal section of the human brain illustrating the location of the corpus callosum and the other commissures

Posterior commissure

Hippocampal commissure

Corpus callosum

Massa intermedia

Anterior commissure

Optic chiasm

FIGURE 17.1 *The cerebral commissures and the hemispheres of the human brain. (Adapted from Sperry, 1964.)*

17.1 Lateralization of Function

In 1836, Marc Dax, an unknown country doctor, presented a short report at a medical society meeting in Montpellier, France. It was his first and only scientific presentation. Dax was struck by the fact that, of the 40 or so brain-damaged patients with speech problems whom he had seen during his career, not a single case had damage restricted to the right hemisphere. His report aroused virtually no interest among those who heard it, and Dax died the following year unaware that he had anticipated one of today's most important areas of neuropsychological research: the study of lateralization of function.

Aphasia and Unilateral Brain Damage

It is not surprising that Dax's paper had so little impact, considering that the dominant view of the time was that the brain acted as whole and that specific functions could not be attributed to particular parts of it. But this view began to change 25 years later when Paul Broca reported the results of the *postmortem examination* of the brains of two aphasic patients. **Aphasia** is a general term used to refer to brain-damage-produced deficits in the ability to produce or comprehend language. Broca found that both of his aphasic patients had a left-hemisphere lesion that seemed to center on an area in the frontal cortex just in front of what we now know to be the "face area" of *primary motor cortex* (see Chapter 9). Broca at first did not realize that there was a relation between the aphasia of his two patients and the side of their brain damage; he had not heard of Dax's paper. However, by

1864 Broca had performed postmortem examinations on seven more cases, and he was struck by the fact that, like his first two cases, they all had damage that involved the *inferior (lower) prefrontal cortex* (that portion of frontal cortex in front of the motor area) of the left hemisphere—which by then had become known as **Broca's area** (see Figure 17.2).

Because of the interest generated in the lateralization of speech by Broca's findings, it was soon discovered that the left hemisphere plays the dominant role in language functions in general—not just in speech. Patients with left-hemisphere damage were found also to be much more likely to have difficulty in reading, writing, and understanding speech than were those with comparable right-hemisphere damage. Next, the relation between left-hemisphere damage and **apraxia** was discovered. Apraxic patients are those who have great difficulty performing movements with either side of the body when asked to perform them (see Chapter 9), even though they have no difficulty performing the same responses when they are not thinking about what they are doing. Although the symptoms of apraxia are *bilateral* (involving both sides of the body), they are usually produced by left hemisphere lesions.

The combined impact of the evidence that the left hemisphere plays a special role in both language and voluntary movement led to the notion of cerebral dominance. According to this view, one hemisphere—usually the left—assumed the dominant role in the control of all complex behavioral and cognitive processes. Consequently, the left hemisphere was dubbed the **dominant hemisphere** and the right hemisphere was called the **minor hemisphere**.

Speech Laterality and Handedness

With the publication of two large-scale studies, one in 1959 and one in 1961, it became apparent that the likelihood of a unilateral lesion producing aphasia was related to the handedness of the individual. One study was of military personnel who suffered unilateral brain damage in World War II

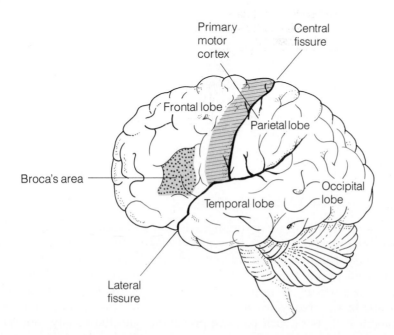

FIGURE 17.2 *The location of Broca's area in the inferior left prefrontal cortex.*

(Russell & Espir, 1961), and the other was of neurological patients who underwent unilateral excisions for the treatment of neurological disorders (Penfield & Roberts, 1959). In both studies, approximately 60% of right-handers (**dextrals**) with left-hemisphere lesions and 2% of those with right-hemisphere lesions were diagnosed as aphasic, and the comparable figures for left-handers (**sinestrals**) were about 30% and 24%, respectively. These results suggest that the left hemisphere is dominant for speech in almost all right-handers and in the majority of left-handers (see Annett, 1978; Benson, 1985).

The Sodium Amytal Test

The **sodium amytal test** is a test of language lateralization that is often given to patients prior to neurosurgery. The neurosurgeon uses the results of the test to decide what tissue to remove—every effort is made to avoid damaging areas of the cortex likely to be involved in language. The sodium amytal test involves the injection of a small amount of sodium amytal into the *carotid artery* on one side of the neck, which anesthetizes the hemisphere on that side for a few minutes, thus allowing the capacities of the other hemisphere to be assessed. During the test, the patient is asked to recite well-known series (i.e., letters of the alphabet, days of the week, months of the year, etc.) and to name well-known objects. Then an injection is administered to the other side, and the test is repeated. When the anesthetized hemisphere is the one dominant for speech, the subject is rendered completely mute for a minute or two, and once the ability to talk returns, errors of serial order and naming are common. In contrast, when the minor hemisphere is anesthetized, mutism often does not occur at all, and errors are few. Because the sodium amytal test involves a comparison of the speech abilities of the left and right hemispheres of each subject, it has proven to be a particularly valuable basis for studying speech lateralization. Milner (1974) found that almost all of the right-handed patients were left-hemisphere dominant for speech (92%), that most of the left-handed and ambidextrous patients without early left-hemisphere damage were left-hemisphere dominant for speech (69%), and that early left-hemisphere damage greatly decreased left-hemisphere dominance in left-handed and ambidextrous patients (30%). In evaluating these results, it is important to remember that sodium amytal tests are administered to only people who are experiencing brain dysfunction, that early brain damage can cause the lateralization of speech to shift, and that many more people are left-hemisphere dominant to start with. Considered together, these points suggest that Milner's findings likely underestimate the proportion of left-hemisphere dominant individuals among healthy members of the general population.

The Dichotic Listening Test

The main shortcoming of unilateral lesion and sodium amytal studies of speech lateralization is that they are studies of brain-damaged patients. Accordingly, Kumura's (1961) demonstration that the dichotic listening test can be used to measure the lateralization of language in healthy subjects ranks as a particularly important contribution. In the standard **dichotic listening test**, three pairs of spoken digits are presented through earphones; the digits of each pair are presented simultaneously, one to each ear. For example, a subject might hear the sequence 3, 9, 2 through one ear and at the same time 1, 6, 4 through the other. The subject is then asked to report all of the digits that she or he heard. Kimura found that most people report more of the digits presented to the right ear than to the left ear. On the basis of these observations, Kimura hypothesized that the right-ear superiority of most people for the recall of spoken digits on the dichotic listening test was attributable to the fact that most people are left-hemisphere dominant for language. She argued that, although the sounds from each ear are projected to both hemispheres, the contralateral connections are stronger and take precedence when two different sounds are simultaneously competing for access to the same cortical auditory centers. In support of her hypothesis, she found that 13 patients who were shown by the sodium amytal test to be right-hemisphere dominant for language all performed better with the left ear than the right.

In a subsequent study, Kimura (1964) compared the performance of 20 right-handers on the standard, digit version of the dichotic listening test with their performance on a version of the test involving the dichotic presentation of melodies. In the melody version of the test, Kimura simultaneously played two different melodies—one to each ear—and then she asked the subjects to identify the two that they had just heard from four that were subsequently played individually to both ears. Because Milner (1962) had shown that right temporal lobe lesions are more likely to disrupt music discriminations than are left temporal lobe lesions, Kimura hypothesized that there would be a left ear superiority for melodic stimuli on the dichotic listening test. This proved to be the case.

Other Tests of Language Laterality in Healthy Subjects

Since the development of the dichotic listening test, several other tests of laterality appropriate for healthy subjects have been developed. One such test is based on a comparison of the ability of subjects to identify words presented in their left or right visual fields. The subject fixates on the center of a screen, and then a word is flashed on the screen for less than 0.1 second (see Figure 17.3); this is just long enough to allow some of the subjects to recognize the word, but not long enough for eye movements to be initiated. The words are often presented vertically to control for the fact that English-speaking subjects have a tendency to scan from left to right. The usual finding of such tests is a slight tendency for words presented in the right visual field to be recognized more readily than those presented in the left. This right-field advantage is attributed to the fact that information in the right visual field is transmitted directly to the left hemisphere, which is the dominant language hemisphere in most subjects. Supporting this interpretation is the fact that there is no corresponding right-field advantage for the identification of nonlanguage material (e.g., faces).

Another strategy used to study language lateralization has been to study the asymmetry of motor movements accompanying speech. Because fine motor movements are under contralateral control, it is assumed that their prevalence on one side of the body indicates lateralization of speech on the other side. For example, Kimura (1973) reported that the gestures of the hands that accompany speech tend to be made with the hand contralateral to the dominant hemisphere for speech as determined by the dichotic

Visual input to one visual field goes directly to the contralateral hemisphere, and from there it reaches the ipsilateral hemisphere via the corpus callosum.

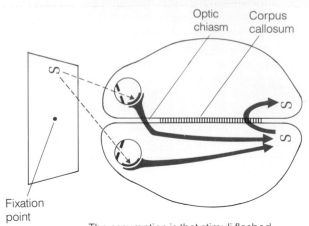

The assumption is that stimuli flashed on a screen in front of the subject will be recognized more readily when they are flashed into the field contralateral to the hemisphere specialized for perceiving them. Language-related material is identified more readily when it is presented in the right visual field than when it is presented in the left.

FIGURE 17.3 *The method of studying lateralization of language abilities in the visual system. (Adapted from Springer & Deutsch, 1981.)*

listening test. Such movements rarely accompany nonverbal oral activities such as humming. It has also been reported that right-handed subjects tend to make larger movements with the right side of the mouth than with the left (e.g., Graves, Goodglass, & Landis, 1982). Wolf and Goodale (1987) and Wylie and Goodale (1988) reported that the same movement asymmetry occurred during complex nonverbal mouth movements, thus leading them to conclude that the left hemisphere is specialized for the control of all complex motor movements, of which speech movements are but one example (see Kimura & Archibald, 1974).

Sex Differences in Lateralization of Function

Interest in the possibility that the brains of females and males differ in their degree of lateralization has been stimulated by a series of papers by McGlone (e.g., 1977, 1980). She proposed on the basis of her studies with victims of unilateral strokes that the brains of males are more lateralized than those of females. Key in supporting this hypothesis were two observations: that left-hemisphere lesions are much more likely to produce language-related deficits in males than in females, and that males are three times more likely to become aphasic after unilateral brain injury than are females. McGlone's hypothesis has led to the suggestion that a gender difference in lateralization might be the basis for the slight tendency for females to perform better on verbal tasks and males to perform better on visuospatial tasks.

McGlone's interesting hypotheses have not received universal support from other researchers (see Kolb & Whishaw, 1989). For example, Inglis and Lawson (1982) found that left-hemisphere lesions were just as likely to disrupt the performance of language-related tests in females as in males, and Hier and Kaplan (1980) and De Renzi (1980) found the incidence of aphasia to be only slightly greater (about 12% greater) in males than in females. Accordingly, although there is some suggestion of a gender difference in lateralization of function, a clear pattern of results in support of this hypothesis has yet to emerge.

17.2 Studying Lateralization of Function in Split-Brain Subjects

In the early 1950s, the corpus callosum constituted a paradox of major proportions. Its size (an estimated 200 million axons) and its central position (right between the two cerebral hemispheres) implied that it performed an extremely important function, yet research in the 1930s and 1940s seemed to suggest that it did nothing at all. The corpus callosum had been cut in monkeys and in several other laboratory species, but the animals seemed no different after the surgery than they had been before. Similarly, human patients born without a corpus callosum seemed perfectly normal. In the early 1950s, Roger Sperry and his colleagues were attracted by this paradox.

> As recently as 1951 the psychologist Karl S. Lashley, director of the Yerkes Laboratories of Primate Biology, was still offering his own jocular surmise that the corpus callosum's purpose "must be mainly mechanical . . . i.e., to keep the hemispheres from sagging." The curious capacity of the brain to carry on undisturbed after the destruction of what is by far its largest central fiber system came to be cited rather widely in support of some of the more mystical views in brain theory.
>
> Intrigued by the problem of the great cerebral commissure and the theoretical implications of this problem, my colleagues and I began an intensive investigation of the matter . . . (Sperry, 1964, p. 42)

The Groundbreaking Experiment of Myers and Sperry

The answer to the puzzle of the corpus callosum was provided in 1953 by an experiment on cats by Myers and Sperry. It made two astounding theoretical points. First, it showed that one function of the corpus callosum was to transfer learned information from one hemisphere to the other. Second, it showed that when the corpus callosum was cut, each hemisphere could function independently—amazingly, each split-brain cat appeared to have two brains. If you find the thought of a cat with two brains provocative, you will almost certainly be bowled over by similar observations in split-brain humans. But I am getting ahead of myself. Let's first consider the research on cats.

In their experiment, Myers and Sperry trained cats to perform a simple visual discrimination. On each trial, each cat was confronted by two panels, one with a circle on it and one with a square on it. The relative positions of the circle and square (right or left) were varied randomly from trial to trial, and the cats had to learn which symbol to press in order to get a food reward. Myers and Sperry correctly surmised that the key to split-brain research was to develop procedures for teaching and testing one hemisphere at a time. Figure 17.4 illustrates the method that they used to

To isolate visual information in one hemisphere of a cat, Myers and Sperry:

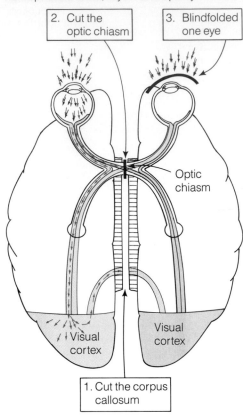

2. Cut the optic chiasm

3. Blindfolded one eye

Optic chiasm

Visual cortex

Visual cortex

1. Cut the corpus callosum

Regardless of how the eyes move, when both the corpus callosum and the optic chiasm have been sectioned and one eye blindfolded, visual input is restricted to the hemisphere opposite the blindfold.

FIGURE 17.4 *Cutting the optic chiasm and putting a patch on one eye isolates visual information in one hemisphere of a split-brain cat.*

STAGE 1

STAGE 2

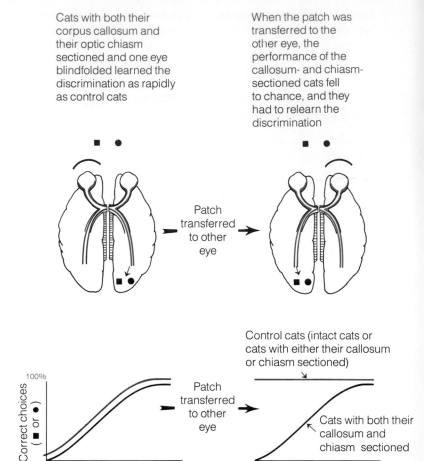

Cats with both their corpus callosum and their optic chiasm sectioned and one eye blindfolded learned the discrimination as rapidly as control cats

When the patch was transferred to the other eye, the performance of the callosum- and chiasm-sectioned cats fell to chance, and they had to relearn the discrimination

Patch transferred to other eye

Correct choices (■ or ●)

100%

50%

Trials

Patch transferred to other eye

Control cats (intact cats or cats with either their callosum or chiasm sectioned)

Cats with both their callosum and chiasm sectioned

Trials

FIGURE 17.5 *Schematic illustration of the results of Myers and Sperry's (1953) split-brain experiment.*

isolate visual discrimination learning in one hemisphere of their cats. There are two routes by which visual information can cross from one eye to the contralateral hemisphere: It can cross via the corpus callosum or via the optic chiasm. Accordingly, Myers and Sperry *transected* (cut completely through) both the optic chiasm and the corpus callosum of each cat in their key experimental group; then they put a patch on one eye in order to restrict all incoming visual information to the hemisphere on the same side as the unpatched eye.

The results of Myers and Sperry's experiment are illustrated schematically in Figure 17.5. In the first phase of the study, the cats in the key experimental group (i.e., the cats with both their optic chiasm and corpus callosum transected) learned the simple discrimination with a patch on one eye as rapidly as unlesioned control cats, despite the fact that cutting the optic chiasm produced a **scotoma** (an area of blindness; see Chapter 7) in the medial half of each retina. This suggested that one hemisphere working alone can learn simple tasks as rapidly as two hemispheres working together. Even more surprising were the results of the second phase of the experiment, during which the patch was transferred to the other eye. This transfer had no effect on the performance of intact control cats or of cats with either their optic chiasms or their corpus callosums transected; these subjects continued to perform the task with close to 100% accuracy. In contrast, transferring the eye patch had a devastating effect on the performance of the experimental cats. In effect, it blinded the hemisphere that had originally learned the task and tested the knowledge of the other hemisphere, which had been blinded during initial training. When the patch was transferred, the performance of the experimental cats dropped immediately to baseline (50% correct), and then they relearned the task with no savings whatsoever, as if they had never seen it before. Myers and Sperry concluded that each cat brain has the capacity to act as two separate brains and that the function of the corpus callosum is to transmit information between them.

Myers and Sperry's startling conclusions about the fundamental duality of the brain and the information-transfer function of the corpus callosum have been confirmed many times in a variety of species using a variety of tests. For example, it has been shown that monkeys with their corpus callosums transected cannot perform tasks requiring fine tactual discriminations (e.g., rough versus smooth) or fine motor responses (e.g., unlocking a puzzle) with their right hands if they have learned them with only their left hands (and vice versa), provided that they were not allowed to watch their hands during the original training. There is no transfer of fine tactual and motor information in split-brain monkeys because the somatosensory and motor fibers involved in fine sensory and motor discriminations with the right hand all project from or to the left hemisphere, and those from the left hand all project from or to the right hemisphere (see Chapters 8 and 9). Thus, fine tactual and motor tasks performed by the one hand of a split-brain monkey are controlled entirely by the contralateral hemisphere.

Commissurotomy in Human Epileptics

In the first half of this century, when the function of the corpus callosum still remained a mystery, it was well known that it served as a conduit through which epileptic discharges originating in one hemisphere could spread into the other. This fact, and the fact that cutting the corpus callosum had no obvious detrimental effects on performance outside of contrived laboratory testing situations, led two neurosurgeons, Vogel and Bogen, to initiate a program of **commissurotomy** for the treatment of intractable and particularly debilitating cases of epilepsy. The rationale underlying their treatment—which entailed transecting the corpus callosum as well as the *anterior commissure,* and the *hippocampal commissure*—was that the severity of the patient's convulsions might be reduced if the discharges could be limited to the hemisphere of their origin. However, the therapeutic benefits of commissurotomy were even greater than anticipated. Despite the fact that commissurotomy is performed in only the most severe cases, many commissurotomized patients never experienced another convulsion after their operation.

The evaluation of the split-brain patient's neuropsychological status was placed in the capable hands of Sperry and his associate Gazzaniga. They immediately set up a battery of tests based on the same general methodological strategy that had proven so informative in their previous studies of laboratory animals; that is, they developed procedures for delivering information to one hemisphere while keeping it out of the other. They could not use the same visual discrimination procedure used in studies of split-brain laboratory animals (i.e., cutting the optic chiasm and blindfolding one eye) because cutting the optic chiasm produces blindness on the nasal half of each retina. Instead, they employed the testing procedure illustrated in Figure 17.6. Each patient was asked to *fixate* on (to stare at with eyes as motionless as possible) the center of a display screen; then visual stimuli were flashed onto the left or right side of the screen for only 0.1 second. (The 0.1 second exposure time was long enough for the subjects to perceive the stimuli, but short enough to preclude the confounding effects of eye movement.) As shown in Figure 17.7, all visual stimuli presented in the left visual field are transmitted to the right visual cortex, and all stimuli presented in the right visual field are transmitted to the left visual cortex (see Chapter 7). In Sperry and Gazzaniga's tests, fine tactual and motor tasks were performed by the hands under a ledge so that the nonperforming hemisphere could not gain access to the fine tactual and motor information via the visual system.

The results of the tests on the initial group of split-brain patients confirmed the previous research with split-brain laboratory animals in one major respect, but not in another. Like the split-brain laboratory animals, the human split-brain patients seemed to have two independent brains, each with its own stream of consciousness, abilities, memories, and emotions (e.g., Gazzaniga, 1967; Gazzaniga & Sperry, 1967; Sperry, 1964). But unlike the brains of the split-brain laboratory animals, the brains of the split-brain patients proved to be far from equal in their ability to perform certain tasks. The most obvious difference between the abilities of the hemispheres of the split-brain patients was that the left hemisphere was capable of speech, whereas the right hemisphere was not—all of the patients in the initial series were right-handed.

Before I recount some of the key results of the tests on split-brain humans, let me give you some advice. Some students become confused by the results of these tests because their tendency to think of the human

FIGURE 17.6 *The testing arrangement commonly used to evaluate the neuropsychological status of split-brain patients.*

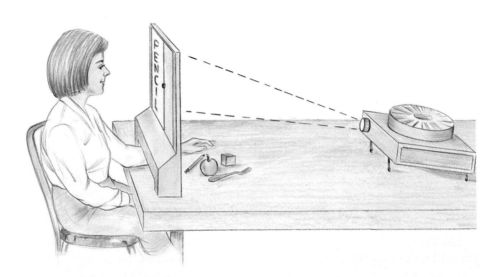

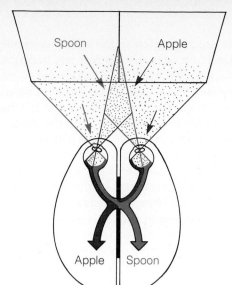

FIGURE 17.7 *The paths of visual information in human split-brain patients.*

brain as a single unitary organ is so deeply engrained in them. If you become confused, stop and think of each split-brain patient as two separate subjects: Mr. or Ms. Right Hemisphere, who understands a few simple instructions but cannot speak, who receives sensory information from the left visual field and left hand, and who controls the fine motor responses of the left hand; and Mr. or Ms. Left Hemisphere, who is verbally adept, who receives sensory information from the right visual field and right hand, and who controls the fine motor responses of the right hand. In everyday life, the behavior of each split-brain subject is reasonably normal because the two brains go through life together and acquire much of the same information; however, in the neuropsychological laboratory, major discrepancies in what the two hemispheres learn can be created, and this has some interesting consequences.

Evidence that the Hemispheres of Split-Brain Patients Function Independently

If a picture of a spoon is flashed in the right visual field of a split-brain patient, the left hemisphere can do one of two things to indicate that it has received and stored the information. Because it is the hemisphere that speaks, the left hemisphere can simply tell the experimenter that it saw a picture of a spoon. Or, the patient can reach under the ledge with his or her right hand, feel the test objects that are there, and pick out the spoon. Similarly, if the spoon is presented to the left hemisphere by placing it in the patient's right hand, the left hemisphere can indicate to the experimenter that it was a spoon either by saying so or by putting the spoon down and picking out another spoon with the right hand from the test objects under the ledge. If, however, the nonspeaking, right hemisphere is asked to indicate the identity of an object presented to left hemisphere, it cannot do so. Although objects presented to the left hemisphere can be accurately identified with the right hand, performance is no better than chance with the left hand.

When test objects are presented to the right hemisphere either visually (in the left visual field) or tactually (in the left hand), the pattern of responses is entirely different. If the patient is asked to name an object flashed in the left visual field, he or she is likely to claim that nothing appeared on the screen. (Remember that it is the left hemisphere who is talking and the right hemisphere who has seen the stimulus.) If the patient is asked to name an object placed in the left hand, he or she is usually aware that something is there (presumably because of the crude tactual information carried by ipsilateral somatosensory fibers; see Chapter 8), but is unable to say what it is. Amazingly, all the while the patient is claiming (i.e., all the while that the left hemisphere is claiming) that he or she cannot identify a test object presented in the left visual field or left hand, the left hand (i.e., the right hemisphere) can identify the correct object. Imagine how confused the patient (the left hemisphere) must become when in trial after trial, the left hand can feel an object and then fetch another just like it from a collection of test items under the ledge, while the left hemisphere is vehemently claiming that it does not know the identity of the test object.

In one particularly interesting test, it was demonstrated that emotional experiences can also be limited to one hemisphere of a split-brain patient. A picture of a nude human figure was flashed into the left visual field during the course of a routine test, and the subject was asked to describe the object. Although the left hemisphere claimed nothing had been presented, the right hemisphere was clearly amused. A sly smile spread over the patient's face, and she began to chuckle. Asked what she was laughing about, she (the left hemisphere) replied "I don't know . . . nothing . . . oh—that funny machine."

Cross-Cuing

Although the two hemispheres of a split-brain subject have no means of direct neural communication, they sometimes communicate with each other indirectly by a method called **cross-cuing.** An example of cross-cuing occurred during a series of tests designed to determine whether the left hemisphere could respond to colors presented in the left visual field. To test this possibility, a red or a green light was flashed in the left visual field, and the subject was asked to verbally report the color: red or green. At first the patient performed at a chance level on this task (i.e., 50% correct), but after several trials performance improved appreciably, thus suggesting that the color information was somehow being transferred over neural pathways from the right hemisphere to the left. However, this proved not to be the case.

> We soon caught on to the strategy the patient used. If a red light was flashed and the patient by chance guessed red, he would stick with that answer. If the flashed light was red, and the patient by chance guessed green, he would frown, shake his head and then say, "Oh no, I meant red." What was happening was that the right hemisphere saw the red light and heard the left hemisphere make the guess "green." Knowing that the answer was wrong, the right hemisphere precipitated a frown and a shake of the head, which in turn cued in the left hemisphere to the fact that the answer was wrong and that it had better correct itself! . . . The realization that the neurological patient has various strategies at his command emphasizes how difficult it is to obtain a clear neurological description of a human being with brain damage (Gazzaniga, 1967, p. 27).

Most of my classes seem to have at least one student who fits the following stereotype. It is usually a male who sits—or rather sprawls—near the back of the class and who, despite good grades, tries to create the impression that he is above it all by occasionally making pointed, slightly sarcastic comments designed to amuse the class. I mention this here because just such a comment recently triggered an interesting discussion about the split brain in one of my classes. The comment went something like this: "If getting my brain cut in two could create two separate brains, perhaps I should get it done so that I can study for two different exams at the same time."

The question raised by this comment is a good one. If the two hemispheres of a split-brain patient are capable of total independence, then they should be able to learn two different things at the same time. Can they? Remarkably, they can. For example, in one test two different visual stimuli appeared simultaneously on the test screen—let's say a pencil in the left visual field and an apple in the right visual field. Then the subject was asked to simultaneously reach into two bags—one with each hand—and grasp in each hand the object that was on the screen. After grasping the objects, but before withdrawing them, the subject was asked to tell the experimenter what was in the two hands, and the subject (the left hemisphere) replied "two apples." However, much to the bewilderment of the verbal left hemisphere, when the hands were withdrawn, there was an apple in the right hand and a pencil in the left. The two hemispheres of the split-brain subject had learned two different things at exactly the same time.

In another test in which two visual stimuli were presented simultaneously—again let's say a pencil to the left visual field and an apple to the right—the subjects were asked to pick up the presented object from an assortment of objects, which were on the table in full view. As the right hand reached out to pick up the apple under the direction of the left hemisphere, the right hemisphere saw what was happening and thought that an error was being made (remember that the right hemisphere saw a pencil). As a result, in a few cases, the left hand shot out, grabbed the right hand away from the apple, and redirected it to the pencil. This response is called the **helping-hand phenomenon.**

Yet another example of simultaneous learning in the two hemispheres involves the phenomenon of **visual completion.** As you may recall from Chapter 8, subjects with scotomas (i.e., areas of blindness in their visual fields) are often unaware of them because their brains have the capacity to fill them in (i.e., to complete them) by using information from the surrounding areas of the visual field. In a sense, each hemisphere of a split-brain patient is a subject with a scotoma covering her or his entire ipsilateral visual field. The ability of each hemisphere of a split-brain subject to simultaneously and independently engage in completion has been demonstrated in studies using the **chimeric figures test**—named after *Chimera*, a mythical monster composed of the combined parts of different animals. Levy, Trevarthen, and Sperry (1972) flashed photographs composed of the fused half faces of two different people onto the center of a screen in front of their split-brain subjects. The subjects were then asked to describe what they saw or to point to what they saw from a series of normal photographs. Amazingly, each subject (i.e., each left hemisphere) reported seeing a complete, bilaterally symmetrical face, even when asked such leading questions as, "Did you notice anything peculiar about what you just saw?" When the subjects were asked to describe what they saw, they usually described a completed version of the half that had been presented to the right visual field (left hemisphere). In contrast, when the subjects were asked to point out the correct face from a series of possibilities, they usually pointed to the completed version of the half that had been presented to the left visual field (right hemisphere), regardless of which hand was used for pointing. Pointing is a crude motor response, which can be controlled either from the contralateral or ipsilateral hemisphere. Clearly, each hemisphere of a split-brain patient is capable of visual completion, and each can see a different face in exactly the same place at exactly the same time.

Comparing the Abilities of the Left and Right Hemispheres of Split-Brain Subjects

Once it was firmly established that the two hemispheres of each split-brain patient can function independently, it became clear that the study of split-brain patients provided a unique opportunity to compare the abilities of left and right hemispheres. However, early studies of the lateralization of function in split-brain patients were limited by the fact that visual stimuli requiring more than 0.1 second to perceive could not be studied using the conventional method for restricting visual input to one hemisphere. This methodological barrier was eliminated by Zaidel in 1975. Zaidel developed a lens that limits visual input to one hemisphere of split-brain patients while they scan complex visual material such as pages of a book. As illustrated in Figure 17.8, the **Z lens,** as it has been termed (after Zaidel), is a contact lens that is opaque on one side. Because it moves with the eye, it permits visual input to enter only one hemisphere, irrespective of eye movement. Zaidel used the Z lens to compare the ability of the left and right hemispheres of split-brain patients to perform tests that had been developed to assess the verbal abilities of children and aphasic patients. Because each ear projects to both hemispheres, it is not possible to present spoken words to only one hemisphere. Thus, to assess the ability of a hemisphere to comprehend spoken words or sentences, he presented

FIGURE 17.8 *The Z-lens system developed by Zaidel to study functional asymmetry in split-brain patients. (Adapted from Springer & Deutsch, 1981.)*

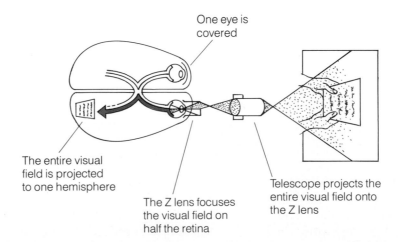

One eye is covered

The entire visual field is projected to one hemisphere

The Z lens focuses the visual field on half the retina

Telescope projects the entire visual field onto the Z lens

them to both ears, and then he asked the subject to pick the correct answer or to perform the correct response under the direction of visual input to only that hemisphere. For example, to test the ability of the right hemisphere to understand the oral commands of the *token test* (see Chapter 4), the subjects were given an oral instruction (such as, "put the green square under the red circle"), and then the right hemisphere's ability to comprehend the direction was tested by allowing only the right hemisphere to observe the colored tokens while the task was being completed. These studies (see Zaidel, 1983) revealed a surprising degree of verbal comprehension ability in the right hemisphere—"surprising" because experts had assumed that because the right hemisphere could not speak that it had no language-related ability whatsoever. Zaidel found that the disconnected right hemisphere could understand common spoken and written words, and simple grammatical and syntactical principles. Although it is impossible to characterize the comprehension abilities of the right hemisphere in any simple way, the level of competence of the right hemisphere in many tests of language comprehension was comparable to that of a normal child between 3 and 6 years old (Zaidel, 1985).

The old concept of left-hemisphere dominance (the idea that the left hemisphere dominates the right in all important activities) was put to rest by the discovery that the right hemisphere is generally superior to the left at tasks that involve spatial ability. For example, Levy (1969) placed a three-dimensional block of a particular shape in either the right hand or the left hand of her split-brain subjects, and then after they had thoroughly *palpated* it (tactually investigated it), she asked them to point to the two-dimensional test stimulus that best represented what the three-dimensional block would look like if it were made of cardboard and unfolded. Not only did she find a striking superiority of the right hemisphere on this task, but she also discovered that the two hemispheres seemed to go about the task in entirely different ways. The performance of the left hand and right hemisphere was rapid and silent, whereas the performance of the right hand and left hemisphere was hesitant and often accompanied by a running verbal commentary that was difficult for the subjects to inhibit. Levy concluded that the left hemisphere thinks in a verbal, analytic mode and that thinking in the right hemisphere is direct, perceptual, and synthetic. The superiority of the right hemisphere of split-brain patients at spatial and pattern tasks is consistent with the finding that patients with right parietal lesions have greater difficulty on the *block-designs test* (see Chapter 9) than do those with equivalent left-hemisphere lesions (Piercy, Hécaen, & Ajuriaguerra, 1962).

Two Theories of Cerebral Asymmetry

Several theories have been proposed to explain why cerebral asymmetry evolved. The two most prominent theories of lateralization of function are based on the premise that there are advantages for areas of the brain that perform similar functions to be located in the same hemisphere. One of these theories (see Levy, 1969; Sperry, 1974, 1985) is that there are two basic modes of thinking, an *analytic mode* and a *synthetic mode,* and that the neural circuitry required for each is intrinsically different. As a result, those functions that benefit from the analytic and synthetic modes of treatment have become segregated during the course of evolution, the analytic mechanisms in the left hemisphere and the synthetic mechanisms in the right.

In the words of Harris (1978),

> The left hemisphere operates in a more logical, analytical, computer-like fashion, analyzing stimulus information input sequentially, abstracting out the relevant details to which it attaches verbal labels; the right hemisphere is primarily a synthesizer, more concerned with the overall stimulus configuration, and organizes and processes information in terms of gestalts or wholes (p. 463).

Kimura (1979) proposed the second major theory of cerebral asymmetry. She hypothesized that, although speech is the most well-known and highly lateralized ability of the human left hemisphere, the left hemisphere is not specialized for the control of speech per se but for the control of fine motor movements, of which speech is only one, albeit particularly notable, example. Kimura offered two major lines of evidence in support of her theory. First, lesions of the left hemisphere selectively disrupt voluntary oral movements whether they are related to speech or not. And second, the degree of disruption of voluntary nonspeech facial movements produced by left-hemisphere lesions is positively correlated with the degree of aphasia that they produce. Kimura believes that verbal communication evolved from a stage of communication that was primarily gestural with a few vocal components to one that is primarily vocal with a few gestural components.

Lateralization of Function and Split-Brains: Fact or Fiction?

> Recently, one of us received a phone call from a well-known Hollywood actress who related an argument with a friend concerning left-hemisphere-right-hemisphere differences. She had read that left-right brain differences are real, pervasive, and the subject of intense scientific studies. Her companion said they were pseudoscientific, popularized stuff, the fad of the decade. Who was right? (Zaidel, 1985, p. 307).

In a sense, both were. On one hand, there is no question that the study of the lateralization of function is one of the most important and productive lines of research in neuropsychology. It has led to the development of a successful treatment for epilepsy; it has provided data that have greatly facilitated the diagnosis and treatment of brain damage; and it has changed the way that we think about ourselves. On the other hand, the broad dissemination and popular appeal of this research has led to major distortions and abuses. Slight hemispheric differences have been transformed by the popular press into clear-cut, all-or-none dichotomies that have been used to account for everything from baseball batting averages to socioeconomic class.

17.3 The Cortical Localization of Language

So far, this chapter has focused on the functional asymmetry of the brain, with a heavy emphasis on the lateralization of language-related functions. At this point, it shifts course slightly, from language lateralization to language localization. In contrast to *language lateralization,* which refers to the relative control of language-related functions by the left and right hemispheres, *language localization* refers to the location within the hemispheres of the circuits participating in language-related activities.

The following treatment of language localization is orthodox in one respect, but not in another. Like most introductions to the topic, the following discussion revolves around the **Wernicke-Geschwind model,** which has dominated the teaching of the neuropsychology of language for 25 years. However, unlike the usual introductions to language lateralization, the ensuing coverage does not suggest that the Wernicke-Geschwind model provides an adequate explanation of the neuropsychology of language. In fact, you will learn that the Wernicke-Geschwind model is consistent with few of the findings of the research that it has stimulated.

You may be wondering right now why I have organized this section of the chapter around the Wernicke-Geschwind model if it is, as I have just pointed out, inconsistent with most of the data. The reason is that the Wernicke-Geschwind model, despite its inaccuracy, has been the primary stimulus for most research and debate about the cortical localization of language. Because most of the research that is described in this section was conducted and interpreted within the context of the Wernicke-Geschwind model, the model provides you with a means of integrating, evaluating, and remembering most of what you are about to read. Reading about the localization of language without a basic understanding of the Wernicke-Geschwind model would be like watching a game of chess without knowing the rules—not a very fulfilling experience.

Historic Antecedents of the Wernicke-Geschwind Model

The history of the localization of language and the history of the lateralization of function began at the same point, with Broca's assertion that a small area in the inferior portion of the left prefrontal cortex (subsequently called **Broca's area**) is the center for speech production. Broca hypothesized that programs of articulation are stored within this area and that speech is produced when these programs activate the adjacent portion of the precentral gyrus, which controls the muscles of the face and oral cavity. According to this theory, damage restricted to Broca's area should disrupt speech production without producing deficits in language comprehension.

The next major chapter in the story of the cerebral localization of language came in 1874, when Wernicke (pronounced VER ni key) claimed to have identified, on the basis of 10 clinical cases, a second cortical language center, which later became known as **Wernicke's area.** He contended that the area in the left temporal lobe just posterior to the primary auditory cortex (see Chapter 8) is the center for language comprehension (see Figure 17.9). In Wernicke's experience, lesions to Broca's area produce a syndrome of aphasia—termed **Broca's aphasia**—that is primarily **expressive,** characterized by speech that retains its meaningfulness, but is slow, labored, disjointed, and poorly articulated. In contrast, he claimed that the deficits produced by lesions of Wernicke's area are primarily **receptive.** According to Wernicke, people with damage to Wernicke's area have difficulty understanding language, and their speech has the superficial structure, rhythm, and intonation of proper speech. However, despite its superficial similarity to proper speech, it is incomprehensible—a veritable **word salad.**

Wernicke reasoned that damage to the pathway connecting Broca's area and Wernicke's area should produce a third type of aphasia, one that he

The seven components of the Wernicke - Geschwind model

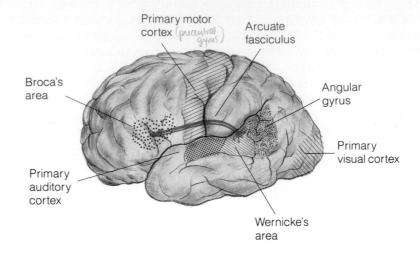

How the Wernicke - Geschwind model works

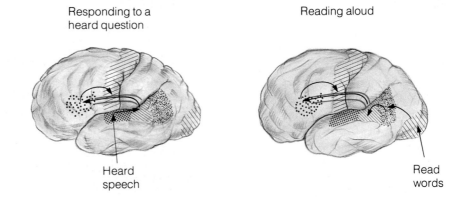

FIGURE 17.9 *Components of the Wernicke-Geschwind model. (Adapted from Geschwind, 1979.)*

called **conduction aphasia.** He argued that comprehension and spontaneous speech would be intact in patients with damage to this pathway, but that there would be a difficulty in repeating words that were heard. The major pathway connecting Wernicke's and Broca's areas was subsequently identified and termed the left **arcuate fasciculus** (see Figure 17.9).

The following are examples of the kinds of speech presumed to be associated with localized damage to Broca's and Wernicke's areas, respectively (Geschwind, 1979).

Broca's Aphasia: A patient asked about a dental appointment said hesitantly and indistinctly: "Yes . . . Monday . . . Dad and Dick . . . Wednesday nine o'clock . . . 10 o'clock . . . doctors . . . and . . . teeth."
Wernicke's Aphasia: A patient who was asked to describe a picture that showed two boys stealing cookies behind a woman's back reported: "Mother is away here working her work to get her better, but when she's looking the two boys looking in the other part. She's working another time." (p. 181)

Another cortical area presumed to be important for language was identified by Dejerine in 1892 on the basis of the postmortem examination of
one patient who suddenly became alexic and agraphic, that is, lost his
ability to read and write in the absence of any gross visual or motor deficits.
The case was particularly valuable because the **alexia** and **agraphia** were
relatively pure in the sense that they occurred in the absence of major
deficits in the production or comprehension of speech. Dejerine's postmortem examination revealed damage in the pathways connecting the visual
cortex to the left **angular gyrus** (see Figure 17.15), an area of left temporal
and parietal cortex just posterior to Wernicke's area. Dejerine concluded
that the left angular gyrus is responsible for comprehending language-
related visual information received directly from the adjacent left visual
cortex and indirectly from the right visual cortex via the corpus callosum.

During the era of Broca, Wernicke, and Dejerine, there were many
influential scientists who opposed their attempts to localize various
language-related abilities to specific neocortical areas (e.g., Head, Freud,
Marie). In fact, these advocates of a more holistic approach to brain function gradually gained the upper hand, and interest in the localization of
language waned. However, in 1965, Geschwind revived the old localizationist ideas of Broca, Wernicke, and Dejerine and melded them into a
powerful theory that emphasized that damage to the language areas of the
left hemisphere or to the connections between them was the major cause of
aphasia and other language-related disorders. This *Wernicke-Geschwind
model*, as it became known, spurred a resurgence of interest in the neuropsychology of language.

The Wernicke-Geschwind Model

The seven components of the Wernicke-Geschwind model are illustrated in Figure 17.9: primary visual cortex, angular gyrus, primary auditory cortex, Wernicke's area, the arcuate fasciculus, Broca's area, and the
primary motor cortex—all in the left hemisphere. The following two examples illustrate how this model is presumed to function. First, when you are
having a conversation, the auditory signals triggered by the speech of the
other person are received by your primary auditory cortex and conducted
to Wernicke's area, where they are comprehended. If a response is in
order, Wernicke's area generates the neural representation of the thought
underlying the reply, and it is transmitted to Broca's area via the arcuate
fasciculus. In Broca's area, this signal activates the appropriate program of
articulation that drives the appropriate orofacial neurons of the primary
motor cortex and ultimately your muscles of articulation. Second, when
you are reading aloud, the signal received by your primary visual cortex is
transmitted to the angular gyrus, which translates the visual form of the
word into its auditory code and transmits it to Wernicke's area for comprehension. Wernicke's area then triggers the appropriate responses in the
arcuate fasciculus, Broca's area, and motor cortex, respectively, to elicit the
appropriate speech sound.

From these two examples, it is clear that the Wernicke-Geschwind
model is a **serial model;** that is, it involves a chain of responses that are
triggered in linear sequence, like a single line of falling dominoes. In
contrast, **parallel models** involve two or more routes of activity (see
Chapter 9).

Before proceeding to an evaluation of the Wernicke-Geschwind model, complete the following exercise to confirm that you understand its fundamentals. According to the Wernicke-Geschwind model:

1. The ___angular___ gyrus translates the visual form of a read word into meaningful auditory code,

2. The __primary motor (precentral gyrus)__ cortex controls the muscles of articulation,

3. The ___visual___ cortex receives the written word,

4. ___Wernicke's___ area is the center for language comprehension,

5. The ___auditory___ cortex receives the spoken word,

6. ___Broca's___ area contains the programs of articulation, and

7. The left ___arcuate fasciculus___ carries signals from the center of language comprehension to the center that contains the programs of articulation.

Evaluation of the Wernicke-Geschwind Model

You should have digested the preceding description of the Wernicke-Geschwind model with some degree of skepticism—unless you are reading this text from back to front. By this point in the text, you will almost certainly recognize that any model of a complex cognitive process that involves a few highly localized neocortical centers joined in a linear fashion by a few arrows, although appealingly simple, is sure to have major shortcomings. You have learned in almost every chapter that the brain—and especially the neocortex—is not divided into neat little compartments whose functions conform to vague concepts such as language comprehension, speech motor programs, and conversion of written language to auditory language.

The evidence offered by advocates of the Wernicke-Geschwind model is composed almost entirely of selected case studies of patients with strokes, tumors, and penetrating brain injuries. Damage in such cases is almost always diffuse, and it inevitably encroaches on underlying myelinated fiber systems that are coursing through the lesion site to other areas of the brain. Clearly, such case studies are a questionable basis for deriving a strictly localizationist theory (cf. Bogen & Bogen, 1976). For example, pictured in Figure 17.10 is an estimate of the damage to the cortical surface in one of the two cases on which Broca based his original claim that a discrete area of frontal cortex (i.e., Broca's area) controls speech programming.

Correct answers to the questions on the preceding page: (1) angular, (2) primary motor, (3) primary visual, (4) Wernicke's, (5) primary auditory, (6) Broca's, and (7) arcuate fasciculus.

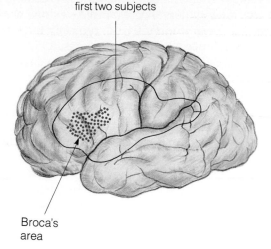

Damage observed in
one of Broca's
first two subjects

Broca's
area

FIGURE 17.10 *The extent of
damage in one of Broca's two
original patients. (Adapted from
Mohr, 1976.)*

The ultimate test of a theory's validity is the degree to which its predictions are consistent with the empirical evidence. The remainder of the chapter reviews several lines of research that have tested predictions of the Wernicke-Geschwind model. But first, two confusing points concerning the use of the terms "Broca's aphasia" and "Wernicke's aphasia" must be clarified. The first is that Broca's and Wernicke's aphasia probably does not exist in their pure forms as defined by Wernicke and Geschwind—or if they do, they are extremely rare. Broca's and Wernicke's aphasia are predictions of the Wernicke-Geschwind model, rather than descriptions of the dysfunctions commonly experienced by aphasic patients. Almost all aphasic patients have a complex mixture of both expressive and receptive symptoms (Benson, 1985), and even in those few reported cases that appear to closely comply with specific deficits predicted by the model, one has to wonder whether other deficits may have been revealed by more extensive testing. Accordingly, the terms of Broca's and Wernicke's aphasia are generally used to designate aphasic disorders that are primarily—not completely—expressive and receptive, respectively. The second confusing point about the terms "Broca's aphasia" and "Wernicke's aphasia" is that they do not—as their names imply—necessarily result from damage to Broca's and Wernicke's areas. This is another prediction of the model, not a description of the evidence.

The Effects of Brain Damage on Language-Related Abilities

Surgical Removal of Cortical Tissue   In view of the fact that the Wernicke-Geschwind model grew out of the study of patients with cortical damage, it is appropriate to begin evaluating it by assessing its ability to predict the language-related deficits produced by damage to various parts of the cortex. The study of patients in whom discrete areas of cortex have been surgically removed has proven particularly informative in this regard because the extent of their lesions is so well known. Unfortunately, the study of patients in whom the Wernicke-Geschwind language areas have been surgically removed has not confirmed the predictions of the model by any stretch of the imagination. For example, lesions that destroy all of Broca's area, but little surrounding tissue, typically have no lasting effects on language-related abilities (Penfield & Roberts, 1959; Rasmussen & Milner, 1975; Zangwill, 1975). There is often some aphasia after such a discrete lesion, but its temporal course suggests that it results from postsurgical *edema* (swelling) in the surrounding neural tissue, rather than from the *excision* (cutting out) of Broca's area per se. The patient typically has no speech problems immediately after Broca's area has been excised; speech deficits develop several hours later and gradually subside in the ensuing weeks. Similarly, permanent speech difficulties are not produced by discrete surgical lesions to the arcuate fasciculus, and permanent alexia and agraphia are not produced by surgical lesions restricted to the cortex of the angular gyrus (Rasmussen & Milner, 1975). The consequences of the surgical removal of Wernicke's area are less well documented; surgeons have been hesitant to remove it in light of Wernicke's dire predictions. Nevertheless, in some cases, a good portion of Wernicke's area has been removed without lasting language-related deficits (e.g., Ojemann, 1979; Penfield & Roberts, 1959). Figure 17.11 summarizes the language-related effects of six cortical excisions performed by Penfield and Roberts (1959).

Supporters of the Wernicke-Geschwind model argue that, despite the precision of surgical excision, negative evidence obtained from the study of the effects of brain surgery should be discounted because the brain pathology that warranted the surgery may have reorganized the control of language by the brain.

Accidental or Disease-Related Brain Damage Hécaen and Angelergues (1964) rated the articulation, fluency, comprehension, naming ability, ability to repeat spoken sentences, reading, and writing of 214 right-handed patients with small, medium, or large accidental or disease-related lesions to the left hemisphere. The extent and location of the damage in each case was estimated by either postmortem histological examination or visual inspection during subsequent surgery. Hécaen and Angelergues found that small lesions to Broca's area seldom produced lasting language deficits and that those restricted to Wernicke's area sometimes did not. Medium-sized lesions did produce some deficits, but in contrast to the predictions of the Wernicke-Geschwind model, problems of articulation were just as likely to occur following medium-sized parietal or temporal lesions as they were following comparable lesions in the vicinity of Broca's area. All other symptoms associated with medium-sized lesions were more likely to appear following parietal or temporal lesions than following frontal damage. The only observation from this study consistent with the Wernicke-Geschwind model came from the analysis of the effects of large lesions (i.e., those involving three lobes). Large lesions of the anterior brain were more likely to be associated with articulation problems than were large lesions of the posterior brain. It is noteworthy that not one of the 214 subjects displayed the specific syndromes of expressive (Broca's aphasia) or receptive (Wernicke's aphasia) aphasia predicted by the Wernicke-Geschwind model. The effects of lesions to the frontal, temporal, parietal, or occipital lobes, or to the area of the central fissure are summarized in Figure 17.12.

Case J.M. No speech difficulties for 2 days after his surgery, but by Day 3 he was almost totally aphasic; 18 days after his operation he had no difficulty in spontaneous speech, naming, or reading, but his spelling and writing were poor.

Case P.R. He had no immediate speech difficulties; 2 days after his operation, he had some language-related problems but they cleared up.

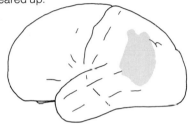

Case D.H. This operation was done in two stages; following completion of the second stage, no speech-related problems were reported.

Case A.D. He had no language-related problems after his operation, except for a slight deficit in silent reading and writing.

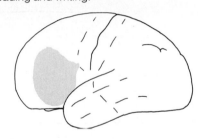

Case J.C. There were no immediate speech problems; 18 hours after his operation he became completely aphasic, but 21 days after surgery, only a mild aphasia remained.

Case H.N. After his operation, he had a slight difficulty in spontaneous speech, but 4 days later he was unable to speak; 23 days after surgery, there were minor deficits in spontaneous speech, naming and reading aloud, and a marked difficulty in oral calculation.

FIGURE 17.11 *The negligible permanent disruption of language-related abilities after surgical excision of the classic Wernicke-Geschwind language areas. (Adapted from Penfield & Roberts, 1959.)*

CAT Scans of Neuropsychological Patients with Language-Related Problems Mazzocchi and Vignolo (1979) and Naeser, Hayward, Laughlin, and Zatz (1981) took CAT scans (see Chapter 4) of the brains of neuropsychological patients with language-related problems. None was found with damage restricted to the classic Broca's and Wernicke's areas, and none was found without subcortical damage. However, both studies confirmed that large anterior lesions of the left hemisphere were more likely to produce deficits in language expression than were large posterior lesions, and that large posterior lesions were more likely to

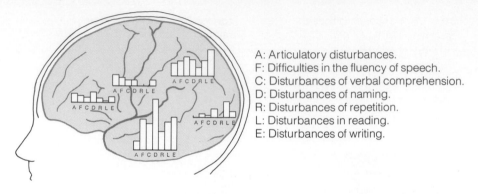

A: Articulatory disturbances.
F: Difficulties in the fluency of speech.
C: Disturbances of verbal comprehension.
D: Disturbances of naming.
R: Disturbances of repetition.
L: Disturbances in reading.
E: Disturbances of writing.

FIGURE 17.12 *The effects of damage to various cortical areas on language-related abilities. (Adapted from Hécaen & Angelergues, 1964.)*

produce deficits in language comprehension than were large anterior lesions. In both studies, **global aphasia,** an almost total elimination of all language-related abilities, was associated with very large left-hemisphere lesions that involved both the anterior and posterior cortex.

Cortical Stimulation and the Localization of Language

The first brain-stimulation studies of humans were conducted by Penfield and his colleagues in the 1940s at the Montreal Neurological Institute (see Feindel, 1986). One purpose of the studies was to map the language areas of each patient's brain so that tissue involved in language could be avoided during the surgery. The mapping was done by assessing the responses of conscious patients under local anesthetic to stimulation applied to various points on the cortical surface. The description of the effects of stimulation were dictated to a stenographer—this was before the days of tape recorders—and then a tiny numbered card was dropped on the stimulation site for subsequent photography. Figure 17.13 illustrates some of the sites at which the brain of a 37-year-old, right-handed Marine was stimulated just prior to excision. He had started to have seizures about 3 months after receiving a blow to the head, and at the time of his operation in 1948, he had been suffering from seizures for 6 years, despite efforts to control them with medication. The following were the responses of the patient to stimulation of the indicated sites (paraphrased from Penfield & Roberts,

FIGURE 17.13 *An illustration of the left hemisphere of a 37-year-old epileptic Marine prior to surgery. The numbered cards were placed on the brain to indicate the sites where brain stimulation had been applied.*

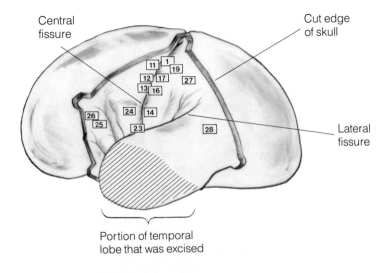

Central fissure

Cut edge of skull

Lateral fissure

Portion of temporal lobe that was excised

1959). In considering these responses, remember that the cortex just posterior to the central fissure is primary somatosensory cortex (see Chapter 8), and that the cortex just anterior to the central fissure is primary motor cortex (see Chapter 9).

1— Tingling in the right thumb and a slight movement

19— Sensation in lower lip

17— Sensation in right upper lip

16— Tingling in right side of tongue

14— Sensation in the jaw and lower lip

11— Feeling in the throat

12— Quivering of the jaw in a sidewise manner

13— Pulling of jaw to right

23— Stimulation applied while the patient was talking, stopped his speech. After cessation of stimulation, he said that he had been unable to speak despite trying.

23— Stimulation applied while the patient was not talking had no observable effect.

24— The patient tried to talk, his mouth moved, but he made no sound.

25— The patient had initial difficulty, but eventually he named a picture of a butterfly.

26— The patient said, "Oh, I know what it is" in response to a picture of a foot. "That is what you put in your shoes." After termination of the stimulation, he said, "foot."

27— Unable to name the picture of a tree, which was being shown to him, he said, "I know what it is." When the current was turned off, he said, "tree."

28— The patient became unable to name the pictures as soon as the electrode was placed here. When asked why he was not cooperating, he said, "no." The EEG revealed that seizure activity had been elicited in the temporal lobe by the stimulation. When the seizure discharges stopped, the patient spoke at once. "Now I can talk," he said, and he correctly identified the picture of a butterfly. He was asked why he had not been able to name the picture, and he replied, "I couldn't get that word 'butterfly', and then I tried to get the word 'moth'."

Such early clinical observations suggested that it might be possible to determine the cortical organization of the control of speech by systematically assessing the nature of the speech disturbances produced by stimulation to various parts of the cortex. Because mild brain stimulation is a much more local event than a brain lesion, Penfield and Roberts (1959) thought that the procedure might provide strong support for the Wernicke-Geschwind model. But it did not. Illustrated in Figure 17.14 is the wide distribution of sites in the left hemisphere at which stimulation produced a complete cessation of speech or various speech disturbances (distortion of speech, confusion of numbers while counting, inability to name with retained ability to speak, misnaming). Aphasia-like responses from the right hemisphere were rare.

Ojemann and his colleagues (see Ojemann, 1983) assessed naming, reading of simple sentences, short-term verbal memory, ability to mimic orofacial movements, and the ability to recognize **phonemes** (individual speech sounds) during cortical stimulation. In contrast to the predictions of

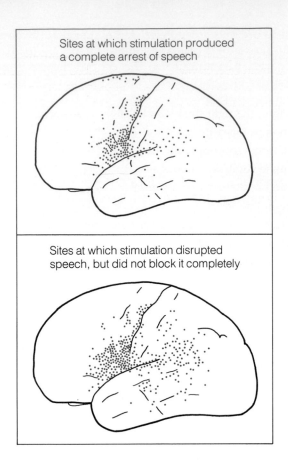

Sites at which stimulation produced
a complete arrest of speech

Sites at which stimulation disrupted
speech, but did not block it completely

FIGURE 17.14 *Distribution of left hemisphere sites where stimulation eliminated the ability to speak and those at which it disrupted speech without eliminating it completely. (Adapted from Penfield & Roberts, 1959.)*

the Wernicke-Geschwind model, they found that the areas of the cortex at which stimulation could disrupt language extended far beyond the boundaries of the Wernicke-Geschwind language areas; they found that all of the language abilities that they assessed were represented at both anterior and posterior sites; and they found that there was considerable difference in the organization of these language abilities in different subjects. Because the disruptive effects of stimulation at a particular site were frequently quite specific (disrupting only a single test), Ojemann (1983) suggested that the language cortex might be organized like a mosaic, with those discrete columns of tissue performing a particular function being widely distributed throughout the language area of the cortex.

Among the most interesting of the modern cortical stimulation studies are those involving bilingual subjects. All have revealed at least some sites at which stimulation disrupts naming in one language, but not the other (e.g., Rapport, Tan, & Whitaker, 1983). In one such study (Ojemann & Whitaker, 1978), the number of cortical sites at which stimulation disrupted naming in the secondary language was found to be much greater than the number at which naming in the primary language was disrupted.

Language Laterality and Neuroanatomical Asymmetry

There are numerous structural differences between the two hemispheres (see Kolb & Whishaw, 1989). Although the first reports of neuroanatomical asymmetries of the human brain were published in the

1800s (see von Bonin, 1962), they were largely ignored until Geschwind and Levitsky (1968) reported that the **planum temporale** in the left hemisphere is larger than that in the right hemisphere in 65% of human brains. This stimulated great interest, because the planum temporale is considered to be part of Wernicke's area. It is tucked in the lateral fissure just behind **Heschl's gyrus,** which is the site of primary auditory cortex. As illustrated in Figure 17.15, to compensate for the smaller planum temporale on the right, the right temporal lobe sometimes has two Heschl's gyri. The finding that this asymmetry is present in many fetal brains (Wada, Clarke, & Hamm, 1975) suggested that the left hemisphere may be structurally specialized for language-related activities even before the development of speech. The research on language and neuroanatomical asymmetry was further stimulated by the observation that the total area of the **frontal operculum** (the location of Broca's area in the left hemisphere) also tends to be greater on the left than the right (Falzi, Perrone, & Vignolo, 1982). It should be emphasized, however, that there is no evidence that people with asymmetric brains are more likely to have highly lateralized language functions—remember that, although about 95% of the population are left-hemisphere dominant for speech, only about 65% have a larger left planum temporale.

Cognitive Neuropsychology and Reading Aloud

Cognitive neuropsychology is an approach to the study of the neural basis of cognitive processes that focuses on the study of brain-damaged subjects. Cognitive neuropsychology is based on the **assumption of modularity,** the assumption that cognitive processes are produced by the combined activity of several specialized neural subsystems or modules, each of which performs a specific function. The basic research strategy of cognitive neuropsychologists is to determine the clusters of specific cognitive functions that tend to be disturbed or spared as a group in brain-damaged individuals, and to infer from these clusters the nature of the neural systems underlying various cognitive processes (see Kosslyn, 1988; Posner, Petersen, Fox, & Raichle, 1988).

Since the emergence of the cognitive-neuropsychological approach in the 1960s, it has focused on the analysis of the cognitive processes involved in reading aloud (see Coltheart, 1985; Marin, Schwartz, & Saffran, 1979). Most models of reading aloud that have emerged from these studies are

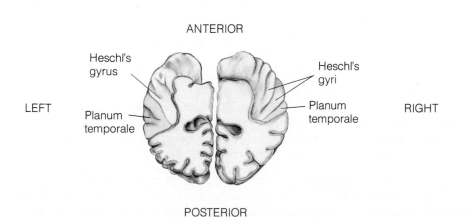

FIGURE 17.15 *The location of the planum temporale. (Adapted from Geschwind, 1972.)*

based on the hypothesis that there are two different systems for reading aloud: one called a **lexical procedure,** based on stored information that we have acquired about the pronunciation of specific written words in our vocabulary and another called a **nonlexical procedure,** based on the general rules of pronunciation that influence our pronunciation of unfamiliar words or nonwords such as "spleemer" and "twiple." Reports of neurological patients who have difficulty with one reading process and not the other provide the strongest support for these **dual-route models** (models of a cognitive process that are based on the premise that the process is mediated by two different pathways of neural activity). Several authors (e.g., Patterson, 1982; Shallice & Warrington, 1980) have reported cases in which nonlexical reading is specifically impaired. For example, W.B., a left-hemisphere stroke victim (Funnell, 1983), scored 0 out of 20 on a list of pronounceable nonwords, whereas his ability to read real words remained intact. In contrast, there have been numerous reports (e.g., Coltheart, Masterson, Byng, Prior, & Riddoch, 1983; Shallice & Warrington, 1980) of a disorder called **surface dyslexia** in which the nonlexical procedure remains intact, but there is a great difficulty in pronouncing words whose pronunciation is exceptional (e.g., yacht, sew). For example, M.P., a woman who was hit by a motor vehicle at the age of 59, subsequently lost her ability to read exceptional words, while her ability to read regular words and nonwords remained normal. Moreover, most of the incorrect responses that she made while reading exceptional words involved the correct application of common rules of English pronunciation: "have," "lose," "own," and "steak" were pronounced as if they rhymed with "cave," "hose," "down," and "beak." Such support for dual-route models of reading seriously challenges **serial models** (i.e., *single-route models*) such as the Wernicke-Geschwind model.

Measurement of Blood Flow During Language-Related Activities

There are increases in the flow of blood to those areas of the brain that are particularly active. This relation between neural activity and flow of blood has made it possible to estimate the activity of various areas of cortex by measuring the blood flow to them. The first generation of blood flow measurement techniques were two-dimensional. An inert radioactive gas was injected into the carotid artery, and then its subsequent dispersal through the ipsilateral cortex was assessed by a bank of *scintillation counters* (devices for measuring radioactivity) placed next to the head (see Chapter 9). Such measurements taken while subjects engaged in various language-related activities have yielded several interesting findings (see Ingvar, 1983).

The second generation of blood flow measurement techniques was developed by Petersen and his colleagues (Petersen, Fox, Mintun, Posner, & Raichle, 1988; Petersen, Fox, Posner, Mintun, & Raichle, 1988). Their technique features four important innovations (see Raichle, 1987). First, rather than using a bank of scintillation counters to obtain a two-dimensional map of the surface of the cortex, they use a PET-scan (see Chapter 4) method that provides a three-dimensional picture of blood flow in all parts of the brain. Second, rather than injecting a radioactive gas, they inject radioactive water. The advantage of water over the gas is that it quickly passes from the bloodstream, thus making it possible for several tests to be given to each subject, one every 10 minutes. Third, injections of the radioactive material are made intravenously rather than into the carotid artery. This allows the material to be dispersed equally to both hemispheres so that they can be studied simultaneously. Fourth, Petersen and his colleagues use a computer program to subtract the changes in blood flow during one activity from those observed during another. The utility of this subtraction procedure will become apparent as I describe their experiments.

The blood flow of each subject was measured under two sets of conditions: visual and auditory. Both sets comprised four conditions of progressively increasing complexity. In the four visual conditions, the subjects were asked to do the following: (1) to fixate on (i.e., to stare at) a crosshair on a display screen, (2) to fixate on the crosshair while printed nouns were being presented, (3) to fixate on the crosshair while repeating aloud the printed nouns, and (4) to fixate on the crosshair while saying an appropriate verb to go with the printed noun (e.g., cake:eat, radio:listen). The four auditory conditions were identical to the four visual conditions except that the nouns were presented auditorily while the subjects stared at the crosshair.

Three levels of subtraction were performed on the images recorded during these two sets of tests. The activity during the fixation-only condition was subtracted from that during the passive-noun condition to get a measure of the activation produced by passively observing or hearing the nouns. The activity during the passive-noun condition was subtracted from that during the saying-noun condition to get a measure of the activation produced by saying the noun. And the activity during the saying-noun condition was subtracted from that during the verb-association condition to get a measure of the activation produced by the cognitive processes involved in forming the association. The results of these three subtractions in both the visual and auditory conditions are summarized in Figure 17.16.

It is apparent in Figure 17.16 that the mere presentation of printed nouns produced activation in the secondary visual cortex (see Chapter 8) which was not present when the subjects just stared at the crosshair, and auditory noun presentation produced bilateral activity in both the primary and secondary auditory cortex, which was not present when they stared at the crosshair in silence. Regardless of whether the nouns were presented in printed or auditory form, repeating them aloud activated the same general cortical areas that were not activated in the passive-word conditions; activation occurred along the central fissures of both hemispheres and along the lateral fissure of the right hemisphere. Similarly, regardless of whether the words were presented in a printed or auditory form, the verb-association condition added activity in the prefrontal cortex of the left hemisphere just in front of Broca's area and in the medial cortex just above the front portion of the corpus callosum. The computer-generated images of these same subtracted patterns of cortical activation (averaged over all of the subjects) are presented in Figure 17.17.

What type of model do these impressive results support? Certainly not the Wernicke-Geschwind model. There was no evidence of activation in either Wernicke's area or in the angular gyrus during the visual tests, and

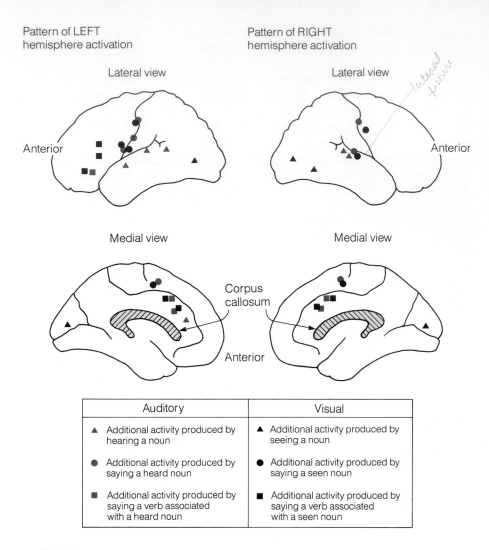

Auditory	Visual
▲ Additional activity produced by hearing a noun	▲ Additional activity produced by seeing a noun
● Additional activity produced by saying a heard noun	● Additional activity produced by saying a seen noun
■ Additional activity produced by saying a verb associated with a heard noun	■ Additional activity produced by saying a verb associated with a seen noun

FIGURE 17.16 *A summary of the results of Petersen et al.'s (1988) PET-scan, subtraction tests of language localization. (Adapted from Petersen et al., 1988.)*

the semantic processing of verb association appeared to occur in frontal and medial cortex rather than in Wernicke's area. Moreover, the activity in the right hemisphere and in the midline areas of both hemispheres was not predicted by the Wernicke-Geschwind model. On a more general level, these results challenge any serial model of language. When subjects were repeating words, input seemed to move directly from the respective secondary sensory areas to the output areas of the central fissure. When the task involved semantic processing (verb association), the signals seemed to follow an alternative route from secondary sensory areas, to frontal cortex, to the central fissure motor areas.

Patterns of Activity
Identified by the
Three Auditory Subtractions

Patterns of Activity
Identified by the
Three Visual Subtractions

525
Lateralization,
Language,
and the Split Brain

Additional activity produced by
hearing a noun:

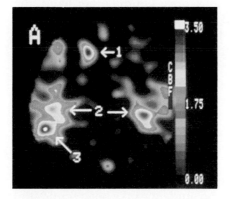

Additional activity produced by
seeing a noun:

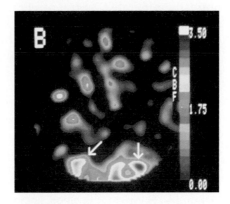

Additional activity produced by
saying a heard noun:

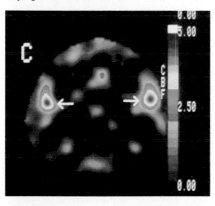

Additional activity produced by
saying a seen noun:

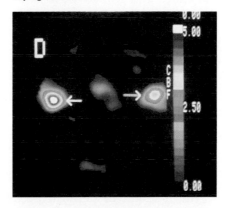

Additional activity produced by
saying a verb associated with a
heard noun:

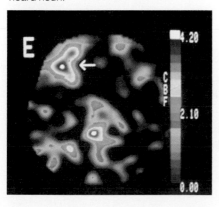

Additional activity produced by
saying a verb associated with a
seen noun:

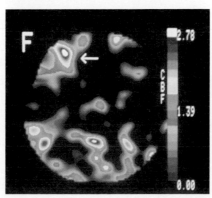

FIGURE 17.17 *PET-scan computer printouts of the subtracted patterns of blood flow from the experiment of Petersen et al. (1988). Each printout represents a horizontal section of the brain averaged over all of the subjects in that condition. Anterior is toward the top of the page; posterior is toward the bottom. The right hemisphere is on your right; the left hemisphere is on your left. As indicated by the adjacent scales, the highest levels of activity are indicated by yellow, orange, red, and white (the very highest). (Courtesy of Steve Petersen.)*

Conclusion

Chapter 17 is the story of two theories: one largely right and one largely wrong, but both extremely important. On the one hand, Sperry's theory of brain duality and asymmetry has withstood the empirical challenge of the research that it has generated. Study after study has confirmed and extended its basic tenets: that the two hemispheres of the human brain can function independently and that they possess different capacities that are normally integrated by the cerebral commissures. On the other hand, the empirical evidence has not been so kind to the strict localizationist theories of language organization proposed by Broca, Wernicke, and Geschwind. Lesion, brain-stimulation, CAT-scan, and PET-scan tests have all failed to confirm its predictions.

The juxtaposition of these two theories illustrates a frequently misunderstood point: Theories are important because they are useful, and to be useful they do not have to be right. Both Sperry's theory of the dual brain and the Wernicke-Geschwind model of language localization have dominated their respective fields for over a quarter of a century, but only one is consistent with the evidence. The strengths of the Wernicke-Geschwind model lie not in its accurate predictions, but in its clarity and testability. Because it is clear, scientists and students alike have found it to be a useful vehicle for organizing their thinking about the localization of language. And because it is so eminently testable, its predictions have stimulated and guided much of the research in the field. Considering that it is only the first step toward the solution of an extremely difficult problem, it is not at all surprising that it has proven to be flawed, but it is the mass of research that it has generated—not its accuracy—that stands as the ultimate testimonial to its worth.

__ Food for Thought

1. Design an experiment to show that it is possible for a human split-brain student to study for an English and a geometry exam at the same time by using the Z lens.

2. The decision to perform prefrontal lobotomies on epileptic patients turned out to be a good one; the decision to perform frontal lobotomies on mental patients (see Chapter 1) did not. Was this just the luck of the draw? Discuss.

ADDITIONAL READING

I recommend two volumes written about lateralization of brain function. The first is a collection of chapters written by prominent researchers on various specific subtopics, and the second provides a readable introduction to the topic.

Bensen, D. F., & Zaidel, E. (Eds.). (1985). *The dual brain: Hemispheric specializations in humans.* New York: Guilford Press.

Springer, S. P. & Deutsch, G. (1981). *Left brain, right brain.* San Francisco: W.H. Freeman.

A good introduction to the cerebral localization of language is contained in the following neuropsychology text:

Kolb, B., & Whishaw, I. Q. (1989). *Fundamentals of human neuropsychology.* New York: Freeman (3rd edition).

To help you study the material in this chapter, all of the key terms—those that have appeared in bold type—are listed and briefly defined here.

Agraphia. A selective disruption of the ability to write.

Alexia. A selective disruption of the ability to read.

Angular gyrus. A gyrus of the posterior cortex at the boundary between the temporal and parietal lobes; the angular gyrus of the left hemisphere is thought to play a role in reading.

Aphasia. Any brain-damage-produced disturbance in the ability to use or comprehend language.

Apraxia. A condition in which patients have great difficulty performing movements with either side of the body when asked to do so out of context, even though they have no trouble performing the same responses when they are not thinking about what they are doing.

Arcuate fasciculus. The major neural pathway between Wernicke's area and Broca's area.

Assumption of modularity. The assumption that cognitive processes are produced by an assembly of specialized neural subsystems or modules, each of which performs a specific function.

Broca's aphasia. A disorder of speech production with no deficits in language comprehension; it is doubtful if such cases exist in the strict sense of the term; all cases of aphasia involve both expressive and receptive deficits.

Broca's area. The area of the inferior prefrontal cortex of the left hemisphere hypothesized by Broca to be involved in speech production.

Cerebral commissures. Tracts that connect the left and right cerebral hemispheres; the corpus callosum is the largest cerebral commissure.

Chimeric figures test. A test of visual completion in split-brain subjects that uses pictures composed by left and right halves of two different faces.

Cognitive neuropsychology. An approach to the study of the neural basis of cognitive processes; cognitive neuropsychologists infer the nature of the neural systems underlying cognitive processes by identifying the clusters of specific cognitive functions that tend to be disturbed together in brain-damaged subjects.

Commissurotomy. Severing the cerebral commissures.

Conduction aphasia. Aphasia that was hypothesized to result from damage to the neural pathway between Wernicke's area and Broca's area; however, surgical transection of this pathway produces no permanent aphasia.

Cross-cuing. Nonneural communication between hemispheres separated by commissurotomy.

Dextrals. Right-handers.

Dichotic listening test. A sequence of three pairs of spoken digits is presented simultaneously to each ear, and the subject is asked to report all of the digits that he or she heard.

Dominant hemisphere. A term used in the past to refer to the left hemisphere; it is based on the incorrect assumption that the left hemisphere is dominant in all complex activities.

Dual-route models. Models of a cognitive process that are based on the premise that the process is mediated by two different pathways of neural activity.

Expressive. Referring to the generation of speech (i.e., writing or talking).

Frontal operculum. The neuroanatomical designation for the area of prefrontal cortex that in the left hemisphere roughly corresponds to Broca's area.

Global aphasia. Almost total elimination of all language-related abilities.

Helping-hand phenomenon. When one hand of a split-brain patient redirects the other hand.

Heschl's gyrus. A temporal-lobe gyrus that is the site of primary auditory cortex.

Lateralization of function. When the two hemispheres of the brain differ in their functions.

Lexical procedure. A procedure for reading aloud based on stored information that we have acquired about the pronunciation of specific written words.

Minor hemisphere. A term used in the past to refer to the right hemisphere; it is based on the incorrect assumption that the left hemisphere is dominant in all complex activities.

Nonlexical procedure. A procedure for reading aloud that is based on the general rules of pronunciation.

Parallel models. Models involving two or more routes of activity (e.g., the dual-route model).

Phonemes. Individual speech sounds.

Planum temporale. An area of the temporal lobe, which in the left hemisphere roughly corresponds to Wernicke's area.

Receptive. Referring to the comprehension of speech.

Scotoma. An area of blindness in the visual field.

Serial model. A model that involves a chain of responses that are triggered in linear sequence; a single-route model.

Sinestrals. Left-handers.

Sodium amytal test. A test of speech lateralization administered to some patients before neurosurgery; each hemisphere is anesthetized with sodium amytal so that the speech abilities of the other hemisphere can be assessed.

Split-brain patients. Commissurotomized patients.

Surface dyslexia. A deficit in lexical reading out loud that is not accompanied by deficits in nonlexical reading.

Visual completion. When the brain completes or fills in a scotoma.

Wernicke's area. An area of the left temporal cortex hypothesized by Wernicke to be the center of language comprehension.

Wernicke-Geschwind model. A serial model of language localization.

Word salad. Speech that has the overall sound and flow of fluid speech, but is totally incomprehensible.

Z lens. A contact lens that is opaque on one side and thus allows visual input to enter only one hemisphere of a split-brain subject, irrespective of eye movement; developed by, and named after, Zaidel.

Epilogue

Biopsychology is a fascinating discipline. I have tried to let you see this for yourself by peeling away its complexities and serving up the remaining fundamentals with big helpings of clear writing, good humor, and personal implication. If you liked this approach, let your instructor know; and please do not hesitate to write me (Department of Psychology, University of British Columbia, Vancouver, B.C., Canada V6T 1Y7) if you have any comments, questions, or suggestions. Like good friends, we have shared good times and bad. We have experienced the fun and wonder of pleasure circuits in the brain, Rhonda the dextrous cashier, the Nads basketball team, people who rarely sleep, the MAMAWAWA, split brains, Freddie the Finn, and neurotransplants. Together we have been touched by the personal tragedies of Alzheimer's disease, MPTP poisoning, the lost mariner, H.M., and the man who mistook his wife for a hat. Thank you for allowing me to share *Biopsychology* with you. I wish you luck.

John P.J. Pinel

Appendices

The Autonomic Nervous System

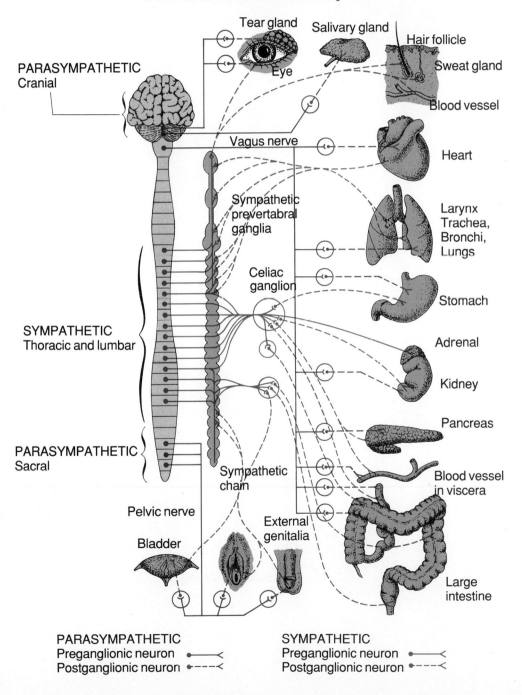

Tear gland

Salivary gland

Hair follicle

PARASYMPATHETIC
Cranial

Sweat gland

Eye

Blood vessel

Vagus nerve

Heart

Sympathetic
prevertabral
ganglia

Larynx
Trachea,
Bronchi,
Lungs

Celiac
ganglion

Stomach

SYMPATHETIC
Thoracic and lumbar

Adrenal

Kidney

Pancreas

Sympathetic
chain

Blood vessel
in viscera

PARASYMPATHETIC
Sacral

Pelvic nerve

External
genitalia

Bladder

Large
intestine

PARASYMPATHETIC	SYMPATHETIC
Preganglionic neuron ●———<	Preganglionic neuron ●———<
Postganglionic neuron ●----<	Postganglionic neuron ●----<

529

The Cranial Nerves

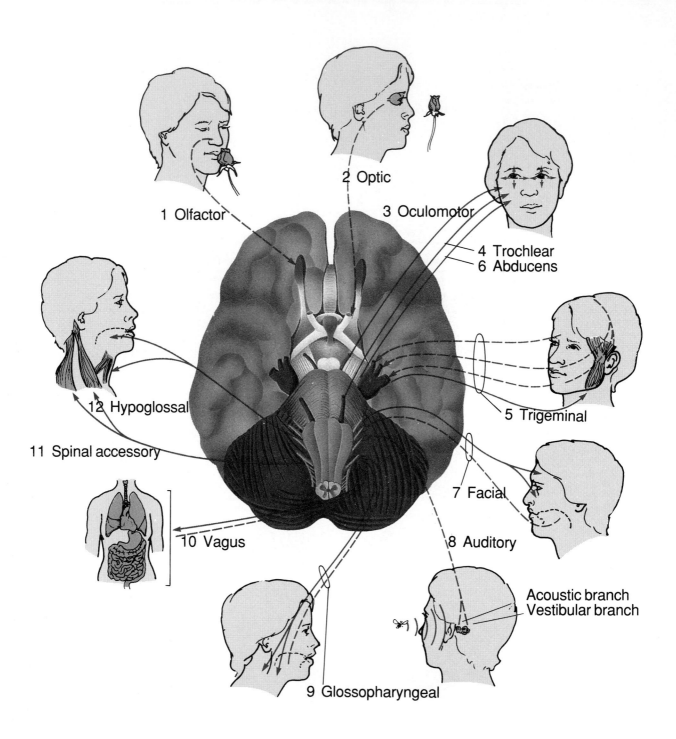

1 Olfactor

2 Optic

3 Oculomotor

4 Trochlear
6 Abducens

5 Trigeminal

12 Hypoglossal

11 Spinal accessory

10 Vagus

7 Facial

8 Auditory

Acoustic branch
Vestibular branch

9 Glossopharyngeal

Nuclei Composing the Left Lobe of the Thalamus

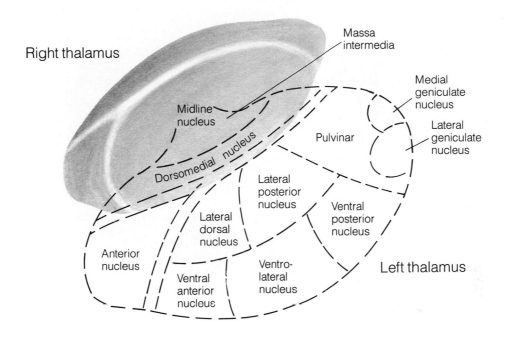

The Nuclei of the Hypothalamus

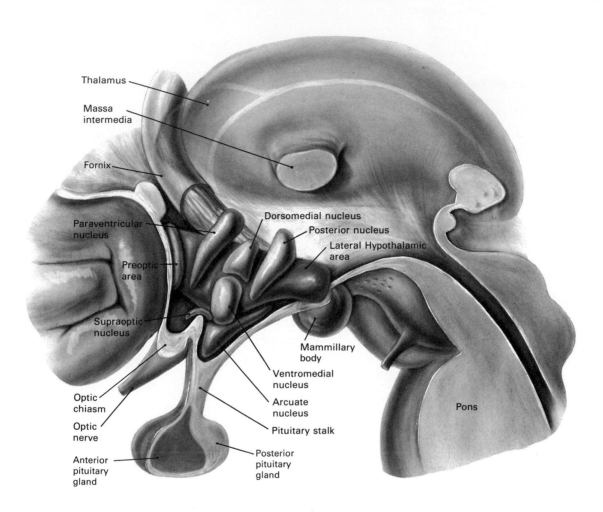

Thalamus

Massa intermedia

Fornix

Paraventricular nucleus

Preoptic area

Supraoptic nucleus

Optic chiasm

Optic nerve

Anterior pituitary gland

Dorsomedial nucleus

Posterior nucleus

Lateral Hypothalamic area

Mammillary body

Ventromedial nucleus

Arcuate nucleus

Pituitary stalk

Posterior pituitary gland

Pons

Appendix V

Peptides Released by Mammalian Neurons

Pituitary Peptides

Corticotropin

Growth hormone

Lipotropin

α-Melanocyte stimulating hormone

Oxytocin

Prolactin

Vasopressin

Gut Peptides

Cholecystokinin

Gastrin

Motilin

Pancreatic polypeptide

Secretin

Substance P

Vasoactive intestinal polypeptide

Hypothalamic Peptides

Luteinizing hormone-releasing hormone

Somatostatin

Thyrotropin-releasing hormone

Opioid Peptides

Dynorphin

β-Endorphin

Met Enkephalin

Leu Enkephalin

Miscellaneous Peptides

Angiotensin

Bombesin

Bradykinin

Carnosine

Glucagon

Insulin

Neuropeptide Y

Neurotensin

Proctolin

Phases of the Human Menstrual Cycle

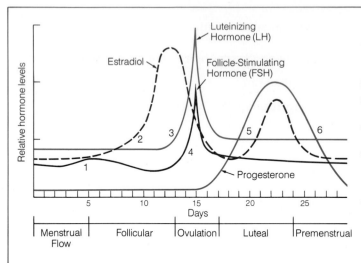

Phases of the human menstrual cycle

1. In response to an increase in FSH, small spheres of cells called ovarian follicles begin to grow around individual egg cells (ova).

2. The follicles begin to release estrogens such as estradiol.

3. The estrogens stimulate the hypothalamus to increase the release of LH and FSH from the anterior pituitary.

4. In response to the LH surge, one of the follicles ruptures and releases its ovum.

5. The ruptured follicle under the influence of LH develops into a corpus luteum (yellow body) and begins to release progesterone, which prepares the lining of the uterus for the implantation of a fertilized ovum.

6. Meanwhile, the ovum is moved into the fallopian tube by the rowing action of ciliated cells. If the ovum is not fertilized, progesterone and estradiol levels fall and the walls of the uterus are sloughed off as menstrual flow and the cycle begins once again.

References

Abramson, H. A. (1974). Editorial: Respiratory disorders and marijuana use. *Journal of Asthma Research, 11,* 97.

Acker, W., Ron, M. A., Lishman, W. A., & Saw, G. K. (1984). A multivariate analysis of psychological, clinical and CT scanning measures in detoxified chronic alcoholics. *British Journal of Addiction, 79,* 293–301.

Adair, E. R., Casby, J. U., & Stolivijk, J. A. J. (1970). Behavioral temperature regulation in the squirrel monkey: Changes induced by shifts in hypothalamic temperature. *Journal of Comparative and Physiological Psychology, 72,* 17–27.

Adolph, E. F. (1947). Urges to eat and drink in rats. *American Journal of Physiology, 151,* 110–125.

Aggleton, J. P. (1985). One-trial object recognition by rats. *Quarterly Journal of Experimental Psychology, 37b,* 279–294.

Aggleton, J. P., & Mishkin, M. (1983). Visual recognition impairment following medial thalamic lesions in monkeys. *Neuropsychologia, 21,* 189–197.

Aggleton, J. P., Nicol, R. M., Huston, A. E., & Fairbairn, A. F. (1988). The performance of amnesic subjects on tests of experimental amnesia in animals: Delayed matching-to-sample and concurrent learning. *Neuropsychologia, 26,* 265–272.

Aguayo, A. J. (1987). Regeneration of axons from the injured central nervous system of adult mammals. In G. Adelman (Ed.), *Encyclopedia of Neuroscience* (pp. 1040–1043). Boston: Birkhauser.

Åkerstedt, T., & Gillberg, M. (1981). The circadian variation of experimentally displaced sleep. *Sleep, 4,* 159–169.

Albert, D. J., & Chew, G. L. (1980). The septal forebrain and the inhibitory modulation of attack and defense in the rat: A review. *Behavioral and Neural Biology, 30,* 357–388.

Albert, D. J., Dyson, E. M., & Walsh, M. L. (1987). Competitive behavior: Intact male rats but not hyperdefensive males with medial hypothalamic lesions share water with females. *Physiology & Behavior, 41,* 549–553.

Albert, D. J., Nanji, N., Brayley, K. N., & Madryga, F. J. (1979). Hyperreactivity as well as mouse killing is induced by electrical stimulation of the lateral hypothalamus in the rat. *Behavioral and Neural Biology, 27,* 59–71.

Albert, D. J., & Walsh, M. L. (1984). Neural systems and the inhibitory modulation of agonistic behavior: A comparison of mammalian species. *Neuroscience & Biobehavioral Reviews, 8,* 5–24.

Albert, D. J., Walsh, M. L., Gorzalka, B. B., Siemens, Y., & Louie, H. (1986). Testosterone removal in rats results in a decrease in social aggression and a loss of social dominance. *Physiology & Behavior, 36,* 401–407.

Albert, D. J., Walsh, M. L., Siemens, Y., & Louie, H. (1986). Spontaneous mouse killing rats: Gentling and food deprivation result in killing behavior almost identical of that of rats with medial hypothalamic lesions. *Physiology & Behavior, 36,* 1197–1199.

Albert, D. J., Walsh, M. L., Zalys, C., & Dyson, E. (1986). Defensive aggression toward an experimenter: No differences between males and females following septal, medial accumbens, or medial hypothalamic lesions in rats. *Physiology & Behavior, 38,* 11–14.

Albert, D. J., Walsh, M. L., Zalys, C., & Dyson, E. (1987). Maternal aggression and intermale social aggression: A behavioral comparison. *Behavioral Processes, 14,* 267–275.

Albert, D. J., & Wong, R. C. K. (1978). Hyperactivity, muricide, and intraspecific aggression in the rat produced by infusion of local anesthetic into the lateral septum or surrounding areas. *Journal of Comparative and Physiological Psychology, 92,* 1062–1073.

Albert, D. J., & Wong, R. C. K. (1978). Interanimal aggression and hyperreactivity following hypothalamic infusion of local anesthetic in the rat. *Physiology & Behavior, 20,* 755–761.

Albert, M. L., Sparks, R., von Stockert, T., & Sax, D. (1972). A case study of auditory agnosia: Linguistic and non-linguistic processing. *Cortex, 8,* 427–443.

Alberts, J. R. (1978). Huddling by rat pups: Group behavioral mechanisms of temperature regulation and energy conservation. *Journal of Comparative and Physiological Psychology, 92,* 231–245.

Alpers, B. J. (1937). Relation of the hypothalamus to disorders of personality. *Archives of Neurology, 38,* 291–303.

Amoore, J. E., Johnston, J. W., & Rubin, M. (1964). The stereochemical theory of odor. *Scientific American, 210,* 42–49.

Anand, B. K., & Brobeck, J. R. (1951). Localization of a "feeding center" in the hypothalamus of the rat. *Proceedings of the Society for Experimental Biology and Medicine, 77,* 323–324.

Andersson, B., Gale, C. C., Hokfelt, B., & Larsson, B. (1965). Acute and chronic effects of preoptic lesions. *Acta Physiologica Scandinavica, 65,* 45–60.

Andreassi, J. L. (1980). *Psychophysiology: Human behavior and physiological response.* New York: Oxford University Press.

Angrist, B., Rotrosen, J., & Gershon, S. (1980). Responses to apomorphine, amphetamine, and neuroleptics in schizophrenic subjects. *Psychopharmacology, 72,* 17–19.

Angst, J., Weis, P., Grof, P., Baastrup, P. G., & Schou, M. (1970). Lithium prophylaxis in recurrent affective disorders. *British Journal of Psychiatry, 116,* 604–614.

Annett, J. (1985). Motor learning: A review. In H. Heuer, U. Kleinbeck, & K. H. Schmidt (Eds.), *Motor behavior: Programming, control, and acquisition* (pp. 188–212). Berlin: Springer-Verlag.

Annett, M. (1978). Genetic and nongenetic influences on handedness. *Behavior Genetics, 8,* 227–249.

Arbour, K. J., & Wilkie, D. M. (1988). Rodents' (*Rattus, Mesocricetus,* and *Meriones*) use of learned caloric information in diet source. *Journal of Comparative Psychology, 102,* 177–181.

Arimura, A., & Schally, A. V. (1971). Augmentation of pituitary responsiveness to LH-releasing hormone (LH-RH) by estrogen. *Proceedings of the Society for Experimental Biology and Medicine, 136,* 290–293.

Asberg, M., Träskman, L., & Thorén, P. (1976). 5-HIAA in the cerebrospinal fluid: A biochemical suicide predictor? *Archives of General Psychiatry, 33,* 1193–1197.

Aschoff, J., & Wever, R. (1976). Human circadian rhythms: A multioscillatory system. *Federation of American Societies for Experimental Biology, 35,* 2326–2332.

Aserinsky, E., & Kleitman, N. (1953). Regularly occurring periods of eye motility and concomitant phenomena, during sleep. *Science, 118,* 273–274.

Attardi, D. G., & Sperry, R. W. (1963). Preferential selection of central pathways by regenerating optic fibers. *Experimental Neurology, 7,* 46–64.

Ax, A. F. (1955). The physiological differentiation between fear and anger in humans. *Psychosomatic Medicine, 15,* 433–442.

Axelrod, J. (1974). Neurotransmitters. *Scientific American, 230,* 120–131.

Baastrup, P. C., & Schou, M. (1967). Lithium as a prophylactic agent. *Archives of General Psychiatry, 16,* 162–172.

Babor, T. F., Mendelson, J. H., Greenberg, I., & Kuehnle, J. C. (1975). Marijuana consumption and tolerance to physiological and subjective effects. *Archives of General Psychiatry, 32,* 1548–1552.

Bachevalier, J., & Mishkin, M. (1986). Visual recognition impairment follows ventromedial but not dorsolateral prefrontal lesions in monkeys. *Behavioral Brain Research, 20,* 249–261.

Backlund, E. O., Granberg, P. O., Hamberger, B., Sedvall, G., Seiger, A., & Olson, L. (1985). Transplantation of adrenal medullary tissue to striatum in Parkinsonism. In A. Björklund & U. Stenevi (Eds.), *Neuronal grafting in the mammalian CNS* (pp. 551–556). Berlin: Elsevier.

Bailey, C. H., & Chen, M. C. (1983). Morphological basis of long-term habituation and sensitization in *Aplysia. Science, 220,* 91–93.

Bailey, C. H., & Chen, M. C. (1988). Long-term memory in *Aplysia* modulates the total number of varicosities of single identified sensory neurons. *Proceedings of the National Academy of Sciences (USA), 85,* 2373–2377.

Bailey, C. H., Hawkins, R. D., & Chen, M. C. (1983). Uptake of [3H]-serotonin in the abdominal ganglion of *Aplysia californica:* Further studies on the morphological and biochemical basis of presynaptic facilitation. *Brain Research, 272,* 71–81.

Baker, R. R. (1982). *Migration: Paths through time and space.* New York: Holmes & Meier.

Baker, T. B., & Tiffany, S. T. (1985). Morphine tolerance as habituation. *Psychological Review, 92,* 78–108.

Balaban, E., Teillet, M. A., & Le Douarin, N. (1988). Application of the quail-chick chimera system to the study of brain development and behavior. *Science, 241,* 1339–1342.

Ballard, P. A., Tetrud, J. W., & Langston, J. W. (1985). Permanent human parkinsonism due to 1-methyl-4-phenyl-1,2,3,6-tetrahydropyridine (MPTP): Seven cases. *Neurology, 35,* 949–956.

Bartus, R. T., Dean, R. L., Beer, B., & Lippa, A. S. (1982). The cholinergic hypothesis of geriatric memory dysfunction. *Science, 217,* 408–417.

Basbaum, A. I., Clanton, C. H., & Fields, H. L. (1976). Opiate and stimulus-produced analgesia: Functional anatomy of a medullospinal pathway. *Proceedings of the National Academy of Sciences (USA), 73,* 4685–4688.

Basbaum, A. I., & Fields, H. L. (1978). Endogenous pain control mechanisms: Review and hypothesis. *Annals of Neurology, 4,* 451–462.

Bash, K. W. (1939). An investigation into a possible organic basis for the hunger drive. *Journal of Comparative Psychology, 28,* 109–134.

Baskin, D. G., Woods, S. C., West, D. B., van Houten, M., Posner, B. I., Dorsa, D. M., & Porte, D., Jr. (1983). Immunocytochemical detection of insulin in rat hypothalamus and its possible uptake from cerebrospinal fluid. *Endocrinology, 113,* 1818–1825.

Bastiani, M. J., Doe, C. Q., Helfand, S. L., & Goodman, C. S. (1985). Neuronal specificity and growth cone guidance in grasshopper and *Drosophila* embryos. *Trends in Neuroscience, 8,* 257–266.

Baudry, M., & Lynch, G. (1987). Properties and substrates of mammalian memory systems. In H. Y. Meltzer (Ed.), *Psychopharmacology: The third generation of progress* (pp. 449–462). New York: Raven Press.

Bauer, R. M., & Rubens, A. B. (1985). Agnosia. In K. M. Heilman & E. Valenstein (Eds.), *Clinical neuropsychology* (2nd ed.). (pp. 187–241). New York: Oxford University Press.

Baum, M. J. (1979). Differentiation of coital behavior in mammals: A comparative analysis. *Neuroscience and Biobehavioral Reviews, 3,* 265–284.

Bazett, H. C., McGlone, B., Williams, R. G., & Lufkin, H. M. (1932). Sensation: I. Depth, distribution, and probable identification in the prepuce of sensory end-organs concerned in sensations of temperature and touch: Thermometric conductivity. *Archives of Neurology and Psychiatry, 27,* 489–517.

Beecher, H. K. (1959). *Measurement of subjective responses: Quantitative effects of drugs.* New York: Oxford University Press.

Bell, D. S. (1973). The experimental reproduction of amphetamine psychosis. *Archives of General Psychiatry, 29,* 35–40.

Bender, M. B., & Feldman, M. (1972). The so-called "visual agnosias." *Brain, 95,* 173–186.

Bennett, E. L., Diamond, M. C., Krech, D., & Rosenzweig, M. R. (1964). Chemical and anatomical plasticity of brain. *Science, 146,* 610–619.

Benson, D. F. (1985). Aphasia. In K. M. Heilman & E. Valenstein (Eds.), *Clinical neuropsychology* (pp. 17–47). New York: Oxford University Press.

Benson, D. F., & Greenberg, J. P. (1969). Visual form agnosia. *Archives of Neurology, 20,* 82–95.

Benson, D. F., & Zaidel, E. (Eds.). (1985). *The dual brain: Hemispheric specialization in humans.* London: The Guilford Press.

Bentley, D., & Keshishian, H. (1982). Pioneer neurons and pathways in insect appendages. *Trends in Neuroscience, 5,* 354–358.

Benton, A. (1985). Visuoperceptual, visuospatial, and visuoconstructive disorders. In K. M. Heilman & E. Valenstein (Eds.), *Clinical neuropsychology* (pp. 151–185). New York: Oxford University Press.

Berger, R. J., & Oswald, I. (1962). Effects of sleep deprivation on behaviour, subsequent sleep, and dreaming. *Journal of Mental Science, 106,* 457–465.

Berlucchi, G., Maffei, L., Moruzzi, G., & Strata, P. (1964). EEG and behavioral effects elicited by cooling of medulla and pons. *Archives Italiennes de Biologie, 102,* 372–392.

Bernard, C. (1878). *Leçons sur les phenomènes de la vie communs aux animaux et aux vegetaux. 1,* 111–114, 123–124. Paris: Baliere.

Bernstein, I. L., & Webster, M. M. (1980). Learned taste aversion in humans. *Physiology & Behavior, 25,* 363–366.

Berridge, V., & Edwards, G. (1981). *Opium and the people: Opiate use in nineteenth-century England.* New York: St. Martin's Press.

Berthoud, H. R., Bereiter, D. A., Trimble, E. R., Siegel, E. G., & Jeanrenaud, B. (1981). Cephalic phase, reflex insulin secretion. *Diabetologia, 20,* 393–401.

Bertler, A., & Rosengren, E. (1959). Occurrence and distribution of dopamine in brain and other tissues. *Experientia, 15,* 10–11.

Bewley, T. H. (1974). Treatment of opiate addiction in Great Britain. In S. Fisher & A. M. Freeman (Eds.), *Opiate addiction: Origins and treatment* (pp. 141–161). New York: John Wiley & Sons.

Bielajew, C., & Shizgal, P. (1986). Evidence implicating descending fibers in self-stimulation of the medial forebrain bundle. *Journal of Neuroscience, 6,* 919–929.

Bigelow, W. G., Lindsay, W. K., Harrison, R. C., Gordon, R. A., & Greenwood, W. F. (1950). Oxygen transport and utilization in dogs at low body temperatures. *American Journal of Physiology, 160,* 125–137.

Bindra, D. (1978). How adaptive behavior is produced: A perceptual-motivational alternative to response-reinforcement. *Behavioral and Brain Sciences, 1,* 41–91.

Birkmayer, W., & Hornykiewicz, O. (1962). Der L-Dioxyphenylalanin (L-DOPA)—Effekt beim Parkinson-Syndrom des Menschen: Zur Pathogenese und Behandlung der Parkinson-Akinese. *Archiv für Psychiatrie und Zeitschrift f. d. ges. Neurologie, 203,* 560–574.

Bishop, M. P., Elder, S. T., & Heath, R. G. (1963). Intracranial self-stimulation in man. *Science, 140,* 394–396.

Bishop, P. O., Henry, G. H., & Smith, C. J. (1971). Binocular interaction fields of single units in the cat striate cortex. *Journal of Physiology, 216,* 39–68.

Bishop, P. O., & Pettigrew, J. D. (1986). Neural mechanisms of binocular vision. *Vision Research, 26,* 1587–1600.

Björklund, A., Dunnett, S. B., Lewis, M. E., & Iversen, S. D. (1980). Reinnervation of the denervated striatum by substantia nigra transplants: Functional consequences as revealed by pharmacological and sensorimotor testing. *Brain Research, 199,* 307–333.

Björklund, A., & Lindvall, O. (1986). Catecholaminergic brainstem regulatory systems. In V. B. Mountcastle, F. E. Bloom, & S. R. Geiger (Eds.), *Handbook of physiology: The nervous system* (Vol. 4, pp. 155–236). Bethesda, MD: American Physiological Society.

Björklund, A., Segal, M., & Stenevi, U. (1979). Functional reinnervation of rat hippocampus by locus coeruleus implants. *Brain Research, 170,* 409–426.

Björklund, A., & Stenevi, U. (1979). Reconstruction of the nigrostriatal dopamine pathway by intracerebral nigral transplants. *Brain Research, 177,* 555–560.

Blackshear, P. J. (1979). Implantable drug-delivery systems. *Scientific American, 241,* 66–73.

Blanchard, D. C., & Blanchard, R. J. (1984). Affect and aggression: An animal model applied to human behavior. In D. C. Blanchard & R. J. Blanchard (Eds.), *Advances in the study of aggression* (pp. 1–62). Orlando, FL: Academic Press.

Blanchard, D. C., & Blanchard, R. J. (1988). Ethoexperimental approaches to the biology of emotion. *Annual Review of Psychology, 39,* 43–68.

Blanchard, R. J., Blanchard, D. C., & Takahashi, L. K. (1977). Reflexive fighting in the albino rat: Aggressive or defensive behavior. *Aggressive Behavior, 3,* 145–155.

Blass, E. M., & Epstein, A. N. (1971). A lateral preoptic osmosensitive zone for thirst in the rat. *Journal of Comparative and Physiological Psychology, 76,* 378–394.

Bleuler, M. (1978). *The schizophrenic disorders.* New Haven, CT: Yale University Press.

Bliss, T. V. P., & Gardner-Medwin, A. R. (1973). Long-lasting potentiation of synaptic transmission in the dentate area of the unanaesthetized rabbit following stimulation of the perforant path. *Journal of Physiology, 232,* 357–374.

Bliss, T. V. P., & Lømo, T. (1973). Long-lasting potentiation of synaptic transmission in the dentate area of the anaesthetized rabbit following stimulation of the perforant path. *Journal of Physiology (London), 232,* 331–356.

Bloom, F. E. (Ed.). (1986). *Handbook of physiology: Nervous system IV.* Bethesda, MD: American Physiological Society.

Bogen, J. E., & Bogen, G. M. (1976). Wernicke's region—Where is it? *Annals of the New York Academy of Science, 280,* 834–843.

Bolles, R. C. (1980). Some functionalistic thought about regulation. In F. M. Toates & T. R. Halliday (Eds.), *Analysis of motivational processes* (pp. 63–75). London: Academic Press.

Bolles, R. C., Hayward, L., & Crandall, C. (1981). Conditioned taste preferences based on caloric density. *Journal of Experimental Psychology: Animal Behavior Processes, 7,* 59–69.

Booth, D. A. (1981). The physiology of appetite. *British Medical Bulletin, 37,* 135–140.

Booth, D. A., Fuller, J., & Lewis, V. (1981). Human control of body weight: Cognitive or physiological? Some energy-related perceptions and misperceptions. In L. A. Cioffi (Ed.), *The body weight regulatory system: Normal and disturbed systems* (pp. 305–314). New York: Raven Press.

Booth, J. E. (1977). Sexual behaviour of male rats injected with the anti-oestrogen MER-25 during infancy. *Physiology & Behavior, 19,* 35–39.

Borbély, A. A. (1981). The sleep process: Circadian and homeostatic aspects. *Advances in Physiological Sciences, 18,* 85–91.

Borbély, A. A. (1982). Sleep regulation: Circadian rhythm and homeostasis. In D. Ganten & D. Pfaff (Eds.), *Sleep: Clinical and experimental aspects* (pp. 83–103). Berlin: Springer-Verlag.

Borbély, A. A. (1983). Pharmacological approaches to sleep regulation. In A. R. Mayes (Ed.), *Sleep mechanisms and functions in humans and animals* (pp. 232–261). Wokingham, England: Van Nostrand Reinhold.

Borbély, A. A. (1984). Sleep regulation: Outline of a model and its implications for depression. In A. Borbély & J. L. Valatx (Eds.), *Sleep mechanisms* (pp. 272–284). Berlin: Springer-Verlag.

Borbély, A. A., Baumann, F., Brandeis, D., Strauch, I., & Lehmann, D. (1981). Sleep deprivation: Effect on sleep stages and EEG power density in man. *Electroencephalography and Clinical Neurophysiology, 51,* 483–493.

Boulos, Z., & Terman, M. (1980). Food availability and daily biological rhythms. *Neuroscience and Biobehavioral Reviews, 4,* 119–131.

Boyd, E. S., & Gardiner, L. C. (1962). Positive and negative reinforcement from intracranial stimulation of teleost. *Science, 136,* 648–649.

Bozarth, M. A. (1987). Intracranial self-administration procedures for the assessment of drug reinforcement. In M. A. Bozarth (Ed.), *Methods of assessing the reinforcing properties of abused drugs* (pp. 173–187). Berlin: Springer-Verlag.

Bozarth, M. A. (1987). Ventral tegmental reward system. In J. Engel & L. Oreland (Eds.), *Brain reward systems and abuse* (pp. 1–17). New York: Raven Press.

Bozarth, M. A., & Wise, R. A. (1981). Heroin reward is dependent on a dopaminergic substrate. *Life Sciences, 29,* 1881–1886.

Bozarth, M. A., & Wise, R. A. (1982). Localization of the reward-relevant opiate receptors. In L. S. Harris (Ed.), *Problems of drug dependence, 1981* (pp. 158–164). Washington, D.C.: National Institute on Drug Abuse.

Brady, J. V., & Nauta, W. J. H. (1955). Subcortical mechanisms in emotional behavior: The duration of affective change following septal and habenular lesions in the albino rat. *Journal of Comparative and Physiological Psychology, 48,* 412–420.

Bray, G. M., Vidal-Sanz, M., & Aguayo, A. J. (1987). Regeneration of axons from the central nervous system of adult rats. In F. J. Seil, E. Herbert, & B. M. Carlson (Eds.), *Progress in brain research* (Vol. 71, pp. 373–378). New York: Elsevier.

Brayley, K. N., & Albert, D. J. (1977). Suppression of VMH-lesion induced reactivity and aggressiveness in the rat by stimulation of lateral septum but not medial septum or cingulate cortex. *Physiology & Behavior, 18,* 567–571.

Brecher, E. M. (1972). *Licit and illicit drugs.* Boston: Little, Brown & Co.

Bremer, F. (1936). Nouvelles recherches sur le mécanisme du sommeil. *Comptes Rendus de la Société de Biologie, 122,* 460–464.

Bremer, F. (1937). L'activité cérébrale au cours du sommeil et de la narcose. Contribution à l'étude du mécanisme du sommeil. *Bulletin de l'Académie Royale de Belgique, 4,* 68–86.

Bremer, J. (1959). *Asexualization.* New York: Macmillan Publishing Co.

Brill, N. Q., & Christie, R. L. (1974). Marijuana use and psychosocial adaptation. *Archives of General Psychiatry, 31,* 713–719.

Brinkman, C. (1984). Supplementary motor area of the monkey's cerebral cortex: Short- and long-term deficits after unilateral ablation and the effects of subsequent callosal section. *Journal of Neuroscience, 4,* 918–929.

Brinkman, C., & Porter, R. (1983). Supplementary motor area and premotor area of monkey cerebral cortex: Functional organization and activities of single neurons during performance of a learned movement. In J. E. Desmedt (Ed.), *Motor control mechanisms in health and disease* (pp. 393–420). New York: Raven Press.

Brion, S., & Mikol, J. (1978). Atteinte du noyau lateral dorsal du thalamus et syndrome de Korsakoff alcoolique. *Journal of Neurological Science, 38,* 249–261.

Brobeck, J. R. (1955). Neural regulation of food intake. *Annals of the New York Academy of Sciences, 63,* 44–55.

Brobeck, J. R., Tepperman, J., & Long, C. N. H. (1943). Experimental hypothalamic hyperphagia in the albino rat. *Yale Journal of Biology and Medicine, 15,* 831–853.

Brooks, P. L., Frost, B. J., Mason, J. L., & Gibson, D. M. (1986). Continuing evaluation of the Queen's University tactile vocoder: II Identification of open set sentences and tracking narrative. *Journal of Rehabilitation Research and Development, 23,* 129–138.

Brooks, V. B. (1986). *The neural basis of motor control.* New York: Oxford.

Brou, P., Sciascia, T. R., Linden, L., & Lettvin, J. Y. (1986). The colors of things. *Scientific American, 255,* 84–91.

Brown, M. C., & Ironton, R. (1977). Motor neurone sprouting induced by prolonged tetrodotoxin block of nerve action potentials. *Nature, 265,* 459–461.

Brown, P. J., & Konner, M. (1987). An anthropological perspective on obesity. *Annals of the New York Academy of Sciences, 449*, 29–46.

Brudny, J. (1982). Biofeedback in chronic neurological cases: Therapeutic electromyography. In L. White & B. Tursky (Eds.), *Clinical biofeedback: Efficacy and mechanisms* (pp. 249–275). New York: The Guilford Press.

Brundin, P., & Björklund, A. (1987). Survival, growth and function of dopaminergic neurons grafted to the brain. In F. J. Seil, E. Herbert, & B. M. Carlson (Eds.), *Progress in brain research* (Vol. 71, pp. 293–307). New York: Elsevier.

Buggy, J., Fisher, A. E., Hoffman, W. E., Johnson, A. K., & Phillips, M. I. (1975). Ventricular obstruction: Effect on drinking induced by intracranial injection of angiotensin. *Science, 190*, 72–74.

Burns, R. S., Chiueh, C. C., Markey, S. P., Ebert, M. H., Jacobowitz, D. M., & Kopin, I. J. (1983). A primate model of Parkinsonism: Selective destruction of dopaminergic neurons in the pars compacta of the substantia nigra by N-methyl-4-phenyl-1,2,3,6-tetrahydropyridine. *Proceedings of the National Academy of Sciences (USA), 80*, 4546–4550.

Bushnell, M. C., Goldberg, M. E., & Robinson, D. L. (1981). Behavioral enhancement of visual responses in monkey cerebral cortex: I. Modulation in posterior cortex related to selective visual attention. *Journal of Neurophysiology, 46*, 755–772.

Byrne, J. H. (1974). *Mrs. Byrne's dictionary of unusual, obscure, and preposterous words.* Secaucus, NJ: Citadel Press.

Bryne, J. H. (1987). Cellular analysis of associative learning. *Physiological Reviews, 67*, 329–437.

Cabanac, M. (1971). Physiological role of pleasure. *Science, 173*, 1103–1107.

Cade, J. F. J. (1949). Lithium salts in treatment of psychotic excitement. *Medical Journal of Australia, 2*, 349–352.

Caggiula, A. R. (1970). Analysis of the copulation-reward properties of posterior hypothalamic stimulation in male rats. *Journal of Comparative and Physiological Psychology, 70*, 399–412.

Calne, S., Shoenberg, B., Martin, W., Uitti, R. J., Spencer, P., & Calne, D. B. (1987). Familial Parkinson's disease: Possible role of environmental factors. *Canadian Journal of Neurology, 14*, 303–305.

Camhi, J. M. (1984). *Neuroethology: Nerve cells and the behavior of animals.* Sunderland, MA: Sinauer Associates, Inc.

Campfield, L. A., Brandon, P., & Smith, F. J. (1985). On-line continuous measurement of blood glucose and meal pattern in free-feeding rats: The role of glucose in meal initiation. *Brain Research Bulletin, 14*, 605–616.

Cannon, W. B., & Washburn, A. L. (1912). An explanation of hunger. *American Journal of Physiology, 29*, 441–454.

Capaldi, E. D., Campbell, D. H., Sheffer, J. D., & Bradford, J. P. (1987). Conditioned flavor preference based on delayed caloric consequences. *Journal of Experimental Psychology: Animal Behavior Processes, 13*, 150–155.

Carew, T. J., Castellucci, V. F., & Kandel, E. R. (1971). Analysis of dishabituation and sensitization of the gill-withdrawal reflex in *Aplysia. International Journal of Neuroscience, 2*, 79–98.

Carew, T. J., Hawkins, R. D., & Kandel, E. R. (1983). Differential classical conditioning of a defensive withdrawal reflex in *Aplysia californica. Science, 219*, 397–400.

Carew, T. J., Pinsker, H. M., & Kandel, E. R. (1972). Long-term habituation of a defensive withdrawal reflex in *Aplysia. Science, 175*, 451–454.

Carew, T. J., & Sahley, C. L. (1986). Invertebrate learning and memory: From behavior to molecules. *Annual Review of Neuroscience, 9*, 435–487.

Carew, T. J., Walters, E. T., & Kandel, E. R. (1981). Associative learning in *Aplysia*: Cellular correlates supporting a conditioned fear hypothesis. *Science, 211*, 501–503.

Carlisle, H. J. (1969). Effect of preoptic and anterior hypothalamic lesions on behavioral thermoregulation in the cold. *Journal of Comparative and Physiological Psychology, 60*, 391–402.

Carlson, A. J. (1912). Contributions to the physiology of the stomach: II. The relation between the contractions of the empty stomach and the sensation of hunger. *American Journal of Physiology, 31*, 175–192.

Carlson, N. R. (1986). *Physiology of behavior* (3rd ed.). Boston, MA: Allyn and Bacon.

Carlsson, A. (1959). The occurrence, distribution and physiological role of catecholamines in the nervous system. *Pharmacological Review, 11*, 490–493.

Carlsson, A. (1987). Monoamines of the central nervous system: A historical perspective. In H. Y. Meltzer (Ed.), *Psychopharmacology: The third generation of progress* (pp. 39–48). New York: Raven Press.

Carlsson, A., & Linqvist, M. (1963). Effect of chlorpromazine or haloperidol on formation of 3-methoxytyramine and normetanephrine in mouse brains. *Acta Pharmacologica et Toxicologica, 20*, 140–144.

Carlsson, A., Linqvist, M., & Magnusson, T. (1957). 3,4-dihydroxyphenylalanine and 5-hydroxytryptophan as reserpine antagonists. *Nature, 180*, 1200.

Carlsson, A., Linqvist, M., Magnusson, T., & Waldeck, B. (1958). On the presence of 3-hydroxytyramine in brain. *Science, 122*, 471.

Carlton, P. L., & Wolgin, D. L. (1971). Contingent tolerance to the anorexinergic effects of amphetamine. *Physiology & Behavior, 7*, 221–225.

Carpenter, W. T., Heinrichs, D. W., & Alphs, L. D. (1985). Treatment of negative symptoms. *Schizophrenia Bulletin, 11*, 440–452.

Carr, G. D., Fibiger, H. C., & Phillips, A. G. (1989). Conditioned place preference as a measure of drug reward. In J. M. Liebman & S. J. Cooper (Eds.), *The neuropharmacological basis of reward* (pp. 264–319). Oxford: Clarendon Press.

Carroll, D. (1984). *Biofeedback in practice.* New York: Longman Group.

Castellucci, V., & Kandel, E. R. (1974). A quantal analysis of the synaptic depression underlying habituation of the gill-withdrawal reflex in *Aplysia. Proceedings of the National Academy of Sciences (USA), 71*, 5004–5008.

Castellucci, V., & Kandel, E. R. (1976). Presynaptic sensitization as a mechanism for behavioral sensitization in *Aplysia. Science, 194*, 1176–1178.

Castellucci, V., Pinsker, H., Kupfermann, I., & Kandel, E. R. (1970). Neuronal mechanisms of habituation and dishabituation of the gill-withdrawal reflex in *Aplysia. Science, 167*, 1745–1748.

Castro-Vazquez, A., & McCann, S. M. (1975). Cyclic variations in the increased responsiveness of the pituitary to luteinizing hormone-releasing hormone (LHRH) induced by LHRH. *Endocrinology, 97*, 13–19.

Cermak, L. S., Uhly, B., & Reale, L. (1980). Encoding specificity in the alcoholic Korsakoff patient. *Brain and Language, 11*, 119–127.

Chang, F. L., Greenough, W. T. (1984). Transient and enduring morphological correlates of synaptic activity and efficacy change in the rat hippocampal slice. *Brain Research, 309*, 35–46.

Chen, C. S. (1968). A study of the alcohol-tolerance effect and an introduction of a new behavioral technique. *Psychopharmacology, 12*, 433–440.

Cheney, P. D. (1985). Role of cerebral cortex in voluntary movements. *Physical Therapy, 65*, 624–635.

Chorover, S. L., & Schiller, P. H. (1965). Short-term retrograde amnesia in rats. *Journal of Comparative and Physiological Psychology, 59*, 73–78.

Chusid, J. G. (1985). *Correlative neuroanatomy & functional neurology.* Los Altos, CA: Lange Medical Publications.

Cohen, D. B. (1979). *Sleep and dreaming: Origins, nature and functions.* Oxford: Pergamon Press.

Cohen, H., & Squire, L. R. (1980). Preserved learning and retention of pattern-analysing skill in amnesia: Dissociation of knowing how and knowing that. *Science, 210*, 207–210.

Cohen, S., & Stillman, R. C. (Eds.) (1976). *The therapeutic poten-*

tial of marihuana. New York: Plenum Medical Book Company.

Coindet, J., Chouvet, G., & Mouret, J. (1975). Effects of lesions of the suprachiasmatic nuclei on paradoxical sleep and slow wave sleep circadian rhythms in the rat. *Neuroscience Letters, 1*, 243–247.

Coleman, R. M. (1986). *Wide awake at 3:00 A.M.* New York: W. H. Freeman.

Collier, G. H. (1980). An ecological analysis of motivation. In F. M. Toates & T. R. Halliday (Eds.), *Analysis of motivational processes* (pp. 125–151). London: Academic Press.

Collingridge, G. L., & Bliss, T. V. P. (1987). NMDA receptors—Their role in long-term potentiation. *Trends in Neuroscience, 10*, 288–293.

Coltheart, M. (1985). Cognitive neuropsychology and the study of reading. In M. I. Posner & O. S. M. Marin (Eds.), *Attention and performance: Vol. 11* (pp. 3–37). Hillsdale, NJ: Erlbaum.

Coltheart, M., Masterson, J., Byng, S., Prior, M., & Riddoch, J. (1983). Surface dyslexia. *Quarterly Journal of Experimental Psychology, 35A*, 469–496.

Connell, P. H. (1958). Amphetamine psychosis. *Maudsley Monograph* No. 5, London: Chapman and Hall.

Cooper, K. E., Cranston, W. I., & Honour, A. J. (1967). Observations on the site and mode of action of pyrogens in the rabbit brain. *Journal of Physiology, 191*, 325–337.

Coons, E. E., Levak, M., & Miller, N. E. (1965). Lateral hypothalamus: Learning of food-seeking response motivated by electrical stimulation. *Science, 150*, 1320–1321.

Corbett, D., & Wise, R. A. (1980). Intracranial self-stimulation in relation to the ascending dopaminergic systems of the midbrain: A moveable electrode mapping study. *Brain Research, 185*, 1–15.

Corcoran, M. E., McCaughran, J. A., Jr., & Wada, J. A. (1973). Acute anti-epileptic effects of Δ^9-Tetrahydrocannabinol in rats with kindled seizures. *Experimental Neurology, 40*, 471–483.

Coren, S., & Ward, L. M. (1989). *Sensation and perception* (3rd ed.). New York: Harcourt Brace Jovanovich.

Corkin, S. (1968). Acquisition of motor skill after bilateral medial temporal-lobe excision. *Neuropsychologia, 6*, 255–265.

Corkin, S., Milner, B., & Rasmussen, R. (1970). Somatosensory thresholds. *Archives of Neurology, 23*, 41–59.

Costall, B., & Naylor, R. J. (1977). Mesolimbic and extrapyramidal sites for the mediation of stereotyped behaviour patterns and hyperactivity by amphetamine and apomorphine in the rat. In E. H. Ellinwood, Jr. & M. M. Kilbey (Eds.), *Cocaine and other stimulants* (pp. 47–76). New York: Plenum Press.

Costanzo, R. M., & Becker, D. P. (1986). Smell and taste disorders in head injury and neurosurgery patients. In H. Meiselman & R. S. Rivlin (Eds.), *Clinical measurement of taste and smell* (pp. 565–578). New York: Macmillan Publishing Co.

Cotman, C. W., Monoghan, D. T., & Ganong, A. H. (1988). Excitatory amino acid neurotransmission: NMDA receptors and Hebb-type synaptic plasticity. *Annual Review of Neuroscience, 11*, 61–80.

Cotman, C. W., Nieto-Sampedro, M., & Harris, E. W. (1981). Synapse replacement in the nervous system of adult vertebrates. *Physiological Reviews, 61*, 684–784.

Cowan, W. M. (1979). The development of the brain. *Scientific American, 241*, 113–133.

Cowey, A. (1981). Why are there so many visual areas? In F. O. Schmitt, F. G. Worden, G. Adelman, & S. G. Dennis (Eds.), *The organization of the cerebral cortex* (pp. 395–413). Cambridge, MA: MIT Press.

Coyle, J. T. (1987). Alzheimer's disease. In G. Adelman (Ed.), *Encyclopedia of neuroscience* (pp. 29–31). Boston: Birkhauser.

Coyle, J. T., Price, D. L., & DeLong, M. R. (1983). Alzheimer's disease: A disorder of cortical cholinergic innervation. *Science, 219*, 1184–1190.

Cragg, B. G. (1975). The development of synapses in kitten visual cortex during visual deprivation. *Experimental Neurology, 46*, 445–451.

Craig, J. C. (1977). Vibrotactile pattern perception: Extraordinary observers. *Science, 196*, 450–452.

Craig, K. D., & Patrick, C. J. (1985). Facial expression during induced pain. *Journal of Personality and Social Psychology, 48*, 1080–1091.

Crawshaw, L. I., Moffitt, B. P., Lemons, D. E., & Downey, J. A. (1981). The evolutionary development of vertebrate thermoregulation. *American Scientist, 69*, 543–550.

Creese, I., Burt, D. R., & Snyder, S. H. (1976). Dopamine receptor binding predicts clinical and pharmacological potencies of antischizophrenic drugs. *Science, 192*, 481–483.

Crews, D. (1988). The problem with gender. *Psychobiology, 16*, 321–334.

Crow, T. J. (1972). A map of the rat mesencephalon for electrical self-stimulation. *Brain Research, 36*, 265–273.

Crow, T. J. (1980). Molecular pathology of schizophrenia: More than one disease process. *British Medical Journal, 12*, 66–68.

Crowell, C. R., Hinson, R. E., & Siegel, S. (1981). The role of conditional drug responses in tolerance to the hypothermic effects of ethanol. *Psychopharmacology, 73*, 51–54.

Cumming, G. D. (1978). Eye movements and visual perception. In E. C. Carterette & M. P. Friedman (Eds.), *Handbook of perception* (Vol. 9, pp. 221–255). New York: Academic Press.

Currier, R. D., & Eldridge, R. (1982). Possible risk factors in multiple sclerosis as found in a national twin study. *Archives of Neurology, 39*, 140–144.

Daan, S., & Lewy, A. J. (1984). Scheduled exposure to daylight: A potential strategy to reduce "jet lag" following transmeridian flight. *Psychopharmacology Bulletin, 20*, 566–568.

Damasio, A. R. (1985). Prosopagnosia. *Trends in Neuroscience, 8*, 132–135.

Damasio, A. R., Damasio, H., & Van Hoesen, G. W. (1982). Prosopagnosia: Anatomic basis and behavioral mechanisms. *Neurology, 32*, 331–341.

Damassa, D. A., Smith, E. R., Tennent, B., & Davidson, J. M. (1977). The relationship between circulating testosterone levels and male sexual behavior in rats. *Hormones and Behavior, 8*, 275–286.

Dartnall, H. J. A., Bowmaker, J. K., & Mollon, J. D. (1983). Microspectrophotometry of human photoreceptors. In J. D. Mollon & L. T. Sharpe (Eds.), *Colour vision: Physiology and psychophysics* (pp. 69–80). New York: Academic Press.

Das, G. D., & Altman, J. (1971). Transplanted precursors of nerve cells: Their fate in the cerebellums of young rats. *Science, 173*, 637–638.

Das, G. D., Hallas, B. H., & Das, K. G. (1980). Transplantation of brain tissue in the brain of rat: I. Growth characteristics of neocortical transplants from embryos of different ages. *American Journal of Anatomy, 158*, 135–145.

David, S., & Aguayo, A. J. (1981). Axonal elongation into peripheral nervous system "bridges" after central nervous system injury in adult rats. *Science, 214*, 931–933.

Davidson, J. M., Camarga, C. A., & Smith, E. R. (1979). Effects of androgen on sexual behavior in hypogonadal men. *Journal of Clinical Endocrinology and Metabolism, 48*, 955–958.

Davidson, J. M., Kwan, M., & Greenleaf, W. J. (1982). Hormonal replacement and sexuality in men. *Clinics in Endocrinology and Metabolism, 11*, 599–623.

Davis, H. P., Rosenzweig, M. R., Becker, L. A., & Sather, K. J. (1988). Biological psychology's relationships to psychology and neuroscience. *American Psychologist, 43*, 359–371.

Davis, J. M. (1974). A two factor theory of schizophrenia. *Journal of Psychiatric Research, 11*, 25–29.

DeBold, J. F., & Miczek, K. A. (1984). Aggression persists after ovariectomy in female rats. *Hormones and Behavior, 18*, 177–190.

de Castro, J. M. (1981). Feeding patterns and their control mechanisms. *Behavioral and Brain Sciences, 4*, 581.

de Kruif, P. (1945). *The male hormone*. New York: Harcourt, Brace and Co.

DeLong, M. (1974). Motor functions of the basal ganglia: Single unit activity during movement. In F. O. Schmitt & F. G. Worden (Eds.), *The neurosciences: The third study program* (pp. 319–326). Cambridge, MA: MIT Press.

Demellweek, C., & Goudie, A. J. (1983). An analysis of behavioural mechanisms involved in the acquisition of amphetamine anorectic tolerance. *Psychopharmacology, 79,* 58–66.

Dement, W. C. (1960). The effect of dream deprivation. *Science, 131,* 1705–1707.

Dement, W. C. (1978). *Some must watch while some must sleep.* New York: W. W. Norton.

Dement, W. C., & Kleitman, N. (1957). The relation of eye movement during sleep to dream activity: An objective method for the study of dreaming. *Journal of Experimental Psychology, 53,* 339–553.

Dement, W. C., Milter, M., & Henriksen, S. (1972). Sleep changes during chronic administration of parachlorophenylalanine. *Revue Canadienne de Biologie, 31,* 239–246.

Dement, W. C., & Wolpert, E. A. (1958). The relation of eye movements, body motility and external stimuli to dream content. *Journal of Experimental Psychology, 55,* 543–553.

Dennerstein, L., & Burrows, G. D. (1982). Hormone replacement therapy and sexuality in women. *Clinics in Endocrinology and Metabolism, 11,* 661–679.

Denny-Brown, D., & Chambers, R. A. (1958). The parietal lobes and behavior. *Research Publications of the Association for Research in Mental Disease, 36,* 35–117.

De Renzi, E. (1980). The influence of sex and age on the incidence and type of aphasia. *Cortex, 16,* 627–630.

De Renzi, E. (1982). *Disorders of space exploration and cognition.* New York: Wiley.

Deuel, R. K. (1977). Loss of motor habits after cortical lesions. *Neuropsychologia, 15,* 205–215.

Deutsch, J. A., Young, W. G., & Kalogeris, T. J. (1978). The stomach signals satiety. *Science, 21,* 165–167.

DeValois, R. L., & DeValois, K. K. (1980). Spatial vision. *Annual Review of Psychology, 31,* 309–341.

Dewsbury, D. A. (1967). A quantitative description of the behavior of rats during copulation. *Behavior, 29,* 154–178.

Diamond, J. (1982). Modelling and competition in the nervous system: Clues from sensory innervation of skin. *Current Topics in Developmental Biology, 17,* 147–205.

Diamond, J. (1986). I want a girl just like the girl. . . . *Discover, 7,* 65–68.

DiCara, L. V. (1970). Learning in the autonomic nervous system. *Scientific American, 222,* 30–39.

Dixson, A. F. (1980). Androgens and aggressive behavior. *Aggressive Behavior, 6,* 37–67.

Dobelle, W. H., Mladejovsky, M. G., & Girvin, J. P. (1974). Artificial vision for the blind: Electrical stimulation of visual cortex offers hope for a functional prosthesis. *Science, 183,* 440–444.

Doty, R. L. (1986). Gender and endocrine-related influences on human olfactory perception. In H. Meiselman & R. S. Rivlin (Eds.), *Clinical measurement of taste and smell* (pp. 377–413). New York: Macmillan Publishing Co.

Doty, R. L., Ford, M., Preti, G., & Huggins, G. R. (1975). Changes in the intensity and pleasantness of human vaginal odors during the menstrual cycle. *Science, 190,* 1316–1318.

Doty, R. L., Green, P. A., Ram, C., & Yankell, S. L. (1982). Communication of gender from human breath odors: Relationship to perceived intensity and pleasantness. *Hormones and Behavior, 16,* 13–22.

Doty, R. L., Snyder, P. J., Huggins, G. R., & Lowry, L. D. (1981). Endocrine, cardiovascular, and psychological correlates of olfactory sensitivity changes during the human menstrual cycle. *Journal of Comparative and Physiological Psychology, 95,* 45–60.

Dowling, J. E. (1979). Information processing by local circuits: The vertebrate retina as a model system. In F. O. Schmitt & F. G. Worden (Eds.), *The neurosciences fourth study program* (pp. 163–181). Cambridge, MA: MIT Press.

Drachman, D. A., & Arbit, J. (1966). Memory and the hippocampal complex. *Archives of Neurology, 15,* 52–61.

Drachman, D. A., & Leavitt, J. (1974). Human memory and the cholinergic receptor. *Archives of Neurology, 30,* 113–121.

Drucker-Collin, R., Aguilar-Roblero, R., & Arankowsky-Sandoval, G. (1985). Re-evaluation of the hypnogenic factor notion. In A. Wauquier, J. M. Gaillard, J. M. Monti, & M. Radulovacki (Eds.), *Sleep: Neurotransmitters and neuromodulators* (pp. 291–304). New York: Raven Press.

Dunant, Y., & Israël, M. (1985). The release of acetylcholine. *Scientific American, 252,* 58–66.

Duvoisin, R. C., Heikkila, R. E., Nicklas, W. J., & Hess, A. (1986). Dopaminergic neurotoxicity of MPTP in the mouse: A murine model of parkinsonism. In S. Fahn, C. D. Marsden, P. Jenner, & P. Teychenne (Eds.), *Recent developments in Parkinson's disease* (pp. 147–154). New York: Raven Press.

Dworkin, B. R., & Miller, N. E. (1986). Failure to replicate visceral learning in the acute curarized rat preparation. *Behavioral Neuroscience, 100,* 299–314.

Dykes, R. W. (1983). Parallel processing of somatosensory information: A theory. *Brain Research Reviews, 6,* 47–115.

Easter, S. S., Jr., Purves, D., Rakic, P., & Spitzer, N. C. (1985). The changing view of neural specificity. *Science, 230,* 507–511.

Edwards, D. A. (1969). Early androgen stimulation and aggressive behavior in male and female mice. *Physiology & Behavior, 4,* 333–338.

Egger, M. D., & Flynn, J. P. (1963). Effects of electrical stimulation of the amygdala on hypothalamically elicited attack behavior in cats. *Journal of Neurophysiology, 26,* 705–720.

Ehrhardt, A. A., Epstein, R., & Money, M. (1968). Fetal androgens and female gender identity in the early-treated androgenital syndrome. *Johns Hopkins Medical Journal, 122,* 160–167.

Ehrhardt, A. A., & Meyer-Bahlberg, H. F. L. (1975). Psychological correlates of abnormal pubertal development. *Clinical Endocrinology and Metabolism, 4,* 207–222.

Ehrhardt, A. A., & Meyer-Bahlberg, H. F. L. (1981). Effects of prenatal sex hormones on gender-related behavior. *Science, 211,* 1312–1317.

Ehringer, H., & Hornykiewicz, O. (1960). Verteilung von Noradrenalin und Dopamin (3-Hydroxytyramin) im gehirn des Menschen und ihr Verhalten bei Erkrankungen des Extrapyramidalen Systems. *Klinische Wochenschrift, 38,* 1236–1239.

Eikelboom, R., & Stewart, J. (1982). Conditioning of drug-induced physiological responses. *Psychological Review, 89,* 507–528.

Engen, T. (1982). *The perception of odors.* New York: Academic Press.

Epstein, A. N. (1982). The physiology of thirst. In D. W. Pfaff (Ed.), *The physiological mechanisms of motivation* (pp. 165–214). New York: Springer-Verlag.

Epstein, A. N. (1987). Drinking behavior. In G. Adelman (Ed.), *Encyclopedia of neuroscience* (pp. 340–342). Boston: Birkhauser.

Epstein, A. N., & Milestone, R. (1968). Showering as a coolant for rats exposed to heat. *Science, 160,* 895–896.

Epstein, A. N., Spector, D., Samman, A., & Goldblum, C. (1964). Exaggerated prandial drinking in the rat without salivary glands. *Nature, 201,* 1342–1343.

Epstein, A. N., & Teitelbuam, P. (1962). Regulation of food intake in the absence of taste, smell, and other oropharyngeal sensations. *Journal of Comparative and Physiological Psychology, 55,* 753–759.

Eränkö, O. (1955). Distribution of fluorescing islets, adrenaline and noradrenaline in the adrenal medulla of the cat. *Acta Endocrinologica, 18,* 180–188.

Ettlinger, G., & Kalsbeck, J. (1962). Changes in tactile discrimination and in visual teaching after successive and simultaneous bilateral posterior parietal ablations in the monkey. *Journal of Neurology, Neurosurgery, and Psychiatry, 25,* 256–268.

Evans, E. F., Ross, H. F., & Whitfield, I. C. (1965). The spatial distribution of unit characteristic frequency in the primary auditory cortex of the cat. *Journal of Physiology, 179,* 238–247.

Evarts, E. V. (1981). Functional studies of the motor cortex. In

F. O. Schmitt, F. G. Worden, G. Adelman, & S. G. Dennis (Eds.), *The organization of the cerebral cortex* (pp. 263–283). Cambridge, MA: MIT Press.

Fadem, B. H., & Barfield, R. J. (1981). Neonatal hormonal influences on the development of proceptive and receptive feminine sexual behavior in rats. *Hormones and Behavior, 15,* 282–288.

Falck, B., Hillarp, N. A., Thieme, G., & Torp, A. (1962). Fluorescence of catechol amines and related compounds condensed with formaldehyde. *Journal of Histochemistry and Cytochemistry, 10,* 348–364.

Falk, J. L. (1964). Production of polydipsia in normal rats by an intermittent food schedule. *Science, 133,* 195–196.

Falzi, G., Perrone, P., & Vignolo, L. A. (1982). Right-left asymmetry in anterior speech region. *Archives of Neurology, 39,* 239–240.

Faris, P. L., & Olney, J. W. (1985). Suppression of food intake in rats by microinjection of cholecystokinin (CCK) to the paraventricular nucleus (PVN). *Society for Neuroscience Abstracts, 2,* 39.

Faust, I. M., Johnson, P. R., & Hirsch, J. (1977). Adipose tissue regeneration following lipectomy. *Science, 197,* 391–393.

Feder, H. H. (1981). Perinatal hormones and their role in the development of sexually dimorphic behaviors. In N. T. Adler (Ed.), *Neuroendocrinology of reproduction: Physiology and behavior* (pp. 127–157). New York: Plenum Press.

Feder, H. H. (1984). Hormones and sexual behavior. *Anual Review of Psychology, 35,* 165–200.

Feindel, W. (1986). Electrical stimulation of the brain during surgery for epilepsy—historical highlights. In G. P. Varkey (Ed.), *Anesthetic considerations for craniotomy in awake patients* (pp. 75–87). Boston: Little, Brown and Company.

Feldman, S. M., & Waller, H. J. (1962). Disassociation of electrocortical activation and behavioural arousal. *Nature, 196,* 1320–1322.

Fentress, J. C. (1973). Development of grooming in mice with amputated forelimbs. *Science, 179,* 704–705.

Fibiger, H. C., LePiane, F. G., Jakubovic, A., & Phillips, A. G. (1987). The role of dopamine in intracranial self-stimulation of the ventral tegmental area. *Journal of Neuroscience, 7,* 3888–3896.

Fibiger, II. C., Murray, C. L., & Phillips, A. G. (1983). Lesions of the nucleus basalis magnocellularis impair long-term memory in rats. *Society for Neuroscience Abstracts, 9,* 332.

Fibiger, H. C., & Phillips, A. G. (1986). Reward, motivation, cognition: Psychobiology of mesotelencephalic dopamine system. In V. B. Mountcastle, F. E. Bloom, & S. R. Geiger (Eds.), *Handbook of physiology: The nervous system. Vol. 4. Intrinsic systems of the brain* (pp. 647–675). Bethesda, MD: American Physiological Society.

Fibiger, H. C., & Phillips, A. G. (1987). Role of catecholamine transmitters in brain reward systems: Implications for the neurobiology of affect. In J. Engel & L. Oreland (Eds.), *Brain reward systems and abuse* (pp. 61–74). New York: Raven Press.

Fields, H. L., & Basbaum, A. I. (1984). Endogenous pain control mechanisms. In P. D. Wall & R. Melzack (Eds.), *Textbook of pain* (pp. 142–152). Edinburgh: Churchill Livingstone.

Fillion, T. J., & Blass, E. M. (1986). Infantile experience with suckling odors determines adult sexual behavior in male rats. *Science, 231,* 729–731.

Fine, A. (1986). Transplantation in the central nervous system. *Scientific American, 255,* 52–58.

Finger, S., & Almli, C. R. (1985). Brain damage and neuroplasticity: Mechanisms of recovery or development? *Brain Research Reviews, 10,* 177–186.

Fitzsimons, J. T. (1961). Drinking by rats depleted of body fluid without increase in osmotic pressure. *Journal of Physiology, 159,* 297–309.

Fitzsimons, J. T. (1972). Thirst. *Physiological Reviews, 52,* 468–561.

Fitzsimons, J. T., Epstein, A. N., & Johnson, A. K. (1978). Peptide antagonists of the renin-angiotensin system in the char-

acterisation of receptors for angiotensin-induced drinking. *Brain Research, 153,* 319–331.

Fitzsimons, J. T., & LeMagnen, J. (1969). Eating as a regulatory control of drinking in the rat. *Journal of Comparative and Physiological Psychology, 67,* 273–283.

Fitzsimons, J. T., & Simons, B. J. (1969). The effect on drinking in the rat of intravenous infusion of angiotensin, given alone or in combination with other stimuli of thirst. *Journal of Physiology, 203,* 45–57.

Flannelly, K. J., Kemble, E. D., Blanchard, D. C., & Blanchard, R. J. (1986). Effects of septal-forebrain lesions on maternal aggression and maternal care. *Behavioral and Neural Biology, 45,* 17–30.

Forth, A., Hart, S., Hare, R., & Harpur, T. (1988, October). *Event-related brain potentials and detection of deception.* Paper presented at the Annual Meeting of the Society for Psychophysiological Research, San Francisco, CA.

Foulkes, D., & Rechtschaffen, A. (1964). Presleep determinants of dream content: Effects of two films. *Perceptual and Motor Skills, 49,* 983–1005.

Freed, W. J., de Medinaceli, L., & Wyatt, R. J. (1985). Promoting functional plasticity in the damaged nervous system. *Science, 227,* 1544–1552.

Freed, W. J., Perlow, M., Karoum, F., Seiger, A., Olson, L., Hoffer, B. J., & Wyatt, R. J. (1980). Restoration of dopaminergic function by grafting of fetal rat substantia nigra to the caudate nucleus: Long-term behavioral, biochemical, and histochemical studies. *Annals of Neurology, 8,* 510–519.

Friedman, J., Globus, G., Huntley, A., Mullaney, D., Naitoh, P., & Johnson, L. (1977). Performance and mood during and after gradual sleep reduction. *Psychophysiology, 14,* 245–250.

Friedman, M. I. (1981). Metabolic elements of eating behavior. *Behavioral and Brain Sciences, 4,* 583–584.

Friedman, M. I., & Stricker, E. M. (1976). The physiological psychology of hunger: A physiological perspective. *Psychological Review, 83,* 409–431.

Fritsch, G., & Hitzig, E. (1870). Über die elektrische Erregbarkeit des Grosshirns. *Archiv für Anatomie Physiologie und Wissenschaftlichen Medicin, 37,* 300–332. In G. von Bonin (Trans.), (1960). *Some papers on the cerebral cortex* (pp. 73–96). Springfield, IL: Charles C. Thomas.

Funnell, D. (1983). Phonological processes in reading: New evidence from acquired dyslexia. *British Journal of Psychology, 74,* 159–180.

Furedy, J. J. (1983). Operational, analogical and genuine definitions of psychophysiology. *International Journal of Psychophysiology, 1,* 13–19.

Galef, B. G. (1989). Laboratory studies of naturally-occurring feeding behaviors: Pitfalls, progress and problems in ethoexperimental analysis. In R. J. Blanchard, P. F. Brain, D. C. Blanchard, & S. Parmigiani (Eds.), *Ethoexperimental approaches to the study of behavior.* (pp. 51–77). Dordrecht, The Netherlands: Kluwer Academic Publishers.

Galef, B. G., & Clark, M. M. (1972). Mother's milk and adult presence: Two factors determining initial dietary selection by weanling rats. *Journal of Comparative and Physiological Psychology, 78,* 220–225.

Galef, B. G., & Sherry, D. F. (1973). Mother's milk: A medium for transmission of cues reflecting the flavor of mother's diet. *Journal of Comparative and Physiological Psychology, 83,* 374–378.

Gallistel, C. R., Gomita, Y., Yadin, E., & Campbell, K. A. (1985). Forebrain origins and terminations of the medial forebrain bundle metabolically activated by rewarding stimulation or by reward-blocking doses of pimozide. *Journal of Neuroscience, 5,* 1246–1261.

Garcia, J., & Koelling, R. A. (1966). Relation of cue to consequence in avoidance learning. *Psychonomic Science, 4,* 123–124.

Garcia-Arraras, J. E., & Pappenheimer, J. R. (1983). Site of action of sleep-inducing muramyl peptide isolated from human urine: Microinjection studies in rabbit brains. *Journal of Neurophysiology, 49,* 528–533.

Garrigues, A. M., & Cazala, P. (1983). Central catecholamine metabolism and hypothalamic self-stimulation behaviour in two inbred strains of mice. *Brain Research, 265,* 265–271.

Garrow, J. S. (1974). *Energy balance and obesity in man.* (pp. 210–217). New York: Elsevier Publishing Company.

Gaze, R. M. (1974). Neuronal specificity. *British Medical Bulletin, 30,* 116–121.

Gaze, R. M., Keating, M. J., Ostberg, A., & Chung, S. H. (1979). The relationship between retinal and tectal growth in larval *Xenopus:* Implications for the development of the retino-tectal projection. *Journal of Embryology and Experimental Morphology, 53,* 103–143.

Gaze, R. M., & Sharma, S. C. (1970). Axial differences in the reinnervation of the goldfish optic tectum by regenerating optic nerve fibres. *Experimental Brain Research, 10,* 171–181.

Gazzaniga, M. S. (1967). The split brain in man. *Scientific American, 217,* 24–29.

Gazzaniga, M. S., & Sperry, R. W. (1967). Language after section of the cerebral commissure. *Brain, 90,* 131–148.

Geiselman, P. J. (1987). Carbohydrates do not always produce satiety: An explanation of the appetite- and hunger-stimulating effects of hexoses. *Progress in Psychobiology and Physiological Psychology, 12,* 1–46.

Gerbino, L., Oleshansky, M., & Gershon, S. (1978). Clinical use and mode of action of lithium. In M. A. Lipton, A. DiMascio, & K. F. Killam (Eds.), *Psychopharmacology: A generation of progress* (pp. 1261–1275). New York: Raven Press.

Geschwind, N. (1972). Language and the brain. *Scientific American, 226,* 76–83.

Geschwind, N. (1979). Specializations of the human brain. *Scientific American, 241,* 180–199.

Geschwind, N., & Levitsky, W. (1968). Human brain: Left-right asymmetries in temporal speech region. *Science, 161,* 186–187.

Ghez, C. (1985). Voluntary movement. In E. R. Kandel & J. H. Schwartz (Eds.), *Principles of neuroscience* (pp. 487–501). New York: Elsevier.

Gibbs, C. (1985). Voluntary movement. In E. R. Kandel & J. H. Schwartz (Eds.), *Principles of neuroscience* (pp. 487–501). New York: Elsevier.

Gibbs, J., Maddison, S. P., & Rolls, E. T. (1981). Satiety role of the small intestine examined in sham-feeding rhesus monkeys. *Journal of Comparative and Physiological Psychology, 95,* 1003–1015.

Gilbert, C. D. (1977). Laminar differences in receptive field properties of cells in cat primary visual cortex. *Journal of Physiology, 268,* 391–421.

Gilman, A. (1937). The relation between blood osmotic pressure, fluid distribution and voluntary water intake. *American Journal of Physiology, 120,* 323–328.

Glickman, S. E., & Schiff, B. B. (1967). A biological theory of reinforcement. *Psychological Review, 74,* 81–109.

Goddard, G. V., McIntyre, D. C., & Leech, C. K. (1969). A permanent change in brain function resulting from daily electrical stimulation. *Experimental Neurology, 25,* 295–330.

Goddard, G. V., & Morrell, F. (1971). Chronic progressive epileptogenesis induced by focal electrical stimulation of brain. *Neurology, 21,* 393.

Goeders, N. E., Lane, J. D., & Smith, J. E. (1984). Self-administration of methionine enkephalin into the nucleus accumbens. *Pharmacology Biochemistry & Behavior, 20,* 451–455.

Gold, R. M. (1973). Hypothalamic obesity: The myth of the ventromedial nucleus. *Science, 182,* 488–490.

Gold, R. M., Jones, A. P., Sawchenko, P. E., & Kapatos, G. (1977). Paraventricular area: Critical focus of a longitudinal neurocircuitry mediating food intake. *Physiology & Behavior, 18,* 1111–1119.

Gold, R. M., & Simson, E. L. (1982). Perturbations of serum insulin, glucagon, somatostatin, epinephrine, norepinephrine and glucose after obesifying hypothalamic knife-cuts. In B. G. Hoebel & D. Novin (Eds.). *The neural basis of feeding and reward.* Brunswick, MN: Haer Institute.

Goldberg, M. E., & Bushnell, M. C. (1981). Behavioral enhancement of visual responses in monkey cerebral cortex: II. Modulation in frontal eye fields specifically related to saccades. *Journal of Neurophysiology, 46,* 773–787.

Goldgaber, D., Lerman, M. I., McBride, W., Saffiotti, U., & Gajdusek, D. C. (1987). Characterization and chromosomal localization of cDNA encoding brain amyloid of Alzheimer's disease. *Science, 235,* 877–880.

Goldman, B. (1984). *Death in the locker room: Steroids and sports.* South Bend, IN: Icarus Press.

Goldstein, M. H., Abeles, M., Daly, R. L., & McIntosh, J. (1970). Functional architecture in cat primary auditory cortex: Tonotopic organization. *Journal of Neurophysiology, 33,* 188–197.

Gollin, E. S. (1960). Developmental studies of visual recognition of incomplete objects. *Perceptual Motor Skills, 11,* 289–298.

Gollinick, P. D., & Hodgson, D. R. (1986). The identification of fiber types in skeletal muscle: A continual dilemma. *Exercise and Sport Sciences Reviews, 14,* 81–104.

Goodale, M. A. (1983). Neural mechanisms of visual orientation in rodents: Targets versus places. In A. Hein & M. Jeannerod (Eds.), *Spatially oriented behavior* (pp. 36–61). New York: Springer-Verlag.

Goodenough, D. R., Shapiro, A., Holden, M., & Steinschriber, L. (1959). A comparison of "dreamers" and "nondreamers": Eye movements, electroencephalograms, and the recall of dreams. *Journal of Abnormal and Social Psychology, 59,* 295–303.

Goodenough, D. R., Witkin, H. A., Koulack, D., & Cohen, H. (1975). The effects of stress films on dream effect and on respiration and eye-movement activity during rapid-eye-movement sleep. *Psychophysiology, 12,* 313–320.

Goodglass, H., & Kaplan, E. (1979). Assessment of cognitive deficit in the brain-injured patient. In M. S. Gazzaniga (Ed.), *Handbook of behavioral neurobiology: Vol. 2. Neuropsychology* (pp. 3–22). New York: Plenum Press.

Gormezano, I. (1972). Classical conditioning: Investigations of defense and reward conditioning in the rabbit. In A. H. Black & W. R. Prokasy (Eds.), *Classical conditioning II* (pp. 151–181). New York: Appleton-Century-Crofts.

Gorski, R. A. (1971). Gonadal hormones and the perinatal development of neuroendocrine function. In L. Martini & W. F. Ganong (Eds.), *Frontiers in neuroendocrinology* (pp. 237–290). New York: Oxford University Press.

Gorski, R. A. (1980). Sexual differentiation in the brain. In D. T. Krieger & J. C. Hughes (Eds.). *Neuroendocrinology* (pp. 215–222). Sunderland, MA: Sinauer.

Gorski, R. A. (1985). The 13th J. A. Stevenson Memorial Lecture: Sexual differentiation of the brain: Possible mechanisms and implications. *Canadian Journal of Physiology and Pharmacology, 63,* 577–594.

Gorski, R. A., Harlan, R. E., & Christensen, L. W. (1977). Perinatal hormonal exposure and the development of neuroendocrine regulatory processes. *Journal of Toxicology and Environmental Health, 3,* 97–121.

Gottlieb, D. I. (1988). GABAergic neurons. *Scientific American, 258,* 82–89.

Gould, S. J. (1980). *The panda's thumb.* New York: W. W. Norton and Co.

Gouras, P., & Kruger, J. (1979). Responses of cells in foveal visual cortex of the monkey to pure color contrast. *Journal of Neurophysiology, 42,* 850–860.

Goy, R. W. (1970). Experimental control of psychosexuality. *Philosophical Transactions of the Royal Society of London, (B), 259,* 149–162.

Goy, R. W. (1978). Development of play and mounting behaviour in female rhesus virilized prenatally with esters of testosterone or dihydrotestosterone. In D. J. Chivers & J. Herbert (Eds.), *Recent advances in primatology* (pp. 449–462). London: Academic Press.

Goy, R. W., & McEwen, B. S. (1980). *Sexual differentiation of the brain.* Cambridge, MA: MIT Press.

Grady, K. L., Phoenix, C. H., & Young, W. C. (1965). Role of the developing rat testis in differentiation of the neural tissues mediating mating behavior. *Journal of Comparative and Physiological Psychology, 59,* 176–182.

Graf, P., & Schacter, D. J. (1985). Implicit and explicit memory for new associations in normal and amnesic subjects. *Journal of Experimental Psychology: Learning, Memory, and Cognition, 11,* 501–518.

Graf, P., & Schacter, D. J. (1987). Selective effects of interference on implicit and explicit memory for new associations. *Journal of Experimental Psychology: Learning, Memory, and Cognition, 13,* 45–53.

Graf, P., Squire, L. R., & Mandler, G. (1984). The information that amnesic patients do not forget. *Journal of Experimental Psychology, Learning, Memory, and Cognition, 10,* 164–178.

Graff-Radford, N., Damasio, H., Yamada, T., Eslinger, P. J., & Damasio, A. R. (1985). Nonhaemorrhagic thalamic infarction. *Brain, 108,* 485–516.

Graves, R., Goodglass, H., & Landis, T. (1982). Mouth asymmetry during spontaneous speech. *Neuropsychologia, 20,* 371–381.

Gray, T. S., & Morley, J. E. (1986). Minireview: Neuropeptide Y: Anatomical distribution and possible function in mammalian nervous system. *Life Sciences, 38,* 389–401.

Greenough, W. T., Carter, C. S., Steerman, C., & Devoogd, T. J. (1977). Sex differences in dendritic patterns in hamster preoptic area. *Brain Research, 126,* 63–72.

Greenough, W. T., & Volkmar, F. R. (1973). Pattern of dendritic branching in occipital cortex of rats reared in complex environments. *Experimental Neurology, 40,* 491–504.

Griffith, J. D., Cavanaugh, J., Held, J., & Oates, J. A. (1972). Dextroamphetamine. *Archives of General Psychiatry, 26,* 97–100.

Grillner, S. (1985). Neurobiological bases of rhythmic motor acts in vertebrates. *Science, 228,* 143–149.

Grinspoon, L. (1977). *Marijuana reconsidered.* Cambridge, MA: Harvard University Press.

Groos, G. (1983). Regulation of the circadian sleep-wake cycle. *Sleep 1982, 6th European Congress on Sleep Research* (Zurich, 1982) (pp. 19–29). Basel: Karger.

Groos, G. (1984). The physiological organization of the circadian sleep-wake cycle. In A. Borbély & J. L. Valatx (Eds.), *Sleep mechanisms* (pp. 241–257). Berlin: Springer-Verlag.

Groos, G., & Hendricks, J. (1982). Circadian rhythms in electrical discharge of rat suprachiasmatic neurones recorded in vitro. *Neuroscience Letters, 34,* 283–288.

Gross, C. G., Desimone, R., Albright, T. D., & Schwarz, E. L. (1985). Inferior temporal cortex and pattern recognition. In C. Chagas, R. Gattass, & C. Gross (Eds.), *Pattern recognition mechanisms* (pp. 179–201). Berlin: Springer-Verlag.

Grossman, S. P. (1967). *A textbook of physiological psychology.* New York: John Wiley & Sons, Inc.

Groves, P. M., & Thompson, R. F. (1970). Habituation: A dual process theory. *Psychological Reviews, 77,* 419–450.

Grudin, J. T. (1983). Error patterns in skilled and novice transcription typing. In W.E. Cooper (Ed.), *Cognitive aspects of skilled typewriting* (pp. 121–144). New York: Springer.

Grunt, J. A., & Young, W. C. (1952). Differential reactivity of individuals and the response of the male guinea pig to testosterone propionate. *Endocrinology, 51,* 64–75.

Guieu, J. D., & Hardy, J. D. (1970). Effects of heating and cooling of the spinal cord on preoptic unit activity. *Journal of Applied Physiology, 29,* 675–683.

Gunne, L. M., Ånggård, E., & Jönsson, L. E. (1972). Clinical trials with amphetamine-blocking drugs. *Psychiatria, Neurologia, Neurochirurgia, 75,* 225–226.

Haber, S., Barchas, P. R., & Barchas, J. D. (1981). A primate analogue of amphetamine-induced behavior in humans. *Biological Psychiatry, 16,* 181–195.

Hallas, B. H., Oblinger, M. M., & Das, G. D. (1980). Heterotopic neural transplants in the cerebellum of the rat: Their afferents. *Brain Research, 196,* 2442–2446.

Halmi, K. A., Ackerman, S., Gibbs, J., & Smith, G. (1987). Basic biological overview of the eating disorders. In H. Y. Meltzer (Ed.), *Psychopharmacology: The third generation of progress* (pp. 1255–1266). New York: Raven Press.

Hammel, H. T., Caldwell, F. T., & Abrams, R. M. (1967). Regulation of body temperature in the blue-tongued lizard. *Science, 156,* 1260–1262.

Hammond, P. H., Merton, P. A., & Sutton, G. G. (1956). Nervous gradation of muscular contraction. *British Medical Bulletin, 12,* 214–218.

Han, P. J., Feng, L. Y., & Kuo, P. T. (1972). Insulin sensitivity of pair-fed, hyperlipemic, hyperinsulinemic, obese hypothalamic rats. *American Journal of Physiology, 223,* 1206–1209.

Hardy, J. D. (1980). Body temperature regulation. In V. B. Mountcastle (Ed.), *Medical physiology, II* (pp. 1417–1456). St. Louis, C. V. Mosby Co.

Harnet, R. M., Pruitt, J. R., & Sias, F. R. (1983). A review of the literature concerning resuscitation from hypothermia: Part 1. The problem and general approaches. *Aviation Space and Environmental Medicine, 54,* 425–435.

Harris, G. W. (1955). *Neural control of the pituitary gland.* London: Edward Arnold (Pub.) Ltd.

Harris, G. W., & Jacobsohn, D. (1952). Functional grafts of the anterior pituitary gland. *Proceedings of the Royal Society of London (B), 139,* 1951–1952.

Harris, G. W., & Levine, S. (1965). Sexual differentiation of the brain and its experimental control. *Journal of Physiology, 181,* 379–400.

Harris, L. J. (1978). Sex differences in spatial ability: Possible environmental, genetic, and neurological factors. In M. Kinsbourne (Ed.), *Asymmetrical function of the brain* (p. 463). Cambridge: Cambridge University Press.

Harris, L. J., Clay, J., Hargreaves, F. J., & Ward, A. (1933). Appetite and choice of diet: The ability of the vitamin B deficient rat to discriminate between diets containing and lacking the vitamin. *Proceedings of the Royal Society of London, (B), 113,* 161–190.

Hartmann, E. (1980). Effects of psychotropic drugs on sleep: The catecholamines and sleep. In M. A. Lipton, A. DiMascio, & K. F. Killam (Eds.), *Psychopharmacology: A generation of progress* (pp. 711–728). New York: Raven Press.

Hartmann, E. L. (1973). *The functions of sleep.* Westford, MA: Murray Printing Company.

Haseltine, F. P., & Ohno, S. (1981). Mechanisms of gonadal differentiation. *Science, 211,* 1272–1277.

Haupt, H. A., & Revere, G. D. (1984). Anabolic steroids: A review of the literature. *American Journal of Sports Medicine, 12,* 469–484.

Hawkins, R. D. (1983). Cellular neurophysiological studies of learning. In J. A. Deutsch (Ed.), *The physiological basis of memory* (pp. 71–120). New York: Academic Press.

Hawkins, R. D., Abrams, T. W., Carew, T. J., & Kandel, E. R. (1983). A cellular mechanism of classical conditioning in *Aplysia:* Activity-dependent amplification of presynaptic facilitation. *Science, 219,* 400–405.

Hawkins, R. D., Castellucci, V. F., & Kandel, E. R. (1981). Interneurons involved in mediation and modulation of gill-withdrawal reflex in *Aplysia.* II. Identified neurons produce heterosynaptic facilitation contributing to behavioral sensitization. *Neurophysiology, 45,* 315–326.

Hawkins, R. D., Clark, G. A., & Kandel, E. R. (1987). Cell biological studies of learning in simple vertebrate and invertebrate systems. In F. Plum (Ed.), *Handbook of neurophysiology* (Vol. 6, pp. 25–83). Bethesda, MD: American Physiological Society.

Hebb, D. O. (1949). *The organization of behavior.* New York: John Wiley & Sons, Inc.

Hécaen, H., & Angelergues, R. (1964). Localization of symptoms in aphasia. In A. V. S. de Reuck & M. O'Connor (Eds.), *CIBA foundation symposium on the disorders of language* (pp. 222–256). London: Churchill Press.

Heilman, K. M., & Watson, R. T. (1977). The neglect syndrome—A unilateral defect of the orienting response. In S. Harnad, R. W. Doty, L. Goldstein, J. Jaynes, &

G. Krauhamer (Eds.), *Lateralization in the nervous system* (pp. 285–302). New York: Academic Press.

Heilman, K. M., Watson, R. T., & Valenstein, E. (1985). Neglect and related disorders. In K. M. Heilman & E. Valenstein (Eds.), *Clinical neuropsychology* (pp. 243–293). New York: Oxford University Press.

Helmholtz, H. L. F. (1852). *On the sensation of tone* (2nd Eng. ed.). New York: Dover (1954).

Hendrickson, A. E., Wagoner, N., & Cowan, W. M. (1972). Autoradiographic and electron microscopic study of retinohypothalamic connections. *Zeitschrift für Zellforschung und Mikroskopische Anatomie, 125*, 1–26.

Herbert, J. (1977). The neuroendocrine basis of sexual behaviour in primates. In J. Money & H. Musaph (Eds.), *Handbook of sexology* (pp. 449–459). Amsterdam: Exerpta Medica.

Hering, E. (1878). Der Raumsinn und die Bewegungen des Auges. In L. Hermann (Ed.), *Handbuch der Physiologie, Band III* (pp. 343–601). T. I. Leipzig: F. C. W. Vogel.

Hetherington, A. W., & Ranson, S. W. (1940). Hypothalamic lesions and adiposity in the rat. *Anatomical Record, 78*, 149–172.

Heuser, J. E. (1977). Synaptic vesicle exocytosis revealed in quick-frozen frog neuromuscular junctions treated with 4-aminopyridine and given a single electrical shock. In W. M. Cowan & F. A. Ferrendelli (Eds.), *Society for neuroscience symposia: Approaches to the cell biology of neurons* (Vol. 11, pp. 215–239). Bethesda, MD: Society for Neuroscience.

Hier, D. B., & Kaplan, J. (1980). Are sex differences in cerebral organization clinically significant? *Behavioral and Brain Sciences, 3*, 238–239.

Hillyard, S. A., & Kutas, M. (1983). Electrophysiology of cognitive processing. *Annual Review of Psychology, 34*, 33–61.

Hirst, W., Spelke, E. S., Reaves, C. C., Canarack, G., & Neisser, U. (1980). Dividing attention without alteration or automaticity. *Journal of Experimental Psychology: General, 109*, 98–117.

Hochner, B., Klein, M., Schacher, S., & Kandel, E. R. (1986). Action-potential duration and the modulation of transmitter release from the sensory neurons of *Aplysia* in presynaptic facilitation and behavioral sensitization. *Proceedings of the National Academy of Sciences (USA), 83*, 8410–8414.

Hodgkin, A. L., & Keynes, R. D. (1955). Active transport of cations in giant axons from *Sepia* and *Loligo*. *Journal of Physiology, 128*, 28–60.

Hoebel, B. G., Monaco, A. P., Hernandez, L., Aulisi, E. F., Stanley, B. G., & Lenard, L. (1983). Self-injection of amphetamine directly into the brain. *Psychopharmacology, 81*, 158–163.

Hoebel, B. G., & Teitelbaum, P. (1961). Hypothalamic control of feeding and self-stimulation. *Science, 135*, 375–377.

Hoffman, S., & Edelman, G. M. (1983). Kinetics of homophilic binding by embryonic and adult forms of the neural cell adhesion molecule. *Proceedings of the National Academy of Sciences (USA), 80*, 5762–5766.

Hollyday, M., & Hamburger, V. (1976). Reduction of the naturally occurring motor neuron loss by enlargement of the periphery. *Journal of Comparative Neurology, 170*, 311–320.

Holm, H., Hustvedt, B. E., & Lovo, A. (1973). Protein metabolism in rats with ventromedial hypothalamic lesions. *Metabolism, 22*, 1377–1387.

Holman, G. L. (1968). Intragastric reinforcement effect. *Journal of Comparative and Physiological Psychology, 69*, 432–441.

Holzman, P. S., Solomon, C. M., Levin, S., & Waternaux, C. S. (1984). Pursuit eye movement dysfunctions in schizophrenia. *Archives of General Psychiatry, 41*, 136–139.

Hopkins, W. G., & Brown, M. C. (1984). *Development of nerve cells and their connections*. Cambridge: Cambridge University Press.

Horel, J. A. (1978). The neuroanatomy of amnesia: A critique of the hippocampal memory hypothesis. *Brain, 101*, 403–445.

Horne, J. A. (1976). Recovery sleep following different visual conditions during total sleep deprivation in man. *Biological Psychology, 4*, 107–118.

Horne, J. A. (1983). Mammalian sleep function with particular reference to man. In A. R. Mayes (Ed.), *Sleep mechanisms and functions in humans and animals* (pp. 262–312). Wokingham, England: Van Nostrand Reinhold.

Horne, J. A. (1983). Interacting functions of mammalian sleep. In I. Tobler & J. Horne (Chairs), *Sleep 1982. 6th European Congress on Sleep Research* (Zurich, 1982) (pp. 130–134). Basel: Karger.

Hoyle, G. (1984). The scope of neuroethology. *Behavioral and Brain Sciences, 7*, 367–412.

Hubel, D. H. (1982). Exploration of the primary visual cortex. *Nature, 299*, 515–524.

Hubel, D. H., & Wiesel, T. N. (1979). Brain mechanisms of vision. *Scientific American, 249*, 150–162.

Hubel, D. H., Wiesel, T. N., & LeVay, S. (1977). Plasticity of ocular dominance columns in the monkey striate cortex. *Philosophical Transactions of the Royal Society of London, 278*, 377–409.

Hubel, D. H., Wiesel, T. N., & Stryker, M. P. (1977). Orientation columns in macaque monkey visual cortex demonstrated by the 2-deoxyglucose autoradiographic technique. *Nature, 269*, 328–330.

Hudspeth, A. J. (1983). The hair cells of the inner ear. *Scientific American, 248*, 54–64.

Hudspeth, A. J. (1985). The cellular basis of hearing: The biophysics of hair cells. *Science, 230*, 745–752.

Hughes, J., Smith, T. W., Kosterlitz, H. W., Fothergill, L. A., Morgan, B. A., & Morris, H. R. (1975). Identification of two related pentapeptides from the brain with potent opiate agonist activity. *Nature, 258*, 577–581.

Hume, K. I., & Mills, J. N. (1977). Rhythms of REM and slow-wave sleep in subjects living on abnormal time schedules. *Waking and Sleeping, 1*, 291–296.

Humphrey, D. R. (1979). On the cortical control of visually directed reaching: Contributions by nonprecentral motor areas. In R. E. Talbot & D. R. Humphrey (Eds.), *Posture and movement* (pp. 51–112). New York: Raven Press.

Huppert, F. A., & Piercy, M. (1978). Dissociation between learning and remembering in organic amnesia. *Nature, 275*, 317–318.

Huppert, F. A., & Piercy, M. (1979). Normal and abnormal forgetting in organic amnesia: Effect of locus of lesion. *Cortex, 15*, 385–390.

Hustvedt, B. E., & Løvø, A. (1972). Correlation between hyperinsulinemia and hyperphagia in rats with ventromedial hypothalamic lesions. *Acta Physiologica Scandinavica, 84*, 29–33.

Iacono, W. G. (1985). Psychophysiologic markers in psychopathology: A review. *Canadian Psychology, 26*, 96–111.

Iacono, W. G., & Koenig, W. G. R. (1983). Features that distinguish the smooth-pursuit eye-tracking performance of schizophrenic, affective-disorder, and normal individuals. *Journal of Abnormal Psychology, 92*, 29–41.

Iacono, W. G., & Patrick, C. J. (1987). What psychologists should know about lie detection. In I. B. Weiner & A. K. Hess (Eds.), *Handbook of forensic psychology* (pp. 460–489). New York: John Wiley & Sons.

Ibuka, N., Inouye, S. I., & Kawamura, H. (1977). Analysis of sleep-wakefulness rhythms in male rats after suprachiasmatic nucleus lesions and ocular enucleation. *Brain Research, 122*, 33–47.

Ichikawa, S., & Fujii, Y. (1982). Effect of prenatal androgen treatment on maternal behavior in the female rat. *Hormones and Behavior, 16*, 224–233.

Inglis, J., & Lawson, J. S. (1982). A meta-analysis of sex-differences in the effects of unilateral brain damage on intelligence test results. *Canadian Journal of Psychology, 36*, 670–683.

Ingvar, D. H. (1983). Serial aspects of language and speech related to prefrontal cortical activity. *Human Neurobiology, 2*, 177–189.

Inouye, S. I., & Kawamura, H. (1982). Characteristics of a circadian pacemaker in the suprachiasmatic nucleus. *Journal of Comparative Psychology, 146*, 153–160.

Ironton, R., Brown, M. C., & Holland, R. L. (1978). Stimuli to intramuscular nerve growth. *Brain Research, 156,* 351–354.

Iversen, L. L. (1987). Neurotransmitters. In G. Adelman (Ed.), *Encyclopedia of neuroscience* (pp. 856–858). Boston: Birkhauser.

Iversen, L. L., Iversen, S. D., & Snyder, S. H. (1982). *Handbook of psychopharmacology,* Vol. 17. New York: Plenum Press.

Iversen, S. D., & Koob, G. F. (1977). Behavioral implications of dopaminergic neurons in the mesolimbic system. In E. Costa & G. L. Gessa (Eds.), *Nonstriatal dopaminergic neurons: Advances in biochemical psychopharmacology* (pp. 209–214). New York: Raven.

Jackson, J. H. (1884). The Croonian Lectures. On evolution and dissolution of the nervous system. *British Medical Journal, 1,* 591–593, 660–663, 703–707.

Jacobs, W., Blackburn, J. R., Buttrick, M., Harpur, T. J., Kennedy, D., Mana, M. J. MacDonald, M. A., McPherson, L. M., Paul, D., & Pfaus, J. G. (1988). Observations. *Psychobiology, 16,* 3–9.

Jacobson, M. (1968). Development of neuronal specificity in retinal ganglion cells of *Xenopus. Developmental Biology, 17,* 202–218.

Jacobson, M., & Hunt, R. K. (1973). The origins of nerve-cell specificity. *Scientific American, 228,* 26–35.

Jacoby, L. L. (1982). Knowing and remembering: Some parallels in the behavior of Korsakoff patients and normals. In L. S. Cermack (Ed.), *Human memory and amnesia.* Hillsdale, NJ: Erlbaum.

Jacoby, L. L. (1984). Incidental versus intentional retrieval: Remembering and awareness as separate issues. In L. R. Squire & N. Butters (Eds.), *Neuropsychology of memory* (pp. 145–156). New York: Guilford Press.

Jaeger, C. B., & Lund, R. D. (1981). Transplantation of embryonic occipital cortex to the brain of newborn rats: A Golgi study of mature and developing transplants. *Journal of Comparative Neurology, 200,* 213–230.

Janosky, D. S., Huey, L., & Storms, L. (1977). Psychologic test responses and methylphenidate. In E. H. Ellinwood, Jr. & M. M. Kilbey (Eds.), *Cocaine and other stimulants* (pp. 675–688). New York: Plenum Press.

Janowitz, H. D., & Grossman, M. I. (1949). Some factors affecting the food intake of normal dogs and dogs with esophagostomy and gastric fistulae. *American Journal of Physiology, 159,* 143–148.

Jenner, P., Rose, S., Boyce, S., Kelly, E., Kilpatrick, G., Rupniak, N. M. J., Briggs, R., & Marsden, C. D. (1986). Induction of parkinsonism in the common marmoset by administration of 1-methly-4-phenyl-1,2,3,6-tetrahydropyridine. In S. Fahn, C. O. Marsden, P. Jenner, & P. Teychenne (Eds.), *Recent developments in Parkinson's disease* (pp. 137–146). New York: Raven Press.

Jewett, D. L., Romano, M. N., & Williston, J. S. (1970). Human auditory evoked potentials: Possible brain stem components detected on the scalp. *Science, 167,* 1517–1518.

Jewett, D. L., & Williston, J. S. (1971). Auditory-evoked far fields averaged from the scalp of humans. *Brain, 94,* 681–696.

Johnson, P. (1984). The acquisition of skill. In M. M. Smith & A. M. Wing (Eds.), *The psychology of human movement* (pp. 215–240). London: Academic Press.

Jones, H. W., & Park, I. J. (1971). A classification of special problems in sex differentation. In D. Bergsma (Ed.) The clinical delineation of birth defects: Part X: The endocrine system (pp. 113–121). Baltimore: The Williams and Wilkins Company.

Jones, H. S., & Oswald, I. (1966). Two cases of healthy insomnia. *Electroencephalography and Clinical Neurophysiology, 24,* 378–380.

Jones, R. T. (1987). Tobacco dependence. In H. Y. Meltzer (Ed.), *Psychopharmacology: The third generation of progress* (pp. 1589–1596). New York: Raven Press.

Jordan, H. A. (1969). Voluntary intragastric feeding: Oral and gastric contributions of food intake and hunger in man. *Journal of Comparative and Physiological Psychology, 68,* 498–506.

Joseph, M. H., Fillenz, M., MacDonald, I, A., & Marsden, C. A. (1984). *Monitoring neurotransmitter release during behavior.* Deerfield Beech, FL: Ellis Horwood Health Sciences Series.

Jost, A. (1972). A new look at the mechanisms controlling sex differentiation in mammals. *Johns Hopkins Medical Journal, 130,* 38–53.

Jouvet, M. (1967). The states of sleep. *Scientific American, 216,* 329–336.

Jouvet, M., & Renault, J. (1966). Insomnie persistante après lésions des noyaux du raphé chez le chat. *Comptes Rendus de la Société de Biologie (Paris), 160,* 1461–1465.

Julesz, B. (1965). Texture and visual perception. *Scientific American, 212,* 182–194.

Julesz, B. (1986). Stereoscopic vision. *Vision Research, 26,* 1601–1612.

Julien, R. M. (1981). *A primer of drug action.* San Francisco: W. H. Freeman.

Kass, J. H., Nelson, R. J., Sur, M., & Merzenich, M. M. (1981). Organization of somatosensory cortex in primates. In F. O. Schmitt, F. G. Worden, G. Adelman, & S. G. Dennis (Eds.), *The organization of the cerebral cortex* (pp. 237–261). Cambridge, MA: MIT Press.

Kalat, J. W. (1985). *Introduction to psychology.* Belmont, CA: Wadsworth Publishing Company.

Kallman, F. J. (1946). The genetic theory of schizophrenia: An analysis of 691 schizophrenic twin index families. *American Journal of Psychiatry, 103,* 309–322.

Kandel, E. R. (1985). Cellular mechanisms of learning and the biological basis of individuality. In E. R. Kandel & J. H. Schwartz (Eds.), *Principles of neural science* (2nd ed.) (pp. 816–833). New York: Elsevier.

Kandel, E. R., & Schwartz, J. H. (Eds.) (1985). *Principles of neural science.* New York: Elsevier.

Kandel, E. R., & Siegelbaum, S. (1985). In E. R. Kandel and J. H. Schwartz (Eds.), *Principles of neural science* (2nd ed.) (pp. 89–107). New York: Elsevier.

Kapp, B. S., Schwaber, J. S., & Driscoll, P. A. (1985). Frontal cortex projections to the amygdaloid central nucleus in the rabbit. *Neuroscience, 15,* 327–346.

Karacan, I., Goodenough, D. R., Shapiro, A., & Starker, S. (1966). Erection cycle during sleep in relation to dream anxiety. *Archives of General Psychiatry, 15,* 183–189.

Karacan, I., Williams, R. L., Finley, W. W., & Hursch, C. J. (1970). The effects of naps on nocturnal sleep: Influence on the need for stage-1 REM and stage-4 sleep. *Biological Psychiatry, 2,* 391–399.

Karadžić, V. T. (1973). Physiological changes resulting from total sleep deprivation. *1st European Congress on Sleep Research* (Basel, 1972), (pp. 165–174). Basel: Karger.

Karsch, F. J. (1987). Central actions of ovarian steroids in the feedback regulation of pulsatile secretion of luteinizing hormone. *Annual Review of Physiology, 49,* 365–382.

Keesey, R. E., & Powley, T. L. (1975). Hypothalamic regulation of body weight. *American Scientist, 63,* 558–635.

Keesey, R. E., & Powley, T. L. (1986). The regulation of body weight. *Annual Review of Psychology, 37,* 109–133.

Kelso, S. R., & Brown, T. H. (1986). Differential conditioning of associative synaptic enhancements in hippocampal brain slices. *Science, 232,* 85–87.

Kendler, K. S. (1987). The genetics of schizophrenia: A current perspective. In H. Y. Meltzer (Ed.), *Psychopharmacology: The third generation of progress* (pp. 705–713). New York: Raven Press.

Kendler, K. S., & Gruenberg, A. M. (1984). An independent analysis of the Danish adoption study of schizophrenia: VI. The relationship between psychiatric disorders as defined by DSM-III in the relatives and adoptees. *Archives of General Psychiatry, 41,* 555–564.

Kendrick, K. M., & Baldwin, B. A. (1987). Cells in temporal cortex of conscious sheep can respond preferentially to the sight of faces. *Science, 236,* 448–450.

Kennedy, G. C. (1953). The role of depot fat in the hypothalamic control of food intake in the rat. *Proceedings of the Royal Society of London, 140,* 578–592.

Kephalas, T. A., Kiburis, J., Michael, C. M., Miras, C. J., & Papadakis, D. P. (1976). Some aspects of cannabis smoke chemistry. In G. G. Nahas (Ed.), *Marihuana: Chemistry, biochemistry, and cellular effects* (pp. 39–49). New York: Springer-Verlag.

Kety, S. S. (1979). Disorders of the human brain. *Scientific American, 241,* 202–214.

Keynes, R. D. (1958). The nerve impulse and the squid. *Scientific American, 199,* 83–90.

Keynes, R. J. (1987). Schwann cells during neural development and regeneration: Leaders or followers? *Trends in Neuroscience, 10,* 137–138.

Kimura, D. (1961). Some effects of temporal-lobe damage on auditory perception. *Canadian Journal of Psychology, 15,* 156–165.

Kimura, D. (1964). Left-right differences in the perception of melodies. *Quarterly Journal of Experimental Psychology, 16,* 355–358.

Kimura, D. (1973). The asymmetry of the human brain. *Scientific American, 228,* 70–78.

Kimura, D. (1977). Acquisition of a motor skill after left-hemisphere damage. *Brain, 100,* 527–542.

Kimura, D. (1979). Neuromotor mechanisms in the evolution of human communication. In H. E. Steklis & M. J. Raleigh (Eds.), *Neurobiology of social communication in primates* (pp. 197–219). New York: Academic Press.

Kimura, D., & Archibald, Y. (1974). Motor functions of the left hemisphere. *Brain, 97,* 337–350.

King, H. E. (1961). Psychological effects of excitation in the limbic system. In D. E. Sheer (Ed.), *Electrical stimulation of the brain* (pp. 477–486). Austin, TX: University of Texas Press.

King, M. B., & Hoebel, B. G. (1968). Killing elicited by brain stimulation in rats. *Communications in Behavioral Biology, Part A, 2,* 173–177.

Klein, M., & Kandel, E. R. (1978). Presynaptic modulation of voltage-dependent Ca^{2+} current: Mechanism for behavioral sensitization in *Aplysia californica. Proceedings of the National Academy of Sciences (USA), 75,* 3512–3516.

Klein, M., Shapiro, E., & Kandel, E. R. (1980). Synaptic plasticity and the modulation of the Ca^{2+} current. *Journal of Experimental Biology, 89,* 117–157.

Kleitman, N. (1922). Studies on the visceral sensory nervous system: XI. The action of cocaine and aconitine on the pulmonary vagus in the frog and in the turtle. *American Journal of Physiology, 60,* 203–218.

Kleitman, N. (1960). Patterns of dreaming. *Scientific American, 203,* 337–343.

Kleitman, N. (1963). *Sleep and wakefulness.* Chicago: University of Chicago.

Kling, A. (1972). Effects of amygdalectomy on social-affective behavior in non-human primates. In B. E. Eleftherlou (Ed.), *The neurobiology of the amygdala* (pp. 536–551). New York: Plenum Press.

Kolb, B., & Milner, B. (1981). Performance of complex arm and facial movements after focal brain lesions. *Neuropsychologia, 19,* 491–503.

Kolb, B., & Whishaw, I. Q. (1989). *Fundamentals of human neuropsychology* (3rd edition). New York: Freeman.

Kollar, E. J., & Fisher, C. (1980). Tooth induction in chick epithelium: Expression of quiescent genes for enamel synthesis. *Science, 207,* 993–995.

Kolodny, R. C., Masters, W. H., Kolodner, R. M., & Toro, G. (1974). Depression of plasma testosterone levels after chronic intensive marihuana use. *New England Journal of Medicine, 290,* 872–874.

Koob, G. F., & Bloom, F. E. (1988). Cellular and molecular mechanisms of drug dependence. *Science, 242,* 715–723.

Koob, G. F., Pettit, H. O., Ettenberg, A., & Bloom, F. E. (1984). Effects of opiate antagonists and their quaternary derivatives on heroin self-administration in the rat. *Journal of Pharmacology and Experimental Therapeutics, 229,* 481–487.

Koob, G. F., Vaccarino, F., Amalric, M., & Bloom, F. E. (1987). Positive reinforcement properties of drugs: Search for neural

substrates. In J. Engel & L. Oreland (Eds.), *Brain reward systems and abuse* (pp. 35–50). New York: Raven Press.

Koolhaas, J. M., Schuurman, T., & Wiepkema, P. R. (1980). The organization of intraspecific agonistic behaviour in the rat. *Progress in Neurobiology, 15,* 247–268.

Koopmans, H. S. (1981). The role of the gastrointestinal tract in the satiation of hunger. In L. A. Cioffi, W. B. T. James, & T. B. Van Italie (Eds.), *The body weight regulatory system: Normal and disturbed mechanisms* (pp. 45–55). New York: Raven Press.

Kornetsky, C. (1977). Animal models: Promises and problems. In I. Hanin & E. Usdin (Eds.), *Animal models in psychiatry and neurology.* Oxford: Pergamon Press.

Kornhuber, H. H. (1974). Cerebral cortex, cerebellum, and basal ganglia: An introduction to their motor functions. In F. O. Schmitt & F. G. Worden (Eds.), *The neurosciences: The third study program* (pp. 267–280). Cambridge, MA: MIT Press.

Kosambi, D. D. (1967). Living prehistory in India. *Scientific American, 216,* 105–114.

Kosslyn, S. M. (1988). Aspects of a cognitive neuroscience of mental imagery. *Science, 240,* 1621–1626.

Kowalaska, D. M., Bachevelier, J., & Mishkin, M. (1984). Inferior prefrontal cortex and recognition memory. *Society for Neuroscience Abstracts, 10,* 385.

Kozlowski, S., & Drzewiecki, K. (1973). The role of osmoreception in portal circulation in control of water intake in dogs. *Acta Physiologica Polonica, 24,* 325–330.

Kraemer, H. C., Becker, H. B., Brodie, H. K. H., Doering, C. H., Moos, R. H., & Hamburg, D. A. (1976). Orgasmic frequency and plasma testosterone levels in normal human males. *Archives of Sexual Behavior, 5,* 125–132.

Kraly, F. S., & Gibbs, J. (1980). Vagotomy fails to block the satiating effect of food in the stomach. *Physiology & Behavior, 24,* 1007–1010.

Kraly, F. S., Gibbs, J., & Smith, G. P. (1975). Disordered drinking after abdominal vagotomy in rats. *Nature, 258,* 226–228.

Kraly, F. S., & Smith, G. P. (1978). Combined pregastric and gastric stimulation by foods is sufficient for normal meal size. *Physiology & Behavior, 21,* 405–408.

Krieger, D. T., & Hughes, J. C. (1980). *Neuroendocrinology.* Sunderland, MA: Sinauer.

Krueger, J. M. (1985). Endogenous sleep factors. In A. Wauquier, J. M. Gaillard, J. M. Monti, & M. Radulovacki (Eds.), *Sleep: Neurotransmitters and neuromodulators* (pp. 319–331). New York: Raven Press.

Krueger, J. M., Pappenheimer, J. R., & Karnovsky, M. L. (1982). The composition of sleep-promoting factor isolated from human urine. *Journal of Biological Chemistry, 257,* 1664–1669.

Kruk, M. R., Meelis, W., Van der Poel, A. M., & Mos, J. (1981). Electrical stimulation as a tool to trace physiological properties of the hypothalamic network in aggression. In P. F. Brain & D. Benton (Eds.), *The biology of aggression* (pp. 383–395). Alphen ann den Rijn: Sijthoff & Noordhoff.

Kruk, M. R., Van der Laan, C. E., Meelis, W., Phillips, R. E., Mos, J., & van der Poel, A. M. (1984). Brain-stimulation induced agonistic behaviour: A novel paradigm in ethopharmacological aggression research. In K. A. Miczek, M. R. Kruk, & B. Oliver (Eds.), *Progress in clinical and biological research,* (Vol. 167, pp. 157–177). New York: Alan R. Liss.

Kuffler, S. W. (1953). Discharge patterns and functional organization of mammalian retina. *Journal of Neurophysiology, 16,* 37–68.

Kuffler, S. W., Nicholls, J. G., & Martin, A. R. (1984). *From neuron to brain: A cellular approach to the function of the nervous system.* Sunderland, MA: Sinauer Associates, Inc.

Kuwada, J. Y. (1986). Cell recognition by neuronal growth cones in a simple vertebrate embryo. *Science, 233,* 740–746.

Laguzzi, R., & Adrien, J. (1980). Effets des antagonistes de la serotonine sur le cycle veille-sommeil au rat. *Journal de Physiologie et Pathologie, 76,* 20A.

Lamb, A. H. (1984). Motoneuron death in the embryo. *Critical Reviews in Clinical Neurobiology, 1,* 141–173.

Lance-Jones, C., & Landmesser, L. (1980). Motoneuron projection patterns in the chick hind limb following early partial spinal cord reversals. *Journal of Physiology, 302*, 559–580.

Lance-Jones, C., & Landmesser, L. (1984). Pathway selection by embryonic chick motoneurons in an experimentally altered environment. *Proceedings of the Royal Society of London [B], 214*, 19–52.

Land, E. H. (1977). The retinex theory of color vision. *Scientific American, 237*, 108–128.

Landmesser, L. (1978). The development of motor projection patterns in the chick hind limb. *Journal of Physiology, 284*, 391–414.

Langston, J. W. (1985). MPTP and Parkinson's disease. *Trends in Neuroscience, 8*, 79–83.

Langston, J. W. (1986). MPTP-induced parkinsonism: How good a model is it? In S. Fahn, C. P. Marsden, P. Jenner, & P. Teychenne (Eds.), *Recent developments in Parkinson's disease* (pp. 119–126). New York: Raven Press.

Langston, J. W., Forna, L. S., Robert, C. S., & Irwin, I. (1984). Selective nigral toxicity after systemic administration of 1-methyl-4-phenyl-1,2,3,6-tetrahydropyridine (MPTP) in the squirrel monkey. *Brain Research, 292*, 390–394.

Lashley, K. S. (1941). Patterns of cerebral integration indicated by the scotomas of migraine. *Archives of Neurology and Psychiatry, 46*, 331–339.

Latimer, D., & Goldberg, J. (1981). *Flowers in the blood.* New York: Franklin Watts.

Lawrence, D. G., & Kuypers, H. G. J. M. (1968). The functional organization of the motor system in the monkey: I. The effects of bilateral pyramidal lesions. *Brain, 91*, 1–14.

Lawrence, D. G., & Kuypers, H. G. J. M. (1968). The functional organization of the motor system in the monkey: II. The effects of lesions of the descending brain-stem pathways. *Brain, 91*, 15–36.

Lê, A. D., Poulos, C. X., & Cappell, H. (1979). Conditioned tolerance to the hypothermic effects of ethyl alcohol. *Science, 206*, 1109–1110.

Le Douarin, N. M. (1982). *The neural crest.* New York: Cambridge University Press.

Leech, C. K., & McIntyre, D. C. (1976). Kindling rates in inbred mice: An analog to learning? *Behavioral Biology, 16*, 439–452.

Leibowitz, S. F., Hammer, N. J., & Chang, K. (1981). Hypothalamic paraventricular nucleus lesions produce overeating and obesity in the rat. *Physiology & Behavior, 27*, 1031–1040.

Leinonen, L., Hyvärinen, J., Nyman, G., & Linnankoski, I. (1979). Functional properties of neurons in lateral part of associative area 7 in awake monkeys. *Experimental Brain Research, 34*, 299–320.

Leinonen, L., & Nyman, G. (1979). Functional properties of cells in anterolateral part of area 7 associative face area of awake monkeys. *Experimental Brain Research, 34*, 321–333.

LeMagnen, J. (1969). Peripheral and systemic actions of food in the caloric regulation of intake. *Annals of the New York Academy of Science, 157*, 1126–1157.

LeMagnen, J. (1981). The metabolic basis of dual periodicity of feeding in rats. *Behavioral and Brain Sciences, 4*, 561–607.

Lemberger, L., & Rowe, H. (1975). Clinical pharmacology of nabilone, a cannabinol derivative. *Clinical Pharmacology and Therapeutics, 18*, 720–726.

Lennox, W. G. (1960). *Epilepsy and related disorders.* Boston: Little, Brown and Co.

Lepkovsky, S. (1977). The role of the chemical senses in nutrition. In M. R. Kare & O. Maller (Eds.), *The chemical senses and nutrition* (pp. 413–428). New York: Academic Press.

Lester, G. L. L., & Gorzalka, B. B. (1988). Effect of novel and familiar mating partners on the duration of sexual receptivity in the female hamster. *Behavioral and Neural Biology, 49*, 398–405.

LeVay, S., Hubel, D. H., & Wiesel, T. N. (1975). The pattern of ocular dominance columns in Macaque visual cortex revealed by a reduced silver stain. *Journal of Comparative Neurology, 159*, 559–576.

LeVay, S., Stryker, M. P., & Shatz, C. J. (1978). Ocular dominance columns and their development in layer IV of the cat's visual cortex: A quantitative study. *Journal of Comparative Neurology, 179*, 223–244.

Levi-Montalcini, R. (1952). Effects of mouse tumor transplantation on the nervous system. *Annals of the New York Academy of Science, 55*, 330–344.

Levi-Montalcini, R. (1975). NGF: An uncharted route. In F. G. Worden, J. P. Swazey, & G. Adelman (Eds.), *The neurosciences: Paths of discovery* (pp. 245–265). Cambridge, MA: MIT Press.

Levin, H. S., Papanicolaou, A., & Eisenberg, H. M. (1984). Observations on amnesia after non-missile head injury. In L. R. Squire & N. Butters (Eds.), *Neuropsychology of memory* (pp. 247–257). New York: Guilford Press.

Levine, D. G. (1974). "Needle freaks": Compulsive self-injection by drug users. *American Journal of Psychiatry, 131*, 297–301.

Levine, D. N. (1982). Visual agnosia in monkey and in man. In D. J. Ingle, M. A. Goodale, & R. J. W. Mansfield (Eds.), *Analysis of visual behavior* (pp. 629–670). Cambridge, MA: MIT Press.

Levy, J. (1969). Possible basis for the evolution of lateral specialization of the human brain. *Nature, 224*, 614–615.

Levy, J., Trevarthen, C., & Sperry, R. W. (1972). Perception of bilateral chimeric figures following hemispheric deconnection. *Brain, 95*, 61–78.

Liebling, D. S., Eisner, J. D., Gibbs, J., & Smith, G. P. (1975). Intestinal satiety in rats. *Journal of Comparative and Physiological Psychology, 89*, 955–965.

Liebman, J. M., & Cooper, S. J. (Eds.). (1989). *The neuropharmacological basis of reward.* Oxford: Clarendon Press.

Liepmann, H. (1914). Bemerkungen zu v. Monakows Kapitel "Die Lokalisation der Apraxie". *Monatsschr. Psychiatr. Neurol., 35*, 490–516.

Lincoln, J. S., McCormick, D. A., & Thompson, R. F. (1982). Ipsilateral lesions prevent learning of the classically conditioned nictitating membrane eyelid response. *Brain Research, 242*, 190–193.

Lindauer, M. (1961). *Communication among social bees.* Cambridge, MA: Harvard University Press.

Linden, W., & Estrin, R. (1988). Computerized cardiovascular monitoring: Method and data. *Psychophysiology, 25*, 227–234.

Lindsay, P. H., & Norman, D. A. (1977). *Human information processing* (2nd ed.). New York: Academic Press.

Lindsey, D. B., Bowden, J., & Magoun, H. W. (1949). Effect upon the EEG of acute injury to the brain stem activating system. *Electroencephalography and Clinical Neurophysiology, 1*, 475–486.

Lipton, J. M. (1968). Effects of preoptic lesions on heat-escape responding and colonic temperature in the rat. *Physiology & Behavior, 3*, 165–169.

Lipton, J. M. (1987). Temperature regulation. In G. Adelman (Ed.), *Encyclopedia of neuroscience Vol. II* (pp. 1193–1194). Boston: Birkhauser.

Lipton, J. M., & Trzcinka, G. P. (1976). Persistence of febrile response to pyrogens after PO/AH lesions in squirrel monkeys. *American Journal of Physiology, 231*, 1638–1648.

Livingstone, M. S., & Hubel, D. H. (1984). Anatomy and physiology of a color system in the primate visual cortex. *Journal of Neuroscience, 4*, 309–356.

Llinas, R. R. (1982). Calcium in synaptic transmission. *Scientific American, 247*, 56–65.

Lloyd, E. L. (1986). "Near miss" sudden infant death and hypothermia. *British Medical Journal (Clinical Researches), 293*, 1241–1242.

Loewi, O. (1921). Ueber die Beziehungen zwischen Herzmittel—und physiologischer Kationenwirkung. IV. Ueber Nichtelektrolytwirkung auf das Herz. *Arch f. d. ges. exper. Med., 1921*, 263–268.

Loftus, E. F., & Palmer, J. C. (1974). Reconstruction of automobile destruction: An example of the interaction between language and memory. *Journal of Verbal Learning and Verbal Behavior, 13*, 585–589.

Lømo, T. (1966). Frequency potentiation of excitatory synaptic activity in the dentate area of the hippocampal formation. *Acta Physiologica Scandinavica, 68,* (Suppl. 227), 128.

Loomis, A. L., Harvey, E. N., & Hobart, G. (1936). Electrical potentials of the human brain. *Journal of Experimental Psychology, 19,* 249–279.

Losonczy, M. F., Davidson, M., & Davis, K. L. (1987). The dopamine hypothesis of schizophrenia. In H. Y. Meltzer (Ed.), *Psychopharmacology: The third generation of progress* (pp. 715–726). New York: Raven Press.

Lucas, F., Bellisle, F., & Di Maio, A. (1987). Spontaneous insulin fluctuations and the preabsorptive insulin response to food ingestion in humans. *Physiology & Behavior, 40,* 631–636.

Ludwig, A. M., & Wikler, A. (1974). "Craving" and relapse to drink. *Quarterly Journal of Studies on Alcohol, 35,* 108–130.

Lund, R. D., & Harvey, A. R. (1981). Transplantation of tectal tissue in rats: I. Organization of transplants and pattern of distribution of host afferents within them. *Journal of Comparative Neurology, 201,* 191–209.

Lykken, D. T. (1959). The GSR in the detection of guilt. *Journal of Applied Psychology, 43,* 385–388.

Lynch, G., Halpain, S., & Baudry, M. (1982). The biochemistry of memory: A new and specific hypothesis. *Science, 224,* 1057–1063.

Lynch, J. C., Mountcastle, V. B., Talbot, W. H., & Yin, T. C. T. (1977). Parietal lobe mechanisms for directed visual attention. *Journal of Neurophysiology, 40,* 362–389.

MacDonald, R. M., Ingelfinger, F. J., & Belding, H. W. (1947). Late effects of total gastrectomy in man. *New England Journal of Medicine, 237,* 887–896.

Mackay, A. V. P., Iversen, L. L., Rossor, M., Spokes, E., Bird, E., Arregui, A., Creese, I., & Snyder, S. H. (1982). Increased brain dopamine and dopamine receptors in schizophrenia. *Archives of General Psychiatry, 39,* 991–997.

MacLusky, N. J., & Naftolin, F. (1981). Sexual differentiation of the central nervous system. *Science, 211,* 1294–1302.

MacNichol, E. F., Jr. (1964). Three-pigment color vision. *Scientific American, 211,* 48–67.

Maddison, S., Wood, R. J., Rolls, E. T., Rolls, B. J., & Gibbs, J. (1980). Drinking in the rhesus monkey: Peripheral factors. *Journal of Physiology, 272,* 365–374.

Madrazo, I., Drucker-Colin, R., Diaz, V., Martinez-Mata, J., Torres, C., & Becerril, J. J. (1987). Open microsurgical autograft of adrenal medulla to the right caudate nucleus in two patients with intractable Parkinson's disease. *New England Journal of Medicine, 316,* 831–834.

Magni, F., Moruzzi, G., Rossi, G. F., & Zanchetti, A. (1957). EEG arousal following inactivation of the lower brain stem by selective injection of barbiturate into the vertebral circulation. *Archives Italiennes de Biologie, 95,* 33–46.

Mahut, H., Moss, M., & Zola-Morgan, S. (1981). Retention deficits after combined amygdalo-hippocampal and selective hippocampal resections in the monkey. *Neuropsychologia, 19,* 201–225.

Malmo, R. B., & Malmo, H. P. (1979). Responses of lateral preoptic neurons in the rat to hypertonic sucrose and NaCl. *Electroencephalography and Clinical Neurophysiology, 46,* 401–408.

Malsbury, C. W., Kow, L. M., & Pfaff, D. W. (1977). Effects of medial hypothalamic lesions on the lordosis response and other behaviors in female golden hamsters. *Physiology & Behavior, 19,* 223–237.

Mansfield, J. G., & Cunningham, C. L. (1980). Conditioning and extinction of tolerance to the hypothermic effects of ethanol in rats. *Journal of Comparative and Physiological Psychology, 94,* 962–969.

Marchbanks, R. M. (1982). Biochemistry of Alzheimer's dementia. *Journal of Neurochemistry, 39,* 9–15.

Marin, O. S. M., Schwartz, M. F., & Saffran, E. M. (1979). Origins and distribution of language. In M. I. Gazzaniga (Ed.), *Handbook of behavioral neurobiology: Vol. 2. Neuropsychology* (pp. 179–213). New York: Plenum Press.

Mark, V. H., & Ervin, F. R. (1970). *Violence and the brain.* New York: Harper & Row, Publ.

Mark, V. H., Ervin, F. R., & Yakolev, P. I. (1962). The treatment of pain by stereotaxic methods. *1st International Symposium on Stereoencephalotomy (Philadelphia, 1961), Confinia Neurologica, 22,* 238–245.

Marks, W. B., Dobelle, W. H., & MacNichol, E. F. (1964). Visual pigments of single primate cones. *Science, 143,* 1181–1183.

Marler, P. (1984). Song learning: Innate species differences in the learning process. In P. Marler & H. S. Terrace (Eds.), *The biology of learning* (pp. 289–309). New York: Springer-Verlag.

Marques, D. M., Malsbury, C. W., & Daood, J. (1979). Hypothalamic knife cuts dissociate maternal behaviors, sexual receptivity, and estrous cyclicity in female hamsters. *Physiology & Behavior, 23,* 347–355.

Marshall, F. H. A. (1937). On the changeover in the oestrous cycle in animals after transference across the equator, with further observations on the incidence of the breeding seasons and the factors controlling sexual periodicity. *Proceedings of the Royal Society of London, (B), 122,* 413–428.

Marshall, N. B., Barnett, R. J., & Mayer, J. (1955). Hypothalamic lesions in gold thioglucose injected mice. *Proceedings of the Society for Experimental Biology and Medicine, 90,* 240–244.

Marshall, W. A., & Tanner, J. M. (1969). Growth and physiological development during adolescence. *Annual Review of Medicine, 19,* 283–301.

Marslen-Wilson, W. D., & Teuber, H. L. (1975). Memory for remote events in anterograde amnesia: Recognition of public figures from newsphotographs. *Neuropsychologia, 13,* 353–364.

Martin, B. J. (1986). Sleep deprivation and exercise. In K. B. Pandolf (Ed.), *Exercise and Sport Sciences Reviews* (pp. 213–229). New York: Macmillan Pub. Co.

Martin, J. B. (1987). Molecular genetics: Applications to the clinical neurosciences. *Science, 238,* 765–772.

Martin, J. E., Tyrey, L., Everett, J. W., & Fellows, R. E. (1974). Variation in responsiveness to synthetic LH-releasing factor (LRF) in proestrous and diestrous-3 rats. *Endocrinology, 94,* 556–562.

Martin, J. H. (1985). Receptor physiology and submodality coding in the somatic sensory system. In E. R. Kandel & J. H. Schwartz (Eds.), *Principles of neuroscience* (pp. 287–300). New York: Elsevier.

Martin, R. L., Roberts, W. V., & Clayton, P. J. (1980). Psychiatric status after a one-year prospective follow-up. *JAMA, 244,* 350–353.

Mattson, S. N., Barron, S., & Riley, E. P. (1988). The behavioral effects of prenatal alcohol exposure. In K. Kuriyama, A. Takada, & H. Ishii (Eds.), *Biomedical and social aspects of alcohol and alcoholism* (pp. 851–853). Tokyo: Elsevier.

Mayer, D. J., & Liebeskind, J. C. (1974). Pain reduction by focal electrical stimulation of the brain: An anatomical and behavioral analysis. *Brain Research, 68,* 79–93.

Mayer, J. (1955). Regulation of energy intake and the body weight: The glucostatic theory and the lipostatic hypothesis. *Proceedings of the New York Academy of Sciences, 63,* 15–43.

Mayer, J., & Marshall, N. B. (1956). Specificity of gold thioglucose for ventromedial hypothalamic lesions and hyperphagia. *Nature, 178,* 1399–1400.

Mazzocchi, F., & Vignolo, L. A. (1979). Localisation of lesions in aphasia: Clinical-CT scan correlations in stroke patients. *Cortex, 15,* 627–654.

McAuliffe, W. E., Feldman, B., Friedman, R., Launer, E., Magnuson, E., Mahoney, C., Santangelo, S., Ward, W., & Weiss, R. (1986). Explaining relapse to opiate addiction following successful completion of treatment. In F. M. Tims & C. G. Leukefield (Eds.), *Relapse and recovery in drug abuse: National Institute on Drug Abuse Research Monograph Series* (Vol. 72, pp. 136–156). Rockville, MA.

McBurney, D. H. (1986). Taste, smell, and flavor terminology: Taking the confusion out of fusion. In H. Meiselman & R. S. Rivlin (Eds.), *Clinical measurements of taste and smell* (pp. 117–125). New York: Macmillan Publishing Co.

McClintock, M. K. (1971). Menstruation synchrony and suppression. *Nature, 229,* 244–245.

McClintock, M. K. (1984). Group mating in the domestic rat as a context for sexual selection: Consequences for the analysis of sexual behavior and neuroendocrine responses. In J. S. Rosenblatt, C. Beer, M. C. Busnel, & P. C. Slater (Eds.), *Advances in the study of behavior*, (Vol. 14, pp. 2–50). New York: Academic Press, Inc.

McCormick, D. A., & Thompson, R. F. (1984). Neuronal responses of the rabbit cerebellum during acquisition and performance of a classically conditioned nictitating membrane-eyelid response. *Journal of Neuroscience, 4,* 2811–2822.

McDonald, W. I. (1984). Multiple sclerosis: Epidemiology and HLA associations. *Annals of the New York Academy of Sciences, 436,* 109–117.

McEwen, B. S. (1981). Neural gonadal steroid actions. *Science, 211,* 1303–1311.

McEwen, B. S., Davis, P. G., Parsons, B., & Pfaff, D. W. (1979). The brain as a target for steroid hormone action. *Annual Reviews in Neuroscience, 2,* 65–112.

McEwen, B. S., Lieberburg, I., Chaptal, C., & Krey, L. C. (1977). Aromatization: Important for sexual differentiation of the neonatal rat brain. *Hormones and Behavior, 9,* 249–263.

McFarland, H. F., Greenstein, J., McFarlin, D. E., Eldridge, R., Xu, X. H., & Krebs, H. (1984). Family and twin studies in multiple sclerosis. *Annals of the New York Academy of Sciences, 436,* 118–124.

McGinty, D. J., & Sterman, M. B. (1968). Sleep suppression after basal forebrain lesions in the cat. *Science, 160,* 1253–1255.

McGlone, J. (1977). Sex differences in the cerebral organization of verbal functions in patients with unilateral brain lesions. *Brain, 100,* 775–793.

McGlone, J. (1980). Sex differences in human brain asymmetry: A critical survey. *Behavioral and Brain Sciences, 3,* 215–263.

McHugh, P. R., & Moran, T. H. (1985). The stomach: A conception of its dynamic role in satiety. In J. M. Sprague & A. N. Epstein (Eds.), *Progress in psychobiology and physiological psychology, 11,* 197–232.

McKim, W. A. (1986). *Drugs and behavior: An introduction to behavioral pharmacology.* Englewood Cliffs, NJ: Prentice-Hall.

McLoon, S. C., & Lund, R. D. (1980). Identification of cells in retinal transplants which project to host visual centers: A horseradish peroxidase study in rats. *Brain Research, 197,* 491–495.

Meadows, J. C. (1974). The anatomical basis of prosopagnosia. *Journal of Neurology, Neurosurgery, and Psychiatry, 37,* 489–501.

Meaney, M. J., & Stewart, J. (1981). Neonatal androgens influence the social play of prepubescent rats. *Hormones and Behavior, 15,* 197–213.

Meddis, R. (1977). *The sleep instinct.* London: Routledge & Kegan Paul.

Mehiel, R., & Bolles, R. C. (1988). Learned flavor preferences based on calories are dependent of initial hedonic value. *Animal Learning & Behavior, 16,* 383–387.

Mello, N. K., & Mendelson, J. H. (1972). Drinking patterns during work-contingent and noncontingent alcohol acquisition. *Psychosomatic Medicine, 34,* 139–165.

Meltzer, H. Y. (Ed.). (1987). *Psychopharmacology: The third generation of progress.* New York: Raven Press.

Melzack, R., & Wall, P. D. (1965). Pain mechanisms: A new theory. *Science, 150,* 971–979.

Melzack, R., & Wall, P. D. (1982). *The challenge of pain.* Harmondsworth, England: Penguin Books.

Mendelson, J. H. (1987). Marijuana. In H. Y. Meltzer (Ed.), *Psychopharmacology: The third generation of progress* (pp. 1565–1571). New York: Raven Press.

Mendelson, S. D., & Gorzalka, B. B. (1987). An improved chamber for the observation and analysis of the sexual behavior of the female rat. *Physiology & Behavior, 39,* 67–71.

Merzenich, M. M., & Kaas, J. H. (1980). Principles of organization of sensory-perceptual systems in mammals. In J. M. Sprague & A. N. Epstein (Eds.), *Progress in psychobiology and physiological psychology, 9,* 1–42.

Merzenich, M. M., Knight, P. L., & Roth, G. L. (1974). Repre-

sentation of cochlea within primary auditory cortex in the cat. *Journal of Endocrinology, 61,* 231–249.

Meyer-Bahlburg, H. F. L. (1981). Androgens and human aggression. In P. F. Brain & D. Benton (Eds.), *The biology of aggression* (pp. 263–290). Alpen ann den Rijn: Sijthoff & Noordhoff.

Michael, C. R. (1978). Color vision mechanisms in monkey striate cortex: Dual-opponent cells with concentric receptive fields. *Journal of Neurophysiology, 41,* 572–588.

Miller, N. E. (1957). Experiments on motivation: Studies combining psychological, physiological, and pharmacological techniques. *Science, 126,* 1271–1278.

Miller, N. E. (1960). Motivational effects of brain stimulation and drugs. *Federation Proceedings, 19,* 846–854.

Miller, N. E. (1969). Learning of visceral and glandular responses. *Science, 163,* 434–445.

Miller, N. E., Bailey, C. J., & Stevenson, J. A. F. (1950). Decreased "hunger" but increased food intake resulting from hypothalamic lesions. *Science, 112,* 256–259.

Milner, A. D., Ockleford, E. M., & Dewar, W. (1977). Visuospatial performance following posterior parietal and lateral frontal lesions in stumptail macaques. *Cortex, 13,* 350–360.

Milner, B. (1962). Laterality effects in audition. In V. B. Mountcastle, (Ed.), *Interhemispheric relations and cerebral dominance.* (pp. 177–195). Baltimore, MA: The Johns Hopkins Press.

Milner, B. (1965). Memory disturbances after bilateral hippocampal lesions. In P. Milner & S. Glickman (Eds.), *Cognitive processes and the brain* (pp. 104–105). Princeton, NJ: D. Van Nostrand Co. Inc.

Milner, B. (1971). Interhemispheric differences in the localization of psychological processes in man. *British Medical Bulletin, 27,* 272–277.

Milner, B. (1974). Hemispheric specialization: Scope and limits. In F. O. Schmitt & F. G. Worden (Eds.), *The neurosciences: Third study program* (pp. 75–89). Cambridge, MA: MIT Press.

Milner, B., Corkin, S., & Teuber, H. L. (1968). Further analysis of the hippocampal amnesic syndrome: 14-year follow-up study of H.M. *Neuropsychologia, 6,* 317–338.

Milner, P. M., & White, N. M. (1987). What is physiological psychology? *Psychobiology, 15,* 2–6.

Milstein, C. (1980). Monoclonal antibodies. *Scientific American, 243,* 66–74.

Mishkin, M. (1957). Effects of small frontal lesions on delayed alternation in monkeys. *Journal of Neurophysiology, 20,* 615–622.

Mishkin, M. (1978). Memory in monkeys severely impaired by combined but not by separate removal of amygdala and hippocampus. *Nature, 273,* 297–298.

Mishkin, M. (1979). Analogous neural models for tactual and visual learning. *Neuropsychologia, 17,* 139–151.

Mishkin, M. (1982). A memory system in the monkey. *Philosophical Transactions of the Royal Society of London [Biol.], 298,* 85–95.

Mishkin, M., & Appenzeller, T. (1987). The anatomy of memory. *Scientific American, 256,* 80–89.

Mishkin, M., & Manning, F. J. (1978). Nonspatial memory after selective prefrontal lesions in monkeys. *Brain Research, 143,* 313–323.

Mistlberger, R., Bergmann, B., & Rechtschaffen, A. (1987). Period-amplitude analysis of rat electroencephalogram: Effects of sleep deprivation and exercise. *Sleep, 10,* 508–522.

Mlinar, E. J., & Goodale, M. A. (1984). Cortical and tectal controls of visual orientation in the gerbil: Evidence for parallel channels. *Experimental Brain Research, 55,* 33–48.

Mohr, J. P. (1976). Broca's area and Broca's aphasia. In H. Whitaker & H. A. Whitaker (Eds.), *Studies in neurolinguistics: Volume 1* (pp. 201–235). New York: Academic Press.

Moll, L., & Kuypers, H. G. J. M. (1977). Premotor cortical ablations in monkeys: Contralateral changes in visually guided reaching behavior. *Science, 198,* 318–319.

Moore, J. G., & Motoki, D. (1979). Gastric secretory and humoral responses to anticipated feeding in five men. *Gastroenterology, 76,* 71–75.

Moore, R. Y. (1982). The suprachiasmatic nucleus and the organization of a circadian system. *Trends in Neuroscience, 5,* 404–407.

Moore, R. Y., & Eichler, V. B. (1972). Loss of a circadian adrenal corticosterone rhythm following suprachiasmatic lesions in the rat. *Brain Research, 42,* 201–206.

Moore, R. Y., & Lenn, N. J. (1972). A retinohypothalamic projection in the rat. *Journal of Comparative Neurology, 146,* 1–14.

Money, J. (1975). Ablatio penis: Normal male infant sex-reassigned as a girl. *Archives of Sexual Behavior, 4,* 65–186.

Money, J. (1987). Sin, sickness, or status? Homosexual gender identity and psychoneuroendocrinology. *American Psychologist, 42,* 384–399.

Money, J., & Ehrhardt, A. A. (1972). *Man & woman boy & girl.* Baltimore: Johns Hopkins University Press.

Monnier, M., Dudler, L., Gaechter, R., Maier, P. F., Tobler, H. J., & Schoenenberger, G. A. (1975). The delta sleep inducing peptide (DSIP): Comparative properties of the original and synthetic nonapeptide. *Experientia, 33,* 548–552.

Mora, F., Rolls, E. T., & Burton, M. J. (1976). Modulation during learning of the responses of neurons in the lateral hypothalamus to the sight of food. *Experimental Neurobiology, 53,* 508–519.

Morgan, C. T., & Morgan, J. D. (1940). Studies in hunger: II. The relation of gastric denervation and dietary sugar to the effect of insulin upon food-intake in the rat. *Journal of Genetic Psychology, 57,* 153–163.

Morgane, P. J., & Panksepp, J. (Eds.). (1980). *Behavioral studies of the hypothalamus.* New York: Marcel Dekker.

Morris, R. G. M. (1981). Spatial localization does not require the presence of local cues. *Learning and Motivation, 12,* 239–260.

Moruzzi, G., & Magoun, H. W. (1949). Brain stem reticular formation and activation of the EEG. *Electroencephalography and Clinical Neurophysiology, 1,* 455–473.

Moscovitch, M. (1982). Multiple disassociations of function in amnesia. In L. S. Cermak (Ed.), *Human memory and amnesia* (pp. 337–370). Hillsdale, NJ: Erlbaum.

Moskowitz, H., Hulbert, S., & McGlothin, W. H. (1976). Marihuana: Effects on simulated driving performance. *Accident Analysis and Prevention, 8,* 45–50.

Motter, B. C., & Mountcastle, V. B. (1981). The functional properties of the light-sensitive neurons of the posterior parietal cortex studied in waking monkeys: Foveal sparing and opponent vector organization. *Journal of Neuroscience, 1,* 3–26.

Mouret, J., Bobillier, P., & Jouvet, M. (1968). Insomnia following parachlorophenylalanin in the rat. *European Journal of Pharmacology, 5,* 17–22.

Mucha, R. F., Van der Kooy, D., O'Shaughnessy, M., & Bucenieks, P. (1982). Drug reinforcement studied by the use of place conditioning in rat. *Brain Research, 243,* 91–105.

Mullaney, D. J., Johnson, L. C., Naitoh, P., Friedman, J. K., & Globus, G. G. (1977). Sleep during and after gradual sleep reduction. *Psychophysiology, 14,* 237–244.

Mumby, D. G., Pinel, J. P. J., & Wood, E. R. (1989). *The effect of hippocampal and amygdalar lesions on nonrecurring-items delayed nonmatching-to-sample in rats.* Paper presented at the Canadian Spring Conference on Behavior and Brain, Banff, Alberta.

Mumby, D. G., Pinel, J. P. J., & Wood, E. R. (1989). A rat model of medial temporal lobe amnesia: Nonrecurring-item delayed nonmatching-to-sample. *Society for Neuroscience Abstracts, 15.*

Murphy, M. R., & Schneider, G. E. (1970). Olfactory bulb removal eliminates mating behavior in the male golden hamster. *Science, 157,* 302–304.

Myers, R. D., & Knott, P. J. (Eds.). (1986). *Voltammetry and push-pull perfusion.* New York: New York Academy of Science.

Myers, R. E., & Sperry, R. W. (1953). Interocular transfer of a visual form discrimination habit in cats after section of the optic chiasma and corpus callosum. *American Association of Anatomists: Abstracts of Papers from Platform,* p. 351.

Nachman, M. (1963). Learned aversion to the taste of lithium chloride and generalization of other salts. *Journal of Comparative and Physiological Psychology, 56,* 343–349.

Nadel, E. R., Bullard, R. W., & Stolwijk, J. A. J. (1971). Impor-

tance of skin temperature in the regulation of sweating. *Journal of Applied Physiology, 31,* 80–87.

Naeser, M. A., Hayward, R. W., Laughlin, S. A., & Zatz, L. M. (1981). Quantitative CT scan studies in aphasia. *Brain and Language, 12,* 140–164.

National Commission on Marijuana and Drug Abuse (1972). R. P. Schafer, Chairman. *Marijuana: A signal of misunderstanding.* New York: New American Library.

Nauta, W. J. H., & Feirtag, M. (1979). The organization of the brain. *Scientific American, 241,* 88–100.

Nauta, W. J. H., & Feirtag, M. (1986). *Fundamental neuroanatomy.* New York: W. H. Freeman & Co.

Neff, W. D. (1977). The brain and hearing: Auditory discriminations affected by brain lesions. *Annals of Otology, Rhinology, and Laryngology, 86,* 500–506.

Nelson, T. O. (1978). Detecting small amounts of information in memory: Savings for nonrecognized items. *Journal of Experimental Psychology: Human Learning and Memory, 4,* 453–468.

Netter, F. H. (1962). *The CIBA collection of medical illustrations: Vol. 1. The nervous system.* New York: CIBA.

Newman, E. A., & Hartline, P. H. (1982). The infrared "vision" of snakes. *Scientific American, 246,* 116–127.

Niazi, S. A., & Lewis, F. J. (1958). Profound hypothermia in man. *Annals of Surgery, 147,* 264–266.

Nicholaidis, S., & Rowland, N. (1975). Regulatory drinking in rats with permanent access to a bitter fluid source. *Physiology and Behavior, 14,* 819–824.

Nicholaidis, S., & Rowland, N. (1977). Intravenous self-feeding: Long-term regulation of energy balance in rats. *Science, 195,* 589–591.

Norman, R. J., Buchwald, J. S., & Villablanca, J. R. (1977). Classical conditioning with auditory discrimination of the eyeblink in decerebrate cats. *Science, 196,* 551–553.

Oakley, B. (1986). Basic taste physiology. In H. Meiselman & R. S. Rivlin (Eds.), *Clinical measurement of taste and smell* (pp. 5–18). New York: Macmillan Publishing Co.

O'Brien, C. P., Chaddock, B., Woody, G., & Greenstein, R. (1974). Systematic extinction of addiction-associated rituals using narcotic antagonists. *Psychosomatic Medicine, 36,* 458.

O'Brien, C. P., Ternes, J. W., Grabowski, J., & Ehrman, R. (1981). Classically conditioned phenomena in human opiate addiction. *National Institute for Drug Research Monograph Series, 37,* 107–115.

O'Brien, D. F. (1982). The chemistry of vision. *Science, 218,* 961–966.

O'Callaghan, M. A. J., & Carroll, D. (1982). *Psychosurgery: A scientific analysis.* Ridgewood, NJ: George A. Bogdaen & Son, Inc.

Ojeda, S. R., Kalra, P. S., & McCann, S. M. (1975). Further studies on the maturation of the estrogen negative feedback on gonadotropin release in the female rat. *Neuroendocrinology, 18,* 242–255.

Ojemann, G. A. (1979). Individual variability in cortical localization of language. *Journal of Neurosurgery, 50,* 164–169.

Ojemann, G. A. (1983). Brain organization for language from the perspective of electrical stimulation mapping. *Behavioral and Brain Sciences, 2,* 189–230.

Ojemann, G. A., & Whitaker, H. A. (1978). The bilingual brain. *Archives of Neurology, 35,* 409–412.

Olds, J., & Milner, P. (1954). Positive reinforcement produced by electrical stimulation of septal area and other regions of rat brain. *Journal of Comparative and Physiological Psychology, 47,* 419–427.

Olds, M. E., & Olds, J. (1963). Approach-avoidance analysis of rat diencephalon. *Journal of Comparative Neurology, 120,* 259–295.

Oliveras, J. L., Besson, J. M., Guilbaud, G., & Liebeskind, J. C. (1974). Behavioral and electrophysiological evidence of pain inhibition from midbrain stimulation in the cat. *Experimental Brain Research, 20,* 32–44.

Olton, D. S., & Samuelson, R. J. (1976). Remembrance of places: Spatial memory in rats. *Journal of Experimental Psychology: Animal Behavior Processes, 2,* 97–116.

Paletta, M. S., & Wagner, A. R. (1986). Development of context-

550

specific tolerance to morphine: Support for a dual-process interpretation. *Behavioral Neuroscience, 100,* 611–623.

Panksepp, J. (1971). Aggression elicited by electrical stimulation of the hypothalamus in albino rats. *Physiology & Behavior, 6,* 321–329.

Panksepp, J. (1975). Metabolic hormones and regulation of feeding: A reply to Woods, Decke, and Vaselli. *Psychological Review, 82,* 158–164.

Panksepp, J., & Trowill, J. A. (1967). Intraoral self-injection: II. The simulation of self-stimulation phenomena with a conventional reward. *Psychonomic Science, 9,* 407–408.

Pappenheimer, J. R., Koski, G., Fencl, V., Karnovsky, M. L., & Krueger, J. (1975). Extraction of sleep-promoting factor S from cerebrospinal fluid and from brains of sleep-deprived animals. *Journal of Neurophysiology, 38,* 1299–1311.

Park, I. J., & Jones, K. L. K. (1971). Testicular feminization syndrome. In D. Bergsma (Ed.), *The Third Conference on the Clinical Delineation of Birth Defects: Part X. The Endocrine System* (p. 309). Baltimore, MD: The Williams and Wilkins Company.

Parker, G. H. (1919). *The elementary nervous system.* Philadelphia: J. B. Lippincott.

Patrick, C. J. (1987). *The validity of lie detection with criminal psychopaths.* Unpublished doctoral dissertation, University of British Columbia, Vancouver.

Patterson, K. E. (1982). The relation between reading and phonological coding: Further neuropsychological observations. In A. W. Ellis (Ed.), *Normality and pathology in cognition functions* (pp. 77–111). London: Academic Press.

Pavlov, I. P. (1927). *Conditioned reflexes: An investigation of the physiological activity of the cerebral cortex.* New York: Dover Publishing Inc.

Peck, J. W., & Blass, E. M. (1975). Localization of thirst and antidiuretic osmoreceptors by intracranial injections in rats. *American Journal of Physiology, 228,* 1501–1509.

Peck, J. W., & Novin, D. (1971). Evidence that osmoreceptors mediating drinking in rabbits are in the lateral preoptic area. *Journal of Comparative and Physiological Psychology, 74,* 134–147.

Penfield, W., & Boldrey, E. (1937). Somatic motor and sensory representations in cerebral cortex of man as studied by electrical stimulation. *Brain, 60,* 389–443.

Penfield, W., & Rasmussen, T. (1950). *The cerebral cortex of man: A clinical study of the localization of function.* New York: Macmillan Pub. Co.

Penfield, W., & Roberts, L. (1959). *Speech and brain mechanisms* (pp. 133–191). Princeton, NJ: Princeton University Press.

Penot, C., Vergnes, M., Mack, G., & Kempf, E. (1978). Interspecific aggression and reactivity in the rat: Compared effects of electrolytic raphé lesions and intraventricular 5,7 DHT administration. *Biology of Behavior, 3,* 71–85.

Percival, J. E., Horne, J. A., & Tilley, A. J. (1983). Effects of sleep deprivation on tests of higher cerebral functioning. *Sleep 1982. 6th European Congress on Sleep Research* (Zurich, 1982). (pp. 390–391). Basel: Karger.

Perlow, M. J., Freed, W. J., Hoffer, B. J., Seiger, A., Olson, L., & Wyatt, R. J. (1979). Brain grafts reduce motor abnormalities produced by destruction of nigrostriatal dopamine system. *Science, 204,* 643–647.

Perrett, D. I., Rolls, E. T., & Caan, W. (1982). Visual neurones responsive to faces in the monkey temporal cortex. *Experimental Brain Research, 47,* 329–342.

Petersen, S. E., Fox, P. T., Mintun, M. A., Posner, M. I., & Raichle, M. E. (1989). Studies of the processing of single words using averaged positron emission tomographic measurements of cerebral blood flow change. *Journal of Cognitive Neuroscience,* Vol. 1, pp. 153–170.

Petersen, S. E., Fox, P. T., Posner, M. I., Mintun, M., & Raichle, M. E. (1988). Positron emission tomographic studies of the cortical anatomy of single-word processing. *Nature, 331,* 585–589.

Petrides, M., & Iversen, S. D. (1979). Restricted posterior parietal lesions in the rhesus monkey and performance on visuospatial tasks. *Brain Research, 161,* 63–77.

Pfeiffer, C. A. (1936). Sexual differences of the hypophyses and their determination by the gonads. *American Journal of Anatomy, 58,* 195–225.

Phelps, M. E., & Mazziotta, J. C. (1985). Positron emission tomography: Human brain function and biochemistry. *Science, 288,* 782–799.

Phillips, A. G., & Fibiger, H. C. (1989). Neuroanatomical bases of intracranial self-stimulation: Untangling the Gordian knot. In J. M. Leibman & S. J. Cooper (Eds.), *The neuropharmacological basis of reward* (pp. 66–105). Oxford: Clarendon Press.

Phillips, A. G., & LePiane, F. G. (1980). Reinforcing effects of morphine microinjection into the ventral tegmental area. *Pharmacology Biochemistry & Behavior, 12,* 965–968.

Phillips, A. G., Spyraki, C., & Fibiger, H. C. (1982). Conditioned place preference with amphetamine and opiates as reward stimuli: Attenuation by haloperidol. In B. G. Hoebel & D. Novin (Eds.), *The neural basis of feeding and reward* (pp. 455–464). Brunswick, MN: Haer Institute.

Phillips, M. I., & Felix, D. (1976). Specific angiotensin II receptive neurons in the cat subfornical organ. *Brain Research, 109,* 531–540.

Phoenix, C. H., Goy, R. W., Gerall, A. A., & Young, W. C. (1959). Organizing action of prenatally administered testosterone proprionate on the tissues mediating mating behavior in the female guinea pig. *Endocrinology, 65,* 369–382.

Piercy, M., Hécaen, H., & Ajuriaguerra, J. de (1960). Constructional apraxia associated with unilateral cerebral lesions—left and right sided cases compared. In V. B. Mountcastle (Ed.), *Interhemispheric relations and cerebral dominance* (pp. 225–242). Baltimore, MD: The Johns Hopkins Press.

Pilar, G., Landmesser, L., & Burstein, L. (1980). Competition for survival among developing ciliary ganglion cells. *Journal of Neurophysiology, 43,* 233–254.

Pinel, J. P. J. (1969). A short gradient of ECS-produced amnesia in a one-trial appetitive learning situation. *Journal of Comparative and Physiological Psychology, 68,* 650–655.

Pinel, J. P. J. (1981). Spontaneous kindled motor seizures in rats. In J. A. Wada (Ed.), *Kindling 2* (pp. 179–192). New York: Raven Press.

Pinel, J. P. J., & Cheung, K. F. (1977). Controlled demonstration of metrazol kindling. *Pharmacology Biochemistry & Behavior, 6,* 599–600.

Pinel, J. P. J., Gorzalka, B. B., & Ladak, F. (1981). Cadaverine and putrescine initiate the burial of dead conspecifics in rats. *Physiology & Behavior, 27,* 819–824.

Pinel, J. P. J., & Huang, E. (1976). Effects of periodic withdrawal on ethanol and saccharin selection in rats. *Physiology & Behavior, 16,* 693–698.

Pinel, J. P. J., Kim, C. K., Paul, D. J., & Mana, M. J. (1988). Contingent tolerance and cross-tolerance to anticonvulsant drug effects: Pentobarbitol and ethanol. *Psychobiology, 17,* 165–170.

Pinel, J. P. J., & Mana, M. J. (1989). Adaptive interactions of rats with dangerous inanimate objects: Support for a cognitive theory of defensive behavior. In R. J. Blanchard, P. F. Brain, D. C. Blanchard, & S. Parmigiani (Eds.), Ethoexperimental approaches to the study of behavior (pp. 137–150). Dordrecht, The Netherlands: Kluwer Academic Publishers.

Pinel, J. P. J., Mana, M. J., & Kim, C. K. (1989). Effect-dependent tolerance to ethanol's anticonvulsant effect on kindled seizures. In R. J. Porter, R. H. Mattson, J. A. Cramer, & I. Diamond (Eds.), Alcohol and seizures: Basic mechanisms and clinical implications. Philadelphia: F. A. Davis.

Pinel, J. P. J., & Mucha, R. F. (1980). Increased susceptibility to kindled seizures following brief exposure to alcohol. In K. Erikson, J. D. Sinclair, & K. Kiianma (Eds.), *Animal models in alcohol research* (pp. 413–418). New York: Academic Press.

Pinel, J. P. J., & Mumby, D. G. (1989, April). *The Mumby-box paradigm: Nonrecurring-items delayed nonmatching-to-sample in rats.* Paper presented at the Canadian Spring Conference on Behavior and Brain, Banff, Alberta.

Pinel, J. P. J., Pfaus, J. G., & Christensen, B. K. (1988). Contingent tolerance to the disruptive effects of alcohol on the sexual behavior of male rats. Paper read at the *Fourth Congress of the International Society for Biomedical Research on Alcoholism*, Kyoto, Japan.

Pinel, J. P. J., & Rovner, L. I. (1977). Saccharin elation effect. *Bulletin of the Psychonomic Society, 9,* 275–278.

Pinel, J. P. J., & Treit, D. (1978). Burying as a defensive response in rats. *Journal of Comparative and Physiological Psychology, 92,* 708–712.

Pinel, J. P. J., Treit, D., & Rovner, L. I. (1972). Temporal lobe aggression in rats. *Science, 197,* 1088–1089.

Pinsker, H. M., Hening, W. A., Carew, T. J., & Kandel, E. R. (1973). Long-term sensitization of a defensive withdrawal reflex in *Aplysia. Science, 182,* 1039–1042.

Pirozzolo, F. J. (1978). Disorders of perceptual processing. In E. C. Carterette & M. P. Friedman (Eds.), *Handbook of perception* (Vol. 9, pp. 359–383). New York: Academic Press.

Plapinger, L., McEwen, B. S., & Clemens, L. E. (1973). Ontogeny of estradiol-binding macromolecule. *Endocrinology, 93,* 1129–1139.

Pohl, W. (1973). Dissociation of spatial discrimination deficits following frontal and parietal lesions in monkeys. *Comparative and Physiological Psychology, 82,* 227–239.

Polivy, J., & Herman, C. P. (1985). Dieting and binging: A causal analysis. *American Psychologist, 40,* 193–201.

Pons, T. P., Garraghty, P. E., Friedman, D. P., & Mishkin, M. (1987). Physiological evidence for serial processing in somatosensory cortex. *Science, 237,* 417–420.

Pope, H. G., & Katz, D. L. (1987). Bodybuilder's psychosis. *Lancet, 1(8537),* 863.

Poppelreuter, W. (1917). *Die psychischen Schädigungen durch Kopfschuss im Kriege 1914–1916: die Störungen der niederen und höheren Sehleistungen durch Verletzungen des Okzipitalhirns.* Leipzig: Voss.

Porrino, L. J. (1987). Cerebral metabolic changes associated with activation of reward systems. In J. Engel & L. Oreland (Eds.), *Brain reward systems and abuse* (pp. 51–60). New York: Raven Press.

Porrino, L. J., Esposito, R. U., Seeger, T. F., Crane, A. M., Pert, A., & Sokoloff, L. (1984). Metabolic mapping of the brain during rewarding self-stimulation. *Science, 224,* 306–309.

Porte, D., Jr., & Woods, S. C. (1981). Regulation of food intake and body weight by insulin. *Diabetologia, 20,* 274–280.

Posner, M. I., Petersen, S. E., Fox, P. T., & Raichle, M. E. (1988). Localization of cognitive operations in the human brain. *Science, 240,* 1627–1631.

Poulos, C. X., & Hinson, R. E. (1984). A homeostatic model of Pavlovian conditioning: Tolerance to scopolamine-induced adipsia. *Journal of Experimental Psychology: Animal Behavioral Processes, 10,* 75–89.

Powley, T. L., Opsahl, C. A., Cox, J. E., & Weingarten, H. P. (1980). The role of the hypothalamus in energy homeostasis. In P. J. Morgane & J. Panksepp (Eds.), *Handbook of the Hypothalamus—3A: Behavioral studies of the hypothalamus* (pp. 211–298). New York: Marcel Dekker Inc.

Pritchard, R. M. (1961). Stabilized images on the retina. *Scientific American, 204,* 72–78.

Pujol, J. F., Buguet, A., Froment, J. L., Jones, B., & Jouvet, M. (1971). The central metabolism of serotonin in the cat during insomnia: A neurophysiological and biochemical study after administration of P-chlorophenylalanine or destruction of the raphé system. *Brain Research, 29,* 195–212.

Purves, D., & Lichtman, J. W. (1985). *Principles of neural development.* Sunderland, MA: Sinauer.

Quinn, W. G. (1984). Work in invertebrates in the mechanisms underlying learning. In P. Marler & H. S. Terrace (Eds.), *The biology of learning* (pp. 197–246). Berlin: Springer-Verlag.

Raboch, J., & Starka, L. (1973). Reported coital activity of men and levels of plasma testosterone. *Archives of Sexual Behavior, 2,* 309–315.

Racine, R. J. (1972). Modification of siezure activity by electrical stimulation: II. Motor seizure. *Electroencephalography and Clinical Neurophysiology, 32,* 281–294.

Racine, R. J. (1978). Kindling: The first decade. *Neurosurgery, 3,* 234–252.

Racine, R. J., & Burnham, W. M. (1984). The kindling model. In P. A. Schwartzkroin & H. Wheal (Eds.), *Electrophysiology of epilepsy* (pp. 153–171). London: Academic Press.

Racine, R. J., Burnham, W. M., Gartner, J. G., & Levitan, D. (1973). Rates of motor seizure development in rats subjected to electrical brain stimulation: Strain and interstimulation interval effects. *Electroencephalography and Clinical Neurophysiology, 35,* 553–556.

Racine, R. J., & deJonge, M. (1988). Short-term and long-term potentiation in projection pathways and local circuits. In P. W. Landfield & S. A. Deadwyler (Eds.), *Long-term potentiation: From biophysics to behavior* (p. 167). New York: Liss.

Racine, R. J., Livingston, K., & Joaquin, A. (1975). Effects of procaine hydrochloride, diazepam, and diphenylhydantoin on seizure development in cortical and subcortical structures in rats. *Electroencephalography and Clinical Neurophysiology, 38,* 355–365.

Racine, R. J., Milgram, N. W., & Hafner, S. (1983). Long-term potentiation phenomena in the rat limbic forebrain. *Brain Research, 260,* 217–233.

Raichle, M. E. (1987). Circulatory and metabolic correlates of brain function in normal humans. In J. B. Brookhart & V. B. Mountcastle (Eds.), *Handbook of physiology: The nervous system V* (643–674). Bethesda, MD: American Physiological Society.

Raisman, G., & Field, P. M. (1971). Sexual dimorphism in the neuropil of the preoptic area of the rat and its dependence on neonatal androgens. *Brain Research, 54,* 1–29.

Raisman, G., Morris, R. J., & Zhou, C. F. (1987). Specificity in the reinnervation of adult hippocampus by embryonic hippocampal transplants. In F. J. Seil, E. Herbert, & B. M. Carlson (Eds.), *Progress in Brain Research* (Vol. 71, pp. 325–333). New York: Elsevier.

Rakic, P. (1974). Neurons in rhesus monkey visual cortex: Systematic relation betweeen time of origin and eventual disposition. *Science, 183,* 425–427.

Rakic, P., Stensas, L. J., Sayre, E. P., & Sidman, R. L. (1974). Computer-aided three-dimensional reconstruction and quantitative analysis of cells from serial electron microscopic montages of foetal monkey brain. *Nature, 250,* 31–34.

Ramsay, D. J., Rolls, B. J., & Wood, R. J. (1977). Body fluid changes which influence drinking in the water deprived rat. *Journal of Physiology, 266,* 453–469.

Rankin, C. H., & Carew, T. J. (1987). Development of learning and memory in *Aplysia:* II. Habituation and dishabituation. *Journal of Neuroscience, 7,* 133–143.

Rankin, C. H., & Carew, T. J. (1988). Dishabituation and sensitization emerge as separate processes during development in *Aplysia. Journal of Neuroscience, 8,* 197–211.

Rankin, C. H., Nolen, T. G., Marcus, E. A., Stopfer, M., & Carew, T. J. (1988). The development of sensitization in *Aplysia.* In P. W. Kalivas & C. D. Barnes (Eds.), *Sensitization in the nervous system* (pp. 1–26). Caldwell, NJ: Telford Press.

Rapport, R. L., Tan, C. T., & Whitaker, H. A. (1983). Language function and dysfunction among Chinese- and English-speaking polyglots: Cortical stimulation, Wada testing, and clinical studies. *Brain and Language, 18,* 342–366.

Rasmussen, T., & Milner, B. (1975). Excision of Broca's area without persistent aphasia. In K. J. Zulch, O. Creutzfeldt, & G. C. Galbraith (Eds.), *Cerebral localization* (pp. 258–263). New York: Springer-Verlag.

Ratliff, F. (1972). Contour and contrast. *Scientific American, 226,* 90–101.

Rawson, R. O., Quick, K. P., & Coughlin, R. F. (1969). Thermoregulatory responses to intra-abdominal heating of sheep. *Science, 169,* 919–920.

Reame, N., Sauder, S. E., Kelch, R. P., & Marshall, J. C. (1984). Pulsatile gonadotropin secretion during the human menstrual cycle: Evidence for altered frequency of gonadotropin releasing hormone secretion. *Journal of Clinical Endocrinology and Metabolism, 59,* 328.

Rebec, G. V., & Bashore, T. R. (1984). Critical issues in assessing the behavioral effects of amphetamine. *Neuroscience and Biobehavioral Reviews, 8,* 153–158.

Rechtschaffen, A., Gilliland, M. A., Bergmann, B. M., & Winter, J. B. (1983). Physiological correlates of prolonged sleep deprivation in rats. *Science, 221,* 182–184.

Rechtschaffen, A., & Kales, A. (1968). *A manual of standardized terminology, techniques and scoring systems for sleep stages of human subjects.* Washington, DC: U. S. Government Printing Office.

Rechtschaffen, A., Wolpert, E. A., Dement, W. C., Mitchell, S. A., & Fisher, C. (1963). Nocturnal sleep of narcoleptics. *Electroencephalography and Clinical Neurophysiology, 15,* 599–609.

Reeves, A. G., & Plum, F. (1969). Hyperphagia, rage, and dementia accompanying a ventromedial hypothalamic neoplasm. *Archives of Neurology, 20,* 616–624.

Reh, T. A., & Constantine-Paton, M. (1984). Retinal ganglion cell terminals change their projection sites during larval development of *Rana pipiens. Journal of Neuroscience, 4,* 442–457.

Revusky, S. H., & Garcia, J. (1970). Learned associations over long delays. In G. H. Bower & J. T. Spence (Eds.), *The psychology of learning and motivation* (Vol. 4, pp. 1–85). New York: Academic Press.

Reynolds, D. V. (1969). Surgery in the rat during electrical analgesia induced by focal brain stimulation. *Science, 164,* 444–445.

Richter, C. P. (1967). Sleep and activity: Their relation to the 24-hour clock. *Proceedings of the Association for Research on Nervous and Mental Disorders, 45,* 8–27.

Richter, C. P. (1971). Inborn nature of the rat's 24-hour clock. *Journal of Comparative and Physiological Psychology, 75,* 1–14.

Ridley, R. M., & Ettlinger, G. (1975). Visual discrimination performance in the monkey: The activity of single cells in infero-temporal cortex. *Brain Research, 55,* 179–182.

Risner, M. E., & Jones, B. E. (1980). Intravenous self-administration of cocaine and norcocaine by dogs. *Psychopharmacology, 71,* 83–89.

Roberts, D. C. S., Corcoran, M. E., & Fibiger, H. C. (1977). On the role of ascending catecholaminergic systems in intravenous self-administration of cocaine. *Pharmacology Biochemistry & Behavior, 6,* 615–620.

Roberts, D. C. S., & Koob, G. F. (1982). Disruption of cocaine self-administration following 6-hydroxydopamine lesions of the ventral tegmental area in rats. *Pharmacology Biochemistry & Behavior, 17,* 901–904.

Roberts, D. C. S., Koob, G. F., Klonoff, P., & Fibiger, H. C. (1980). Extinction and recovery of cocaine self-administration following 6-hydroxydopamine lesions of the nucleus accumbens. *Pharmacology Biochemistry & Behavior, 12,* 781–787.

Roberts, D. C. S., & Zito, K. A. (1987). Interpretation of lesion effects on stimulant self-administration. In M. A. Bozarth (Ed.), *Methods of assessing the reinforcing properties of abused drugs* (pp. 87–103). New York: Springer-Verlag.

Roberts, W. W., & Martin, J. R. (1977). Effects of lesions in central thermosensitive areas on thermoregulatory responses in rat. *Physiology & Behavior, 19,* 503–511.

Robinson, B. W. (1964). Forebrain alimentary responses: Some organizational principles. In M. J. Wayner (Ed.), *Thirst: Proceedings of the First International Symposium on Thirst in the Regulation of Body Water* (pp. 411–427). New York: Macmillan.

Robinson, B. W., Alexander, M., & Bowne, G. (1969). Dominance reversal resulting from aggressive responses evoked by brain telestimulation. *Physiology & Behavior, 4,* 749–752.

Rogers, P. J., & Blundell, J. E. (1980). Investigation of food selection and meal parameters during the development of dietary induced obesity. *Appetite, 1,* 85–88.

Roland, P. E., & Larsen, B. (1976). Focal increase of cerebral blood flow during stereognostic testing in man. *Archives of Neurology, 33,* 551–558.

Roland, P. E., Larsen, B., Lassen, N. A., & Skinhøj, E. (1980). Supplementary motor area and other cortical areas in organization of voluntary movements in man. *Journal of Neurophysiology, 43,* 118–136.

Roland, P. E., Skinhøj, E., Lassen, N. A., & Larsen, B. (1980). *Journal of Neurophysiology, 43,* 137–150.

Rolls, B. J., & Rolls, E. T. (1982). *Thirst.* Cambridge: Cambridge University Press.

Rolls, B. J., Rolls, E. T., Rowe, E. A., & Sweeney, K. (1981). Sensory specific satiety in man. *Physiology & Behavior, 27,* 137–142.

Rolls, B. J., Wood, R. J., & Rolls, R. M. (1980). Palatability and body fluid homeostasis. *Physiology & Behavior, 20,* 15–19.

Rolls, E. T. (1981). Central nervous mechanisms related to feeding and appetite. *British Medical Bulletin, 37,* 131–134.

Rolls, E. T. (1985.). Neuronal activity in relation to the recognition of stimuli in the primate. In C. Chagas, R. Gattass, & C. Gross (Eds.), *Pattern recognition mechanisms* (pp. 203–213). Berlin: Springer-Verlag.

Rolls, E. T., & Rolls, B. J. (1982). Brain mechanisms involved in feeding. In L. M. Barker (Ed.), *The psychobiology of human food selection* (pp. 33–65). Westport, CT: AVI Pub. Co.

Rolls, E. T., Sanghera, M. K., & Roper-Hall, A. (1979). The latency of activation of neurons in the lateral hypothalamus and substantia innominata during feeding in the monkey. *Brain Research, 164,* 121–135.

Rolls, E. T., Wood, R. J., & Stevens, R. M. (1978). Effects of palatability on body fluid homeostasis. *Physiology & Behavior, 20,* 15–19.

Rosendorff, C., & Mooney, J. J. (1971). Central nervous system sites of action of a purified leucocyte pyrogen. *American Journal of Physiology, 220,* 597–603.

Rosenthal, D., Wender, P. H., Kety, S. S., Welner, J., & Schulsinger, F. (1980). The adopted-away offspring of schizophrenics. *American Journal of Psychiatry, 128,* 87–91.

Rothblat, L. A., & Hayes, L. L. (1987). Short-term object recognition memory in the rat: Nonmatching with trial-unique junk stimuli. *Behavioral Neuroscience, 101,* 587–590.

Rothwell, J. C., Traub, M. M., Day, B. L., Obeso, J. A., Thomas, P. K., & Marsden, C. D. (1982). Manual motor performance in a deafferented man. *Brain, 105,* 515–542.

Rothwell, N. J., & Stock, M. J. (1979). A role for brown adipose tissue in diet-induced thermogenesis. *Nature, 281,* 31–35.

Rothwell, N. J., & Stock, M. J. (1982). Energy expenditure derived from measurements of oxygen consumption and energy balance in hyperphagic, 'cafeteria'-fed rats. *Journal of Physiology, 324,* 59–60.

Routtenberg, A., & Malsbury, C. (1969). Brainstem pathways of reward. *Journal of Comparative and Physiological Psychology, 68,* 22–30.

Rovasio, R. A., Delouvée, A., Yamada, K. M., Timpl, R., & Thiery, J. P. (1983). Neural crest cell migration: Requirements for exogenous fibronectin and high cell density. *Journal of Cell Biology, 96,* 462–473.

Rowland, N. (1981). Feeding behaviour: Caused by, or just correlated with, physiology? *Behavioral and Brain Sciences, 4,* 589–590.

Rowland, N. (1981). Glucoregulatory feeding in cats. *Physiology & Behavior, 26,* 901–903.

Rummelhart, D. E., & Norman, D. A. (1982). Simulating a skilled typist: A study of skilled cognitive motor performance. *Cognitive Science, 6,* 1–36.

Rusak, B. (1979). Neural mechanisms for entrainment and generation of mammalian circadian rhythms. *Proceedings of the Federation of American Societies for Experimental Biology, 38,* 2589–2595.

Rusak, B., & Groos, G. (1982). Suprachiasmatic stimulation phase shifts rodent circadian rhythms. *Science, 215,* 1407–1409.

Rusak, B., & Zucker, I. (1979). Neural regulation of circadian rhythms. *Psychological Reviews, 59,* 449–526.

Rushton, W. A. H. (1962). Visual pigments in man. *Scientific American, 207,* 120–132.

Russek, M. (1975). Current hypotheses in the control of feeding behaviour. In G. J. Mogenson & F. R. Calaresu (Eds.),

Neural integration of physiological mechanisms and behaviour (pp. 128–147). Toronto: University of Toronto Press.

Russek, M. (1981). Current status of the hepatostatic theory of food intake control. *Appetite, 2,* 137–143.

Russell, W. R., & Espir, M. I. E. (1961). *Traumatic aphasia—a study of aphasia in war wounds of the brain.* London: Oxford University Press.

Rutishauser, U., Acheson, A., Hall, A. K., Mann, D. M., & Sunshine, J. (1988). The neural cell adhesion molecule (NCAM) as a regulator of cell-cell interactions. *Science, 240,* 53–57.

Sachar, E. J. (1985). Disorders of thought: The schizophrenic syndromes. In E. R. Kandel & J. H. Schwartz (Eds.), *Principles of neural science* (2nd ed.). (pp. 704–715). New York: Elsevier.

Sacks, O. (1985). *The man who mistook his wife for a hat and other clinical tales.* New York: Summit Books.

St. George-Hyslop, P., Tanzi, R. E., Polinsky, R. J., Haines, J. L., Nee, L., Watkins, P. C., Myers, R. H., Feldman, R. G., Pollen, D., Drachman, D., Growdon, J., Bruni, A., Foncin, J. F., Salmon, D., Frommelt, P., Amaducci, L., Sorbi, S., Piacentini, S., Stewart, G. D., Hobbs, W. J., Conneally, P. M., & Gusella, J. F. (1987). The genetic defect causing familial Alzheimer's disease maps on chromosome 21. *Science, 235,* 885–889.

Salmimies, P., Kockott, G., Pirke, K. M., Vogt, H. J., & Shill, W. B. (1982). Effects of testosterone replacement on sexual behavior in hypogonadal men. *Archives of Sexual Behavior, 11,* 345–353.

Salmon, D. P., Zola-Morgan, S., & Squire, R. L. (1987). Retrograde amnesia following combined hippocampus-amygdala lesions in monkeys. *Psychobiology, 15,* 37–47.

Sanders, D., & Bancroft, J. (1982). Hormones and the sexuality of women—the menstrual cycle. *Clinics in Endocrinology and Metabolism, 11,* 639–659.

Satinoff, E. (1982). Are there similarities between thermoregulation and sexual behavior? In D. W. Pfaff (Ed.), *The physiological mechanisms of motivation* (pp. 217–251). New York: Springer-Verlag.

Satinoff, E., Valentino, D., & Teitelbaum, P. (1976). Thermoregulatory cold-defense deficits in rats with preoptic/anterior hypothalamic lesions. *Brain Research Bulletin, 1,* 553–565.

Sawchenko, P. E., Eng, R., Gold, R. M., & Simson, E. L. (1977). *Effects of selective subdiaphragmatic vagotomies on knife cut induced hypothalamic hyperphagia.* Paper presented at the Sixth International Conference on the Physiology of Food and Fluid Intake, Paris, France.

Schacter, D. L. (1987). Implicit memory: History and current status. *Journal of Experimental Psychology: Learning, Memory and Cognition, 13,* 501–518.

Schallert, T., Whishaw, I. Q., & Flannigan, K. P. (1977). Gastric pathology and feeding deficits induced by hypothalamic damage in rats: Effects of lesion type, size, and placement. *Journal of Comparative and Physiological Psychology, 91* (3), 598–610.

Schally, A. V. (1978). Aspects of hypothalamic regulation of the pituitary gland. *Science, 202,* 18–28.

Schally, A. V., Kastin, A. J., & Arimura, A. (1971). Hypothalamic follicle-stimulating hormone (FSH) and luteinizing hormone (LH)-regulating hormone: Structure, physiology, and clinical studies. *Fertility and Sterility, 22,* 703–721.

Scherschlicht, R. (1983). Pharmacological profile of delta sleep-inducing peptide (DSIP) and a phosphorylated analogue, (Ser-PO$_4$) DSIP. *Sleep 1982, 6th European Congress for Sleep Research, Zurich, 1982* (pp. 109–111). Basel, Karger.

Scherschlicht, R., & Marias, J. (1983). Effects of oral and intravenous midazolam, trizolam and flunitrazepam on the sleep-wakefulness cycle of rabbits. *British Journal of Clinical Pharmacology, 16* (Supplement 1), 29S–35S.

Schiller, P. H. (1986). The central visual system. *Vision Research, 26,* 1351–1386.

Schiorring, E. (1979). An open-field study of stereotyped locomotor activity in amphetamine-treated rats. *Psychopharmacology, 66,* 281–287.

Schleidt, M., Hold, B., & Attili, G. (1981). A cross-cultural study on the attitude towards personal odors. *Journal of Chemical Ecology, 7,* 19–31.

Schnapf, J. L., & Baylor, D. A. (1987). How photoreceptor cells respond to light. *Scientific American, 256,* 40–47.

Schneider, G. E. (1969). Brain mechanisms for localization and discrimination are dissociated by tectal and cortical lesions. *Science, 163,* 895–902.

Schneider-Helmert, D. (1985). Clinical evaluation of DSIP. In A. Wauquier, J. M. Gaillard, J. M. Monti, & M. Radulovacki (Eds.), *Sleep: Neurotransmitters and neuromodulators* (pp. 279–289). New York: Raven Press.

Schoenenberger, G. A., & Graf, M. V. (1985). Effects of DSIP and DSIP-P on different biorhythmic parameters. In A. Wauquier, J. M. Gaillard, J. M. Monti, & M. Radulovacki (Eds.), *Sleep: Neurotransmitters and neuromodulators* (pp. 265–277). New York: Raven Press.

Schou, M., Juel-Neilsen, N., Stromberg, E., & Voldby, H. (1954). The treatment of manic psychoses by the administration of lithium salts. *Journal of Neurology, Neurosurgery and Psychiatry, 17,* 250–260.

Schwartz, G. E., Fair, P. L., Salt, P., Mandel, M. R., & Klerman, G. L. (1976). Facial muscle patterning to affective imagery in depressed and nondepressed subjects. *Science, 192,* 489–491.

Schwartz, J. H. (1980). The transport of substances in nerve cells. *Scientific American, 242,* 152–171.

Schwartz, J. H. (1987). Molecular aspects of postsynaptic receptors. In E. R. Kandel & J. H. Schwartz (Eds.), *Principles of neural science* (pp. 159–168). New York: Elsevier.

Schwartz, W. J., & Gainer, H. (1977). Suprachiasmatic nucleus: Use of 14-C-labelled deoxyglucose uptake as a functional marker. *Science, 197,* 1089–1091.

Sclafani, A. (1980). Dietary obesity. In A. J. Stunkard (Ed.), *Obesity* (pp. 166–181). Philadelphia: W. B. Saunders Company.

Sclafani, A. (1981). Correlation and causation in the study of feeding behavior. *Behavioral and Brain Sciences, 4,* 590–591.

Scott, J. W. (1986). The olfactory bulb and central pathways. *Experientia, 42,* 223–231.

Scoville, W. B., & Milner, B. (1957). Loss of recent memory after bilateral hippocampal lesions. *Journal of Neurology, Neurosurgery and Psychiatry, 20,* 11–21.

Seeman, P. (1980). Brain dopamine receptors. *Pharmacological Reviews, 32,* 229–313.

Selmanoff, M. K., Brodkin, L. D., Weiner, R. I., & Siiteri, P. K. (1977). Aromatization and 5-alpha-reduction of androgens in discrete hypothalamic and limbic regions of the male and female rat. *Endocrinology, 108,* 841–848.

Semmes, J., Weinstein, S., Ghent, L., & Teuber, H. L. (1963). Correlates of impaired orientation in personal and extrapersonal space. *Brain, 86,* 747–772.

Shaffer, L. H. (1981). Performances of Chopin, Bach and Bartok: Studies in motor programming. *Cognitive Psychology, 13,* 326–376.

Shallice, T., & Warrington, E. K. (1980). Single and multiple component central dyslexic syndromes. In M. Coltheart, K. E. Patterson & J. C. Marshall (Eds.), *Deep dyslexia* (pp. 119–145). London: Routledge & Kegan Paul.

Shapiro, B. H., Levine, D. C., & Adler, N. T. (1980). The testicular feminized rat: A naturally occurring model of androgen independent brain masculinization. *Science, 209,* 418–420.

Shelton, R. C., & Weinberger, D. R. (1987). Brain morphology in schizophrenia. In H. Y. Meltzer (Ed.), *Psychopharmacology: The third generation of progress* (pp. 773–781). New York: Raven Press.

Sherman, S. M. (1985). Functional organization of the W-, X-, and Y-cell pathways in the cat: A review and hypothesis. In J. M. Sprague & A. N. Epstein (Eds.), *Progress in psychobiology and physiological psychology* (Vol. 11, pp. 233–314). New York: Academic Press.

Shettleworth, S. J. (1983). Memory in food-hoarding birds. *Scientific American, 248,* 102–110.

Shipley, J. E., & Kolb, B. (1977). Neural correlates of species-typical behavior in the Syrian golden hamster. *Journal of Comparative and Physiological Psychology, 91*, 1056–1073.

Shizgal, P., & Murray, B. (1989). Neuronal basis of intracranial self-stimulation. In J. M. Liebman & S. J. Cooper (Eds.), *The neuropharmacological basis of reward* (pp. 106–163). Oxford: Clarendon Press.

Shore, P. A., Silver, S. L., & Brodie, B. B. (1955). Interaction of reserpine, serotonin, and lysergic acid diethylamide in brain. *Science, 122*, 284–285.

Shuttlesworth, D., Neill, D., & Ellen, F. (1984). Current issues: The place of physiological psychology in neuroscience. *Physiological Psychology, 12*, 3–7.

Sidman, M., Stoddard, L. T., & More, J. P. (1968). Some additional quantitative observations of immediate memory in a patient with bilateral hippocampal lesions. *Neuropsychologia, 6*, 245–254.

Siegel, J. M. (1983). A behavioral approach to the analysis of reticular formation unit activity. In T. E. Robinson (Ed.), *Behavioral approaches to brain research* (pp. 94–116). New York: Oxford University Press.

Siegel, S. (1978). Tolerance to the hyperthermic effect of morphine in the rat is a learned response. *Journal of Comparative and Physiological Psychology, 92*, 1137–1149.

Siegel, S. (1983). Classical conditioning, drug tolerance, and drug dependence. In Y. Israel, F. B. Graser, H. Kalant, W. Popham, W. Schmidt, & R. G. Smart (Eds.), *Research advances in alcohol and drug problems*. (Vol. 7, pp. 207–246). New York: Plenum.

Siegel, S., Hinson, R. E., Krank, M. D., & McCully, J. (1982). Heroin "overdose" death: Contribution of drug-associated environmental cues. *Science, 216*, 436–437.

Simpson, J. B., Epstein, A. N., & Camardo, J. S. (1978). Localization of receptors for the dipsogenic action of angiotensin II in the subfornical organ of rat. *Journal of Comparative and Physiological Psychology, 92*, 581–608.

Sinclair, D. (1981). *Mechanisms of cutaneous sensation*. New York: Oxford University Press.

Sinclair, J. D. (1972). The alcohol-deprivation effect: Influence of various factors. *Quarterly Journal of Studies on Alcohol, 33*, 769–782.

Singer, M., Nordlander, R. H., & Egar, M. (1979). Axonal guidance during embryogenesis and regeneration in the spinal cord of the newt: The blueprint hypothesis of neuronal pathway patterning. *Journal of Comparative Neurology, 185*, 1–22.

Sitaram, N., Weingartner, H., & Gillin, J. C. (1978). Human serial learning: Enhancement with acetylcholine and choline and impairment with scopolamine. *Science, 201*, 271–276.

Skakkebaek, N. E., Bancroft, J., Davidson, D. W., & Warner, P. (1980). Androgen replacement with oral testosterone undecanoate in hypogonadal men: A double blind controlled study. *Clinical Endocrinology, 41*, 49–61.

Skelton, R. W., Scarth, A. S., Wilkie, D. M., Miller, J. J., & Phillips, A. G. (1987). Long-term increases in dentate granule cell responsivity accompany operant conditioning. *Journal of Neuroscience, 7*, 3081–3087.

Sladek, J. R., Jr., Redmond, D. E., Jr., Collier, T. J., Haber, S. N., Elsworth, J. D., Deutch, A. Y., & Roth, R. H. (1987). Transplantation of fetal dopamine neurons in primate brain reverses MPTP induced parkinsonism. In F. J. Seil, E. Herbert, & B. M. Carlson (Eds.), *Progress in brain research* (Vol. 71, pp. 309–323). New York: Elsevier.

Slaunwhite, W. R., III, Goldman, J. K., & Bernardis, L. L. (1972). Sequential changes in glucose metabolism by adipose tissue and liver of rats after destruction of the ventromedial hypothalamic nuclei: Effect of three dietary regimes. *Metabolism, 21*, 619–631.

Snyder, S. H. (1976). The dopamine hypothesis of schizophrenia: Focus on the dopamine receptor. *American Journal of Psychiatry, 133*, 197–202.

Snyder, S. H. (1978). Neuroleptic drugs and neurotransmitter receptors. *Journal of Clinical and Experimental Psychiatry, 133*, 21–31.

Snyder, S. H. (1984). Drug and neurotransmitter receptors in the brain. *Science, 224*, 22–31.

Snyder, S. H. (1985). The molecular basis of communication between cells. *Scientific American, 253*, 132–141.

Snyder, S. H. (1986). *Drugs and the brain*. New York: Scientific American Books.

Sochurek, H., & Miller, P. (1987). Medicine's new vision. *National Geographic, 171*, 2–41.

Sperry, R. W. (1943). Effect of 180 degrees rotation of the retinal field on visuomotor coordination. *Journal of Experimental Zoology, 92*, 263–279.

Sperry, R. W. (1963). Chemoaffinity in the orderly growth of nerve fiber patterns and connections. *Proceedings of the National Academy of Sciences (USA), 50*, 703–710.

Sperry, R. W. (1964). The great cerebral commissure. *Scientific American, 210*, 42–52.

Sperry, R. W. (1974). Lateral specialization in the surgically separated hemispheres. In F. O. Schmitt & F. G. Worden (Eds.), *The neurosciences: Third study program* (pp. 5–19). Cambridge, MA: MIT Press.

Sperry, R. W. (1985). Consciousness, personal identity, and the divided brain. In D. F. Benson & E. Zaidel (Eds.). *The dual brain: Hemispheric specialization in humans* (pp. 11–26). New York: Guilford Press.

Spreen, O., Benton, A. L., & Fincham, R. W. (1965). Auditory agnosia without aphasia. *Archives of Neurology, 13*, 84–92.

Springer, S. P., & Deutsch, G. (1981). *Left brain, right brain*. San Francisco: W. H. Freeman and Company.

Squire, L. R. (1982). Comparisons between forms of amnesia: Some deficits are unique to Korsakoff's syndrome. *Journal of Experimental Psychology: Learning, Memory, and Cognition, 8*, 560–571.

Squire, L. R. (1982). The neuropsychology of human memory. *Annual Review of Neuroscience, 5*, 241–273.

Squire, L. R. (1986). Mechanisms of memory. *Science, 232*, 1612–1619.

Squire, L. R. (1987). *Memory and brain* (p. 193). New York: Oxford University Press.

Squire, L. R., & Cohen, N. (1979). Memory and amnesia: Resistance to disruption develops for years after learning. *Behavioral and Neural Biology, 25*, 115–125.

Squire, L. R., & Moore, R. Y. (1979). Dorsal thalamic lesion in a noted case of human memory dysfunction. *Annals of Neurology, 6*, 503–506.

Squire, L. R., Nadel, L., & Slater, P. C. (1981). Anterograde amnesia and memory for temporal order. *Neuropsychologia, 19*, 441–445.

Squire, L. R., Slater, P. C., & Chace, P. M. (1975). Retrograde amnesia: Temporal gradient in very long term memory following electroconvulsive therapy. *Science, 187*, 77–79.

Squire, L. R., Slater, P. C., & Chace, P. M. (1976). Retrograde amnesia following electroconvulsive therapy. *Nature, 260*, 775–777.

Squire, L. R., & Spanis, C. W. (1984). Long gradient of retrograde amnesia in mice: Continuity with the findings in humans. *Behavioral Neuroscience, 98*, 345–348.

Squire, L. R., & Zola-Morgan, S. (1985). The neuropsychology of memory: New links between humans and experimental animals. *Annals of the New York Academy of Sciences, 444*, 137–149.

Squire, L. R., Zola-Morgan, S., & Chen, K. (1988). Human amnesia and animal models of amnesia: Performance of amnesic patients on tests designed for the monkey. *Behavioral Neuroscience, 102*, 210–221.

Stellar, E. (1954). The physiology of motivation. *Psychological Review, 61*, 5–22.

Stephan, F. K., & Nunez, A. A. (1977). Elimination of circadian rhythms in drinking, activity, sleep, and temperature by isolation of the suprachiasmatic nucleus. *Behavioral Biology, 20*, 1–16.

Stephan, F. K., & Zucker, I. (1972). Circadian rhythms in drinking behaviour and locomotor activity of rats are eliminated by hypothalamic lesions. *Proceedings of the National Academy of Science (USA), 60*, 1583–1586.

Steriade, M., & Hobson, J. A. (1976). Neuronal activity during the sleep-waking cycle. *Progress in Neurobiology, 6,* 155–376.

Sterman, M. B., & Clemente, C. D. (1962). Forebrain inhibitory mechanisms: Cortical synchronization induced by basal forebrain stimulation. *Experimental Neurology, 6,* 91–102.

Sterman, M. B., & Clemente, C. D. (1962). Forebrain inhibitory mechanisms: Sleep patterns induced by basal forebrain stimulation in the behaving cat. *Experimental Neurology, 6,* 103–117.

Sternbach, L. H. (1983). The benzodiazepine story. *Journal of Psychoactive Drugs, 15,* 15–17.

Stewart, J., de Wit, H., & Eikelboom, R. (1984). Role of unconditioned and conditioned drug effects in the self-administration of opiates and stimulants. *Psychological Review, 91,* 251–268.

Stewart, J., & Eikelboom, R. (1982). Conditioned drug effects. In L. L. Iversen, S. D. Iversen, & S. H. Snyder (Eds.), *Handbook of psychopharmacology: Volume 19. New directions in behavioral pharmacology* (pp. 1–57). New York: Plenum Press.

Strick, P. L., & Preston, J. B. (1983). Input-output organization of the primate motor cortex. In J. E. Desmedt (Ed.), *Motor control mechanisms in health and disease* (pp. 321–327). New York: Raven Press.

Stricker, E. M. (1973). Thirst, sodium appetite, and complementary physiological contributions to the regulation of intravascular fluid volume. In A. N. Epstein, H. R. Kissileff, & E. Stellar (Eds.), *The neuropsychology of thirst: New findings and advances in concepts* (pp. 73–98). Washington, D. C.: Winston.

Stricker, E. M. (1981). Factors in the control of food intake. *Behavioral and Brain Sciences, 4,* 591–592.

Stricker, E. M., Rowland, N., Saller, C. F., & Friedman, M. I. (1977). Homeostasis during hypoglycemia: Central control of adrenal secretion and peripheral control of feeding. *Science, 196,* 79–81.

Stripling, J. S., & Ellinwood, E. H., Jr. (1976). Cocaine: Physiological and behavioral effects of acute and chronic administrations. In S. J. Mule (Ed.), *Cocaine: Chemical, biological, clinical, social and treatment aspects.* Cleveland, OH: CRC Press.

Stromberg, I., Herrera-Marschitz, M., Ungerstedt, U., Ebendal, T., & Olson, L. (1985). Chronic implants of chromaffin tissue into the dopamine-denervated striatum: Effects of NGF on graft survival, fiber growth and rotational behavior. *Experimental Brain Research, 60,* 335–349.

Strömgren, E. (1987). Schizophrenia. In G. Adelman (Ed.), *Encyclopedia of neuroscience* (pp. 1072–1074). Boston: Birkhauser.

Strubbe, J. H., & Steffens, A. B. (1977). Blood glucose levels in portal and peripheral circulation and their relation to food intake in the rat. *Physiology & Behavior, 19,* 303–307.

Stunkard, A. J. (Ed.). (1980). *Obesity.* Philadelphia: W. B. Saunders.

Summers, W. K., Majovski, L. V., Marsh, G. M., Tachiki, K., & Kling, A. (1986). Oral tetrahydroaminoacridine in long-term treatment of senile dementia, Alzheimer type. *The New England Journal of Medicine, 315,* 1241–1245.

Sumner, D. (1964). Post-traumatic anosmia. *Brain, 87,* 107–120.

Sutton, S., Teuting, P., Zubin, J., & John, E. R. (1967). Information delivery and the sensory evoked potentials. *Science, 155,* 1436–1439.

Svaetichin, G. (1956). Spectral response curves from single cones. *Acta Physiologica Scandinavica, 39,* 17–46.

Svare, B. (1977). Psychobiological determinants of maternal aggressive behavior. In E. C. Simmel, M. E. Hahn, & J. K. Walters (Eds.), *Aggressive behavior: Genetic and neural approaches* (pp. 129–146). Hillsdale, NJ: Lawrence Erlbaum Associates.

Swaab, D. F., & Fliers, E. (1985). A sexually dimorphic nucleus in the human brain. *Science, 118,* 1112–1115.

Sweet, W. H. (1982). Cerebral localization of pain. In R. A. Thompson & J. R. Green (Eds.), *New perspectives in cerebral localization* (pp. 205–242). New York: Raven Press.

Tanaka, A. (1972). A progressive change of behavioral and elec-troencephalographic response to daily amygdaloid stimulations in rabbits. *Fukuoka Acta Medica, 63,* 152–163.

Tanji, J., & Kurata, K. (1983). Functional organization of the supplementary motor area. In J. E. Desmedt (Ed.), *Motor control mechanisms in health and disease* (pp. 421–431). New York: Raven Press.

Tanzi, R. E., Gusella, J. F., Watkins, P. C., Bruns, G. A. P., St. George-Hyslop, P., Van Keuren, M. L., Patterson, K., Pagan, S., Kurnit, D. M., & Neve, R. L. (1987). Amyloid beta protein gene: cDNA, mRNA distribution and genetic linkage near the Alzheimer locus. *Science, 235,* 880–884.

Taub, E. (1976). Movement in nonhuman primates deprived of somatosensory feedback. *Exercise and Sport Sciences Reviews, 4,* 335–374.

Tees, R. C. (1968). Effect of early visual restriction on later visual intensity discrimination in rats. *Journal of Comparative and Physiological Psychology, 66,* 224–227.

Tees, R. C., & Cartwright, J. (1972). Sensory preconditioning in rats following early visual deprivation. *Journal of Comparative and Physiological Psychology, 81,* 12–20.

Teitelbaum, P. (1957). Random and food-directed activity in hyperphagic and normal rats. *Journal of Comparative and Physiological Psychology, 50,* 486–490.

Teitelbaum, P. (1961). Disturbances in feeding and drinking behavior after hypothalamic lesions. In M. R. Jones (Ed.), *Nebraska Symposium on Motivation* (pp. 39–69). Lincoln, NB: University of Nebraska Press.

Teitelbaum, P., & Campbell, B. A. (1958). Ingestion patterns in hyperphagic and normal rats. *Journal of Comparative and Physiological Psychology, 51,* 135–141.

Teitelbaum, P., & Epstein, A. N. (1962). The lateral hypothalamic syndrome: Recovery of feeding and drinking after lateral hypothalamic lesions. *Psychological Review, 69,* 74–90.

Terman, G. W., Shavit, Y., Lewis, J. W., Cannon, J. T., & Liebeskind, J. C. (1984). Intrinsic mechanisms of pain inhibition: Activation by stress. *Science, 226,* 1270–1277.

Teuber, H. L., Battersby, W. S., & Bender, M. B. (1960). *Visual field defects after penetrating missile wounds of the brain.* Cambridge, MA: Harvard University Press.

Teuber, H. L., Milner, B., & Vaughan, H. G. Jr. (1968). Persistent anterograde amnesia after stab wound of the basal brain. *Neuropsychologia, 6,* 267–282.

Teyler, T. J. (1986). Electrophysiology of memory. In J. L. Martinez, Jr., & R. P. Kesner (Eds.), *Learning and memory: A biological view* (pp. 237–265). Orlando, FL: Academic Press.

Teyler, T. J., & DiScenna, P. (1984). Long-term potentiation as a candidate mnemonic device. *Brain Research Reviews, 7,* 15–28.

Thauer, R. (1970). Thermosensitivity of the spinal cord. In J. D. Hardy, A. P. Gagge, & J. A. J. Stolwijk (Eds.), *Physiological and behavioral temperature regulation* (pp. 472–492). Springfield, IL: Charles C Thomas, Publisher.

Thompson, R. F. (1986). The neurobiology of learning and memory. *Science, 233,* 941–947.

Tilles, D., Goldenheim, P., Johnson, D. C., Mendelson, J. H., Mello, N. K., & Hales, C. A. (1986). Marijuana smoking as cause of reduction in single-breath carbon monoxide diffusing capacity. *American Journal of Medicine, 80,* 601–606.

Tinkelberg, J. R. (1974). Marijuana and human aggression. In L. L. Miller (Ed.), *Marijuana, effects on human behavior* (pp. 339–358). New York: Academic Press.

Toates, F. M. (1981). The control of ingestive behaviour by internal and external stimuli—A theoretical review. *Appetite, 2,* 35–50.

Toates, F. M., & Halliday, T. R. (Eds.). (1980). *Analysis of motivated processes.* New York: Academic Press.

Tranel, D., & Damasio, A. R. (1985). Knowledge without awareness: An autonomic index of facial recognition by prosopagnosics. *Science, 228,* 1453–1454.

Trayhurn, P., & James, W. P. T. (1981). Thermogenesis: Dietary and non-shivering aspects. In L. A. Cioffi, W. P. T. James, & T. B. Vanltalie (Eds.), *The body weight regulatory system: Normal and disturbed mechanisms* (pp. 97–105). New York: Raven Press.

Traynor, A. E., Schlapfer, W. T., & Barondes, S. J. (1980). Stimulation is necessary for the development of tolerance to a neural effect of ethanol. *Journal of Neurobiology, 11,* 633–637.

Treit, D. (1987). RO 15-1788, CGS 8216, picrotoxin, and pentylenetetrazol: Do they antagonize anxiolytic drug effects through an anxiogenic action? *Brain Research Bulletin, 19,* 401–405.

Tsukahara, N. (1981). Sprouting and the neuronal basis of learning. *Trends in neuroscience, 4,* 234–240.

Tuck, R. R., Brew, B. J., Britton, A. M., & Loewy, J. (1984). Alcohol and brain damage. *British Journal of Addiction, 79,* 251–259.

Turek, F. W., & Losee-Olson, S. (1986). A benzodiazepine used in the treatment of insomnia phase-shifts the mammalian circadian clock. *Nature, 321,* 167–168.

Turner, A. M., & Greenough, W. T. (1983). Synapses per neuron and synaptic dimensions in occipital cortex of rats reared in complex, social, or isolation housing. *Acta Stereologica, Vol. 2, Suppl. 1,* 239–244.

Ungerleider, L. G., & Brody, B. A. (1977). Extrapersonal spatial orientation: The role of posterior parietal, anterior frontal, and inferotemporal cortex. *Experimental Neurology, 56,* 265–280.

Ungerleider, L. G., & Mishkin, M. (1982). Two cortical visual systems. In D. J. Ingle, M. A. Goodale, & R. J. W. Mansfield (Eds.), *Analysis of visual behavior* (pp. 549–586). Cambridge, MA: MIT Press.

Ursin, R. (1983). Endogenous sleep factors. In R. Ursin & A. A. Borbély (Chairs), *Sleep 1982, 6th European Congress on Sleep Research* (Zurich, 1982) (pp. 106–125). Basel: Karger.

Ursin, R. (1984). Endogenous sleep factors. *Experimental Brain Research, Supplement 8,* 118–131.

Valenstein, E. S. (1973). *Brain Control.* New York: John Wiley and Sons.

Valenstein, E. S. (1980). *The psychosurgery debate: Scientific, legal, and ethical perspectives.* San Francisco: W. H. Freeman and Co.

Valenstein, E. S., & Campbell, J. F. (1966). Medial forebrain bundle-lateral hypothalamic area and reinforcing brain stimulation. *American Journal of Physiology, 210,* 270–274.

Valverde, F. (1971). Rate and extent of recovery from dark rearing in the visual cortex of the mouse. *Brain Research, 33,* 1–11.

Van Buren, J. M., Ajmone-Marsan, C., Mutsuga, N., & Sadowsky, D. (1975). Surgery of temporal lobe epilepsy. In D. P. Purpura, J. K. Penry, & R. D. Walter (Eds.), *Advances in neurology: Volume 8. Neurosurgical management of the epilepsies* (pp. 155–196). New York: Raven Press.

Van der Kooy, D. (1987). Place conditioning: A simple and effective method for assessing the motivational properties of drugs. In M. A. Bozarth (Ed.), *Methods of assessing the reinforcing properties of abused drugs* (pp. 229–240). New York: Springer-Verlag.

Vanderwolf, C. H., & Robinson, T. E. (1981). Reticulo-cortical activity and behavior: A critique of the arousal theory and a new synthesis. *Behavioral and Brain Sciences, 4,* 459–514.

Van Essen, D. C., & Maunsell, J. H. R. (1983). Hierarchical organization and functional streams in the visual cortex. *Trends in neuroscience, 6,* 370–375.

Veale, W. L., & Cooper, K. E. (1975). Comparison of sites of action of prostaglandin E and leucocyte pyrogen in brain. *Temperature Regulation and Drug Action, Proceedings of the Symposium* (Paris, 1974), 218–226.

Vergnes, M., & Karli, P. (1969). Effects of stimulation of the lateral hypothalamus, amygdala, and hippocampus on interspecific rat-mouse aggressive behavior. *Physiology & Behavior, 4,* 889–894.

Vertes, R. P. (1983). Brainstem control of the events of REM sleep. *Progress in Neurobiology, 22,* 241–288.

Vessie, P. R. (1932). On the transmission of Huntington's Chorea for 300 years—the Bures family group. *The Journal of Nervous and Mental Disease, 76,* 553–573.

Victor, M., Adams, R. D., & Collins, G. H. (1971). *The Wernicke syndrome* (p. 22). Philadelphia: F. A. Davis.

von Bonin, G. (1962). Anatomical asymmetries of the cerebral hemispheres. In V. B. Mountcastle, (Ed.), *Interhemispheric relations and cerebral dominance* (pp. 1–6). Baltimore, MD: The Johns Hopkins Press.

von Cramon, D. Y., Hebel, N., & Schuri, U. (1985). A contribution to the anatomical basis of thalamic amnesia. *Brain, 108,* 993–1008.

Wada, J. A. (1949). A new method for the determination of the side of cerebral speech dominance. *Igaku to Seibutsugaku, 14,* 221–222.

Wada, J. A., Clarke, R., & Hamm, A. (1975). Cerebral hemispheric asymmetry in humans. *Archives of Neurology, 32,* 239–246.

Wada, J. A., Osawa, T., Wake, A., & Corcoran, M. E. (1975). Effects of taurine on kindled amygdaloid seizures in rats, cats, and photosensitive baboons. *Epilepsia, 16,* 229–234.

Wada, J. A., & Sato, M. (1974). Generalized convulsive seizures induced by daily electrical stimulation of the amygdala in cats: Correlative electrographic and behavioral features. *Neurology, 24,* 565–574.

Wada, J. A., Sato, M., & Corcoran, M. E. (1974). Persistent seizure susceptibility and recurrent spontaneous seizures in kindled cats. *Epilepsia, 15,* 465–478.

Wald, G. (1964). The receptors of human color vision. *Science, 145,* 1007–1016.

Wald, G. (1968). The molecular basis of visual excitation. *Nature, 219,* 800–807.

Walk, R. D., & Walters, C. P. (1973). Effect of visual deprivation on depth discrimination of hooded rats. *Journal of Comparative and Physiological Psychology, 85,* 559–563.

Walker, D. W., Barnes, D. E., Zornetzer, S. F., Hunter, B. E., & Kubanis, P. (1980). Neuronal loss in hippocampus induced by prolonged ethanol comsumption in rats. *Science, 209,* 711–713.

Wangensteen, O. H., & Carlson, H. A. (1930). Hunger sensations in a patient after total gastrectomy. *Proceedings of the Society for Experimental Biology and Medicine, 28,* 545–547.

Wauquier, A., Ashton, D., & Melis, W. (1970). Behavioral analysis of amygdaloid kindling in beagle dogs and the effects of clonazepam, diazepam, phenobarbital, diphenylhydantoin, and flunarizine on seizure manifestion. *Experimental Neurology, 64,* 579–586.

Waxenberg, S. E., Drellich, M. G., & Sutherland, A. M. (1959). The role of hormones in human behavior: I. Changes in female sexuality after adrenalectomy. *Journal of Clinical Endocrinology, 19,* 193–202.

Webb, W. B. (1968). *Sleep: An experimental approach.* New York: Macmillan Co.

Webb, W. B. (1973). Selective and partial deprivation of sleep. In W. P. Koella & P. Levin (Eds.), *Sleep: Physiology, biochemistry, psychology, pharmacology, clinical implications* (pp. 176–204). Basel: Karger.

Webb, W. B., & Agnew, H. W. (1967). Sleep cycling within the twenty-four hour period. *Journal of Experimental Psychology, 74,* 167–169.

Webb, W. B., & Agnew, H. W. (1970). Sleep stage characteristics of long and short sleepers. *Science, 163,* 146–147.

Webb, W. B., & Agnew, H. W. (1974). The effects of a chronic limitation of sleep length. *Psychophysiology, 11,* 265–274.

Webb, W. B., & Agnew, H. W. (1975). The effects on subsequent sleep of an acute restriction of sleep length. *Psychophysiology, 12,* 367–370.

Wechsler, D. (1981). *Wechsler adult intelligence scale—revised.* New York: The Psychological Corporation.

Weerts, T. C., & Roberts, R. (1976). The physiological effects of imagining anger-provoking and fear-provoking scenes. *Psychophysiology, 13,* 174.

Weingarten, H. P. (1983). Conditioned cues elicit feeding in sated rats: A role for learning in meal initiation. *Science, 220,* 431–433.

Weingarten, H. P. (1984). Meal initiation controlled by learned cues: Basic behavioral properties. *Appetite, 5,* 147–158.

Weingarten, H. P. (1985). Stimulus control of eating: Implications for a two-factor theory of hunger. *Appetite, 6,* 387–401.

Weingarten, H. P., Chang, P. K., & Jarvie, K. R. (1983). Reactivity of normal and VMH-lesion rats to quinine-adulterated foods: Negative evidence for negative finickiness. *Behavioral Neuroscience, 97,* 221–233.

Weinrich, M., & Wise, S. P. (1982). The premotor cortex of the monkey. *Journal of Neuroscience, 2,* 1329–1345.

Weisinger, R. S. (1975). Conditioned and pseudoconditioned thirst and sodium appetite. In G. Peters, J. T. Fitzsimons, & L. Peters-Haefeli (Eds.), *Control Mechanisms of Drinking* (pp. 149–154). New York: Springer-Verlag.

Weiskrantz, L., & Warrington, E. K. (1979). Conditioning in amnesic patients. *Neuropsychologia, 17,* 187–194.

Weiskrantz, L., Warrington, E. K., Sanders, M. D., & Marshall, J. (1974). Visual capacity in the hemianopic field following a restricted occipital ablation. *Brain, 97,* 709–728.

Weiss, B., & Laties, V. G. (1961). Behavioral thermoregulation. *Science, 133,* 1338–1344.

Wenger, J. R., Tiffany, T. M., Bombardier, C., Nicholls, K., & Woods, S. C. (1981). Ethanol tolerance in the rat is learned. *Science, 213,* 575–577.

Wever, R. A. (1979). *The circadian system of man.* Andechs: Max-Planck-Institut fur Verhaltensphysiologie.

Whalen, R. E., & Rezek, D. L. (1974). Inhibition of lordosis in female rats by subcutaneous implants of testosterone, androstenedione or dihydrotestosterone in infancy. *Hormones and Behavior, 5,* 125–128.

Whishaw, I. Q., Kolb, B., & Sutherland, R. J. (1983). The analysis of behavior in the laboratory rat. In T. E. Robinson (Ed.), *Behavioral approaches to brain research* (pp. 141–211). New York: Oxford University Press.

White, N., Sklar, L., & Amit, Z. (1977). The reinforcing action of morphine and its paradoxical side effect. *Psychopharmacology, 52,* 63–66.

Whitehouse, P. J., Price, D. L., Struble, R. G., Clark, A. W. Coyle, J. T., & DeLong, M. R. (1982). Alzheimer's disease and senile dementia: Loss of neurons in the basal forebrain. *Science, 215,* 1237–1239.

Whitelaw, V., & Hollyday, M. (1983). Position-dependent motor innervation of the chick hindlimb following serial and parallel duplications of limb segments. *Journal of Neuroscience, 3,* 1216–1225.

Wickelgren, W. A. (1968). Sparing of short-term memory in an amnesic patient: Implications for strength theory of memory. *Neuropsychologia, 6,* 235–244.

Wikler, A. (1980). *Opioid dependence: Mechanisms and treatment.* New York: Plenum Press.

Wilhelm, P. (1983). *The Nobel prize.* London: Springwood Books.

Wilkinson, D. A. (1982). Examination of alcoholics by computed tomographic (CT) scans: A critical review. *Alcoholism: Clinical and Experimental Research, 6,* 31–45.

Wilkinson, R. T. (1965). Sleep deprivation. In O. G. Edholm & A. L. Bacharach (Eds.), *The physiology of human survival* (pp. 399–430). London: Academic Press.

Wilson, J. D., George, F. W., & Griffin, J. E. (1981). The hormonal control of sexual development. *Science, 211,* 1278–1284.

Wilson, J. D., & Griffin, J. E. (1980). The use and misuse of androgens. *Progress in Endocrinology and Metabolism, 29,* 1278–1295.

Winocur, G., Kinsbourne, M., & Moscovitch, M. (1981). The effects of cuing on release from proactive interference in Korsakoff amnesia patients. *Journal of Experimental Psychology: Human Learning and Memory, 1,* 56–65.

Winocur, G., Oxbury, S., Roberts, R., Agnetti, V., & Davis, C. (1984). Amnesia in patients with bilateral lesions to the thalamus. *Neuropsychologia, 22,* 123–143.

Winokur, G. (1978). Mania and depression: Family studies and genetics in relation to treatment. In M. A. Lipton, A. DiMascio, & K. F. Killam (Eds.), *Psychopharmacology: A generation of progress* (pp. 1213–1221). New York: Raven Press.

Wirtshafter, D., & Davis, J. D. (1977). Set points, settling points, and the control of body weight. *Physiology & Behavior, 19,* 75–78.

Wise, R. A. (1987). The role of reward pathways in the development of drug dependence. *Pharmac. Ther., 35,* 227–263.

Wise, R. A., & Bozarth, M. A. (1984). Brain reward circuitry: Four circuit elements "wired" in apparent series. *Brain Research Bulletin, 12,* 203–208.

Wise, R. A., & Bozarth, M. A. (1987). A psychomotor stimulant theory of addiction. *Psychological Review, 94,* 469–492.

Wolf, M. E., & Goodale, M. A. (1987). Oral asymmetries during verbal and non-verbal movements of the mouth. *Neuropsychologia, 25,* 375–396.

Wolf, S., & Wolff, H. G. (1947). *Human gastric function* (2nd ed.), London: Oxford University Press.

Wood, E. R., Mumby, D. G., Pinel, J. P. J., & Phillips, A. G. (1989). Ischemia-induced damage to the rat hippocampus produces deficits in nonrecurring-items delayed nonmatching to sample. *Society for Neuroscience Abstracts, 15.*

Wood, R. J., Rolls, B. J., & Ramsay, D. J. (1977). Drinking following intracarotid infusions of hypertonic solutions in dogs. *American Journal of Physiology, 1,* R88–R91.

Woods, J. W. (1956). "Taming" of the wild Norway rat by rhinencephalic lesions. *Science, 178,* 869.

Woods, S. C., Lotter, E. C., McKay, L. D., & Porte, D., Jr. (1979). Chronic intracerebroventricular infusion of insulin reduces food intake and body weight of baboons. *Nature, 282,* 503–505.

Woods, S. C., & Porte, D., Jr. (1977). Relationship between plasma and cerebrospinal fluid insulin levels of dogs. *American Journal of Physiology, 233,* E331–E334.

Woods, S. C., Taborsky, G. J., & Porte, D., Jr. (1986). Central nervous system control of nutrient homeostasis. In V. B. Mountcastle & F. E. Bloom (Eds.), *Handbook of physiology: The nervous system IV: Intrinsic regulatory systems of the brain* (pp. 365–411). Bethesda, MD: American Physiological Society.

Woods, S. C., Vasselli, J. R., Kaestner, E., Szakmary, G. A., Milburn, P., & Vitiello, M. V. (1977). Conditioned insulin secretion and meal feeding in rats. *Journal of Comparative and Physiological Psychology, 91,* 128–133.

Woodworth, C. H. (1971). Attack elicited in rats by electrical stimulation of the lateral hypothalamus. *Physiology & Behavior, 6,* 345–353.

Woolsey, C. N. (1960). Organization of cortical auditory system: A review and a synthesis. In G. L. Rasmussen & W. F. Windle (Eds.), *Neural mechanisms of the auditory and vestibular systems* (pp. 165–180). Springfield, IL: Charles C Thomas.

Wurtman, R. J. (1985). Alzheimer's disease. *Scientific American, 252,* 62–74.

Wylie, D. R., & Goodale, M. A. (1988). Left-sided oral asymmetries in spontaneous but not posed smiles. *Neuropsychologia, 26,* 823–832.

Wyrwicka, W. (1969). Sensory regulation of food intake. *Physiology & Behavior, 4,* 853–858.

Xuereb, M. M. L., Pritchard, P. M., & Daniel, P. M. (1954). The arterial supply and venous drainage of the human hypophysis cerebri. *Quarterly Journal of Experimental Physiology, 39,* 199–229.

Yadin, E., Guarini, V., & Gallistel, C. R. (1983). Unilaterally activated systems in rats self-stimulating at sites in the medial forebrain bundle, medial prefrontal cortex, or locus coeruleus. *Brain Research, 266,* 39–50.

Yeo, C. H., Hardiman, M. F., Glickstein, M., & Steele-Russell, I. (1982). Lesions of cerebellar nuclei abolish the classically conditioned nictitating membrane response. *Society for Neuroscience Abstracts, 8,* 22.

Yeung, J. C., & Rudy, T. A. (1978). Sites of antinociceptive action of systemically injected morphine: Involvement of supraspinal loci as revealed by intracerebroventricular injection of naloxone. *Journal of Pharmacology and Experimental Therapeutics, 215,* 626–632.

Yokel, R. A. (1987). Intravenous self-administration: Response rates, the effects of pharmacological challenges, and drug preference. In M. A. Bozarth (Ed.), *Methods of assessing the reinforcing properties of abused drugs* (pp. 1–33). New York: Springer-Verlag.

Yoon, M. (1971). Reorganization of retinotectal projection following surgical operations on the optic tectum in goldfish. *Experimental Neurology, 33,* 395–411.

Young, T. (1802). The Bakerian Lecture: On the theory of light and colours. *Philosophical Transactions of the Royal Society of London,* 12–48.

Zaidel, E. (1975). A technique for presenting lateralized visual input with prolonged exposure. *Vision Research, 15,* 283–289.

Zaidel, E. (1983). Disconnection syndrome as a model for laterality effects in the normal brain. In J. B. Hellige (Ed.), *Cerebral hemisphere asymmetry: Method, theory, and application* (pp. 95–151). New York: Praeger Press.

Zaidel, E. (1985). Introduction. In F. D. Benson & E. Zaidel (Eds.), *The dual brain: Hemispheric specialization in humans* (pp. 47–63). London: The Guildford Press.

Zangwill, O. L. (1975). Excision of Broca's area without persistent aphasia. In K. J. Zulch, O. Creutzfeldt, & G. C. Galbraith (Eds.), *Cerebral localization* (pp. 258–263). New York: Springer-Verlag.

Zatz, M., & Herkenham, M. A. (1981). Intraventricular carbachol mimics the phase-shifting effect of light on the circadian rhythm of wheel-running activity. *Brain Research, 212,* 234–238.

Zelman, D. C., Tiffany, S. T., & Baker, T. B. (1985). Influence of stress on morphine induced pyrexia: Relevance to a pavlovian model of tolerance development. *Behavioral Neuroscience, 99,* 122–144.

Zeman, W., & King, F. A. (1958). Tumors of the septum pellucidum and adjacent structures with abnormal affective behavior: An anterior midline structure syndrome. *Journal of Nervous and Mental Diseases, 127,* 490–501.

Zola-Morgan, S., Dabrowska, J., Moss, M., & Mahut, H. (1983). Enhanced preference for perceptual novelty in the monkey after section of the fornix but not after ablation of the hippocampus. *Neuropsychologia, 21,* 433–454.

Zola-Morgan, S., & Squire, L. R. (1982). Two forms of amnesia in monkeys: Rapid forgetting after medial temporal lesions but not diencephalic lesions. *Society for Neuroscience Abstracts, 8,* 24.

Zola-Morgan, S., & Squire, L. R. (1984). Preserved learning in monkeys with medial temporal lesions: Sparing of motor and cognitive skills. *Journal of Neuroscience, 4,* 1072–1085.

Zola-Morgan, S., & Squire, L. R. (1985). Medial temporal lesions in monkeys impair memory on a variety of tasks sensitive to human amnesia. *Behavioral Neuroscience, 99,* 22–34.

Zola-Morgan, S., & Squire, L. R. (1985). Two forms of amnesia in monkeys: Rapid forgetting after medial temporal lesions but not diencephalic lesions. *Society for Neuroscience Abstracts, 8,* 24.

Zola-Morgan, S., Squire, L. R., & Amaral, D. G. (1986). Human amnesia and the medial temporal region: Enduring memory impairment following a bilateral lesion limited to field CA1 of the hippocampus. *Journal of Neuroscience, 6,* 2950–2967.

Zola-Morgan, S., Squire, L. R., & Mishkin, M. (1982). The neuroanatomy of amnesia: Amygdala-hippocampus versus temporal stem. *Science, 218,* 1337–1339.

Zusho, H. (1983). Posttraumatic anosmia. *Archives of ontolaryngology, 4,* 252–256.

Name Index

Subject Index

Neurosecretory cells, 275, 301
Neurotoxic effect, 9, 22
Neurotoxins, 114, 122–123, 310
Neurotransmission, concept of, 152–153
Neurotransmitters, 28, 61
  amino acid, 150–151
  catecholamine, 389
  classes of, 150–155
  deactivation of, 74
  definition for, 51, 79
  identification of, 144
  located in CNS, 147–150
  monoamine, 151
  putative, 142, 144, 167
  release of, 72, 73, 77
  study of, 143–150
  universally recognized, 167
Neurotransmitter synthesis, 145, 146
Neurotransplantation, 458–461
Neurotropic, definition for, 139
Nicotine, 473, 493
Nicotinic receptors, 153, 167
Nictitating membrane, 452, 465
Nictitating-membrane reflex, circuit mediating,
Nictitating-membrane response, in rabbits,
  451–454
Nigrostriatal bundle, 463
Nigrostriatal pathway, 129, 139, 488
Nissl stain, 28, 47, 51
N-Methyl-D-asparate (NMDA), 451
N-Methyl-D-asparate (NMDA) receptor, 451,
  465
Nocturnal animals, 373, 394
Nocturnal myoclonus, 390, 394
Nonlexical procedure, for reading aloud, 522,
  527
Nonmatching-to-sample task, nonrecurring-
  items delayed, 416–417, 421, 422, 426,
  428
Nootropics, 411, 428
Noradrenaline, 141
Norepinephrine, 141, 147, 151
Nuclei
  in CNS, 32
  definition for, 31, 51
  dorsal column, 219, 234
  gustatory, 234
  medial septal, 410
  mediodorsal, 428
  paraventricular, 332
  Raphé, 347, 349, 384, 385, 394
  sexual dimorphic, 284, 285, 302
  suprachiasmatic, 386–387
  vestibular, 268
Nutritive density, 306, 332
Nutritive density, definition for, 332

Obesity
  problem of, 318
  produced by VHM lesions, 324
  and VMH satiety center, 312–313
Observational methods, 15–17
Occipital lobe, 42
Odors, reaction to, 228
Off-center cells, 187, 199
Olfaction (smell), 201
  behavior and, 227
  primary function of, 226
Olfactory bulbs, 228, 235
Olfactory cortex, 44, 228
Olfactory nerves, 24, 231
Olfactory system, 227–228
Oligoendroglia, 33, 51, 461, 465
Ommatidia, 185, 199
On-center cells, 187
  definition for, 199
  lateral inhibition in, 188
Open-field test, 108, 114
Operant conditioning, 110, 114
Opiate antagonists, 225
Opiate reward, neural substances of, 489–490
Opiates
  abuse of, 478–481

analgesic effect of, 224
  definition for, 493
Opium, 154, 479, 494
Opponent-process theory, of color vision, 193–
  194, 199
Optic chasm, 41, 284, 387
Optic disk, 172, 199
Optic nerves
  cutting of, 387
  in neural development, 438
Optic tectum, 435
  definition for, 465
  in neural development, 438
Orchidectomy, 281, 296, 301
Orientation columns, 192
Orthodromic, definition for, 79
Oscilloscope, 56, 79
Osmoreceptors, 336, 361, 363
Osmotic pressure, 335, 363
Ossicles, of ear, 211, 235
Oval window, 211, 235. See also Ear
Ovariectomy, 281, 296, 301
Ovaries, 271
  definition for, 301
  fetal development of, 280–282, 283
Ovulation, 277, 278, 301
Oxytocin, 275, 301

Pacinian corpuscle, 216–217, 235
Pain, 216
  gate-control theory of, 224, 234
  neural basis of, 224
  paradoxes of, 223–224
Pain control, mechanisms of, 224–226
Paired-associate test, of memory, 100, 114
Palatability
  effects of variety on, 317–318
  and incentive properties, 327
  influence on eating of, 316–317
Paleocortex, 44, 51
Pancreas, 332
Pancreatitis, 475
Pantropic, definition for, 139
Papillae, of tongue, 229
Parabiotic preparation, 389, 394
Parachlorophenylalanine (PCPA), 384, 394
Paradoxical sleep, 368, 394
Parallel models, 232, 513
Parallel processing, 235, 527
Parasympathetic nerves, 24, 51
Paraventricular nuclei, 275, 301
Parietal cortex, posterior, 219, 235, 239–243,
  268
Parietal lobe, 42, 207
Parkinson's disease, 45, 128, 129, 157, 161, 250
  cause of, 143
  definition for, 139
  dopaminergic transmission in, 158
  L-DOPA in, 145
  MPTP model of, 136–137
  surgery for, 462–463
Paresis, general, 122, 139
Partial seizure, 126
  complex, 138
  definition for, 139
  simple, 139
Patellar tendon reflex, 259–261, 268
Pattern approach, 103–104
Pavlovian conditioning, 110, 447–448
  definition for, 115, 465
  discriminated, 464
Penile erections, during sleep, 371
Penis, ablatio, 292–293
Peptides, 72, 79, 152, 167
Perception
  audition, 209–216
  definition for, 202, 235
  edge, 183–192
  of motion, 16
  sensation and, 202–203
  of sound, 210
Perceptual-motor function, tests of, 101–105
Perforant path, 449, 465

Periaqueductal gray (PAG) area, 224, 235
Perimetry, definition for, 235
Perimetry test, 204–205
Peripheral nervous system (PNS), 24
  definition for, 51
  and spinal cord, 37
Peristaltic contractions, 306, 332
Perseveration, 103, 115
Personal orientation test, 101
Petit mal, 128, 139
PET-scan, 522, 524, 525, 526
Phagocytes, 457, 465
Phagocytosis, 457, 465
Phenothiazines, 160, 167
Phenylketonuria (PKU), 124, 139
Pheromones, 226–227, 235
Phonemes, 519, 527
Photons, 169
Photopic sensitivity, 177, 199
Phototopic system, 175
Pia mater, 25, 51
Piloerection, 356, 363
Pioneer growth cones, 436, 465
Pituitary gland, 41
  anterior, 273, 275, 300
  hormones of, 273
  hypothalamic control of, 275
  neural control of, 274, 275
  posterior, 273, 275, 301
Pituitary stalk, 273, 301
Planum temporale, 521, 527
Plateau phase, of fever, 359, 363
Plethysmography, 92, 115
Pneumoencephalography, 82, 115
Poikilotherms, 354, 355, 363
Polydipsia, 344
  definition for, 363
  schedule-induced, 345, 364
Polygraph, 115
Polygraphy, 104
Polypeptides, 152, 167
Pons, 39
Pontine nuclei, 454
Positive feedback, 277, 301
Positron emission tomography (PET), 85
  definition for, 115
  scans, 522, 524, 525, 526
Posterior, definition for, 51
Postsynaptic cell, 144
Postsynaptic inhibition, 75, 79
Postsynaptic membranes, 78, 144
Postsynaptic potentials, 61–62
  generation of, 73–74
  integration of, 62–66
Posttraumatic amnesia (PTA), 411–412
Potassium ions (K+)
  during action potentials, 66
  and membrane potentials, 58–60
Prefrontal cortex, inferior, 497
Premotor cortex, 243–245, 245–246
Preoptic and anterior hypothalamus (POAH),
  357, 362
  definition for, 363
  fever and, 360
Preoptic area
  definition for, 301
  lateral, 337, 338
Prestriate cortex, 207, 235
Presynaptic facilitation, 445, 465
Presynaptic inhibition, 75, 79
Presynaptic neurons, 78
Primary motor cortex
  location of, 246
  somatotopic layout of, 274
Priming, definition for, 494
Proactive interference, 409, 428
Procaine, 477
Procedural memories, 423–424
Proceptive, definition for, 301
Proceptive behavior, 287
Progesterone, 272, 278, 287, 301
Progestins, 272, 301
Prosopagnosia, 208, 235
Proteins, 152, 167